CARING
for children

NURTURING
children's development

GUIDING
children's behavior

Essential
parenting
skills are the
focus of this
completely
revised text.

GLENCOE

THE PROGRAM

Parenting: Rewards and Responsibilities

helps your students build skills in decision-making, family relations, and nuturing children's development. Emphasis is on both the joys and challenges of parenthood.

STUDENT TEXTBOOK

Content stresses all aspects of parenting and helps your students understand the responsibilities and rewards of parenting.

TEACHER'S ANNOTATED EDITION

Detailed lesson plans for every chapter in the bound-in Teacher's Manual save you valuable preparation time. Teaching Annotations on every page help you reinforce and expand text content.

STUDENT WORKBOOK

More options for increasing students' learning include a study guide and two or more additional activities for every chapter. A special Teacher's Annotated Edition of the Student Workbook provides you with answers to every worksheet.

TEACHER'S CLASSROOM RESOURCES

This complete package of resource materials now makes your preparation easier than ever. You will find activities to reteach, enrich, and extend learning. Includes special components for teen parenting, decision-making, cooperative learning, and practicing parenting.

Parenting: Rewards and Responsibilities
Dr. Verna Hildebrand

Parenting: Rewards and Responsibilities
Dr. Verna Hildebrand

STUDENT WORKBOOK
Parenting: Rewards and Responsibilities
Dr. Verna Hildebrand

TEACHER'S ANNOTATED STUDENT WORKBOOK
Parenting: Rewards and Responsibilities
Dr. Verna Hildebrand

IVE LEARNING ACTIVITIES

Parenting:
Rewards and
Responsibilities

TEEN PARENTING

Parenting:
Rewards and
Responsibilities

Dr. Verna Hildebrand

TESTING PROGRAM

Parenting:
Rewards and
Responsibilities

Dr. Verna Hildebrand

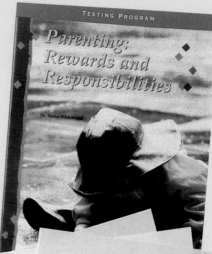

REPRODUCIBLE LESSON PLANS

Parenting:
Rewards and
Responsibilities

Dr. Verna Hildebrand

SUCCESSFUL BABYSITTING

TENSION ACTIVITIES

enting:
ards and
ponsibilities

DECISION-MAKING ACTIVITIES

Parenting:
Rewards and
Responsibilities

Dr. Verna Hildebrand

ENRICHMENT ACTIVITIES

Parenting:
Rewards and
Responsibilities

Dr. Verna Hildebrand

COLOR TRANSPARENCY PACKET

Parenting:
Rewards and
Responsibilities

Dr. Verna Hildebrand

RETEACHING ACTIVITIES

arenting:
ewards and
esponsibilities

Dr. Verna Hildebrand

PRACTICING PARENTING

Parenting:
Rewards and
Responsibilities

Dr. Verna Hildebrand

Parenting:
Rewards and
Responsibilities

Dr. Verna Hildebrand

Teacher's Classroom Resources

STUDENT TEXT

At last, a text with more emphasis on parenting and families! The completely revised Student Text now includes the topics you asked for: teen parenting, parenthood and it's obligations, guiding and encouraging children, and strengthening the role of family.

ILLUSTRATION PROGRAM

Photography, illustrations, and graphics combine to create an inviting text that your students will enjoy using.

TEACHING FEATURES

Objectives and vocabulary set the stage for learning. An opening "story" captures your student's interest at the beginning of each chapter. Boxed features highlight essential information.

CHAPTER 13

Understanding Infants

Objectives

This chapter will help you to:
- Summarize the physical development of infants.
- Identify important goals for emotional and social development during infancy.
- Explain how infants use their senses to learn.
- Describe how language develops in infants.

Vocabul

maturation
physical deve
reflexes
fontanels
motor skills
emotional de
social develo
stranger anxi
separation a
temperamen
attachment
behavior

A muffled little cry accompanied by a slight shudder signals that baby Timmy, age two weeks, is waking up. Timmy's parents, Melody and Arnie, turn away from the TV program and peek in the bassinet. They smile at each other and realize that at any moment the action will start. Arnie squeezes Melody's hand. They both like anticipating what Timmy will do.

In a few minutes the little cry becomes more pronounced. Arnie gets up and brings Timmy to the couch. Both parents look lovingly at the baby and touch his little hands. They both start talking to him—almost in unison. They laugh together, amused.

The baby is uniting Melody and Arnie as they had never imagined. They agree that this new stage of life is very satisfying.

Growt

Infants
and devel
to an incre
family me
growth. Y
saying to
you've gr

Develo
physical,
ities. In t
growth a
a baby's

Matu
growth
process
have pr
for a five
ally, this

Around the World

What's in a Name?

In some cultures, certain customs influ-
e the name a parent chooses for a
d.

hildren in Burma are named for the
of the week on which they are born.
day of the week is assigned a different
letters from the alphabet. For exam-
children were born on a Sunday, their
begins with a vowel. If they were
n a Monday, their name begins with
ng. If they were born on a Tuesday,
name begins with s, z, or ny.
ese children, the day of the week
ch they are born is more important
e actual birth date. Many Burmese
that a person's character is deter-
y the day of birth. People born on
are thought to be stingy. Those
Monday are considered jealous.
rn on Tuesday are supposedly

ezuela, most of the people are
atholic. Children are usually
er the saint whose feast day
eir birth date. This means that
ren with the same name cele-
irthday on the same day.

ewish religion, children are
r a deceased relative or el se
e family. Th

When criticisms are directed at children's
efforts or tasks rather than children's personality or character, their self-esteem is preserved. In this way, children learn that even
though they have done something wrong,
they are still loved as a person.

If parents and caregivers criticize the child
rather than his or her actions, they make the
child feel guilty and unworthy. Compare the
following comments on the same incident:
"You really made a mess. Now you can help
clean it up."

"How could you be so clumsy? Now look at
what I have to do."

As children grow older, some do not
always do well in school. Poor grades often
bring discouragement and shame. A parent
who nags, punishes, or threatens such a child
will probably find that the child does worse
instead of better. Rather than helping the
child, the withdrawal of parental approval
often has a discouraging effect.

At times like this, children need additional
support and encouragement from parents as
well as from teachers. When children know
others are genuinely concerned about them,
they have more self-confidence about trying
again. They are able to direct their efforts
toward learning rather than toward trying to
compensate for their academic failures.

Self-Esteem

Parents and other caregivers should encourage children to try again when they experience failure. Adults should also recognize
children's efforts when they succeed. Children
who receive encouragement, guidance, and
love usually develop a positive self-concept.
Those who are neglected, rejected, and often
punished usually develop a negative view of
themselves.

Praising Efforts and Accomplishments

Praise is most effective when directed at
children's efforts or accomplishments. This
focuses on their attempts to succeed or to
carry out certain tasks successfully. When
praise is aimed at their personality, it has less
impact.

For example, Tad's mother told him she
liked the way he cleaned up the spill from the
glass of milk he tried to pour. If she had told
him he was a good boy for wiping up the
spill, the result might have been different. Tad
knows whether he was good or not. Maybe
he was misbehaving when he spilled the
milk. In that case, he might have become confused if his mother had told him he was a
good boy for cleaning up the spill. He might
even have misbehaved again to get future
praise. Instead, Tad's mother praised his
efforts, not him.

When children are praised for their efforts
and accomplishments, they are encouraged
to keep trying. For example, Isako's dad told
her he was pleased that she tasted her broccoli
even though she did not eat all of it. When
Jake's mother told him he had really worked
hard to tie his shoelaces, he beamed with joy.
Even though he did not succeed, she praised
his efforts.

A "high five" is one of many ways that parents can
acknowledge childrens's efforts and accomplishments.

Praise can take many forms. It is up to parents to find the most effective approach in
nurturing each child's confidence and self-
esteem. Praising the child's efforts and accomplishments should be an important part of
that approach.

Handling Mistakes and Failures

Sometimes children make mistakes or fail
to achieve a task. Mistakes are a part of the
process of trying various alternatives to see
what works best. Children learn by experiencing the consequences of their actions.

DECISIONS ◆ ◆ DECISIONS

Clara, age three, uses her whole fist to
grasp a spoon. She handles crayons and
small blocks in the same way. She is
adept at handling these objects, and her
parents think she is ready for a more
advanced level of coordination. How
might Clara's parents encourage her to
learn new skills?

---

cognitive
development
sensorimotor
stage

Development

e many stages of growth
Growth, you recall, refers
e or weight. Friends and
ten talk about children's
bly remember someone
can't believe how much

ers to an increasing skill in
l, social, or cognitive abil-
r you will learn about the
opment that occurs during

the process of reaching full
elopment. It is an internal
d by age and genetics. You
ard people say, "She's short
d" or "He's immature." Usu-
hat some part of a person's

AROUND THE WORLD

This special feature helps your
students develop appreciation for
parenting in our culturally diverse
world.

SELF-ESTEEM

These boxes present your students with a variety of ways to
enhance children's self-esteem.

DECISIONS, DECISIONS

These short case studies allow
your students to practice the caregiver's role.

HEALTH AND SAFETY

This feature emphasizes topics
such as lead poisoning, Rh factor,
crib safety, failure to thrive syndrome, high-tech pregnancies,
and neonatal intensive care.

CHAPTER 22

Encouraging Children

Objectives

This chapter will help you to:
- Explain the relationship between encouragement, motivation, and praise.
- Describe how parents and caregivers can provide guidance for children.
- List and give examples of effective communication skills.
- Discuss the importance of love for children.

Vocabulary

encouragement
motivation
communication
active listening

Terri and her father were at the playground in the park. She always enjoyed the swings. As she was swinging back and forth, she watched the other children climbing the slide and sliding down. As the swing slowed, Terri jumped off. She went to the slide but hesitated. Perhaps the children's shouts and their fast pace, along with the height of the slide, gave Terri a moment of fear.

Terri's father noticed her hesitation. He went near her but waited to see what she would do. She looked at him, then back at the slide. "I'll stand right here," said her father. He moved closer to the slide so he could reach Terri if necessary.

Her father continued, "You can hold on tight as you climb the steps. I know you can do it, and then you can slide down." He let her think about the situation for a moment. A few children passed her and climbed the steps.

At last Terri made her decision. She climbed up the stairs. At the top she said, "Look Daddy! See how high I am." Then she slid down and ran to the steps again. Her father had given her just the right amount of encouragement.

Chapter Opener. Ask students to read the opening scenario to the chapter. Ask these questions: What conflicting feelings did Terri have at the playground? If her father had handled the situation differently, what might have been the result?

Providing Encouragem

All children need **encouragemen** a message of confidence and faith in ability. Encouragement is important dren at all stages of development them a sense of hope and self-co Encouragement helps children feel i It lets them know someone cares.

Encouragement is one of the mo ways that parents and caregivers can dren develop into healthy and ha viduals. When adults provide encou they nurture children's self-este encouragement leads to the develo more positive self-concept and h esteem. Encouragement also help develop self-confidence in their ab

Motivation

Encouragement is especially when children face new tasks. The ing new skills when they know faith and confidence in their ab

Activity. Ask students to tabulate how many encouraging things to them in the next 24-ho them evaluate how each statement makes th

As people
wrinkle and
early in life ca
Ultraviolet ray
burn and dama
Even worse, e
result in skin ca

All children s
sun, even those
dark skin has ext
some natural pro
ple with a dark co
and skin cancer.

Here are some
from the harmful e

- Use a hat with a
  child's head, bac
  will also help sha

- Apply a sunscree
  an SPF (sun prot
  more to the child
  rated by number
  The number ind

Discuss. What household items cou that would encourage the developr skills? What activities would help coordination?

TEACHING ANNOTATIONS

These bottom-of-page teaching notes provide you with another convenient resource for teaching.

- Quick and easy ACTIVITY suggestions help you introduce topics or reinforce concepts.

- Ideas to DISCUSS help you stimulate discussion or application of the content.

- Other annotations make it easier for you to help your students practice PROBLEM-SOLVING.

- You can tell your students MORE ABOUT the content and provide them with a REFERENCE for further study.

The Teacher's Manual, bound in the front of the Teacher's Annotated Edition, includes a multitude of effective teaching strategies. The detailed lesson plans for every chapter provide multi-level and cross-curricular activities. Answers to the Chapter Reviews are included.

ring Children

n to practice eye-
s' puzzles should
ine large pieces.
t can be placed
to build a tower
toddlers enjoy.
an place over a
y. Parents need
ect different-
yogurt, and
enjoy sorting
l in a box or
n.

Parents can make other toys from items around the home that will help toddlers with small motor skills.

Other items appropriate for toddlers are large crayons, chalk, and paint brushes. Young children generally grasp these with a fist and take large, whole-arm strokes. Toddlers need large sheets of paper for their drawings.

All kinds of puzzles, blocks, erector sets, lacing kits, cars, and dolls stimulate the practice of small motor skills. Many of these objects are more appropriate for four-year-olds

Health & Safety

Protection from the Sun

their skin begins to
er, too much sun
the aging process.
un can cause sun-
yers of skin cells.
n exposure may
ears later.
otected from the
skin. Although
which provides
n sunburn, peo-
an get wrinkles

otect children
sun.

to protect the
lders. The hat
d's eyes.

cream with
or) of 15 or
screens are
to SPF 50.
nscreen's

ability to screen out the ultraviolet rays. Choose a sunscreen recommended for children. Many babies have skin that is sensitive to fragrances and other additives used in products designed for adults. Reapply a sunscreen at least every two hours.

- Be particularly careful when the child is playing outdoors in water or snow. Ultraviolet rays are reflected upward from water, sand, and snow. Even on cloudy days, most of the ultraviolet rays can penetrate through the haze, fog, or clouds.

- See that the child relaxes in the shade— not the sun—at a beach or pool. Remember, however, that a beach umbrella or a leafy tree is no substitute for a sunscreen lotion or cream.

- Use an awning or hood on a stroller or carriage when taking a walk in the sun.

- If possible, keep the child out of the sun between 10:00 A.M. and 2:00 P.M. This is when the ultraviolet rays are strongest.

y with safely
small motor
eye-hand

Activity. Ask students to create a puzzle for toddlers, using heavy cardboard.
Problem Solving. Have students discuss whether or not boys should be encouraged to play with dolls.

Picking up a puzzle piece and placing it in a specific position help children develop small motor skills.

because they demand greater skills than most three-year-olds possess.

Practicing small motor skills is important during the preschool years. These early skills form the basis for the useful skills of writing, drawing, cutting, and pasting at later ages.

Self-Esteem

As children play with others, they get to know themselves better. They form ideas about themselves by the way others play with them. They develop autonomy and a sense of self. Parents can help children develop good feelings about themselves by playing with them and in the process providing compliments and encouragement.

Activity. Have students list as many games and toys as they can on the chalkboard. Then ask them to label each as to which motor skills development would be strengthened most by its use.

Emotional-Social Development

Play can contribute a great deal to children's emotional and social development. The give-and-take of interacting with others is especially important during play. For example, a high school student makes friends and learns new ways to deal with people to make life more satisfying. Toddlers and young children are just getting started on the ladder of social development. They learn and develop socially and emotionally through play.

Learning to relate to others and learning how to handle the emotions involved in relating to others eventually become crucial parts of play. During their first two years or so, infants engage in **solitary play;** that is, they play by themselves. Babies play alone even when other babies are present, though they do seem to enjoy the presence of these others. At this age, babies play as if they were little satellites, each moving around in his or her own universe. If they do interact with others, it is quite by accident.

Between the ages of two and three, children begin to look forward to having another child around when they play. When they are together, they play side by side. This is known as **parallel play.** For instance, they may each zoom a truck around the room at the same time.

After age four, children engage in **cooperative play;** that is, their play actually requires them to do things together. In this kind of play, children make plans, talk things over, and pretend they are people they know from story books, television, or the neighborhood. Language development is obviously a big asset in such activities. Cooperative play helps children practice the social skills of sharing and taking turns. As children learn to share toys and take turns, they develop feelings of concern and respect for each other.

Problem Solving. Have students descri_
playtime might go better.
What

Developed specifically to ease your preparation for teaching, the Teacher's Classroom Resources provides you with hundreds of ready-to-use resources that will save you hours and hours of planning time.

- **TEEN PARENTING** includes teaching tips, activities, and student handout masters for teaching this special population.

- **PRACTICING PARENTING** provides exercises and games, readings, and outstanding activities that involve students in the realities of parenting.

- There are booklets of handouts and activities for **RETEACHING, EXTENSION,** and **ENRICHMENT.**

- Other components provide activities for teaching **DECISION- MAKING** and **COOPERATIVE LEARNING.**

- Glencoe also provides you with **REPRODUCIBLE LESSON PLANS** and a complete **TESTING PROGRAM.**

- A packet of **FULL-COLOR TRANSPARENCIES** completes the program.

PARENTING: REWARDS AND RESPONSIBILITIES

Student Edition	ISBN	0-02-676373-7
Teacher's Annotated Edition		0-02-676374-5
Student Workbook		0-02-676377-X
Teacher's Annotated Workbook*		0-02-676376-1
Teacher's Classroom Resources		0-02-676375-3
Teen Parenting*		0-02-676388-5
Practicing Parenting*		0-02-676389-3
Decision-Making Activities*		0-02-676387-7
Cooperative Learning Activities*		0-02-676383-4
Extension Activities*		0-02-676386-9
Enrichment Activities*		0-02-676385-0
Reteaching Activities*		0-02-676384-2
Testing Program*		0-02-676382-6
Reproducible Lesson Plans*		0-02-676381-8
Color Transparency Packet*		0-02-676378-8

*These components are included in the Teacher's Classroom Resources.

GLENCOE
Macmillan/McGraw-Hill

P.O. Box 503, Blacklick, Ohio 43004-0543
1-800-334-7344

Teacher's Manual

Parenting: Rewards and Responsibilities

Fourth Edition

Verna Hildebrand, Ph.D.
Professor of Family and Child Ecology
Michigan State University

GLENCOE
Macmillan/McGraw-Hill

New York, New York   Columbus, Ohio   Mission Hills, California   Peoria, Illinois

Contributors:

Sue Couch

Julie Massey

Send all inquiries to:
GLENCOE DIVISION
Macmillan/McGraw-Hill
3008 W. Willow Knolls Drive
Peoria, Illinois 61614-1083

ISBN 0-02-676373-7 (Student Edition)
ISBN 0-02-676374-5 (Teacher's Annotated Edition)

Printed in the United States of America

1 2 3 4 5 6 7 8 9 RRW 99 98 97 96 95 94 93

Teaching with *Parenting: Rewards and Responsibilities*

Welcome to the fourth edition of *Parenting: Rewards and Responsibilities.* The program has been updated, rewritten, and redesigned to include more emphasis on parenting and families. Students will learn about all three areas of parenting: caring for children, nurturing children, and guiding children. They will also develop skills for making decisions and thinking critically which they can apply to all areas of their lives.

How has *Parenting: Rewards and Responsibilities* changed? You will find:

- Updated and rewritten text that contains more emphasis on parenting and families, including teenage parenthood.

- High-interest features in every chapter on "Self-Esteem," "Health and Safety," and "Around the World."

- Short case studies, "Decisions, Decisions," in every chapter that promote decision making and problem solving.

- Special "Tips and Topics" features in every unit that illustrate practical information.

- Large, colorful photographs that capture student interest.

- End-of-chapter reviews that contain a summary, review questions, activities, and questions that require higher-level thinking skills.

- New support materials for both teachers and students.

In this fourth edition, the basic goals of *Parenting: Rewards and Responsibilities* are carried out in components that are completely integrated for easy use by students and teachers. The program includes:

- **Student text.** Up-to-date content focuses on nurturing and guiding children, as well as caring for children. New chapters include the role of families, teenage parenthood, parenting skills, adjusting to parenthood, encouraging children, guiding behavior, handling common problems, and strengthening families. The student text has an appealing design, full-color illustrations, and special features in every chapter.

- **Teacher's Annotated Edition.** The special teacher's edition contains annotations at the bottom of each page of the student text. The Teacher's Manual contains teaching strategies and is bound into the front of the teacher's edition.

- **Teacher's Classroom Resources.** This resource box contains individual booklets that provide a wide variety of student activities.

- **Student Workbook.** Each chapter has a study guide and two or more student activities.

❖❖ *The Student Text*

The organization of the student text progresses from a discussion of the difference between parenting and parenthood through the skills needed to care for, nurture, and guide children from infancy through adolescence. The text is very discussion oriented, encouraging students to think about situations, make decisions, and solve problems. It also suggests a wide range of activities that can be done individually or in groups.

Parenting: Rewards and Responsibilities is for students of today who are planning for tomorrow. It is for those interested in being parents, those interested in teaching or caring for young children, and those interested in other child-related careers. The emphasis is on being a caregiver in any of these roles.

Units

The text is divided into six units, each focusing on a different aspect of parenting. Thirty chapters combine to make these units.

Unit 1: Parenting Decisions

Students first take a look at the many decisions involved in parenting. They discuss the difference between parenting and parenthood, as well as the role of a caregiver. They learn about different types of parenthood and the role of the family, including its influence and functions. Then they consider the various rewards and responsibilities of parenthood and how they can decide when they might be ready for parenthood. A separate chapter focuses on the special challenges of teenage pregnancy and parenthood. The unit concludes with an overview of parenting skills.

Unit 2: *Becoming a Parent*

This unit contains important information about reproduction and pregnancy, including updated medical and health concerns. Students learn about genetic counseling, prenatal care, prenatal development, and the stages of labor and delivery. They also discuss ways to maintain physical and emotional health throughout pregnancy and in the months following birth. They learn how both the mother-to-be and father-to-be can be involved in preparing for the baby's arrival and how they can help each other adjust to their new roles as parents.

Unit 3: *A New Baby*

This unit focuses on the growth and development of the infant and how caregivers can meet the infant's needs. Students learn about the different areas of growth and development—physical, emotional, social, and cognitive—and what parents and other caregivers can do to encourage each area of development. A separate chapter looks at special concerns related to health and safety, and then these concerns are woven in throughout the text.

Unit 4: *Nurturing Children*

This unit includes the essentials of growth and development—from early childhood through adolescence. A separate chapter is devoted to each area of development: physical, emotional, social, and cognitive. Students learn not only about the various stages of development but, even more important, how parents and other caregivers can nurture, encourage, and stimulate children's growth in each area. A separate chapter on the value of play discusses how play activities can enhance each area of development. The unit also has a separate chapter on children with special needs. Students learn how parents, teachers, and other caregivers can meet the needs of children with physical, mental, or emotional disabilities; children with learning problems; and gifted children.

Unit 5: *Guiding Children*

This unit focuses on ways to encourage and guide children' s behavior. Students learn about moral development, communication skills, and guidance techniques. They discuss important topics such as values, responsibility, and sexuality. They learn how to handle common behavior problems and why punishment and child abuse are not appropriate guidance techniques. They under-

stand how parenting is much more than just meeting the physical needs of children.

Unit 6: *Family Resources*

This unit examines ways that families can meet challenges, solve problems, select resources, and strengthen their own family life. Students learn about family challenges, from balancing work and parenting to changes in family life-style and structure. Topics such as moving, unemployment, divorce, remarriage, adoption, illness, and death are covered. Two chapters are devoted to selecting child care and selecting early childhood education programs. Students learn about the advantages and disadvantages of various options and ways that parents can evaluate child care and early childhood education programs. The final chapter focuses on careers in child care and other occupations. Students have been brought full-circle in their exploration of the parenting role, as well as the role children might someday play in their own lives. Hopefully, they have gained a greater understanding of children, parents, caregivers, and themselves.

Chapters

This edition of *Parenting: Rewards and Responsibilities* is divided into thirty chapters. Each deals with one major concept or theme, which makes the material flexible for lesson planning. Each chapter includes:

- **Objectives.** To help you define goals for the course, clearly stated behavior objectives begin each chapter. The review questions, activities, tests, and supplemental materials are written to support these objectives.

- **Vocabulary.** The new and significant terms used in the chapter are listed in the order introduced. When each term is first used in the chapter, it appears in boldface type, followed by the definition. Phonetic pronunciation guides are given for difficult words. The terms are also listed and defined in the Glossary.

- **Writing style.** Students will enjoy reading the chapters and features. The information is practical, real-life, anecdotal, and upbeat. The frequent use of headings and lists help maintain interest and readability.

- **Chapter Review.** At the end of each chapter, a full page is devoted to review. This comprehensive section includes:

  Summary—Bulleted list of key concepts in the chapter.

Questions—Objective questions that check students' recall of major concepts in the chapter.

Activities—Independent and group activities that enable students to apply what they have learned. Many of the activities reinforce reading, writing, math, and science skills. Others involve observation and parenting skills.

Think About—Special parenting questions that promote higher-level thinking skills.

Special Features

To support the chapter components, the fourth edition of *Parenting: Rewards and Responsibilities* incorporates special features which promote interest and reinforce learning. These features include:

- **Self-Esteem.** These are specific ways that parents and other caregivers can foster children's self-esteem, as well as their own self-esteem.

- **Decisions, Decisions.** These short case studies present a parenting situation in which a person has to make a decision. These features provide additional opportunities for students to practice problem solving and decision making.

- **Health and Safety.** High-interest topics such as lead poisoning, Rh factor, crib safety, failure to thrive syndrome, and neonatal intensive care extend the health and safety information throughout the text.

- **Around the World.** Children and families from around the world give an international and multicultural approach to parenting topics. Students learn about the similarities and differences in traditions, customs, toys, first words, and many other topics.

- **Tips and Topics.** Special two-page and four-page features illustrate key concepts in the text, such as prenatal development, communication skills, childproofing a home, and child-related careers.

❖ *Teacher's Annotated Edition*

The Teacher's Annotated Edition (TAE) of the *Parenting: Rewards and Responsibilities* text contains the Teacher's Manual, which provides information about the program and all its components. Included in the manual is a Scope and Sequence Chart. It shows how major themes are woven throughout the text. You will find it useful for:

- Planning your course.
- Sequence courses.
- Emphasizing particular course themes.
- Correlating *Parenting: Rewards and Responsibilities* to your curriculum.

The TAE also includes annotations for teacher use printed at the bottom of each text page. They help make the student material more interesting, relevant, and useful. Each annotation has a label to identify its purpose and how you might best use the information on the student page. They will perhaps be most useful as a springboard for your own creative ideas in guiding the work of your students.

The annotations are of six different types:

- **Chapter Opener.** To introduce the chapter, refer to these discussion questions that pertain to the scenario that begins each chapter. After students have read the scenario or you have read it together, use these questions to guide students into thinking about some of the points that will be covered in the chapter.

- **Discussion.** Some ideas for discussion are presented in question format.

- **Activity.** These are activities that can be done individually, in small groups, or as a class. Some may be accomplished in a short time. Others may require outside time and preparation.

- **Problem Solving.** These are questions or activities with a problem theme. Students are asked to evaluate the problem and find solutions.

- **More About.** Additional information is presented that extends chapter content.

- **Reference.** Other chapters and features are referenced within the text.

❖ *Teacher's Classroom Resources*

The *Parenting: Rewards and Responsibilities* Teacher's Classroom Resources (TCR) is a source of reference materials and reproducible masters for classroom use. The box contains individual booklets that provide a wide variety of activities:

- **Reteaching Activities.** These activities allow students who are having difficulty with mastering the major concepts of a lesson to review the concepts from a different perspective. Reteaching activities are provided for every chapter. Answers for the teacher are provided at the back of the booklet.

- **Enrichment Activities.** These activities allow students the opportunity to explore concepts further. There is one activity for each chapter. Answers for the teacher are provided at the back of the booklet.
- **Decision-Making Activities.** These activities give students an opportunity to practice the decision-making process as they consider a variety of hypothetical situations. An activity is provided for each chapter.
- **Cooperative Learning Activities.** These activities give students opportunities to work cooperatively in small groups. They also develop working relationship skills, such as how to listen, respond, agree, disagree, clarify, encourage, and evaluate.
- **Extension Activities.** These activities provide additional information about topics covered in the chapters, as well as related topics. The materials can also be used as handouts.
- **Testing Program.** Chapter tests and unit tests are provided for the program. Answers for the teacher are given at the back of the booklet.

- **Teen Parenting.** This special booklet includes information and activities that can be used in teen parenting programs. Suggestions for developing special teen parenting programs and activities are also included.
- **Practicing Parenting.** This booklet focuses on individual components of good parenting. Activities include exercises, puzzles, and observations. Each activity can stand alone or be used in conjunction with teacher-guided discussions.
- **Color Transparencies.** The transparency packet includes color transparencies plus teaching strategies for use with each transparency.
- **Student Workbook TAE.** A teacher's annotated edition of the student workbook is contained in the TCR box.

◆◆ *Student Workbook*

The student workbook contains a study guide and activities for each of the chapters. A Teacher's Annotated Edition of the student workbook, containing the answers, is found in the TCR box.

Effective Teaching

As an experienced teacher or a new teacher, you will already have ideas and plans for teaching with *Parenting: Rewards and Responsibilities.* Hopefully, many of the suggestions presented in the Teacher's Annotated Edition and the Teacher's Classroom Resources will help you develop content and strategies that will be motivating and effective in the classroom. Here are some additional suggestions for using the teaching materials.

◆◆ *Curriculum Applications*

The *Parenting: Rewards and Responsibilities* program can be used for both one-semester and full-year courses. The chapters provide flexibility in selecting the content that must be covered in the course. In addition, the wealth of support materials enables you to develop lesson plans that will best meet the individual needs of your students.

◆◆ *Teaching Students with Varying Ability Levels and Learning Styles*

Just as in any other course, students taking parenting will demonstrate wide differences in abilities and interests. Providing for individual differences is one of the more challenging tasks in teaching. While the task of adapting the course to individual needs probably will never be totally accomplished, the following suggestions will prove to be helpful.

- Because the content in *Parenting: Rewards and Responsibilities* is so varied, all students will find topics in which they have great interest. Be alert to such interest and capitalize on it by giving every student the opportunity to enter into the discussion, prepare activities, and participate in other ways.

- Vary your teaching methods. Not all students learn in the same way. Some learn readily through reading. Others learn best through problem solving, participating in discussions, listening to interesting speakers, observing parents and children, assembling projects, or completing workbook activities.

- End-of-chapter activities are varied in both type of activity and level of difficulty. Some activities might be assigned to small groups of students working together. Others could be assigned to individual students as extra credit.

- Reteaching and enrichment activities are located in the Lesson Plans for each chapter. These offer specific activities for both slow and fast learners.

- The TCR box contains reteaching and enrichment booklets that support the text content. These activities can be used to reinforce basic concepts or to provide enrichment information.

◆◆ *Teaching Critical Thinking Skills*

Preparing students to think critically requires direct instruction in particular skills. Bloom's Taxonomy of Cognitive Behavior serves as a basic organizational design that places cognitive learning into six major hierarchal classes:

- **Knowledge:** define, recognize, recall, identify, label, understand, examine, show, collect.

- **Comprehension:** translate, interpret, explain, describe, summarize, extrapolate.

- **Application:** apply, solve, experiment, show, predict.

- **Analysis:** connect, relate, differentiate, classify, arrange, check, group, distinguish, organize, categorize, detect, compare, infer.

- **Synthesis:** produce, propose, design, plan, combine, formulate, compose, hypothesize, construct.

- **Evaluation:** appraise, judge, criticize, decide.

Since these skills build on one another, students must learn lower level thinking skills before moving on to higher level thinking skills. The level of complexity (from knowledge to evaluation) is not equal to the level of difficulty. For example, labeling all the parts of the reproductive system may be difficult, but it remains a task at the lowest level of the taxonomy, knowledge.

All students at any age and any ability level can experience thinking at each of the levels of taxonomy. For example, students can be asked to evaluate which toys encourage different types of development and to give supporting reasons.

Parenting: Rewards and Responsibilities helps promote critical thinking skills. For example, the Chapter Review provides questions and activities at all levels. Some of the questions check knowledge and comprehension by requesting recall of information or the organization and selection of facts and ideas. Other questions require the application of facts and principles or ask the student to analyze a situation. The "Think About" questions focus on higher level thinking skills. Students are asked to apply knowledge to develop opinions, judgements, and decisions.

❖ Teaching Decision-Making Skills

Students need to learn how to make wise decisions. *Parenting: Rewards and Responsibilities* uses the five-step decision-making process:

1. **Define the problem.** This sounds easy but it is the most important step. The situation may have different facets or subproblems that confuse the issue.
2. **Identify alternatives.** This is often difficult for adolescents who frequently look at situations from an either/or reference. They do not see that they have other options. When practicing in a classroom, have student brainstorm all possible alternatives. Asking questions such as "What else might you do?" helps them think of other choices.
3. **Analyze the possible consequences.** This step requires seeking additional information. Ask the question "What would happen if...?" Remind students that consequences may be either positive or negative. Encourage students to apply their personal values and goals to each alternative.
4. **Make the decision.** The person who has gone through the process must now accept responsibility for his or her decision. Excuses mean that the person did not do a thorough job at the first three steps.
5. **Evaluate the results.** This is an important step that should not be skipped. Helping adolescents learn from mistakes is important if they are to develop the skill of examining available choices.

A number of skills are necessary in making decisions:

- the ability to identify options,
- the ability to identify priorities,
- the ability to identify and evaluate consequences,
- the ability to make a choice and act on it.

Adolescents are moving from concrete thinking to abstract thinking ability. This is a learned task. In other words, the ability to think abstractly does not just happen. Within any given class, you will have students at various levels of thinking ability. Some will not be able to comprehend and apply the entire process described above. However, by practicing with a variety of examples, they can learn the process and develop the skill.

Within the classroom, students can practice their decision-making skills with real-life situations. These help students develop the ability to examine options and evaluate consequences in an unemotional, unpressured setting. Later, when students are faced with decisions, they are more likely to use this process if they have such practice.

Goals and values are also part of the decision-making process. Students who have set realistic short- and long-term goals can weigh their choices for any given situation with reference to those goals. Having goals also gives people some sense of personal control over their own lives. Values also form a basis for making decisions. When students know what is important to them, they are better able to make wise decisions based on their values.

❖ Reinforcing Basic Skills

Basic skills represent a critical area of learning that can be addressed in all areas of education. Because the home economics curriculum is very discussion- and activity-oriented, it is particularly suited for practicing the basic skills in reading, writing, math, and science.

Here are some additional strategies for incorporating basic skills instruction into the home economics classroom:

Reading

- Students get more out of a reading assignment when the lesson is preceded with background information and followed with discussion.

- Reading comprehension can be divided into three levels: literal, inferential, and applicative. Literal comprehension involves the understanding of what the author said and meant. Inferential comprehension entails understanding what is implied or inferred. Applicative comprehension involves applying what is learned in the reading to situations outside the text.
- A key to promoting independent reading is to make books and other resources easily available in a classroom library.

Writing

- The most effective way to develop writing skills is to present writing assignments as a process of brainstorming, composing, revising, and editing.
- Students learn to write well through frequent practice. A well-structured assignment has a meaningful topic and a clear sense of purpose.
- Good writing assignments should be an extension of class reading, discussion, and activities—not isolated exercises.

Mathematics

- Students learn mathematics more effectively when they use real physical objects or situations as aids in their lessons.
- Students need to learn the skill of estimating answers. When students can make good estimates, it shows they understand the math problem. This skill leads them to reject unreasonable answers and is very practical in everyday situations.

Science

- Students learn science best when they are able to witness demonstrations and conduct experiments.
- Reading about scientific principles is frequently not enough for understanding. Causes and effects are not always obvious, and it may take an experiment to dramatize the principles.
- Scientific explanations sometimes conflict with the way students may suppose that things happen. To clear up misconceptions, students need the chance to predict the results of an experiment. The teacher can then explain why the original intuitive hypothesis was faulty. In this way experiments help students use the scientific method to distinguish facts from opinions and misconceptions.

◆◆ *Using Cooperative Learning Strategies*

Cooperative learning activities require students to work together as they pursue a common goal. Such classroom learning activities in which cooperation replaces competitiveness help students learn effective interpersonal communication skills.

In their efforts to arrive at group goals or objectives, students are given practice in such social skills as listening critically, offering and accepting constructive feedback, consensus building, and conflict resolution. Such skills practiced in the classroom have life-long value in family, work, and community settings.

◆◆ *Teaching Students from Various Cultural and Ethnic Backgrounds*

Parenting, child development, and child care information is influenced by culture, ethnicity, and socioeconomic background. It is important that teachers be sensitive to these differences in students' backgrounds.

Parents, grandparents, and other relatives may have passed on certain parenting and child-rearing beliefs. It is important not to say a student's parents are wrong, but rather reinforce what we presently know as factual parenting, child development, and child care information. Some old wives' tales were based on inadequate information. As scientists learned more about growth and development, information became more accurate. If students are willing to share practices and beliefs unique to their culture, it may help other students better understand the culture and cultural influence on children, parents, and families.

Scope and Sequence	**Chapter 1** **What Is Parenting?**	**Chapter 2** **Role of the Family**	**Chapter 3** **Rewards and Responsibilities**
Communication		• maintaining kinship • the media	• being a nurturer • being a teacher
Cultures	• cultural differences	• changing family • cultural background	• special celebrations
Decision-Making	• features	• functions of the family • features	• features
Families	• types of parenthood	• types of families • family life cycle • changing characteristics • changing roles • functions • influences on the family	• joys of parenting • myths about children
Growth and Development	• theories • ages and stages		• importance of early years
Guidance	• guidance needs	• providing guidance	• being a teacher • being a role model
Health and Safety	• wellness	• fitness	• illness
Nurturing	• nurturing needs	• providing emotional support	• being a nurturer
Parenting Skills	• parenting defined • importance of parenting	• responsibilities of parents • changing roles	• importance of parenting • rewards and responsibilities • meeting financial costs • myths about parenting • realities
Physical Care	• physical needs	• providing care	• being a caregiver
Relationships	• caregiver • types of parenthood	• types of families • family life cycle • changing roles • influences on the family • community and society	• role models
Self-Esteem	• self-concept • self-esteem • feature	• feature	• feature
Sources of Help		• family members	

	Chapter 4 Personal Readiness	Chapter 5 Teenage Parenthood	Chapter 6 Parenting Skills
Communication	• making decisions	• sexual activity	• parenting styles • effective parenting skills
Cultures	• changing roles of fathers	• adolescent fertility	• influence on parenting styles • birth announcements
Decision-Making	• to have or not to have children • readiness for parenthood • decision-making skills • setting goals • features	• sexual activity • abstinence • parenthood options • challenges of teen parenthood • features	• parenting styles • features
Families	• family life-style • personal experiences	• marriage • single parenthood • adoption	• changing parenting styles
Growth and Development	• maturity	• health risks of pregnancy	• process of growth and development • basic human needs
Guidance			• parenting styles
Health and Safety	• physical health • mental health • emotional health	• teenage pregnancy • health risks of pregnancy	• safety needs • pets
Nurturing	• expression of love	• emotional concerns	• esteem needs
Parenting Skills	• substitute parenting	• lack of skills	• needs and parenting skills • parenting styles • effective parenting skills • ineffective parenting practices
Physical Care			• physiological needs
Relationships	• other people's expectations • stability of relationship • social considerations	• teenage relationships • role of teenage fathers	• social needs
Self-Esteem	• emotional health • feature	• teenagers • feature	• esteem needs • positive self-concept • feature
Sources of Help		• parents and family • school nurse and counselor • doctor and clinic • clergy and religious organizations • social worker	• sources of parenting information

	<u>Chapter 7</u> **Planning a Family**	<u>Chapter 8</u> **Pregnancy**	<u>Chapter 9</u> **Prenatal Care**
Communication	• counseling	• with doctor	
Cultures	• population explosion	• midwives	• infant mortality rates
Decision-Making	• planning for parenthood • contraceptives • choosing medical care • features	• discomforts during pregnancy • prenatal tests • features	• choosing healthy foods • avoiding harmful substances • features
Families			
Growth and Development	• human reproduction • genetic birth defects	• prenatal development • principles of development • physical changes during pregnancy • miscarriage	• dangers to fetus
Guidance			
Health and Safety	• reproduction • genetic birth defects • contraception • medically assisted pregnancies • medical specialists • medical costs	• signs of pregnancy • pregnancy tests • characteristics of pregnancy • common discomforts • medical care • Rh factor • high-risk pregnancies • prenatal tests • warning signals	• healthy eating • weight gain and loss • health concerns • exercise • dangers to fetus • pregnancy complications
Nurturing		• emotional support	• emotions during pregnancy
Parenting Skills			
Physical Care	• medical care	• medical care during pregnancy	• prenatal care
Relationships			• sexually transmitted diseases
Self-Esteem	• feature	• feature	• feature
Sources of Help	• genetic counseling • help for infertility	• medical specialists	• Food Guide Pyramid • medical specialists

	Chapter 10 Preparing for Baby's Arrival	**Chapter 11** Birth	**Chapter 12** Adjusting to Parenthood
Communication	• sharing preparations • preparing siblings for baby		• conflicting feelings of new parents
Cultures	• parental leave	• cesarean section	• sleeping arrangements
Decision-Making	• location of birth • choosing a pediatrician • deciding how to feed baby • choosing baby items • features	• features	• sharing responsibilities • managing stress • getting support • features
Families	• parental leaves • child care options	• birthing rooms • bonding	• spending time together
Growth and Development		• premature infants	
Guidance			
Health and Safety	• prepared childbirth training • crib safety	• stages of labor • medication during labor • types of delivery • care of neonate • neonatal intensive care • circumcision	• nutrition • rest and sleep • exercise • physical and emotional adjustments • managing stress
Nurturing		• bonding	• emotional adjustments
Parenting Skills			• new routines • coping strategies
Physical Care	• breast-feeding vs bottle-feeding • obtaining baby items	• care of neonate	• medical checkups
Relationships	• childbirth coach • siblings	• support during labor	• life-style changes • new roles • siblings • relatives • sharing responsibilities
Self-Esteem	• feature	• feature	• feature
Sources of Help	• childbirth courses • support for breast-feeding	• medical specialists	• support for new parents

	Chapter 13 Understanding Infants	Chapter 14 Parenting Infants	Chapter 15 Health and Safety
Communication	• learning to communicate • language development	• language development	
Cultures	• first words	• swaddling	• childhood diseases
Decision-Making	• features	• responding to needs • planning nutritious meals	• calling the doctor • handling emergencies • features
Families	• role in social development		
Growth and Development	• physical growth • reflexes • motor skills • emotional/social development • cognitive development	• emotions • social development • language development	
Guidance		• self-feeding	
Health and Safety	• failure to thrive	• nutrition • cleanliness • safety in bath	• wellness • checkups • immunizations • common illnesses • childproofing rooms • lead poisoning • preventing accidents • first aid
Nurturing	• emotional/social development • developing sense of trust	• encouraging development	
Parenting Skills	• goals for emotional/social development • encouraging language development	• encouraging motor skills • dealing with emotions • encouraging social development • encouraging cognitive development	• handling illnesses • preventing accidents
Physical Care	• teething	• feeding • cleanliness • clothing • rest and sleep	• treating illnesses • first aid
Relationships	• temperament • social development		
Self-Esteem	• developing positive self-esteem • feature	• feature	• feature
Sources of Help			• doctors and clinics

	Chapter 16 Physical Development	Chapter 17 Emotional Development	Chapter 18 Social Development
Communication		• influencing self-esteem • encouraging independence	• interacting with others
Cultures	• breakfast	• birthday celebrations	• rites of passage
Decision-Making	• features	• handling emotional behavior • setting limits • features	• features
Families		• influence on personality	• roles of family members • birth order • parents and siblings • relatives
Growth and Development	• physical growth • motor skill development	• emotional development • personality development	• social development • awareness of self and others
Guidance	• self-feeding • toilet training	• handling emotional behavior • encouraging independence • setting limits	• socialization process • sharing • cooperation and competition • stereotypes and prejudice
Health and Safety	• nutrition • hygiene • health care • chicken pox • hospitalization	• stress • depression and suicide	• contagious infections
Nurturing		• showing affection • influencing self-esteem • offering encouragement • providing reassurance	• self awareness
Parenting Skills	• influencing skill development • providing nutritious meals • selecting clothing • teaching hygiene • providing health care	• handling emotional behavior • influencing self-esteem • encouraging independence • managing stress	• teaching socialization • teaching sharing and cooperation
Physical Care	• food needs • clothing needs • toilet training • bathing • care of teeth • illness		
Relationships		• influence on personality	• importance of relationships • socialization process • family members • playmates and friends
Self-Esteem	• feature	• self-concept and self-esteem • influencing self-esteem • feature	• self-awareness • stereotypes and prejudice • feature
Sources of Help	• doctors and clinics		

	Chapter 19 Cognitive Development	Chapter 20 Value of Play	Chapter 21 Children with Special Needs
Communication	• language development • speech problems • bilingual	• dramatic play • art and music activities	• positive attitude • computer technology
Cultures	• nonverbal communication	• games	• labeling disabilities
Decision-Making	• reasoning and problem solving • features	• choosing toys • features	• locating resources
Families			• impact of child with a disability
Growth and Development	• brain development • cognitive development • concept development • language development	• physical-motor development • emotional-social development • cognitive development	• types of disabilities
Guidance	• reading books • supervising television		• promoting independence • educating children with special needs
Health and Safety	• speech problems	• protection from sun	• types of disabilities • animal companions
Nurturing	• encouraging curiosity and imagination	• encouraging exploration and creativity	• identifying children's strengths
Parenting Skills	• stimulating cognitive development • providing a stimulating environment	• providing appropriate toys and activities • participating in play	• dealing with emotions • identifying children's strengths • promoting independence
Physical Care			• living space adaptations • clothing adaptations
Relationships		• imaginary playmates	• family • classmates
Self-Esteem	• feature	• feature	• promoting self-esteem • feature
Sources of Help	• using computers		• friends and relatives • support groups • national organizations • community services • computer technology

	Chapter 22 Encouraging Children	Chapter 23 Moral Development	Chapter 24 Guiding Behavior
Communication	• communication skills • listening skills • communicating with children	• discussing values • discussing sexuality	• verbal guidance
Cultures	• names	• care of children	• changing expectations
Decision-Making	• features	• stages for moral decisions • values and decisions • features	• guidance techniques • features
Families		• influence on values	
Growth and Development		• moral development • self-responsibility • sexuality	• self-control
Guidance	• providing guidance • being a role model	• values • developing responsibility	• offering choices • setting limits • indirect guidance • direct guidance • physical guidance • verbal guidance • affective guidance
Health and Safety	• mental health	• home alone	• childhood obesity
Nurturing	• providing encouragement • giving praise • acknowledging feelings • importance of love	• encouraging responsibility	• affective guidance
Parenting Skills	• communication skills • showing love	• encouraging moral development	• guidance techniques
Physical Care			• preventing abuse
Relationships		• stages of moral development • influence on values • coworkers	
Self-Esteem	• developing self-esteem • praising efforts and accomplishments • handling mistakes and failures • feature	• feature	• effect of harsh discipline • effect of child abuse • feature
Sources of Help			• child abuse prevention programs

	Chapter 25 Handling Common Problems	**Chapter 26** Strengthening Families	**Chapter 27** Family Challenges
Communication	• communicating with children	• verbal and nonverbal messages • listening skills • resolving conflicts	• helping children cope
Cultures	• infant massage	• Kwanzaa	• international adoption
Decision-Making	• choosing appropriate techniques • features	• resolving conflicts • finding resources	• investigating options
Families		• spending time together • showing respect and trust • expressing understanding and love • establishing traditions	• balancing work and parenting • changes in life-style • changes in family structure • family crises
Growth and Development	• emotional and social development • moral development		
Guidance	• guiding behavior • promoting honesty	• strengthening families	
Health and Safety	• teenage drinking	• crises hot lines	• codependency
Nurturing	• encouraging self-esteem	• showing respect and trust • expressing love and understanding	• helping children cope
Parenting Skills	• handling emotional problems • handling bedtime problems • handling dishonesty	• relationship skills • communication skills	• communication skills • coping skills
Physical Care	• bedwetting		
Relationships	• stranger anxiety • jealousy and sibling rivalry • aggression	• strengthening family relationships • personal support groups	• divorce • blended families • adoption
Self-Esteem	• encouraging self-esteem • feature	• respect and trust • positive communication	• feature
Sources of Help	• counseling	• educational services • youth groups and organizations • health services • human services • religious organizations • crises hot lines	• counseling • support groups • family programs

	Chapter 28 Child Care	**Chapter 29** Early Childhood Education	**Chapter 30** Careers
Communication	• communicating with parents	• showing interest	• writing a resume • interview skills
Cultures	• child care on a kibbutz	• preschools in other countries	• education in other countries
Decision-Making	• hiring a caregiver • evaluating child care services • features	• choosing preschool program • avoiding overscheduling • features	• identifying interests and talents • finding job openings • applying for a job • choosing a job
Families	• need for child care	• parent involvement	
Growth and Development		• learning activities	
Guidance	• philosophy of caregivers	• types of preschool programs • types of activities	• sources of advice and help
Health and Safety	• health and safety standards	• safe play • health and safety standards	• good health
Nurturing	• attention shown by caregivers • activities offered by child care • dealing with separation	• enrichment activities • showing interest • easing transitions	
Parenting Skills	• selecting child care	• parental interest and involvement	• skills needed in workplace
Physical Care	• care provided by child care	• physical activities • safety	
Relationships	• between parent and caregiver	• understanding others • participating with others	• networking for a job • getting along with others
Self-Esteem	• feature	• caring for oneself • feature	• importance of self-esteem • feature
Sources of Help	• NAEYC	• community programs	• personal networking • classified ads • placement services • employment agencies

What Is Parenting?

◆◆ *Introducing the Lesson*

Objectives
This chapter will help you to:
- Discuss the importance of parenting.
- List and describe various types of parenthood.
- Explain how one can learn about children from theories and observations.
- Summarize the focus of this course.

Motivators
1. Ask students to describe the positive feelings, thoughts, and images brought to mind by the word *parent*. Have students write these down on a sheet of paper. Next, ask the students to describe the negative thoughts, feelings, and images brought to mind by the word *parent*. Have students write these down as well. Divide the class into groups to share their lists. Have each group share a collection of thoughts, feelings, and images with the class. Compile a master list on the chalkboard. Use the list as a springboard for introducing the unit.
2. Write the words, *parent* and *parenting* on the chalkboard. Ask the class to explain the difference between the words. Next put the words *parent* and *caregiver* on the chalkboard. Have the class explain the difference between these words. Write the class definitions on newsprint and display them in the classroom for reference later in the chapter. Use this activity to introduce the chapter.

◆◆ *Teaching the Lesson*

Learning Activities
1. Introduce the class to the three basic parenting skills described in the text (providing physical care, nurturing, and giving guidance). Provide three "graffiti" sheets, each labeled with one parenting skill, and have students consider what each basic parenting skill involves. Give students markers to write their ideas on the graffiti sheets. After they have finished writing, discuss the students' ideas. Compare their ideas with the information in the text. Why are these skills considered essential? Do all people

automatically acquire these skills when they become parents? What can be done to help people learn parenting skills? (communication, critical thinking)
2. Lead a brainstorming session on the various ways a person could become a parent. List student's ideas on the chalkboard. Discuss the list, using descriptions from the text. Which form of parenthood do students feel would be especially difficult? What would cause the difficulty? Have students ever considered becoming a parent in any way other than the biological route? Under what circumstances would students consider other forms of parenthood? (critical thinking)
3. Introduce students to the stages of development identified by theorists (infant, toddler, preschool, school-age, adolescent). Provide magazines for the students to use to illustrate each stage of development. Discuss the pictures they selected. What led students to identify the child pictured as being at a particular stage? What are the common characteristics of children in each stage? Next, divide the class into groups and assign each group one stage of development. Instruct each group to use the magazine pictures to create a poster collage of their assigned stage. Display the posters in the classroom (cooperative group work, critical thinking)
4. Explain to the class that much of our current knowledge and understanding of children was acquired through observation of children. Ask the class to list the kinds of information that one can gather through observing children. Compile the students' ideas in a master list on the chalkboard. Compare the students' ideas with the information on observation in the text. Note the difference between the subjective and objective observation descriptions provided in the text. (reading)

Reteaching Activities
1. Invite a foster parent to speak to the class about his or her experiences. Prepare students for the speaker by having them write questions about foster parenting. Ask the speaker to address the following: How many children has the fos-

ter parent cared for? How did this person become involved in foster parenting? What type of assistance does he or she receive as a foster parent? Have students write thank-you notes to the speaker following the visit. (communication, writing)

2. Have students bring in photographs of themselves at each developmental stage outlined in the text. Allow students to share their pictures with class members. Create a class bulletin board display of the photographs.

Enrichment Activities

1. Have students write for information from an adoption agency. They might request pamphlets, information for teen parents, or videos to borrow. Have students write thank-you notes to the agency after the requested information is received. (writing)
2. Arrange for students to observe children who are playing outdoors. Have students select one child to watch and keep a record of everything that the child does and says. After the observation experience, have students summarize what they learned about the child in a written report. Share reflections as a class. Was it difficult to observe the child? (science, writing)

3. Have students find out more about one of the theorists mentioned in the text. After completing their research, students are to write a brief paper about the theorist. Provide time in class for students to read their reports. (reading, writing, communication)

❖ Completing the Lesson

Review

1. Have students define the vocabulary words from the chapter in complete, original sentences.
2. Allow students to work in pairs to develop a crossword puzzle and puzzle key using the vocabulary words and other key concepts from the chapter. Reproduce the puzzles and have students select one done by another pair to complete.

Evaluation

1. Have students answer the questions in the Think About section at the end of the chapter. Go over the questions and answers as a class.
2. Have students use the chapter objectives as an outline to write a three-paragraph summary of the chapter. Allow students to use the textbook if needed.

❖ Answers to Chapter 1 Review Questions

1. Parenting means providing care, support, and love for a child in order to meet the child's needs. Parenthood means to be a father or mother. Many people besides parents use parenting skills.
2. Three skills involved in parenting are providing physical care, nurturing, and giving guidance.
3. Nurturing involves giving children attention, love, and a sense of security.
4. Self-concept is the image of oneself. Self-esteem is one's opinion, belief, or judgement about one's worthiness as a person. Self-esteem involves feelings.
5. A biological parent is one of the two people who conceive a child. An adop-

tive parent legally becomes the parent of a child and raises the child as his or her own. A stepparent is married to a parent who has a child from an earlier relationship. A foster parent provides care and a home for a child in times of emergency.
6. By understanding human development, caregivers know what to expect of a child at various ages. This enables them to use appropriate parenting skills and makes them feel more secure.
7. Developmental theory is a combination of many theories; no one theory explains all aspects of a child's development and behavior.

8. Age categories are: infant, toddler, preschool, school-age, adolescent.
9. (1) Choose only one or two children to observe. (2) Pretend you are only looking on. (3) Describe objectively what you observe. (4) Keep all information confidential.
10. You can expect to learn about children's growth and development, responsibilities of parenthood, and information and skills needed by caregivers. You also will learn more about yourself, the role children may have in your future, and child-related career opportunities.

Chapter **2**
Lesson Plan

Role of the Family

◆◆ *Introducing the Lesson*

Objectives
This chapter will help you to:
- Describe various types of family structures.
- Explain how families have changed in comparison to families in previous generations.
- List various functions of families.
- Discuss the many influences on today's families.

Motivators
1. Have students draw stick-figure pictures of their immediate family and share their "family portraits" with their classmates. Collect the pictures and save them for use in another activity.
2. Have students define the word *family*. Write their definitions on the chalkboard. Are there other ways of defining a family? Compare students' definitions with the definition given in the text.

◆◆ *Teaching the Lesson*

Learning Activities
1. List the different types of families on the chalkboard (nuclear family, single-parent family, blended family, extended family, cooperative family, nonchild family). Have students write the types of families on a piece of paper and define them in their own words. As a class, list definitions for each type of family on the chalkboard. Compare the students' definitions to the descriptions of the various types of families presented in the text. (critical thinking, reading)
2. Redistribute students' "family portraits" (see motivator 1). Have students write a description of their family type according to the textbook definitions. Be sure to have students explain why they labeled their family in the way they did. Have students share information about their family with the class. (writing, communication)
3. Invite the members of an extended family to speak to the class. Ask the family to talk to the class about the advantages as well as the disadvantages of living in an extended family. Have students write thank-you notes to the family after the visit. (writing)
4. Use a visual aid to describe what is meant by the family life cycle. Ask students to identify the stage that their own family is currently experiencing. Have students draw their family life cycle, beginning with their grandparents if necessary for a complete cycle. Display the drawings in the classroom.
5. Divide the class into groups and assign each group one of the functions of the family described in the text (to provide emotional support, economic support, child care and guidance, housekeeping, kinship, and recreation). Have the groups study the text discussion of each of the functions. Appoint spokespersons for the groups and have them teach the class about their group's particular function of the family. Do members of the class feel that there are other functions of the family? If so, what are they? (cooperative group work)
6. Have students consider the six functions of the family described in the text. Ask students to think about their own family and how the functions are reflected in their family life. Have students rank the functions (1 being the most important, 6 being the least important) in order of importance to their own family members. Instruct students to survey their parents concerning the ranking of the functions. Would the parents rank the functions in the same order? Discuss the results of the survey as a class. What are the differences in perceived importance of the functions? (critical thinking)
7. Have students brainstorm influences on family life today. List students' suggestions on the chalkboard. Have students compare this list to the text information about influences of family life today.

Reteaching Activities
1. Read the story of Cinderella to the class. Conduct a class discussion about the way the stepmother is portrayed in the fairy tale. Are stepmothers viewed in a similar way in today's society? What causes relationships with stepparents to be difficult? What are the benefits

of maintaining a positive relationship with a stepparent? (critical thinking)

2. Provide art materials such as construction paper, markers, scissors, wire, and glue for students to use to create a mobile of their family structure. Encourage students to use colors and shapes to represent the members of their family in a meaningful way. Allow time for students to model and explain their mobile, including why they gave each family member a particular color and shape. Hang the mobiles in the classroom. (critical thinking)

3. Provide magazines for students' use, along with paper and scissors. Have students find pictures that they believe illustrate their family's life-style and make a collage of the pictures. Have students share and explain their collage to the class. Display the collages in the classroom. (communication)

Enrichment Activities

1. After discussing the family life cycle, read the book *I'll Love You Forever* to the class. Have students draw a life cycle diagram to illustrate the story. In addition, have students provide a written explanation of how the story illustrates the family life cycle. (writing)

2. Rent the movie *Mr. Mom* and show the video to the class to illustrate the changing roles of parents. Ask students to describe ways in which the video exaggerates role reversal and ways in which the movie points out ways that husbands and wives can share household tasks. (communication)

3. Videotape several segments from a current family-oriented television sitcom. Have students watch the video and analyze the basic messages about family life and the roles of family members found in the sitcom's story line. Are the messages positive ones? Does the television show reflect reality? (critical thinking)

❖ Completing the Lesson

Review

1. Have students define the vocabulary words from the chapter in original sentences.

2. Have students select a classmate to work with to design a word game based on vocabulary words and key concepts from the chapter. The pairs should write incomplete statements for clues (e.g., A _____family is one in which there are stepparents.) and provide a list of the key terms and concepts from which players choose the correct answer.

Evaluation

1. Have students answer the questions in the Think About section at the end of the chapter.

2. Have students use the chapter objectives as an outline to write a four-paragraph composition about the information and knowledge they gained from the chapter.

❖ Answers to Chapter 2 Review Questions

1. A nuclear family is composed of a mother, a father, and one or more biological or adopted children. A blended family consists of two parents, one or both of whom have children from a previous relationship.

2. Single parents do not have a partner to share the responsibilities of children and home. They may have financial problems and little free time for own interests. However, their children may help with household tasks and take on responsibilities at an earlier age.

3. An extended family is made up of all the immediate relatives of a family, such as grandparents, aunts, uncles, and cousins.

4. The six stages of the family life cycle are: beginning, expanding, developing, launching, middle years, retirement years.

5. Families are smaller and the largest percentage live in urban and suburban areas.

6. With more mothers employed outside the home, many parents share parenting responsibilities. Some fathers are the primary caregiver for the children.

7. The six functions of the family are: providing emotional support, providing economic support, providing child care and guidance, housekeeping, maintaining kinship, and providing recreation.

8. Television can provide information and entertainment for families. It can also reduce communication within families and expose children to violence, sex, and crime.

9. The community influences a family through the goods and services it provides and the various standards, regulations, and laws it requires residents to follow.

Rewards and Responsibilities

◆ *Introducing the Lesson*

Objectives

This chapter will help you to:

- Describe what it might be like to be a parent.
- Discuss the various rewards and myths of parenthood.
- List and explain the different responsibilities of being a parent.
- Discuss reasons why parents may have mixed feelings about parenthood.

Motivators

1. Use modeling clay to explain that parenting is much like sculpting a lump of clay. Explain that although babies are born with innate abilities and talents, parents will shape and influence their children's lives in many ways, sometimes without even realizing the influence they have on their children. Lead a class discussion on the magnitude of the responsibility parents have to their children in this respect.

2. Write the following statements on the chalkboard and have students complete them on paper:
   - When I am a parent, I will . . .
   - I like parents who . . .
   - One of the rewards of parenthood that would be great is . . .
   - Children need families who . . .
   - When I think about becoming a parent, I feel . . .

◆ *Teaching the Lesson*

Learning Activities

1. Lead the class in brainstorming rewards of parenthood. Have a student volunteer to record the ideas on the chalkboard. Then have students read about the rewards of parenthood described in the text. After students have read the section, have them make any necessary additions to the list on the chalkboard. (critical thinking, reading)

2. Divide the class into four groups to explore the myths about children outlined in the text.

Assign one myth to each group. Have each group find magazine pictures that illustrate or promote their assigned myth. Have the class create four posters to illustrate the myths about children. Display the posters in the classroom. Did any of the students previously believe any of the myths illustrated? Are there other myths related to children? (cooperative group work)

3. Lead the class in brainstorming responsibilities of parenthood. Ask for a student volunteer to record the ideas on the chalkboard. Then assign reading from the text about the responsibilities of parenthood. Have students make additions to the list on the chalkboard, if necessary, after they have read the text. (critical thinking, reading)

4. On separate sheets of newsprint, write the four main responsibilities of parents (being a caregiver, a nurturer, a teacher, a role model). Hang the sheets around the room and allow students to write their ideas about what each responsibility involves on the appropriate sheet. Discuss each role as a class, using the students' ideas as a basis for the discussion. Compare students' ideas to the text. (critical thinking, reading, communication)

5. Discuss the role of parent as teacher. How do "parent teachers" compare with school teachers? What are the similarities? What are the differences? Ask students to consider the ways their parents socialized them. Lead a class discussion about the process of socialization (e.g., learning manners, behavior guidelines, etc.). Would students handle the same situations differently? What behavior guidelines would students set for their children? (communication)

6. Have students suggest values that are important to them. List the values on the chalkboard. Tell students you are going to conduct an auction of the values and each student will be allowed to spend up to $500 on a set of values. Have students copy the list of values on a piece of paper and consider which ones they would like to purchase and the amount they are willing to spend for it. Conduct the auction, selling the values to the highest bidder. When students run out of money, they must drop out of the game. Continue until all the values are

sold. Ask students to consider the values they purchased. What information does this activity give students about themselves? Would students teach their children these values? Why or why not? (critical thinking)

7. Divide the males and females in the class into separate groups. Give the groups ten minutes to list the specific parenting tasks they would expect their mates to accomplish. Have the groups share their lists. Encourage discussion and debate on the expectations. (cooperative group work, communication)

Reteaching Activities

1. Allow students to work in groups to develop skits about the myths concerning children. Have each group present their skit for the class. (cooperative group work)

2. Have students describe what it might be like to be a parent for 24 hours. (writing)

Enrichment Activities

1. Have students interview their grandparents or other relatives or family friends about their parents as little children. Encourage students to find out something about their parents' favorite activities, their personalities, and at least one funny story about each parent. Provide time for students to share their information with the class. (communication)

2. Ask students to write an essay describing a parent's mixed feelings about parenthood. (writing)

◆◆ *Completing the Lesson*

Review

1. Divide the class into two teams for a review "tug of war." Assign one team the rewards of parenthood and the other group the responsibilities of parenthood. Encourage the teams to think of as many examples as possible to use in the game. Position the teams in two different parts of the room (the rope is optional). Each team must provide an example of a reward or responsibility during their turn. List the examples on newsprint or the chalkboard. For each example given, award a point to the team and allow them to move on step toward the other team's "territory." For each missed turn, deduct a point and make the team move one step backwards. The team with the most points and "territory" wins the game.

2. Lead a class discussion on each of the chapter objectives. After reviewing the responsibilities, rewards, and myths of parenthood, assign a summary paragraph on the reasons parents may have ambivalent feelings about parenthood.

Evaluation

1. Have students answer the questions in the Think About section at the end of the chapter.

2. Allow students to develop, write, and film a video for teenagers titled "This Is Your Life." The theme of the video should be what it might be like to be a parent and should incorporate the major points from the chapter. Once the video is complete, arrange a showing for the class.

◆◆ *Answers to Chapter 3 Review Questions*

1. Parents set the tone for family life and the environment in which children grow and develop. They provide love and security, safety and comfort, spiritual and moral guidance, and serve as role models.

2. A role model shows others how to talk, act, and behave through their own words, attitudes, actions, and behavior.

3. Most parents enjoy watching their child develop, learning from new experiences and adventures, participating in children's activities, experiencing new depths of emotions, and having a new purpose and meaning in life.

4. Common myths include: "Children are sweet and lovable;" they can also be stubborn, unhappy, angry, and messy.

"Children can strengthen a marriage;" they can also create new problems and conflicts. "Children provide companionship and love;" infants require more love than they give and soon grow up. "Children do not cost much money;" total cost of rearing a child to age 18 is tremendous.

5. Children learn by watching and listening to their parents every day. Parents also provide guidance, set rules, and encourage mental development.

6. Parents can be good role models by modeling the behavior they want their child to imitate.

7. Values are beliefs about what is right, worthwhile, or desirable.

8. Financial costs of children include: food, clothing, housing, transportation, health care, child care, education, recreation, toys. Extra costs may result from an illness or accident, medications, special counseling, or tutoring.

9. Guidance probably causes more mixed feelings about parenting because parents can love a child even when they do not like the child's behavior.

10. Parents do not know in advance whether parenthood will provide rewards or regrets. Most have both good and bad experiences and remain optimistic even in times of crisis. The challenges and rewards give meaning to life and provide opportunities to love and nurture children as they grow and develop.

Personal Readiness

◆◆ *Introducing the Lesson*

Objectives
This chapter will help you to:
- Discuss the reasons why people choose to have or not to have children.
- Explain how people can evaluate their personal readiness for parenthood.
- List and describe the five steps of the decision-making process.
- Answer questions about personal readiness for parenthood.

Motivators
1. Tape-record the sound of a clock ticking. Play the recording for the class and ask students to guess the source of the sound. Ask whether they have ever heard someone say, "Her biological clock is ticking"? Have the class explain the meaning of the saying. Is this necessarily a good reason for having children? Explain that this chapter covers personal readiness for parenthood.
2. Have students image that they have just learned they/their girlfriend is pregnant. Ask students to share the feelings they would have about the situation. Does any student feel ready to be a parent? What would help students feel ready to be a parent? Explain that the focus of this chapter is personal readiness for parenthood.

◆◆ *Teaching the Lesson*

Learning Activities
1. Lead a class discussion on what factors are important to consider before having children. When is a person ready to become a parent? Is there a certain "ideal" age for becoming a parent? How does a person know when he or she is ready to become a parent? Have any of the students ever known someone who had a baby but was not ready to become a parent? What behaviors led students to this conclusion? (communication, critical thinking)
2. Have the class brainstorm as many reasons as possible for wanting to become a parent. List the students' ideas on the chalkboard. Have

students read the text section titled "Why People Choose to Have Children." Compare the text discussion with the list of ideas given by students. Make additions to the list if necessary. Which of the reasons are good ones for becoming a parent? Which are poor reasons for becoming a parent? (communication)
3. Write the words *love* and *infatuation* on the chalkboard. Have students suggest definitions for each term. Write these definitions under each term. What are the key differences between love and infatuation? What might be the consequences of parenthood if the relationship between the parents was based on infatuation instead of love? How does one know when he or she is infatuated? What are the signs of genuine love? (critical thinking)
4. Divide students into small groups. Assign one characteristic of personal readiness for parenthood to each group. Have groups present skits or role plays about their specific characteristic. The presentations should include the advantages of possessing the characteristic as well as the disadvantages of not having the characteristic. (cooperative group work, communication)
5. List the five steps of the decision-making process on separate pieces of poster board. Lead a discussion of the decision-making process by having the class suggest examples relating to the decision to have children for each of the steps. Hang the posters around the room to indicate five decision-making stations. Divide the class into "couples." Have each couple role-play the decision to have children by walking through the five stations of the decision-making process and discussing various considerations and factors that would relate to their decision. You may want to make specific assignments regarding outcomes: immediate pregnancy, delayed pregnancy, no pregnancy. (cooperative group work, communication)

Reteaching Activities
1. Invite a panel of parents and nonparents to speak to the class. Have the parents talk to the students about their decision to have children. What factors did they consider before becom-

ing parents? Have the childless couples talk to the class about their decision not to have children. What factors influenced their decision? What have been the reactions of their parents and friends?

2. Have students list and describe the five steps of the decision-making process. (writing)

Enrichment Activities

1. Have the class survey several new parents concerning readiness for parenthood. How did a couple know they were ready to have a baby? What words of advice would the new parents offer high school students about parenthood? (communication)

2. Have students consider their goals for the next five to ten years. What are their career aspirations? What type of life-style do they plan? Have students write one paragraph describing these goals and a second paragraph describing when (if ever) becoming a parent fits in with their goals. What conclusions can students draw about their future plans and parenthood? (critical thinking, writing)

◆◆ *Completing the Lesson*

Review

1. Assign the questions in the text concerning readiness for parenthood for students' application of the chapter to their lives. Have students write a response to each question based on their own situation. Assure students of confidentiality.

2. Divide the class into two groups to debate the proposition that children are a necessary part of family life. Assign one group to support the proposition and the other group to reject it. Following the debate, have students write a summary paragraph about their own personal stance on the issue.

Evaluation

1. Have students answer the questions in the Think About section at the end of the chapter.

2. Have students write a three-paragraph composition using the chapter objectives as an outline. In their papers, students should discuss their understanding of each objective on the basis of the knowledge they gained from the chapter.

◆◆ *Answers to Chapter 4 Review Questions*

1. People have children because of life experiences, expression of love, desire for family life-style, other people's expectations, appeal of children, economic asset, curiosity.

2. Infatuation is an intense but usually short-term feeling of love for someone. It is usually based on appearance, personality, or ability. In contrast, true love is much deeper and longer lasting. It is based on mutual respect, admiration, and trust.

3. People choose not to have children because of long-term goals, freedom, personal experiences, fears.

4. A person's level of maturity reflects physical development, as well as the ability to act reasonably, responsibly, reliably, and independently.

5. Couples need time to adjust to each other before having to adjust to a third family member. They need to develop mutual respect and trust, be sure of their long-term commitment, and establish strong bonds with each other.

6. A person who has good physical health is well-nourished, not involved in harmful behaviors, and free of diseases. Good mental health means recognizing the realities of parenthood. Good emotional health involves high self-esteem and ability to control one's reactions to emotions.

7. Caring for a baby involves a great deal of time and effort, leaving little time for leisure. Parents must make arrangements to take the baby with them or leave the baby with someone else whenever they go out.

8. People who plan ahead for parenthood know how it will fit in with their career, financial, and life-style goals. Those who do not plan ahead may have to pursue goals more slowly or even give up on their goals, resulting in disappointment and resentment.

9. Five steps in the decision-making process are: (1) Define the problem. (2) Identify alternatives. (3) Analyze the possible consequences. (4) Make the decision. (5) Evaluate the results.

Teenage Parenthood

◆◆ *Introducing the Lesson*

Objectives
This chapter will help you to:
- Discuss the issues of sexuality, sexual activity, and abstinence.
- Describe the health risks and emotional concerns associated with teenage pregnancy.
- Compare the parenthood options of marriage, single parenthood, and adoption.
- Explain how teenagers can best meet the challenges of parenthood.

Motivators
1. Have a student volunteer read aloud the chapter-opening scenario about Katrina and Joe. Ask students to imagine themselves in the story as it is read. Ask students to describe how they would feel if they were Katrina or Joe. What would students do in a situation like the one described? How do students feel their parents would react to hearing the news?
2. Create a visual aid with statistics concerning teenage pregnancy and parenthood. Share the information with the class. Ask for students' reactions to the information. Explain that this chapter focuses on teenage parenting.

◆◆ *Teaching the Lesson*

Learning Activities
1. Write the word *sexuality* on the chalkboard. Have students write a definition of the word on a piece of paper. Ask for volunteers to share their definitions. Write these definitions on the chalkboard. (critical thinking)
2. Divide the class into small groups to brainstorm pressures on teens to have sex. List each group's ideas on the chalkboard. Compare students' ideas with the sources of pressure mentioned in the text, and make additions to the list if necessary. How can teens deal positively with the pressures to be sexually active? (cooperative group work, critical thinking)
3. Write the word *consequences* vertically on the chalkboard. Have students write the word on a piece of paper and fill in the possible results of teen-age sexual activity, using the letters as a framework. Have students share their responses. Compile a master list on the chalkboard. Use the activity as a springboard for discussion of the possible consequences of sexual activity. Classify the suggestions according to the area affected: physical, mental, emotional, social. Emphasize that many times the mental, emotional, and social aspects of sexuality are overlooked as areas of risk for sexual activity. (critical thinking)
4. Write the statistics about teen pregnancy provided in the chapter on individual slips of paper and put the slips in a basket. Have students draw the slips from the basket. Explain to the class that they are about to hear some statistics concerning teenage pregnancy. Have student volunteers take turns reading the information printed on their slip. After all the slips have been read, have students write their reactions to the information, including which statistic had the greatest impact on them. (reading, writing)
5. Invite a speaker from an adoption agency to speak to the class about the services available to teenage parents. Prepare the class for the visit by having students write questions for the speaker. Following the visit, have the class write thank-you notes to the speaker expressing their appreciation and listing at least one new piece of information gained from the visit. (communication, writing)

Reteaching Activities
1. Ask for volunteers to bring in examples of popular songs with lyrics that promote sexual activity. Ask volunteers to supply copies of the lyrics as well. Reproduce the lyrics for each student in the class. Play the songs for students and encourage them to listen for the messages promoted in the lyrics. Use the following questions to prompt student discussion of each song: Do the lyrics promote sexual activity? Do the lyrics encourage healthy relationships? Is the message based on love or infatuation? (critical thinking)
2. Provide magazines for students to use to find examples of advertisements that rely on sex

appeal to sell a product. Have students cut out examples of such ads. Have students write an analysis of the underlying message in each ad. Does the ad lead consumers to believe they will become more appealing to the opposite gender if they use the products? Why is sex used to sell products? (critical thinking, writing)

Enrichment Activities

1. Invite a teenage mother to speak to the class about her pregnancy. Prepare the class by having each student submit an anonymous question to be asked of the speaker. Have the speaker share information about her pregnancy and her plans for the future. Also ask her to share any words of advice concerning sexual relationships. Have students write thank-you notes to the speaker expressing support and appreciation for her openness. (communication, writing)

2. Make arrangements for the class to visit a high school parenting program for teenage parents. Have the students find out what services are available to teen parents. Is there on-site child care? What are the requirements for admission? Is there a waiting list for admission? What kinds of classes are offered?

◆ *Completing the Lesson*

Review

1. Have students define the vocabulary words from the chapter. In addition to definitions, have students write original sentences using the vocabulary words.

2. Have students write a letter to the teacher explaining what they have learned from this chapter about teenage sexuality and parenthood. Have the students highlight at least one point they will remember from the chapter.

Evaluation

1. Have students answer the questions in the Think About section at the end of the chapter.

2. Have students divide into small groups and write a hypothetical letter to an advice columnist concerning teen sexuality and teen pregnancy. Place each group's letter in a separate folder. Rotate the folders among the groups. Have each group read the letter in each folder and write a response. The response should be placed inside the folder and sent to the next group. At the end of the activity, have a spokesperson from each group read the original letter and the various written responses to it.

◆ *Answers to Chapter 5 Review Questions*

1. Three possible consequences of sexual activity are: pregnancy, contracting a sexually transmitted disease, loss of self-respect.

2. Some teenagers become pregnant because of inaccurate information about reproduction, unreliable means of contraception, desire for a baby's love and affection, desire for accomplishment or attention, being unaware of the responsibilities of parenthood.

3. Teenage pregnancy is high-risk because the health risks for both mother and child are greatly increased. Young teenage mothers are more likely to have complications during pregnancy; their babies are more likely to have a low birth weight or be born prematurely.

4. Both premature and low birth weight babies may have immature organs, breathing problems, difficulty regulating body systems, physical or mental disabilities, more illness.

5. Prenatal care is regular medical care and supervision prior to the baby's birth. It can help prevent health problems for both the mother and the baby.

6. Courts can take money from his paycheck or bank account if a father refuses to pay regular child support.

7. Advice and help can be obtained from parents and family, school nurse or counselor, doctor or clinic, clergy or religious organization, social worker or family planning counselor.

8. Parenthood options include: Marriage—enables partners to share parenting and household responsibilities, but adjustments and challenges of marriage plus parenthood often are overwhelming. Single parenthood—able to rear a child, but may have problems with finances, balancing responsibilities, getting a job, or continuing school. Adoption—provides a good start in life for the baby and enables teen to achieve future goals, but requires placing the baby with another family.

9. Teenage parents can reach long-term goals by rearranging their priorities, focusing on ways to still achieve goals, and seeking advice and help from others.

Parenting Skills

❖ *Introducing the Lesson*

Objectives
This chapter will help you to:
- Explain how parents and caregivers can benefit from information about growth and development, human needs, and parenting skills.
- Compare the three different types of parenting styles.
- Describe certain characteristics of a successful parent.
- Discuss poor parenting practices and their effect on children.

Motivators
1. Write the term *parenting skills* on the chalkboard. Have students copy the words on a piece of paper and identify behaviors or characteristics that could be considered parenting skills. Have students share their answers for a master list. Tell the class that this chapter focuses on parenting skills.
2. Have students write a brief description of a parent they know. Collect the descriptions and read them aloud to the class. As the descriptions are read, have a student volunteer write key words on the chalkboard under the heading "positive characteristics" or the heading "Negative Characteristics." Discuss the characteristics, and have students explain why the behaviors are classified as listed. Explain that this chapter will help students explore parenting skills.

❖ *Teaching the Lesson*

Learning Activities
1. Draw a large triangle on the chalkboard. Have students copy the triangle on a piece of paper. Develop the triangle into a visual of Maslow's Hierarchy of Needs during a lecture on Maslow's theory. Label each level during the discussion. Ask students for examples of needs at each level. Why is it important to be aware of basic human needs? How can awareness of needs enhance parenting skills? (communication, critical thinking)
2. Lead a brainstorming session on the ways par-

ents can gain information about parenting skills. List students' ideas on the chalkboard. How do most people learn how to be parents? What are some of the most easily accessible sources of information for parents? (critical thinking)

3. Divide the class into three groups. Assign each group a parenting style to investigate (authoritative, democratic, permissive). Provide poster board and markers for each group. Have the groups create a visual aid to assist them in teaching the class about their parenting style. Following the presentations, lead a class discussion based on the following questions: What effect would each parenting style have on children? How would family dynamics be affected if a child's parents had different parenting styles? Which style do students consider to be the most beneficial for children? Display the posters in the classroom. (cooperative group work, communication, critical thinking)

4. Lead a brainstorming session on influences on parenting styles. List students' ideas on the chalkboard. Assign reading from the text on predicting parenting styles. Compare students' ideas with the information presented in the text. Have students write predictions about their own parenting style. Have them provide a rationale for their prediction based on the text or class discussion. (critical thinking, reading, writing)

5. Using information from the text, guide a class discussion on the characteristics of successful parents. For the discussion, develop large cards with the letters *p-a-r-e-n-t-s* written on them. Have student volunteers stand before the class and suggest one characteristic of successful parents per letter (for example, *P* = positive self-concept, patience: *A* = adaptability; *R* = realistic; *E* = emotional health; *N* = nurturing; *T* = team player; *S* = sense of humor). As each letter is presented, have students discuss what is meant by the characteristic. Are there additional characteristics that describe successful parents? (communication, reading)

Reteaching Activities
1. Divide students into groups to develop a set of flashcards relating to a parenting style (author-

itative, democratic, permissive). The flashcards should consist of key words or phrases that describe the particular parenting style. Post large signs for each type of parenting style at the front of the room and shuffle the cards. Pass the cards out randomly to students. Have students place each description card under the matching parenting style. After all cards have been placed, allow students the opportunity to move any cards they feel are misplaced. Provide students with the correct answers. (cooperative group work, critical thinking).

2. Divide the class into groups to develop skits or raps about the characteristics of successful parents as well as ineffective parenting skills. Provide time in class for each group to present their skit or rap. (cooperative group work, communication)

Enrichment Activities

1. Provide art materials for students to use in creating a bulletin board display. The display should illustrate positive and negative characteristics of parents. After the display is finished, have students write an evaluation of their design. Why did they choose to illustrate the particular characteristics they did? (critical thinking, writing)

2. Have students use information from the chapter to develop a survey questionnaire on parenting styles. The questionnaire should include characteristics from each of the three styles. Arrange to have the questionnaire reproduced and distributed to other teachers and administrators in the school. Collect the completed questionnaires and have students tally the results. What is the primary parenting style evident among school personnel? (writing, mathematics)

❖ *Completing the Lesson*

Review

1. Have students use the criteria for successful parenting outlined in the text to rate themselves as a potential parent. Instruct students to list the criteria on a piece of paper and to rate themselves on each criterion on a scale of 1 to 5, with 1 being weakest and 5 being strongest. As a summary, ask students to write about the ways they need to grow and develop before becoming a parent.

2. Have students define the vocabulary words from the chapter. In addition, have students write original sentences using the vocabulary words.

Evaluation

1. Have students answer the questions in the Think About section at the end of the chapter.

2. Have students write a summary composition in response to the first chapter objective. The compositions should demonstrate student comprehension of the information presented in the chapter.

❖ *Answers to Chapter 6 Review Questions*

1. Parents and caregivers benefit from understanding growth and development by knowing what needs and behaviors to expect and by being able to apply appropriate parenting skills. They have more confidence and less misunderstanding and worry.

2. Maslow arranged needs in a hierarchy to show the order in which they most motivate people's behavior.

3. Maslow's hierarchy of human needs are: Physiological needs—food, water, sleep, and shelter are needed for survival. Safety needs—freedom from physical harm; security. Social needs—interaction with others; love, affection, belongingness. Esteem needs—desire for self-esteem and the respect and admiration of others. Self-actualization needs—desire for fulfillment.

4. Physiological refers to the functioning of the body; psychological refers to mental and emotional states.

5. Parents can learn about parenting skills from a parenting course or class, books and magazine articles, relatives and friends, observations of parents and caregivers, actual experience in caring for or working with children.

6. Parenting styles: Authoritarian parents are generally strict in rearing children. Democratic parents generally consider the child's needs and their own point of view when making decisions. Permissive parents generally permit a wide range of behavior.

7. Some parents change their parenting style with different children or when they experience stress or a crisis.

8. Parenting styles are influenced by cultural background, child-rearing goals, personality patterns, role models, the environment.

9. Characteristics of successful parents include: adaptability, sense of humor, maturity, positive self-concept, emotional health, patience, integrity, team effort.

10. Parents should have realistic expectations of children so as not to demand they perform beyond their level of ability. Otherwise children may develop poor self-concept and low self-esteem.

Planning A Family

◆◆ *Introducing the Lesson*

Objectives
This chapter will help you to:
- Summarize how conception occurs.
- Explain how the chromosomes and genes determine an individual's inherited traits.
- Compare the concerns associated with fertility and infertility.
- Discuss the medical care options for prospective parents.

Motivators
1. Have students bring in baby pictures of themselves at the beginning of the unit. Arrange the pictures in a bulletin board display titled "Guess Who?" Students can take turns trying to match classmates with pictures.
2. Rent the movie *Look Who's Talking*. Show the opening scene, which pictures sperm racing toward an egg while being narrated with the thoughts of the sperm. Ask students to guess what the focus of this chapter is. Explain to the students that in this chapter they will be studying how conception occurs.

◆◆ *Teaching the Lesson*

Learning Activities
1. Use visual aids to illustrate the female reproductive system. Explain the process of ovulation and the menstruation cycle. Have students identify and explain the function of the ovaries, fallopian tubes, uterus, cervix, and vagina. (science)
2. Use the visual aids to illustrate the male reproductive system. Explain how sperm are manufactured and the purpose of nocturnal emissions. Have students identify and explain the function of the penis, scrotum, testes, seminal vesicles, prostate gland, urethra, and vas deferens. (science)
3. Obtain a video that shows the moment of conception (*The Miracle of Life* is a good one). Describe the process of ovulation and fertilization. Explain how menstruation occurs if the egg is not fertilized. (science)

4. Explain that our physical appearance is a result of the unique combination of genes that occurs when the egg is fertilized by a sperm. Have students consider traits they inherited from their parents. On a piece of paper, have students set up two columns titled "Traits from Mother" and "Traits from Father." Have students list physical characteristics inherited from each parent. (critical thinking)
5. Gather information on birth defects and set up a classroom display. Have each student select a birth defect to investigate and report on orally to the class. (communication)
6. Record a portion of the television show "Life Goes On" to illustrate the characteristics of individuals with Down syndrome. Supplement the presentation with information about the causes of Down syndrome.
7. Have students break into small groups and discuss myths they have heard about when pregnancy can and cannot occur. Discuss the myths as a class. Emphasize the facts about fertility and when conception is possible. (science, cooperative group work)
8. Obtain information on average medical expenses for prenatal care and delivery in your area. Outline expenses likely to be incurred during pregnancy and birth. (mathematics)
9. Tour the maternity ward of local hospitals and any alternative birth centers in your area to determine the variety of birth options available to local parents.

Reteaching Activities
1. Have students draw pictures of themselves, using markers, crayons, or water colors to show hair, skin, and eye color. Have students label the traits they inherited from their mother and father. Emphasize that genes from the mother and father mix at conception to form new combinations. Ask students what obvious family characteristics they inherited and what is unique about their appearance.
2. Have students bring in pictures of themselves and other family members. Have them identify inherited family characteristics. What traits do members of each family share? What

makes each student unique or different from other members of his or her family (critical thinking)

3. Have students create a memory card game on the reproductive system. Label one set of index cards with the names of the reproductive organs of males and females. On another set of index cards, explain the function of each organ. The index cards should all be the same color. Shuffle the cards and place them blank side up on a table. Have students take turns turning over two cards. The object of the game is to find a match between the description and the name of the organ. If a match is found, the student keeps the two matching cards and takes another turn. Unmatched cards are turned face down again, and the next player takes a turn. The student with the most matches wins the game.

Enrichment Activities

1. Create a wall chart on birth defects, with information on cause, effect or result, treatment or cure, and prevention. Differentiate between chromosomal and environmental birth defects. (writing)
2. Have students create a crossword puzzle on reproduction and pregnancy. (writing)

3. Have students study the advances in fertility treatment and the options available for couples experiencing fertility problems. Topics might include in vitro fertilization, artificial insemination with husband's sperm or donor's sperm, surrogate mothers, egg harvesting, frozen embryos, and the moral and ethical aspects of new technology related to fertility. (reading)

◆ Completing the Lesson

Review

1. Have students define each of the vocabulary words from the chapter.
2. Have students answer the review questions at the end of the chapter.

Evaluation

1. Have students write a letter to a hypothetical couple who have decided to begin their family. The letter should offer insight into what the couple might expect their child to inherit as well as the wide range of options in medical care available during pregnancy and birth.
2. Have students respond to the Think About section at the end of the chapter.

◆ Answers to Chapter 7 Review Questions

1. Conception is the moment when the male and female reproductive cells unite.
2. After fertilization, the cell begins to divide and multiple as it travels down the fallopian tube toward the uterus.
3. Dominant genes are: curly hair, black or brown hair, straight nose, brown eyes, long eyelashes, dimples, full lips, freckles. Recessive genes are: straight hair, blond or red hair, turned-up nose, blue eyes, short eyelashes, smooth cheeks, thin lips, no freckles.
4. The male determines gender. If the sperm contains an X chromosome, the baby is a girl. If it has a Y chromosome, the baby is a boy.

5. Identical twins occur when one fertilized egg splits evenly into two identical cells. Fraternal twins occur when two eggs are fertilized by two sperm.
6. Genetic birth defects include: Down syndrome—child is short and stocky, may have a heart defect, is moderately to severely mentally retarded. Hemophilia—prevents normal blood clotting. Cystic fibrosis—affects mucus glands, causing problems with breathing and digestion. Sickle cell anemia—painful blood disorder that often leads to early death. Tay-Sachs disease—gradual degeneration of the brain, resulting in blindness and weakening muscles. PKU—causes severe retardation if not treated soon after birth.

7. Contraception is the deliberate prevention of conception or pregnancy by any of various drugs, devices, or techniques.
8. A gynecologist is a doctor who specializes in the health of the female reproductive organs. A nurse-midwife is a nurse trained in prenatal care and delivery.
9. Couples should consider the type of specialist and costs when exploring medical care options.

Chapter 8
Lesson Plan

Pregnancy

◆ Introducing the Lesson

Objectives
This chapter will help you to:

- Give examples of early signs of pregnancy.
- Identify and describe the three stages of pre-natal development.
- Explain the changes that occur in a woman's body during pregnancy.
- Discuss the importance of medical care during pregnancy.

Motivators

1. Write on the board, "What are the early signs of pregnancy?" Have students make a list and use their responses to introduce the chapter.
2. Write the word *pregnancy* vertically on the board. For each letter, have students think of words that relate to pregnancy. Ask for student volunteers to write in the words on the chalkboard.
3. List sayings such as "the rabbit died" and "the stork is on the way" on the board. Explain the origins of each saying. Ask students to share other sayings used in relation to pregnancy.

◆ Teaching the Lesson

Learning Activities

1. Follow up on student responses to the question "What are the early signs of pregnancy" by discussing each signal of pregnancy in greater detail. Have students read the beginning of the chapter and add any signs that were missed in the discussion. (reading)
2. Display several over-the-counter pregnancy tests. Demonstrate how the tests are conducted. Explain that home pregnancy tests and those conducted in the doctor's office react to the presence of hormones in the urine. (science)
3. Select a visual aid that shows the process of cell division during the zygote stage. Obtain a model that shows the development of the embryo and fetus. Outline the development of various organs and systems during pregnancy. (science)

4. Create a chart on the chalkboard outlining changes in the woman's body during the trimesters of pregnancy. Divide students into three groups and assign each group a trimester to review. Have a recorder from each group fill in the bodily changes. Have the class copy the chart in their notes. (writing)
5. Ask students to name factors that would cause a pregnancy to be considered high risk. Follow up with a discussion on high-risk pregnancies using the text. (communication)
6. Lead a class discussion on the value of learning about any birth defect a child might have before the child is born. Describe the options available to parents whose child has a birth defect, including time to prepare and adjust to the situation, the opportunity to explore local assistance or institutional care options, and the option of abortion.
7. Obtain a sonogram to share with the class. Challenge the students to identify body parts. Explain that many times a baby's gender can be determined from a sonogram. Ask students if they would want to know the gender of their child before birth. List the pros and cons of knowing this information in advance. (science)
8. Lead a discussion on the causes of miscarriages. Emphasize that many women who experience a miscarriage feel as though they have lost a child and need to go through the grieving process. Emphasize the importance of communicating support during the period of grief ("I'm sorry for your loss." "You must be feeling really sad.") instead of trying to minimize the experience ("You can always have another baby.") (communication)

Reteaching Activities

1. Have students place their hand over their navel. Relate the navel to the umbilical cord by explaining the function of the umbilical cord in attaching the baby to the mother's placenta.
2. Have students study the section on common discomforts. Gather the group into a circle and play "hot potato." Toss a bean bag from student to student. The student must name a common discomfort experienced during preg-

nancy when the bag is tossed to him or her. If the student in unable to answer, he or she must drop out of the game. The last student in the circle is the winner.

3. Have students design cards listing developmental milestones of the baby during the zygote, embryo, and fetus stages of pregnancy. Shuffle the cards and have the students try to match the event to the appropriate stage of pregnancy.

Enrichment Activities

1. Have students create a card game covering changes in a woman's body during pregnancy, prenatal development of the baby, and discomforts during pregnancy. The object of the game is to collect all of the cards that relate to one of the three trimesters. Three students may play per round. The game should be played like "Go Fish." Students will be dealt five cards each and leftover cards placed in a pile in the center of the table. Students may draw from another player, draw from the pile, or discard a card during a turn. The first player to assemble a complete set of trimester characteristics wins the hand.

2. Invite an expectant couple to speak to the class about their experiences with the pregnancy.

Ask them to address the issue of emotional changes during pregnancy. Prepare the class for the guest speakers by having them write questions for the couple. What have they done to prepare for the birth? What difficulties, if any, have been experienced? What are their hopes for their baby? What are their fears, if any? (communication, writing)

◆ *Completing the Lesson*

Review

1. Review the objectives for the chapter. Ask students to discuss information learned relating to each of the objectives.

2. Have students define each of the vocabulary words from the chapter.

Evaluation

1. Have students write a paper detailing the early signs of pregnancy, the physical and emotional changes a pregnant woman might experience, and routine medical care during pregnancy. Evaluate the paper on thoroughness of material covered.

2. Have students respond to the Think About section at the end of the chapter.

◆ *Answers to Chapter 8 Review Questions*

1. Indications of pregnancy are: missing a menstrual period, increase in size of uterus, enlarged and tender breasts, nausea, increased need to urinate.

2. As soon as a woman suspects she is pregnant, she should visit a doctor or clinic to confirm the pregnancy and receive prenatal care.

3. Three stages of prenatal care are: Zygote—develops from a single cell into a ball of cells and attaches to the lining of the uterus. Embryo—different groups of cells begin to form muscle, bone, organs, and other body parts. Fetus—grows in size from a tiny embryo to a full-term baby.

4. The umbilical cord attaches the embryo to the placenta, a flat disk-shaped organ attached to the uterine wall. Nutrients and oxygen pass from the woman's bloodstream to the embryo or fetus through the placenta and umbilical cord; waste products are returned.

5. During first trimester, the breasts enlarge and become tender, the uterus enlarges, the abdomen expands slightly. She gains 2 to 4 pounds, feels sleepy, and may have nausea or emotional swings. During the second trimester, the abdomen enlarges dramatically. She begins to feel fetal movements. During the third trimester, the abdomen continues to enlarge, and she may have discomforts because of the enlarged uterus pressing on the bladder, intestines, or stomach.

6. The father-to-be may find that his partner needs more understanding and support during pregnancy. He may be both excited and concerned about the pregnancy and the responsibilities of becoming a father. He may be jealous of the attention his partner is receiving.

7. During the first medical exam, the doctor gathers information about the woman's medical history and her pre-

sent physical condition, including weight, measurements, urine and blood tests, and pelvic examination.

8. Women age 17 and younger and women over age 35 are more likely to have high-risk pregnancies than other women.

9. An ultrasound image provides information about the developmental process of the fetus. It can reveal certain birth defects, multiple fetuses, and gender.

10. Some miscarriages occur because of chromosomal abnormalities, incorrect implantation in the uterus, or physical problems such as infection and tumors.

11. Warning signs include: bleeding, sudden swelling, vomiting, headaches, poor vision, fever, painful urination, preterm labor, absence of fetal movements, discharge of fluids.

Prenatal Care

◆◆ *Introducing the Lesson*

Objectives

This chapter will help you to:

- Describe the guidelines to follow when choosing nutritious meals and snacks during pregnancy.
- Discuss weight gain during pregnancy.
- Explain the importance of activity and rest during pregnancy.
- List specific substances, diseases, and environmental hazards that can be harmful to the fetus.

Motivators

1. Ask students to name various health factors that couples should consider before they decide to have a baby. List the students' ideas on the chalkboard. After discussing special health considerations with the class, have students list three of their current habits or lifestyle factors that they would need to drop or improve before attempting to become a parent. Ask the students to share at least one of their habits with the class.

2. Write the word *prenatal* vertically down the chalkboard. Tell the class that this chapter covers important aspects of the mother's health and care of herself during pregnancy. For each letter in the word *prenatal*, have students suggest factors or considerations a woman needs to become aware of during pregnancy. List students' suggestions beside each appropriate letter.

◆◆ *Teaching the Lesson*

Learning Activities

1. Use a visual aid to introduce the Food Guide Pyramid. Lead a class discussion about the recommended number of servings from each food group. Note the differences between the Food Guide Pyramid and the Four Food Groups system. Of which foods do we need the most servings daily? Of which foods do we need the least number of servings daily? Have students analyze their current diet in relation to the recommended number of servings specified in the food pyramid. What changes do students need to make in their daily food intake? What are some ways people can be certain to eat the recommended number of servings in each food group? (critical thinking)

2. Go over the recommended number of servings from each food group for pregnant women outlined in the text. Divide students into small groups of three or four. Provide cookbooks for the groups to use to plan a day's menu for a pregnant woman. The menus should be planned to meet the daily requirements for pregnant women as recommended by the Food Guide Pyramid. (cooperative group work)

3. Display a bottle of vitamins for the class to inspect. Discuss the importance of getting enough vitamins and minerals as well as the importance of prenatal care from a doctor or health clinic. Explain why a pregnant woman may need to increase her intake of certain nutrients. Emphasize that medical professionals can guide a woman in selecting any necessary vitamin supplements. (communication)

4. Discuss the importance of exercise and activity during pregnancy. Have the class describe which areas of the body need to be strengthened for pregnancy (back and abdominal muscles). Brainstorm exercises that can be performed to increase strength in these areas. Explain that women can prepare themselves in advance of pregnancy by maintaining strong abdominal and back muscles through proper exercise.

5. Arrange for a field trip to a maternity clothing store. Ask the store clerk to explain and demonstrate the special features found in maternity clothing. What specific pieces of clothing does a woman need during pregnancy? What are some other sources of maternity clothing? Are maternity clothes necessary? (critical thinking)

6. Invite a speaker from the March of Dimes to talk to the class about the potential for harm to the fetus if proper caution is not taken during pregnancy. Have the speaker discuss common birth defects and how they can be avoided. Ask for resource pamphlets available from the

March of Dimes on proper diet, sexually transmitted diseases, alcohol use and smoking, and drug use.

Reteaching Activities

1. Have students draw an empty Food Guide Pyramid on a sheet of paper. Discuss each food group and the recommended number of servings from each group. Have students fill in the information in the appropriate parts of the pyramid and list foods in each category that they enjoy. Share answers as a group and as a way to assist students in becoming more familiar with the Food Guide Pyramid. (writing)

2. Provide cookbooks for students to use to identify recipes for milk-based foods. Divide students into lab groups. Allow each group to choose a recipe to prepare. Have students taste their products and evaluate each product on the basis of taste, appearance, and nutrition. (cooperative group work)

3. Conduct a poster contest on the theme "What can harm the baby?" Have students use the text for information. Provide art materials and poster board for the students' illustrations. Display the posters around the room and invite a panel of judges to award prizes.

Enrichment Activities

1. Have students study the changes that take place in a female during pregnancy. Have the students use this information to prepare a detailed monthly chart of the physical, emotional, social, and mental changes that occur in the pregnant woman. Ask students to share their charts with the class. (writing)

2. Assign research on drug-addicted babies and babies born with AIDS. What are the numbers of children born in the United States with these afflictions? What kinds of physical, mental and emotional problems do these babies experience? What type of medical treatment do these babies need? (reading)

◆◆ Completing the Lesson

Review

1. Have students work in groups to design crossword puzzles using the vocabulary words and other concepts from the chapter. Duplicate the puzzles and distribute them to students to complete.

2. Review each of the chapter objectives with the class. Discuss guidelines and recommendations for prenatal health.

Evaluation

1. Have students work in groups to develop skits about the importance of prenatal care. Allow time for students to perform their skits for the class.

2. Have students answer the questions in the Think About section at the end of the chapter.

◆◆ Answers to Chapter 9 Review Questions

1. Essential nutrients are proteins, carbohydrates, fats, vitamins, minerals, and water.

2. Pregnant and breast-feeding women need three servings of the milk group.

3. A pregnant woman should gain about 2 to 4 pounds in the first trimester and about a pound per week during the second and third trimesters.

4. Physical activity during pregnancy can help strengthen muscles and improve circulation.

5. Smoking pollutes the environment and secondhand smoke can cause respiratory problems for others.

6. Fetal alcohol syndrome is a condition caused by a drinking alcohol during pregnancy. Babies born with FAS may have a very small head, sight and hearing problems, heart and kidney defects, poor coordination, and mental retardation. Later, FAS children may have learning and behavior problems.

7. Use of illegal drugs during pregnancy can cause miscarriage, early labor and premature birth, low birth weight, infant addiction and withdrawal, physical deformities, brain damage, or even death.

8. Chlamydia is the most common sexually transmitted disease. It can cause urethral infection in men, pelvic inflammatory disease in women, and damage the reproductive organs of men and women. Babies often develop eye infections, followed by ear and lung infections that can cause death.

9. HIV can be passed to a fetus or infant by the exchange of blood through the umbilical cord, from infected blood entering a cut on the infant's body during childbirth, or through breast milk during nursing.

10. PIH is a potentially serious condition that involves high blood pressure. If untreated, it can lead to severe convulsions, coma, and death.

Chapter **10**
Lesson Plan

Preparing for Baby's Arrival

◆◆ *Introducing the Lesson*

Objectives

This chapter will help you to:

- Describe prepared childbirth and the training involved.
- Compare the advantages of breast-feeding and bottle-feeding a baby.
- List essential clothing, equipment, and other supplies needed for a baby.
- Discuss parental leaves and child care options for working parents.

Motivators

1. Have students make a list of physical and human resources that will be needed prior to the birth of a baby and for the first few weeks after the baby is born. Use their lists to introduce chapter material.

2. Lead the class in brainstorming ways to include expectant fathers during the pregnancy and the preparation for the arrival of the child. List student ideas on the chalkboard and compare the list with the suggestions given in the chapter.

◆◆ *Teaching the Lesson*

Learning Activities

1. Brainstorm with the class to contrast the preparation a happy couple would make in preparing for the birth of their baby to that of an unmarried teenager who is scared about the prospect of becoming a parent. Help students explore some of the possible long-range effects of each situation. (critical thinking)

2. Lead a class discussion around the question "What is your concept of prepared childbirth?" Use students responses to further explain the methods of prepared childbirth. Ask students' opinions about fathers in the delivery room. Are there other people that students would want to be present? (friends, relatives, children) Take a survey of the female students on whether they would choose natural or medicated childbirth. Following the discussion, list the pros and cons of prepared childbirth on the chalkboard. (critical thinking)

3. Invite three couples who used different methods of childbirth to serve on a panel and discuss the advantages and disadvantages of each method. Possible methods might include Lamaze, cesarean section, and medicated childbirth. (communication)

4. Invite a midwife to talk to the class about at-home births. Prepare the students for the visit by having them write questions for the midwife. Follow the visit by having the class write thank you letters to the speaker. (communication, writing)

5. Display types of bottles and formulas. Discuss the sanitation steps that must be followed when bottle-feeding a baby. Have students suggest the advantages and disadvantages of bottle-feeding a baby. Then describe the benefits of breast-feeding for the class. Use written information or a video on breast-feeding to supplement the discussion. Have students suggest the advantages and disadvantages of breast-feeding a baby. (science, critical thinking)

6. Divide the class into pairs of "parents." Provide "birth certificates" and have students determine the gender and name of their child as well as birth date, weight, and length. Have the couples discuss whether to breast-feed or bottle-feed their newborn baby. When they have chosen a feeding method, provide them with paper and markers to design an advertisement promoting their chosen method. Display the advertisements in the classroom. (cooperative group work, decision making)

7. Provide the class with a list of items needed for a layette. Have the class discuss the various ways the items may be obtained. Provide catalogs for pairs of "parents" to use to select items for their baby's layette. Instruct the class to list the price of every item chosen. (decision making)

8. Assign a cost study of the different options for diapers. Remind students that approximately 10,000 diapers will be used. Have them record this information in chart form for easy reference and discuss findings. (mathematics)

9. Display the items needed to bathe a baby. Then demonstrate the proper way to bathe a baby. Allow the class to practice using dolls.

10. After the class has read the section on parental leave, have the students write a paper on what they expect for themselves in terms of combining a career and parenthood. Which option appeals most to them? (writing)

Reteaching Activities

1. Have students ask their parents if they were bottle-fed or breast-fed. Then have them decide how they would feed their own baby if they became a parent.

2. Teach the class how to fold a cloth diaper and have the class practice diapering dolls.

Enrichment Activities

1. Divide students into three groups. Have each group consult with a couple who has recently had a baby and ask them to respond to the following questions: "What changes have occurred in your life-style since the birth of your baby?" "What preparations did you make to get ready for your baby?" "What is one aspect of being a parent that you were not prepared for?" Have students list the responses and note the similarities and differences among the responses. (critical thinking)

2. Plan a field trip to a hospital to see the labor and delivery area, birthing rooms, and newborn nursery area.

3. Obtain items that would be included in a baby's layette. Play a "baby shower" game where the objective is to be able to correctly name the layette item displayed. Students who name the item correctly "receive" the item for their layette. Students who are unable to name the item are out of the game. The student who "receives" the most items wins the game.

◆◆ Completing the Lesson

Review

1. Review the objectives of this chapter. Discuss the physical preparations necessary for the arrival of a baby. Explore how this event will affect the lives of the parents and any siblings.

2. Have students define the vocabulary words from the chapter.

Evaluation

1. Have students plan a hypothetical baby shower for a couple expecting their first child. Have students suggest gift ideas to guests that would help the couple with preparations for the birth of their child.

2. Have students respond to the Think About section at the end of the chapter.

◆◆ Answers to Chapter 10 Review Questions

1. Prepared childbirth training helps parents understand the birth process, control the pain through breathing and relation techniques, and take an active part in the birth process.

2. She should ask a friend or relative to be her coach during classes, labor, and delivery.

3. A delivery room is a sterile hospital room that is specifically used for delivering babies and is equipped for surgery and emergency procedures. A birthing room is used for both labor and delivery, has many home comforts, and family members can stay throughout the childbirth process.

4. A pediatrician is a doctor who specializes in the treatment of infants and young children.

5. The advantages of breast-feeding include: being a perfect food, providing health benefits for baby and mother, promoting bonding, providing convenience, being economical.

6. When selecting a crib, check for safety standards such as width of slats, height of posts, locking mechanism, plastic covering on rail, height and fit of mattress, no rough edges or exposed bolts, no lead paint.

7. Home-laundered diapers are the least expensive option but must be washed and dried and used with plastic pants. Diaper-service diapers are less likely to cause diaper rash and are laundered by the service, but they are expensive, must be used with plastic pants, and are not available in every area. Disposable diapers are convenient and waterproof, but they are costly and present a disposal problem.

8. Parental leave provides time for a parent to develop an emotional attachment with a new child and learn to care for the child without job pressures. The child develops a sense of security and love.

9. Child care options include: relatives, friends or neighbors, trained caregiver, child care center. Work options include: not working and caring for the child, returning to work full- or part-time when child is older, flexible work schedules, part-time work, work at home.

10. Parents should talk to siblings about the new baby, read books, involve siblings in preparation plans, and make arrangements for siblings during the time of birth.

Chapter 11 Lesson Plan — Birth

◆ Introducing the Lesson

Objectives
This chapter will help you to:
- Summarize the three stages of labor.
- Identify problems that might occur during delivery.
- Describe the mother's recovery after labor.
- List important care procedures for the newborn.

Motivators
1. Have students work in groups to plan and present a role-play situation of first-time parents preparing to go to the hospital for the birth of their baby.
2. Ask the class the definition of the term *labor*. Some examples might include work or exertion. Why is childbirth referred to as labor? What are some other common phrases that include the word *labor*? (labor force, labor of love). Explain to the class that this chapter will focus on childbirth.
3. Ask the students to describe what is meant by the term *bonding*. What kinds of activities can promote bonding between parents and newborns?

◆ Teaching the Lesson

Learning Activities
1. Give each student a chance to report on an interesting or an unusual happening that occurred during their birth. This assignment will need to be made the previous day so that students can discuss the event with their parents. Start the discussion by sharing an interesting story about your own birth.
2. Ask the students how a woman knows she is in labor? Explain the two signs of labor to the class.
3. Show a video that portrays childbirth. Have the students identify the three stages of labor. Ask students to write questions for a Question Box before viewing the video and to answer the questions afterward. (writing)
4. Draw a diagram of circles representing the size of the cervix during various stages of labor (before labor begins, 2 cm, 4 cm, 6 cm, 8 cm, and 10 cm). Explain that the widening of the cervix occurs during the second stage of labor. The third stage of labor (the delivery of the baby) will begin after the cervix has dilated to 10 centimeters and there is room for the baby's head to move down the birth canal.
5. Conduct a class discussion on the different birthing options available to women today. Include the traditional hospital arrangement of different rooms for labor, delivery, and recovery; the LDR (labor-delivery-recovery) hospital rooms where a woman is able to stay in the same bed for the birth; alternative birthing centers; and at-home births. Which options would the class choose? Do the students know anyone who has used the options discussed? (decision making)
6. Explain to the class that many hospitals allow newborns to stay in the mother's room. This is referred to as rooming-in. Lead the class in brainstorming on the advantages and disadvantages of rooming-in. Record the students' ideas on the chalkboard. (critical thinking)
7. Invite a Lamaze teacher to speak to the class about prepared childbirth. What are the advantages of breathing techniques and relaxation exercises during labor? What are the disadvantages of the Lamaze method? (critical thinking)
8. Obtain pictures of premature babies and conduct a class discussion on the characteristics of premature babies. Define the criteria for premature birth and describe some of the potential health problems of premature babies. Was anyone in the class born prematurely?
9. Describe the activities that are conducted to evaluate and ensure the health of the newborn. Include a description of the Apgar scale by writing the word *Apgar* vertically on the board and filling in the letters horizontally with the words describing the procedures used to evaluate infants.

Reteaching Activities

1. Have students divide into small groups and discuss types of anesthesia available for women during labor. What type of anesthesia would they choose or advise a woman to choose? Students should be prepared to defend their choice. Discuss the recommendations as a class. (decision making, cooperative group work)

2. Invite a group of mothers to talk to the class about their experiences with labor and childbirth. Include women whose experiences have been different (vaginal birth, cesarean birth, natural childbirth, medicated birth). (communication)

Enrichment Activities

1. Invite a midwife to speak to the class. Prepare the class for the visit by having them write questions for a Question Box. Ask the midwife to describe the role of the midwife during labor and delivery and any unusual experiences he or she may have experienced. (writing)

2. Arrange to tour the labor and delivery ward of a local hospital. Ask the tour guide to explain what takes place at each stage of childbirth. If possible, tour an alternative birthing center.

3. Secure admittance forms from a local hospital. Let students practice filling out the forms. Have the students investigate the medical costs associated with having a baby.(writing)

4. The excessive number of cesarean births in recent years has become a controversial issue. Have students research this topic for a paper. The paper should present both the rationale for the increase in numbers of cesarean births and the concern over the increase on the part of many medical experts. (writing)

◆◆ *Completing the Lesson*

Review

1. Play a matching game with the class to review the three stages of labor. Call out clues or events that occur during the labor process. Have the students label each clue 1, 2, or 3 to represent the correct stage of labor. Go over the correct answers as a group.

2. Have students define the vocabulary words from the chapter and use each word in an original sentence related to the main concepts from the chapter.

Evaluation

1. Have students answer the questions in the Think About section.

2. Have students design a pamphlet titled "What You Should Know About Labor and Delivery." Information in the pamphlet should cover the main topics from the chapter.

◆◆ *Answers to Chapter 11 Review Questions*

1. The two signs of labor are: progressing contractions and rupture of the amniotic sac.

2. During the first stage, contractions dilate the cervix. During the second stage, contractions push the baby through the birth canal. During the third stage, the placenta is expelled. During the fourth stage, called recovery, the mother's condition is stabilized.

3. The father can help the mother concentrate on breathing and relaxing techniques; massage her arms, legs, and back; soothe and encourage her; and support her back during pushing contractions.

4. An episiotomy is a small cut made at the opening of the vagina to make it easier for the baby's head to come out and to prevent any tearing of the opening.

5. A breech birth occurs when the baby's buttocks or feet emerge first instead of the head.

6. A cesarean section is performed if complications occur for either the mother or child.

7. During the recovery period, the new mother may be thirsty and hungry, may feel cramps as the uterus contracts, and may have some discomfort with an episiotomy.

8. Apgar scale rates: appearance or skin color, pulse or heart rate, grimace or reflex response, activity or muscle tone, respiration or breathing.

9. Premature infants require special care because their prenatal development is incomplete. They may have a low birth weight and a variety of health problems.

10. A birth certificate serves as proof of age, relationships, and citizenship.

Adjusting to Parenthood

◆◆ *Introducing the Lesson*

Objectives

This chapter will help you to:

- Explain the physical and emotional adjustments that take place after birth.
- Describe how a new baby can change the parents' life-style.
- Discuss how relationships can be affected by a new baby.
- Give examples of coping strategies that can help new parents.

Motivators

1. Ask a student to read the chapter-opening story about Tom and Megan aloud to the class. Then have the class discuss the range of thoughts and feelings both Tom and Megan may have had following the birth of their daughter. Note students' ideas on the chalkboard. Use the story and the discussion as a way to introduce the chapter.

2. Ask the students to imagine that they are about to become a parent. Have them think about the changes in their life-style that would be necessary after the baby arrived. What would be different in their lives? What would stay the same? Ask each student to write a paragraph about the changes. Explain that this chapter will enable them to understand more fully the adjustments required of new parents.

◆◆ *Teaching the Lesson*

Learning Activities

1. Lead the class in a brainstorming session on the changes in life-style a couple has to make after a baby is born. List the students' ideas on the chalkboard. Are all of the changes necessary? What would be the consequences for the child if the parents were unwilling to make the changes listed on the board? Are most teenagers ready to make these types of adjustments in life-style? (critical thinking)

2. Invite a mother who has recently had a baby to speak to the class about the impact of motherhood on her life. Have the class prepare questions for the new mother. Ask the speaker to respond to the question, "What changes have occurred in your life-style since the birth of your baby?" Have students write thank-you notes to the mother after her visit. (communication, writing)

3. Lead a class discussion about postpartum blues. Explain the physical reasons why many women experience postpartum blues. Have any of the students ever known someone who experienced postpartum blues? If so, ask the students to share their impressions with the class. (communication)

4. Provide the class with copies of *Parenting Magazine* or other magazines for parents. Have each student select an issue and read articles or columns related to the adjustments required of new parents. Ask students to write a two-paragraph summary of the issue or problem discussed and the solutions or advice given. Would students consider the periodicals helpful if they were new parents? (reading, writing)

5. Select a children's book written to help children prepare and adjust to the birth of a sibling. Read the book to the class. In what ways would the book be helpful? How can children's literature help older brothers or sisters accept a new baby? What are some other ways parents can help children with the adjustment to a new sibling? (critical thinking, communication)

6. Create three large "graffiti sheets" on which students are to write strategies new parents might use to adjust to parenthood. Label one sheet "Sharing Responsibilities", the second sheet "Managing Stress", and the third "Getting Support." Provide the class with markers and allow several minutes for students to write suggestions for carrying out each coping strategy. After everyone has had an opportunity to write something on each sheet, discuss the suggestions as a class. Compare students' suggestions and ideas with the text. (critical thinking, writing)

Reteaching Activities

1. Rent an exercise video for expectant mothers and mothers recovering from childbirth. Have students exercise along with the video. After exercise, discuss the differences students noticed in the exercises for expectant mothers and exercises the students may do. What precautions must pregnant women take when exercising? What muscle groups were targeted in the exercise video? Why might these muscles need strengthening? (communication)

2. Have students design a matching card game for ways to manage stress. Using the text, students should create at least three example cards for each of the following: relax, exercise, plan, set priorities.

Enrichment Activities

1. Have students survey new parents for their feelings and attitudes toward becoming parents. What is the most difficult aspect of being a parent? The most enjoyable? The most unexpected? Share results of the survey as a class. (communication)

2. Allow students to plan menus for new mothers according to recommended dietary guidelines. Have students look for recipes and prepare at least one item from their menu. Conduct a "taste-off" for the entire class. Determine class favorites and publish a recipe booklet for new mothers. (science, writing)

◆◆ *Completing the Lesson*

Review

1. Have students define the vocabulary words from the chapter and write a two-paragraph summary of the chapter using the vocabulary words in original sentences.

2. Review the objectives of the chapter with the class. Have students give examples of something they learned for each objective.

3. Divide the class into small groups. Have each group write a story for children about getting a new brother or sister. Provide paper and art supplies for students. Have each group design and illustrate their story in an appropriate form for young children. Donate the stories to a children's library.

Evaluation

1. Divide students into groups. Have each group write a letter to an advice columnist from a new mother or father who is struggling to adjust to the role of parent. Scramble the letters and place each one in a separate folder. Ask each group to select a folder, read the letter inside, and write a reply to the parent. After placing a written answer in the folder, the groups should trade folders until every letter has been answered by each group. Allow groups to read each other's replies only after their response has been placed in a folder.

2. Have students answer the questions in the Think About section found at the end of the chapter.

◆◆ *Answers to Chapter 12 Review Questions*

1. A new mother needs rest, nutritious meals, and exercise to help her maintain her energy and return to her pre-pregnancy condition. A new father also needs rest to help him cope with demands of baby, home, and work.

2. Good nutrition is needed for breastfeeding and to provide energy needed for the baby's care.

3. A new mother should lose weight gradually by combining a healthy diet with moderate physical activity.

4. Possible causes of postpartum blues include: change in hormone levels, body fatigue and soreness, lack of rest and sleep, physical discomfort, anxiety, disappointment, adjustment problems of father or siblings.

5. A new father may feel jealous because his needs and interests are being overlooked. He should participate more in the baby's care to help him overcome these feelings.

6. New parents can no longer make last-minute plans. Whenever they go out, they must arrange to take the baby or leave the baby with a responsible caregiver. They may develop new friendships with other parents and adjust to extra financial responsibilities.

7. New parents should discuss their problems so they can be resolved before becoming major conflicts.

8. Bonding between siblings can be nurtured by having the siblings help care for the baby.

9. Stress is tension caused by important events or changes in one's life. To manage stress: try to relax, get some exercise, plan ahead, set priorities, remember that no parent is perfect.

10. New parents can turn to their parents, relatives, other new parents, doctors or other health professionals, books, and organizations for advice and support.

Chapter 13
Lesson Plan

Understanding Infants

❖ *Introducing the Lesson*

Objectives

This chapter will help you to:

- Summarize the physical development of infants.
- Identify important goals for emotional and social development during infancy.
- Explain how infants use their senses to learn.
- Describe how language develops in infants.

Motivators

1. Have students list ways in which a father can be involved with his infant during the early stages of development. Use these lists as a springboard for beginning the chapter.

2. Provide students with pictures of newborn babies and an index card. Have the students study the pictures and write a description of a newborn baby on the card. Mount the pictures and students' descriptions on a bulletin board.

❖ *Teaching the Lesson*

Learning Activities

1. Have students estimate the average weight and length of a newborn. Provide the class with the correct information and reward the students with the closest answers with stickers. Use a ruler or tape measure to show students the average length of a newborn. Pack a paper sack with 7 to 8 pounds of flour and pass the sack around the room for students to handle. (mathematics)

2. Have students define *reflexes* and give an example. Use the chart provided in the chapter to discuss the types of reflexes babies have at birth. (reading, communication)

3. Draw the figure of an infant on a poster or transparency film to use in discussing the body of a newborn. Following the information in the chapter, discuss the various parts of an infant's body with the class. Create a handout similar to the drawing for students to use to take notes.

4. Describe the phenomenon of head to toe development in infants. Explain that this is the reason why babies are able to use their hands and arms before their legs and feet (for example, sitting before crawling, crawling before walking). (communication)

5. Have students reflect on babies they know. Ask them to describe the characteristics in babies they have observed that would illustrate each temperament. Do the students know what their temperament was as a baby? Follow with a discussion of temperament and the importance to parents of identifying and accepting temperament in their children. (communication)

6. Discuss the five goals for social and emotional development in infancy. Write each of the goals on the chalkboard during the discussion. Brainstorm with the students to create an activity that would help an infant reach each of these five goals. List the students' ideas on the chalkboard under the appropriate goal. (critical thinking)

7. Divide the chalkboard in half. Label one side "Positive Self-Concept" and the other side "Negative Self-Concept." Have students brainstorm on ways parents could make positive contributions to a child's self-concept. List the ideas on the chalkboard. Have students brainstorm ways parents make a negative impact on a child's self-concept. List the ideas on the board. Divide the class into buzz groups to discuss ways negative parental behaviors could be redirected into behaviors that build positive self-concept in children. Discuss ideas as a group. (critical thinking, communication)

8. Have students write a paragraph on the idea that parents who say "don't touch" are in essence saying "don't learn." Do students agree or disagree with the statement? Why might this be true? In what ways is this reasoning false? (writing, critical thinking)

9. Introduce students to Piaget's stages of development by explaining typical behavior of children in each stage. Provide boards labeled with the different stages of development according to Piaget. Have students use markers to write examples of behaviors that would take place in each stage of development. Use the boards as a springboard for further discussion on development. (writing)

Reteaching Activities

1. Have students focus on one or two senses at a time (for example, touch and taste, smell and taste, sight, and hearing) by providing students with interesting tastes, objects to touch, music or noises for listening. Explain that infants learn about their world through their senses and that this type of learning continues until a child is about seven years old. Given this information, what can parents and caregivers do to encourage learning and development in babies and small children? (critical thinking)

2. Provide construction paper and markers and have students create a matching game for the stages of development. Students could create cards with typical infant behaviors at various stages and match these to an age range. Laminate the game for use with other classes.

Enrichment Activities

1. Invite mothers with infants of various ages to visit the classroom. Allow the students to interact with the babies and observe their behaviors and temperaments. Ask the mothers to describe their baby's temperament according to the three temperaments described in the chapter. Use the list of typical aspects of growth in the mental ability of infants to determine the stages of development of the visiting babies. What differences in development did students notice between the infants? (critical thinking, communication)

2. Have students ask parents or relatives for information about themselves as infants. If possible, have students obtain their baby books and pictures of themselves as infants. Have students write a report about their infancy, including milestones such as first smile, first words, first steps, etc. (writing)

3. Have students plan to care for a group of infants for a brief period of time. Students will need to plan for the types of equipment needed, sleeping arrangements for infants, various toys, etc. Arrange for students to provide free babysitting services for infants during a school function. After the experience, have students evaluate their plans and make observations about infants. (writing, communication)

❖ Completing the Lesson

Review

1. Review the objectives and purpose of this chapter along with the physical, intellectual, emotional, and social development of infants. Discuss how parents can maximize development of their babies.

2. Have students define the vocabulary words from the chapter by writing an original sentence using each word in context.

Evaluation

1. Have students complete the Think About section at the end of the chapter.

2. Have students write one or two paragraphs in response to the statement "In this chapter, I learned that infants..."

❖ Answers to Chapter 13 Review Questions

1. A newborn is about 20 inches long and weighs about 7 pounds. Compared to an adult, the newborn's head is very large (and may be elongated), the abdomen is large, and the arms and legs are proportionately small.

2. Reflexes help an infant respond automatically to a stimulation, such as sucking or grasping.

3. Motor skills are the ability to use and control the muscles of the body.

4. Babies express emotions through cooing, crying, and body movements.

5. Stranger anxiety is the fear of people you do not know. Separation anxiety is the fear of being away from familiar people or environment.

6. Parents and caregivers can build a baby's sense of trust by responding warmly to the baby's physical, emotional, and social needs. This is done by feeding, comforting, cuddling, and loving.

7. Babies use sensory exploration—looking, listening, tasting, smelling, and touching—to learn through direct experience.

8. Sensorimotor stage of cognitive development is when infants learn to use their senses and to control their muscles. This stage lasts from birth until about two years of age.

9. Parents and other caregivers can encourage language development by talking to the baby regularly and by responding to the baby with smiles, nods, and verbal replies.

10. A six-month-old can sit with support, roll over, put objects in mouth, reach for objects, hold a bottle, switch objects from hand to hand, hold out arms, laugh out loud, babble, call for help, scream when annoyed.

11. A twelve-month-old can stand, perhaps walk, climb, drop and throw toys, express affection, remember events, use trial and error to solve problems, say simple words; also prefers using one hand, fears strange people and places.

Chapter 14
Lesson Plan
Parenting Infants

◆◆ *Introducing the Lesson*

Objectives
This chapter will help you to:
- Suggest ways to meet infants' physical needs.
- Explain how to deal with babies' emotions.
- Describe how to encourage sociability.
- List ways to provide a stimulating environment.

Motivators
1. Ask students to imagine they have just become the parent of a new baby. Have students share what image first comes to mind when thinking about parenting an infant. Use the discussion as a way to introduce the chapter.
2. Write the word *infants* vertically on the chalkboard. Have students do the same on a piece of paper. Tell students to think of one word per letter that relates to parenting infants and providing for their needs. Have students share their ideas as you fill in each letter on the chalkboard.

◆◆ *Teaching the Lesson*

Learning Activities
1. Demonstrate sterilization methods for bottles and nipples. Discuss the importance of proper preparation of a bottle with the class. Demonstrate different types of bottles and allow the students to practice preparing a bottle.
2. Display a variety of baby food and cereals, toasts, junior foods, and juices. Explain that these foods are considered solid foods and may be given to the baby around six months of age or when directed by the pediatrician. Allow students to taste the baby foods. Have them compare at least two labels for nutritional content.
3. Display pictures of babies feeding themselves. Ask students what is happening in babies' development when they are feeding themselves? Why is it important to allow babies to feed themselves in spite of the mess? (critical thinking)

4. Divide students into groups to explore the information about nutrition found in the chapter. Assign each group a different nutrient group to investigate. Have each group report to the class about their assigned nutrient group and its importance in a baby's diet. (cooperative group work, reading)
5. Survey the class for how many students sucked their thumbs as babies. Why is thumb sucking necessary for many babies? Why is thumb sucking an issue for many parents? (critical thinking)
6. Discuss the pros and cons of using cloth or disposable diapers. Divide the class into two teams and hold a debate over the issue. Each team should advocate the use of one type of diaper instead of the other. (communication)
7. Display several types of clothing for babies and discuss the clothing needs of infants with the class. Ask the class to describe features of baby clothes that they would consider important to parents. (decision making)
8. Tape-record the coos and cries of an infant. Play the recording for the class. For each cry, ask the students to write down what the baby is attempting to communicate. Explain that babies communicate through crying and cooing and that most parents will grow to understand their infant's cries. (writing)
9. Ask students to find out what their first words were as babies. Did anyone have special names for siblings or grandparents? Have students share with the class. Why do so many young children have special nicknames for people in their world? What can parents do to encourage language development in their infants? How does language development relate to sociability? (critical thinking)
10. Explain to the class that infants have feelings and express emotions just as other people do. Ask students to think about times they may have been around an infant who was angry, scared, or happy. How did they know what the infant was feeling? What can parents do to deal with an infant's emotions? (critical thinking)

Reteaching Activities

1. Allow students to prepare different formulas. Have students rate the formulas from most satisfactory to least satisfactory according to nutritional quality, price, ease of preparation, storage, etc. (critical thinking)
2. Have students develop a set of flash cards with descriptions of the various nutrient groups. Allow the students to use the flash cards in small groups to review nutritional information. (cooperative group work)
3. Demonstrate how to bathe a baby using a plastic doll. Provide the necessary equipment and allow students to practice bathing the doll.

Enrichment Activities

1. Allow students the opportunity to prepare homemade baby foods using blender, food processor, and strainer. Let the students demonstrate at least one method of preparing baby food for the class. Have students compare the homemade product to a similar store-bought variety in terms of appearance, taste, smell, preparation time and cost. Students should evaluate their lab by preparing a written justification about their choice of baby foods. (writing)
2. Arrange to take the class to the supermarket. Assign half the class to investigate the cost of different kinds of baby foods and baby formulas available. Have the other half of the class check the disposable diapers for brands, sizes, costs, etc. After returning from the field trip, have the class calculate the cost of feeding and diapering a one-year old infant for one month. (mathematics)
3. Have students develop a skit about a parenting class in which the instructor is answering questions from new parents. Content in the skit should cover the main points in this chapter. Arrange to video tape the skit. (communication)

❖❖ Completing the Lesson

Review

1. Have students define the vocabulary words from the chapter. Have a discussion on how these relate to chapter objectives.
2. Develop a crossword puzzle using ideas and concepts from the chapter. Have students work in groups to complete the puzzle.

Evaluation

1. Have students complete the Think About section at the end of the chapter.
2. Have students write a paragraph to explain the statement "Parenting is a full-time job." The paragraph should include information gleaned from the chapter.

❖❖ Answers to Chapter 14 Review Questions

1. Self-demand feeding is feeding babies when they seem to be hungry rather than according to a fixed schedule.
2. When babies are held and cuddled while being fed they develop a sense of trust and security.
3. Formula temperature should be checked by dropping a bit of milk on the palm side of the wrist. Warming a bottle of formula can cause the milk to become hotter than the bottle.
4. New foods should be offered one at a time in order to identify any that cause a rash or upset stomach.
5. Cradle cap is a dirty-looking, patchy scalp condition that may be prevented by washing a baby's scalp every day.
6. Toys with knobs to pull, buttons to press, and handles to turn, as well as rings, bars, balls, and pull toys, encourage motor development.
7. A fussy baby may be soothed by being held, carried, rocked, pushed in a stroller, or given a pacifier or favorite item. Gentle talking or singing may also help comfort the baby.
8. Colic often causes loud and prolonged crying at about the same time each day, often in the evening. Colic usually begins about the second or third week after birth and disappears within a month or two.
9. Through such play, a baby learns that relating to others is enjoyable.
10. Parents should provide lots of items to see, hear, and touch; opportunities to explore and be with others; and outings in the community.
11. Infants communicate by crying in various ways, smiling, gurgling and trying to imitate sounds, and saying simple first words.

Chapter 15 Lesson Plan Health and Safety

◆◆ *Introducing the Lesson*

Objectives
This chapter will help you to:
- Describe ways to maintain a child's good health.
- Explain procedures to follow when a child becomes ill.
- Identify safety precautions to protect children.
- Demonstrate the steps to follow in an emergency situation.

Motivators
1. Hold up a Band-Aid box in front of the class. Ask, "When is this item necessary?" Explain that the purpose of this chapter is to explore health and safety for children.
2. Ask the class to explain the old saying "Feed a fever; starve a cold." Is this sound advice? Explain that although parents sometimes use age-old remedies to care for their children, accurate and up-to-date health and safety information is available to parents today. What might be some sources of health and safety information for parents?

◆◆ *Teaching the Lesson*

Learning Activities
1. Discuss the concept of wellness with the class. Explain the influence of each aspect of health and wellness. What role does stress play in illness? How do positive relationships with friends and family help people stay well? (communication)
2. Display a baby book for the class. Show the sections in the book where health information can be recorded. Why is it important to keep accurate records of a child's health?
3. Ask the class to share childhood memories about getting vaccinations. Have students check their immunization records to see when they last received their boosters and when the next one is due.
4. Ask students to recall times when they pretended to be ill. What did they do to convince a parent that they were sick? Use the discussion as a way to review the general signs and symptoms of illness. (science)

5. Invite a pediatric nurse to speak to the class about routine medical care for children. Ask him or her to describe the special techniques used to give immunizations to children and how medical professionals handle other medical tests. (communication)
6. Survey the class for students who suffer from allergies. Check to see whether these students have had allergy tests or whether they simply suspect they are allergic to something. What are the signs of an allergic reaction? (science)
7. Using the round-robin method of response, have students report one medical emergency that occurred in their household while they were young. Prepare a list of emergencies that could occur at any time. Give each student one situation and have him or her answer the question "How would you handle this emergency if you were the babysitter?" (critical thinking)
8. Ask students to research the emergency telephone numbers for fire, police, ambulance, and poison control in your community. Have students design posters displaying the numbers for the classroom. Award prizes to students who memorize the numbers. (communication)
9. Arrange to set up a CPR training session at your school. Give students credit for passing the CPR exam, including infant and child CPR. Have students write an article for the school newspaper about the training, listing names of students who participated. (writing, science)
10. Arrange a tour of a local hospital. Before the tour, have students describe their own experiences in a hospital emergency room or while being hospitalized. During the tour, ask the guide to explain special procedures used with children in the emergency room or pediatrics ward. Following the tour, ask students to compare and contrast the procedures used with children and adults. What might be the advantages to children and their families of a children's hospital? (communication, critical thinking)

11. Have the class evaluate the classroom using the checklist for childproofing a home found in the text. What improvements would be needed to make the room childproof? Why is childproofing so important? (critical thinking)

Reteaching Activities

1. Have students use concepts from the chapter to make a list of "Rules for Parents" that would help ensure protection and safety for young children. (writing)
2. Challenge students to design a form for emergency information that parents of young children could keep near the telephone. Arrange to have a composite form printed and distributed to parents of young children. (critical thinking)
3. Obtain a copy of Eric Clapton's Award-winning song "Tears in Heaven," and play it for the class. Explain that Clapton wrote the song for his four-year-old son, who fell to his death from a window. Ask students to write about their thoughts and feelings after listening to the song. (writing)

Enrichment Activities

1. Allow students to assemble a model first-aid kit to give to a needy family or a nearby child care center. Have students evaluate the kit, using a checklist for first-aid kits.
2. Assign a research project on sudden infant death syndrome (SIDS). Have students use information and statistics from current periodicals. (writing)

3. Work cooperatively with a biology teacher to obtain germ cultures from clean and dirty hands. Allow students to compare the results and ask them to draw conclusions about the health practice of washing hands frequently. (science, critical thinking)
4. Have students investigate the availability of infant safety seats through loaner programs from local hospitals. Students should determine which hospitals will lend car seats to new parents, the length of the loan, and the terms of the loan. Would it be cheaper to purchase or borrow a seat? (mathematics)

❖ *Completing the Lesson*

Review

1. Have students define the vocabulary words from the chapter. Ask students to use these definitions to create a crossword puzzle covering concepts discussed in the chapter.
2. Have students create health and safety posters promoting concepts discussed in the chapter. Display the posters around the room.

Evaluation

1. Have students answer the questions in the Think About section at the end of the chapter.
2. Develop case studies of various emergency situations involving children. Have students explain what they would do if they were responsible for the child in each situation.

❖ *Answers to Chapter 15 Review Questions*

1. Wellness is achieving and maintaining a state of good health.
2. Babies should have medical checkups every one or two months.
3. Immunizations are given for: DPT (diphtheria, pertussis, and tetanus), OPV (oral polio vaccine), HIB (hemophilus influenza type b), and MMR (measles, mumps, and rubella virus).
4. A baby may be ill if he or she has a high fever, diarrhea, unusual skin rash, loss of appetite, vomiting, or is screaming and pulling at an ear.

5. Croup is a condition marked by a loud, barking cough and difficult breathing. It can be treated by placing the baby in a steamy bathroom or using a cool mist humidifier or vaporizer.
6. SIDS occurs when a seemingly healthy baby is put to bed and later is found dead with no symptoms of an illness or accident.
7. Rooms should be childproofed to protect babies against accidents.
8. A parent bathing a baby should ignore a ringing telephone or doorbell or wrap the baby in a towel and carry the child along to answer the ring.

9. Infants and children should be strapped into a safety seat when riding in a car or truck.
10. If an infant is choking, lay the infant face down on your arm and give four quick blows to the infant's back, then turn the child over and press four times on the chest. Repeat until help arrives. For a child more than one year old, perform the Heimlich maneuver.
11. Parents should call the Poison Control Center or local hospital emergency service immediately if a child has swallowed a poisonous substance.

Helping Children Grow and Develop Physically

◆◆ *Introducing the Lesson*

Objectives

This chapter will help you to:

- Describe how a child's body grows and changes.
- Give examples of activities that help the development of large and small motor skills.
- Explain how parents and caregivers can influence a child's physical development.
- Identify the daily food, clothing, and personal hygiene needs of a child.

Motivators

1. Show the class a picture of a smiling child who has lost one or more baby teeth. What milestone in physical development is illustrated in the picture? What causes baby teeth to fall out?

2. Have a student read the interaction between Jessica and her mother found at the beginning of the chapter. Can students remember wondering or worrying about their physical development as a child? Ask students to write about a time when they had questions or concerns about their physical development.

◆◆ *Teaching the Lesson*

Learning Activities

1. Tape a piece of butcher paper vertically on the wall. Tape two yardsticks vertically along one side of the paper, one above the other. Have students take turns measuring one another's height, making a mark for each person on the paper. Ask students to comment on the activity. How many students' families routinely measured the children in the family? (mathematics)

2. Consult a height and weight chart for adolescents and adults. Have students compare their own height and weight to the chart and draw conclusions about their development. (mathematics)

3. Conduct a class discussion about family traditions for celebrating the childhood milestone of losing a tooth. Did students expect the tooth fairy to leave money in place of the tooth? What other traditions were observed? Why do

parents create special observances for the loss of children's baby teeth? (communication)

4. Reproduce the chart in the text that lists motor skill development. Cut the list into strips and divide the strips among students. Have students arrange the strips according to appropriate age groups. (reading)

5. Ask which students in the class are left-handed. Have any of the left-handed students ever experienced having someone try to change their handedness? How did that make them feel? Are any of the students ambidextrous?

6. Lead the class in brainstorming ways to encourage children's physical activity, and list the ideas on the chalkboard. Have students identify the activities that encourage the development of large motor skills and those that encourage the development of small motor skills. Compare the activities to those listed in the text. (communication)

7. Divide the class into teams and conduct a debate on whether or not children should be required to clean their plate at meals. Have the teams justify their answers. Conclude the debate by having students consult the text on the issue. (communication, reading)

8. Divide the class into small groups to explore the mealtime goals discussed in the text. Prepare slips of paper with individual goals written on them and allow one person from each group to draw a goal. Each group should discuss the goal drawn and be prepared to elaborate on it for the class. (cooperative group work)

9. Post sheets of butcher paper around the classroom with one guideline for selecting children's clothing written on each sheet. Instruct the students to write comments under each guideline explaining its meaning. After everyone has had the opportunity to write, discuss each guideline. Use the text for additional information. (writing)

10. Invite several parents of toddlers to speak to the class about their experiences with toilet training. Have students take notes about the techniques and routines described by the

speakers. Following the visit, ask students to compare the information shared by the parents with the information about toilet training found in the text. Why might some parents use different techniques? (reading, critical thinking)

Reteaching Activities
1. Display several wooden puzzles with various numbers of puzzle pieces. Allow students to play with the puzzles. What kind of physical development do puzzles enhance?
2. Have students work in groups to illustrate the guidelines from the text about children's food preferences. Provide poster board, markers, magazines, scissors, and glue for the activity. Display the posters in the classroom. (cooperative group work)
3. Arrange to have students observe a group of toddlers playing. Have the students list the children's physical movements and actions. Discuss the students' observations as a class. Determine which activities involved small motor skills and which involved large motor skills. (communication)

Enrichment Activities
1. Have students work in groups to write menus for children. Ask students to justify their selections according to recommended daily food guides for children. Allow students to plan and prepare their menus. Invite groups of children to visit the classroom to sample the food. Have students evaluate their menus, food preparation skills, and the children's responses to the food. (cooperative group work, science, writing)
2. Assign a consumer experience related to children's bath products. Have students investigate soaps, hair products, and bath toys for children. Ask students to report on types, brands, variety, and price. Are all these products necessary? What factors seem to influence price? (critical thinking)

◆ Completing the Lesson
Review
1. Have students define the vocabulary words from this chapter in original sentences.
2. Review the objectives of the chapter with the class. Discuss ways a child's body grows and how parents and caregivers can enhance children's physical development.

Evaluation
1. Have students design games or activities that would help strengthen large or small motor skills. Arrange to take the class to a child care center to try out the games or activities with the children there. After the visit, have students evaluate the experience. How did the children respond to the games or activities? Which ones captured the children's interest? Why?
2. Have students answer the questions in the Think About section at the end of the chapter.

◆ Answers to Chapter 16 Review Questions

1. Height and weight charts tell a child's doctor and parents whether the child is in the normal range.
2. During infancy, a baby's arms and legs are short in comparison to the head and trunk. Then there is rapid growth of arms, legs, and lower body during the toddler years. Preschoolers and school-age children become straighter and slimmer, with flatter abdomen, wider shoulders, and longer legs.
3. Large motor skills are involved in the control and use of large muscles in the arms and legs. Small motor skills are involved in the control and use of small muscles in the hands and fingers. Large motor skills develop first.
4. Walking, climbing, jumping, running, throwing, catching, pedaling, and skating develop large motor skills. Blocks, puzzles, crayons and markers, scissors, building sets, lacing kits, small cars, dolls, keyboards, model building, and handicrafts develop small motor skills.
5. Dexterity is the skilled use of the hands.
6. Parents can place the high chair next to the table, put newspaper or plastic under the chair, put a plastic apron on the child, fill cup only half full, give small amounts of food, wipe fingers and hands after eating, and plan bath time for after the meal.
7. Clothing with elastic waistbands, large buttons and snaps, zippers with big tabs, front openings, and Velcro closings are easier for children to use.
8. Children are ready for toilet training when they are physically and emotionally mature enough to control elimination, recognize the need to use the toilet, and are interested in being dry.
9. Brushing and checkups help protect the baby teeth which are needed for proper speech development and eating. They also help establish important habits.
10. Three- and four-year-olds need a medical checkup twice a year; school-age children need an annual checkup.

Chapter 17 Lesson Plan — Helping Children Develop Emotionally

◆ Introducing the Lesson

Objectives

This chapter will help you to:

- Describe the emotional characteristics of children at different ages.
- Explain how parents and caregivers influence children's self-esteem.
- List ways to help children develop independence.
- Discuss how children can cope with stress.

Motivators

1. Let students work in groups to list as many ways as they can to say, "Good!" Combine their lists to form a master list. Use this activity to introduce the importance of positive feedback in helping children develop emotionally.

2. Have the class consider the vignette about Corey found at the beginning of the chapter. Do the students agree with the way Corey's mother handled his emotions? How can parents help their children's emotional development?

◆◆ Teaching the Lesson

Learning Activities

1. Discuss with the class the emotional changes that occur during adolescence. Emphasize that it is normal to feel a wide range of emotions and to experience mood swings during this period. Have students write about the mood swings they experience. Reassure them that their papers will be confidential. (writing)

2. Lead the class in a brainstorming session on all the ways parents show affection toward children. List the ideas on the chalkboard. Ask the students to consider the ways affection is shown in their family Divide the class into small groups to discuss the display of affection within families. (communication)

3. Ask students to explain what they think is meant by the label "terrible two's." Use the students' responses as a lead-in to the concept of negativism and a toddler's budding independence. (critical thinking)

4. Lead a class discussion on anger. How do students handle their own anger? What do they do when angry? How do they react to anger in other people? How do their parents act when angry? Are there similarities between students' reactions to anger and their parents' reactions? Explain that children often respond to anger in the same manner as their parents. (critical thinking, communication)

5. Have students write a paragraph about a fear they had as a child. What did they do when they felt afraid? Did they overcome the fear? If so, what did they do to overcome it? If the fear remains, how do they respond when the feeling occurs? (writing)

6. Divide the class into discussion groups. Assign each group a method of learning mentioned in the text. Have each group explore ways children can learn emotions according to the particular method described. What are some examples of ways emotions can be learned by that method? Share answers and examples as a class. (cooperative group work, communication)

7. Divide the class into groups to discuss the effects of physical growth and development on self-concept. The groups should discuss both positive and negative effects. How can parents help children accept their body and physical appearance? (cooperative group work)

8. Ask students to describe how they react under stress. What do they do to handle the stress? Are the methods positive or negative? Ask the class to consider how children react to stress. What might be sources of stress for children? Does having several extracurricular activities add to children's stress? Brainstorm ways that parents can shelter children from too much stress. Compare the list to suggestions given in the text. (communication)

9. Lead a class discussion on sibling rivalry. What causes siblings to fight with or compete against one another? Are parents' actions ever a contributing factor? Have the class write about sibling rivalry in their family or in a family they know. (writing)

Reteaching Activities

1. Have the class design a bulletin board display illustrating the three A's of parenting for building self-esteem in children (attention, acceptance, active parenting). Divide the class into three groups and assign each group one A to illustrate. Provide magazines, scissors, markers, and other materials. (cooperative group work)

2. Have students draw stick people to illustrate Erikson's positive stages of personality development (trust, autonomy, initiative, industry, identity). Allow time for students to share and explain their illustrations. (communication)

Enrichment Activities

1. Arrange for students to observe a group of kindergarten children in a play situation for approximately 30 minutes. Students should note the most sought after child, the most isolated child, and the children who fall in the middle. Discuss students' observations as a class. What accounts for popularity? How can teachers help children who are not sought out socially by other children? (communication)

2. Have students research and report on childhood stress. (David Elkind's book *The Hurried Child* is a good resource.) Reports should include information for parents who notice their child beginning to exhibit warning signs for stress. (reading, writing)

◆◆ *Completing the Lesson*

Review

1. Write the word *emotions* vertically on the chalkboard. Have students suggest words or phrases for each letter of the word that describe ways that parents or caregivers can help children develop self-esteem.

2. Have students define the vocabulary words from the chapter and write an original sentence using each word.

Evaluation

1. Have students answer the questions in the Think About section at the end of the chapter. Discuss the answers as a class.

2. Provide paper and art materials for students. Have them create a book for school-age children about dealing with emotions. The book should cover the main points given in the chapter.

◆◆ *Answers to Chapter 17 Review Questions*

1. Egocentric means self-centered or viewing things only in relation to oneself. Toddlers who become furious when they cannot have what they want are exhibiting egocentric behavior.

2. The best response to a temper tantrum is for the parent to pay no attention to the behavior and not to give in to the child's demands. The parent should remain calm and objective.

3. Sibling rivalry, a form of jealousy, is competition among brothers and sisters for parents' attention.

4. The positive outcomes of Erikson's five stages of personality development are trust, autonomy, initiative, industry, and identity.

5. Relationships greatly influence personality development because they help children develop either positive or negative outcomes, such as trust or mistrust, at each stage.

6. Self-concept is one's image of oneself. Self-esteem differs somewhat because it involves feelings—one's opinion, belief, or judgement about his or her worthiness as a person.

7. Children with high self-esteem feel they are worthwhile. They like themselves, can make choices, can give and accept affection, are not overwhelmed by feelings, can accept their strengths and weaknesses, have confidence to try new things, and interact well with others.

8. The words and actions of parents and caregivers influence children's self-esteem. Attention, acceptance, and active parenting contribute to children's high self-esteem.

9. Parents and caregivers can encourage independence by providing both security and freedom. They also should be patient, offer encouragement, provide reassurance, set limits, and relinquish control.

10. Signs of stress in children include: boasts, complaints, urge to be clean, ear tugging or hair twisting, cruelty, downgrading of self, jumpiness or fears, extreme worry or nervousness, headaches, lying or stealing, nightmares, teeth grinding, thumb sucking, unusual shyness, poor eating or sleeping habits, explosive crying or screaming.

Chapter 18
Lesson Plan

Helping Children Get Along with Others

❖ *Introducing the Lesson*

Objectives

This chapter will help you to:

- Define the socialization process.
- Discuss how family members influence a child's social development.
- Explain how children learn to share and cooperate with other children.
- Describe how children become aware of gender and ethnic differences.

Motivators

1. Have students write a description of a special friend from their kindergarten days. What do they remember about the friend? What kinds of games did they play together?

2. Develop a series of cards that depict a child being taught socially appropriate behavior (for example, a child burps and her mother instructs her to say excuse me; a father tells his children to put their napkins in their laps). Allow students to draw a card and have them read the situations aloud. Ask the class what they think this chapter will discuss.

❖ *Teaching the Lesson*

Learning Activities

1. Lead a class discussion on the process of socialization. Ask the students to name factors that contribute to the socialization process. Have volunteers describe the person or factor that they feel has had the most influence on their own socialization. Is there a particular event or lesson that stands out in their mind? (communication)

2. Discuss the general rules of conduct for your school. Why is it important to learn to respect the rights of others? How do school rules contribute to the students' continuing socialization? Which rules or expectations do the students agree with? disagree with? What additional rules would they like to see in place? (communication, critical thinking)

3. Define *role* for the class. Tell the students that in recent years traditional roles have been changing. Ask students to give examples. (working mothers, at-home fathers, single parents) As a society, do we socialize boys differently than girls? How? How is this changing? (critical thinking)

4. Have students consider all the roles they hold. Ask volunteers to share their different roles. What influences their roles? How did they learn about their roles?

5. Survey the students for birth order. Hold a class discussion on the information provided in the chapter about the influence of birth order on personality. Then divide the class into groups according to birth order. Have each group create a description for their position in the family birth order. Each group should select a spokesperson to report to the class. (cooperative learning, communication)

6. Ask students to describe behaviors they have learned from peers. Explain that peers play an important part in each person's socialization from an early age. Have students write about a lesson they learned from peers. (writing)

7. Explain that children often learn gender roles from the toys they are given to play with. Ask the class to list some examples of toys that are given to boys and toys given to girls. Discuss the advantages and disadvantages of this practice. What impact do gender-specific toys have on social development? How would children benefit by having toys based on their interests rather than their gender? (critical thinking)

8. Lead the class in brainstorming for ways a single parent could expose his or her children to role models of the opposite sex. Why is this important for a child's social development?

9. Divide the class into buzz groups. Ask students to discuss different stereotypes and prejudices they have heard about or that they may hold. Have each group share a few of their examples and discuss as a class. How do stereotypes limit people? How are stereotypes formed? What makes people prejudiced? How are stereotypes and prejudices passed along to children? What is the result of stereotypes and prejudices? (communication, critical thinking)

10. Lead the class in brainstorming a list of games that would promote cooperation and social development in children. Conduct a discussion about the differences between competitive games and cooperative games. What are the advantages and disadvantages of each of these types of games? How does it feel to lose? to win? How does it feel to be the last one picked for a team?

Reteaching Activities

1. Have students diagram the various roles they play. (son, daughter, sister, brother, student, basketball player, etc.) In the center of a sheet of paper, students should write their name and circle it. From the circle, have the students draw and label spokes representing each different role in their life. Have the students write a description of their diagram, including the kind of socialization they received about each role. (writing, critical thinking)

2. Arrange for students to observe children in a child care or early childhood education program. Have students record examples of social behavior observed among the children. Share observations as a class.

Enrichment Activities

1. Have students develop an advertising campaign designed to eliminate stereotypes and prejudices. Provide art materials for students to make posters to display in the school. A series of brief announcements could be written to accompany the posters. (communication, writing)

2. Have students study the comic section of the newspaper and find cartoons that illustrate social development or behavior. Allow students to clip the cartoons and mount them on colored paper. Have the students analyze what is taking place in each cartoon in a written paragraph. Mount the paragraph on the back of each cartoon. Arrange to have the cartoons laminated. Display the cartoons on a bulletin board titled "A Comic View of Social Behavior." (critical thinking, writing)

◆◆ *Completing the Lesson*

Review

1. Read each of the objectives and have students give examples from the lesson that helped them master the objective.

2. Have students define the vocabulary words from the chapter.

Evaluation

1. Have students answer the questions in the Think About section at the end of the chapter.

2. Ask students to write a summary paper about what they learned in this chapter about social development. The paper should list learning related to each of the chapter objectives.

◆◆ *Answers to Chapter 18 Review Questions*

1. Relationships with others provide children with love, affection, a feeling of security, acceptance, and approval.

2. Socialization is the process by which people acquire the attitudes, beliefs, and behavior patterns of a society. It helps children get along with others in our society.

3. Birth order affects how the family treats the child. Oldest children receive lots of attention, may become more independent and competitive, but may need to keep proving themselves. Middle children may feel less pressure but also receive less attention. Youngest children may be given privileges at an earlier age, may be more sociable and self-confident, but may be treated as the baby. Only children usually receive a great deal of attention and support,

develop self-confidence, but may feel pressured to succeed.

4. Children can maintain close relationships with grandparents or other relatives who live far away through letters, cards, telephone calls, and videotapes.

5. Parents can give children a chance to play with other children through a child care or preschool program, visiting a playground, inviting children over, or setting up a play group.

6. Peer pressure is the strong influence of friends or others of the same age to make someone do whatever the group does.

7. Parents can teach children to share by helping them feel good about themselves, letting them make decisions about what toys to share, and encouraging them to share.

8. Competition encourages children to do their best, helps them feel good about themselves when they win, and helps some children become leaders. Competition also creates losers, can damage self-esteem, and causes stress.

9. Gender roles have changed in several ways: all adults members of many families work outside the home, both men and women hold many of the same jobs, both parents take care of the children, housework is done by both genders.

10. Stereotypes are harmful because they cause people to act differently toward others; prejudice hurts self-esteem because people are judged on the basis of something they cannot change, such as gender or skin color.

Helping Children Learn

◆◆ *Introducing the Lesson*

Objectives

This chapter will help you to:

- List and describe Piaget's stages of cognitive development.
- Explain various ways that children learn.
- Describe how children develop language skills.
- Give examples of ways that parents and caregivers can stimulate a child's cognitive development.

Motivators

1. Ask half the class to write a description of an environment that would stimulate intellectual development. Have the other half describe an environment lacking stimuli to promote intellectual development. Use these descriptions to introduce the chapter.

2. Have students make two lists identifying the following:

   - Ways parents can provide stimulating activities at home for their children.
   - Ways parents can provide stimulating activities for their children outside the home environment.

   Record and display final lists on poster board. Use these lists to introduce the chapter.

◆◆ *Teaching the Lesson*

Learning Activities

1. Lead the class in brainstorming about conditions that could keep a child from reaching his or her maximum intellectual potential. List the students' ideas on the chalkboard. (communication)

2. Have students give examples of ways in which each of the five senses can stimulate mental growth and development.

3. Define the term *operation* as it is used in Jean Piaget's theory. Ask students to think of misconceptions or inaccurate information expressed by young children that would illustrate their misunderstanding of some concept. (critical thinking)

4. Demonstrate Piaget's concept of classification by displaying a group of objects such as buttons, colored blocks, or pieces of fabric. Ask for volunteers from the class to sort the objects into categories. Are there other ways to sort the objects? Explain that according to Piaget, a child between the ages of two and seven years is unable to reverse his or her thinking to classify the objects in another way. (critical thinking)

5. Explain that children who are in the preoperational stage begin to be able to think symbolically; thus, a large amount of pretend play occurs at this time. Have students write about a pretend play theme from their childhood. What did they pretend? What props did they use? Have the students share their compositions. (writing, communication)

6. Demonstrate the property of conservation. Display two glasses of different heights and widths. Pour water from the shorter, wider glass into the taller, narrower glass and back into the shorter glass. Ask the students which glass contained more water. Explain that children in the preoperational stage of Piaget's theory would focus on the height of the glasses and believe that the taller one held more water. Once children move from the preoperational stage into the stage of concrete operations, they realize that the amount of water contained in either glass is the same. (science)

7. Encourage students to remember a field trip they took in early elementary school. What did they learn from that trip? Instruct students to make a list of places in their community that children could visit on field trips that would contribute to intellectual development. Call on students to share their lists in class.

8. Discuss the issues surrounding bilingual education with students. Divide the class into two groups to study and debate the pros and cons of bilingual education. (communication)

Reteaching Activities

1. Have students read Dr. Seuss books to get a feel for wordplay and its importance for young children who are developing speech. If desired, provide additional children's books for students to read. Then ask them to write reviews of the books, focusing on the devel-

opment of language and cognitive abilities in children. (reading, writing)

2. Provide art materials for an art lab. Divide students into small groups to explore several activities, such as working with play dough, finger paint, and water colors. After the lab, have students write about their feelings during the activities, as well as how they think children would respond to such activities. How do art experiences benefit children? (writing, cooperative group work)

3. Ask students to watch a specific television show. Then have a class discussion on the following: What was the theme? What was positive? What was negative? What was advertised? Should young children be allowed to watch the program? Why or why not? (communication)

Enrichment Activities

1. Have students work in groups to design a game that could teach a special skill or concept. Examples might include a math game showing objects that are similar and dissimilar and flash cards showing words and definitions. Allow the groups the opportunity to share their game with the class. (cooperative learning)

2. Assign research on the right and left hemispheres of the brain. Have students investigate the type of learning that occurs in each of the two sides of the brain. (reading, writing, science)

3. Invite a school counselor to speak to the class about intelligence testing. Have the speaker address the ways intelligence is measured and the current questions concerning the validity of intelligence tests for various cultures.

❖ Completing the Lesson

Review

1. Review the objectives of this chapter. Discuss ways in which adults can stimulate cognitive development. Describe the stages of cognitive development and the acquisition of language. Explain how learning to recognize and respond to teachable moments can further a child's developmental progress.

2. Have students work in pairs to design a word game or puzzle made up of the chapter vocabulary words. After everyone is finished, have each pair exchange their game or puzzle with that of another pair and play or complete it.

Evaluation

1. Have students respond to the Think About section at the end of the chapter.

2. Have students plan a series of learning activities that would promote kindergartners' cognitive and language development. The plans should include an explanation of how each learning activity would enhance cognitive development.

❖ Answers to Chapter 19 Review Questions

1. The two halves of the brain are called the right hemisphere and left hemisphere. The right hemisphere specializes in spatial relationships, colors, designs, music skills, and controls the left side of the body. The left hemisphere specializes in language functions and controls the right side of the body.

2. Piaget's four stages of cognitive development are: Sensorimotor stage—use the senses to explore the environment. Preoperational stage—egocentric and irreversible thinking, classification based on one characteristic, seriation, symbolic thinking. Concrete operations—think about actions without actually doing them, classification based on several characteristics, conservation, reversibility. Formal operations—abstract and hypothetical thinking.

3. Object permanence is understanding that objects continue to exist even when they are out of sight.

4. Toddlers begin to learn concept of size by matching pegs to holes and putting smaller boxes into larger ones.

5. Parents should listen to and answer questions to help children learn how and why things happen as they do. If their questions are not answered, children's curiosity will be dampened.

6. The four steps of the reasoning process are: (1) Make a careful analysis of a situation. (2) Think through possible solutions. (3) Choose a solution. (4) Evaluate that solution.

7. Children develop productive language by imitating the speech of family members and others around them.

8. Bilingual children learn languages quickly, often have good math skills, often are very skilled in both languages, and can communicate with more people throughout the world.

9. Parents encourage children to read by reading to them when they are toddlers and by reading themselves.

10. Parents should supervise television viewing in order to monitor programs, answer questions, and soothe fears. Children need to learn by hands-on activities, not just passive viewing.

Value of Play

◆ *Introducing the Lesson*

Objectives
This chapter will help you to:
- Relate the value of play to children's physical, emotional, social, and cognitive development.
- List factors to consider when choosing toys for children.
- Explain how different play activities can contribute to a child's learning.
- Discuss ways that parents and caregivers can guide children's play activities.

Motivators
1. Have students think of a favorite toy from their childhood and describe the toy in a paragraph. How old were they when they had the toy? Why was that toy their favorite? What kinds of games did they play using the toy? Have students take turns sharing their memories.
2. Display a group of toys. Explain that different types of toys are appropriate for different ages of children. Have students divide the toys into groups according to ages of children (infants, toddlers, preschoolers, elementary children). Why did students group the toys as they did? What makes one toy appropriate for an infant and inappropriate for a school-age child?

◆ *Teaching the Lesson*

Learning Activities
1. Explain to students what is meant by large and small motor activities. Have students list on the chalkboard as many types of motor activities as possible. Categorize the activities by ages of children. (critical thinking)
2. Have students think of children's games and activities. Create a list on the chalkboard using students' suggestions. Review the following terms: large motor skills development, small motor skills development, cognitive development, and social development. As a class, identify games that would aid children in each area of development.
3. Ask each student to bring a toy to class. Have the class evaluate each toy for durability,

safety, and versatility. Emphasize that non-specific toys allow children to use their imagination more readily than do task-specific toys. (critical thinking)
4. Arrange for students to observe children in a preschool classroom. Have students select one child to watch during the observation. Have each student keep a record of the toys the child uses during the hour. What skills was the child developing by playing with each toy? (writing)
5. Bring to class several items that may be used for children's dramatic play (hats, ties, dress-up clothes, shoes). Allow the students to experiment with the items to create an imaginary character. How do props encourage children to use their imagination? What is the value of dramatic play for children?
6. Conduct a classroom debate on the issue of gender-specific toys (such as dolls for girls, trucks for boys). How would students feel about giving their son a doll? How would they feel about their daughter playing with a truck? (communication)
7. Have students write about a pretend or dramatic play theme that they enjoyed as a child. Who did they pretend to be? Did they use props? Divide the students into groups and ask them to share information about their play themes. (communication, writing)
8. Obtain a recording and the words of songs for children. Practice songs and fingerplays with the class. After learning basic songs, include simple instruments in the experience of music learning. What do children learn by participating in music activities? What is learned by using an instrument? What other activities might accompany music activities?

Reteaching Activities
1. Ask students to demonstrate small and large motor skills. Each student should demonstrate a different skill.
2. Lead the class in several children's games (Hokey Pokey, Mother May I, I Spy, Simon Says). What skills are children developing as they play these games?

3. Allow students to experiment with various art mediums used by children (finger paint, markers, clay, soft dough, crayons, etc.). Lead a class discussion about age-appropriate art materials. Point out typical behaviors of children of various ages when using art materials.

Enrichment Activities

1. Conduct a lab in which students create a child's toy that could be used to enhance at least three areas of development. What age child would play with the toy? How much does it cost to construct/create? Could parents make this toy at home? Create instructions for the newly designed toy. Arrange to display the toys in a display case, school library, or in the community. (writing, math)

2. Have students develop a recipe booklet of art recipes for parents to use with children. Allow the students to create the art mediums in the booklet and invite a group of children to use them. Arrange to distribute them at a parent-teacher organization meeting. (writing)

3. Have students develop a list of safety rules for children's toys. Submit the list to the newspaper with an article about the project. (writing)

❖ *Completing the Lesson*

Review

1. Have students define each of the vocabulary words from the chapter.

2. Have students answer the review questions at the end of the chapter.

Evaluation

1. Have students respond to the Think About section at the end of the chapter.

2. Have students select an age group of children and plan three activities that would be appropriate for the children. Students should identify the skills children would be developing through the activities, the materials needed to conduct the activities, and the preparation involved for the activities.

3. Tell students they have been selected as a parent's consultant for a local toy store. The role of the consultant is to give advice on factors to be considered when buying toys for children, as well as what children will learn from the toys. Following those criteria, students should respond to questions about toys for several ages and stages of children.

❖ *Answers to Chapter 20 Review Questions*

1. Play is any activity that people choose to do, usually because they enjoy it. Through play, children practice their developing physical, emotional, social, and cognitive abilities. Play uses energy and reduces tension.

2. Play enhances physical development when children practice motor skills. It enhances social and emotional development as children learn how to relate to others and handle their emotions. It enhances cognitive development by challenging their knowledge, memory, and reasoning skills.

3. Wagons, kiddie cars, tricycles, skates, bicycles, pull toys, balls, jump ropes, and climbing equipment encourage children to practice large motor skills.

4. Blocks, puzzles, nesting cans or cubes, stacking rings, crayons, chalk, paint brushes, erector sets, lacing kits, cars, and dolls help children practice small motor skills.

5. In solitary play, babies play alone, even when other babies are present. In parallel play, children between the ages of two and three play side by side. In cooperative play, after age four, children actually do things together.

6. Toys should be durable and strong, safe to use, age appropriate, usable in different ways and in different places, and reasonably priced.

7. Dramatic play benefits children by providing an outlet for inner thoughts and feelings, offering ways to make contact with other children, teaching about roles in society, stimulating the imagination, providing practice for language skills, and teaching rules of social interaction.

8. The first stage is scribbling. The second stage is connecting a circle to make a human face, usually with features. The third stage is representing things children see around them.

9. Computer and electronic games help children become familiar with the equipment and technology, however they take time that might be better spent on reading or playing with other children.

10. Yes, parents should be involved. They can provide toys, equipment, materials, and space; set aside time for daily play; think about the meaning of the child's play; provide a playmate; encourage language use; and avoid dominating the child's play.

Chapter **21**
Lesson Plan

Children with Special Needs

❖ *Introducing the Lesson*

Objectives

This chapter will help you to:

- Identify different types of physical, emotional, cognitive, and learning disabilities.
- Discuss how parents and caregivers can meet the special needs of children with disabilities.
- Describe methods used to help educate children with special needs.
- Suggest ways to meet the special needs of gifted children.

Motivators

1. Share a list of labels often applied to children who have special needs (slow learner, handicapped, differently abled, talented, retarded, gifted, behavior problem, and so on). Have the class tell what words or images come to mind when they hear these labels. List these words next to each label. Explain to the class that this chapter will help them better understand children with special needs.

2. Number students from 1 to 10. Have each student with the number 1 stand. Explain that one in every ten families has a child with a disability.

❖ *Teaching the Lesson*

Learning Activities

1. List common handicapping conditions on a large poster board. Ask students which area of development (physical, emotional, mental, or social) is affected by each condition. Have students use the chapter to determine the cause of each condition. List causes on the board and display it on the wall. (reading, writing)

2. Have students suggest ways that parents can promote the development of independent behavior in children with a disability. Discuss the suggestions as a class. Why might it be difficult for parents to promote independence of such children? In what ways are the suggestions the same as and different from ways parents promote independent behavior in children without disabilities? (critical thinking)

3. Discuss the concept of including children with disabilities in the regular classroom. Also discuss the federal legislation requiring inclusion or mainstreaming. On the chalkboard, list the positive and negative (if any) aspects of inclusion for children with disabilities. (critical thinking)

4. Conduct a debate on the issue of institutionalizing children with serious or multiple disabilities. Prepare students for the debate by asking them to thoughtfully consider what they would do if they had a child with a disability. (cooperative group work, critical thinking, communication)

5. Invite a school counselor and a special education teacher to speak to the class about students with learning disabilities and attention-deficit hyperactivity disorder. Ask the speakers to address how schools identify and work with these students. What are the most common learning disorders? How can they be managed or overcome? What are the recommendations to teachers and students for making the school experience more successful?

6. Lead a class discussion on why parents of special needs children should not ignore their own physical, emotional, and social needs. What are some things these parents can do to meet their own needs? (communications)

7. Have the class summarize information in the text on the needs of gifted children. Then have them prepare a pamphlet for parents of gifted children. What precautions should be taken to ensure that giftedness does not hinder a child's development? Submit copies of the pamphlet to the PTA for distribution. (writing, reading)

Reteaching Activities

1. Obtain a wheelchair for students to use. Have them evaluate the school for easy access by wheelchair-bound students. Are all entrances accessible by wheelchair? Are bathrooms equipped for a person in a wheelchair? Is an elevator provided in multilevel buildings? Summarize the findings as a class and submit them to the school administration. (critical thinking)

2. Place students in pairs to lead each other in a trust walk. One person in each pair is to blindfold and lead the other throughout the school. After the tour, reverse the roles so that the leader becomes the blindfolded partner. After the trust walk, have students share their feelings about being unable to see and having to trust another person to lead them. Use a children's book to tell the story of Helen Keller and her amazing ability to overcome her handicaps and lead a full life. (cooperative group work)

3. Invite the parent of a child with a disability to speak to the class about his or her experiences. Ask the parent to describe his or her feelings when the child's disorder was first discovered, the treatment received by the child, and the impact the disorder has had on family life. Have students write thank-you notes to the parent expressing their appreciation. (writing)

Enrichment Activities

1. Have students study the Americans with Disabilities Act and write a report summarizing the legislation. What are the requirements of the act? How do people with disabilities benefit from the legislation? How does the law affect businesses and other public places? (reading, writing)

2. Have students study clothing for children and adults with physical disabilities. What adjustments need to be made in clothing for a person on crutches, in braces, in a wheelchair, or bedridden? How can clothing be adapted to promote greater independence of people with a disability? Have students make helpful adaptations to one or more articles of clothing. (critical thinking)

3. Show a movie that portrays a person with a disability. Have students evaluate the effect of the disability on the person, the family, and other relationships. Have students write a short reaction paper on the film. (writing)

❖ *Completing the Lesson*

Review

1. Have students create a wall chart listing genetic disorders and environmental disorders. Students should classify handicapping conditions discussed in this chapter under the appropriate heading and include a brief description of each.

2. Have students use the vocabulary words from the chapter in a two-paragraph composition that addresses information learned from the chapter.

Evaluation

1. Write a series of case studies about families who have a child with a disability. Have students work in groups to evaluate each case in terms of adjustments in housing, clothing, responsibilities, and expectations.

2. Have students answer the questions in the Think About section at the end of the chapter.

❖ *Answers to Chapter 21 Review Questions*

1. Environmental causes of disabilities include exposure to drugs, alcohol, rubella, or STDs while in the womb; a very high fever; or an injury, illness, or chronic health impairment.

2. Chronic health conditions include asthma, congenital heart defect, kidney disorders, cystic fibrosis, and cancer.

3. Autism is characterized by lack of communication, extreme concern with oneself, and detachment from reality.

4. Children with attention-deficit hyperactivity disorder (ADHD) are inattentive, overactive, and impulsive. Children with dyslexia have difficulty interpreting information they see and hear.

5. Learning as much as possible about the disability can help parents know what to expect in terms of development and behavior. Then they can help the child understand and deal with the disability.

6. Parents can promote independence by teaching children to care for themselves, by providing clothing that is easy to put on and take off, by adapting living space, and by encouraging tasks and responsibilities.

7. Support groups help parents explore and accept their situation and locate helpful resources.

8. Inclusion provides an environment more like the community, enables others to interact with special needs students, enables students with disabilities to model social behavior, helps people overcome uncomfortable feelings, and provides new support for parents.

9. Some gifted children feel a lot of pressure because they set very high standards for themselves or may worry about family or world problems over which they have no control.

Encouraging Children

◆◆ *Introducing the Lesson*

Objectives

This chapter will help you to:

- Explain the relationship between encouragement, motivation, and praise.
- Describe how parents and caregivers can provide guidance for children.
- List and give examples of effective communication skills.
- Discuss the importance of love for children.

Motivators

1. Write the word *encouragement* on the chalkboard. Ask the class to explain the importance of encouragement in the development of children. Why is it important for parents, caregivers, and teachers to encourage children? Explain that this chapter will cover the ways adults can express encouragement, guidance, and love for children.

2. Ask students to describe for the class one teacher from their past who gave them encouragement and the motivation to study and work hard. Then discuss with the class the qualities that these adults had in common. What lessons can people learn from thinking about encouraging individuals from their past? How can people develop those qualities in themselves?

◆◆ *Teaching the Lesson*

Learning Activities

1. Instruct students to write a paragraph about a time when they were highly motivated to accomplish a task. Ask them to describe precisely what it was that motivated them (a person, a promised reward, intrinsic satisfaction). Allow students to take turns sharing information about the experience in small groups or with the class. (writing, communication)

2. Lead a class discussion about the importance of praise. What are some of the things people say to communicate praise to someone else? Start a round robin letter entitled "Good Job!" around the room. Each time the letter comes to a student, he or she must add a different "praise phrase." When a student runs out of

ideas, he or she must drop out of the game. The last student to write a praise phrase wins a prize. Post the letter in the classroom. Encourage students to make it a point to encourage each other more often. (critical thinking, communication)

3. Write the word *guidance* vertically down a sheet of newsprint or on the chalkboard. Using the letters of the word *guidance* as a framework, have students think of words or actions that are used by adults to guide children. List students' ideas that begin with each letter as the class discusses common guidance techniques. (communication)

4. Ask students to take a moment to consider the hobbies or activities that they enjoy. Which hobbies or activities did they acquire by observing an adult or by spending time with a parent, relative, or other adult friend? Ask students to write a paragraph describing one of their hobbies and how they learned about it. Have students share what they wrote with the class. (writing, communication)

5. Have each student write down ten commands that adults commonly give to children. Instruct students to skip two lines between each example. Then have students exchange papers and rewrite any negative commands to make them positive by stating what the child should do rather than not do. (critical thinking, writing)

6. Explain the formula for "I" messages to the class. Have students practice using "I" messages by writing five sentences that follow the basic formula. Have students read their sentences aloud to the class; correct any mistakes in form as each sentence is read. What is the value of using "I" messages? How can "I" messages be helpful in parent-child communication? (writing, critical thinking)

7. Have students write a paragraph about the ways that love is communicated in their family. Encourage students to think beyond saying "I love you" to other ways that let them know they are loved. (writing)

Reteaching Activities

1. Have student think about a person who has influenced their life. Ask students to share information about the person and explain

what made the person so influential. Provide students with writing paper to write thank-you notes to the people who have served as role models for them. Arrange to have the notes mailed. (communication, writing)

2. Have three students assume the role of adults communicating with children. Instruct the three to stand on chairs. Have one student play the role of a child asking the adults for assistance. The child should stand before each chair, look up at the adult, and ask for help. Each adult is to brush the child away or talk down to the child, ignoring his or her request. Allow enough time for the activity so that everyone has the opportunity to take the role of the child and an adult. (It may be necessary to divide the class into smaller groups for this activity.) After the activity, lead a class discussion about the feelings of students as they played the part of the child. Was it intimidating to approach the adults? How did it feel to look up at the adults? How did the adults feel while standing on the chairs? What conclusions can be drawn about communication with children? (communication, critical thinking)

Enrichment Activities

1. Have students work in pairs to practice active listening skills. Allow each student five minutes to talk about something important to him or her. The listening partner is not to interrupt or converse but simply to listen and reflect on what the speaker is saying. After each partner has had the opportunity to listen, discuss the exercise as a class. Which role was more diffi-cult, speaker or listener? Why was the role difficult? (communication, critical thinking)

2. Allow students to use a video camera to create a video of tips for positive communication with children and teenagers. Have students incorporate concepts from the chapter. Arrange to show the video at a meeting of the parent-teacher organization. (communication)

❖ *Completing the Lesson*

Review

1. Have students demonstrate their understanding of the vocabulary words from the chapter by using the words appropriately in original written sentences. Have students read their sentences aloud for the class to assist in review.

2. Develop a "Jeopardy" type of review game in which the chapter objectives are the categories. Have students write questions for each category. Scramble the questions within each category before beginning the game. Allow each student to select a category from which to receive a review question. If the question is answered correctly, award points. The student with the highest number of points wins a prize.

Enrichment

1. Have students answer the questions in the Think About section at the end of the chapter.

2. Have students write a four-paragraph composition summarizing the main points of the chapter. Suggest that they use the chapter objectives as an outline for their paper.

❖ *Answers to Chapter 22 Review Questions*

1. Encouragement is a message of confidence and faith in another person's ability. When children receive this message, they become self-confident and try to do their best. This gives them motivation to behave or act in a certain way.

2. It is better to criticize children's undesirable actions than them because this preserves their self-esteem and lets them know they are still loved even when they do something wrong.

3. Guidance is the words and actions used to influence behavior. It can help children develop a positive self-concept and high self-esteem, grow in independence, learn to get along with others, and gain self-control.

4. Role models should demonstrate the kind of behavior they would like to see children imitate.

5. Parents can encourage children to express positive and negative feelings by asking questions and talking to children about how parents feel when they are happy or angry or sad. This helps children deal with feelings and not hold them inside, creating stress.

6. "Getting on the child's level" means sitting or kneeling to communicate face-to-face. It also means using simple words and short sentences that the child can understand.

7. Positive statements tell children what they should do.

8. "I" messages clarify what action or behavior bothers a parent, the parent's feelings about the behavior, and the consequences of the behavior. These messages usually get more positive responses than "you" messages, which are filled with blame and criticism.

9. Parents can express love by holding, hugging, kissing, cuddling, and rocking children. Parents also show love by using a kind voice, listening to them, tucking them in bed, reading stories to them, helping them feel secure, and remaining calm and loving even when they make mistakes.

Chapter **23**
Lesson Plan

Guiding Moral Development

✦✦ *Introducing the Lesson*

Objectives

This chapter will help you to:

- Compare the various stages of moral development.
- Discuss the importance of values.
- Explain how parents can help children develop responsibility.
- Describe how parents should handle questions about sexuality.

Motivators

1. Write the word *morals* on the chalkboard. Have students suggest definitions for the word. Explain to the class that this chapter explores moral development throughout childhood and adolescence.

2. Show the class a picture of a person with an angel on one shoulder and a devil on the other. Have students describe what kind of struggle is being portrayed in the picture. What does the angel represent? (conscience) What does the word *conscience* mean? What is meant by the saying "The devil made me do it"? Explain that this chapter provides information about how parents and caregivers can guide children's moral development.

3. Ask students to describe what comes to mind when they hear the phrase "the birds and the bees." Tell students that in this chapter they will learn about ways that parents can handle their children's questions about sexuality.

✦✦*Teaching the Lesson*

Learning Activities

1. Lead a class discussion about the various levels of moral development as proposed by Kohlberg. Create a large visual of Kohlberg's theory on newsprint during the discussion. Label each level and have students suggest examples for each level of moral development. (Refer to the text if necessary.) Which level do students see as their present level of moral development? Do students know other people who characterize each level of moral development? How can one tell if a person has achieved moral maturity? (communication, critical thinking)

2. Have the class discuss why it is important for children to be taught to respect the rights of others. How can parents help children learn to think about others' rights? How do students feel when they are around people who do not respect other people? What might be some of the consequences for people who do not learn to respect others? (critical thinking, communication)

3. Have students recall playing games as young children. Ask students to write a paragraph describing an incident that stands out in their mind about games or sports when they were young. Were students very concerned about everyone playing fairly? Were students involved in making and enforcing game rules? Lead a class discussion based on the following questions: What happens in sporting events when one team appears to be cheating? How can adults help children learn to abide by the rules of games and other activities? How does learning to follow rules in games help a child develop self-control? (writing, critical thinking, communication)

4. Divide the chalkboard into two columns labeled "positive" and "negative." Have students suggest influences on personal values for each category. How can parents maximize the positive influences on values and minimize the negative influences on values? (communication, critical thinking)

5. Have students write about one particular influence on their values. Was the influence a positive one or a negative one? (writing)

6. Lead the class through a discussion and explanation of the guidelines provided in the text for determining and expressing values in daily life. Have students apply these guidelines to a peer pressure situation they or a friend have had to face. What values were involved? (communication, critical thinking)

7. Guide a class discussion about the importance of instilling a sense of responsibility in children. Have students share examples of their responsibilities at home. Are students' responsibilities reasonable? Would students require

their children to have the same responsibilities? (communication)

8. Ask students who received an allowance when they were younger to raise their hand. Have the class discuss the following question: should children receive an allowance? If so, what should the money be used for? Should children be paid for doing specific chores around the home? (communication)

9. Divide the class into small groups to discuss the kind of sex education they received as children. Have the students share childhood memories of learning about sexuality. Did students' parents have a formal talk about sex with them, or were students' questions answered as they came up? How do students plan to teach their children about sexuality? Have a reporter from each group share with the class some of the memories of group members. (communication)

Reteaching Activities

1. Obtain several books written for children about sexuality and reproduction. Divide the class into small groups to study the books. Are these types of books helpful for parents to use with children? Did students' own parents use a book to tell them about sexuality and reproduction? (reading, cooperative group work, critical thinking)

2. Have students develop a bulletin board display about Kohlberg's theory of moral development. Have them illustrate each stage of moral development with magazine pictures, artwork, and other objects. (cooperative group work, critical thinking)

Enrichment Activities

1. Assign a research paper on Kohlberg's theory of moral development. Have students not only discuss the different stages of moral development within the paper but also the influences on Kohlberg's formulation of the theory. (reading, writing)

2. Use several stories depicting moral dilemmas with the class. After reading each story to the students, have them discuss what they would have done in the same situation. What do students' answers reveal about their own level of moral development? (reading, critical thinking, communication)

❖ Completing the Lesson

Review

1. Have students divide into small groups and develop crossword puzzles that review the main concepts from the chapter. Arrange to have the puzzles duplicated. Have the groups work through each other's puzzles.

2. Have students define the vocabulary words from the chapter in original sentences.

Evaluation

1. Have students answer the questions in the Think About section at the end of the chapter.

2. Have students write a four-paragraph paper summarizing the information in the chapter. Students should use the chapter objectives as an outline for their paper.

❖ Answers to Chapter 23 Review Questions

1. Moral development is the process of learning standards of right and wrong.

2. A conscience makes people feel obligated to do what is right or good and helps them control their behavior.

3. At the preconventional level, children try to avoid punishment and receive rewards. At the conventional level, children want approval of others and abide by rules. At the postconventional level, people grasp the notion of human rights, develop a true conscience, and make decisions based on ethical principles.

4. Values help develop a person's character and help people make decisions about what is important to them. Values form the basis of our society.

5. Parents communicate values to children through their words, their actions, and the way they feel toward other people and society.

6. Parents can help children deal with peer pressure by encouraging them to decide what values are important, to feel comfortable expressing those values, and to behave in ways that are consistent with those values.

7. Parents should talk to the child about the task, show the child how to do it, and then let the child carry out the task in his or her own way.

8. Holding a job can help teenagers learn to balance responsibilities of home, school, and work; to manage money; to learn a skill; to get along with others; and to learn more about themselves.

9. Parents should answer questions about reproduction and sexuality so young children can understand what concerns them at the moment and so they develop a healthy attitude.

Chapter **24**
Lesson Plan

Guiding Children's Behavior

◆◆ *Introducing the Lesson*

Objectives
This chapter will help you to:
- Explain why parents should have realistic expectations for children's behavior.
- Describe how parents can help children develop self-control.
- Compare the techniques used for indirect guidance and direct guidance.
- Discuss the causes and effects of child abuse.

Motivators
1. Have students imagine a highway where there are no speed limits, no white lines dividing lanes, and no law officers. Would students want to drive on this highway? What might one expect of drivers on this highway? Explain to the class that just as traffic laws are designed for the safety of drivers and passengers, guidance limits and rules help protect children from dangers.
2. Write the word guidance on the chalkboard. What does this word mean? What is the goal of guidance? How can parents help children reach this goal?

◆◆ *Teaching the Lesson*

Learning Activities
1. Divide the class into four groups to discuss the guidelines for helping parents evaluate misbehavior. Assign one guideline to each group and have them develop a brief presentation of the guideline for the class. Have each group elect a spokesperson to share the group's thoughts. Why are these guidelines important for parents to consider before reacting to a child's misbehavior? (reading, cooperative group work, communication)
2. Divide the class into three groups to explore the three indirect guidance techniques discussed in the text (childproofing the home, arranging schedules, planning children's activities). Have each group prepare a skit or role play for the class about their assigned technique. After the presentations, lead a class discussion based on these questions: How do

indirect guidance methods work to guide children's behavior? What is required of parents when they use indirect guidance techniques? (reading, cooperative group work, communication, critical thinking)
3. Divide the class into small groups to create charts that explain direct guidance and indirect guidance. Allow students to use the textbook if necessary. (cooperative group work)
4. Create posters for the various direct guidance techniques. Have students suggest examples for each method, and list students' ideas on the appropriate posters. Then divide the class into groups and have them illustrate each poster. Review direct guidance techniques as you display the posters around the classroom. What is the main difference between indirect guidance and direct guidance? Which type of guidance is most effective with young children? (communication, cooperative group work)
5. Have students develop a matching game for unacceptable guidance techniques. Divide the chalkboard into four columns; label the first column "Withholding Love," the second column "Bribing and Promising," the third "Threatening," and the fourth "Inflicting Physical Punishment." Pass out four index cards to each student. State the name of each unacceptable technique, provide a brief explanation of it, and have students write down an example of a parent's use of each technique on a different index card. Collect all of the cards and shuffle them. Read students' examples and have the class tell which guidance technique is being illustrated. Post each example in the correct column. Have students write the examples down in their class notes. (critical thinking, communication)
6. Have students research community services available in their area that could be helpful to abused children and their family. Ask students to create a display of the information they obtained. Arrange for the display to be placed in the lobby of the school.

Reteaching Activities
1. Have students work with a partner to evaluate the safety of the classroom for small chil-

dren. Ask the pairs to submit written suggestions on what changes would have to be made to make the classroom childproof. (critical thinking, cooperative group work, writing)

2. Invite a child protection case worker to speak to the class about his or her job. Have the students prepare questions for the speaker in advance. Ask the speaker to tell the class how many cases of child abuse are reported in your state and area each year. What are the most commonly reported kinds of cases? What does the state agency do when a case is reported? After the case worker has spoken to the class, have students write a paragraph reacting to the information he or she provided. Select several paragraphs to copy and send to the speaker. (writing, communication)

Enrichment Activities

1. Assign a research paper on child abuse. Allow students time to conduct their research in the school or local public library. Have students include information on the causes of child abuse and the effects of abuse on children's future lives in their paper. (writing)

2. Divide the students into groups to prepare skits or role plays on ways parents can help children learn self-control. Have students use the text as a reference in depicting parents giving children choices, setting limits, and enforc-

ing limits and rules. Have each group give a brief introduction about what they are going to portray and then present their skit for the class. Following each presentation, have the class discuss what took place and offer any other suggestions they might have for handling the situation. (cooperative group work, communication)

◆◆ Completing the Lesson

Review

1. Have students define the vocabulary words from the chapter in original sentences.

2. Have students work in small groups to develop a list of signs of child abuse and neglect. Provide art materials for students to develop posters illustrating warning signals. Display the posters in the classroom.

Evaluation

1. Have students answer the questions in the Think About section at the end of the chapter. Have volunteers share their answers with the class.

2. Have students write a four-paragraph paper summarizing the chapter. Students should use the chapter objectives as an outline.

◆◆ Answers to Chapter 24 Review Questions

1. Only when parents understand a child's developmental level can they know what to expect of the child's behavior and how to guide it.

2. Positive reinforcement is any action that encourages a certain behavior. It helps children associate a particular behavior with praise so they are less motivated to seek attention in negative ways.

3. Parents can evaluate behavior according to the child's age, whether the behavior was intentional or unintentional, whether the child knows right from wrong, and whether the child can learn from the consequences of the behavior.

4. Children should be given opportunities to make choices so they can learn to make decisions and develop responsibility.

5. Limits are guidelines and boundaries to which children must adhere. Limits help children learn what is acceptable and safe to do.

6. Indirect guidance is any method of arranging the environment to help children behave in an acceptable or desired way. It includes childproofing the home, arranging schedules, and planning activities for children.

7. Physical guidance involves direct contact with children, such as helping, showing, or leading. Verbal guidance is the use of words to influence behavior. Affective guidance involves expressing emotions or feelings to influence behavior.

8. Punishment is not effective in guiding behavior because it is often unrelated to the behavior that prompted it, does not help children know what to do to improve their behavior, may challenge children to repeat the misbehavior to get attention, may damage children's self-concept and self-esteem.

9. Potential signs of child abuse include: repeated injuries; hunger, poor hygiene, inappropriate clothing; genital bruises, pain, itching, blood; passive, withdrawn behavior; emotional problems; talk about a "friend" who is abused.

Chapter 25
Lesson Plan
Handling Common Problems

◆ *Introducing the Lesson*

Objectives
This chapter will help you to:
- Explain why some behavioral problems should be discussed with a child and others ignored.
- Describe ways that parents can handle emotional problems such as temper tantrums, fears, sibling rivalry, and aggression.
- Discuss common problems associated with bedtime.
- Describe how parents should handle dishonest behavior.

Motivators
1. Ask students to share stories about times when they got into trouble as a young child. How did students' parents handle their misbehavior? Explain that this chapter provides information on how to handle common problems with children.
2. Use a comic strip such as "Dennis the Menace" or "Nancy," showing a child getting into trouble to introduce the chapter's focus on dealing with misbehavior. What are some common ways parents and caregivers deal with children's behavioral problems?

◆ *Teaching the Lesson*

Learning Activities
1. Have students brainstorm reasons why babies and children cry. List students' ideas on the chalkboard. Have students read the text discussion on crying and then make any necessary adjustments or additions to their original list. (reading, communication)
2. Have students share stories about temper tantrums they have witnessed at home or in public places. How did the parents handle the situation? What does the text suggest about handling temper tantrums? Have student volunteers role-play some of the suggestions given in the text for handling temper tantrums. (reading, communication)
3. Ask students to recall a childhood fear they had. Have them write a paragraph describing

the fear, what their parents did to help them deal with the fear, and how they were able to overcome the fear. Have students share their paragraphs with the class. (reading, communication)
4. Divide the class into three groups to investigate ways the text suggests handling separation anxiety, stranger anxiety, and imaginative fears. Assign one type of fear to each group and ask them to prepare an explanation of the reasons for the fear and ways parents and caregivers can deal with it. Have each group elect a spokesperson to deliver their explanation in a brief oral report to the class. (cooperative group work, communication, reading)
5. Have students recount their experiences with sibling rivalry for the class. Why do students think siblings tend to fight among themselves? What should parents or caregivers do about sibling rivalry? Have students read the text discussion on sibling rivalry and explain any changes they would make in their answers to the foregoing questions. (communication, reading)

Reteaching Activities
1. Obtain a copy of the book *Where the Wild Things Are* by Maurice Sendak. Read the story to the class, and have students discuss the way the child in the book dealt with his fears. Would this be a helpful book to use with young children who are experiencing some imaginary fears? (reading, critical thinking)
2. Have students review children's books designed to help with bedtime routines. After reading a book, students are to write a paragraph summarizing the story line and describing how the book would be helpful in putting children to bed. (reading, writing, critical thinking)

Enrichment Activities
1. Have students develop a handbook of tips on how parents can handle common behavior problems in positive ways. The handbook should cover sibling rivalry, physical aggression, biting, bedtime problems, lying, cheating, stealing, and shoplifting. Arrange to have the handbook duplicated, and make copies

available for parents of children attending a local child care center. (cooperative group work, reading, writing)

2. Have students interview parents of young children about the problems outlined in the chapter. How often do the parents encounter such situations with their own children? Have students collect a list of suggestions from the parents about what works with their children when they have problems. Publish the suggestions on a tip sheet for parents. Make arrangements to distribute the tips to parents of young children. (communication, writing)

❖ Completing the Lesson

Review

1. Play a "hot potato" review game. Toss a beanbag to a student and have the student give an example for one of the chapter's objectives. Continue tossing the beanbag until each chapter objective has been thoroughly illustrated.

2. Develop a list of problems discussed in the chapter. Duplicate the list and have students write suggestions for handling each problem, using knowledge gained from the chapter. Have students share their ideas with the class while classmates add the suggestions to their list.

Evaluation

1. Have students write a four-paragraph paper summarizing the main ideas in the chapter. Have students use the chapter objectives as an outline for their composition.

2. Have students answer the questions in the Think About section at the end of the chapter.

❖ Answers to Chapter 25 Review Questions

1. Parents should ignore some behavioral problems because they are a normal part of growth and development and will pass if little attention is paid to them.

2. Parents should meet the physical needs of a crying baby by providing food or changing a diaper. Then they should try to comfort the baby by holding, walking, rocking, playing soft music, offering a pacifier, swaddling, or other comforting techniques.

3. Parents should not ignore a temper tantrum when the child becomes physically violent. At this point, parents should gently but firmly restrain the child and take him or her to a new location.

4. Parents should always prepare a child for a separation by saying good-bye and not slipping away.

5. Parents can cope with sibling rivalry by understanding that such behavior is normal, by accepting children's expressions of jealousy, by not comparing children, by not encouraging competition between siblings, by giving children the opportunity to continue friendships and activities, by reassuring children that they are loved, and by treating each child as an individual.

6. Children who are afraid of the dark need reassurance from parents—holding the child's hand, looking around the room, talking with the child, and possibly leaving on a dim light.

7. Enuresis is lack of bladder control or bedwetting. It can be helped by having the child urinate before bedtime, not giving large amounts of liquids in the evening, encouraging the child to get up during the night, not scolding or shaming the child, and seeking professional help.

8. Parents can help promote honesty by modeling honest words and actions and by encouraging children to tell the truth about their feelings and behavior.

9. Parents should make it absolutely clear that stealing is unacceptable behavior, emphasize that there are stiff penalties for stealing, and talk with the child about his or her reasons for stealing.

Strengthening Families

◆◆ *Introducing the Lesson*

Objectives
This chapter will help you to:
• Describe ways that parents and children can enrich family life.
• Explain how family members can communicate more effectively.
• List community resources for families.
• Discuss how families can develop support groups.

Motivators
1. On the chalkboard, write "Quality vs. Quantity." Ask the students to explain the meaning of the phrase with regard to families. After hearing their responses, explain that this chapter will focus on ways to strengthen family life.
2. Play a tape of Christmas carols as students are arriving for class. Ask students to write on a piece of paper several examples of traditions observed by their family at special holidays. Take turns sharing family traditions. Explain that traditions are one way to strengthen family life, which is the topic of this chapter.

◆◆ *Teaching the Lesson*

Learning Activities
1. Lead the class in brainstorming ways that busy families can spend time together. List students' ideas on the chalkboard.
2. Divide the students into groups. Ask them to discuss ways families can show respect and trust to one another. Students should not only consider how parents can show respect and trust to their children but how children can show respect and trust to parents and siblings. Have each group elect a spokesperson to report the group's ideas to the rest of the class. How might respect and trust strengthen families? How does lack of respect and trust affect family life? (critical thinking, communication)
3. Ask students to list ways that communication is stifled and what makes them afraid to communicate. Next, ask the class to list ways to encourage communication and when they are

most willing to communicate. Then ask students to describe the ways they communicate with family members at home. (writing)
4. Demonstrate several common nonverbal behaviors for the class (such as yawning, raised eyebrows and open mouth, arms crossed in front of body) and invite them to guess your message. Divide students into small groups to create role plays where a person communicates nonverbally. Have each small group perform their role play. Invite the class to guess what the actor is trying to convey. How did they know what was being expressed? What is the importance of nonverbal communication? (communication)
5. Lead a class discussion on conflict in the family. Ask students to share how families resolve conflicts and make decisions. Do the students think their methods are effective?
6. Write the five steps of conflict resolution from the chapter on separate slips of paper. Divide the class into five buzz groups and give a different step to each group. Ask the groups to discuss several ways their step could be accomplished. Allow time for sharing and class discussion for methods of conflict resolution. (communication)
7. Explain the various methods of conflict resolution (consensus, compromise, accommodation, deciding not to decide). Ask the class to give examples of times each of the styles of resolving conflict would be appropriate. Have students ever used one of these methods for resolving conflict? What was the result? How did they feel about the process?
8. Lead the class in brainstorming available resources for helping families in need. Provide students with the broad categories of educational services, youth groups and organizations, health services, human services, mental health services, recreation services, religious organizations, and emergency shelters. Students should think of examples for each of the categories. Write the students' ideas on the board. Discuss the resources listed in the chapter and expand the list on the board if necessary.

Reteaching Activities
1. Have students create a flyer listing ideas for quality family time. Use a computer program with graphic capabilities to enhance the layout. Reproduce the flyer and arrange to have it distributed as a resource at a parent-teacher meeting. (writing)
2. Lead the class in a game of charades. Explain that we all communicate nonverbally and receive nonverbal messages from others everyday. How does a simple game like charades relate to communication? Why is it important to pay special attention to nonverbal communication? (communication)

Enrichment Activities
1. Have students create a pamphlet listing the community resources available in your area to help families in need of assistance. Arrange to print and distribute the pamphlet. (writing)
2. Invite a panel of speakers from social service groups to speak to the class about the services provided by their organizations. Prepare the students by discussing different crises faced by families. Have students present hypothetical situations to the panel to determine what assistance could be given to the family by each organization represented. Evaluate the panel presentation by having students write a reaction paper describing what they have learned about community services for families in need. (writing, communication)

❖ *Completing the Lesson*
Review
1. Allow students to select a partner, then pose this question to each pair: "If you and your spouse were having difficulty, what steps would you take to resolve the conflict?" Pairs are free to tailor the problem according to their imagination, but the activity should be used for a review of the main concepts presented in the chapter. Evaluate the work on the basis of information used from the chapter.
2. Write this open-ended sentence on the board: "In my own family, I hope to strengthen family life by...." Have students write a paragraph to complete this phrase. They should apply all the things that were discussed in this chapter to their lives. Use the paragraphs as a means for reviewing the major concepts from the chapter.

Evaluation
1. Have students plan an FHA-sponsored family event that involves games and activities for all age groups and provides a relaxing, fun-filled evening. Have students write a summary paper of the event, explaining how family recreation time strengthens family life.
2. Have students answer the questions in the Think About section at the end of the chapter.

❖ *Answers to Chapter 26 Review Questions*

1. Family members can show respect for each other by being thoughtful and polite, being considerate of each other's possessions and privacy, paying attention to and showing concern for each other, and not belittling each other's opinions.
2. Traditions create a special identity for families, help them celebrate their ethnic or cultural background, and allow them to look forward to and later remember special times together.
3. Nonverbal messages are expressed through appearance and actions rather than words. They include facial expressions, eye contact, posture, and body movements.
4. Steps to follow in dealing with conflicts: (1) Identify the problem. (2) Talk it over. (3) Keep calm. (4) Keep to the point. (5) Seek outside help if necessary.
5. Compromise is when each person gives up something in order to come to an agreement that satisfies everyone.
6. Human services departments regulate licensing of child care programs, supervise foster care and adoption programs, oversee programs for people with disabilities, and provide financial aid to families.
7. People can locate resources and programs through the telephone directory, local offices, toll-free numbers, and through recommendations from friends, relatives, medical professionals, and school administrators.
8. Families can develop a personal support group by reaching out to others, sharing information, asking advice, and donating time.

Chapter **27**
Lesson Plan
Family Challenges

❖ *Introducing the Lesson*

Objectives
This chapter will help you to:
- Discuss how parents can balance work and parenting responsibilities.
- Describe how changes in life-style can affect family members.
- Explain how divorce, remarriage, and adoption can affect children.
- Suggest ways that parents can help children cope with family crises.

Motivators
1. Lead the class in a brainstorming session to list various challenges and difficulties faced by families today.
2. Have students remember a particularly challenging or stressful time in the life of their family. Ask the students to write about what was happening in the family and how it made them feel. Invite volunteers to share what they have written. Be prepared to share an experience from the life of your family.
3. Make newspapers or magazines available for students to use in class. Have each student locate an article that deals with stress in the family. Help the class relate each incident to how it would affect a young child.

❖ *Teaching the Lesson*

Learning Activities
1. Divide the class into buzz groups. Have each group come up with a list of challenges that dual career parents and/or families face. Compile the answers collectively on the chalkboard. (cooperative group work)
2. List each of the work options mentioned in the chapter (flexible schedules, part-time work, working at home, and postponing work) on the chalkboard. Have students explain the benefits and the drawbacks of each work option. Ask students to give examples of each of these situations in their own lives.
3. Conduct a class debate on whether a parent should stay at home with the children while

they are young. Is it always in the best interest of the children for a parent to stay at home? Should the at-home parent always be the mother? Follow up the debate by having the students write a reaction paper to the arguments they heard presented. Students should state their own position on the issue and indicate what they would like to do as a parent. (critical thinking, communicating, writing)
4. Explain what the term *preplanning* means. Emphasize its usefulness as a management tool. Ask students to list examples of preplanning that working parents can do to manage their tasks. What are some examples of preplanning from students' own families? (communication)
5. Have students share situations that cause them stress. Ask the class for ideas on constructive ways to relieve stress. What do students do when they feel pressured or under stress?
6. Ask students to describe any experience they might have had with moving to another community or school. What kinds of feelings were experienced during the move? How did it feel to be a new student in school? How can moving be especially stressful to families? (critical thinking)
7. Provide the class with information relating to alcohol and drug addiction, including the signals that there is a problem and the effects of alcohol and drugs on the body. Provide information about the local chapters of Alcoholics Anonymous, Alateen, and Al-Anon.
8 Describe the various forms of child abuse, including physical, sexual, emotional/verbal, and neglect. Emphasize the laws about reporting child abuse and provide the telephone number of the child abuse hot line.
9. Explain the stages of grief as outlined by Elizabeth Kübler-Ross. Emphasize that the feelings in each stage are normal and to be expected. Additionally, explain that grieving occurs for all types of losses, not just death.

Reteaching Activities
1. Introduce students to a job rotation chart for sharing household duties. Work with the stu-

dents to come up with a list of tasks that must be performed in the classroom. Allow the students to create a job rotation chart designed to involve members of the class in completing the tasks. How might a job rotation chart facilitate household chores at home? (writing)

2. Lead the class in a relaxation exercise. Have students close their eyes and listen to your instructions. Tell students to begin relaxing every muscle in their body, starting with their feet and working up to the head. Progress through each group of muscles slowly, and encourage the students to breathe deeply. After the exercise, have students open their eyes, stand up, stretch, and breathe deeply. Inform the class that relaxation exercises during stressful times can be helpful.

3. Videotape a portion of a television situation comedy that illustrates family relationships. Discuss the problems and challenges of the television family and how they are different from or similar to those of real families.

Enrichment Activities

1. Invite a psychologist to speak to the class about adjustments families face because of divorce, separation, or remarriage. Prepare the students for the speaker by having them write questions they would like answered.

2. Rent the movie *Kramer vs. Kramer* and show selected clips to illustrate the pressure put on a child when parents divorce and fight for custody of the children. Have students write a reaction paragraph after watching the movie. (writing)

❖ Completing the Lesson

Review

1. Have students define each vocabulary word from the chapter and tell how it relates to the theme of the chapter, "Family Challenges."

2. Draw a balancing scale on the chalkboard. In one dish of the scale, write the words *career, work responsibilities, job pressure*. Have students provide suggestions to balance the other side of the scale with family-related topics.

Evaluation

1. Have students answer the questions in the Think About section at the end of the chapter.

2. Create two or three different scenarios related to challenges a family has encountered. Write them in the form of a letter to an advice columnist. Divide the class into small groups and give each group a different letter. Have the group come to a consensus about the advice to give the family. Have each group elect a spokesperson to report to the class.

❖ Answers to Chapter 27 Review Questions

1. Some companies allow parents to work on flexible schedules, to work part-time, or to work at home.

2. Parents can balance work and family life by doing lots of preplanning, simplifying tasks, sharing responsibilities, learning to compartmentalize, scheduling special time for children, building a support system, and minimizing stress.

3. Parents can talk about the move in advance with children, show or describe the new home and community, encourage questions, let children help pack, and then help children make new friends.

4. Some children cope quite well; others react with anger, hostility, or depression. They may long for the absent parent, hope their parents will get back together, think they are the cause of the divorce, deny the reality of the divorce, and worry about its causes and effects.

5. Parents can help children cope with divorce by being honest with themselves, giving lots of love and understanding, talking honestly and frankly, encouraging questions, encouraging a positive relationship with the other parent, talking about future arrangements, and never using the children to get revenge against the other parent.

6. Blended families may take a long time to become a family unit because they must establish new relationships, household routines, and family traditions.

7. Parents might explain that adoption is one very special way that a child comes into a family. The birth parents made arrangement for someone else to care for the child but the adoptive parents will never give them away.

8. Family members often feel ashamed and experience anxiety about what will happen if they tell anyone about the violence. Some think they have no choice but to suffer the abuse.

9. Children under age three deal with death as a separation or absence. Between ages three and five, they do not understand that death is permanent. Between ages five and nine, they understand that a particular person is dead and will not return. Around age nine or ten, they begin to understand that everyone eventually dies. Between ages ten and twelve, children come to terms with their fears.

Chapter 28
Lesson Plan

Selecting Child Care

❖ *Introducing the Lesson*

Objectives

This chapter will help you to:

- Discuss the need for supplemental child care.
- Compare home-based child care and center-based child care.
- List the characteristics of a high-quality child care program.
- Describe the concerns that parents may have regarding child care.

Motivators

1. Survey the class regarding the type of child care settings the students have experienced. How many students attended day care? How many students went to preschool? How many students spent time in home-care settings? How many students had babysitters in their homes? How many students were latchkey children? Tally the results on the chalkboard. Inform students that in this chapter you will be discussing the various types of child care.

2. Have a student volunteer to read the opening scenario in this chapter. What feelings did Michelle seem to be having as she and her father approached the center? If you were the parent in this situation, how would you feel leaving your child in this center? What qualities of the center would make you feel good about leaving your child?

❖ *Teaching the Lesson*

Learning Activities

1. Design a bar graph to show the percentage of women in the work force in the 1990s as compared with earlier years. Why has the number of working women increased so dramatically? Do students think the trend of increasing numbers of working women will continue? What does this trend say about the need for quality child care? (critical thinking, mathematics)

2. Obtain information from your state licensing agency for child care centers on what parents should look for in a quality child care center. Use this information as a basis for a class discussion on high-quality child care.

3. Divide the students into small groups and have each group investigate one of the various types of child care settings mentioned in the chapter (home-based care, relatives and neighbors, nannies and au pairs, family child care, child care centers, government-sponsored child care centers, employer-sponsored child care centers, school-aged child care). Then provide students with butcher paper and markers, and ask each group to make posters describing the type of child care their group investigated. Have each group elect a reporter to tell the class about their type of child care. Hang the posters around the room and discuss the advantages and disadvantages of each type of child care arrangement. (communication, critical thinking)

4. Read selected portions of *Mary Poppins* to the class. What type of child care is portrayed in the story? What are the characteristics necessary for being a child care provider? List the characteristics on the chalkboard. Have students rate themselves according to these characteristics by listing them on paper and writing yes or no beside each one. (critical thinking)

5. List examples of government-sponsored child care centers, such as Head Start. Provide students with background information about Head Start and explain that it is a tax-supported educational program for children. Have students write to their U.S. representative expressing support for the program. (writing)

6. Discuss the advantages of employer-sponsored child care. Why is the business community moving toward this type of child care? How could employer-sponsored child care be considered a job benefit? (critical thinking)

7. Have students call the NAEYC toll-free number to obtain information on accredited programs in their area. Ask students to report their findings to the class.

8. Have students investigate the different types of child care facilities available in their area and make a list. Display several posters around the room with the various types of child care facilities listed on them. Have students classify the local child care facilities under the appropriate headings.

Reteaching Activities

1. Have students use a computer to develop a checklist of the characteristics of a high-quality child care center for parents to use. Help students design an attractive layout for the checklist, and arrange for the students to publish the checklist for parents in their community. (writing)

2. Have students interview parents whose children are in some type of child care. What were the qualities they looked for in a child care situation? Compile the answers as a class. (communication)

3. Have students work in groups to list architectural features and physical characteristics that are important in a child care facility. Write these on butcher paper. When students have finished their lists, have them compare their features to the minimum standards set by their state.

Enrichment Activities

1. Invite a representative from the agency that licenses child care centers to speak to the class about standards and regulations for operating a child care center. Ask the representative to speak about the various types of licensed child care operations, as well as the qualifications of staff who work in them. Ask for a list of licensed child care centers in your area.

2. Arrange a tour of a local child care facility. Ask the manager to explain the licensing requirements that must be met to operate. Find out what characteristics and background one must have in order to work in the center. Have stu-

dents write thank-you notes to the center following the tour. (writing)

3. Have students design a program to support latchkey children. Students should determine what services will be provided, how to advertise the program, who would be involved, etc. Students should also describe the types of safety information that latchkey children need to know and propose ways to teach them the information. Arrange for the students to present their ideas at a parent-teacher meeting. (critical thinking, writing, communication)

❖ Completing the Lesson

Review

1. Create a crossword puzzle for the vocabulary words found in this chapter. Allow the students to use their books to complete the puzzle.

2. Review the objectives from the chapter with the class. Conduct an oral review of the information found in the chapter that addresses each objective.

Evaluation

1. Write examples of parental concerns regarding child care on index cards. Have students draw a card and write a response to the concern on the basis of knowledge gained from this chapter. Have students take turns sharing their situation and response.

2. Have students answer the questions in the Think About section at the end of the chapter.

❖ Answers to Chapter 28 Review Questions

1. Supplemental child care is needed because of the increasing numbers of mothers of young children who work outside the home.

2. Child care should be suitable, affordable, and dependable.

3. If a relative or neighbor provides child care, the child knows the person and can remain in familiar surroundings, cost may be low, and the parent may not have to take or pick up the child. However the relative or neighbor may not have enough energy, may not be familiar with appropriate learning activities, or may not encourage the child to play with other children.

4. A nanny is a live-in caregiver who is generally on call 24 hours a day.

5. Family child care is usually provided by a mother in her own home.

6. Some businesses sponsor child care programs as an employee benefit. Parents do not have to worry about finding child care. They work more effectively, miss fewer days, and take shorter parental leaves.

7. Latchkey children are those who must take care of themselves before and after school. Some communities have child care programs for school-age children.

8. A high quality child care program should meet standards and be accredited by NAEYC, have a high staff-child ratio, provide a variety of developmentally appropriate activities and equipment, and communicate with parents.

9. Parents should gather information about available child care programs, check licensing, visit unannounced, observe staff and children, and compare advantages of disadvantages of each program before making a choice.

10. Ideally, a child should be introduced gradually to a child care center.

Early Childhood Education

❖ *Introducing the Lesson*

Objectives
This chapter will help you to:
- Compare various types of preschool facilities and programs.
- Describe the types of activities offered in kindergarten.
- Discuss the advantages and disadvantages of enrichment activities.
- Explain how parents can become involved in their children's early education.

Motivators
1. Have students list as many classroom learning centers as they can think of that would be meaningful to a kindergarten child. Under each center, have them list items that would promote learning in that center. Use the students' lists to introduce the chapter.
2. Survey the class for students who attended a preschool program. Ask the students who attended a preschool to describe their memories of it for the class.

❖ *Teaching the Lesson*

Learning Activities
1. Explain to the class the difference between a preschool program and a child care center. Brainstorm with the class about the reasons parents might place their child in a preschool program. Write students' ideas on the chalkboard. (critical thinking)
2. Divide the class into eight groups and instruct each group to study one type of early childhood program described in the text (infant-parent classes, play groups, preschool programs, parent cooperative nursery schools, Head Start programs, public education programs, child development laboratory programs, Montessori preschools). As a class, create a chart comparing the various types of programs according to purpose or benefit for children, parents' roles, and general organization. Discuss the similarities and differences among the programs as the chart is being cre-

ated. (cooperative group work, writing, critical thinking)
3. Lead a class discussion on the advantages and disadvantages of preschool programs for young children. Would a child who had attended a preschool program have an advantage over a child who had not? Why or why not? Ask the students whether they feel a preschool program would be important for their children. (critical thinking)
4. Have students make a list of ways that parents can become involved in their child's early education. Ask students to share their lists. How were students' own parents involved in their early education? Why is parental involvement important? (writing)
5. Have students explore the educational and background requirements for preschool and kindergarten teachers in your state. What standards must preschool programs meet? Why do states have requirements and standards for preschool teachers and programs? (critical thinking)
6. Have students plan a half-day schedule of activities for children in a preschool program. Compare this schedule with sample schedules from other sources. Why is a consistent routine important for children in a preschool environment? (writing)
7. On the chalkboard, make a list of the types of enrichment activities in which students participated as children. Ask for the types of enrichment activities in which students are currently involved. What skills can be gained from enrichment activities? What are negative aspects of being involved in enrichment activities? (critical thinking)

Reteaching Activities
1. Invite a kindergarten teacher to speak to the class about his or her program. What are the educational goals for kindergarten children? What is a typical day's schedule? What types of activities occur every day? Have students write a paper about new information they learned from the speaker. In what ways were their ideas about kindergarten challenged? (writing, critical thinking)

2. Arrange for students to observe preschool or kindergarten children in their classroom. What types of activities occurred? What kinds of teacher-child interaction did students observe? Was there evidence of a schedule? (critical thinking)

3. Have students create a bulletin board display illustrating ways that parents can become involved in their children's early education experiences. (cooperative group work)

Enrichment Activities

1. Have students investigate the different types of child-care facilities available in your area. Help them find out which facilities use the instructional approach and which use the discovery approach. Assign groups of students to visit a center in your community. Have the groups report their findings to the class. (cooperative group work, communication)

2. Arrange with a kindergarten teacher to allow students to plan and carry out learning activities for the children. Divide students into small groups to plan and prepare a learning center in advance. As a follow-up, have students evaluate their learning center and the children's responses to the activities. (cooperative group work, critical thinking)

◆◆ Completing the Lesson

Review

1. Play a review game in the form of "Jeopardy," using the chapter objectives as general categories. In small groups, have students develop questions and answers for each of the categories. Play the review game as a class.

2. Have students use the vocabulary words from the chapter in two paragraphs that summarize what they learned about early childhood education. Have students take turns reading their summaries aloud for the class.

Evaluation

1. Have students answer the Think About questions at the end of the chapter.

2. Have students write a four-paragraph paper about the advantages of a preschool or kindergarten program for children.

◆◆ Answers to Chapter 29 Review Questions

1. Early childhood education programs are most appropriate for families in which one parent is home at least part of the time. Most programs are only offered for part of a day for several days a week between September and May.

2. Parent cooperatives enable parents to assist in the classroom. Head Start offers activities, nutritious meals, medical care, and parent participation. Public education preschools help prepare at-risk students, or all students, for elementary school. Child development labs offer low-cost care since students observe or work with the children. Montessori schools emphasize cognitive skills and independent learning.

3. Head Start is an early childhood education program funded by the federal government for low-income and disadvantaged preschoolers.

4. Children gain literacy skills by expressing their ideas, enjoying poetry and songs, looking at books, relating pictures to words, recognizing names, recognizing shapes, writing their names, and orally relating their experiences.

5. Learning centers contain supplies and enough room for a few children to work independently or together on an activity.

6. Children need free time to play and enjoy life. Overscheduling can create a great deal of stress.

7. Parents can become involved by joining a parents' organization and attending school events, workshops, and conferences.

8. Parents can ease the transition by having the child visit the new school and classroom, helping the child feel ready for the new experience, and not stressing what the child should do or not do in school.

Chapter 30
Lesson Plan

Exploring Careers in Child Care and Other Occupations

❖ *Introducing the Lesson*

Objectives
This chapter will help you to:

- List some advantages and disadvantages of child care careers.
- Identify ways to learn more about various occupations.
- Describe the steps involved in finding and applying for a job.
- Discuss the personal characteristics that contribute to success on the job.

Motivators
1. Have the class brainstorm as many careers as possible that would involve working with children. List the ideas on the chalkboard. Have students take note of the jobs for later use.
2. Have students list the following on a sheet of paper: things they like to do, their personality traits, their talents. Use the lists to introduce the chapter's focus on career exploration. Emphasize that an accurate assessment of oneself is important when considering a career. Collect the lists to become better acquainted with the students.
3. Ask the class to describe their responses to adults who inquire about their future plans. How can the adults in their life be helpful to them in their preparation and search for a career?

❖ *Teaching the Lesson*

Learning Activities
1. Have students make a list of the qualities a person would need in a child-related career. Compile the students' answers on a sheet of newsprint and share the list with the class. (critical thinking)
2. Model the correct form of a resume for the class. Have students evaluate an incorrectly written resume. How could the resume be improved? Help each student prepare a resume that he or she could use when trying to secure a job. (critical thinking, writing)
3. Divide the class into groups. Ask half of the groups to write role-play situations in an employment office that demonstrate the correct things to do during an interview. Have the other half write role-play situations that demonstrate how *not* to act during an interview. Ask the groups to perform their role plays in class. (cooperative group work, communication)
4. Invite a panel of people who have child-related careers to speak to the class on how they got started in the field and the positive and negative aspects of their jobs. Assign students to small groups to give an oral summary of the career panel following the speakers' presentation. Have students write thank-you notes to the speakers as a follow-up activity. (communication, writing)
5. Have students brainstorm ways to gain experience with children in the community. Emphasize that volunteer work experience may be used on a resume if a person does not yet have a paying job. Why may volunteer work experiences and extracurricular activities impress employers? (critical thinking)
6. Have students choose two child-related jobs to investigate from the list of jobs given near the beginning of the chapter. Provide copies of the *Occupational Outlook Handbook* for students' research. Have students determine the requirements for both jobs, salary ranges, and possibilities for advancement. Conduct a class discussion on the findings. (reading, writing)
7. Model the correct way to write a letter of application for a job. Have students choose a job opening from the "help wanted" section of a newspaper and practice writing a letter of application. (reading, writing)
8. Discuss questions that are frequently asked during an interview. Arrange for another adult to interview the students individually for practice. Have the interviewer prepare some general comments for the class about his or her observations of students' interviews. (communication)
9. Obtain sample application forms for students to practice filling out. Advise them to read the forms carefully and to be sure their responses are properly placed. (reading, writing)

Reteaching Activities

1. Invite a representative from the state employment commission to speak to the class about successful job searches. Ask the speaker to highlight the services offered by the state to assist people in finding employment. Prepare the class for the presentation by having students write questions for the speaker. (writing)

2. Show a video about interviewing skills that contrasts appropriate and inappropriate ways to participate in an interview. Following the video, divide the class into small groups to develop role plays of poor interviewing techniques. Following each role play, have the audience critique the situation portrayed and identify the preferred techniques to use. (cooperative group work, critical thinking)

Enrichment Activities

1. Arrange for students to "shadow" a person working in a child-related career of interest to them. Ask them to determine what they would have to do to obtain a similar position and progress to the next level on the career ladder. Ask each student to present an oral report to the class on the experience. (communication)

2. Have students interview several young mothers who work outside the home concerning problems they have encountered relating to child care and child care facilities. Have students prepare a brief report listing these problems. For each problem listed, ask them to recommend at least one possible solution. (communication, writing, critical thinking)

3. Invite your school vocational counselor to administer an aptitude test to your students that would help them in the career decision-making process. Encourage students to investigate at least two possible careers requiring strengths that are evident from their test results.

◆◆ Completing the Lesson

Review

1. For each chapter objective, have students list three points they learned about careers in child care. Allow students to use their text and notes. (writing)

2. Have students write two paragraphs using the chapter vocabulary words in original sentences.

Evaluation

1. Have students form pairs or small groups and create a tip sheet for other high school students on how to conduct a job search.

2. Have students answer the Think About questions at the end of the chapter.

◆◆ Answers to Chapter 30 Review Questions

1. An entrepreneur is a person who starts and manages his or her own business.

2. Advantages of a career in child care include: on-the-job learning, never boring, opportunity to fill a need, daily interaction with people, practical application of knowledge, opportunity to strengthen families, flexible schedule, opportunity for advancement, application of job experience to own family life, worldwide professional opportunities. Disadvantages include: low paying, physically demanding, limited interaction with adults, need for patience, lack of appreciation.

3. A personal inventory helps identify interests, personality traits, and talents so you can look for work you will enjoy and can perform successfully.

4. People can gain experience in caring for children by playing or reading to children, volunteering in a children's program, teaching at church or synagogue, helping a teacher after school, babysitting, tutoring, or working in a child-related store.

5. Parents should leave the telephone numbers of where they can be reached, the doctor or hospital, and a close relative or friend.

6. You can find job openings by contacting people who might know of an opening; reading the help wanted ads; checking with school job placement services, referral services, employment agencies, and government employment offices; and directly contacting employers through a letter, telephone call, or visit.

7. A resume is a detailed summary of your education, work experience, and job-related volunteer activities. It is needed when applying for professional, technical, managerial, clerical, and some service jobs.

8. An application form usually requests social security number, education, employment, and references.

9. Interview tips include: dress appropriately; go alone; arrive early; be positive, interested, and enthusiastic; sit comfortably and speak slowly and clearly; use complete sentences; answer questions about your past record; ask questions; wait until salary is brought up; thank the interviewer.

10. Employers look for a person who is responsible, cooperative, punctual, courteous, honest and trustworthy, and who uses good communication skills, maintains a good appearance, follows rules and procedures, sets high standards, and always tries to do his or her best.

Activities Across the Curriculum

Language Arts

- Have students read books or short stories about families and children.
- Have students write a short story from the viewpoint of a fetus, a newborn, an infant, or a toddler.
- Have students write a fictitious first-person story about a parenting experience.
- Have students describe another person who possesses certain qualities that are admirable as a parent, teacher, role model, spouse, or best friend.
- Ask students to gather newspaper and magazine ads on a specific topic. Have them evaluate the ads.
- Have students write an advice column for the school newspaper on teen-related topics.
- Have students write and present a radio or TV script about a parenting skill that could be used as a public service announcement. Then have students tape the announcement.
- Ask students to develop a variety of positive statements to communicate directions to a child. Have them present their statements to the class.
- Have students write a poem about children. Encourage them to use poetic tools such as imagery, metaphor, alliteration, rhyme, or free verse.

Mathematics

- Have students create graphs or pie charts illustrating statistics.
- Ask students to compare the costs of two or more items or services.
- Have students calculate calories consumed from various foods and calories burned during various activities.
- Have students find out the average costs of different medical procedures. Then have them compute the total estimated health-care expenditures of a person during a 75-year life span.
- Have students prepare family budgets using various incomes and expenses.
- Have students compare an individual's height and weight to growth charts.
- Have students research various costs, such as prenatal care and delivery, child care, and education.
- Have students gather data from a survey. Then have them make a bar graph of the information.

Social Studies

- Have students research family life-styles in different cultures.
- Have students prepare reports on how diseases or war affects people in the past and today.
- Ask students to research their ethnic or cultural background.
- Have students research organizations engaged in offering child-related services all over the world.
- Have students select one country and gather information about families and child-rearing practices.
- Have students compare types of education offered in different countries.
- Have students prepare meals from different cultures. Ask them to identify the nutrients and servings provided.
- Have students research teenage parenthood in different cultures.
- Ask students to discuss the influence of cultural background on parents' expectations of children and their techniques used in rearing children.
- Ask students to discuss prejudice and civil rights in the United States.
- Have students collect articles about crisis situations, such as famine or floods, for families around the world.

Science

- Have students research the debate of nature versus nurture.
- Have students research prenatal development.
- Using a microscope, have students look at slides of an ovum and sperm.
- Have students research various medicines and their advantages and disadvantages.
- Have students prepare a report on a disease, including symptoms, methods of treatment, and long-term effects.
- Invite a doctor, nurse, therapist, or psychologist to speak to the class.
- Have students research various types of tests done during pregnancy.
- Ask students to gather the latest information on STDs, including HIV and AIDS.
- Have students research the latest information on genetic and environmental causes of birth disorders and defects.
- Ask students to investigate the causes of lead poisoning and its effect on children.
- In small groups, have students investigate the benefits of a particular vitamin, the problems causes by the lack of it, and the foods rich in it.
- Have students research the cycle of ovulation and menstruation.
- Have students conduct a test to determine their blood type.

Art

- Have students study prints or photographs of famous artworks that show children and families.
- Have students create sketches, posters, murals, collages, or other forms of art to represent a specific topic.
- Ask students to experience various art mediums by working with finger paints, play dough, poster paints, and so on.
- Ask students to design an age-appropriate toy for a child.
- Have students create an advertisement for a product, service, group, or idea.
- Have students create a picture book for toddlers.
- Ask students to take photographs of children involved in various activities.

Music

- Have students listen to songs that describe emotions and relationships.
- Have students learn favorite lullabies, children's songs, and finger plays.
- Have students write lyrics to a song.
- Play a variety of different types of music for the class. Have students discuss the effect on children and parents and which music they would prefer to listen to during different types of activities.

Drama

- Have students role play various parenting situations.
- Have students write and perform skits that deal with relationships for an audience of peers, children, or parents.
- Have students develop a pantomime about feelings or communication.
- Invite a professional actor/actress to speak about the techniques used to communicate on stage.

Technology/Industrial Arts

- Have students evaluate safety factors within the home.
- Have students make adaptations in the home to meet the needs of a family member with a physical disability.

Physical Education/Health

- Have students learn physical exercises and activities that help reduce stress.
- Have students learn physical exercises that help strengthen back and abdominal muscles.
- Have students determine their heart rate before, during, and after aerobic activity. Have them determine the rate that would give them optimal benefit.
- Have students learn first aid and CPR.
- Have students research body systems, including reproductive, digestive, cardiovascular, and respiratory.
- Have students gather information about all three areas of health: physical, mental, and emotional.
- Have students research different types of medicines and their effects.
- Have students research communicable and noncommunicable diseases.
- Have students investigate health services available in your community.

Parenting: Rewards and Responsibilities

Teacher's Annotated Edition

Parenting: Rewards and Responsibilities

Teacher's Annotated Edition

Fourth Edition

Verna Hildebrand, Ph.D.
Professor of Family and Child Ecology
Michigan State University

GLENCOE
Macmillan/McGraw-Hill

New York, New York   Columbus, Ohio   Mission Hills, California   Peoria, Illinois

Send all inquiries to:
GLENCOE DIVISION
Macmillan/McGraw-Hill
3008 W. Willow Knolls Drive
Peoria, Illinois 61614-1083

ISBN 0-02-676373-7

Printed in the United States of America

1 2 3 4 5 6 7 8 9 RRW 99 98 97 96 95 94 93

Contributors and Reviewers

Debbie Baldwin
A.R.N.P.
Yakima Pediatrics Associates
Yakima, Washington

Susie Ball
Genetic Counselor
Yakima Valley Memorial Hospital
Yakima, Washington

Carol Barany
Childbirth Educator
Yakima Valley Memorial Hospital
Yakima, Washington

Pat Brodeen
Teacher, Teen Parent Coordinator
Theodore Roosevelt High School
San Antonio, Texas

Nancy Elizabeth Buchtel
Coordinator, School-Age Parent
  Program
Carrollton, Farmers Branch I.S.D.
Carrollton, Texas

Nancy Harris Eshelman
Teacher, Child Care and
  Development
Buckhannon-Upshur High School
Buckhannon, West Virginia

Sharon Frankenbery
Teacher, Home Economics
Fredonia High School
Fredonia, Kansas

Kay L. Kummerow
Beginning Parenthood Program
School District U-46
Elgin, Illinois

Joyce Ramsey Marshall
Teacher, Home Economics
Robert E. Lee High School
San Antonio, Texas

Karen J. Misner
Instructor
Pinellas Technical Education
  Center
Clearwater, Florida

Petra E. Pershall
HOEC Instructor
Yellville-Summit Schools
Yellville, Arkansas

Carole J. Ralston
Teacher, Home Economics
Buckhannon-Upshur High School
Buckhannon, West Virginia

Shirley H. Rice
Project Specialist
Kern High School District
Bakersfield, California

Pam F. Smith
Teacher, Home Economics and
  Health
Jonesport-Beals High School
Jonesport, Maine

Susan M. Todd
Teenage Parent Resource Teacher
Pinellas County Schools
Largo, Florida

Contents

◆◆ Unit 6 Family Resources ... 494

Parenting Decisions

CHAPTERS

What Is Parenting?

Objectives

This chapter will help you to:
- Discuss the importance of parenting.
- List and describe various types of parenthood.
- Explain how one can learn about children from theories and observations.
- Summarize the focus of this course.

Vocabulary

parenting
caregiver
nurture
guidance
self-concept
self-esteem
biological parent
adoptive parent
stepparent
foster parent

legal guardian
development
theory

Craig, age sixteen, attended a holiday party with some of his relatives. His older cousin Donna brought her eight-month-old daughter to the party. Craig was fascinated by the baby and spent most of the time talking and playing with the little girl.

This was a new experience for Craig since he is the youngest child in his family and none of his neighbors have young children. He asked his cousin many questions about the baby and how Donna liked being a parent.

On the way home, Craig and his family talked about the party. Craig said, "Donna's little girl is such a cute baby! I had so much fun talking to her and getting her to smile. She wanted to put everything in her mouth—toys, fingers, blanket, even my shirt! Donna told me how much she enjoys being a parent, but I had no idea a baby involves so much work!"

Then Craig asked his parents, "What was I like when I was a baby?"

Craig had learned something about parenting that day.

Parenting Defined

What do you think of when you hear the word *parenting*? Like many other people, you may think of parenting as being a parent. That is true, but it is only part of the answer.

Parenting means providing care, support, and love in a way that leads to a child's total development. Parenting includes being responsible for the child's physical needs. It means creating a nurturing environment of attention, encouragement, and love for the child. It also means providing guidance for the child. Thus parenting involves meeting the child's physical, mental, emotional, and social needs.

Many people besides parents can love, care for, and guide a child. The term for such a person is a **caregiver.** Some caregivers are relatives, such as grandparents, older brothers and sisters, and aunts and uncles. Other caregivers may be nonrelatives, such as babysitters, teachers, coaches, scout leaders, and professional child care providers. For example, a grandparent may care for a child while the parents are at work. A babysitter may comfort a child who cries when the parents go out for dinner. A teacher may provide guidance for a child who is having trouble with an assignment. All of these caregivers use various parenting skills.

❖ Parenting Skills

Parenting is not the same as parenthood, which means to be a father or a mother. All people who care for children, whether on a full- or part-time basis, use parenting skills. Let's take a look at the three basic skills involved in parenting: providing physical care, nurturing, and giving guidance.

Providing Physical Care

All children have certain basic needs. These include the need for food, clothing, shelter, health, and safety. Children are unable to satisfy these needs for themselves. They are

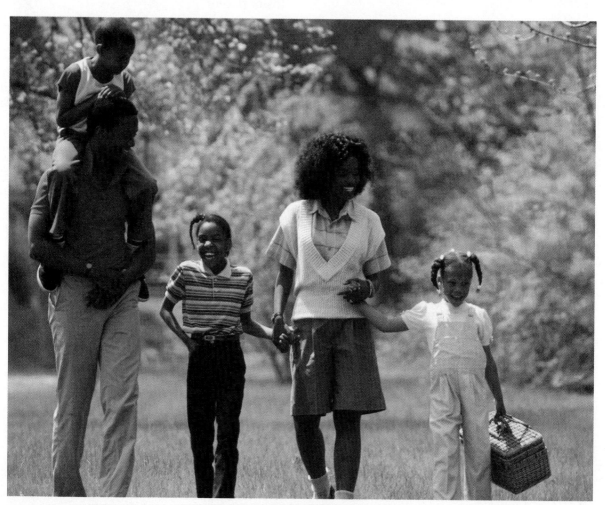

Many adults find that parenting is one of life's most satisfying experiences.

Activity. Ask students to write a description of the best caregiver they know. How has this person fulfilled the three essential elements of parenting for a child?

Problem Solving. Bring in current newspaper articles that describe accidents involving young children. Have students identify preventive measures which could have been taken by parents or other caregivers.

totally dependent upon caregivers to meet these needs.

Children need nutritious food that will help them grow and develop. They need clothing and shelter for warmth and protection. They need to be washed and given medical care. Children are not aware of the dangers in their environment, such as hot pans, medicine bottles, and busy streets. Parents and other caregivers must watch children carefully and protect them from accidents and harm.

Nurturing

To **nurture** means to support and encourage. Nurturing involves giving children attention, love, and a sense of security. Children need encouragement and praise when they try various tasks. They need comforting when they are upset or hurt. Above all, they need to know that their parents and other caregivers really care about them. Nurturing helps bring out the best in children.

Providing Guidance

Parenting also involves **guidance.** This refers to the words and actions that adults use to influence children's behavior. Guidance helps children understand what type of behavior is acceptable and what type is unacceptable. It also helps children learn the difference between right and wrong.

As parents and other caregivers interact with young children, they help the children learn social and emotional skills. For example, children must learn how to get along with others. They must also learn how to express their emotions in acceptable ways. By using effective guidance techniques, parents can help children become responsible and independent individuals.

❖ The Importance of Parenting

A child's education begins at birth. Through everyday activities such as caring for, nurturing, and guiding a baby, parents and other caregivers help the baby learn. The child learns many skills and facts, as well as how to learn.

During these early years, children also learn about themselves. They develop an image of themselves from how others treat them. This image of oneself is called **self-concept.** Children also sense whether or not they are important to others. This feeling about oneself is called **self-esteem.** It is a person's opinion, belief, or judgment about his

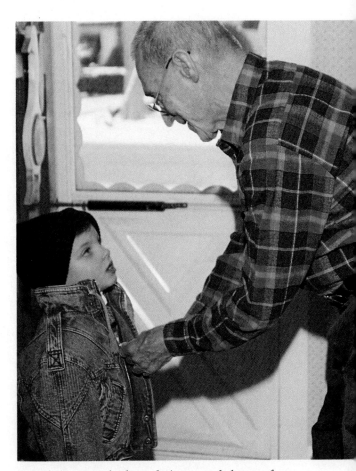

Grandparents and other relatives may help care for a child on a part-time basis. However, the parents remain the primary caregiver.

or her worthiness as a person. Self-esteem differs somewhat from self-concept because it involves feelings.

A person's self-concept and self-esteem begin to develop in infancy. These images and feelings about oneself have lifelong effects. For example, children's behavior is strongly influenced by the positive or negative images and feelings they have of themselves.

Parents and other caregivers can help shape and mold a child by doing the following:

- Building up the child's self-esteem.
- Satisfying the child's physical needs for food, clothing, shelter, security, and safety.
- Providing guidance for the child's behavior.

- Showing faith and confidence in the child's abilities.
- Taking time to listen to what the child wants to say.
- Encouraging the child to try new things, understanding when the child fails, and comforting the child in times of sadness.
- Giving the child affection and love.

Parents and other caregivers should practice all three essential dimensions of parenting: providing physical care, nurturing, and guiding. This leads to a healthy, happy, confident child with a positive self-concept and high self-esteem. If parents and caregivers fail to provide the necessary physical care, the child may not grow and develop properly. If they fail to provide nurturing, the child may feel ignored, unloved, or worthless. If they fail to provide guidance, the child may grow up with little self-discipline. All three aspects of parenting are essential.

Teachers and coaches use parenting skills as they help nurture and guide children.

Types of Parenthood

There are many types of parenthood today. How a person becomes a parent is less important than the role of a parent. Thus the two people who create a child may or may not provide the regular daily care and guidance of the child. A parent is the person who accepts the role of parenting and provides a meaningful relationship with the child.

People can become biological, adoptive, step-, or foster parents.

◆◆ Biological Parenthood

A **biological parent** is one of the two people who conceive a child. A biological parent is sometimes called a birth parent. A child's biological parents may or may not serve in the role of mother or father to the child.

◆◆ Adoptive Parenthood

Some people become parents through adoption. An **adoptive parent** legally becomes the parent of a child and raises the child as his or her own. Adoptive parents assume the same responsibilities as biological parents.

Adopted children are not the biological children of their parents. However, some children are adopted by relatives after their biological parents' death. Adopted children usually take the last name of their adoptive parents and have all the legal rights of biological children.

Some couples who adopt children have physical conditions that prevent them from becoming biological parents. Others have health disorders that might be inherited by their offspring. This influences their decision not to have a biological child. Still other couples realize that many children in the world need families. They adopt infants or older

children in need of homes. In the past, only married couples were considered suitable to adopt a child. However, mature single men and women can now become adoptive parents.

Today, many of the children available for adoption are no longer babies. Some of these older children have physical, emotional, or mental disabilities. Others are brothers and sisters who want to be adopted by the same family and not separated. People who are considering adoption should have an understanding of themselves and their reasons for wanting children. This will help them decide whether becoming adoptive parents is a good option for themselves.

Adoptive parents become the legal parents of a child and raise the child as their own. The adopted child has all the legal rights of a biological child.

Discuss. What are advantages and disadvantages of each type of parenthood? How could any disadvantages be minimized?
Activity. Invite an attorney to speak on the legal aspects of different types of parenthood.

Reference. See pages 95 and 525-526 for more information on adoption.
Activity. Have students gather information about different types of adoption procedures that are currently available.

❖ Step Parenthood

Parenthood comes immediately when an individual without children marries a person with children. The individual then becomes a **stepparent** to his or her spouse's children from an earlier relationship. The children become stepchildren to the stepparent. Some stepparents choose later to legally adopt the children of their marriage partner.

In many cases, both individuals who marry are parents with children. Thus each parent is a biological parent as well as a stepparent. The children of one parent become stepbrothers or stepsisters to the children of the other parent. You will learn more about stepfamilies in Chapter 2.

❖ Foster Parenthood

A **foster parent** is a person who provides a home to children in times of emergency. Some children are placed in foster homes because their parents cannot provide adequate care for them due to illness or family crisis. Others are placed with foster parents because they cannot get along with their own parents. Still other children are placed in foster homes because of abuse, neglect, or abandonment. Children may stay in a foster home for a short time or for several years.

Foster parents are carefully selected by state or city agencies and monitored by social workers. This is to ensure that the children receive adequate care. Foster parents receive

This couple became foster parents after their own children were grown. They now care for children who need a temporary home due to a family emergency or crisis.

Reference. See pages 39 and 523–524 for more information on stepparents and stepchildren.

Activity. Have students research how people can become foster parents in your state or community. What are some of the rewards and challenges of being a foster parent? What financial assistance is available?

a payment from the government for the children's expenses.

Being a foster parent can be very satisfying. Foster parents provide care and understanding to children who may be experiencing a problem or crisis. However, some of the children pose special challenges because of severe emotional or behavioral problems.

Foster parents must understand that the children are in their care only temporarily. Eventually, the children will return to their own family or to an adoptive family. However, foster parents occasionally decide to adopt a foster child.

❖ Legal Guardianship

A **legal guardian** is a person appointed by a court to provide parenting for a child. This is often done when a child's parents die. The legal guardian is usually a relative or close friend of the family. He or she is responsible for taking care of the child and may take on the parenting role. Unlike the case in adoption, the child does not take the last name of the legal guardian.

DECISIONS ◆ ◆ DECISIONS

Lindsey, age sixteen, is babysitting for a neighbor's four-year-old son, Taylor. She reminds him that it is almost bedtime and that he should start putting away his toys before she reads him a story. Suddenly Taylor says, "You can't tell me what do do. You're not my mommy! Only my mommy and daddy can tell me what to do." As a caregiver for Taylor, what should Lindsey say to him?"

Around the World

One World, Many Points of View

For centuries, people have argued whether heredity or environment is more important in determining a person's personality traits. This argument is called the nature-nurture controversy. *Nature* refers to heredity, or inherited characteristics. *Nurture* refers to the environment—all the care, upbring, training, and education that influence a person's inherited potential.

Most experts believe that a child's personality is the result of many factors. Some traits are part of the child's genetic makeup. Others are influenced by the way the child is reared.

One of the strongest influences on how children are reared is cultural heritage. People of different nationalities, ethnic groups, and religions have different beliefs about parenting children. For example, some cultures are very permissive about how small children should behave. Other cultures are stricter about social behavior and emphasize discipline. Some cultures put a high value on education and hard work. Other cultures place greater emphasis on family relationships.

Parents usually rear their children according to the particular customs of their own cultural group. Their expectations of how children should behave will influence the child from a very young age.

Cultural differences are very noticeable in the United States, where people come from a wide variety of backgrounds. This is why many school systems are helping children understand and respect their cultural differences.

Activity. Have students ask their parents if they have a will. If so, have they designated a legal guardian for their children?

Activity. Invite a panel of biological, adoptive, step, and foster parents to talk about their experiences. Ask them to share some of the joys and frustrations of parenthood. Have students identify the similarities in the parents' experiences.

Learning About Children

Good parenting skills are based on knowledge of how children grow and develop. This information helps parents and other caregivers understand why certain parenting skills are considered appropriate.

Human development occurs in the same sequence in all people. **Development** refers to an increasing skill in one or a combination of abilities. These include physical, emotional, social, and mental skills. All human babies learn to walk and talk in much the same way. Although there are differences in hair and skin color, language, and family styles, children all over the world are more alike than different.

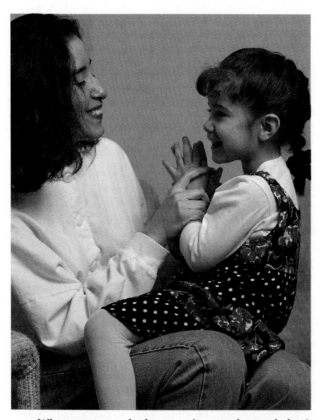

When parents and other caregivers understand physical, emotional, mental, and social development, they are better able to meet children's needs.

A basic knowledge of human development and practice with parenting skills will make you more likely to enjoy children. Someone who does not understand a child's action may be bothered by it. For example, a newborn baby cries loudly when his or her clothes are removed. This happens because the infant's immature nervous system reacts to slight drops in temperature. Knowing this, a parent or other caregiver can take steps to keep the infant covered during diaper changes instead of becoming worried or angry about the baby's crying. The adult also knows that this behavior will disappear as the baby's nervous system develops. Then it is not always necessary to keep the child covered during changes.

This kind of know-how makes both the child and the caregiver feel more secure. Their experiences together will be more rewarding as they build a stronger relationship.

Parents and other caregivers can learn about human development in two ways: from theories and from observations.

❖ Theories About Children

A **theory** is an organized set of suggestions about facts or events that is developed through study and observation. Good theories contain carefully defined terms and are tested in controlled studies. Test results are published in journals so that anyone can read, critique, and further test the theories.

A theory is not a fact. Once it becomes a fact it is no longer called a theory. For example, most people once believed that the world is flat. However, others had a theory that the world is round. They observed and tested that theory, published and discussed their ideas, and eventually proved that the world is round. They did this by observing that ships disappear over the horizon. You can now prove the fact that the world is round by looking at photos taken from outer space.

Over the centuries, many researchers have focused on children's growth and development. They have organized, stated, tested, and published theories to help explain children's growth and development. These theories are helpful to parents, teachers, counselors, physicians, and others.

The theories you will read about in this book are currently being tested. None is yet a perfect theory or fact. Scientists are still attempting to find a theory that is always true for all humans. However, it is difficult to study human beings for several reasons. Some studies need to be done over a period of many years to follow the growth and development of individuals. Sometimes the human subjects move away from the researchers. In addition, some tests are inappropriate or unethical to use on humans. Thus human developmental facts are difficult to obtain.

Some of these theorists are famous for their work. Their theories are discussed throughout this book. See pages 26–27 for brief sketches of several of these people and their ideas.

DECISIONS ◆ ◆ DECISIONS

Kelsey and Bill are discussing whether parents, teachers, and other caregivers could learn more about children from developmental theories or from personal observations. Bill says that theories could be more helpful because they have been developed by researchers who spent many years studying children. Ann replies that observations could be more beneficial because all children do not behave the same way in similar situations. Now they turn to you and ask your opinion. What will you say?

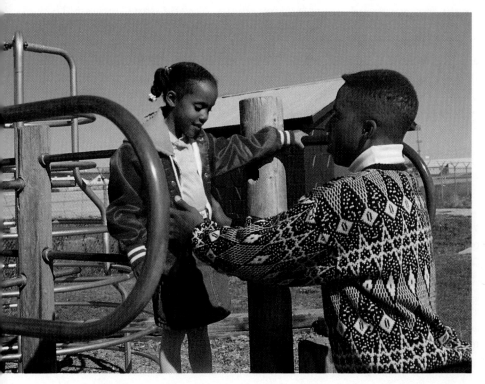

You can use child development and parenting information whenever you are around children—in your family, neighborhood, or job.

Activity. Ask students to select one child development theorist and research his or her work. Have them prepare an oral or written report.

Activity. Have students make wall charts of child development theories. Charts should include name of theorist, developmental area, and specific stages of development. Throughout the course have students refer to the charts and compare theories.

Child Development Theorists

Observers of Children

The earliest studies of children involved making, recording, and analyzing observations. This method of study continues to provide important ideas about child development.

Jean Piaget (1896–1980) was a Swiss psychologist and educator. He researched and defined the mental, or cognitive, skills that children learn. Piaget began by observing his own three children in their day-to-day activities and growth. From these observations, he developed a sequence of how a child's intellect unfolds and how thought develops at each stage from infancy through adolescence. He described these stages in great detail.

Piaget was also interested in the development of moral reasoning, which is how decision making and behavior relate to social values. He believed that moral reasoning, like thought, occurs in stages.

Margaret Mahler (1897–1985), an educator and child psychoanalyst, was the first to describe psychological stages in a child's development. A psychoanalyst is a professional who studies the human mind as it affects behavior and tries to help people understand their mental and behavioral problems. Mahler discovered that normal children and psychotic children develop in parallel ways. For example, normal children establish a oneness with their mother during infancy and use this for security. Psychotic children do not establish this close relationship and lack the security to act with confidence.

Erik Erikson (1902–   ) studied children from a psychosocial point of view. The term *psychosocial* refers to the relationship between one's view of oneself and one's social world. In his theory, called the "Eight Stages of Man," Erikson describes the important stages of personality development from birth to old age. He believes that people acquire lasting personality characteristics at each stage. According to Erikson, the successful or unsuccessful mastery of a central emotional task at each stage can determine a person's emotional health as he or she grows older.

Sigmund Freud (1856–1939) offered a psychosexual theory of child development. This refers to a child's ability to satisfy basic physical and emotional needs such as those for food, love, warmth, and security. Freud believed that the pleasure and pain that infants associate with the sensory experiences of feeding and toilet training influence the development of their personality.

Albert Bandura (1925–   ), a social psychologist, believes that a person's behavior can be explained by knowing the other individuals around that person. Children, in particular, imitate the models around them.

Lawrence Kohlberg (1927–1987) studied the development of moral reasoning in adolescents. His theory describes developmental stages that occur in a set order. The lowest stage is related to obedience, and the highest stage is related to conscience or principle. Kohlberg used an all-male sample in his studies. Now researchers are using female subjects to test his theory.

B. F. Skinner (1904–1990) believed that a system of rewards and punishments explains much of human behavior. He believed that to change a behavior parents must reward or punish an existing behavior. To encourage children to use the toilet, for example, parents can reward the child's efforts with smiles, praise, or treats. To stop children from handling items at a check-out counter, parents should not reward that behavior by purchasing one of the items.

Information on Skinner's theory is useful in a number of parenting situations. However, many experts believe that the theory is too simplistic to apply to many of the complex tasks children must learn.

Maria Montessori (1870–1952), an Italian physician and educator, believed that all young children have the ability and desire to learn words. She developed a teaching method to help them with that learning. The Montessori method of teaching is designed to increase mental development in young children. It emphasizes the use of the five senses to develop cognitive and social skills.

Testers of Children

Some people test and measure children's development. They devise tests to see how well a child has mastered the many tasks that are important to succeed and fully participate in life. Some tests measure mental development. Others use children's drawings to measure the children's awareness of themselves and their environment.

Robert Havighurst (1900–1991) organized into a series the developmental tasks that he believed to be most easily learned at certain ages. These developmental tasks are requirements that an individual must accomplish at each stage of life before proceeding to the next developmental level. Havighurst suggested three sources for these tasks: growth and development, the society in which the individual lives, and the individual's personal attitudes, values, and belief system.

Alfred Binet (1857–1911) devised the original testing scale for measuring intelligence. His work was the first to show the relationship between chronological age and thought processes. His revised scale, called the Stanford-Binet Intelligence Scale, is often referred to as the IQ (intelligence quotient) test.

Nancy Bayley (1899–) used longitudinal studies to follow groups of the same children over more than 20 years. The findings of longitudinal studies are thought to be more reliable than the findings of studies of children seen only once. Bayley studied how each child scored on tests of mental and motor skills over time. The scores were compared according to the children's gender, birth order, and race and the education of their parents. The results of Bayley's studies demonstrate the effects of attention and stimulation in infancy.

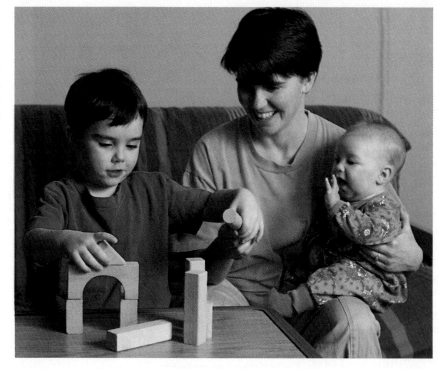

A baby's education begins at birth. Parents help nurture and guide their children's development from infancy to adulthood.

◆◆ Developmental Theory

Developmental theory is a combination of many theories that describe in various ways how children grow and develop. Developmental theory is what most people who work with children follow. No one theory is completely satisfactory for helping explain all aspects of a child's development and behavior. For example, Piaget's theories help explain cognitive and language development. Erikson's theory deals with personality development, and Kohlberg's focuses on moral development. In trying to assess development, one must look at each child and determine where he or she is on many developmental scales: physical-motor, emotional, social, moral, cognitive, and language.

Ages and Stages

The theories created by researchers trace child growth and development through distinct ages and stages during which major changes occur. Age refers to the actual chronological age of children from the year of birth. Stage means one of several periods of development that children pass through as they grow.

Throughout this text, children are discussed in terms of various age categories:

- Infant—from birth until age one.
- Toddler—from age one to age three.
- Preschool—from age three to age five.
- School-age—from age five to puberty.
- Adolescent—from puberty to adulthood.

When planning activities for a child at home or school, it is important for caregivers to be familiar with the many developmental stages. That is, at what age do children typically smile, walk, hold a spoon, or say two-word sentences? It is unreasonable to expect any child to act in a certain way, such as taking turns with other children, when neither the child's body nor mind is ready for the task.

More About. Non-scientific people, such as parents, teachers, and other caregivers, can verify many of the theories from their own experiences with children.

Emphasize. Parents and other caregivers should not expect children to perform or behave in a way that is above their current level of physical, emotional, social, cognitive, or moral development.

❖ Observing Children

As you study parenting, you may want to find ways to observe and work with children. This will help you understand parenting concepts and remember them more vividly.

Many parenting and child development courses provide opportunities for students to observe children in a child care setting. Neighbors and relatives, community centers, and playgrounds also offer opportunities to gain experience with one or more children. Some teenagers enjoy volunteering in after-school or summer child care programs. Others tutor a child or become involved in children's sports programs. Churches and synagogues offer opportunities to work in child care programs, as well as special religious education programs. Still other teenagers work with children in dancing, gymnastics, or swimming programs.

In many of these situations, you may have the opportunity to talk to parents about what it is like to care for, nurture, and guide a child. Most parents will be happy to talk to you about their daily experiences. They may also give you valuable advice regarding preparation for parenting and parenthood.

Purposes of Observing Children

Child research involves observing children in natural settings. This means that the observer does not change any of the conditions surrounding the children.

Observation helps us do the following:

- Learn how children grow and accomplish developmental tasks.
- Provide ideas for planning appropriate activities for children.
- Find out how a child feels about himself or herself and determine the effect of a particular activity.
- Recognize children's distress signals.

Observing or working with children will help you understand parenting concepts.

Discuss. Where in the community might teenagers be able to observe or work with young children?
Activity. Have students ask their parents to describe what they were like as a baby and toddler. Questions might include: When did I get my first tooth? When did I walk? What was my favorite toy? What made me angry? Have students share their findings with classmates.

Through skillful observation, you can analyze behavior and understand the principles of growth and development.

Guidelines for Observing Children

Skillful observation involves more than simply looking and watching. Here are some guidelines. First, choose one or two children to observe at a time rather than many children at once.

Second, pretend that you are only looking on rather than observing. Children will behave more normally if they do not think adults are watching them carefully.

Third, write a description of what you have observed. The description should be objective. In other words it should not be influenced by judgments or interpretations. Explain what the child does and what you actually see.

For example, an observer writes the following: "Ben, age three, is playing with small blocks and a truck. Melissa, age four, runs up, takes the truck from Ben, and goes away with it. Ben's eyes are wide, and he looks at his empty hand. His lips pucker up. He says, 'I want my truck.'"

An inexperienced observer might have recorded, "Ben did not cry. He did not scream." This would have been judgmental or nonobjective. The "did not" phrase indicates that the observer expected the child to cry or scream.

Finally, keep all information confidential. Observers should not discuss children and their behavior outside the classroom.

Activity. Using various resources, have students develop an observational checklist or other means of observing and recording children's behavior. Throughout the course, revise checklists to include topics for specific ages and stages.

More About. Arrange to have children of different ages brought to class throughout the course so students can observe their development and behavior. Have classroom set up to resemble a child care center with age-appropriate toys and activities.

Analyzing Observations

Analyzing your observations is an important part of developing skills. To analyze the behavior you observe, you need to recognize and understand the principles of growth and development in the behavior of children. Following are ways to develop analyzing skills:

- Look for behavior that is repeated.
- Look for the circumstances under which the repeated behavior occurs.
- Ask yourself how the observed behavior

affects the child's learning and relationships with others.

- Look for specific efforts that the child makes to satisfy needs and accomplish developmental tasks. Are the efforts appropriate? Are they getting results?
- Listen carefully to the conversations of the children, noting their questions.
- Look in resource books to see what others say about the behavior you have observed for a child of this age.

◆◆ *Health & Safety* ◆◆

Wellness

Being a parent requires energy and physical stamina, as well as patience and a sense of humor. Although parenting may appear easy, there are times in every parent's life when it is very difficult. Being in good health is one way to help ease the pressures.

Good health means much more than not being sick. To be well, a person needs to have good physical, mental, and social health. This means having a healthy body, a healthy mind, and a positive attitude toward life. The process of becoming and remaining healthy is called wellness.

How do you know whether you are healthy? The signs of physical good health usually relate to your appearance, your energy, and the absence of disease. A parent in good physical health has the energy and stamina to care for children during the day, as well as at night. Physical health also includes greater resistance to disease. This is particularly important for parents when their children enter a child care or preschool program. Children bring home all sorts of illnesses, which they can pass on to family members.

Good mental health involves liking, accepting, and feeling good about yourself. You are able to express your emotions in acceptable ways. You can deal with problems and frustrations without becoming overwhelmed by them. People with good mental health enjoy learning and developing their thinking skills. Good mental health helps parents deal with daily demands and challenges. It helps parents remain patient and calm. It enables them to nurture and guide their children's emotional and mental development.

Good social health means being able to get along with other people. It involves making and keeping friends, communicating well, and cooperating with others at home and work. Good social health enables parents to teach their children how to get along with others.

All three areas of health—physical, mental, and social—are important for wellness. Your state of wellness affects how you look, feel, and act. It also affects how parents care for, nurture, and guide their children.

More About. To analyze means to break down into component parts for a better understanding.

Activity. Have students record observations of children's behavior and then analyze their observations. What can you learn from the observations?

Focus of This Course

All children are different. You have probably already noticed this in children you have seen, whether they were infants, toddlers, preschoolers, or school-age children. Have you ever wondered why children are different? What makes one child pleasant to be around and another child difficult? *Parenting: Rewards and Responsibilities* will help answer these questions. This course in parenting, child development, and caregiving is designed to help you do the following:

- Think more deeply about children.
- Follow a child's growth and development.
- Begin to understand the responsibilities of parenthood.
- Learn and use the information and the skills needed to serve as a caregiver to children.
- Learn more about yourself by recalling your own childhood.
- Reflect on whether children will have a major or a minor place in your future.
- Examine the opportunities for a career in child development, child care, or related fields.

Do you remember the various stages of your own childhood? The more you understand children, the more you will enjoy being with them.

◆ ◆ Self-Esteem ◆ ◆

Parenting involves many commitments and responsibilities. Perhaps the greatest of these is helping a child develop a positive self-concept and high self-esteem. With these assets, a child will be better able to make wise decisions, relate well to others, and assume responsibility for his or her own life.

Learning about children teaches you about yourself. As you learn about children, you will remember events and feelings from your own childhood. This leads to increased self-awareness and a better understanding of what you value and how you react. You will discover ways of nurturing that are easy and natural for you. You may also find that you gain insight into your own parents and the ways your family interacts.

Using what you learn in this course, you can practice your parenting skills with children in your family, in your neighborhood, or in a child care center. This practice is important. It will help you learn whether the role of parent or caregiver is right for you.

Discuss. What careers are in the field of child development and child care? What other careers work closely with children? **Reference.** See pages 570–573 for a list of child-related careers.

Activity. Survey students about the following: How many think they will be a parent some day? How many children do they think they want? How many would like to work in a child-related field? What do they hope to gain from this course?

CHAPTER 1 REVIEW

Summary

- Parenting involves meeting a child's physical, mental, emotional, and social needs.
- Parenting skills include physically caring for a child, nurturing the child, and guiding the child's behavior.
- A person's self-concept and self-esteem begin to develop in infancy.
- There are several types of parenthood, including biological, adoptive, step, and foster parenthood, as well as legal guardianship.
- Many researchers have studied children and formulated, tested, and published theories on children's growth and development.
- Most developmental theories trace children's growth and development through specific ages and stages during which major changes occur.
- We can learn many things about children by observing them objectively and analyzing our observations.
- Learning more about children helps us learn more about ourselves.

Questions

p. 17 **1.** What is the difference between parenting and parenthood?

p. 18 **2.** What three skills are involved in parenting?

p. 19 **3.** What does nurturing involve?

p. 19 **4.** Define and compare self-concept and self-esteem.

p. 21 **5.** List and describe four types of parents.

p. 24 **6.** Why is it helpful for caregivers to have a basic knowledge of human development?

p. 28 **7.** Why do most people who work with children follow developmental theory?

p. 28 **8.** Into what five age categories are children divided in this book?

p. 30 **9.** Name four guidelines to remember when observing children.

p. 32 **10.** What can you expect to learn from this course?

Activities

1. Write a description of yourself as a five-year-old. Ask your parents, other relatives, neighbors, or a teacher what you were like at that age. Also use your own memories to describe yourself and your development at age five.

2. List all the people who have served as caregivers for you throughout childhood. Compare your list with other classmates' lists.

3. During this course, it will be helpful to be in contact with children and their parents. Identify three children from your family, neighborhood, or a children's center. Each child should be from a different age category: infant, toddler, preschooler, school-age child. Talk to the parent or parents of each child. Ask whether you may occasionally observe, play with, or help care for the child during this course.

Think About

1. What qualities do you think all parents should have?

2. Make a list of questions about parenting, child development, and child care that you hope this course will answer.

Reference. See the Teacher's Manual in the front of the Teacher's Annotated Edition for complete answers to the chapter review questions.

Role of the Family

Objectives

This chapter will help you to:
- Describe various types of family structures.
- Explain how families have changed in comparison to families in previous generations.
- List various functions of families.
- Discuss the many influences on today's families.

Vocabulary

roles
nuclear family
single-parent family
blended family
extended family
cooperative family
family life cycle
life-style

Jennifer, age five, drew a picture of her family. She drew her father first—including his beard and eyeglasses. She stated, "That's my dad," as she carefully printed "Dad" under the figure.

"Here's Mommy," she said, as she made a large triangle and head at the top.

Next she drew herself, using another triangle for a dress.

Finally, she drew her little sister under the edge of her mother's skirt. She added her sister's arms reaching out toward the parents. Jennifer then drew identical smiles on all the figures.

"This is my family—me, my dad, my mom, and my sister, Heather. I like my family," Jennifer proclaimed.

What Is a Family?

Jennifer is growing up in a family. A family has been a social unit throughout the world for centuries. What is a family? Dictionaries include many different definitions, ranging from "parents and their children" to "a group of people who share common attitudes, interests, or goals."

The U.S. Census Bureau describes a family as "two or more persons related by birth, marriage, or adoption who reside in the same household." Some courts have defined family characteristics as a long-term relationship, emotional and financial commitment, and dependence upon one another for daily services. Others have described a family as "a group who love and care for each other."

Chapter Opener. Ask students to read the opening scenario to the chapter. Ask these questions: What does Jennifer's drawing tell you about her family? How does she perceive each member of her family? How do you know she likes her family?

Activity. Have students draw a picture of their own family.
Activity. Ask students to write down the first word or phrase they think of when they hear the word *family*. Have them share their responses.

The family has been a social unit throughout the world for centuries. Each family is as unique as the people in it.

Each member of a family has certain **roles,** or parts one plays when interacting with others. These roles are defined within the family and within society.

Whatever the definition, each family is as unique as the people in it. Some people grow up in very large families, others in small families. No simple pattern exists among families in our society.

❖ Types of Families

There are more than 66 million families in the United States. Some families consist of only two people—one parent and a child.

Other families consist of many people—with various combinations of relatives or even unrelated friends all living together under the same roof.

Until children are about six or seven years old, they believe that all families are like their own. They do not reason that other families could be different. However, some children live with one parent; others live with two parents. Still others live with a stepparent or are cared for by a grandparent.

Let's take a look at the various types of family structure. Each type has distinct advantages and disadvantages. Each also has its own challenges and concerns for those in the parenting role.

Activity. On the chalkboard, have students list the roles of each member of their family. Then ask them to compare the lists for similarities and differences between families. How are roles determined within families? Within society?

Discuss. What are examples of different types of families that are portrayed in television shows, movies, and books? What images of families do viewers and readers gain from these? Do you think these images are accurate? Why or why not?

Nuclear Family

Jennifer, in the chapter-opening story, is growing up in a **nuclear** (NOO-klee-ur) **family.** This is a family that consists of a mother, a father, and one or more children. The children may be biological or adopted. The size of Jennifer's family is near the statistical average of families in the United States today—two adults plus 1.8 children. This was called a traditional family in the past, but the number of nuclear families has been steadily declining.

There are many advantages to a nuclear family structure. In this family type, two people share the parenting responsibilities. The parents usually have more time to spend with the children because they can share the tasks of running the household. If both parents work outside the home, they can also share financial responsibilities.

A two-parent family provides examples of both male and female roles. The children are able to learn how their parents share responsibilities. They also see how couples communicate, make decisions, and solve problems on a daily basis.

However, some nuclear families actually have only one parent at home a large part of the time. For example, one parent may be in the military and be assigned to duty far away from home. The remaining parent must care for the children almost as a single parent. This situation also occurs when one parent must travel extensively for his or her job. The parent may be absent from the family for one or more weeks, returning home only on weekends. A parent who works long hours or commutes long distances may have to leave early and arrive home late. As a result, young children may see little of the parent. Thus not all parents in nuclear families are able to share parenting and household responsibilities.

A nuclear family consists of a mother, a father, and one or more biological or adopted children.

Activity. Divide the class into the six family types: nuclear, single-parent, blended, extended, cooperative, and non-child. Ask each group to research the advantages and disadvantages of their family type. Then have the groups present their findings in the form of a skit, role play, or debate.

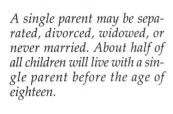

A single parent may be separated, divorced, widowed, or never married. About half of all children will live with a single parent before the age of eighteen.

Single-Parent Family

A **single-parent family** consists of only one parent and one or more children. Some single-parent families result from legal separation, desertion, or divorce. Others are due to the death of one parent. Still others are the result of unmarried people becoming parents through birth or adoption.

The number of single parents has increased dramatically in recent years. About 25 percent of all families in the United States are single-parent families. Most of these families are headed by mothers. However, single fathers head about 16 percent of single-parent families. It is estimated that one-half of all children will live with a single parent before they are eighteen years old.

Parenting is a big job to do alone. Single parents must balance all the responsibilities of parenting, managing a household, and probably holding a job. They have no one with whom to share the challenges or problems of rearing children. As a result, they usually have less free time to spend on their own interests.

Many single parents are totally responsible for their family's expenses. They do not receive any financial support from their child's other parent. As a result, many single parent families, especially those headed by women, have financial problems. This is because men generally have higher-paying jobs than women in our society.

Single parents may be concerned about their children having few opportunities to interact with adults of the opposite gender from the parent. However, single parents can arrange for their children to spend time with adult relatives, neighbors, and friends in order to learn about gender roles.

Although the role of single parent is difficult, it also has rewards. Children of single parents often participate in more household tasks and take on responsibilities at an earlier age. This helps them learn to be responsible, dependable, and independent.

Children who grow up in single-parent families can have happy and full lives. In fact, dedicated single parents can provide a high level of care, security, and love for their children. Children in a happy single-parent family are often more stable than those living in an unhappy two-parent family.

Blended Family

The **blended family** consists of two parents, one or both of whom have children from a previous relationship. Each becomes a stepparent to the other's children. The children become stepbrothers or stepsisters. If the parents then have a child of their own, the children from the previous marriages are half brothers and half sisters to the new child.

A blended family enables the adults to share the family responsibilities. It may also improve the financial situation of a single parent and children.

However, both the parents and children in a blended family may have problems in establishing a new family unit. It may take a great deal of patience and understanding before stepparents and stepchildren learn to get along with each other. Each person must adjust to new family members, new roles, and new habits. Eventually, most members of a blended family gain each other's respect.

Some of the problems associated with blended families are merging different family customs, developing new daily routines, and establishing new rules of behavior. Members of a blended family must learn to respect the possessions and privacy of others. They also have to establish bonds with the new family as well as maintain relationships with members of their former family.

The background of the family members affects the smoothness of the transition to a new family unit. If either or both of the spouses were divorced or widowed, memories and habits from the former marriages will influence the new marriage. Children may still be dealing with the emotional effects of their parents' divorce or the death of a parent. Family members may need some counseling to help smooth the transition from one family structure to the other.

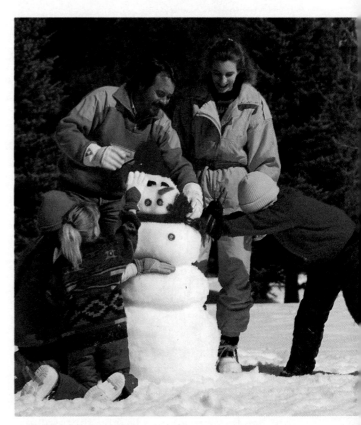

A blended family is formed when a couple—one or both whom have children from a previous relationship— marry. Both the stepparents and stepchildren must make many adjustments to new family relationships.

Activity. On the chalkboard, have students list the challenges and problems that parents and children encounter in a blended family. Then have them consider how many of these challenges and problems occur in other types of families.

Discuss. What routines of family members might need to be altered in a new blended family? What family customs and traditions might need to be changed? How could parents help children adjust to these changes?

All the immediate relatives of a family make up the extended family. Several generations of an extended family may live together in the same household.

Extended Family

The **extended family** is made up of all the immediate relatives of a family, such as grandparents, aunts, uncles, and cousins. Sometimes the members of an extended family live together or near each other.

Years ago, it was very common for many members of an extended family to live together under one roof. More recently, most families have chosen to live by themselves rather than with relatives. However, the trend is now reversing. For example, Allen and Marcy Weber have her elderly parents living

with them. Recently their divorced daughter returned home, along with her two children. Now four generations are living together. Family life experts predict that this trend will continue as more people live longer and family structures continue to change.

Members of an extended family, just as in a blended family, may have difficulty getting along together. Older or younger relatives who move into the home may resent having to give up their own home and independence. Conflicts may arise about how to divide up various household responsibilities from han-

More About. When relatives live near but not with each other, the family may be called a modified extended family.
Activity. Have students create a family tree of their extended family.

Discuss. What adjustments would each member of the Weber family have to make when all four generations began living together? Which family member(s) do you think would have to make the greatest adjustment? Why?

dling finances to preparing meals to doing the laundry. It is important for family members to discuss their problems with each other. It may also be necessary to establish specific rules and responsibilities for the various relatives to achieve family harmony.

On the other hand, living in an extended family has many advantages. Grandparents and other adult relatives can help care for the children and share household tasks. They can offer advice to other family members. They can also be very supportive in times of family emergencies or crises.

However, members of an extended family must strike a happy balance between offering help and advice and maintaining their own lives and independence. Parents should not automatically assume that relatives will help out with child care or other day-to-day tasks. At the same time, grandparents, aunts, and uncles should offer only as much advice and help as is requested. It is important for parents to maintain the main responsibility for rearing their children and managing their immediate family.

Cooperative Family

The **cooperative family** consists of nonrelated people who get together to rear their children in one household. They are able to share living expenses and household chores. They also are able to share the responsibilities of caring for the children.

◆ ◆ Self-Esteem ◆ ◆

All children need at least one person whom they love and who loves them. When parents or other family members give children a hug or words of encouragement—especially when unexpected—children feel loved and valued.

Often two best friends who are single parents with children will move in together to form a cooperative family. They help each other as in an extended family, even though they are not related. Some elderly people also live together and cooperate as a family. They are able to share housing, meals, companionship, expenses, and care.

Family Without Children

A married couple without children are also considered a family. Some couples are unable to have children; others choose to remain childless.

In the past, married couples were expected to have children. This attitude is changing as many couples decide to delay parenting or decide against becoming parents. Some couples prefer to spend their time and energy on career goals. Others do not want to limit their freedom or assume the financial responsibilities of rearing children. Still others choose to focus on their own growth and development, both as individuals and as a couple.

Some couples without children take an active interest in the children of relatives and friends. Others become involved in children's programs in the community.

❖ Living in More Than One Type of Family

As children grow up, they may live in several different types of family. For example, they may be born into a nuclear family. Then, if their parents divorce or one parent dies, they will live in a single-parent family. This may be followed by a blended family if the parent remarries. If a grandparent arrives to live with the family, the children will experience an extended-family situation. Thus the structure of the same family may change over the years.

Activity. Divide class into small groups. Have each group compare living expenses for two different types of families, using average costs of rent, utilities, food, transportation, child care, etc. for your area. Ask groups to share their findings.

Problem Solving. Have students identify adjustments a child would have to make as the family changed from a nuclear (as a toddler) to a single-parent (as a preschooler) to a blended (as a school-age child) to an extended family (as an adolescent).

◆◆ The Family Life Cycle

Although there are many different types of families, all families go through a series of stages. These are called the **family life cycle.** This pattern of change includes the following stages:

- Beginning—two people marry, establish a home, and adjust to living together as a couple.

- Expanding—the couple have one or more children and adjust to the role and responsibilities of parents.

- Developing—the parents focus on rearing their children from infancy through the teenage years and adjust to the changing needs of the children.

- Launching—the parents help their children move out on their own.

- The Middle Years—the couple adjust to an empty nest, develop new interests, plan for retirement, and become grandparents.

- The Retirement Years—the couple retire, enjoy more leisure time, and adjust to aging.

The cycle continues as members of the next generation form their own families, become parents, and rear their children. It must be remembered, however, that the family life cycle has many variations. Some couples never have children; others may adopt an older child. Single parents and stepparents may skip some of the stages.

At each stage of the family life cycle, parents have to adjust to different roles as the children grow and develop. For example, infants are totally dependent on parents to meet all their needs. Toddlers and preschoolers slowly become less dependent as they develop new skills and confidence. Once children go to school, they develop many relationships outside the family. By the teenage years, children are seeking independence as they approach adulthood. Throughout these stages, parents must provide encouragement, understanding, and guidance to help their children develop into mature adults. Finally, most parents are able to enjoy their adult children and grandchildren without being responsible for them.

At the same time, the couple must adjust to changes in their own relationship. For example, they must learn new roles as parents. They have more responsibilities and demands on their time and energy. However, by the time the last child has left home, the couple may want to develop new interests such as hobbies, travel, or volunteer work. For the first time in many years they may have more time to spend together. Then as grandparents, they have a second chance to enjoy the rewards of parenting.

When children marry or move away, parents enter the stage of "empty nest."

The Changing Family

As you have learned, families are very different. They differ by type and by their stage in the family life cycle. Today's families are also experiencing many changes from families of previous generations.

✦✦ Changing Family Characteristics

Families in our society have become smaller, averaging about two children per family. This contrasts with the average size of families in earlier generations. Then larger families were an economic asset because the children could help out on the farm or in the family business. Moreover, many children did not live into adulthood. They died of childhood diseases that can now be prevented or treated successfully.

The largest percentage of families now live in urban and suburban areas. Only a small percentage live on farms or in rural areas. Today, with the aid of modern equipment, farms can be run by far fewer people than were needed in the past.

Today's families move more frequently than did those of earlier generations. As a result, parents often live far from relatives and the communities in which they grew up. Instead of asking nearby relatives for help in caring for children and the home, many parents now reach out to friends and neighbors. Community organizations and government services also provide advice and support that used to be provided by relatives.

The average family is smaller than previous generations—3.8 persons. They live in an urban or suburban area, usually far away from relatives.

✦✦ Changing Roles of Parents

Years ago, the husband was considered the economic provider for the family. The wife stayed home and cared for the children and the household. However, this so-called traditional family is no longer typical.

Today about two-thirds of all married women with children under age eighteen are in the work force. This is more than double the rate of 1960. Now more than half of all

Around the World

The Changing Family Internationally

In nineteenth-century China, the average family had as many as 80 members. They all lived on one tract of land in several connecting houses. Everyone in the family, from grandparents to aunts, uncles, and cousins, helped farm the land.

In Africa, extended families have lived in houses built around a central courtyard for generations. This living arrangement is called a compound.

In Colonial America, it was very common for grandparents, parents, and children to live in the same house, usually on a farm. These pioneer families lived together because it was safer and because they could share the hard work of establishing their farms.

Today in the United States, large families are no longer necessary for economic survival. Families do not need to grow their own food or make the things they use. Families have become smaller, and in many families, only two generations live together. There are also more people living alone. In fact, the one-person household is the fastest growing type of household. One out of five households in the United States consists of a person living alone.

Family patterns are continuing to change around the world as well. In Japan, families are much smaller today than they were in the past. In the Scandinavian countries, many unrelated people form various types of living arrangements.

Throughout history, family structures and living arrangements have continually changed to meet the needs of family members. Experts now predict that more families will again become multigenerational as people live longer. What type of family structure do you think you will be living in 10, 20, or 50 years from now?

---

mothers of infants work outside the home. This increase in the number of employed mothers has had an impact on both the workplace and the family.

In the past, most mothers were responsible for caring for and nurturing the children. Fathers were involved primarily in guiding behavior and disciplining the children. These roles have also been changing. Today many mothers and fathers share parenting responsibilities. As a result, fathers have become much more involved in the physical care of their children as well as in providing love and affection. In fact, some fathers are the primary caregiver for the children. In these families the traditional roles have been reversed. The mother is employed outside the home, and the father is responsible for the care of the children and the household.

Changing roles can be confusing for some parents. When both parents work outside the home, they usually have less time to be with each other and with their children. At the same time, they want to provide a stable and nurturing environment in which to rear their children. The modern-day dilemma for many parents is how to create a balance between the responsibilities of work and family life.

Reference. See "The Modern Father" on page 73 for information about the changing roles of fathers in our society.
Problem Solving. Although many dual-income couples agree that family tasks should be shared, the female usually assumes the major responsibility for the care of the children and the household. How might a couple create a better balance of these responsibilities?

Functions of the Family

Most people believe that the family performs very special functions that no other social unit can perform. Family sociologists have studied American families and what they do to get the work of the family done. Kathleen Galvin and Bernard Brommel, in their book *Family Communication,* have identified several functions of a family. Let's look briefly at each of these.

• **Providing emotional support.** This function is at the heart of the role of families. The family members offer each other affection and companionship. They may express feelings of frustration or anger yet still find understanding, concern, and continuing love. Husbands and wives grow closer as they listen to each other's and their children's problems. They support each other and become stronger individuals. The parents accept their children's individuality. The children know the family is always there to listen and pro-

vide guidance. As a result, they feel secure enough to push for independence. Emotional support nurtures the self-esteem of all family members.

• **Providing economic support.** Another major function of families is to satisfy the family's economic needs. In previous generations, this function was considered primarily the man's responsibility. Today a majority of women are also in the work force. In many two-parent families, both parents are employed outside the home. In single-parent families, the parent must often be the sole provider.

• **Providing child care and guidance.** This function may also be called the parenting function. Some experts believe that it is the most important function of the family. Parenting requires keeping children physically and psychologically safe. It involves teaching children many roles, both formally and informally. It also involves teaching behaviors, skills, and information that children must learn to function adequately in the world outside the family.

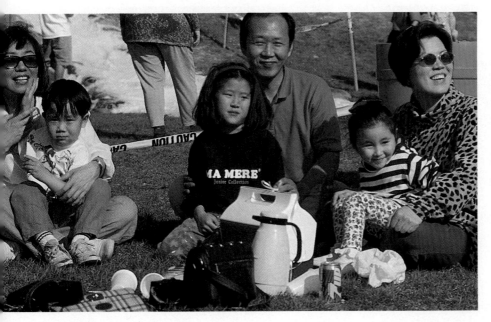

Families provide special functions for their members. These range from economic and emotional support to parenting and recreation.

Activity. List the functions of the family on the chalkboard. Ask each student to prioritize the functions, in writing, according to how they believe their parents rank them at this stage of the life cycle. Then have them compare how the functions were ranked when they were young children. Would they prioritize the functions in a similar way for their own family of the future? Why or why not?

Parenting was once the sole responsibility of mothers. Now this function is also considered the responsibility of fathers.

- **Housekeeping.** This function includes making a pleasant, healthful, and protective environment for the family. In the past, the wife traditionally performed the housekeeping function—cooking, cleaning, and maintaining the home. Today women are taking on more of the economic function, and men are becoming involved in the housekeeping function. As a result, all family members should share household responsibilities, such as cooking, shopping, cleaning, and other tasks.

- **Maintaining kinship.** The kinship function involves maintaining the family network with relatives. This may include parents, children, sisters, brothers, grandparents, aunts, uncles, and cousins of several generations on both sides of the family. It is through this kinship network that cultural and religious traditions are expressed. As families have decreased in size, so have kinship networks. For example, families with eight children have

many relatives within two generations. The average family network today is smaller in comparison. Yet today's family network is larger than one might expect because people are living longer. It is not uncommon for children to know their great-grandparents.

- **Providing recreation.** Recreation includes nonwork activities done for relaxation, fun, and self-development. Doing things as a family may mean playing games, going to the park, or taking a yearly vacation together. The recreation function is very important to most families because it provides time for family members to play, laugh, and relax together.

Within families, parents determine which functions get higher priority than others. They base their decisions on their values, goals, knowledge, ability, energy, and available resources. Because these factors differ, it is sometimes difficult for a family to balance the family functions. In addition, various functions are affected by the age and stage of the children in the family. They are also affected by the roles of the parents.

Children learn particular interests, activities, and customs from their family, neighbors, and friends. These children enjoy baking cookies from an old family recipe with their mother and grandmother.

Activity. Have students describe how the kinship function is maintained in their family. Who is primarily responsible for maintaining the kinship network? What benefits does kinship provide for their family?

Discuss. What recreational activities can be enjoyed by families in your community that are free or cost less than $5 per person?

Influences on the Family

There are many influences on today's families. Some of these influences come from the parents' own cultural, religious, or ethnic background. Others come from outside sources such as the media and technology. All help shape the family and their attitude toward parenting. As a result, children learn particular attitudes, beliefs, customs, and behaviors from a variety of sources.

❖ Cultural Background

A parent's cultural background has a significant influence on the family. People's background includes their ethnic heritage, religion, social status, economic level, and education. Couples who come from similar backgrounds usually have similar attitudes and goals. Thus they may have many of the same ideas about families, children, and parenting.

Today, however, many couples come from different backgrounds. They may be from different ethnic groups, have completed different levels of education, or come from families with vastly different incomes. As a result, they may have different ideas and beliefs about parenting children. These differences can lead to disagreements that can seriously affect the family. Parents need to deal realistically with their differences so that both parents and children can avoid conflicts.

Many families have recently moved to the United States from another country. As immigrants, they may have to learn a new language, accept a different job, and develop new skills. They may face discrimination and prejudice from others in the new community. Immigrants may find it difficult to maintain certain family traditions and ways of living in this country. For example, some immi-

Cultural background has a strong influence on families. It helps shape family roles, attitudes, and life-style.

grants must adjust to a lower social position and less income than they had in their native country. Children may seek a different way of life according to what they learn at school or from television and the movies. As a result, conflicts may occur between generations as the parents try to maintain certain family traditions and the children seek new directions.

The struggles of today's immigrants are similar to those of previous generations. Each is seeking a better life for his or her children and family. The contributions of generations of immigrants have helped make America a very diverse and strong nation that values individual rights and freedoms.

Activity. Ask students to talk to parents, grandparents, or other relatives about their cultural background and any challenges they faced because of it. Have them bring to class a special item (food, clothing, book, decoration, etc.) that represents their family's cultural background. Ask students to describe the item and its role in their family life.
Activity. Invite parents or grandparents born in another country to talk to the class about their cultural background.

❖ Relationships

The types of relationships that a family has with relatives, friends, and neighbors can influence the family's social and emotional life. For example, some families have little contact with relatives outside the nuclear family. Others feel strong kinship ties and see their relatives often.

Both relatives and friends can serve as part of the family support system. These people may help parents with child care during the family's early stages and with friendship and companionship during the later years.

❖ Life-Style

The term **life-style** is widely used to describe how individuals and families choose to live. A family's life-style consists of a number of factors. These include location, activities, priorities, and goals. As a result, every family has a life-style that is in some ways different from that of other families.

For example, a family who lives in the city may live in an apartment building that is home to many other families. This family may not own a car because family members can walk or take a bus or subway to get around

---

◆ *Health & Safety* ◆

Facts About Fitness

Everybody—children, teenagers, and adults—can benefit from regular exercise. Even as little as 30 minutes of exercise three times a week can be beneficial. The best exercise is an aerobic activity, which requires the heart and lungs to function at an increased rate. Familiar aerobic activities include walking, jogging, swimming, bicycling, and aerobic dancing.

Here are some of the benefits of a regular exercise program.

- Exercise is good for your heart and lungs. When you exercise vigorously, your muscles require more oxygen. This means you must breathe more deeply to fill your lungs with air. As a result, your heart must beat faster and harder to pump blood to your muscles. This makes the heart stronger and more resilient.
- Exercise can help you maintain or even lose weight. Even when two people weigh the same amount, an active person

looks trimmer than a person who does not exercise.
- A regular exercise program can help reduce tension and stress. It is a healthy outlet for feelings of anger and frustration. It also helps relieve boredom.
- Exercise helps you sleep better and improves your concentration. As a result, you feel less fatigue and are more mentally alert.
- Different types of exercise can improve the body's strength, endurance, or flexibility. This helps to reduce stiffness and improve coordination.
- Exercise also contributes to your self-esteem. People who exercise generally look good and feel good about themselves.
- A lifetime program of regular exercise can provide physical, mental, and social benefits. It is a way to relax and take care of yourself at the same time.

---

town. This type of life-style is very different from that of a family that lives in a rural area. There a family may live in a house on a large piece of land. They may have to drive to all the stores and other community services.

Jobs are another major influence on a family's life-style. Some jobs require family members to spend a great deal of time commuting to and from work. Other jobs require long hours or travel. This means the parent will have less time to spend with the family.

Interests and hobbies also influence family life-style. Some families enjoy camping; others like visiting museums. Some enjoy casual picnics; others prefer dining in ethnic restaurants. Family hobbies range from stamp collecting to gardening, from biking to boating, from refinishing old furniture to playing chess.

Some families enjoy becoming involved in community activities. They may serve on committees or volunteer their time to environmental projects or helping the homeless. Other families prefer to spend their time with their own immediate family or a few close friends.

Sometimes families consciously select their life-style. They may change jobs or move from a large city to the country in order to live a less hectic life. Others mold their life-style into one that best suits their members. Their life-style evolves gradually on the basis of the interests and decisions of the members.

You will discover that families are as unique as the people in them. No one life-style is best for everyone in similar situations.

❖ The Media and Entertainment

Family members are exposed to many influences from the media, which include television, radio, magazines, and newspapers. Some of these offer good information and advice on topics ranging from consumer

products to relationship skills. For example, educational television programs can help children learn to read or learn about different cultures. Advertisements and commercials let families know which products are on sale in various stores. Newspaper and magazine articles inform families about topics ranging from politics to sports.

However, the media and entertainment world also relay a variety of sensational events and life-styles that may be confusing to children. For example, some movies and television programs feature violence, sex, or crime. Many talk shows highlight relationships or behavior that is unusual or bizarre. Some song lyrics are degrading to certain groups of people.

As a result, parents should talk with their children about what they see and hear in the media and entertainment world. Children need to learn how to distinguish between reality and fantasy, true and false, and good and bad. Unfortunately, the life-styles of most families never make the news.

DECISIONS ◆ ◆ DECISIONS

Jerry and Laurie have two young children, ages three and six. The parents try to limit the children's television viewing to educational or family programs. However, Jerry and Laurie sometimes give in to the children's pleas to stay up and watch television shows and movies with their parents. Now Jerry and Laurie are concerned that the children may be influenced by the swearing, violence, and sex that some of these shows include. Laurie and Jerry have asked you for your advice. What will you tell them?

❖❖ Technology

Technology has a very important influence on today's families. Just consider these contributions: television, microwave ovens, home computers and fax machines, cellular telephones, video cameras, and VCRs.

All of these modern inventions can have a positive or a negative effect on individuals and families. For example, television can bring knowledge and entertainment to family members. However, it can also reduce communication within the family. If a family has more than one television set, then different family members may watch separate programs by themselves.

Technology has influenced the foods we eat, the clothes we wear, and the homes we live in. It has also influenced health and medical care, transportation, communication, and education. What advantages and disadvantages do you think technology has had for families in each of these areas?

❖❖ The Community and Society

Every family lives in some type of community, whether it is large or small. Within this community may be schools, churches, stores, recreation facilities, libraries, fire and police departments, and a hospital. All of these influence families through the services they provide.

Communities also have various standards, regulations, and laws that families and individuals must follow. For example, children of a certain age must attend school. Store owners must follow certain safety and health regulations. Parents must not abuse or neglect their children.

Ultimately, the well-being of families is important to every society. Family issues are debated and discussed by politicians, religious leaders, sociologists, and business leaders. Articles appear in magazines and newspapers. Debates are held on television and radio programs. Experts predict that family issues will grow in importance in the coming decade.

Many people believe that families are the foundation of a society. Although family structures and parental roles may continue to change, the family unit provides the love and care its members need.

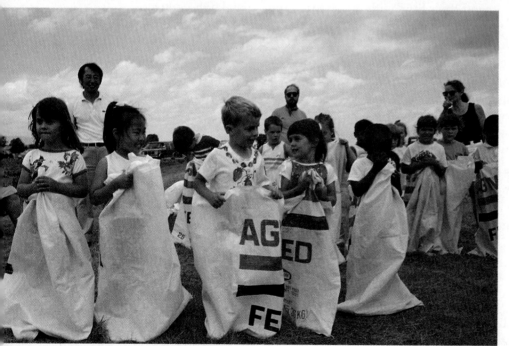

Society needs strong and healthy families. Families make up communities, which influence our nation and the world.

Discuss. What advantages and disadvantages has technology had on families? What inventions have been most beneficial? Least beneficial? Why?
Reference. See pages 505–509 for lists of community resources.

Problem Solving. Have students discuss what family issues are currently important in your community and in society. How might these issues be resolved? Do you think family issues will grow in importance in the future? Why or why not?

CHAPTER 2 REVIEW

Summary

- Types of families include nuclear, single-parent, blended, extended, cooperative, and nonchild families. Each has advantages and disadvantages.
- All families go through certain stages, which make up the family life cycle.
- U.S. families are becoming smaller. More live in urban and suburban areas and move more frequently than families in the past.
- As mothers enter the work force, an increasing number of fathers are assuming more child care responsibilities.
- Families serve a number of basic functions, which include providing emotional and economic support, child care and guidance, housekeeping, kinship, and recreation.
- Families are influenced by their cultural background, relationships with others, life-style, the media, technology, and the community and society.

Questions

p. 37 **1.** How does a nuclear family differ from a blended family?

p. 38 **2.** What are the advantages and disadvantages of being a single parent?

p. 40 **3.** What is an extended family?

p. 42 **4.** List the six stages of the family life cycle.

p. 43 **5.** How have families changed in size and location compared to earlier generations?

p. 43 **6.** How has the increased number of employed mothers affected parental roles?

p. 45 **7.** Name the six functions of the family.

p. 49 **8.** Suggest one positive and one negative effect television might have on a family.

p. 50 **9.** How does the community influence a family?

Activities

1. Define the word *family.* Then discuss various classmates' definitions and agree upon one definition as a group.

2. Take a class poll to answer the following questions. In what different types of families are class members now living? What is the average number of children per family? What percentage of families have relatives living in the same community or nearby? How many times have class members moved? What percentage of students' mothers work outside the home? Compare answers with national statistics.

3. Using a television programming guide, highlight programs that would be good for young children to watch. Identify programs which might be confusing or unsuitable for children. Give reasons for your selections.

Think About

1. Why do you suppose the U.S. Census Bureau makes no specific mention of children in their definition of a family?

2. Do you believe the changing characteristics of families in our society are making families stronger or weaker than families were when your grandparents were children? Defend your answer.

Reference. See the Teacher's Manual in the front of the Teacher's Annotated Edition for complete answers to the chapter review questions.

CHAPTER
3

Rewards and Responsibilities

Objectives

This chapter will help you to:

- Describe what it might be like to be a parent.
- Discuss the various rewards and myths of parenthood.
- List and explain the different responsibilities of being a parent.
- Discuss reasons why parents may have mixed feelings about parenthood.

Vocabulary

role models
values
ambivalence

Grandmother Wilson is looking through her photo album with two of her grandchildren. As she turns each page of the album, they talk excitedly about seeing their father as a child.

"Look at Daddy's curly hair," says Sarah. "It's just like mine!"

"Yes," replies her grandmother. "I loved your daddy's curls when he was a little boy, but he hated them. He wanted to have straight hair."

When they reach the last page, Jonathan asks, "Grandma, what was it like having five children? Did they ever get in trouble?"

Grandmother Wilson lays down the album and smiles. "Well, there sure was lots of activity around our household. After school, some of the children would bring friends home and my kitchen would be filled with kids. I never realized how much work there would be in having five children."

She continues: "We had many, many happy times together. I remember all the fun we had going camping. One time, the children tossed your grandpa into the lake with all his clothes on but that never happened again! There were sad times, too. Like the year your grandpa was out of work, and the summer your daddy was in a car accident. We didn't know whether he'd be able to walk again."

Sarah says, "Tell us more, Grandma."

Grandma Wilson smiles and says, "Each of our children had special qualities, just like each of you. Grandpa and I were so proud when they reached important milestones, such as graduation, getting jobs, and having their own families. We only hope that you bring as much joy and happiness to your parents."

Chapter Opener. Ask students to read the opening scenario to the chapter. Ask these questions: What did Sarah and Jonathan learn about their family from their grandmother? What rewards and responsibilities of parenthood has Grandmother Wilson had over the years? What role can she now play in her grandchildren's lives?

What Is It Like to Be a Parent?

Having a child is a lifetime adventure. Everyday brings a new experience. Being a parent is not always as you think it might be. Some days are good, and some are not so good. You may have heard grandparents say they are able to enjoy their grandchildren more than their children because when things get rough the grandchildren can be sent back home. It is one thing to have children for an evening or a weekend but something else to live with them on an everyday basis. Many prospective parents do not really understand the lifetime commitment that goes with being a parent.

❖ Importance of the Early Years

Parents help shape the world by the way they bring up their children. This is a great and awesome responsibility. It is true that by the time children are four or five years old, many factors outside the family begin to influence their lives. For the first few years, however, children are influenced mainly by their parents and what goes on in the home.

We can easily see the physical growth of a baby because the changes are so rapid. By toddlerhood, the child has developed from a helpless infant to a child who is beginning to walk and get around with little help from others. The surroundings in which babies and toddlers grow have a profound effect on their physical and emotional health.

Children need plenty of nutritious food, rest, and active play. They need warm and loving care. They need the assurance that they can always count on their parents for encouragement. Children who feel emotionally secure during infancy and toddlerhood have a better chance of facing the world beyond the family. Thus, the first few years of childhood are crucial in setting the stage for all of life to follow.

Parents set the tone for family life and the environment in which children grow and develop. They are responsible for providing love and security, safety and comfort, and

Being a parent is an adventure. Everyday brings new rewards and challenges.

Parents are responsible for their child's welfare—not just for a few years, but for many years. Parenthood is a lifetime commitment.

spiritual and moral guidance. They set guidelines for children's behavior. In addition, they serve as **role models** for their children. This means they show children how to talk, act, and behave through their own words, attitudes, actions, and behavior. By setting good examples, role models help children learn appropriate behavior.

Children have no choice in the matter of who their parents are or what kind of parents they have. In a sense, children come into this world taking a chance on the people who gave them their start in life. A good beginning for any child is to be wanted and loved.

❖ Once a Parent, Always a Parent

Some people think that once a child is old enough for school, their task as a parent is more than half over. Others recognize that their duties continue until the child is mature and can take care of himself or herself. Few understand that parenting is a lifetime occupation. Talk to any grandparent and you will find a parent who is still interested and concerned about an adult child.

With each new stage in a child's development, parents and other caregivers meet with a fresh set of rewards and challenges. Reading about the ages and stages of development can give you some idea of these rewards and challenges. Yet until you actually take care of a child—as a babysitter, child care provider, or parent—it is hard to understand all that the job involves. It is also hard to understand what your feelings about being a parent or caregiver are likely to be.

No caregiver is perfect. Those who take on the awesome task of rearing or working with children must be prepared to give much of themselves.

Activity. Have students write a short essay on "If I were a parent, I would..."
Problem Solving. Divide class into small groups. Ask half of the groups to write a child's bill of rights. Ask the others to write a parent's bill of rights. Then compare the bills of rights for similarities and differences. What might be sources of conflict between the rights of parents and children? How could these be successfully resolved?

Rewards of Parenthood

If you have ever had a bad experience babysitting or taking care of a younger brother or sister, you may have wondered why adults keep having children. One of the reasons is that most of the time being a parent is very satisfying.

Parents feel an overwhelming tenderness toward their children that few other experiences equal. There is the thrill of watching a human being develop. The baby's first smile, step, or word brings happiness and pride. Then, as the child grows older, parents have a continuing influence on his or her development. They also help their youngster explore the world.

❖ Joys of Parenting

For many people, parenthood brings great joy. As parents watch their child develop through the various stages, they can feel a sense of achievement. They are happy when the baby smiles and coos. They are proud when the toddler takes his or her first steps. They feel content when the preschooler sleeps peacefully after a day filled with activities. Day by day they are able to watch their child become a unique and special individual with their help and guidance.

Parenthood also provides many new experiences and adventures. Parents need to learn all sorts of things: how to make the home safe for an exploring child, how to evaluate a child care program, how to buy a bicycle, and how to say no and handle the period of anger that may result. They learn to answer questions such as "Why is the sky blue?" and "Where did I come from?" Later, parents may learn to coach a Little League team or be the leader of a scout troop.

At the same time, parents can enjoy the special pleasures of childhood along with their children. They can help build a tower of blocks, soar on a swing, or romp in the snow. This helps them capture the sense of unin-

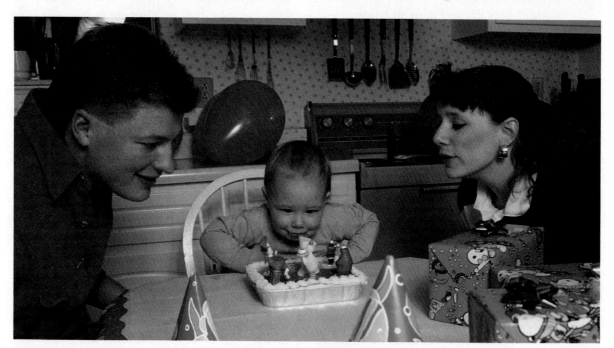

These parents experience a thrill as they watch their child celebrate his first birthday.

Activity. Have students ask their parents what special joys they experienced at each stage of their son's or daughter's development.

Discuss. What types of positive experiences can parenthood provide for mothers and fathers?

hibited joy and spontaneity that children express. Such experiences often bring back happy memories of the parents' own childhood.

Parenthood also provides new depths of emotions for many parents. They may be surprised by the intensity of their love for their child. For example, parents react instinctively to save a child from danger. They feel compassion when a child is sick. They become worried when a child does not arrive home on time. They cherish a child's smile or sense of humor. They feel protective of a child who is bullied by a classmate. They also have a sense of satisfaction and success when their child attains a certain goal.

Many parents say that their children have given their lives new purpose and meaning. They now have an important long-term goal—to nurture and guide their children so they are able to reach their fullest potential. The parents' reward is a strong sense of accomplishment and pride when their children become happy, responsible, and independent adults. As parents broaden their focus to the next generation, they see continuity between their own parents, themselves, and their children. This gives people and families a sense of immortality.

Around the World

Special Celebrations for Children

Families around the world celebrate many different types of holidays. Here are a few that are mainly for children.

- In the Agona district in Ghana, adults celebrate the Yam Festival for only one week, but the children get to celebrate it for two weeks. The festival is held in early August, at the end of the rainy season. People celebrate because vegetables and other crops are now ready for harvest and the hungry days of May, June, and July are over. During the Yam Festival, children under twelve years of age collect foodstuffs. They gather in an open place where girls cook the food and then invite all the other children to eat with them. After the meal, everyone plays special games.
- In India, on the fifth day of the Hindu new year, brothers and sisters celebrate their relationship. If the sister does not earn any money, she usually gives her brother a gift of food. A brother might give his sister jewelry, a sari, or money.

If a boy does not have a sister, his mother usually invites a cousin or the daughter of a friend to be his "sister."

- In the region around Florence, Italy, there is a spring celebration called the Cricket Festival. Long ago, children used to catch their own crickets in the garden. Today, crickets in tiny painted cages are sold in the stores. Part of the fun is selecting your cricket, then showing it off to everyone. The crickets chirp loudly in their cages, adding their song to the festivities.
- In the Indian villages of Bolivia, a special party is held when a baby first gets a full head of hair. The party is called *Las Cintas,* or "the ribbons." The baby's hair is tied in tiny bunches with ribbons. These ribbons are gifts from the people at the party. During the party, the baby's hair is cut off close to the scalp. Each ribbon, along with the lock of hair, is returned to the person who gave the ribbon. In exchange, that person must give the baby a gift.

Activity. Have students list their short- and long-term goals for their own children.

Emphasize. When parents have realistic expectations about parenthood, they are more likely to enjoy their children at each stage of development.

Parents feel a sense of pride and accomplishment as children reach certain milestones in life, such as graduation from high school.

◆◆ Myths About Parenting

There are many myths about parenthood and children. Some of these may have begun as true stories, but they have been exaggerated and altered so that they are no longer true. If people believe these myths, they will probably be disappointed when they face the realities of parenthood.

Some common myths are reinforced by television programs and advertisements. These almost always show parents and children smiling, having fun, and interacting successfully. Rarely do they show children who are crying, angry, or sick. Yet, in real life, children do not always play quietly or carry on meaningful conversations with parents and other relatives. Some of these images are based more on wishful thinking and fantasies than on reality.

People need to have realistic expectations about children and parenting. Let's take a look at some of the common myths in our society.

- **Myth: Children are sweet and lovable.** In real life, children are stubborn and unhappy at times. They cry, scream, and have temper tantrums. They say no and misbehave. They can be very messy and unable to pick up after themselves. They spit up and soil their diapers. Caring for children can be frustrating and tiring at times. Parents and other caregivers need plenty of patience as well as a sense of humor to help them through the rough times.

- **Myth: Children can strengthen a marriage.** Some people believe that having a baby can save a troubled marriage. In real life, the added responsibilities and demands of caring for a baby more often create new problems in a relationship. The addition of a child brings about many changes, which can cause further conflicts that never existed before. Couples should first solve the existing problems in their relationship before having a child.

- **Myth: Children provide companionship and love.** Babies cannot cure loneliness or unhappiness. In fact, young babies need to receive a great deal of care and love in the early months—a time when they do not know how to return that love. The demands of caring for a baby can actually isolate parents. They may no longer be able to join their friends in many social activities because of child care responsibilities. Children also grow up quickly. They soon develop friends and interests outside the family. The person who wants to have a child only for the opportunity to care for a cuddly baby will be disappointed. The period of infancy and toddlerhood is short in comparison to the long-term commitment of parenthood. Being a parent involves caring for, nurturing, and guiding children through all the different stages of growth and development.

- **Myth: Children do not cost much money.** Children need food, clothing, and shelter. They need medical care, toys, and books. Parents are responsible for meeting their children's needs. As children grow up, their needs increase. The costs of satisfying these needs also increase. The total cost of rearing a child for 18 or more years is tremendous.

Parenthood has many joys and rewards. However, the expectations about parenting children must be realistic. If they are not, parents will be disappointed when they realize that rearing children to adulthood is a long-term commitment that includes many obligations and responsibilities.

DECISIONS ◆
◆ DECISIONS

Marie and Ramon have been married for over a year. However, their relationship has problems, and the couple argue constantly. Marie thinks that a baby would help pull her and Ramon together. Instead of arguing with each other, they could enjoy taking care of a cute little baby. Marie is confident that a baby would save their marriage. Do you think Marie's ideas are realistic? Why or why not?

Parenthood has many rewards. However, children are not always happy, sweet, and loving. Parents should have realistic expectations about both the joys and responsibilities of parenthood.

Problem Solving. On the chalkboard, have students list children's stories and fairy tales that include children and/or parents. Then discuss whether or not each story portrays a realistic image of children and parenting. If not, what myths do the stories reinforce?

Reference. See pages 64–65 for information about the financial costs of rearing children.

Responsibilities of Parenthood

Good parenting means meeting many responsibilities. These responsibilities change along with the stages of a child's life. During early childhood, parents do most of the giving, and children do most of the receiving. Babies need food, clothing, medical attention, love, and affection. They need to be kept clean and warm. Without someone to satisfy these needs, babies could die.

A baby turns life upside down. New parents lose freedom and privacy. At the beginning, a baby requires so much of the parents' time that they may feel isolated from friends or work. If the baby cries a great deal or becomes sick, parents often become anxious. Infants also require a lot of equipment. Suddenly parents find themselves bumping into the crib or playpen that clutters a small apartment.

Becoming a parent brings legal and moral responsibilities as well. If parents fail to provide for a child's basic needs, they can be punished legally. Federal legislation enables states to track absent parents to collect payment of child support. Parents also have a moral obli-gation to love and cherish their children and to bring them up to be useful members of society.

The responsibilities of parenthood include being a caregiver, a nurturer, a teacher, and a role model. They also include meeting the financial costs of rearing children.

◆◆ Being a Caregiver

Being a caregiver means meeting children's physical needs. Among these needs are shelter, food, clothing, rest, and medical care.

Babies must be held, fed, carried from place to place, and put to bed. They cannot tell a parent when they are hungry, tired, or sick except by crying. Although toddlers can climb into a high chair and feed themselves, they need someone to prepare their food and clean up after them. Someone must dress them appropriately for the weather. Preschoolers are more independent than toddlers. Usually they can dress and go to the bathroom by themselves. However, all young children must be protected from harmful situations. They do not understand the dangers of crawling near stairways, running into the street, or playing with matches.

Each day parents must make decisions that affect the health and well-being of their children. They make choices regarding a baby's routines for eating and sleeping. They must arrange for child care when they will be away. They are responsible for the safety and comfort of the home. They must also decide where and when to seek help when things go wrong.

◆◆ Being a Nurturer

Children also have emotional needs. They require lots and lots of love. They need to know they are loved for their own special qualities. This helps them gain a sense of security. In turn, this security helps children develop high self-esteem and self-confidence.

◆ ◆ Self-Esteem ◆ ◆

Parents should pay more attention to children when they practice good behavior than when they misbehave. This positive attention makes children feel good about themselves and what they do. It also helps motivate children to repeat appropriate behavior. In contrast, when parents pay more attention to misbehavior, children may repeat the inappropriate behavior to get desired attention—even if in includes reprimands or punishment.

Activity. Before students read this section, have them list the responsibilities of parenthood on the chalkboard. Then categorize the list into caring, nurturing, teaching, role modeling, and financial. Which categories have the most examples?

Discuss. How do the caregiving responsibilities change as a child goes from being an infant to a toddler to a preschooler to a school-age child? Which stage do you think involves the most responsibilities? Why?

Some of the responsibilities of parenthood include meeting children's physical and emotional needs, as well as helping children learn.

Parents nurture their children's emotional development by picking up, holding, and cuddling them when they are very young. Parents show love and affection through smiles, hugs, and tender words. As children grow older, parents still need to provide reassurance and affection. A pat on the back, a hug, or the words "I love you" are important to children of all ages.

❖ Being a Teacher

Parents are the most effective teachers their children will ever have. For better or for worse, children learn from their parents in very natural ways. This learning takes place every day.

Children learn by watching and listening to their parents and by helping them do things around the home. For example, they learn how to hold a spoon, brush their teeth, and tie their shoelaces. They learn where to store their toys, how to set the table, and when to wash their hands. As they grow older, they can learn to prepare a meal or do the laundry. These are skills they will need when they are living on their own or forming their own family.

Parents also teach children how to act in various situations. They do this by providing guidance as to appropriate and inappropriate behavior. For example, parents may remind children to say please, excuse me, and thank you. They encourage children to share their toys and take turns when playing with other children. They also demonstrate ways of expressing emotions, such as love, anger, or fear.

Most parents establish certain guidelines and rules for children to follow. Some guidelines and rules relate to watching television, eating snacks, putting away toys, and being home on time. These help children understand what kind of behavior their parents expect of them. Other guidelines and rules help children learn how to get along with others. For example, parents may tell children not to hit or bite other children. Guidance is also necessary to protect children from certain dangers. Parents teach children to look both ways before crossing the street and never to talk to strangers.

Parents also have a responsibility to encourage their children's mental development. Adults can help children learn about the world by pointing out objects, describing situations, and answering questions. They can provide appropriate toys and stimulating play experiences for children. They can read books to young children and encourage older children to read on their own. Above all, parents can stress the importance of getting an education.

Learning should be an ongoing experience throughout life. When parents encourage children to express their ideas, ask questions, and safely explore their environment, they help promote children's learning. Parents should also help children learn to make good choices and decisions. The skills involved can be developed through practice. Even young children can make choices about which outfit to wear or which activity to do. Then as they grow older and become more independent, they will be better able to make wise decisions on their own.

◆ Health & Safety ◆

When Illness Strikes

One of the responsibilities of parenting is taking care of children when they are ill. When children do not feel well, they often have difficulty describing their symptoms. They usually do not understand the reasons for various medications or treatments. In addition, they require more reassurance and companionship during illness than adults do. This means that nursing a sick child can be very demanding. Following are some tips to make it easier.

Viral infections, ear infections, and strep throat are the most common causes of fever in children. Although a fever should never be ignored, it is important to know that high fevers are much more common in children than in adults. While a high fever is not necessarily a cause for alarm, parents should check with the child's doctor.

To help keep a fever under control, encourage the child to drink plenty of liquids. Keep clothing and bed coverings to a minimum. If necessary, sponge the child's face, neck, and the inside of the arms and legs with a damp washcloth and lukewarm water. Never give a child aspirin. Instead, give

acetaminophen, in the dosage recommended for the child's age and weight.

Most medications can be mixed with food or liquids. Juice, soda, and applesauce can be used to disguise the taste of many medicines. Check with the doctor or pharmacist. Even if the medicine is supposed to be taken on an empty stomach, sometimes a small amount of food is permissible.

Do not bribe a child to take medication by promising a treat. Even worse, never tell a child that the medicine is candy. It is important that children do not confuse medicine with candy or other sweets.

Check with the doctor about whether or not the child can infect other children. Some illnesses are contagious only at the beginning stage, while others continue to be contagious for several days. Although visits from others can cheer a child, no one wants to be exposed to a contagious disease.

Unless children are very sick, it is difficult to keep them quiet and occupied. A new coloring book and crayons, a special tape, some books, or a few small toys that are tucked away for sick days may help.

Activity. Ask students to compile a list of questions they hear children ask adults and older children. How was each question answered? How would you have answered it?

Discuss. What are the benefits to children of the following: Reading to young children? Encouraging older children to read on their own? Stressing the importance of education?

❖ Being a Role Model

Parents serve as role models for their children to imitate. As a result, children reflect many of the attitudes and behaviors of their parents. Sometimes parents may wish their children would not copy everything they see and hear. However, children view their parents as authority figures or very important people and want to follow their examples. By being good role models, parents can help children learn appropriate behavior.

Watch children at play and you will often see what they have learned from their parents. For example, children will use many of the same words and mannerisms that their parents use. Children also play with their dolls in the same way their parents take care

of them or their younger brothers or sisters. Some children will be kind and loving and handle their dolls with care. Others will be mean and bossy or spank their dolls. These behaviors reflect their own parent-child experiences. Parents who watch their children at play often "see themselves."

Children first learn about getting along with other people by observing how their mother and father interact with each other and with the children in the family. When the family gets together with relatives and friends, children learn more about relationships, roles, and social interaction. Parents can best reinforce their teachings about behavior by modeling the appropriate behavior for their children. Children always learn better from seeing appropriate behavior than from being told what to do.

Parents have the additional responsibility of helping their children develop **values.** These are beliefs about what is right, worth-

Parents serve as role models for their children. Thus parents should always model the behavior they want their children to imitate.

DECISIONS ◆ ◆ DECISIONS

Leon is watching his two young children playing house with some friends. He hears his four-year-old son, Jaime, shout angrily at his teddy bear, "No! No! Don't you ever do that again! You are a bad, bad boy." Then Jaime starts spanking the stuffed animal. Leon is surprised at the anger that his son is showing. He does not want Jaime to treat others in this manner. Suddenly, Leon remembers that these are the same words and tone of voice that he used with Jaime last week. Now he can't even remember why he got so angry at his son. Do you think Leon should be concerned about Jaime imitating his angry behavior? Why or why not?

Activity. On the chalkboard, have students list the behaviors and attitudes of parents that children often imitate. Then ask students to identify which behaviors and attitudes they would *not* want their own child to imitate.

Problem Solving. Ask students to keep a journal of their activities, habits, language, attitudes, and emotions for one week. Then have students write an evaluation of what kind of role model they would have been for a young child.

while, or desirable. Each family has their own set of values that give meaning and direction to their lives. Most parents hope that their children will come to value certain qualities, such as honesty, respect, responsibility, and a concern for others. Although parents can talk to children about different values, values are best taught by example. When parents are always honest, children are more likely to be honest. When parents show respect for other people and their possessions, children are likely to do the same.

◆◆ Meeting the Financial Costs

Parents should expect to spend a large portion of their income on children. Some expenses can be planned for in advance. These include food, clothing, toys, child care, regular medical care, schooling, transportation, and recreation. However, there are unexpected expenses that may emerge without notice. These may include the costs of an unexpected illness or accident, medications, and special counseling or tutoring.

Parents may also want to provide additional educational opportunities, such as music lessons, sports programs, or art workshops, for their children. This may result in the need for special clothing or equipment for these activities. For example, a child may need athletic shoes, dance costumes, sports equipment, or a musical instrument. All of these are extra costs. Many parents also want to set aside money for future expenses, such as a college education or job training.

Obviously, then, children are very expensive. The U.S. Department of Agriculture has studied how much it costs to rear a child to age eighteen in each of four regions of the United States.

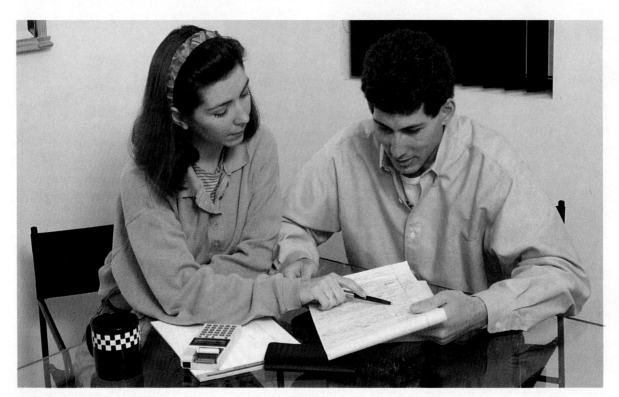

Children cost lots of money. Couples need to plan their finances so they can meet regular expenses, as well as save for unexpected and future costs.

Reference. See pages 442–445 for information about the importance of values and how they are influenced.
Discuss. What are five values that you hope your children would learn from you?

Activity. Have students research the first year's cost of having a child. Expenses should include the cost of prenatal care and delivery, food, clothing, diapers, equipment and supplies, health care, toys, and child care.

Total Cost to Raise a Child Birth to Age 18*

West	$124,530
Midwest	$118,410
South	$122,280
Northeast	$123,780

*Urban moderate budget in 1990 dollars.

The researchers classified family budgets as economy, low, moderate, and liberal. They found that urban family budgets are about 10 percent higher than rural family budgets. The report shows that an urban midwestern family on a moderate budget has the following expenses when raising a child to age eighteen:

Midwest Urban Moderate Budget*

Food	$21,300
Clothing	$10,530
Housing	$38,040
Transportation	$21,000
Health Care	$ 5,070
Child care, education, other	$22,470
TOTAL:	$118,410

*Per child to age 18 years.

Source: U.S. Department of Agriculture, 1991. *Economic Review*, March 1991.

These are average figures. They give only a very general idea of the expense of rearing a child. Parents have to add the cost of medical care and delivery, which was about $4,500 in 1991. If a child decides to go to college, parents have to add about $19,000 a year for tuition fees, room, and board for one year at a private university or about $5,000 a year at a public university in their home state. Looking at these numbers, you can understand how raising children costs a great deal of money.

Mixed Feelings About Parenthood

When you review the rewards and responsibilities of parenting, you will find a number of each. This can lead to a feeling of **ambivalence** (am-BIV-ah-lahns), which means being drawn both toward and away from something. It explains why mothers and fathers usually have mixed feelings about children and the parenting role.

◆ Long-Term Challenges of Parenthood

Because parenthood is a long-term commitment, parents' emotions about their children are not constant. They may adore their baby daughter when she giggles happily in the tub. However, they probably will dislike it when she talks back as a teenager. Parents may glow when their son gets an A in history and be horrified when he impulsively breaks streetlights with his friends.

Parents may love their children while disliking the demands they make. For example, one father enjoyed buying his nine-year-old son a bright yellow bicycle for his birthday. The boy was happy and proud of it. Less than a week after he received the bicycle, he left it overnight on the school playground. It was promptly stolen. The boy then asked his father to buy him a new bicycle. Another set of parents willingly gave up buying a home they had wanted and used the money to send their child to college. They were hurt and angry when the child dropped out of school, saying flippantly, "I never wanted to go, anyway."

Guidance probably causes more mixed feelings about parenting than anything else. This happens because most people confuse love with liking and respect. If parents are mature, they probably always love their children. However, there will be times when they do not like their children's behavior. In turn, their children will not always like the decisions their parents make. It is important for parents to let children know that they are still loved even when their behavior is wrong. This helps children maintain their self-esteem while learning the difference between appropriate and inappropriate behavior.

To guide children effectively, it is important for parents to know how they feel about a great many issues. For example, parents must decide how they will deal with bedtime, television, chores, friends, homework, movies, part-time jobs, driving, smoking, drugs and alcohol, and sex. These are only some of the things people will have to make decisions about if they become parents.

◆◆ Realities of Parenthood

What, then, are the realities of parenthood? While parenting brings rewards and happiness for many parents, it may mean disappointment and sorrow for other parents. Parents usually feel proud and rewarded when their children become happy, confident, and productive adults. On the other hand, parents usually experience unhappiness and regret when their children do not meet their expectations.

Some parents may not find the parenting role to be what they had expected it to be. One of the realities is that people do not know ahead of time if the experience will be positive or negative for them. For most people, however, parenting is filled with both good and bad experiences. Because the final results cannot be predicted, they remain optimistic and hopeful even in times of crisis.

Children challenge parents to be the best they can be. They enable parents to use the knowledge, experience, and skills they have spent a lifetime acquiring. Children provide a sense of meaning and continuity to parents' lives. They enable parents to express their need to love, nurture, and cherish. Even though children can be demanding and challenging, the joy of watching children grow and develop can be one of life's most satisfying experiences.

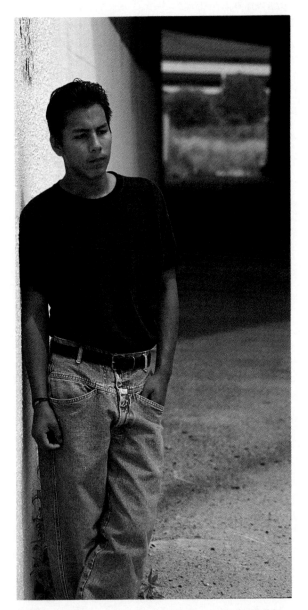

Young people may have mixed feelings about children and parenthood.

CHAPTER 3 REVIEW

Summary

- Parents set the tone for family life and the environment in which children grow and develop.
- Parenthood is a lifetime commitment that brings both rewards and responsibilities.
- Among the joys of parenting are watching a new human being grow and develop, experiencing new adventures and depths of feeling, and gaining a sense of continuity.
- When people believe the myths about parenthood, they may be disappointed by the realities of parenthood.
- The responsibilities of parenthood include being a caregiver, nurturer, teacher, and role model, as well as meeting the financial costs.
- Many people feel ambivalent about parenthood because of its long-term challenges and its daily ups and downs.

Questions

p. 54   **1.** Why do parents play such an important role in a child's early years?

p. 55   **2.** What is a role model?

p. 56   **3.** What are three rewards of parenthood that most parents enjoy?

p. 58   **4.** State two common myths about parenting and children. Explain why each is at least partially untrue.

p. 61   **5.** Why are parents such influential teachers for their children?

p. 63   **6.** How can parents be good role models for their children?

7. What are values?   p. 63

8. List at least six categories of expenses that may be part of the financial costs of rearing a child.   p. 64

9. Why does guidance probably cause more mixed feelings about parenting than anything else?   p. 65

10. Describe some of the realities of parenthood.   p. 66

Activities

1. Ask five parents what rewards and responsibilities they have experienced as parents. Write down their exact answers. Then look over the answers to see whether there are more similarities or differences among them. Share your findings with the class.

2. Research the latest findings of the Bureau of Statistics for the current average cost of raising a baby born today to age eighteen.

3. Write a job description of a parent for a "Help Wanted" advertisement.

Think About

1. Why is the tone parents set for family life and the environment so important during a child's early years?

2. If you became a parent, what values would you want your children to develop?

Reference. See the Teacher's Manual in the front of the Teacher's Annotated Edition for complete answers to the chapter review questions.

67

CHAPTER

4

Personal Readiness

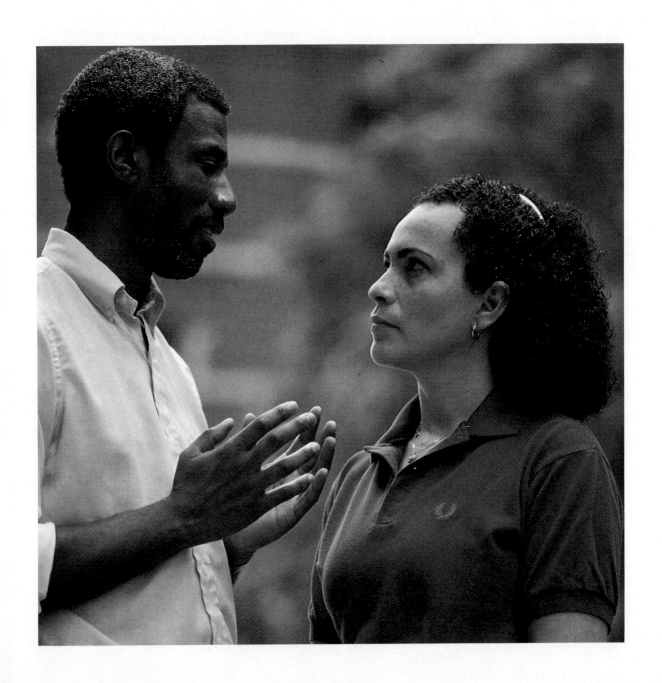

Objectives

This chapter will help you to:
- Discuss the reasons why people choose to have or not to have children.
- Explain how people can evaluate their personal readiness for parenthood.
- List and describe the five steps of the decision-making process.
- Answer questions about your personal readiness for parenthood.

Vocabulary

condition
infatuation
maturity
prioritize

Diana and Ryan have been married for two years. They have each achieved an important personal goal. Diana, age twenty-four, has just received her nursing degree. She worked part-time at the local hospital while completing her education. Now she has been offered a full-time nursing position at the hospital. Ryan, age twenty-five, is employed as a salesperson for a computer software company. His career is finally on track.

Diana and Ryan have postponed starting a family to pursue their education and career goals. Now they are considering whether it is time for them to have a child.

Diana says, "I've been looking forward to being a nurse for as long as I can remember. If I become pregnant now, I may have to stop working to care for the baby. Since I'm just getting started in my career, it might be difficult later on to find another job that I like as much as this one. On the other hand, I've always wanted children. Maybe I could work part-time at the hospital and find someone to take care of the baby when I'm at work."

Ryan replies, "Now that we both have full-time jobs, we can start saving money to buy a house someday. Yet it sure would be fun to buy a little boat and go fishing on weekends. We've both been so busy working and going to school that we haven't had time to do some of the things we like to do. It would also be fun to teach our children how to fish! Maybe we could arrange our work hours so that one of us would always be home to care for a baby."

Diana and Ryan continue discussing the pros and cons of having a child. They agree that they both want to have children. The question now is: Are they ready to become parents?

Chapter Opener. Ask students to read the opening scenario to the chapter. Ask these questions: What are the pros and cons of having a child for Diana and for Ryan? How can they decide whether or not they are ready to become parents? What should they do if they disagree on when to have a child? Is there a "best" time for a couple to have a baby?

To Have or Not to Have Children

Becoming a parent changes a person's life. Some people recognize that the decision to become a parent is one of the most important decisions they will ever make. Other people do not give the matter serious thought until the baby arrives, alive and wiggling.

Parenthood brings many changes and new responsibilities to parents' lives. Some of the frustrations and challenges of parenting can be avoided when parents are personally ready for parenthood.

Couples need to talk about parenthood and their readiness for the role of parents. Some people may decide that they will not be ready to be a parent for a few years. Others will need more time. Still others may feel they will never choose to become parents.

➡ Why People Choose to Have Children

Let's take a look at some of the reasons why people decide to have children. There are almost as many reasons for having children as there are people. Some people's reasons are carefully thought out and logical. Others' reasons are very emotional and difficult to describe. In some cases they are based on unrealistic expectations.

Life Experiences

Everyone first experiences life as a child. It is a role every adult has played. A past or present experience can **condition,** or affect, people's attitudes and actions for a lifetime. Thus their feelings about parenthood are conditioned by their experiences as children.

If you stop and think for a moment, your own childhood memories can come flooding back. Perhaps you remember the first time you were left behind with a babysitter. You may relive the joy of getting exactly what you wanted for your ninth birthday. Perhaps you recall a large holiday party with plenty of food, songs, and games. If your feelings about childhood are mostly positive, you probably have positive feelings about parenthood. If your feelings are negative, however, then you may view parenthood in a negative way.

Your personal experiences with children affect your feelings about having your own child. The personal experiences of your

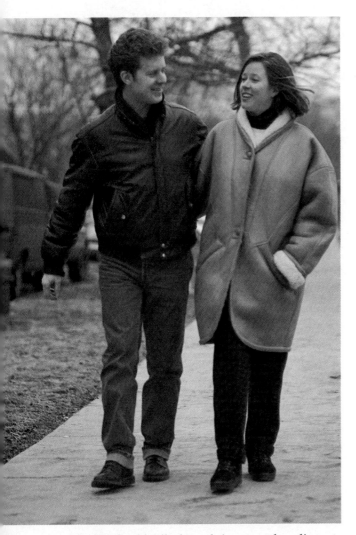

Couples should talk about their personal readiness to become parents.

Activity. Divide class into small groups. Have each group list all the reasons why people become parents. Ask them to decide which reasons are *positive* and which are *negative*. Then have them explain how they made their decisions.

Discuss. Choosing to become a parent is relatively new in our society. What changes have occurred over the years that have made parenthood more of a choice for couples than an assumption or obligation?

friends or people you have read about also influence your feelings about children.

Expression of Love

The desire to have children comes from a basic, powerful, natural urge—love between adults. At its best, adult love is a combination of physical desire and friendship. It is a feeling that produces extraordinary closeness between a man and a woman. An infant is the living, tangible expression of this love.

Unfortunately, some people confuse infatuation and love. **Infatuation** is an intense but usually short-term feeling of love for someone. It is most often based on characteristics such as physical appearance, personality, or a certain ability. In contrast, true love is much deeper and longer lasting. When couples truly love each other, they share mutual respect, admiration, and trust. They are interested in each other's ideas and attitudes.

Desire for Family Life-Style

For many people, the joy of day-to-day family life is essential to their own lives. They want to continue the family experience that began when their parents had them. These people enjoy watching children play, going on family outings, and being involved in activities with other family members. They are happy when their home is filled with relatives for celebrations such as Thanksgiving, anniversaries, and birthdays.

For example, Kenneth had a very happy childhood. He says, "My family was warm and supportive. I always wanted to have kids and raise them in a family like my own." Connie, on the other hand, did not have a happy childhood. Yet she says, "I have lots of love inside me. I want to have a loving family for my own kids."

Other People's Expectations

Married adults have traditionally been expected to produce children. This expectation is as old as the history of human beings. Reproduction is necessary for the human species to survive. Today, adults who choose not to have children may find that society puts subtle pressures on them to become parents.

Sometimes pressure to have children comes from potential grandparents. They may have a strong desire to see the family line continue. They may want grandchildren to carry on the family name and traditions. Grandchildren can also provide another opportunity for grandparents to experience the joys of parenting.

Appeal of Children

Babies are very appealing to most people. Have you ever noticed how much attention they receive in a room full of adults? Parents become part of their children's limelight, too.

Most adults act spontaneously with babies and young children. They feel free to laugh, act silly, and express the childlike parts of their personality. They experience the warmth of their caring and nurturing selves. They are touched by the affection and trust that children demonstrate. Many people want this joy to be a part of their lives.

DECISIONS ◆ ◆ DECISIONS

Janelle has been feeling lonely. Her brother has moved out of the house, and her mother is usually at work. Janelle has a boyfriend, but their romance seems stale. Lately, Janelle has been dreaming about having a baby to love and cherish. She has told you her idea and asked your opinion. What will you tell her?

Discuss. Is there a difference between adult love and the love experienced by teenagers?
Activity. Invite a marriage counselor to talk about infatuation, love, relationships, and marriage. How can couples know if they love each other? What decisions should they make before marriage? How can they strengthen their marriage?
Problem Solving. How could you tactfully tell another person to stop pressuring you to become a parent?

Economic Asset

In a number of developing countries, adults want children because they can eventually go to work and contribute to the family's income. This reason was prominent in the United States several generations ago and may still be true in a few areas today.

Some people want children so that the children will take care of them when they become elderly. In some cultures, the eldest son assumes the responsibility of caring for his elderly parents. In our society, social security, pensions, and other benefits help provide economic support for older people. However, older parents may still need assistance and support from their adult children.

Curiosity

Some people have children out of sheer curiosity. They wonder what a child of theirs might be like. They also wonder what type of parent they would be. These people may have heard that being a parent is a central experience in life. They fear that they will miss an important experience if they do not have children.

◆◆ Why People Choose Not to Have Children

Many people are taking a close look at the long-term commitment that having children requires. Some feel that their lives will be better if they postpone having children until a later time. Others decide not to have children at all.

Long-Term Goals

Some people are concerned that children will limit their long-term goals. These people may want to focus on getting an education or becoming established in a career. Perhaps they want to travel, pursue hobbies, or save money to buy a home.

Freedom

Some adults get great satisfaction from developing their own physical and mental abilities and do not want to take the time to rear children. Others enjoy doing things on the spur of the moment. These people do not want the responsibilities or life-style changes that parenthood creates.

Parenthood changes people's life-styles. Parents have less time to go out with friends than they did before they had children.

Discuss. Are children an economic asset to most families in the U.S. today? Are you an economic asset or liability?
Activity. Have students research which cultures encourage large families and which encourage small families. What factors contribute to these cultural differences?
Discuss. If you discovered you would become a parent tomorrow, how would it change your present life-style and your long-term goals?

Furthermore, some adults feel that they have such a good one-to-one relationship as a couple that they are content with their lives without children. As one such couple said, "We are our own family."

Personal Experiences

Some people decide to postpone or not to have children on the basis of their own experiences. Some adults did not have a happy childhood and believe they might inflict the same bad experiences they had on their own youngsters. Others have been responsible for the care of younger brothers or sisters and feel they have done their share of child rearing.

Some people cannot imagine themselves tied to a long-term relationship. They have never had one and do not think such relationships work. Others cannot picture themselves as parents.

Fears

Other reasons for not having children center around certain fears. Some women fear the physical changes of pregnancy. Others worry about the possible pain of delivery. Couples with certain health problems or hereditary conditions may decide to remain childless because they do not want to pass the health or medical problem on to a child.

Both men and women may worry about their ability to care for and support a child. Do they have enough patience to deal with a baby? Can they afford a child? Would they be able to manage the responsibilities of children, home, and work? Some couples wonder how a child would change their relationship with each other.

If people are uncertain or hesitant about having children, they should postpone parenthood or choose to remain childless. Children suffer when they are brought into homes where they are unwanted.

Around the World

The Modern Father

If you had been born a hundred years ago, you might have a different image of the father's role in a family. At the beginning of the twentieth century, most families were *patriarchal.* This term means that the family authority is vested in the father.

The father was the unquestioned head of the household. He held all the economic power. Since he was the only income earner, or at least the main income earner, how well the family lived depended on how much money he made. If he could not afford a doctor, sick children stayed sick or died. If he deserted them, they could starve. The father was the sole guardian of his children. If he decided to divorce his wife and forbid her to see the children, the law would support him.

Years ago, most children viewed their father as a remote authority figure. Fathers seldom were actively involved in day-to-day child rearing. Their role was primarily to discipline the children.

The modern image of the ideal father is of one who participates in all areas of family life, from caring for the children to preparing meals. Many fathers equally share the responsibilities of parenting. They change diapers, give baths, take walks, and read stories to their children. In divorced families, many fathers continue their relationship with their children. Some choose to rear their children.

Today, most families depend economically on both mothers and fathers being wage earners. Government programs are available to help families in a crisis. If parents divorce, the custody of the children no longer automatically goes to the father. Instead the court tries to determine what arrangement would be best for the children.

Discuss. What other reasons might people have for not wanting to be a parent?
Problem Solving. Have students suggest ways that specific fears about having children could be overcome or eliminated.

Emphasize. If people have doubts about becoming a parent, they should postpone having children.

When Are You Ready for Parenthood?

Creating a new life is one of the most exciting and rewarding experiences a couple can have. It means that two adults are ready to accept a long-term responsibility that will alter the way they live.

The right time for parenthood varies from person to person and from couple to couple. However, there are guidelines to help people decide whether they are personally ready for parenthood.

◆◆ Level of Maturity

A good measure of how ready someone is to be a parent is the person's level of **maturity.** This is the condition in which a person's body is fully developed and he or she thinks and acts reasonably, responsibly, reliably, and independently. Overall maturity does not depend only on how old a person is. However, most people are better able to manage their lives as they become older.

Mature women and men can take care of themselves. They have good judgment and make wise decisions. They are able to put the needs of others ahead of their own.

Elizabeth, for example, thinks she wants to have a baby. However, she likes to go out with her friends almost every night. Her social activities are important to her. She is probably not ready to be a mother because she might resent staying home with a child.

Now consider Bruce. He does not handle responsibilities well. It is hard for him to hold the same job for more than a year or to remember details such as having his car serviced regularly. He is probably not ready for the many responsibilities and constant care that a baby requires.

◆◆ Stability of Relationship

Parenthood can put a strain on relationships. Couples need time together to develop a meaningful relationship before they are ready to have children. They need opportunities to share their love and concern for each other and to establish strong, lasting bonds. It takes many months—and sometimes even years—to test feelings and thoughts, develop mutual respect and trust, and form a strong basis for building a family.

Couples need to be sure of their commitment before they have children. Some people think that having a child will cause their partner to fall in love with them. Others think that a baby will solve their relationship problems. However, the birth of a child poses challenges to a couple. Instead of giving stability to a shaky marriage, it can create additional problems and conflicts.

Most couples go through a period of adjustment in their relationship after the birth of a first child. They must add the demanding role of parents to their role of partners. This usually takes some time. It always takes mature insights and decisions. As one parent pointed out: "It's not just a matter of how the two of us are going to adjust to the baby. It's a whole new ball game. Now it's a matter of how these three people are going to relate to each other."

The early months and years of marriage allow partners time to get used to living together. They learn how to share their feelings and how to settle differences. They develop a comfortable rhythm and flow to their lives. They build strong bonds of marriage that will enable them to withstand the hardships and disappointments that life may bring. Their marriage will have a greater chance for success if children do not come along too soon. Also, the children will benefit from a happy and stable marriage.

On the other hand, many couples do have children early in their marriage and still maintain a happy marriage. Usually, these parents are successful because they are self-confident and mature individuals.

◆◆ Physical, Mental, and Emotional Health

Before becoming parents, individuals should evaluate their physical, mental, and emotional health. All three areas of health are important for successful parenting.

Physical Health

Ideally, both partners should be in good physical health before becoming parents. They should be well-nourished and not involved in behaviors, such as smoking, drinking, and drug use, that could affect the development of their baby. They should also be free of any diseases that could be passed along to the child.

The woman should be sure that her body is healthy enough to carry the baby for the nine months of pregnancy. Her reproductive system should have reached its mature growth. Her skeletal structure should provide enough room for the developing child. Her age must also be considered. Women younger than seventeen or older than thirty-five years of age run a greater risk of health problems during pregnancy than other women.

Mental Health

Thinking realistically is a sign of good mental health. Babies are not dolls. They cannot be everything their parents might wish them to be. Babies also grow up. They do not remain cuddly little infants for long. People who are mentally ready for parenthood rec-

ognize the realities of parenthood. They understand that children can be dirty, sick, or naughty, just as they can be clean, healthy, and well behaved. Predicting what a baby will be like is impossible. Most babies are a mixture of the delightful and the difficult. To deal with both, parents need to be mentally mature.

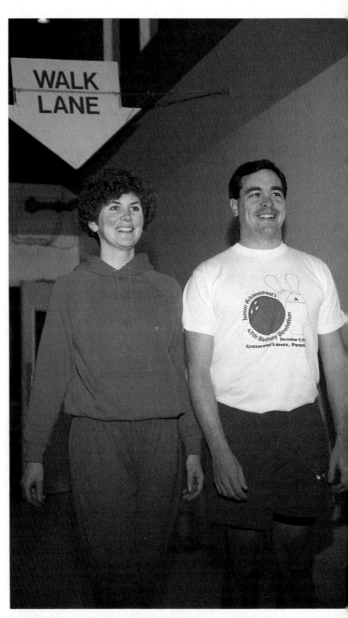

The total health of prospective parents is important—physical, mental, and emotional health.

Reference. See pages 87–90 and 155–170 for information about wellness and health risks during pregnancy.

Emphasize. A parent who is rested and well-nourished is better able to cope emotionally with the demands of a baby or young child.

Emotional Health

Individuals with good emotional health have high self-esteem. They feel confident about facing new tasks, such as parenting. They have a good understanding of themselves. They are able to give love without expecting a great deal in return. Babies bring much emotional satisfaction to parents. Yet babies are unable to respond to an adult's need for emotional support. Parents who yearn for someone to love them and understand how they feel may be disappointed when the baby is unable to fulfill these expectations. Having a child cannot give parents permanent feelings of self-esteem. This is something that individuals must secure for themselves, before the birth of a child.

Good emotional health also involves the ability to control one's reactions to emotions. For example, a baby who cries and cries can cause feelings of frustration and even anger in parents. Emotionally mature parents are able to control their feelings of frustration and respond calmly to their child's needs. These parents are able to cope with the many responsibilities of parenting, even when things go wrong.

DECISIONS ◆
◆ DECISIONS

Dominic often babysits for neighborhood children. Usually, he enjoys it. One toddler, however, has been making Dominic uneasy. The toddler does the opposite of whatever she is asked. She whines and cries a lot. At times, Dominic feels like spanking the child. That worries him and makes him wonder whether he might be an abusive parent someday. He wonders whether he should become a parent at all. What do you think?

To be emotionally ready for parenthood, both partners should want to have a child. This is an essential ingredient in making parenthood a joyful experience. However, even those who want and plan a pregnancy can have moments of doubt. Couples who are emotionally healthy are able to express their feelings of doubt or worry. They know that anxiety about parenthood is natural.

◆◆ Social Considerations

Parenthood can significantly change a couple's social life. The care of a baby involves a great deal of time and effort. New parents discover that they have little, if any, leisure time. They are no longer able to go out every night with friends or join in spur-of-the-moment activities. This sometimes leads to feelings of loneliness or isolation.

When parents plan to go out—whether for a few minutes or for several hours—they must make arrangements for the baby's care. Children must never be left alone. Sometimes parents want to take the baby with them. This often requires packing a supply of bottles, diapers, toys, and a change of clothes if the family will be away for several hours. They may need an infant carrier, stroller, or car seat. At other times, parents may prefer to leave the child with a caregiver. However, reliable caregivers are sometimes difficult to find, and they add to the cost of having a child. If the baby gets sick or the caregiver is unable to come, plans must be canceled.

Parents often find that their social activities change after the baby arrives. They may discover they have more similar interests with friends who have children than with those who are childless. Gradually, they may spend more and more time with other parents in child-centered activities. They may also spend more time with relatives and at family gatherings.

✧ Financial Considerations

Romantics may believe that "two can live as cheaply as one." However, the truth is that each person added to a family increases expenses. The more children in a family, the more money the family needs for food, clothing, shelter, and medical care.

Financial readiness for parenthood includes providing for the costs of medical care during pregnancy and birth. Once the baby is born, financial readiness includes having an adequate place to live. Although babies do not take up much space, their equipment does. Couples with enough room for their child have an easier time adjusting to the constant demands of parenthood. Prospective parents should take the time to plan a budget. This is not as simple as it sounds. Although many costs can be estimated beforehand, others may be unexpected. If either parent stops working after the baby arrives, the family will have to live on a reduced income.

Many couples must change their life-style after becoming parents. Money that used to be spent on entertainment, clothing, and travel may now have to be used to pay for medical expenses, child care services, and other necessities. Most parents also want to save for long-range goals, such as a larger home or college education for their children.

◆ ◆ Self-Esteem ◆ ◆

Accepting yourself, with your various strengths and weaknesses, is a first step toward maturity. If you can look in the mirror and say, "I like the person I see," then you will find it easier to accept others. Self-acceptance and self-esteem go hand in hand. If you like and feel good about yourself, your self-esteem will flourish.

Reference. See pages 64–65 for information about the financial costs of rearing children.
Activity. Ask students to research the child care options for infants in your community. Have them prepare a chart show-

✧ Career Plans

When you have only yourself to think about, deciding what job or career you want may be relatively easy. If you decide to marry, you have to integrate two lives and possibly two careers. A baby complicates matters because a newborn requires full-time attention from someone.

People need to make decisions about getting enough education or training for the job or career of their choice. They must also decide how children will fit into this career. For a person who places importance on being a family member and parent, some careers may be more attractive than others. For example, some jobs allow people to go home after regular working hours, while others require a great amount of travel away from home. Some jobs require many evening or weekend hours. Others require a person to be "on call," ready to leave home on a few moments notice.

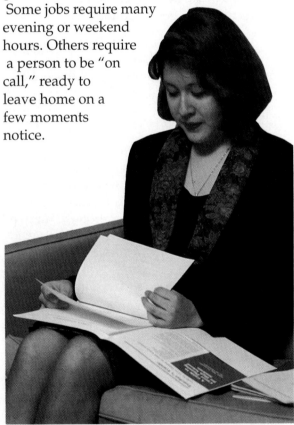

Parenthood can affect career goals. Some jobs are easier to combine with parenthood than others.

ing the costs.
Discuss. How would a child fit in with your present career plans? What careers would be difficult to combine with being a parent? Why?

It is also important for people to decide how important a career is to them. Would they be able or willing to work part-time or take time off to care for a child? If so, for how long? If both parents work full-time, what child care options are available? The answers to these questions can help couples decide about career plans.

❖ Goals

Couples need to talk about their long-term goals. Do they want to continue their education? What career goals does each partner have? What financial goals do they both have? Do they agree about if and when to have children? Have they discussed how many children they would like to have?

Couples also need to talk about their social and recreational goals. Do they like to enter-tain frequently or go out with friends? Do they want to travel? What hobbies and activities do they enjoy? How do they want to spend their leisure time?

Many people become parents without planning ahead. As a result, they may have fewer options than those who prepare for parenthood. Some are able to pursue their goals, but more slowly and with more hardships. Others become disappointed and even resentful because their parenting responsibilities prevent them from pursuing their goals in life. Still others find the task of parenting so demanding that they give up their goals. There are, of course, those who manage to accomplish their personal goals while being very successful parents.

People can quit a job or turn their backs on a career. However, they can neither stop being a parent nor turn their backs on their children.

◆ ◆ *Health & Safety* ◆ ◆

Substitute Parenting

People who love children do not always have children of their own. Some are not able to conceive a baby. Others may have difficulty adopting a child. Still others have careers or obligations that keep them from wanting to be full-time parents. Sometimes people want to be parents in the future but are not yet ready to become parents.

If these people enjoy the company of children, here are some ways they can interact with them:

- "Adopt" the children of a close friend or relative. Take the children places or just spend time reading, playing, and relaxing with them. Become a part of their holidays and other joyous events.

- Get involved in a Big Brother or Big Sister program. These programs pair an adult with a school-age child or teenager who can benefit from the guidance of a same-gender adult. The "big brother" or "big sister" develops a one-on-one relationship with the child.

- Volunteer to help various community organizations that work with children. Become a scout leader, coach a team, teach a Sunday school class, or tutor children. Most community organizations welcome volunteer help.

These activities also help people discover whether or not they are ready for full-time parenthood.

Activity. Conduct an egg-baby or flour-baby project. Have students draw for gender and special situations (twins, preemies, disabilities). Students are responsible for their "baby" for one week and must arrange for child care if they work or are in activities. They must keep a journal of their experiences, emotions, frustrations, and adjustments to the responsibilities of parenthood and note other people's comments. Students can be accused of neglect, abuse, or kidnapping in "court."

Decision-Making Skills

Depending on religious beliefs, people today are able to decide whether they want to become parents. They should make this decision only after carefully weighing the pros and cons of parenthood in relation to their own lives. Joint discussions between the partners are essential in making wise family decisions. The lives of both parents will be affected, and both will be legally responsible for the outcome. One partner should never pressure the other about important decisions.

◆◆ The Decision-Making Process

Choosing to become a parent should be based on an informed decision. People need to find out as much as possible about what it is like to be a parent. They need to examine their motives and clarify their feelings. They also need to consider the kind of life they want to lead. This information will help them make a decision that best meets their life goals.

The decision-making process involves five basic steps:

1. **Define the problem.** Both partners should understand what they are considering.
   Problem: "Should we have a child?"

2. **Identify alternatives.** The couple should consider all the various options they have at this time.
   Alternatives:
   Try for pregnancy immediately.
   Delay pregnancy.
   Do not have a child.

3. **Analyze the possible consequences.** The couple should evaluate the possible results of each alternative and compare their advantages and disadvantages.

Consequences of pregnancy: The couple would be able to start a desired family, but a child would dramatically change their lives and create many challenges.
Consequences of delaying pregnancy: The couple could achieve desired goals before having a child, but they might have difficulty having a child later.
Consequences of not having a child: The couple could focus on their careers and each other, but they would not experience the rewards of parenting.

4. **Make the decision.** In order to make the best decision, the couple should **prioritize** their goals. This means to rank them in order of importance. Then they should decide which option will best help them meet their goals. It is important that both partners agree on their final choice.

5. **Evaluate the results.** Options to postpone or not to have a child can be reevaluated on a regular basis. As time goes on, situations change and couples may decide to reevaluate their original decision. However, the option of having a child is a permanent one. It should be selected only after careful evaluation of the advantages and disadvantages of having children.

Sometimes the responsibility of decision making can seem overwhelming. In some situations, people may be tempted to let fate take over the direction of their life. However, the decision to become a parent will affect every aspect of a person's life. It should not be made without careful thought.

In the long run, people retain a sense of control when they make the important choices in their life. This enables them to stay in charge of their life. When they wake up and stumble groggily over to their infant's crib for a middle-of-the-night feeding, it will be comforting to know that they undertook this role with a full awareness of what they were getting into. They chose to be a parent.

Activity. Working in "couples," have students go through the decision-making process for other situations: Should we get married? Where could we live? Should we continue our education? **Reference.** See pages 501–505 for communication skills.

Problem Solving. Have students discuss how a relationship might be affected if one person wanted to become a parent but the other did not. What problems might arise if the woman did become pregnant? How might they be resolved?

What Do You Think?

Now it is your turn to think personally about parenthood. So far, your experiences have probably been on only one side of the parent-child equation. Here are some important questions for you to answer some day. They will help you determine your personal readiness for parenthood.

- Do you and your partner agree that you are both ready to become parents?
- How will a baby fit in with your long-term goals?
- Are you and your partner physically and emotionally mature?
- Do you have a stable relationship?
- Do you have enough income to support a child?
- Would you be willing to give up something you wanted to get something for your child?
- Are you and your partner healthy?
- Are you patient? Can you control your emotions in times of stress?
- Are you willing to spend less time with your friends in order to care for a child?
- Will a child change your career plans?
- Could you manage school or a job and parenting?
- Have you spent much time babysitting or caring for children? If so, do you enjoy it? Are you good at it? If not, do you intend to get experience taking care of children?
- What kind of parents would you and your partner be?
- Do you really want to be a parent?

People's feelings about parenthood are influenced by the memories of their own childhood and family.

Discuss. Do you agree that having a baby can affect every aspect of a person's life? Why or why not?
Activity. Have students write a short essay entitled "Am I Ready to Become a Parent?"

Emphasize. Important decisions that have long-lasting effects on your life should not be made quickly or carelessly.

CHAPTER 4 REVIEW

Summary

- Couples need to talk about parenthood and their readiness for the role of parents.
- Reasons why people choose to have children include life experiences, expression of love, desire for family life-style, other people's expectations, appeal of children, economic asset, and curiosity.
- Some people choose not to have children because of long-term goals, loss of freedom, personal experiences, and fears.
- Guidelines for parenthood readiness include level of maturity, stability of relationship, health, social and financial considerations, career plans, and goals.
- By following the five steps of the decision-making process, couples can make an informed decision about when or whether to have a child.

Questions

p. 70 **1.** What are five reasons why people choose to have children?

p. 71 **2.** What is infatuation? How does it differ from true love?

p. 72 **3.** List four reasons why people decide not to have children.

p. 74 **4.** Why is a person's level of maturity a good measure of personal readiness for parenthood?

p. 74 **5.** Why should a couple avoid having a baby early in their relationship?

p. 75 **6.** Describe a person who has good physical, mental, and emotional health.

7. How does parenthood change a couple's social life? p. 76

8. Why do people who plan ahead for parenthood usually have more options than people who do not? p. 78

9. List the five steps in the decision-making process. p. 79

Activities

1. Take a few minutes to answer the questions on page 80. Then determine the areas in which you are and are not presently ready for parenthood.

2. Use the decision-making process to help you make a decision about a current problem in your life. Identify as many alternatives and possible consequences as possible. Explain how the process enabled you to decide which option to select.

3. Research and report the views of two child psychologists on the subject of spacing children within a family. What do these experts suggest as the best age for the first child to be before the next child is born. Do you agree or disagree with these findings? Explain your answer.

Think About

1. When might some people feel pressured to have a child? By whom? Why?

2. If you suddenly became a parent, how would your upcoming weekend plans be affected? Your long-term plans?

CHAPTER 5

Teenage Parenthood

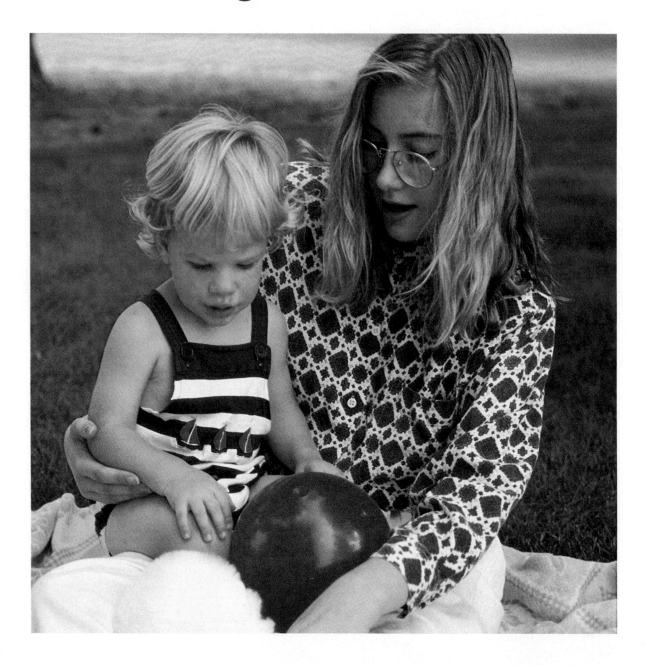

Objectives

This chapter will help you to:

- Discuss the issues of sexuality, sexual activity, and abstinence.
- Describe the health risks and emotional concerns associated with teenage pregnancy.
- Compare the parenthood options of marriage, single parenthood, and adoption.
- Explain how teenagers can best meet the challenges of parenthood.

Vocabulary

consequences
sexuality
puberty
hormones
abstinence
sexually transmitted
    disease (STD)
low birth weight
premature

prenatal care
open adoption

Katrina and Joe are returning from the local health clinic where Katrina's pregnancy has been confirmed. The teenage couple have been going together for six months. Now they are bewildered at this sudden turn of events in their lives.

Katrina says, "What are we going to do, Joe? How are we going to tell our parents? My mom and dad want me to graduate so I can get a good job. Now I don't know how I'll even be able to finish this year. How could this have happened? I'm not ready to have a baby. I'm really scared!"

Joe replies, "Somehow we'll manage, Katrina. Do you want to get married? I don't know how we can afford to live on our own. Maybe I can get another part-time job to help support the baby. Gosh, there are so many things to think about. I promise I'll stay with you and help you."

Katrina sighs, "I wish we could talk to someone. I never thought this would happen to us."

Katrina and Joe are experiencing many confusing emotions. What decisions do they have to make? Where can they get advice and support? How can they face the challenges of pregnancy and parenthood?

Teenage Relationships

Katrina and Joe have been sexually active. One of the **consequences**—the results or outcomes—of such activity can be pregnancy. Teenage pregnancy is a controversial topic in our society. Many adults are critical of early teenage pregnancy and parenthood for various reasons. They know that being a parent demands a great deal of an individual's time, effort, and money. No matter how mature a teenager is physically, he or she is almost never emotionally, mentally, or financially prepared for parenthood. Most teenagers are still learning to be responsible for themselves. They are not ready to assume the responsibility for the life of another person.

Chapter Opener. Ask students to read the opening scenario to the chapter. Ask these questions: What emotions do Katrina and Joe have? What decisions do they have to make? Where can they get advice? What challenges do they face?

Activity. Have students research the latest statistics on teenage pregnancy in your city or county, your state, and the nation. Have the numbers been increasing or decreasing for different ages?

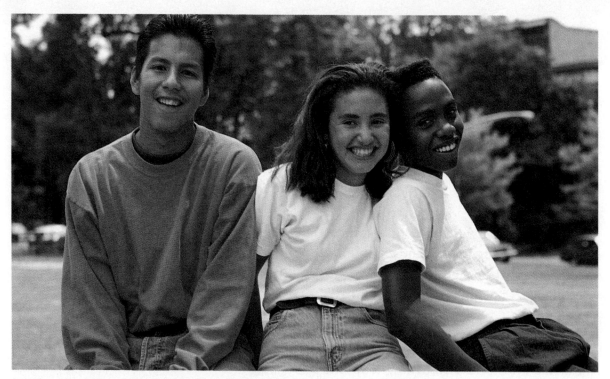

The teenage years are a time of growth and development when adolescents should gain an education, plan for a career, expand friendships, and learn about themselves.

Some teenagers think that adults exaggerate the challenges and hardships of being a teenage parent. These young people feel that parenthood is a role that they can successfully manage. They have had lots of child care experience. Other teenagers do not think about the role of parents. They are sexually active and become parents not by choice but by accident.

❖ Sexuality

Sexuality refers to a person's concept of himself or herself as a male or a female. Sexuality begins in early childhood as children learn about their own identity and gender differences. People express their sexuality in many ways—in how they move, talk, dress, and laugh. Thus sexuality involves physical, emotional, social, and mental development.

Adolescence is a time of increased awareness of sexuality because of the physical and emotional changes that occur. **Puberty** marks the beginning of adolescence, usually between the ages of eleven and fourteen. However, puberty may occur as young as nine years of age. This is the stage of growth and development when males and females become physically able to reproduce. During puberty, adolescents experience changes in their body shape caused by **hormones,** or body chemicals that stimulate growth. Boys and girls develop the respective physical characteristics of men and women.

Hormones cause emotional changes in adolescents as well. Most adolescents discover that their emotions now change more abruptly than they did in the past. One moment they may feel very confident and sure of themselves. The next moment they

Discuss. Do you think adults exaggerate the challenges and hardships of being a teenage parent? Why or why not?
Activity. Ask students to observe preschoolers at play for specific ways that they have begun to adopt masculine or feminine ways of behaving in our society.
Activity. Have students research the physical and emotional changes that occur during puberty.

may feel confused or unsure. They may also experience emotions more deeply than they did when they were younger.

Adolescence is also a time for many social changes. Having a best friend or belonging to a close group of friends becomes very important to adolescents. There is a strong emphasis on belonging and acceptance. At some point during the adolescent years, most young people begin to feel an attraction or strong emotion toward one or more people of the other gender.

As adolescents learn about their sexuality, they must make important decisions concerning sexual activity. These decisions should be based on their own beliefs, values, and goals, not on the actions of others.

◆◆ Sexual Activity

Why do some adolescents become sexually active? Some are influenced by what they see, hear, and read. Television shows, movies, books, and magazines usually give a very romantic, glamorous, or sophisticated view of sexual involvement. Seldom do they focus on the negative consequences. In addition, advertisements frequently use the theme of sexual attraction to promote their products. This sends a confusing message to young people about sexuality, relationships, and responsibilities.

Some adolescents become sexually active because they feel it will strengthen a relationship. However, a good relationship involves much more than physical closeness. It must include emotional closeness and respect as well. Relationships based solely on sex seldom last.

Some adolescents become sexually active because of pressure from friends. They may think it will make them more accepted by their group. Perhaps they find it difficult to say no to a partner who is pressuring them to

have sex. As a result, some young people become sexually active even when they would prefer not to.

Adolescent couples should talk over their ideas and feelings about sexual activity. They should discuss the consequences of various behaviors. They should make firm decisions about such behaviors beforehand. This eliminates the need to make a sudden decision in the heat of passion. The decision-making process can help adolescents sort out what really matters to them—not just for now but for the future as well.

Teenage couples need time to get to know one another. Relationships should be based on mutual caring and respect.

❖ Abstinence

Many adolescents choose not to become sexually involved. **Abstinence** (AB-stuh-nuns) means refraining from sexual intercourse. It is the result of a decision that is usually based on a person's values, beliefs, and goals. It is the decision encouraged by adults.

Pressure from others is easier to resist if young people have high self-esteem, a clear set of values, and goals for the future. It is also easier to resist when relationships are based on mutual feelings of caring and respect rather than pleasure or prowess.

Many adolescents choose abstinence because of the possible consequences of sexual activity. Pregnancy is one possible consequence. A female can become pregnant anytime a couple have intercourse, even if it is the first time or if they use birth control

methods. The only 100 percent effective method of avoiding pregnancy is abstinence.

Another possible consequence of sexual activity is contracting a **sexually transmitted disease (STD).** This is a disease that is transmitted by sexual contact. You will learn more about pregnancy and STDs in Unit 2.

Sexual activity for adolescents can also result in loss of self-respect. When people do something they feel uncomfortable about or unprepared for just to be liked or accepted, they often suffer emotionally. Instead of feeling good about themselves afterward, they have lower self-esteem. Sexual activity can also strain teenagers' relationships with parents, relatives, and other caregivers. Often teenagers who are sexually active feel they must hide their behavior from adults. As a result, they may become more secretive in their actions and feelings.

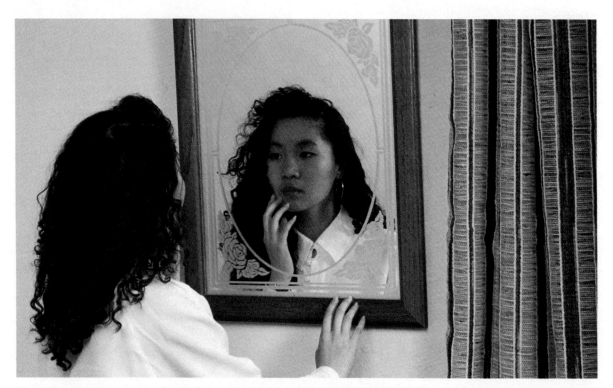

Teenagers may become confused about relationships. They need to think about their values and goals because pregnancy can change a teenager's life.

Problem Solving. Using the decision-making process on page 79, ask students to chart the steps for deciding, "Should I be sexually active *now?*" Have students work individually, then in pairs, then in small groups, then as a class to chart all the choices, consequences, and pros and cons of sexual activity. **Discuss.** What beliefs, values, and goals could be in conflict or hindered by sexual activity during adolescence?

❖ Teenage Pregnancy

Why do teenagers become pregnant? There are many reasons. Some adolescents are uninformed about reproduction and the consequences of sexual activity. They may be embarrassed to discuss these topics or do not know where to get accurate information. Some teenagers think that pregnancy cannot occur because they are young, not in love, or have intercourse only once. None of these can prevent a pregnancy.

Other adolescents use unreliable means to prevent a pregnancy, or the method fails. Many teenagers are hesitant to talk to their partner about birth control. However, one of the signs of a mature relationship is the ability to share feelings and concerns with each other.

Still other teenagers think that a baby will give them love and affection. They believe that having their own child can give purpose and meaning to their own life. These teenagers often have low self-esteem or a feeling of hopelessness. They may seek a sense of accomplishment and attention from being a parent that they have not received before.

DECISIONS ◆ ◆ DECISIONS

Josie, age fifteen, is trying to decide whether to have sex with her boyfriend, Mark. He has been pressuring her for several weeks, saying, "Everyone's doing it! If you really loved me, you'd do it too!" Josie does not feel that she is ready to become sexually active. However, she doesn't want to lose Mark. She has asked you for your opinion. What will you tell her?

Discuss. What is the process of reproduction? What misconceptions do some teenagers have about the process?
Reference. See pages 119–121 and 126–128 for information about reproduction and contraception.

For some, conceiving a child may be a sign of manhood or womanhood. They have focused their attention more on the accomplishment of having a child than on the responsibilities involved in rearing a child.

Others seem unaware of the risks and challenges of teenage pregnancy and parenthood. They may not realize the changes that a child makes in parents' lives. They may not have considered the impact a baby makes on schooling, jobs, finances, and independence. Knowing someone else who is pregnant or a teenage parent does not always give a complete picture of the responsibilities involved in bringing a child into the world.

❖ Concerns About Teenage Pregnancy

Many people are concerned about the problems teenage parents and their children face. Let's take a look at some of the current statistics:

- Four out of ten girls become pregnant before they are twenty years old.
- Over 500,000 teenagers give birth each year.
- Almost 13 percent of all U.S. births are to teenage girls.
- Two-thirds of all teenage mothers are unmarried.
- Babies born to teenage mothers have a higher risk of serious health problems. They are more than twice as likely to die than babies born to women in their twenties.
- Teenagers who become pregnant and drop out of school are less likely to return and complete high school. As a result, they usually lack job skills. They may remain financially dependent on their family or on welfare.

Discuss. What are some other characteristics of a mature relationship? Should embarrassment be one of them?
Discuss. Does conceiving a baby mean that you are a "real man" or a "real woman?" Why or why not?

Health Risks

When a female under seventeen years of age becomes pregnant, the health risks for both mother and child increase sharply. Adolescent girls have not finished their own growth. Pregnancy places extra demands on teenage bodies that are still growing. Young teenagers are more likely than older women to experience complications during pregnancy and birth. See "Health Risks of Teenage Pregnancy" on the next page.

Infants of teenage mothers may also experience serious health problems. The most hazardous is **low birth weight,** a weight of less than 5½ pounds at birth. One out of seven babies born to teenage mothers has a low birth weight. Babies that have a low birth weight are 40 times more likely to die in their first month of life than babies who weigh 7½ pounds or more. Low birth weight is often due to the mother's poor health habits, such as eating an inadequate diet, smoking, or using alcohol or drugs. It may also be due to the baby being born prematurely. A **premature** (pree-muh-CHOOR) baby is one who is born before his or her development is complete.

Premature babies and babies with low birth weight often have immature organs, such as lungs, heart, and brain. They frequently have breathing problems. They have difficulty controlling body temperature and blood sugar levels. They get sick more easily than full-term or normal-weight babies. They are also at greater risk for having one or more physical or mental disabilities.

As a result, pregnant teenagers are considered to be in the high-risk health category. They need good **prenatal care** from the earliest months of pregnancy. This is regular medical care and supervision prior to the baby's birth. Advice about nutrition, exercise, rest, and avoidance of harmful substances is given by a doctor, nurse, or other medical practitioner.

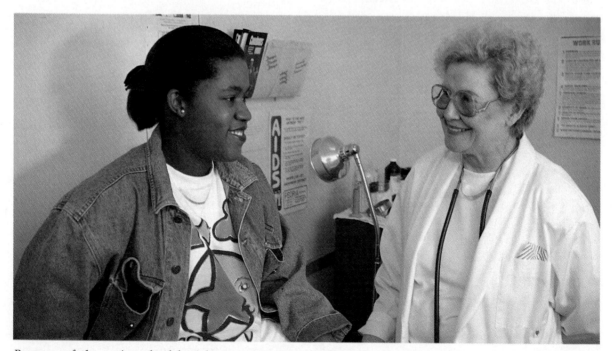

Because of the serious health risks associated with teenage pregnancy, expectant mothers need regular medical care beginning early in the pregnancy.

Reference. See pages 164–170 for information about health risks during pregnancy for the mother-to-be and the fetus.
More About. Premature babies frequently have breathing problems because the lungs are one of the last organs to develop.
Activity. Invite a health care professional to discuss the importance of prenatal care throughout pregnancy.

Many premature and low birth weight babies have not developed sufficiently to survive without medical assistance.

◆◆ Health & Safety ◆◆

Health Risks of Teenage Pregnancy

Pregnancy has certain medical risks at any age, but teenage pregnancy is considered to be especially high risk.

- Both the mother's body and the developing child have to compete for inadequate nutrients if the teenager has poor eating habits. An inadequate diet increases her risk of giving birth to a low birth weight baby.
- If the teenager's bone structure is not fully developed, she can experience problems with her spine and pelvic bones during pregnancy and birth.
- The teenager may develop health problems such as pregnancy induced hypertension (high blood pressure and other complications), which is a potentially fatal condition.
- Depending on the mother's size, her birth canal may be too small for the passage of a full-term baby.

- The teenager is more likely to have premature labor than a woman only a few years older.
- Miscarriage and stillbirth rates are higher for teenagers than for older women.
- The death rate from pregnancy complications is much higher among girls under age fifteen who give birth than among older mothers.

Although teenage girls usually receive less prenatal care than older women, they actually need more because they are in a high-risk category. This is why it is so important for pregnant teenagers to have regular prenatal care during the early months as well as the later months of pregnancy. Prenatal care can help prevent pregnancy complications and improve one's chances of having a healthy baby.

Activity. Have students gather information about certain health risks of pregnancy: iron deficiency anemia, hypertension, toxemia, premature labor, low birth weight, and fetal alcohol syndrome (FAS).

More About. The death rate from pregnancy complications is 60% higher for teens under age 15 and 13% higher for teens between ages 15–19.

Around the World

Adolescent Fertility: A Worldwide Concern

Adolescent fertility means childbearing by females under age twenty. The rate of adolescent fertility is particularly high in undeveloped countries. Organizations such as the United Nations, as well as many world population experts, believe that this is cause for concern. When many adolescents in a society have babies, the result is economic problems that affect the quality of life for everyone.

- Illness and mortality rates are significantly higher for adolescent mothers and their babies than for older mothers. Proper medical care, if available, is usually too expensive for most people in undeveloped countries.

- When parenthood comes too early, the mother's education is interrupted or stopped. Usually the father's is, too. This means a lower future family income. Most babies who are born to teenage parents can expect to grow up poor in undeveloped countries.

- When adolescents have babies, the number of years between each generation is shortened. This means that more babies will be born in a shorter period of time. Most developing countries do not have enough economic resources to support a population that grows so rapidly.

Interestingly, industrialized nations are experiencing some of the same problems associated with adolescent parenthood as undeveloped countries. This is why many concerned people in the United States are urging teenagers to finish their education and delay having children until they are more mature and in a better financial position.

Unfortunately, half of all teenagers who eventually give birth neglect to obtain prenatal care during the first four months of pregnancy. Yet this is the period of time when the unborn child is rapidly developing. Prenatal care throughout pregnancy greatly reduces the health risks to pregnant teenagers and their babies. You will learn more about the importance of prenatal care for all pregnant women in Chapter 9.

Emotional Concerns

Every woman, no matter what her age or situation, experiences various emotions upon learning that she is pregnant. Some of these may be positive, such as happiness and anticipation. Others may be negative, such as anxiety and doubt. It always helps to talk about these emotions with her partner, family, and friends. Doctors, nurses, counselors, and members of the clergy can also provide helpful advice.

Teenagers, in particular, may be confused or frightened when they discover they are pregnant. Some try to ignore any symptoms in the hope that they will disappear. Most are afraid to tell their parents about the pregnancy. Many are uncertain about what to do and where to seek help.

Most pregnant teenagers have many questions: How will my family react? Will the baby's father help me? Do we love each other? Should we get married? What will my friends think? What will pregnancy be like? What will birth be like? Will the baby be all right? Who will pay all the expenses? Will I be able to finish high school? What will my life be like?

It is important for a teenager who learns she is pregnant as well as the potential father to talk to someone they trust as soon as possible. They need help and support to make wise decisions about health, the pregnancy, and their unborn child.

More About. Over 50% of all pregnant teens seek no prenatal care in the first trimester. Others put off getting prenatal care until, in many cases, the actual labor and delivery.
Activity. Have each student answer the following questions:

- How would you feel if you found out you/your girlfriend were pregnant?
- Where would you go or who would you tell first?
- What changes would you have to make in your future goals?

Role of Teenage Fathers

Whenever a teenage girl becomes pregnant, family and friends tend to focus on the mother-to-be rather than the father-to-be. However, a partner is always involved. Usually he, too, is a teenager, but older than the female.

The reactions of teenage boys to their partner's pregnancy vary greatly. Some feel guilty; others feel proud. Some may deny that the baby is their own. Still others seem not to care. Most boys respond to an unwanted pregnancy with the same feelings as their partner—disbelief, anger, and helplessness. Yet teenage boys are not encouraged to talk about their emotions, particularly if the couple do not stay together throughout the pregnancy.

Some unmarried teenage fathers are willing to accept the consequences of their actions. They want to help their partner and be involved in making decisions about the child's future. They provide emotional support for their partner during the pregnancy and delivery. After the birth, they help care for, nurture, and guide the child. They want to contribute financial support for the child.

Unfortunately, some teenage fathers do not want to accept responsibility for the children they conceive. They expect the mother to bear full responsibility for rearing the child. However, states have child support laws that hold fathers legally responsible for the welfare of their children. This means a father must provide financial support for his children on a regular basis, no matter where he lives. If he refuses, the courts can take money from his paycheck or bank account. In many states, he cannot escape legal responsibilities even if he is a minor, is not married, or does not see the mother anymore.

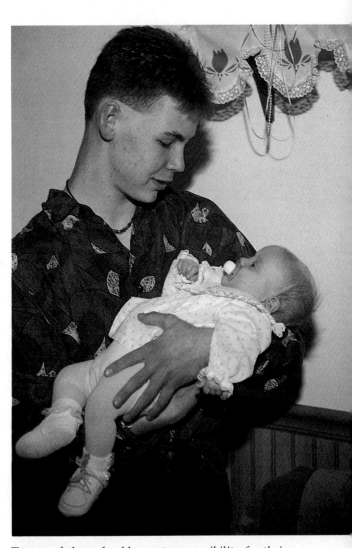

Teenage fathers should accept responsibility for their child. They should provide financial support, as well as help care for and nurture their child.

◆ ◆ *Self-Esteem* ◆ ◆

Teenage parents and parents-to-be cannot go back to the past and change what has happened. Instead, they should look to the future and make wise decisions about their role as parents. Both family and friends can give support and guidance to teenage parents. This will help strengthen their self-esteem and help them to be effective and loving parents.

Activity. Invite an attorney, social worker, or paternity law expert to discuss current paternity laws and the rights and responsibilities of teen parents.

Activity. Have students research DNA tests as proof of paternity.
Discuss. Should the unmarried teenage father have the right to be included in making decisions about the baby's future?

Difficult Choices

Once a teenager knows she is pregnant, she must make decisions about the future. If possible, the potential father should also be involved in the decision-making process. Both partners are equally responsible.

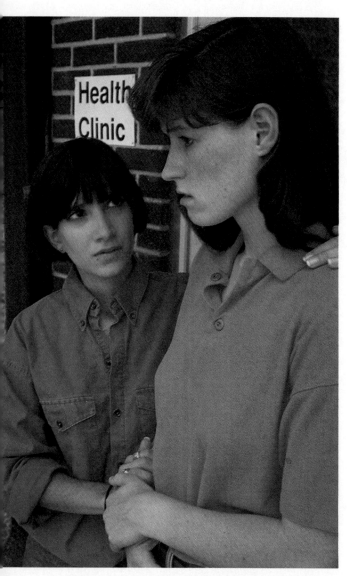

If a female thinks she might be pregnant, she should tell someone—a parent, friend, teacher, or counselor.

❖ Sources of Advice and Support

As soon as a pregnancy is suspected or confirmed, teenagers should seek advice from someone they trust. If they try to ignore or conceal the pregnancy, they will have to face their worries and concerns alone. No teenager should go through such a confusing time without support.

Let's take a look at some of the available sources of advice and help.

- **Parents and family.** Many teenagers are afraid to tell their parents about a pregnancy. However, most parents are far more supportive than expected. Although most parents first react with disbelief or anger, they are eventually able to provide advice, support, and love at a time when their child most needs them. Some teenagers enlist the help of an older brother, sister, or other relative to help break the news to parents. If teenage parents decide to rear their baby, they will need the support of their parents in the coming years. Couples should discuss their options with both the girl's and the boy's family. Both will be the baby's relatives and can help suggest solutions to some of the problems.

- **School nurse or counselor.** Teenagers can ask the school nurse or counselor for information. These professionals can suggest clinics, counseling centers, and community organizations that have programs for pregnant teenagers. They can also help students remain in school during the pregnancy and after the baby is born.

- **Doctor or clinic.** Even though home pregnancy tests are available, they are not as reliable as laboratory tests. Teenagers who get positive results from a home pregnancy test should visit a doctor or clinic to confirm the pregnancy and to receive pre-natal care. Some clinics provide free preg-

Reference. See pages 135–136 for early signs of pregnancy.
More About. Some schools have a Teenage Parent Coordinator, a certified teacher hired by the district, to coordinate programs that minister to the needs of pregnant students. These may include prenatal instruction, counseling, nutrition information, parenting skills, and networking with human services agencies. Coordinator may oversee child care services provided by some school districts.

nancy tests. Doctors and nurses will also answer teenagers' questions about pregnancy and birth. They will explain the importance of prenatal care and discuss any concerns young people may have.

- **Clergy or religious organization.** Ministers, priests, rabbis, and imans can provide guidance as teenagers evaluate their options. Many religious organizations provide special counseling for pregnant teenagers. Some have residence homes where teenagers can stay before and after the baby's birth.

- **Social worker or family planning counselor.** These professionals can explain various options and discuss the community resources available to teenagers. They offer advice on prenatal care, nutrition information, childbirth classes, and parenting skills. They help arrange for financial assistance and recommend support groups. If necessary, they may help teenagers discuss the pregnancy with their parents.

Many organizations also provide pregnancy information or counseling by telephone. Teenagers can usually find the names and telephone numbers of these organizations in their local directory.

◆ Parenthood Options

Those who decide to have the baby have three options. The couple can marry and raise the child together. The mother or the father can raise the child as a single parent. The baby can be placed for adoption.

Marriage

When some teenagers become pregnant, their first reaction is to marry quickly. The couple may have talked of eventually getting married anyway. Sometimes the teenagers' parents push for marriage. However, only

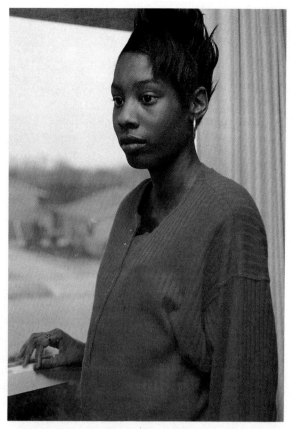

Teenage girls who are expecting a baby must make many decisions that will affect themselves, their families, and their baby.

one-third of the teenagers who become parents before the age of eighteen are married.

Babies need constant attention; they want to be fed, burped, diapered, and cuddled immediately. Having a marriage partner to share the parenting and household responsibilities can be very helpful.

However, statistics show that most teenage marriages do not last long. The freedom some teenagers expect as a married couple actually turns out to be less freedom than they had before. They must make decisions about a new set of considerations, such as where to live and how to pay the bills. Often they live with family members. They must adjust to the role of parents at the same time they are adjusting to the role of marriage partners.

Activity. Have students look through the local telephone directory for organizations that provide pregnancy information. **Discuss.** What additional services could your school or community offer that would benefit teenage parents-to-be? That

would benefit teenage parents and their children? **Discuss.** What are the pros and cons of teenagers marrying because of a pregnancy?

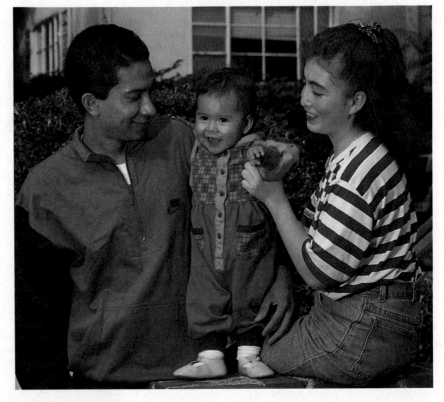

Teenagers who do become parents need to learn how to be good ones.

These challenges can be difficult for older and more mature people with a strong sense of who they are and what they want in life. For adolescents, who are in the midst of discovering their identity and gaining independence, the challenges can be overwhelming. As a result, four out of five teenage couples who marry because of pregnancy divorce within six years.

Of course, some teenage marriages are successful. These couples usually receive a great deal of support from family and friends. They also are very committed to being successful as marriage partners and parents.

Single Parenthood

Most unmarried teenage mothers decide to rear the child alone. The mother and child usually live with the mother's own parents, who may help rear the baby. Sometimes, however, a teenager's parents cannot or will not help. Occasionally, the teenage father chooses to take care of the child.

While money concerns play a large part in most teenage marriages, they are an even greater problem for single parents. Most teenagers have not had enough time to get an education and develop the skills necessary for finding a good job. Teenage workers are twice as likely as other workers to be unemployed. Furthermore, the single parent must arrange for child care if she or he plans to continue schooling, go to work, or enroll in a career training program. Unless free or low-cost child care is available, the parent usually cannot afford to pay for the care.

Some teenagers are able to balance the responsibilities of going to school, holding a job, and taking care of a child. These single parents usually have a great deal of help from their parents and other relatives. Often a teenager's mother will watch the baby while the young parent is at school or at work. Some schools provide child care for teenage students so they can continue their education.

Adoption

A few couples decide to place their baby for adoption. People who make this decision usually have thought long and hard about their baby's needs and their own future. They realize that they are unable to provide their child with a good start in life. They also understand the difficulties that they would face as teenage parents. They decide that, under the circumstances, adoption is the best option for their baby.

Adoptions can be arranged by local, state, religious, and private agencies. Adoption agencies have lists of couples who cannot have their own children but want very much to adopt a child. These couples are carefully screened. They must be financially secure and emotionally able to care for a child. Only those with the potential to be good parents can adopt a child. Teenagers who place their baby with an adoption agency can feel assured that the child will get loving, capable adoptive parents. Agencies also provide counseling for the pregnant teenager.

Some adoptions are arranged independently by attorneys, physicians, and members of the clergy. They match a couple who want to adopt a child with a pregnant woman who wants to have her baby adopted. It is against the law for adoptive parents to give money to a birth parent. However, they can pay for the expectant mother's prenatal care, hospital costs, and other related expenses.

Although adoptions can be informally arranged before birth, the legal arrangements cannot be made until after the baby is born. The birth mother must then sign the adoption papers. Adoption laws vary from state to state, but most require that the father also sign the release forms. If the father cannot be found, there must be legal proof that an effort has been made to locate him.

In the past, adoption was a secret process and all information about the birth parents was sealed. It was thought that children might reject their adoptive parents if they were able to find their birth parents.

Today, some background information is available for both the adoptive parents and the birth parents. For example, an **open adoption** allows the birth and adoptive parents to share information about themselves and the child. Information about the birth parents' health and family background is given to the adoptive parents. Often the birth mother meets the adoptive parents during the pregnancy or after the baby is born. Sometimes adoptive parents send a letter and photographs of the child to the birth mother each year.

Open adoptions have many advantages for everyone involved. The birth parents can know how their child is growing up. The child can know something about his or her biological background. The adoptive parents can answer many of the questions that the child asks about her or his birth parents.

DECISIONS ◆ ◆ DECISIONS

Connor's girlfriend, Ayanna, is expecting a baby in seven months. Although they do not plan to marry, he would like to help her as much as possible. He has saved some money from his part-time job but knows it will not cover all the costs of medical care and baby items. In what ways can Connor help Ayanna during the pregnancy and after their baby is born?

Challenges of Teenage Parenthood

The challenges of teenage parenthood are many. Teenage parents may not be emotionally mature. Most have not finished their education. They usually cannot afford to support themselves, let alone a baby. Many teenagers underestimate the responsibilities involved in parenting even if they have had experience in caring for children. Although they want to be good parents, they may not fully understand the challenges and difficulties that parents often face over many years.

However, with continuing support from parents, friends, and counselors, teenagers can be successful parents. Let's take a look at some of the challenges of rearing a child as a married or unmarried teenager.

❖ Lack of Maturity

Many of the difficulties teenagers have as parents directly relate to lack of maturity. Most teenagers are still developing physically, mentally, and emotionally. They are still learning how to be responsible for themselves.

To be successful parents, teenagers need to learn parenting skills. They need to develop good decision-making skills. They also need to look at the long-range effects of their decisions on the life of their child. They cannot think only of the present.

❖ Loss of Independence

The teenage years can be an exciting time of gaining independence and taking on new responsibilities. This is easier when done gradually, rather than suddenly having the responsibilities of adulthood thrust upon an individual.

Teenage parents must quickly leave childhood behind and assume adult responsibilities. As parents, they are now responsible for caring for, nurturing, and guiding a child that is totally dependent. This responsibility lasts 24 hours a day, seven days a week. Unlike going to school or holding a summer job, parenthood is a full-time career.

An unmarried teenage mother is likely to be dependent on her own parents for a long period of time. This dependence may cause strain within the family. Her parents may be resentful because they had planned to focus on interests other than caring for a young grandchild. If she has younger brothers and sisters, they may be jealous because the family must first attend to the infant's needs rather than to their needs.

Teenage parents need to develop skills that will help them eventually become independent. They should learn how to manage their time and money. They should learn how to care for a child and a home. They need to set long-term goals that they can work toward, such as completing high school and then going on to college or getting a job. Working toward these goals can give teenagers confidence in their ability to achieve the independence and life-style they hope to have some day.

❖ Continuing Education

Pregnant teenagers have the right to continue their education. In some schools, they remain in their regular classes. In other schools, they are enrolled in special classes for pregnant teenagers and teenage parents. These classes help students learn about pregnancy, prenatal care, and parenting skills. A few schools provide a child care center for infants and toddlers of students. Such a center also serves as a laboratory for students taking child development and parenting classes. Meanwhile, the teenage parents are able to complete their education.

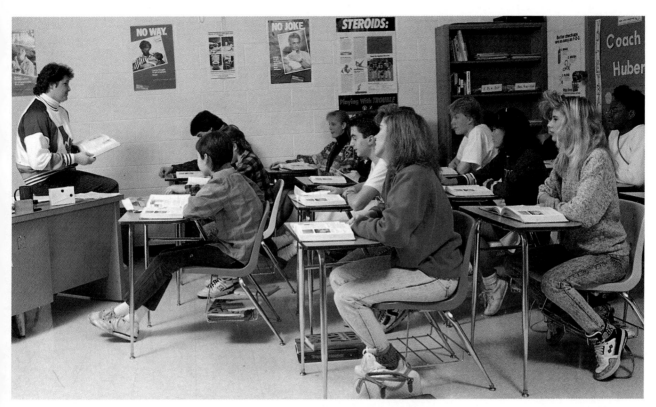

Getting an education can be interrupted or cut short by teenage pregnancy.

It is very important for teenage parents to complete their high school education. This enables them to have more career choices. Teenagers who drop out of school usually discover that they are qualified only for the lowest-paying jobs in the community.

❖ Social Life and Relationships

The teenage years are a time for developing relationships. Yet teenage parents discover that they are rarely able to go to parties or out with friends as they did before they had a child. Instead, they must spend their time caring for a baby. Often, teenage parents discover that they spend more time with their family or other teenage parents than with their childless friends. Their interests and needs have changed.

Couples often grow apart during the teenage years. What attracted them to each other in the beginning may not last because their values, attitudes, and goals are changing as they mature. For example, a fun-loving teenager who likes to party may not make a responsible partner or parent. When couples have a child, their breakup affects not only themselves but also their child. Some teenage parents eventually find the right person to marry when they are older and better able to develop a lasting relationship.

❖ Financial Problems

Teenage parents usually face more financial problems than parents who are older. They lack the education and skills needed to obtain a job that can support a family. Even if

More About. Many teenage mothers may need to make new friends, usually other teenage parents, since they may have fewer common interests and less time and financial resources for socializing with childless friends.

Activity. In small groups, have students calculate the income of a teenage couple who have an infant, attend school, and work 20 hours a week at minimum wage. Subtract costs of an apartment and food for parents and child. How much is left?

How might parenthood change one's life? Are you ready for the many responsibilities involved in rearing a child?

both partners work, they may have difficulty meeting their basic expenses.

Many teenage parents, especially unmarried mothers, must go on welfare. Aid to Families with Dependent Children (AFDC) is a government program that gives financial support to eligible parents and children. Medicare helps families with health costs, while food stamps can be used to purchase food. Women, Infants, and Children (WIC) program provides vouchers to obtain specific foods necessary for adequate prenatal nutrition and for the infant after birth. Even with governmental assistance, however, many teenage parents and their children live below the poverty line.

As already noted, teenagers who are able to complete their high school education generally earn more money than those who drop out of school do. Those who go on for additional training or education generally earn more money than high school graduates earn.

◆◆ Long-Term Goals

Parenthood usually forces teenagers to rearrange their long-term goals. For example, instead of going to college at age eighteen, they may go part-time when they are in their twenties and their child is in school.

It is important to understand that parenthood does not mean teenagers have to give up their goals. Many are able to complete school, get a job, and achieve financial independence while being a parent. To do this, they must focus on ways to achieve their goals, even if doing so takes longer than they originally planned. Often, families and friends can provide emotional and financial support. Counselors can provide information and advice. Organizations and agencies can provide necessary resources. Then it is up to the teenage parents to make a conscientious effort to build the best life possible for themselves and their children.

Activity. Have students research current statistics from Department of Labor that compare the incomes of high school dropouts, high school graduates, vocational school graduates, and college graduates.

Activity. Invite a panel of teenage mothers and fathers to discuss the challenges they have encountered and how they have tried to meet those challenges. What recommendations do they make to other teenagers about teen parenthood?

CHAPTER 5 REVIEW

Summary

- Most teenagers are emotionally, mentally, and financially unprepared for parenthood.
- Peer pressure and the media influence some teenagers to become sexually active.
- Abstinence is the only 100 percent effective method of preventing pregnancy.
- Babies born to teenage mothers have a high risk of health problems.
- Good prenatal care is important for all expectant mothers, especially pregnant teenagers.
- A pregnant teenage girl and the potential father should seek advice and support in making wise decisions.
- Teenagers who decide to have the baby may marry and rear the child together; the mother or father may rear the child alone; or the baby may be placed for adoption.
- Teenage parents face many challenges and benefit from lots of support from parents, friends, and counselors.

Questions

p. 86 1. Name three possible consequences of sexual activity.

p. 87 2. What are three reasons why teenagers become pregnant?

p. 88 3. Why is teenage pregnancy considered high risk for the female?

p. 88 4. What problems do many premature babies and babies with low birth weight have in common?

p. 88 5. What is prenatal care? Why is it important?

p. 91 6. What can the courts do if a father refuses to provide regular financial support for his child?

p. 92 7. Where might a pregnant teenager and the prospective father turn for advice and help?

p. 93 8. What are three parenthood options for couples who decide to have the baby? What is one advantage and disadvantage of each option?

p. 98 9. How can teenage parents still reach their long-term goals?

Activities

1. Evaluate the sexual messages presented in television shows and commercials. Share your findings with the class.

2. Develop specific refusals to the following pressure statements to be sexually active:
   "You would if you loved me."
   "Come on—everyone's doing it."
   "If you won't, I don't want to see you any more."

3. Find out about resources in your community that provide advice and support for pregnant teenagers and teenage fathers-to-be. In a report, include the name, address, and telephone number of each resource, along with the services provided and any fees.

Think About

1. How much responsibility do you think teenage fathers should have in rearing their children?

2. What could you do to organize a "Teenage Pregnancy Prevention" program? Would it be effective? Why or why not?

Reference. See the Teacher's Manual in the front of the Teacher's Annotated Edition for complete answers to the chapter review questions.

99

Parenting Skills

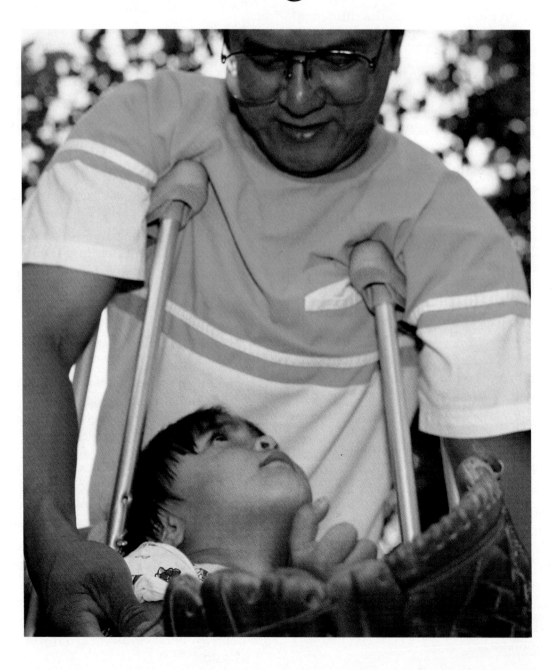

Objectives

This chapter will help you to:

- Explain how parents and caregivers can benefit from information about growth and development, human needs, and parenting skills.
- Compare the three different types of parenting styles.
- Describe certain characteristics of a successful parent.
- Discuss poor parenting practices and their effect on children.

Vocabulary

physiological
self-actualization
psychological
parenting style
authoritarian
democratic
permissive
indulgence

Holly kissed her six-month-old son, Justin, as she bundled him into the carrier. She slipped the straps of the carrier over her shoulders. Then she checked to be sure her son was securely placed on her back. She reached up and held Justin's hand for a moment. "Now, we're ready for our walk," Holly said to her waiting friend. "It takes a while to get ready, but an outdoor walk is good for both of us."

Roger talked to his three-year-old daughter, Kelsey, as he drove across town on an errand. She was securely strapped into her safety seat, which was anchored in the car's rear seat. Roger smiled whenever he looked in his rear-view mirror at Kelsey as they talked. She watched the mirror, where she could see her father's eyes.

Holly and Roger are using various parenting skills as they interact with their children. Each parent is taking the time to be sure of the child's safety. In addition, they are showing love and attention to their children.

What Do Parents and Caregivers Need to Know?

Most people learn about parenting from their own parents. When children grow up, they take with them many of the ways in which their parents cared for them. For some people, their parents were excellent role models of parenting skills. Others, however, may have seen poor examples of how to handle various situations. All people can benefit from learning how to develop the best skills possible.

Parenting skills are learned skills, not inborn traits. This fact gives all people hope and confidence that they, too, can learn good parenting skills.

❖ The Process of Growth and Development

Parents and caregivers should learn all they can about how children grow and develop. Knowing what to expect helps prevent misunderstanding and worry. People who know the facts about child development can apply their parenting skills with confidence. They can identify milestones in their children's development and enjoy the excitement of watching their children grow.

For example, all children go through the same basic step-by-step process of development. Even so, every child progresses at a different rate. Some develop more slowly and some develop more quickly than others. Successful parents accept each child's individuality. They respect each child's uniqueness. They do not compare one child with another or expect children to accomplish certain tasks in exactly the same way.

Parents who know that development follows a pattern can predict a child's needs and anticipate certain behaviors. They can be prepared to help a child meet the challenges ahead. Parents who know what to expect are usually more tolerant when a child goes through a difficult stage of development. For example, infants go through a period when they are afraid of strangers. During this stage, children scream when strangers approach them. Parents who expect this to occur know that it is temporary and that the child will eventually lose this fear. They can tolerate the behavior because they know it is a natural phase of infant development. In fact, fear of strangers is a mark of progress in the child's social and emotional development. Parents who know this are less likely to be embarrassed when the child screams rather than smiles around parents' friends and relatives.

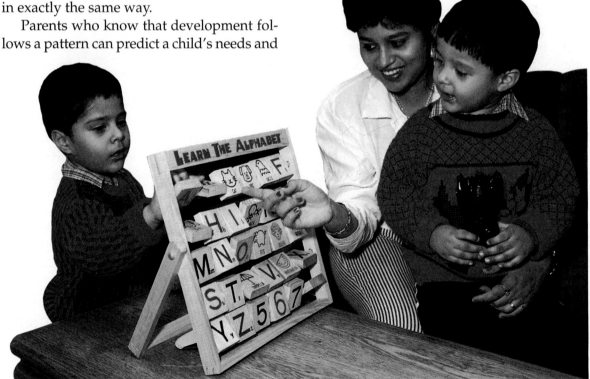

By learning about parenting skills, parents gain confidence in their own ability to be an effective caregiver, nurturer, teacher, and role model.

Activity. Ask each student to write two or three questions about parenting skills. Each day select questions to discuss.
Activity. Have students create a large wall chart for each stage of development. Throughout the course, have students add information about physical, emotional, social, cognitive, and moral development at each stage.
Reference. Fear of strangers is called *stranger anxiety*. See pages 239 and 480 for more information.

Basic Human Needs

To respond to children in the best way possible, it is necessary to figure out what each child needs. Children have many needs that arise during any typical day. Some needs are for personal care. Others are for nurturing and guidance. Psychologist Abraham Maslow created a scale of people's basic needs. These needs apply to all people—adults and children.

Maslow's Hierarchy of Needs

Maslow arranged basic human needs into a hierarchy, placing groups of needs on levels from lowest to highest. He put those needs thought to be most strongly motivating at the lower levels. Lower-level needs must be met before a person can pay attention to needs on the higher levels. The five levels of needs are: physiological, safety, social, esteem, and self-actualization.

Maslow's Hierarchy of Human Needs

Self-Actualization Needs
This is a desire for fulfillment. It is the need to become what one is capable of becoming.

Esteem Needs
This is a desire for self-respect and self-esteem based on real personal capacity and achievement. One type of need is for achievement, strength, adequacy, confidence, and independence. The other is for attention, appreciation, recognition, importance, prestige, and reputation.

Social Needs
These needs are concerned with love, affection, and belongingness.

Safety Needs
These needs refer to freedom from bodily threat and to security in the psychological sense.

Physiological Needs
Among physiological needs are food, clothing, and shelter. These needs are the most potent of all. The person who is hungry has little interest in anything other than food.

Problem Solving. Divide class into five groups and assign one basic human need to each group. Have each group list and discuss ways that parents can provide for the need at each stage of development (infant, toddler, preschooler, school-age, adolescent). Have groups share their lists.
Activity. Prepare a time line for a child from birth through adolescence. Using Maslow's hierarchy of needs, discuss how these needs change with each stage of development.

- **Physiological needs.** At the first level are physiological needs. **Physiological** (fiz-ee-ah-LAHJ-eh-kahl) refers to the functioning of the body. Physiological needs are basic to all humans. These are the needs for food and water, sleep, and shelter. People must satisfy these needs to survive. Parents meet their children's physiological needs by providing food, water, rest, and housing.

- **Safety needs.** After the physiological needs are satisfied, safety needs must be met. People need to feel safe from physical harm. They also need to have a sense of security that their needs will be met. Parents are responsible for protecting their children from danger. Parents provide children with a sense of security when family life is predictable and stable. When children know they are loved, no matter what happens, they can feel secure.

- **Social needs.** At the third tier of Maslow's hierarchy are social needs. These become important after physiological and safety needs are met. The term *social* refers to interaction with other people—family, neighbors, friends, and acquaintances. People need to belong to a family and other groups. They also need to love and be loved. Parents meet children's social needs by talking and playing with them, as well as teaching them how to get along with others. Parents show children that they are loved by providing smiles, hugs, kisses, and words of encouragement.

- **Esteem needs.** At the fourth level are esteem needs. The concerns at this level are for self-esteem and for the respect and admiration of others. People need to value themselves highly, to think of themselves as worthwhile. The love and admiration of parents, teachers, and friends help children build self-esteem. As children are loved and praised, they begin to realize

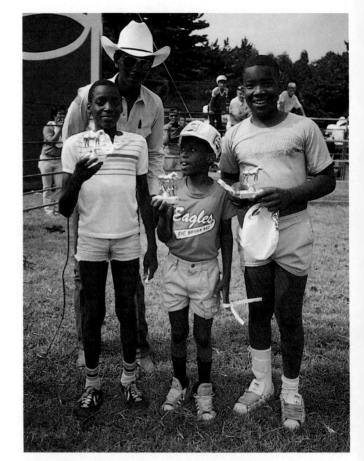

The desire for self-esteem is met by achievement, recognition, and appreciation.

that they are lovable. This helps them feel good about themselves. They gain a sense of achievement, confidence, and independence. Self-esteem needs are also concerned with recognition, appreciation, and reputation. Parents and other caregivers help meet these needs by recognizing and appreciating children's efforts and accomplishments.

- **Self-actualization need.** At the fifth level, according to Maslow, is the need for **self-actualization.** This is the achievement of one's full potential. It is met through creativity, independence, spontaneity, and a grasp of the real world. The need for self-actualization pertains to finally becoming all that one is capable of becoming. Maslow said this level is open only to adults, although not all adults reach it. You might think of your grandparents and other elders in your community in regard to this need.

Needs and Behavior

Both physiological and psychological needs motivate behavior. **Psychological** (sigh-keh-LAHJ-eh-kahl) refers to a person's mental and emotional states. The needs for safety, belonging and love, esteem, and self-actualization are mental or emotional needs. Thus people have more psychological needs than physiological needs.

Which of our needs is most important? Which need motivates behavior most strongly? The level and intensity of human needs vary from person to person. For example, a child who is hungry and has no warm place to sleep is unlikely to be concerned about achievement and recognition. After the child has a secure supply of food and comfortable shelter, he or she can begin to interact with others and seek their admiration.

Needs and Parenting Skills

Maslow's hierarchy of needs helps explain the importance of nurturing as a parenting skill. It also helps parents realize that they must balance their own needs with those of their children. That is, parents cannot overlook their children's needs in order to focus on their own needs. At the same time, parents should not permit their own needs to be overwhelmed by their children's needs.

Ideally, parents should maintain a balance between the needs of their children and their own needs. This may be one of the most demanding tasks of parenthood. Often parents must be in two places at once. They may be torn in at least two directions by the demands of their personal lives and the demands of their children. These conflicts are more common when children are young; they lessen as children become more independent. In whatever way parents resolve conflicting needs, children benefit from knowing that their mother and father are people in their own right. This helps provide healthy role models for children to follow when they become adults.

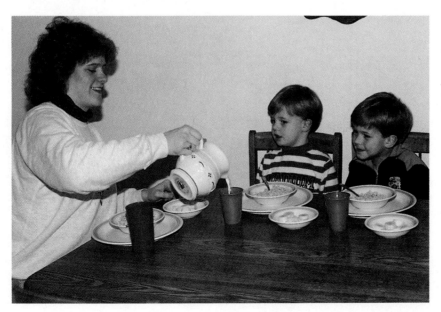

Parents must meet the needs of their children. These include food, clothing, shelter, safety, security, love, affection, and self-esteem.

Activity. Divide class into five groups and assign one basic need to each group. Give students five minutes to decide how they can convince others that their need is the most important. Have each group present and defend their views.

Problem Solving. Parents of young children often feel that they have no time for themselves. Have students suggest ways that parents can arrange time for themselves—alone and as a couple.

◆◆ Sources of Parenting Information

Parenting skills are learned in a variety of ways. Most people learn parenting techniques from their parents and other caregivers. Yet much of parenting is "caught" more often than "taught." Think about the patience needed when teaching a child to tie a shoe, ride a bicycle, or drive a car. Parents seldom tell their children, "You'll need to know how to be patient and understanding when you're a parent." Instead, parents model patience through their attitudes and behavior.

Unfortunately, some people have had a difficult childhood. They may have grown up with parents who were abusive, unloving, or neglectful. Because they are able to recognize their parents' less favorable behavior, they want to rear their own children differently. For these people, childhood experiences can serve as a model for what not to do as parents. They can also educate themselves about effective ways to care for, nurture, and guide children.

The following ways of learning about parenting skills can benefit people who have had positive role models, as well as those who have not.

- Take a parenting course or class.
- Read books and magazine articles about children and parenting.
- Talk to relatives and friends about their experiences in caring for children.
- Observe parents and other caregivers with children.
- Gain experience in caring for or working with children.

People can learn about parenting skills by reading books and magazine articles, talking to and observing parents, and taking a parenting course.

Parenting Styles

A **parenting style** is the particular way that a parent consistently behaves toward children. Style includes the expectations one has of children and the manner in which one treats them. It also includes the type of rules established for children and the method by which the rules are made and enforced.

For example, some parents are strict and others are casual in the way they guide and direct their children's behavior. Some are overly harsh, while others rarely correct their children. Some let their children do things for themselves, while others do too much for them.

Some parents model desirable behavior and expect their children to imitate them. Other parents threaten their children with punishment if they misbehave. Many parents are consistent and do exactly what they say they will do. Others seldom follow through on their promises or threats.

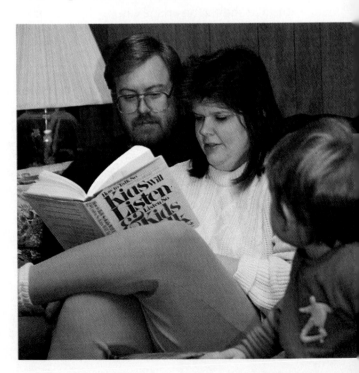

❖ Comparing Parenting Styles

Let's look at three basic parenting styles: authoritarian, permissive, and democratic. Each one can be successful if parents also provide love, care, and support.

Authoritarian

Parents who are **authoritarian** are generally strict in rearing their children. What are some important characteristics of authoritarian parenting?

- Parents decide the rules, inform the children of them, and then enforce them.
- Patterns of parent behavior are predictable. The children can expect their parents to respond in about the same way to similar situations.
- Parents show little or no flexibility in their handling of guidance or discipline.
- Parents see themselves as the authority figures in the family. They require their children to conform to their directions and expectations.

Democratic

Parents who are **democratic** consider both the child's needs and their own point of view when making decisions. This parenting style is also called authoritative. Consider these characteristics of democratic parenting:

- Parents and children work together to set rules. Children are then expected to conform to these rules. If they do not, they help determine the consequences of their behavior.
- Patterns of parent behavior are predictable most of the time. Parents usually respond in similar ways to similar situations.
- Principles of guidance and discipline are generally discussed by parents and children. Both parents and children can suggest changes that may be needed because of changing circumstances.
- Parents see themselves as leaders in helping their children learn to share in the responsibilities for the well-being of family members. Parents view their children as important people who have contributions to make to the family.

Permissive

Parents who are **permissive** generally permit a wide range of behavior. Important characteristics of permissive parenting include the following:

- Parents set few specific rules and allow the children much freedom and self-expression.
- Patterns of parent behavior are somewhat difficult to predict. Parents may respond in different ways to similar situations, depending on the circumstances and the child involved.
- Parents may change their guidance to meet individual situations.
- Parents expect their children to make many choices and face the consequences of their decisions.

DECISIONS ◆
◆ DECISIONS

Priya and Vijay are expecting their first child. They have read about various parenting styles and are confused as to which style is best. Priya's parents were very strict, while Vijay's parents were democratic. Some of their friends had permissive parents. Thus Priya and Vijay are unsure about which style they should use with their own child. They have asked you for advice. What will you tell them?

Activity. On the chalkboard, have students list the advantages and disadvantages of each parenting style for the parent. Then have them list the advantages and disadvantages for the child. Compare the lists.

Discuss. Do you agree with the statement: "Children of democratic parents are more cooperative because they have a feeling of ownership in family decisions"? Why or why not?

◆◆ Changing Parenting Styles

Some parents change their parenting style with different children. For example, many parents are strict with their first child but become more democratic with the next one. By the time the third child arrives, the same parents may take a more permissive approach. Moreover, in some families, the father has one style of parenting and the mother has another.

Some parents are consistent in their style of parenting until they experience a crisis or a great amount of stress. Then their style changes. For example, a parent who is generally democratic may suddenly become very strict when under pressure. Ordinarily this parent is calm and confident. However, when a stressful situation occurs, this same parent may suddenly become very controlling. He or she may make statements such as, "Now, you are going to do exactly what I say and that's final." Sometimes parents under stress resort to using the same type of behavior that their parents used with them in similar situations. If this involves physical punishment, it can be very harmful. Instead, parents need to learn how to remain calm and consistent even in stressful situations.

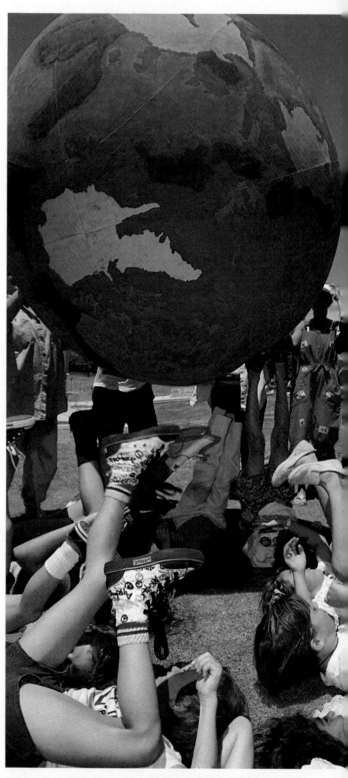

Parenting styles are influenced by cultural background, goals, personality, role models, and environment.

◆ ◆ *Self-Esteem* ◆ ◆

Parents have a dual role. They need to provide a sense of security and belonging for their children. At the same time, parents need to encourage their children to gradually become independent. A popular quotation simply states, "There are only two lasting bequests parents can give their children—one is roots; the other is wings."

Discuss. What can children do to cause parents to change their parenting style (become more strict or allow more privileges)? How might an older sibling influence a parent's guidance of a younger sibling?

Reference. See pages 223–224 for ways to manage stress.

❖ Predicting Parenting Styles

You have probably observed differences in the parenting behavior of your parents compared to that of a friends' parents. When you become a parent, there will be differences between your style of parenting and other parents' styles.

Why do these differences occur? According to various experts, parenting styles are influenced by a number of factors.

- **Cultural background.** Parents within cultural groups tend to have some common expectations and parenting practices. Cultural influences are usually stronger in neighborhoods or communities populated by many families of the same cultural background. In some cultures, children are expected to be quiet and always to defer to their elders. In other cultures, children are encouraged to express their ideas and individualism.

- **Child-rearing goals.** Parents have various goals for their children. These goals may range from personal behaviors to career achievements. For example, parents who want their children to get a good education may have certain expectations and establish certain rules about school work.

- **Personality patterns.** Every parent and every child has a distinct, unique personality. It is influenced by heredity, personal experiences, and interactions with others. As a result, people act and respond in different ways to similar situations. For example, some parents are quiet, controlled, and thoughtful. Others are talkative, easygoing, and carefree. Some children respond with squeals of delight when surprised, while others tremble or cry.

- **Role models.** Most people learn parenting styles from their parents and other caregivers. As a result, couples may disagree about parenting styles because each partner has had different role models. Unless parents resolve their differences about expectations, rules, and guidance techniques, their children will suffer.

- **Environment.** The environment refers to the surroundings in which a family lives. The environment of a large city differs dramatically from that of a rural area. As a result, an urban parent and a rural parent may need to set different rules concerning children's safety.

Other environmental factors, such as the weather, the time of day, and the season of the year, affect children's feelings and behavior. For example, rainy days are often difficult for many parents and children. Instead of being able to play outdoors, the children are confined in a small space where their activities may conflict with those of their parents.

DECISIONS ◆ ◆ DECISIONS

Shawn had a sad and troubled childhood. His memories are of a loveless home, abusive parents, and a constant struggle to feel good about himself. Shawn vows to rear his own children differently than the way he was brought up. However, he wonders whether he could ever be a successful parent because his role models were not positive. He has confided his doubts and fears to you. What advice can you give Shawn?

Activity. Divide class into small groups. Have each group decide which factor has the greatest influence on parenting styles. Have each group explain their choice.
Activity. Have students research the child-rearing practices and goals in different cultures for a report.
Reference. See pages 322–323 for information on personality.
Discuss. What are the pros and cons of rearing children in a city, suburb, small town, or rural area?

Effective Parenting Skills

Throughout this text, you will read about the various skills that successful parents use. Some of the skills are related to caring for children's physical growth and development. Others skills help nurture children's emotional, social, and mental development. Still others are used to guide children's behavior.

Parents serve as caregivers, teachers, and role models. They share their ideas, thoughts, and feelings through their words and actions. They encourage children to try new activities, test new skills, seek new knowledge, and gain independence. Above all, successful parents provide security and love.

◆◆ Characteristics of Successful Parents

Parenting is complex. Therefore, it is helpful for parents and would-be parents to know what generally contributes to successful parenting. The following characteristics are frequently used to describe successful parents.

- **Adaptability.** Successful parents are able to change their ways to improve their parenting skills. They are flexible and can see many ways of doing things. They can respond according to their children's needs.

- **Sense of humor.** Successful parents can laugh about and enjoy the challenges of parenting. They can see the lighter side of

If parents provide lots of love and support, they will be successful in whatever parenting style they use.

life, along with the more stressful aspects. This helps them relax while coping with problems.

- **Maturity.** Successful parents are able to make wise decisions about their children's development and guidance. They are able to promote a healthy parent-child relationship.

- **Positive self-concept.** Parents who see themselves as successful parents will likely perform their role successfully. They are able to view both their strengths and weaknesses without blaming themselves or their children. They are able to fulfill their personal needs without expecting their children to do it for them.

- **Emotional health.** Parents who are emotionally healthy are able to withstand much of the stress that comes with rearing children. They are able to express both positive and negative feelings in acceptable ways. They help their children do the same.

- **Patience.** Successful parents remain calm in times of difficulty or stress. They demonstrate tolerance for children's individual differences. They accept their children at each stage of growth and development.

- **Integrity.** Successful parents make realistic judgments on a consistent basis. They practice honesty. They are willing to accept the responsibility and even the blame when things go wrong.

- **Team effort.** Successful parents work together to set goals for their children and family. They decide together as parents on the ways to best meet their children's varying needs.

◆ *Health & Safety* ◆

A Child's Best Friend?

Pets can provide very valuable experiences for children. However, most authorities believe that children under the age of three are not ready for a pet, such as a dog or cat. Young children do not understand that these animals are living things and not toys. This can be dangerous, both for the child and the pet.

When children are a little older, parents may want to add a pet to the family. Common household pets include cats, dogs, fish, hamsters, and gerbils. When selecting a pet, parents should keep these considerations in mind:

- Choose the type of pet carefully. Consider the age of the child, the size and temperament of the animal, and the type of care the pet needs.

- Teach the child how to treat the animal. For example, say, "Pat Rex gently so you don't hurt him." Then take the child's hand and show him or her how to touch the pet.

- Involve the child in the feeding and care of the pet. This will help the child understand what it means to be responsible for someone else.

- Make sure the child understands the difference between the family pet and other animals. Petting a strange animal is never a good idea, no matter how friendly the animal appears.

- Never give a child a pet as a gift without first discussing it with the child's parents.

Activity. Divide class into small groups and assign each group one characteristic of successful parents. Have them role play parenting situations in which this characteristic is demonstrated.
More About. *Integrity* is defined as uncompromising adherence to moral and ethical principles; soundness of moral character; honesty.
Discuss. What are other characteristics of successful parents?

◆◆ Undesirable Parenting Practices

Unfortunately, some parents seem unable to practice appropriate child-rearing techniques even though they love their children and want the best for them. Inappropriate parenting occurs once in a while in every family. This does not mean that a parent is irresponsible or that the child's development will be hindered. However, ongoing undesirable practices may eventually lead to serious problems.

The following parenting practices should be avoided.

- **Unrealistic expectations.** Parents who expect children to perform beyond their level of ability may actually hinder their development. These parents often demand perfect behavior and high achievement. Children are measured against what they do wrong rather than what they do right. Parents who expect too much often withhold their acceptance of a child when failure occurs. As a result, the child may develop a poor self-concept and negative self-esteem.

When parents understand the process of growth and development they have realistic expectations of children's abilities.

- **Indulgence.** Some parents try to meet their child's needs and wishes even before the child is aware of them. **Indulgence** is the practice of giving children more of everything, such as attention, toys, or food, whether they want it or not. Children who are indulged have little ability to wait for satisfaction or to delay gratification. They are often bored and lack initiative. Overindulged children grow up expecting to get everything they ask for with little or no effort on their part.

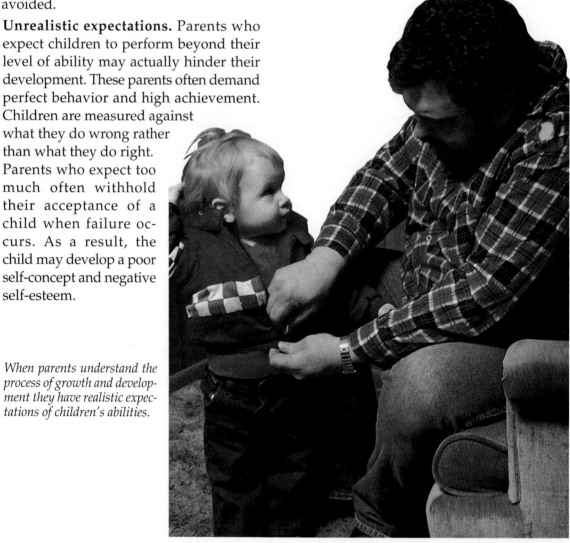

- **Submissiveness.** Parents who are submissive give in to the child's desires or wishes. They fear that the child will not love them if they do not satisfy the child's wants. They have difficulty in setting and enforcing limits. Children of submissive parents often act on impulse, without a sense of responsibility or concern for others.

- **Overprotection.** The overprotective parent does not allow the child to experience everyday life without intervening. These parents have a difficult time letting the child try new tasks without their help. They try to shield the child from difficult or uncertain experiences. As a result, overprotected children often lack the confidence needed to explore and learn for themselves. They have great difficulty making their own decisions.

- **Belittling.** No one likes to feel put down. Belittling does that. It lowers children's sense of self-esteem and self-respect. Parents who belittle their children accuse them of being lazy, stupid, silly, ugly, or bad. Parents also belittle children when they make fun of their accomplishments. As a result, the children may feel insignificant or unworthy.

- **Neglect.** Parents who neglect their children fail to give the necessary time and effort for love and care. These parents ignore children's need for guidance, attention, and encouragement during the various stages of development. Neglected children are insecure and lack a feeling of self-worth. They are often unable to form relationships with others.

- **Rejection.** Parents who reject their children are unwilling or unable to accept responsibility for the children's care and development. Rejection takes many forms, such as ignoring a child's physical needs

Around the World

Birth Announcements

In our culture, it is common to send cards announcing the birth of a baby to relatives and friends. In other cultures, this event is celebrated in very different ways.

- In Ethiopia, shouts echo across the mountains. Five shouts mean "It's a boy," and three shouts mean "It's a girl."

- In Kenya, the Masai mother puts her baby on her back and walks to the place where the village's valuable cattle are kept. Her husband is waiting there, along with the village elders. In this important place, the child is given a name.

- Many families who live in West Africa's cities still celebrate the ancient ceremony of "outdooring." When a baby is eight days old, the mother takes the child out of the house for a first look at the world. Family and friends come along to meet the baby.

- In Egypt, when the baby is seven days old, the birth is celebrated with a special celebration. Older children wear flowers and carry candles. They also sing a song that asks for blessings on the baby.

or avoiding playing and talking with the child. Another form of rejection is abandonment. Rejected children have difficulty developing a positive self-concept. Most do not know why their parents reject them. They become confused and sometimes angry.

Activity. Have students research additional effects on children of one or more negative parenting practices.

Reference. See pages 468–472 for information on unacceptable methods of discipline, including child abuse and neglect.

How Will You Rate as a Parent?

It is helpful to learn about the practices that either contribute to or detract from being a successful parent. With this knowledge, you will have a clearer understanding of what parenting means.

Successful parenting is more than giving birth or adopting a child. It is more than providing a home. Successful parenting means getting in touch with your feelings about being a parent. It means finding ways to build deep and meaningful relationships with your children. Success in parenting is measured more by the child's overall development than by the specific parenting practices.

Here are some good criteria for evaluating your chances of being a successful parent:

- You *feel* good about yourself—who you are and what you are like.
- You *believe* you would make a good parent—or that you are now a good parent.
- You *know* a lot about children's development and about a parent's role in rearing children.
- You *think* of yourself as a caring person.
- You *value* children and family life.
- You *like* the idea of becoming a parent or of being a parent.

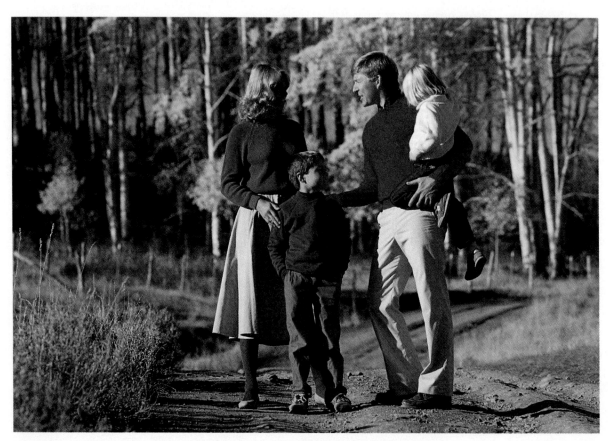

When parents enjoy their children and spend time with them, the children will likely grow up happy, loved, and feeling good about themselves.

Discuss. Mark Twain remarked: "When I was fourteen my father knew nothing, but when I was twenty-one I was amazed at how much the old man had learned in those seven years." **Activity.** Ask students to write a description of the type of parent they hope to be someday. Have them seal their essay inside a labeled envelope. At end of course, distribute envelopes. Have students reread their essays and add additional comments. Encourage them to save their essays.

CHAPTER 6 REVIEW

Summary

- Understanding human growth and development helps parents and caregivers use appropriate parenting skills.
- All people have basic needs, which motivate their behavior.
- One of the most demanding tasks of parenthood is for parents to maintain a balance between attending to their own needs and the needs of their children.
- Parenting skills can be learned from classes, books and articles, talking to others, observations, and experience.
- The three basic parenting styles are authoritarian, democratic, and permissive.
- Parenting styles are influenced by cultural background, child-rearing goals, personality patterns, role models, and environment.
- Most successful parents share certain characteristics.
- Undesirable parenting practices range from expecting too much of a child to neglecting or rejecting a child.

Questions

p. 102 **1.** How do parents and caregivers benefit from knowing about children's growth and development?

p. 103 **2.** Why did Maslow arrange basic human needs into a hierarchy?

p. 104 **3.** List and explain Maslow's five levels of human needs.

p. 105 **4.** What is the difference between physiological and psychological?

p. 106 **5.** How can people learn about effective parenting skills?

p. 107 **6.** Name and compare the three types of parenting styles.

7. Why do some people change their parenting style? p. 108

8. What are four influences on parenting styles? p. 109

9. Identify at least six characteristics that most successful parents share. p. 110

10. Why should parents have realistic expectations for their children? p. 112

Activities

1. Visit your local library or bookstore and prepare a bibliography of at least ten books on parenting. For each book, write the name(s) of the author(s), book title, city where the book was published, name of publisher, and date of publication. As a class, make a bibliography of all books cited.

2. Select a parenting topic of interest to you and read three current magazine articles on the topic. Compare the readings in a written report.

3. Describe how three different parenting styles would handle the following situations: three-year-old refuses to eat peas, six-year-old wants to ride a bike around the neighborhood, thirteen-year-old wants to go to a party with older teens.

Think About

1. Discuss the quotation: "There are only two lasting bequests parents can give their children—one is roots; the other is wings."

2. Using the criteria on page 114, how would you rate your chances of being a successful parent?

Reference. See the Teacher's Manual in the front of the Teacher's Annotated Edition for complete answers to the chapter review questions.

Becoming a Parent

CHAPTERS

Planning a Family

Objectives

This chapter will help you to:
- Summarize how conception occurs.
- Explain how the chromosomes and genes determine an individual's inherited traits.
- Compare the concerns associated with fertility and infertility.
- Discuss the medical care options for prospective parents.

Vocabulary

conception
sperm
ovum
fertilization
ovaries
uterus
testes
chromosomes
genes
genetic counseling
contraception

infertility
obstetrician
gynecologist
nurse-midwife

"Claudia and I wanted our children to be at least three years apart," said Don, father of two. "By spacing them we believe we will be able to give each child more individual attention. Our older child has enjoyed helping with our new baby—an advantage she would not have if she were younger."

"Also, my doctor recommended that I not become pregnant shortly after giving birth to our first child," said Claudia. "She told us that a woman's body can benefit from a period of recovery between pregnancies."

Claudia and Don have made a number of decisions regarding the planning of their family. They have talked about their options, gained medical advice, and made informed decisions based on their values and goals. This chapter focuses on the many considerations involved in becoming biological parents.

Human Reproduction

Prenatal development begins at conception. **Conception** (kahn-SEP-shuhn) refers to the moment when the male and female reproductive cells unite.

All the traits a human inherits come from two tiny cells, one from the father and one from the mother. The male reproductive cell, or **sperm,** is so tiny that a microscope is required to see it. The female reproductive cell, or **ovum,** is somewhat larger—about the size of a tiny speck of dust. The word *ovum* comes from the Latin word meaning *egg*.

Conception brings together the father's sperm and the mother's ovum. Each cell holds one-half of the code for developing a human being. When they unite at conception, the resulting cell develops in nine months into a baby with billions of cells. The union of the sperm and ovum is also called **fertilization** (fert-uhl-uh-ZAY-shuhn).

❖ Female Reproductive System

When a female is born, thousands of ova or egg cells are already stored in her two **ovaries** (OHV-uh-rees), the female reproductive glands. Of all these eggs, about 400 will mature during the woman's reproductive lifetime. During puberty, which usually occurs between the ages of eleven and fourteen years, the eggs begin to mature.

Typically, one or the other ovary releases one mature egg each month. The egg travels down one of the two *fallopian* (fuh-LOH-pee-uhn) *tubes* that connect the ovaries to the uterus. The **uterus** (YOOT-uh-russ), or womb, is the pear-shaped organ in which the future child develops. Each month, the uterus becomes lined with blood vessels and other tissue in preparation for nurturing a fertilized egg.

If the ovum is fertilized by a sperm in the fallopian tube, it then travels into the uterus. Here the fertilized egg attaches to the wall of

The Process of Fertilization

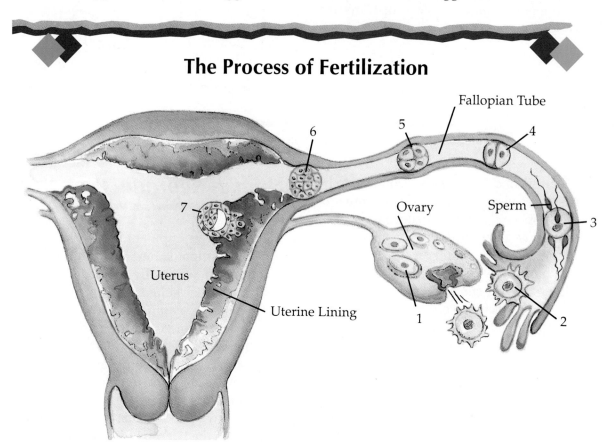

The ovary produces an egg (1) which travels down the fallopian tube (2). Fertilization begins when a single sperm cell unites with an egg (3). The fertilized cell begins to divide into two cells, then four, then eight, and so on (4 and 5). The clump of cells travels down the fallopian tube toward the uterus (6). Two weeks after conception the cells forming the baby are firmly planted in the uterine wall (7).

More About. The lining of the uterus is called the endometrium.

More About. A fertilized egg that becomes implanted in the fallopian tube results in an ectopic or tubal pregnancy. This is an extremely dangerous condition if not detected early because the tube will rupture, causing hemorrhaging and possible death.

the uterus to grow and develop. It will remain in the uterus for nine months. You will learn about prenatal growth and development in Chapter 8.

If the ovum is not fertilized, the uterus casts off the lining in the *menstruation* (men-struh-WAY-shuhn) process. This process is repeated approximately every 28 days during the woman's reproductive lifetime—about 40 years. Menstruation stops when the female becomes pregnant and resumes after childbirth.

❖ Male Reproductive System

Sperm develop when a male reaches puberty. For most boys, this occurs between the ages of twelve and fifteen years. Sperm are produced in the two **testes** (TES-tees), the male reproductive glands. Once a male reaches puberty, he is capable of producing sperm for the rest of his life.

Rather than releasing only a single sperm, the male releases 400 million to 500 million sperm at one time. The sperm are carried in *semen,* a milky liquid, that helps protect the sperm and gives them mobility.

Sperm are released from the male's body through the *urethra* (yu-REE-thruh), a narrow tube in the penis. Although the penis is usually soft and flexible, it becomes erect and firm during sexual arousal. When the many small blood vessels in the penis fill with blood, an erection occurs. If an erection is followed by *ejaculation* (ee-jack-u-LAY-shun), semen is discharged from the penis.

During intercourse, the male penis can deposit sperm near the narrow, lower end of the female's uterus. Each sperm cell has a tail that enables it to swim quickly into the uterus and then into one of the fallopian tubes. If an ovum is present, only one of the millions of sperm cells will fertilize the egg. Once an egg is fertilized, its surface seals out all other sperm. The remaining sperm eventually die.

Inheritance Begins

The reproductive cells carry a biological blueprint, or instruction code. This code will determine the traits and guide the development of a new human being. The new person will be similar to other people but will have some unique features, too. The blueprint determines the child's gender, eye color, hair color, body type, and many other characteristics.

The plan for a new human being is carried by the chromosomes of the reproductive cells. **Chromosomes** (KROH-muh-sohms) are long, threadlike particles in the cell nucleus.

There are 23 chromosomes in each ovum and in each sperm. When the sperm cell from the male combines with the egg cell from the female, the new cell has 46 chromosomes. The chromosomes provide a complete set of instructions for the development of a unique human being.

On the chromosomes are genes. **Genes** (JEENZ) are the chromosome parts that determine the inherited traits that make each individual somewhat different from all others. Genes determine what you have inherited from your parents, grandparents, and other ancestors. Your particular genes were randomly drawn from a large collection of genes contributed by all of those individuals. According to one scientific estimate, the number of possible unique heredity arrangements of genes may be as high as 64 trillion.

❖ Dominant and Recessive Genes

Genes determine a person's inherited features. Into one ovum might go the gene for blue eyes; into another ovum, the gene for hazel eyes; into a third, the gene for brown eyes, and so on. The same process takes place

---

More About. Each sperm is about 1/600th of an inch long (600 sperm = 1 inch) and can swim an inch in 4 to 16 minutes. **Emphasize.** Pregnancy can occur even if the male withdraws before ejaculation because sperm is present in seminal fluid.

More About. Chromosomes are long, threadlike particles of DNA (deoxyribonucleic acid) which is often referred to as the building blocks or building code of life. Each chromosome has thousands of genes.

in the sperm to distribute the male's collection of genes for eye color. Genes for other features are also distributed randomly in the sperm or ovum.

Dominant and Recessive Traits

Dominant	Recessive
curly hair	straight hair
black or brown hair	blond or red hair
straight nose	turned-up nose
brown eyes	blue eyes
long, full eyelashes	short, thin eyelashes
dimples	smooth cheeks
full lips	thin lips
freckles	no freckles

Some genes are *dominant genes,* or stronger than other genes. For example, the stronger gene carrying brown hair is dominant over the *recessive gene,* or weaker gene, for blond hair. When a gene for brown hair and a gene for blond hair are both present, the trait of brown hair is expressed. However, if the parent with brown hair has any ancestors with blond hair, he or she may carry a gene for blond hair. If a sperm with a gene for blond hair and an ovum with a gene for blond hair unite, a blond child results. This is how two parents with brown hair, both carrying recessive genes for blond hair, may produce a child with blond hair.

◈ Gender Determination

Of the 46 chromosomes that unite at conception to form 23 pairs, only one pair determines the gender of the child. These are the

Males have two sex chromosomes: X and Y. Females have X and X. A baby inherits one chromosome from each parent—an X from the mother and either an X or a Y from the father. If the sperm that unites with the ovum contains an X chromosome, the baby is a girl. If it has a Y chromosome, the baby is a boy.

Activity. Have students survey their own inherited characteristics. From whom did they receive their more distinguishable traits? What other relatives have similar physical characteristics?

Discuss. Which parent determines the gender of the child? Can methods be used to assure the conception of a girl or a boy baby? Are these methods medically approved or simply folklore? Why might parents want to have only a girl or a boy?

special chromosomes called X and Y. A sperm has either an X or a Y chromosome. An ovum always has an X chromosome.

If a sperm cell with a Y chromosome unites with the egg cell, the future baby will be a boy. If a sperm with an X chromosome unites with the egg, the baby will be a girl. Thus the father determines the gender of the child. See the illustration on the previous page.

A son inherits an X chromosome from his mother and a Y chromosome from his father. A daughter inherits an X chromosome from each parent.

◆◆ Multiple Births

Some pregnancies result in multiple births. Twins are born about once in every 89 births. Triplets occur about once in 7,900 births, and quadruplets about once in 705,000 births.

Some women may release two or more eggs at one time from either ovary. When two eggs are fertilized by two sperm, fraternal twins begin to develop. Fraternal twins can be the same gender or different genders. They usually look no more alike than regular brothers and sisters. Each fraternal twin has his or her own individual genetic makeup. This occurs because each future child forms from the union of a separate sperm and ovum.

Sometimes one fertilized egg splits evenly into two identical cells. These cells then develop eventually to form identical twins. These twins are the same gender. They look very much alike because they have inherited the same genetic makeup.

Triplets and quadruplets can be fraternal,

identical, or both. They may result from separate eggs, from the division of one egg, or be a combination of fraternal and identical babies.

DECISIONS ◆ ◆ DECISIONS

Roberto and Carmen have just discovered that Carmen is going to have twins. They are excited about being able to dress the babies alike and take them out in a twin stroller. They are thrilled that their first children will have instant playmates. They are sure the twins will be adorable. What practical aspects of having twins have Carmen and Roberto overlooked? What do you think of their present feelings?

Some pregnancies result in multiple births. This mother had quintuplets—one boy and four girls.

Genetic Counseling

Some people worry that they may be a carrier of a genetic defect that they could pass along to their children through the genes. Genetic defects can cause certain diseases or disabilities. Some families may have one or more members who have a genetic birth defect or health problem. Thus they know that some family members are carriers of the genetic disorder. Couples who already have one child with a birth defect or health problem may be concerned about passing the disorder along to additional children.

Some genetic defects are caused by dominant genes. In this case, just one gene can cause a child to inherit the disorder. Other genetic defects are caused by recessive genes. A child would need two recessive genes, one from the mother and one from the father, to be born with the disorder. If the child inher-

its only one recessive gene, he or she will not have the disorder. However, this child will be a carrier and could eventually pass the defect on to future offspring.

Couples who worry that they might pass on genetic defects to their children may want to consult a genetic counselor before they decide to have children. **Genetic counseling** is expert information and explanation about heredity, especially about the risk for disorders to be passed along to children through the genes. Counseling is given by doctors, genetic doctors, and genetic specialists.

Genetic counselors cannot prevent birth defects. They simply inform prospective parents about their chances of having a child with a particular disease or disability. They can also describe how a specific disorder can affect the child and the family. Sometimes medical tests can determine whether a person is a carrier of a specific genetic disorder. By receiving counseling about the specific

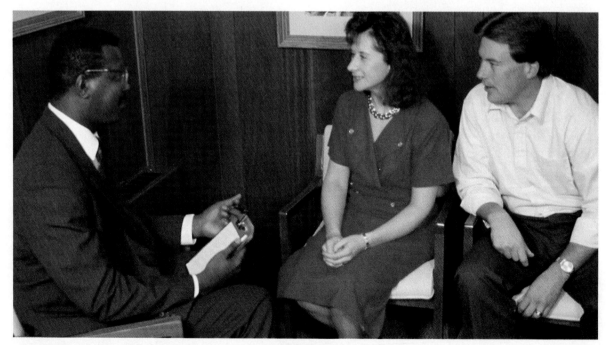

Couples can meet with a genetic counselor to discuss the risks of passing a disease or disability on to future children through the genes.

Activity. Invite a March of Dimes representative, a genetic counselor, or a medical specialist to talk to the students about various types of genetic birth defects and disorders.

Discuss. Would genetics be an exciting field for a career? Why or why not?

risks involved, prospective parents are better able to make decisions about having children.

Some couples who discover they are carriers of a genetic disorder may feel that it would not be right to bring into the world a child who would suffer a serious disease or disability. Many such couples choose to adopt a child. Other couples may decide to take the risk of having a child with a serious birth defect. Today, medical technology and specialized training can help many of these children achieve a long and happy life.

❖ Types of Genetic Birth Defects

Nearly 200 abnormalities of the chromosomes or genes can be detected by medical testing. A description of some disorders caused by such abnormalities follows.

Down Syndrome

One chromosomal disorder is Down syndrome. After conception the fertilized ovum has three, rather than two, number 21 chromosomes. Instead of the normal 46 chromosomes, then, infants with Down syndrome have 47 chromosomes. The condition can be detected by medical tests.

A child with Down syndrome is short and stocky, often has a heart defect, and is moderately to severely mentally retarded. Although there is no cure for Down syndrome, educational training can help those with the disorder lead more normal lives.

Older mothers have a higher risk than younger mothers of having a baby with Down syndrome. This is one reason why physicians offer special tests and precautions when caring for pregnant women who are age thirty-five and older. Researchers indicate that in 97 percent of Down syndrome cases, the syndrome would not occur in another child by the same parents.

An estimated 1 in 600 to 800 infants is born with Down syndrome, a birth abnormality caused by the presence of an extra chromosome.

Hemophilia

Hemophilia (hee-muh-FILL-ee-uh) is a gender-linked genetic disorder that usually affects male offspring. Women who carry the hemophilia gene rarely suffer from the disorder. Hemophilia prevents normal blood clotting. Those with the disorder may need frequent blood transfusions to prevent them from bleeding to death.

Cystic Fibrosis

One of the most common inherited diseases is cystic fibrosis. The recessive disorder affects the mucus glands of the body. Individuals with this disease have problems with breathing and digestion. Although there is no cure for cystic fibrosis, special treatment and exercise can help children with the disease live into early adulthood.

More About. One in every one hundred children has some major chromosomal abnormality. One in six hundred babies is born with Down syndrome.
Emphasize. Individuals must inherit a recessive gene from both parents in order to be affected by a genetic disorder caused by recessive genes. If individuals inherit only one recessive gene for a disorder, they become a carrier but have no symptoms.

Sickle Cell Anemia

Sickle cell anemia is a painful blood disorder that often leads to early death. It is most common among blacks. People may carry the recessive gene for sickle cell anemia but have no symptoms. When both parents carry the gene for this condition, their children have a one-in-four chance of getting sickle cell anemia. So far there is no cure.

Tay-Sachs Disease

Another recessive disorder is Tay-Sachs disease. It is characterized by a gradual degeneration of the brain that results in blindness and weakening muscles. Children with Tay-Sachs disease live only a few years at the most. It is most common among those whose ancestors came from Jewish communities in Central or Eastern Europe. It is similar to sickle cell anemia and cystic fibrosis because both parents must carry the gene to pass on the disease. There is no cure for Tay-Sachs disease.

PKU

Phenylketonuria (fen-uhl-KEET-oh-nuh-ree-uh), or PKU, is another disorder caused by a recessive gene. If detected soon after birth, PKU can be effectively treated by a special diet. If PKU is not detected, severe retardation will occur because of poisons that build up in the baby's body. All states require PKU testing of newborns just after birth.

◆ ◆ *Self-Esteem* ◆ ◆

Every child has the right to be loved, nurtured, and adequately cared for. In addition, every child needs to live in a family that shows genuine love and concern for each individual. In this type of environment, a child develops high self-esteem and a sincere appreciation for others.

Planning for Parenthood

Responsible parents make important decisions concerning their children. Some parents want to limit the number of children they have. Others want to space their children a certain number of years apart. Some couples want to delay parenthood until they complete college, get established in a career, or purchase a home of their own. Thus everyone needs to give careful thought to many factors before making a decision about becoming a parent.

❖ Fertility

Fertility is the ability to produce offspring. For conception to occur, the ovum must be fertilized by a sperm during the first few days after the egg is released from the ovary. Anytime sperm are deposited into a female when there is an ovum in the fallopian tube, a pregnancy can occur.

For many females, it is difficult to determine when an ovum might be in the fallopian tube. For adolescents, who are undergoing many physical changes, it is especially difficult to know when they might be fertile.

It is important to understand that as soon as a female first releases a mature egg from an ovary, she can become pregnant. Thus pregnancy can occur even before she first starts to menstruate. It can occur the first time she has intercourse. Because deposited sperm can live five to seven days in the female body, a female can also become pregnant even if she has intercourse during her menstrual period. Standing up, taking a hot bath, or urinating after intercourse cannot prevent a pregnancy. Even if the male withdraws his penis before releasing semen, sperm can still enter the female body and travel up to the fallopian tubes.

More About. One in ten blacks in U.S. is a carrier of sickle-cell anemia. The sickle-shaped cell is due to the loss of hemoglobin.
Reference. See Chapter 21 for more information about birth defects such as muscular dystrophy and spina bifida.
Problem Solving. Have students list specific goals they have for the future. Then ask them to discuss how an unexpected pregnancy might change their plans for attaining their goals.

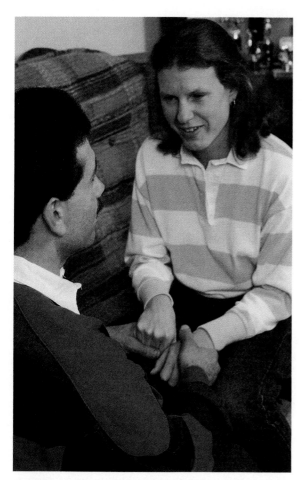

Couples should discuss their thoughts and feelings about parenthood with each other. Then they can make better decisions about whether or when to have children.

❖ Contraception

Contraception (kahn-truh-SEP-shuhn) is the deliberate prevention of conception or pregnancy by any of various drugs, devices, or techniques. Some contraceptives prevent the monthly release of the ovum. Others provide a barrier that prevents sperm from reaching the ovum. Some methods include chemicals that kill sperm. Surgical procedures can seal off the fallopian tubes or block the sperm in the testes.

Each method has certain advantages and disadvantages. Some methods are far more effective in preventing pregnancy than others. See the chart on the next page. Techniques such as withdrawing the penis before semen is released or avoiding intercourse only during what is believed to be the fertile period have a high failure rate. It must be remembered that abstinence is the only method that is 100 percent effective in preventing a pregnancy.

Deciding to use contraceptives and choosing a particular contraceptive method are very personal decisions. It is important for couples to discuss the use of contraceptives with each other and to get advice from a doctor or other health care professional. Many couples base their decision about family planning on their personal values and religious beliefs, age, health, education, and economic situation.

If a couple decides to use a contraceptive method, both partners should feel comfortable about their choice and be committed to its proper use. They can get information, physical examinations, and prescriptions for certain contraceptives at doctors' offices, regular health clinics, and family planning clinics.

❖ Infertility

Although some couples want to avoid a pregnancy, others want to have a child but cannot. **Infertility** (in-fur-TIL-eh-tee) is the inability to have children. If a couple has tried to conceive a child for over a year without success, one or both partners may have a fertility problem.

The cause of infertility varies. Sometimes the cause is physical. Sometimes stress or other emotional factors can be the cause.

Couples who are worried about their inability to conceive should seek medical help. Doctors can conduct a fertility analysis that includes physical and psychological examinations of both partners. Some physi-

Discuss. What incorrect information do some people have about the process of conception? What methods of contraception do some couples use that are completely unreliable? Why can pregnancy occur any time a couple has intercourse?

Activity. Have students research and report on the reasons why males and females may be infertile.

Methods of Contraception

Method	Function	Disadvantages	Effectiveness
Abstinence	No sexual intercourse.	None	100%
Oral Contraceptive: Hormone pill taken daily.	Prevents monthly release of ovum.	Prescription needed. Can cause weight gain, headaches, mood changes. Health risks for women who are over 35, smoke, or have family history of certain diseases.	94–97%
Condom: Latex sheath that fits over penis.	Traps semen. Reduces risk of sexually transmitted diseases.	Can break or slip off. Can only be used once. Damaged by hot or cold and petroleum products.	86–90%
Diaphragm: Dome-shaped latex cup stretched over a flexible ring; inserted into vagina.	Blocks entrance to uterus. Used with spermicide.	Must be fitted by health professional. Must remain in place for at least 6 hours. Increases risk of bladder/urinary infections.	84%
Cervical cap: Small latex or plastic thimble; inserted over cervix (narrow opening of uterus).	Provides barrier by fitting snugly over cervix and blocking entrance to uterus. Used with spermicide.	Must be fitted by health professional. Difficult to insert. Must remain in place for at least 8 hours.	82%
Spermicide: Foams, creams, gels, and vaginal inserts.	Sperm-killing chemical. Used with condom, diaphragm, cervical cap.	Not very effective when used alone. May cause allergic reaction.	74%
Sponge: Small, soft sponge with spermicide; inserted into vagina.	Blocks entrance to uterus and releases sperm-killing chemical.	Must remain in place for at least 6 hours. Can only be used once. May cause allergic reaction.	74%
IUD (Intrauterine device): Small plastic or metal device inserted into uterus.	Prevents pregnancy by interfering with implantation of fertilized ovum.	Doctor must insert. Increases risk of pelvic infection. May increase menstrual flow and cramping.	94%
Hormone implant: Capsules inserted beneath skin in upper arm.	Prevents monthly release of ovum for up to 5 years.	Doctor must insert. May cause irregular bleeding or missed menstrual periods.	99%
Hormone injection: Injection given once every 3 months.	Prevents monthly release of ovum for 3 months.	Doctor must inject. May cause weight gain, headaches, abdominal pain, irregular periods.	99%
Sterilization: Surgical procedures (tubal ligation for female, vasectomy for male).	Clamps or seals fallopian tubes; cuts or ties the vas deferns (tubes carrying sperm to penis).	Minor surgery with some risk of infection. May require major surgery to reverse, often without success.	99%
Natural family planning: System determines when ovum is likely to be released; called "rhythm method."	Prevents pregnancy by avoiding intercourse during fertile period.	Requires accurate record keeping. Illness or irregular menstrual cycle can throw off calculations. Errors easily made.	70–80%

cal problems can be corrected by medication or surgery. For example, the doctor may prescribe fertility drugs for the female or use microsurgery techniques to open the ducts that carry the sperm from the testes. See "Medically Assisted Pregnancies" below. For emotional problems, the couple may benefit from counseling by a trained professional.

Many couples who have fertility problems can be helped to conceive a child. For couples who remain infertile, the emotional experience may be very difficult. Some couples may choose to remain childless. Others may choose to adopt a child. Parents of adopted children experience the same rewards of parenthood as do biological parents.

◆ ◆ *Health & Safety* ◆ ◆

Medically Assisted Pregnancies

In the past, couples who were having difficulty conceiving a baby had to let nature take its course. With today's new technological advances, a doctor can often identify the cause and provide the appropriate medical assistance.

- **Fertility drugs.** These drugs contain the hormones necessary for ova production. They can be helpful if a woman's ovaries do not produce an ovum each month. When a woman takes these drugs, fertilization can occur normally. Because fertility drugs may cause the body to produce two, three, or more ova, the chance of multiple births greatly increases.

- **Microsurgery.** If a female has had a pelvic infection, her fallopian tubes may become blocked. Then the ova will not be able to travel from the ovaries to the uterus. Microsurgery techniques can sometimes be used to reopen these closed tubes. Microsurgery can also be used on males to reopen the ducts that carry the sperm from the testes to the penis.

- **Artificial insemination.** During this procedure, sperm are injected into a woman's uterus with a special surgical syringe. The doctor does this during the woman's fertile period. The sperm may be from the husband or from an unknown male donor.

- **In vitro fertilization.** If a woman's fallopian tubes are damaged, the doctor can remove an ovum from the woman's ovary. Sperm from the husband or donor are mixed with the ovum in a small glass dish. Then the fertilized ovum is inserted into the woman's uterus. If the procedure is successful, a pregnancy can proceed normally. Because in vitro fertilization occurs in a laboratory, the babies are often called test-tube babies.

- **Implanted ovum.** This procedure is used if the woman has a healthy uterus but inactive ovaries. The ovum is provided by a female donor. It is fertilized in the laboratory, using the husband's sperm, then implanted in the wife's uterus.

- **Surrogate mother.** This option may be used if the biological mother has a health problem that prevents her from carrying a baby to term. Her ovum can be fertilized in the laboratory, then inserted into the uterus of another woman, the surrogate. If the wife is infertile, the surrogate can be artificially inseminated with the husband's sperm. This procedure is very controversial and has raised many ethical and legal questions.

Activity. Have students research and report on different infertility tests and procedures that are used to diagnose and treat infertility of males and females.

Discuss. Ask students about the moral implications involved in artificial insemination, in vitro fertilization, and surrogate mothers. What legal and ethical problems may be created by such procedures?

Selecting Medical Care for Pregnancy and Delivery

Most couples have a choice of medical care for the mother-to-be during pregnancy and for the delivery of their baby. The decisions will depend on available options, finances, and personal feelings.

Private doctors practice alone or in partnership with other doctors. In some partnerships, the woman sees only the doctor who plans to deliver her baby. Another doctor in the partnership will deliver the baby only if the woman's regular doctor is not available at the time. In other partnerships, every woman gets to know every doctor. Which doctor delivers the baby depends upon who is on duty at the time. A local hospital or medical society will provide the names of private doctors who are accepting new patients.

Most city and county health clinics offer medical advice for pregnant women. Public health clinics, available for low-income patients, are often staffed by interns from medical colleges. These interns are supervised by licensed doctors. Local health departments have information on the locations and hours of nearby public health clinics.

Before making a decision about medical care, the couple should also talk to friends or relatives who are pregnant or who have young children. Recommendations from friends and relatives can be very helpful.

◆◆ Medical Specialists

A variety of medical specialists deal with pregnancy. These people can help answer questions, provide prenatal medical care, and assist in the delivery of the baby.

- An **obstetrician** (ahb-stuh-TRISH-uhn) is a doctor who specializes in delivering babies. Obstetricians provide pregnant

women with appropriate care before, during, and after childbirth. They are trained to handle any complications or emergencies that may arise.

- A **gynecologist** (gyn-uh-KAHL-uh-juhst) is a doctor who specializes in the health of the female reproductive organs. For example, gynecologists perform routine breast and pelvic examinations that all women should have at least once a year to check for breast and uterine cancer. Many gynecologists are also obstetricians.

- A family practice physician is a doctor who treats patients for all types of conditions, including pregnancy. Family practice physicians can offer prenatal and postnatal care and deliver babies. They may call on obstetricians or gynecologists for advice or assistance if problems arise.

- A **nurse-midwife** is a female or male registered nurse trained in obstetrics and pre-

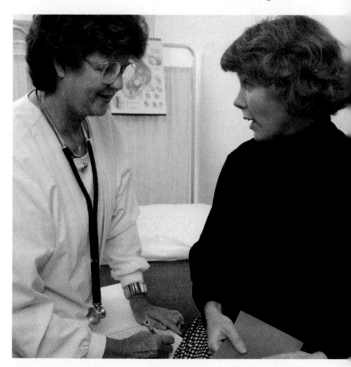

Obstetricians, family practice physicians, and nurse-midwives are all trained to provide prenatal care and assist in the delivery of a baby.

Activity. Invite a medical specialist to talk to the class about his/her career.

Activity. Have students research disorders and diseases of the female reproductive system that gynecologists diagnose and treat.

DECISIONS ◆
◆ DECISIONS

Kay and Mitch have just learned that Kay is pregnant. Before making a decision about medical care, they want to talk to friends who also are pregnant. Mitch's cousin is five months pregnant and highly recommends her obstetrician. Kay's friend, who is six months pregnant, is looking forward to a nurse-midwife delivering her baby. Kay is confused as to which option would be better for her. Mitch thinks they should wait until the other two women give birth before deciding whether to use the obstetrician or nurse-midwife. What recommendations would you make to Kay and Mitch? How could they gain more information about their options?

natal care. Many nurse-midwives provide routine prenatal care under the supervision of a doctor. All of them perform normal deliveries of babies. The majority of nurse-midwives are connected with a delivery program at or near a hospital. Such programs usually require an initial examination by an obstetrician to determine that the woman is in a low-risk pregnancy category. This means that the woman is unlikely to experience any complications in childbirth that may be dangerous to her life or to the baby. However, if any complication in the delivery does occur, a qualified obstetrician is available to handle the birth.

◆◆ Medical Costs

The costs of medical care, hospitalization, and delivery are substantial. Doctors and nurse-midwives typically consider prenatal

care and delivery a total package and charge one fee for all services. However, doctors may charge an additional fee for taking care of serious medical problems that arise during the pregnancy or delivery. Couples can learn what a doctor's or nurse-midwife's fee is by simply asking her or him.

It is both wise and economical to begin seeing a doctor or nurse-midwife early in the pregnancy. Because the costs of office visits are included in the general fee, a woman will not save money by avoiding prenatal care. Also, it is better and less expensive to prevent any potential problems from occurring by visiting the doctor or nurse-midwife early in pregnancy and regularly. Some doctors refuse to accept as patients women who are in their final months of pregnancy. These doctors do so because it is too late to begin preventive measures that ensure the baby's safe delivery. You will learn more about the importance of prenatal care in Chapter 9.

Hospital fees are separate from doctors' or nurse-midwives' fees. Besides the daily hospital room cost, there are charges for the delivery room, for the nursery, and for medication. Most hospitals require that a specialist in administering medication be present in the delivery room. Even if medication is not needed, the patient is charged a standby fee. Some money is saved if the mother stays in a room with one or more roommates. Couples can learn current rates by calling a hospital's accounting department.

Some communities have alternative birth centers. These are in a separate location, though often close to a hospital. They provide services for routine deliveries, usually for a lower fee than hospitals charge. If complications occur, the woman will be transported to a hospital. You will learn more about alternative birth sites in Chapter 10.

It is important for a couple considering parenthood to have a good medical insurance

Activity. Have students develop a list of medical specialists in your community who provide prenatal care and delivery. Which ones are affiliated with a clinic or private office? Hospital or birthing center? What are their fees for prenatal care and delivery?

Problem Solving. Have students compare the costs of medical care provided by the local hospital versus an alternative birth center. Then discuss health insurance and what medical costs are covered by various policies.

Around the World

The Population Explosion

In 1840, there were approximately a billion people in the world. By 1940, just 100 years later, the world's population had grown to 2 billion. By 1965, a mere 35 years later, there were 3 billion people in the world. Sometime in the mid-1990s, approximately 20 years later, the world's population will be more than 5 billion. This is what is meant by the population explosion.

There are many reasons for the population explosion. Improved disease control and health care mean people are living longer. The infant mortality rate—the number of children who die at birth or during infancy—is lower. That means more infants worldwide grow up to have children of their own. In some places, long-established cultural or religious values may encourage large families. In many nonindustrialized countries, for example, people must still grow most of their own food. A big family means more people to help in the fields.

While having children has been considered a personal decision, there is increasing global concern about the population explosion. The consequences of overpopulation include famine, resource depletion, overcrowding, unemployment, and poor family health. Some countries—especially those already experiencing overcrowding—actively encourage family planning. In China, for example, family planning focuses on lowering the birthrate. Government programs encourage Chinese families to limit themselves to one child. In Sweden, family planning means deciding how many children you will have and when you will have them. It includes birth control information, fertility treatments, and adoption services.

plan. Many people with full-time jobs have plans that pay for prenatal care, delivery, and hospitalization. It is important to have a medical plan that also covers the newborn baby. Prospective parents should check to see whether the hospital will accept payment directly from the insurance company. If not, the parents will have to pay the hospital bill themselves and be reimbursed later by the insurance company.

If parents do not have health insurance, they may qualify for government assistance. They should check with the public health clinic, hospital, or social service agency for information about free or special-rate medical care.

⚫ Making a Decision

Expectant parents should try to find out all they can about different medical personnel and medical costs before making their choice. They should visit and talk with each doctor or nurse-midwife they are considering. They should ask questions about labor and delivery. For example: Will the doctor or nurse-midwife be present during most of the labor or only during the delivery? Can the father or a friend be present during labor and delivery? What drugs might be used during labor and delivery? Will the baby stay most of the time with the mother or in the hospital nursery?

A good physician or nurse-midwife takes plenty of time with each patient and answers all questions. Such a professional will not be rushed or act impatient. In addition to evaluating the medical qualifications of a doctor or nurse-midwife, expectant parents should feel comfortable with him or her. It is important for a pregnant woman to like and trust her doctor or nurse-midwife. They must work together throughout the pregnancy to help produce a healthy child.

Discuss. Some experts are greatly concerned about the population explosion. Ask students whether they think governments should encourage family planning. Why or why not?

Activity. Have students make a list of typical questions that expectant parents might ask their health care provider about labor and delivery.

CHAPTER 7 REVIEW

Summary

- Conception occurs when two reproductive cells, a sperm and ovum, unite.
- Ovum are produced in the female's ovaries. Sperm are produced in the male's testes.
- If sperm encounter an ovum in the fallopian tube, a single sperm fertilizes the ovum. The fertilized cell begins to divide and multiply as it travels toward the uterus.
- Genes, which determine inherited traits, are located on the chromosomes of each ovum and sperm. Some genes are dominate; others are recessive.
- Genetic counseling provides information about the risks involved in passing a genetic defect along to future children.
- Birth defects resulting from chromosome abnormalities include Down syndrome, hemophilia, cystic fibrosis, sickle cell anemia, Tay-Sachs disease, and PKU.
- Medical specialists who deal with pregnancy include obstetricians, family practice physicians, and nurse-midwives.
- Expectant parents should learn all they can about medical care options and costs before making a choice.

Questions

p. 119   **1.** What is conception?

p. 120   **2.** What happens after an ovum is fertilized by a sperm cell?

p. 122   **3.** Give four examples of dominant and recessive genes.

4. Who determines what the gender of a baby will be? How?   p. 122

5. How do identical twins occur? Fraternal twins?   p. 123

6. List and describe three types of genetic birth defects.   p. 125

7. What is contraception?   p. 127

8. What is the difference between a gynecologist and a nurse-midwife?   p. 130

9. What are two factors that couples should consider when exploring medical care options?   p. 130

Activities

1. Bring in photos of family members. Look for similar physical characteristics among biological relatives.

2. Contact the March of Dimes for information on birth defects. Select one type of birth defect and prepare a written or oral report, including characteristics, life expectancy, treatment, and current research.

3. Research the current medical costs of having a baby in your community. Include costs of medical care, hospitalization, and delivery.

Think About

1. Why should couples understand that no contraceptive method, other than abstinence, is 100% effective?

2. What might be the advantages or disadvantages of having a nurse-midwife provide medical care during pregnancy and delivery?

Pregnancy

Objectives

This chapter will help you to:
- Give examples of early signs of pregnancy.
- Identify and describe the three stages of prenatal development.
- Explain the changes that occur in a woman's body during pregnancy.
- Discuss the importance of medical care during pregnancy.

Vocabulary

zygote
embryo
placenta
umbilical cord
fetus
Rh factor
anemia
vagina
cervix
Pap smear
ultrasonography
amniocentesis
chorionic villus sampling (CVS)
miscarriage

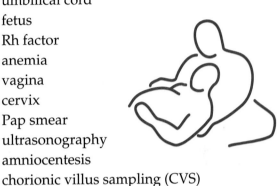

"Honey, I have wonderful news. You're going to be a father!"

"Did you hear? Flora and Manuel are going to have a baby!"

"What? You're pregnant? How can that be?"

Comments such as these often follow the confirmation that a woman is pregnant. Depending on the circumstances, they may be said with joy and happiness or with uncertainty and fear.

By the time a woman knows she is pregnant, many physical changes have begun to take place in her body. Knowing about these changes helps her understand prenatal development and take better care of herself and her developing baby.

Early Signs of Pregnancy

A woman usually does not know right after conception that she is pregnant. However, within a few weeks her body gives several signs that cause her to suspect she is pregnant.

◆ Missing a Menstrual Period

Missing a menstrual period is one of the first signs of pregnancy. It is a very reliable indicator of pregnancy for women who have regularly occurring menstrual periods. Those whose periods do not come at regular intervals may miss two or more periods before suspecting they are pregnant.

In the first two or three months of pregnancy, some women have a slight spotting of blood during the usual time for their period. They may feel mild menstrual-like cramps when their period is due. These exceptions can cause confusion about whether a woman is pregnant.

❖ Other Indications of Pregnancy

After a woman misses the second menstrual period, a doctor can determine whether she is pregnant without performing laboratory tests. An increase in the size of the uterus is an important clue that a doctor will recognize during a routine examination.

Another indication of pregnancy is enlarged and tender breasts. They start to develop to serve the needs of the infant after birth.

Some pregnant women experience nausea. This is commonly called morning sickness, although it may occur at other times of the day. The nausea makes some women think they have the flu or food poisoning. Usually the nausea disappears after the third month of pregnancy.

Increased need to urinate is yet another early sign of pregnancy. Because the uterus and the bladder are close together, the expanding uterus puts pressure on the bladder. The bladder needs to be emptied more often than before the pregnancy.

❖ Pregnancy Tests

A woman who thinks she is pregnant can use a home pregnancy test. Several types are available in drugstores. The home tests can determine pregnancy within a few days of a missed menstrual period. For an accurate indication, the instructions must be followed exactly. However, home pregnancy tests are still not as reliable as laboratory tests. Women

who get positive results from a home pregnancy test should see a doctor to confirm the pregnancy and to receive prenatal care.

A laboratory test ordered by a doctor or other health professional provides the most accurate indication of whether or not a woman is pregnant. The test is done on a sample of blood or urine. The sample is analyzed for hormones that will be present if the woman is pregnant. The results of the laboratory test are usually available within 24 hours and sometimes sooner.

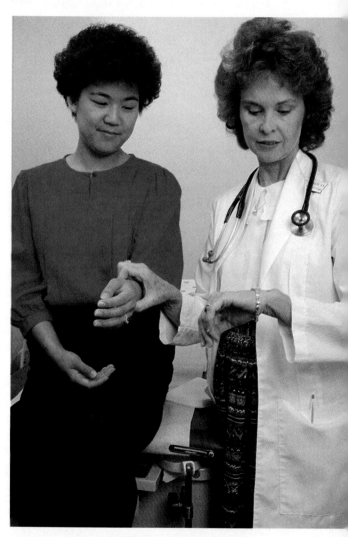

A woman who suspects she is pregnant should see a doctor to confirm the pregnancy and receive prenatal care.

Activity. Have students check local stores for home pregnancy tests and do a cost comparison. If possible, purchase a home pregnancy test and have students read the instructions and accompanying information. Are the tests 100% accurate?

More About. The hormone that will be present if a woman is pregnant is called hCG. It is secreted by a fertilized ovum at 4 days old and spreads in body water to the body's tissues. It can be detected in the blood, and shortly thereafter in the urine.

Prenatal Development

Prenatal development begins at conception and ends at birth. It occurs in three stages: zygote, embryo, and fetus. See "The Months Before Birth" on pages 140-143.

Stage of the Zygote

After the sperm unites with the ovum, the new cell is called a **zygote** (ZY-goht). The zygote divides into two cells, then four, then eight, and so on. Within five days, the zygote is made up of about 500 cells. Within a few more days it travels down the fallopian tube into the uterus, which will be its home for the rest of the prenatal period. The zygote becomes attached to the lining of the uterus, which is richly supplied with blood vessels. By now the zygote has begun to change from a small mass of cells into a ball of cells with a hollow center. The zygote stage lasts about two weeks.

Stage of the Embryo

The second stage of prenatal development lasts from the time the cluster of cells attaches itself to the uterine wall until the eighth week of pregnancy. During this stage, the ball of rapidly multiplying cells is called an **embryo** (EM-bree-oh). Different groups of cells begin to form muscle, bone, organs, and other body

Principles of Development

The following developmental principles will help you understand growth and development as described throughout this book.

- **Development is head to toe.** Humans develop in a head-to-toe direction. In prenatal development, out of the cluster of cells the head forms first. Then the upper body develops, then the legs and feet. Development proceeds in a head-to-toe direction after the baby is born as well. Babies can do many things with their hands before being able to use their legs.

- **Development proceeds in an orderly sequence.** All parts of the body develop in an orderly sequence. For example, the bones in a child's hand become calcified, or hardened, in a specific order. A technician reading an x-ray can tell what stage of growth a child is in by which bones of the hand are fully calcified. All the organs have a similar timetable.

- **Development has individual differences.** There are individual differences in the terminals, or end points, of development. For example, the final height of individuals differs from one person to another.

- **Development is interrelated.** Different areas of development, such as social and emotional development and physical and language development, are interrelated. If development is slow in one area, it is typically slow in the other area as well.

- **Development builds on a foundation.** Early development is a foundation for later development. Growth takes place on a foundation that is already established. During prenatal development, a cluster of cells forms the head. From those cells evolve the eyes, brain, ears, nose, and so forth. A child first learns to crawl, then to walk, and then to run and climb.

More About. When the zygote reaches the uterus, it has changed into a group of cells around a fluid-filled cavity, called a blastocyst. One section contains cells that will produce an embryo; the outer layer of cells will produce the placenta.

Emphasize. Babies develop in a head-to-toe direction, as well as close to the body outward. Thus babies can use their arms prior to hand control and use their hands prior to gaining finger coordination.

Prenatal development progresses rapidly. The fetus receives oxygen and nutrients through the umbilical cord which extends from the placenta to its navel.

parts. In fact, almost all of the internal organs begin to develop during this six-week stage.

The embryo also becomes enclosed in a fluid-filled pouch called the *amniotic* (am-nee-OTT-ik) *sac*. The watery substance in the sac, the amniotic fluid, cushions and protects the developing embryo. Now the embryo literally floats through the prenatal period until just before birth.

Also during the embryonic stage, the tissue connecting the embryo to the uterine wall becomes the **placenta** (pluh-SENT-uh), a flat disk-shaped organ. The **umbilical** (uhm-BILL-ih-kuhl) **cord** attaches the embryo to the placenta. Nutrients and oxygen from the woman's bloodstream pass to the embryo through the placenta and umbilical cord. Waste products return to the woman through the umbilical cord and placenta and are discharged through her body.

More About. During the first three months of prenatal development, all the major organs in the body are formed. By the end of the first trimester, the fetal head is disproportionately large compared with the rest of the body.

◆◆ Stage of the Fetus

At the end of the second month, the embryo passes into the third and final stage of prenatal development. During this stage the unborn child is called a **fetus** (FEE-tus). From a small embryo about the size of a walnut, the fetus increases 50 times in size.

During the next seven months, fetal development is a process of growth and maturation. The body, head, arms, and legs grow rapidly. Organs develop for blood circulation, breathing, and digestion. Nerves and muscles also develop. The heart, eventually the size of a large orange, pumps blood through a long network of veins and arteries. The brain, the most intricate part of the body, develops rapidly. The fetus begins to look like a baby, with eyes, ears, nose, fingernails, and hair. The fetal stage lasts approximately seven months.

More About. The umbilical cord is filled with a substance called Wharton's Jelly, which keeps the cord taut (something like a garden hose). The cord averages 12 to 35 inches in length.

Characteristics of Pregnancy

A woman's body goes through various changes as prenatal development progresses. It is important for a woman to understand these changes so she can take proper care of herself and her developing child throughout pregnancy.

◆ Physical Changes

A pregnancy can be divided into *trimesters*, three equal segments that are each about three months long. During the first trimester of pregnancy, a woman's breasts enlarge and become tender. She may begin to gain weight. The average woman gains 2 to 4 pounds during the first trimester. As the uterus begins to enlarge, her abdomen expands slightly. She may feel sleepy during the day and need to take a daily nap. She may have minor discomforts such as nausea or vomiting that usually disappear by the end of the first trimester. During this period, she may have emotional swings. Sometimes she may feel very happy and excited; other times she may feel anxious or depressed.

During the second trimester, a woman's abdomen begins to enlarge dramatically. By the fourth month, she may need to wear loose clothing or maternity clothes. During the fourth or fifth month, she may first feel the movements of the fetus as light flutters. These fetal movements are called *quickening*. They usually become stronger as the pregnancy progresses. Other people can feel the movements by placing a hand on the woman's abdomen. By the sixth month, fetal kicks can be visible through the woman's clothing. Most women enjoy feeling the vigorous new life move around inside.

During the third trimester, the abdomen continues to enlarge as the fetus grows. The average woman gains about a pound per week during the second and third trimesters. By the eighth month, her abdomen is enlarged considerably. She may experience various discomforts because the uterus puts pressure on the bladder, intestines, and diaphragm. Though most of these discomforts are common during pregnancy, the mother-to-be should discuss them with her doctor or nurse-midwife. During the last month of pregnancy, the fetus drops lower in the pelvis in a process called *lightening*. Usually head down in the uterus, the fetus prepares for birth.

During the third trimester, the woman's abdomen enlarges as the fetus grows. The father-to-be can feel the movements of the fetus and even see its kicks.

Reference. See "The Months Before Birth" on pages 140-143. **Discuss.** Ask students if they have heard any "old wive's tales" about pregnancy. Then have students research to see if the statements are fact or fiction.

Activity. Have students wear an empathy belly which simulates a pregnancy. Have students try bending over, tying a shoe, and getting up from a chair. What thoughts and feelings do they have while wearing the belly?

◆

The Months Before Birth

From the moment of conception to the birth of the baby many changes occur in both the pregnant woman and the developing child. As prenatal development continues, the woman's body changes to accommodate the growth of the baby.

Stage of the Zygote

The first stage of prenatal development is called the stage of the zygote. After conception, the single-celled zygote begins to grow into a ball of cells as it moves through the fallopian tube. At about the fourteenth day, the zygote becomes implanted in the lining of the uterus.

Stage of the Embryo

The second stage of prenatal development is the stage of the embryo. It lasts from the end of the second week of pregnancy through the eighth week. The embryo becomes enclosed in the amniotic sac and receives nutrients and oxygen through the umbilical cord. This cord connects the placenta to the embryo at the navel.

During the third and fourth weeks after conception, the central nervous system begins to develop.

The blood vessels and stomach begin to form, and the beginning of a heart starts to beat. During the fifth week, the brain develops at a rapid pace and begins to form different structures. The beginnings of eyes, lungs, arms, and legs start to emerge. By the end of the eighth week, all the major body systems have begun to develop. The face, arms and legs, and hands and feet are forming. The embryo begins to resemble a human being even though it is not much more than an inch long.

Stage of the Fetus

The third and final stage of prenatal development is the stage of the fetus. This stage lasts from the ninth week after conception until birth.

Third Month

At 12 weeks, the fetus is only 3 inches long and weighs about 1 ounce. Its heartbeat may be heard with an electronic stethoscope. Most of its internal organs are formed, and its gender is evident. The fetus may suck its thumb.

The woman's body is changing. Her breasts enlarge and her abdomen expands slightly. She may have some discomfort, such as nausea, vomiting, and sleepiness. This marks the end of the first trimester.

Fourth Month

At the fourth month, the fetus is 8 inches long and weighs 6 ounces. Its skin is less transparent than it was previously. Fine hair covers the entire body. The eyebrows and eyelashes begin to appear. During this time, the woman may feel the fetus move. Later on, the movements will become stronger.

Fifth Month

During the fifth month, the length of the fetus increases to 10 inches and the weight to about 1 pound. Hair and nails appear. The hands are able to grip. Fat deposits begin to appear beneath the wrinkly skin.

Sixth Month

At six months, the fetus is 12 inches long and weighs about 1½ pounds. The eyes open and close. Muscles in the arms and legs are strong. The woman may feel the fetus kicking against the abdominal wall.

The woman's uterus and abdomen enlarge to hold the growing fetus. Her intestines and bladder are pushed aside to make room for the growth. This marks the end of the second trimester.

Seventh Month

The fetus is about 15 inches long and weighs approximately 2½ pounds by the seventh month. It will gain most of its weight during the last 13 weeks of development. The fetus is covered with a thick white protective coating called vernix. The nervous, circulatory, and other systems have become mature enough to give the fetus a two out of three chance of survival if born now. However, there is a much better chance of survival if it is born at full term.

Eighth Month

At the eighth month, length is 16½ inches. Weight is 4 pounds. The fetus hears sounds and may be startled by sudden noises.

The size of the fetus now makes it more difficult for the woman to carry it. Her abdomen is stretched considerably. The top of the uterus pushes against the woman's diaphragm, causing shortness of breath.

Ninth Month

During the ninth month, an increase in fat under the skin makes the fetus look less wrinkled. The downy fuzz disappears. The weight gain is ½ pound each week. The fetus is now at full term, or ready to be born. Its weight is about 7½ pounds, and its length is approximately 20 inches. However, a normal fetus can range in weight from 5½ pounds to 10 pounds.

During the last month, the fetus settles head down in the uterus. For the woman, breathing becomes somewhat easier, but more pressure is put on the bladder.

Most babies are born about 280 days after the first day of the woman's last normal menstrual period. The approximate birth date is calculated by counting ahead nine months from the first day of the last menstrual period and adding seven days.

◆◆ Common Discomforts

Most healthy women experience only minor discomforts during pregnancy. Some of these are more common during the first trimester of pregnancy, while others occur primarily in the last trimester. Usually the doctor or nurse-midwife can recommend exercises or other techniques to help relieve the discomfort.

- Nausea is a common discomfort for many women during the first trimester of pregnancy. Eating a few dry crackers before getting up in the morning can help prevent the nausea. Also, it may help to wait awhile before drinking any liquids. Some women may feel nauseated in the afternoon or early evening. Small, frequent meals throughout the day are usually better than large ones. For some women, the nausea reaches the point of vomiting. If a woman is so nauseated that she cannot eat, she is unable to nourish herself or to stay hydrated. She and her doctor should find a way to relieve the sickness. Most doctors try to avoid medications because of risk to the developing child.
- An increased need for sleep is another common condition during the first trimester. The woman's body is adjusting to the chemical changes that occur during

pregnancy. During the final months of pregnancy, a woman may experience fatigue from carrying extra weight. She can relieve both sleepiness and fatigue by taking naps or resting during the day.

- Frequent urination is an early sign of pregnancy. It usually occurs again during the third trimester as the expanding uterus presses on the bladder.
- Shortness of breath may occur during the third trimester as the top of the uterus presses against the diaphragm. Breathing usually becomes easier when the fetus settles head down in the uterus.
- Heartburn, a burning sensation in the esophagus, is partly caused by the uterus shifting the position of the stomach. Heartburn can be helped by avoiding large or fatty meals and sitting erect. Sometimes the doctor recommends antacids.
- Muscle cramps may occur in the legs during the last trimester. Some women are awakened at night by a sudden muscle cramp. This usually can be relieved by gentle stretching exercises. Some doctors recommend a calcium supplement to help prevent leg cramps.
- Back pain is usually caused by a change in posture as the pregnancy progresses. To help prevent back pain, women can do special exercises to strengthen the back and abdominal muscles. They should also avoid wearing high-heeled shoes and should bend their knees when lifting heavy objects. This will prevent putting extra strain on the back. If back pain does occur, the doctor or nurse-midwife can recommend specific exercises for backaches.
- Varicose veins can occur in the legs when pressure causes the blood vessels to become enlarged or swollen. It helps to rest with the feet and legs elevated. Support hose can also help prevent the swelling.

DECISIONS ◆
◆ DECISIONS

Danielle was looking forward to having a baby, but now she is worried. She is three months pregnant and feels tired all the time. She often feels sick. Her stomach sometimes hurts when she is hungry, yet she feels too sick to eat. She is terrified that something is wrong. What do you think she should do? Why?

More About. As the fetus grows and the organs become more crowded, the pregnant woman may find it necessary to eat small, frequent meals and snacks to avoid indigestion.

Activity. Have students ask their mothers and grandmothers what they did to prevent or relieve pregnancy discomforts. Ask students to read current articles about the discomforts. Compare past and current methods for similarities and differences.

During pregnancy, a woman must learn to "listen" to her body. She may need to rest or nap during the day, especially during the final weeks of pregnancy.

Remember that almost all of these discomforts disappear as the body adjusts to pregnancy or after the baby is born.

❖ Emotional Changes

Mood swings can occur throughout pregnancy. Even though a woman may be enthusiastic about the pregnancy one day, she may be worried or depressed the next day. These mood swings are caused by the hormonal changes that are taking place in the woman's body. Such swings may also result from normal fears many women have about becoming a parent. For example, a first-time mother-to-be may worry about whether she will be a good parent. A woman who plans to continue working full-time may wonder how she will be able to balance work and family life.

Even though a father-to-be does not personally experience pregnancy, he is affected by his partner's moods and physical condition. He may find that she needs a great deal more understanding and emotional support from him than usual. At the same time, he may be going through mood swings of his own. Although he may be excited about his future child, he may be concerned about his ability to be a good father. He may worry about bearing the full responsibility of supporting his family, at least for awhile. He may not feel qualified to do his share of child care and household chores.

Sometimes the father-to-be may feel left out during the woman's pregnancy. The woman, whose body is changing in such a dramatic way, gets all the attention from family and friends. The man may respond with jealousy or anger. He wants people—especially his partner—to notice that his role as the father is just as important as that of the mother.

Both partners should talk about their feelings with one another. By providing love and support, they can help each other adjust to this new role of parenthood. Sometimes it helps to talk about their feelings with an understanding relative or friend. They should also discuss any concerns or fears with the doctor or nurse-midwife during the woman's regular medical checkups.

Problem Solving. Ask students to suggest ways that an expectant father can be helped to feel an important part of his partner's pregnancy. What can the expectant mother do? What can friends and relatives do? What can the expectant father do?

Activity. Have students ask their parents how they felt both physically and emotionally during the pregnancy. The responses can be shared in class or written in a parenting journal.

Medical Care During Pregnancy

If a woman suspects she is pregnant, she should visit a doctor or health clinic as soon as possible. It is important to receive regular medical care throughout the pregnancy. This helps ensure the health of both the mother-to-be and the developing child.

◆◆ The First Medical Examination

During the first examination, the doctor takes a complete medical history. He or she records information about any previous preg-

During the first medical exam, the doctor will ask questions about the woman's medical history. This information can alert the doctor to any problems that may occur during the pregnancy.

nancies, information about any previous deliveries, chronic health problems, medications, and the woman's general level of activity. Past illnesses and operations and family medical history are also recorded.

After the woman has been weighed and measured, a complete head-to-toe physical examination follows. A urine sample will be checked for sugar and the condition of the kidneys. A technician draws blood for various blood tests that are very important in caring for a pregnant woman and developing child.

One blood test indicates the woman's blood type. It also reveals the Rh factor. The **Rh factor** is a substance that is present in the blood of 85 percent of the population. See "Rh Factor" on the next page.

Another blood test helps the doctor detect **anemia,** a condition caused by a shortage of red blood cells. An anemic woman requires additional iron during pregnancy because iron is necessary for the formation of new red blood cells. Because a baby needs a supply of iron that will last for several months after birth, prospective mothers supply this nutrient through a diet rich in iron. Sometimes the doctor will prescribe vitamin and mineral supplements that contain iron.

The pelvic examination is part of a complete physical examination. The woman dresses in a hospital gown. The nurse drapes her with a sheet. Then, lying on the examining table, the woman places her heels in stirrups that extend out from the table. She drops her knees wide apart to enable the doctor to feel and check the uterus and the vagina. The **vagina** (vuh-JY-nuh) is an elastic, tubular organ that leads from the uterus to the outside of the female body. It is the birth canal through which a baby is delivered.

◆◆ *Health & Safety* ◆◆

Rh Factor

Routine blood tests that are conducted as part of the prenatal medical examination also check for the Rh factor. The presence or absence of this substance is an inherited trait. People with the Rh factor are said to be Rh positive (Rh+). The 15 percent of the population whose blood does not contain this substance are said to be Rh negative (Rh−).

People who are Rh− are perfectly healthy. However, the absence of the Rh factor presents a problem for some pregnant women. If conception results for an Rh− woman and an Rh+ man, the developing child will be Rh+. The Rh+ fetus produces substances that enter the pregnant woman's blood. The woman's body then develops a defense system of antibodies that fights these substances. This defense system can harm the fetus, especially if it is the second pregnancy. Without medical treatment, the fetal red blood cells will be killed. Jaundice, anemia, brain damage, or death of the fetus could result.

Treatment is effective when the doctor knows about the problem ahead of time. For this reason, doctors always test for the Rh factor in pregnant women. A medication called RhoGAM is given to Rh− pregnant women to prevent complications. The vaccine stops Rh− women from producing the antibodies. Women should remind their doctors that they are Rh−, especially if they are dealing with several doctors in a group practice or public clinic.

During the examination, the doctor checks for evidence of an increase in the size of the uterus. Measurements of the pelvis are taken to be sure the bony structure is large enough for a baby's head to pass through during childbirth.

The doctor examines the **cervix,** the narrow lower end of the uterus leading to the vagina. A cancer test, called a **Pap smear,** is also done. This is a test every woman should have at least once a year. It is used to detect the early stage of cancer of the cervix.

From all this questioning, examining, and testing, the doctor determines whether the woman is pregnant and in good physical condition for a pregnancy and delivery. If the woman is pregnant, the doctor will estimate the due date for the birth. This will be about 280 days from the beginning of the pregnant woman's last menstrual period. It is a little more than nine calendar months. However, a due date is only an approximate date. About half of all babies are born within two weeks of this date. The other half are born three to six weeks before or after this date.

High-Risk Pregnancies

Some women fall into a high-risk category of pregnancy. That is, they have certain conditions that could result in problems during pregnancy. If undetected or untreated, these conditions could affect the health or the life of the fetus.

Although some medical problems cannot be predicted in advance, others can be. Here are some factors that can result in high-risk pregnancies:

- Being under age seventeen, since young mothers are more likely to have babies with low birth weight.

More About. Most doctors calculate the duration of a pregnancy based on gestational age, which is measured from the first day of the last menstrual period. This is about two weeks before actual fertilization and is about 9.3 months or 40 weeks.

Problem Solving. Divide class into groups and have each group research a high-risk factor of pregnancy. How serious is the risk to the mother and to the fetus? What tests or treatment may be necessary? How can complications be prevented?

Around the World

Midwives

Sometimes an idea that seems very new is actually quite old. The word *midwife* comes from two Old English words. *Mid* meant "with," and *wif* meant "woman",

In colonial America, men were not usually allowed to deliver babies because of women's modesty. Instead, female midwives were used. As advances were made in medical and surgical procedures, however, doctors in the United States demanded that the job of delivering babies be turned over to them. One reason was that most midwives were not trained in childbirth procedures. By 1930, most states had passed laws restricting the practice of midwifery. In that same year, only 15 percent of all newborns were delivered by midwives. By 1970, midwives delivered less than 1 percent of all babies born in the United States.

In many other countries, midwives have always been preferred for delivering a baby. England, Germany, Sweden, and the Netherlands are just a few of the European countries that rely on midwives who are trained health care professionals. In Asia, Africa, and Latin America, nonprofessional midwives provide care for many women.

Today in the United States, midwives are again becoming popular. Modern midwives are registered nurses with specialized training in obstetrics and prenatal care. Many nurse-midwives prefer to be involved only in low-risk pregnancies. However, a physician can be consulted if complications occur. A nurse-midwife's fee is usually lower than a doctor's. This helps reduce the high cost of a routine delivery. In many cases, nurse-midwives provide a very personal approach to prenatal care and childbirth for mothers-to-be.

- Being over age thirty-five, and especially over forty.
- Being severely underweight or overweight.
- Having a serious medical problem, such as heart disease or diabetes.
- Having a family history of genetic disorders.
- Having an Rh incompatibility with one's partner.
- Having a previous history of pregnancy problems.

It is important for the doctor to identify such factors during the initial medical examination. Then the woman can be carefully monitored throughout the pregnancy. Medical treatment often can prevent serious problems from developing in high-risk pregnancies, so that the woman can give birth to a healthy baby.

❖ Regular Checkups

After the first medical examination, a regular schedule of checkups is planned for the pregnant woman. A common schedule is one checkup per month until the eighth month. Then checkups are usually more frequent. This careful monitoring improves the chances for a safe pregnancy and a healthy baby.

The doctor or nurse-midwife should answer any questions the woman has during the checkups. She or he may also answer questions on the telephone between office visits. If requested, the doctor may suggest the name of a clinic where a public health nurse can answer many questions.

During office visits, the doctor or nurse-midwife provides the mother-to-be with important advice on food and nutrition, exercise, weight gain, and health concerns. Chapter 9 provides more information on prenatal care.

Activity. Have students gather information about the availability of nurse-midwives in your community. How can they be located? Where do they practice? What are their fees?

Emphasize. Regular medical checkups are important throughout pregnancy.
Discuss. Have the class make a list of questions that couples might want to ask during a medical examination.

The father-to-be is also welcome at the doctor's office or clinic during prenatal visits. He, too, can talk to the doctor or nurse-midwife to get a better understanding of the pregnancy. Many men want to be included in the birth of their child. The mother-to-be should make every effort to include her partner in the process. She can share her joys and concerns with him and explain what she is learning about the pregnancy.

◆◆ Prenatal Tests

Some prenatal tests are done routinely to monitor the health of the pregnant woman or the development of the fetus. Others are performed if the doctor suspects a complication or needs more information.

With modern technology, diagnostic tests can be performed on the fetus while it is still in the uterus. These tests can indicate whether the fetus has any type of birth defect. They also help the doctor decide whether special medical treatment might be needed before or after the birth.

Some birth defects are hereditary, as you learned in Chapter 7. Others can be caused by exposure to certain diseases, drugs, radiation, or toxic substances. Even though some of these hazards may not be harmful to the pregnant woman, they can severely damage the fetus. Moreover, the risk of damage is greatest during the first trimester when the woman may not know that she is pregnant. Because early development is the foundation for later development, any damage to the early cells can result in one or more severe defects. You will learn more about health hazards to the developing child in Chapter 9.

Prenatal diagnostic techniques can detect more than 100 birth defects. For many couples, the tests can end their worries by showing that their future child will not be born

with a birth defect. For other couples, the tests can enable treatment to be started even before the child is born. When the tests show that the fetus has severe defects, the couple must use their own moral and religious beliefs to make a decision about continuing the pregnancy.

Three of the more commonly conducted prenatal tests are ultrasonography, amniocentesis, and chorionic villus sampling.

Ultrasonography

Ultrasonography (uhl-truh-suh-NOG-ruh-fee) is a procedure in which high-frequency sound waves are bounced off the developing fetus to produce a video image, or sonogram. The doctor can use this technique to view the developmental progress of the fetus during pregnancy.

The ultrasound image will show whether or not the fetus is developing according to schedule. Certain birth defects, such as those involving the skeleton and internal organs, can be identified. The procedure will also reveal the presence of more than one fetus. If

DECISIONS ◆ ◆ DECISIONS

Aretha is having an ultrasonogram in her doctor's office. Although her pregnancy has been progressing normally, Aretha's health history puts her in the high-risk pregnancy category. After viewing the video image, her doctor says that the fetus is developing according to schedule. Then the doctor asks Aretha whether she and her husband would like to know the gender of their baby. How do you think she should respond? Why?

More About. Around the end of the first trimester, the doctor and parents-to-be can hear the fetal heartbeat with the aid of a special microphone.

Activity. Obtain an ultrasound image of a fetus. Have students study it to see if they can distinguish various parts of the body, the internal organs, and the gender of the fetus.

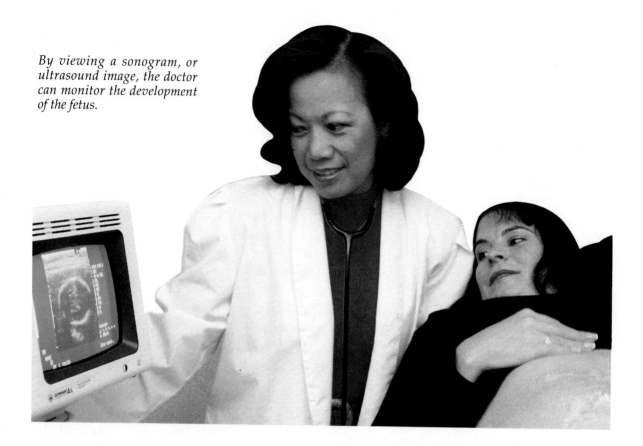

By viewing a sonogram, or ultrasound image, the doctor can monitor the development of the fetus.

there is more than one, parents and the doctor or nurse-midwife can prepare for multiple births. Even the gender of a developing fetus can often be determined.

Ultrasonography is used with other medical procedures, such as amniocentesis. The video image helps guide the doctor when taking test samples from the uterus or even operating on the fetus within the uterus.

Although ultrasonography is considered a safe procedure, it may have some unknown risks. For this reason, scans done without a medical reason are not recommended.

Amniocentesis

Amniocentesis (am-nee-oh-sen-TEE-sis) is a technique that enables doctors to check for abnormal chromosomes in the fetus that might cause birth defects. This test is recommended for pregnant women who are over the age of thirty-five or who have a family history of birth defects. Amniocentesis is performed after the fourteenth week of pregnancy.

In this procedure, the doctor inserts a special needle through the walls of the mother's abdomen and uterus with the aid of ultrasonography. The doctor then withdraws a small amount of the amniotic fluid that surrounds the fetus in the uterus. The fluid contains cells from the fetus. The chromosomes in these cells are checked for genetic defects. The results of the lab work are available within three to four weeks. This procedure can detect certain birth defects, such as Down syndrome, that cannot be identified through

Discuss. Ask students if they would want to know the gender of their child from an ultrasound image or would they rather wait until the actual birth.

More About. Amniocentesis can successfully diagnose the presence of Down syndrome, neurological problems, kidney disorders, and metabolic disorders. It can determine gender which is helpful if there is a risk of a gender-linked disorder.

ultrasonography. Amniocentesis in late pregnancy provides information about fetal lung maturity. This is beneficial if there is a possibility of an early delivery.

Amniocentesis involves some risk to both mother and fetus. As a result, pregnant women who are not in certain high-risk categories do not need to undergo amniocentesis.

Chorionic Villus Sampling

Another technique to test for genetic abnormalities is **chorionic** (KOR-ee-ahn-ik) **villus sampling (CVS).** For this test, ultrasonography is used to guide a catheter, or tubelike device, through the vagina into the uterus. With the catheter, the doctor withdraws a small amount of tissue from the villi. Villi are minute pieces of tissue that protrude from the chorion, the membrane that covers the developing cells. Laboratory analysis of these villi indicates whether any defective chromosomes are present. This procedure can detect the same birth defects that amniocentesis can.

CVS is done at the tenth week of pregnancy. The results of this test are available more quickly than those of amniocentesis.

❖ Termination of a Pregnancy

About one in four pregnancies ends spontaneously, usually during the first trimester. This can result from some defect in the fertilized ovum or from physical problems. A pregnancy also can be terminated by medical procedures.

Miscarriage

Miscarriages are common, especially during the first three months of pregnancy. A **miscarriage** is the body's way of expelling the embryo or fetus before it can fully develop. Sometimes a woman may have a miscarriage before she even knows she is pregnant.

Developing a positive self-concept before one becomes a parent is extremely important to the future parent-child relationship. Adults who can see themselves as successful parents will likely become successful parents. They will be able to apply their parenting skills with confidence and understanding.

Some miscarriages happen because the fertilized ovum does not implant itself correctly in the lining of the uterus. Others result from chromosomal abnormalities. Some women may have physical problems that prevent them from carrying the fetus to full term. Such problems include infection and tumors.

Bleeding or cramps during pregnancy can signal a miscarriage. A woman who thinks she may be having a miscarriage should call her doctor immediately. She may be advised to go to bed and stay there until the bleeding stops. Sometimes, with care, she will be able to carry the fetus to term.

Some women may experience slight bleeding or a dark vaginal discharge during pregnancy. This may be unrelated to a miscarriage. However, a woman who has any type of vaginal bleeding should always check with her doctor.

Bleeding accompanied by severe abdominal cramps is a warning that a miscarriage may occur. The woman's doctor will want to examine her as soon as possible. If she does miscarry, she may have to go to the hospital. Then the doctor will make sure no tissue is left in the uterus. Sometimes the doctor performs a medical procedure called a *D and C* (dilation and curettage). This is performed by scraping the lining of the uterus to remove any remaining fetal tissue.

Having a miscarriage can be a very emotional experience for both partners. They may experience great disappointment and grief upon the loss of their future baby. Talking about their feelings with each other, the doctor, a religious counselor, family, or friends can help them express their sorrow. Most women who have a miscarriage can have successful pregnancies in the future.

Abortion

Some pregnancies are terminated by abortion. Abortion is the removal of an embryo or fetus from the uterus in order to end a pregnancy. A doctor may recommend an abortion because the pregnancy poses a high risk to the woman's health. An abortion that is performed in the first trimester of pregnancy is considered medically safe for the woman. After the twelfth week of pregnancy, abortion involves greater medical risks.

Although abortion is a physical procedure, it can have a great emotional impact as well. Some women may feel very guilty, angry, or sad after choosing to have an abortion. They may become depressed over the loss of the future child. Other women may feel a sense of relief in having the situation resolved.

Abortion is a very controversial topic. Some people believe that abortion should never be allowed. Others believe that women should have the legal option to end a pregnancy. Still others believe that abortion should be permitted only in life-threatening situations.

The decision to end a pregnancy should be carefully considered because abortion is final. The woman and her partner should discuss the options with their families, the doctor, and religious counselor. The decision should be based on one's values and religious beliefs.

◆◆ Warning Signals During Pregnancy

Most women have very few problems during pregnancy, but some do develop complications. Early recognition and treatment improve the chances of a good outcome. A pregnant woman should report any of the following symptoms to her doctor immediately.

- Vaginal bleeding.
- Sudden swelling of the face and hands.
- Severe and persistent vomiting.
- Severe and persistent headaches.
- Dimming or blurring of vision.
- Fever.
- Painful urination.
- Preterm labor, such as a low backache, cramps, or uterine contractions.
- Absence of fetal movements for a six-hour period during the last trimester.
- Discharge of fluids from the vagina.

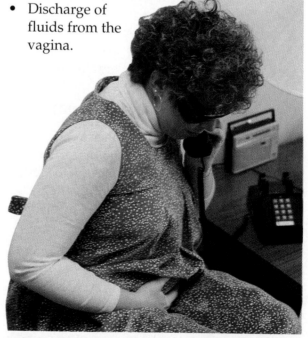

A pregnant woman should report any warning signs immediately to her doctor. Many of these problems can be corrected if treated promptly.

CHAPTER 8 REVIEW

Summary

- Early signs of pregnancy include a missed menstrual period, enlarged breasts, nausea, and increased urination.

- A woman who gets a positive result from a home pregnancy test should visit a clinic or doctor to confirm the pregnancy and receive prenatal care.

- Prenatal development is divided into three stages: zygot, embryo, and fetus.

- A woman experiences body changes, minor discomforts, and possibly mood swings during pregnancy.

- Regular medical checkups throughout pregnancy are important to ensure the health of the pregnant woman and the fetus.

- The first medical examination for a pregnant woman includes a medical history, blood and urine tests, and a pelvic examination.

- Prenatal tests can monitor the development of the fetus and the health of the mother.

- Women experiencing any warning signs of complications in a pregnancy should consult their doctor immediately.

Questions

p. 135 **1.** What are three indications of pregnancy?

p. 136 **2.** What should a woman do as soon as she suspects she is pregnant?

p. 137 **3.** List and describe the three stages of prenatal development.

p. 138 **4.** What purpose does the placenta and umbilical cord serve?

p. 139 **5.** What body changes does a woman experience in each of the three trimesters of pregnancy?

6. How may a father-to-be be affected by his partner's emotional and physical changes during pregnancy? p. 145

7. What information is a doctor seeking during the first medical examination of pregnancy? p. 146

8. At what ages are women most likely to have high-risk pregnancies? p. 147

9. What information can an ultrasound image provide? p. 149

10. Why do some miscarriages occur? p. 151

11. What are some of the danger signs that a pregnant woman should be alarmed about? p. 152

Activities

1. Make a chart showing the development that occurs in each stage of prenatal development.

2. Find out what an ectopic pregnancy is. Then draw a diagram showing where a fertilized ovum implants in a normal pregnancy and where it implants in an ectopic pregnancy.

3. Write what life inside the uterus might be like from the fetus' point of view.

4. Calculate the approximate due date of a pregnant woman whose last menstrual period began on August 14.

Think About

1. Why is prenatal care as important during the early months of pregnancy as during the later months?

2. Why is it helpful to understand the stages of prenatal development and the growth that occurs in each stage?

CHAPTER 9

Prenatal Care

Objectives

This chapter will help you to:
- Describe the guidelines to follow when choosing nutritious meals and snacks during pregnancy.
- Discuss weight gain during pregnancy.
- Explain the importance of activity and rest during pregnancy.
- List specific substances, diseases, and environmental hazards that can be harmful to the fetus.

Vocabulary

nutrients
Food Guide Pyramid
fetal alcohol syndrome (FAS)
rubella
chlamydia
acquired immunodeficiency
    syndrome (AIDS)
pregnancy induced
    hypertension (PIH)

"Ying and I are thinking about having a child," says Jenny Leung. "We both smoke—and I recently read an article that described the harmful effects of tobacco on a developing fetus. I've decided to stop smoking even before I get pregnant. I want Ying to stop smoking, too."

"I'm pleased that Jenny is going to stop smoking," says Ying, "since tobacco can increase the chances of a baby being born too soon. Jenny has been urging me to quit, too—but I think I'll wait until after the baby is born. I don't see how my smoking can harm the baby during Jenny's pregnancy."

"Ying, perhaps we should find out more information about the harmful effects of smoking," replies Jenny. "I want to be sure that our baby will be as healthy as possible."

Ying and Jenny are concerned about health risks to their future child. They know that their own behavior can seriously affect whether or not they have a healthy baby.

A Healthy Pregnancy

At no other time in life is a child as dependent on the mother as during the prenatal period. The health of the developing fetus is directly affected by the health and well-being of the mother. All nourishment for the fetus must come from the mother through the placenta. The placenta also passes along any harmful substances, such as alcohol and drugs, to the fetus.

To have a healthy baby, a pregnant woman should have regular medical checkups throughout her pregnancy. She should eat nutritious meals and snacks, exercise regularly, and get enough rest. Most important, she should avoid substances and diseases that can seriously harm the developing child.

Healthy Eating During Pregnancy

A woman should be healthy and well nourished before she decides to become pregnant. She should be of normal weight for her build and height. A healthy woman is likely to have a healthy baby.

Many women do not have a well-balanced diet because they do not know how to choose nutritious meals and snacks. Others select food unwisely because they want to be thin. Some women consume too many foods that do not provide essential **nutrients** (NOO-tree-

unts). These are chemicals the body must have in order to function, grow, repair itself, and produce energy. Foods such as french fries, potato chips, candy, and soft drinks lack many of the nutrients necessary for good health.

An inadequate diet can cause problems for both the mother and the fetus throughout pregnancy. If the fetus does not receive essential nutrients, its growth can be retarded and even death can occur. Without adequate nutrition, the woman can have medical complications during pregnancy.

The father-to-be plays an active role in good nutrition for the prospective mother and the fetus. A couple who are expecting a child

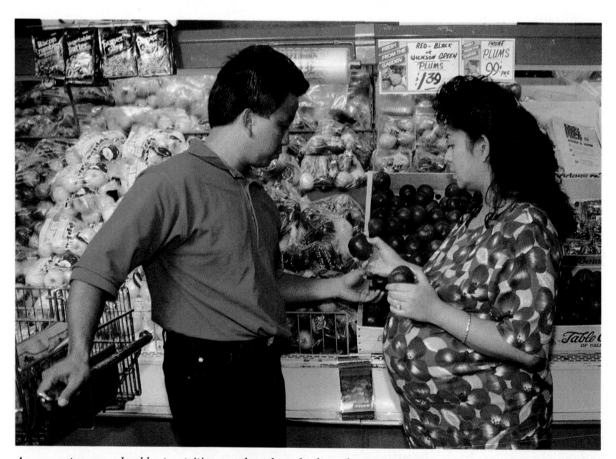

A pregnant woman should eat nutritious meals and snacks throughout pregnancy. This will enable the fetus to get the proper nutrition for growth and development.

Discuss. Ask students to think of conditions that could cause a woman to be malnourished. What about the conditions of anorexia nervosa, bulimia, and excessive dieting? Why are many teens at risk of being malnourished?

Emphasize. "You're eating for two" is a true statement for pregnant women. However, they should choose increased amounts of nutritious meals and snacks, not double their intake of food.

can work together to plan interesting and varied meals that meet the woman's diet requirements. A prospective father might help with the shopping and food preparation. Most important, he can encourage his partner to eat nutritious foods.

❧ A Balanced Diet

Well-balanced meals contain six essential nutrients: proteins, carbohydrates, fats, vitamins, minerals, and water. Being well nourished during pregnancy means following the **Food Guide Pyramid.** This food guide tells how many servings a person should eat from each of the main food groups. See the chart on the next page.

Women who are pregnant or breast-feeding a baby need the following servings each day:

- Bread, Cereal, Rice, and Pasta Group: 6 to 9 servings.
- Vegetable Group: 3 to 4 servings.
- Fruit Group: 2 to 3 servings.
- Milk, Yogurt, and Cheese Group: 3 or more servings.
- Meat, Poultry, Fish, Dry Beans, Eggs, and Nuts Group: 2 to 3 servings.

Some examples of average serving sizes of foods in each group are also given on the chart.

Proteins

Meat, poultry, fish, eggs, beans, and milk contain proteins. Proteins are needed for the growth of new cells in the fetus as well as in the mother's body. A lack of protein during pregnancy increases the chances of physical and mental retardation in the developing infant. A woman who is pregnant needs about 50 percent more protein per day than she needs when she is not pregnant.

Carbohydrates

Breads, cereals, fruits, and vegetables contain carbohydrates. These are good sources of energy. A woman should increase her carbohydrate intake somewhat during pregnancy.

Carbohydrates are also found in "empty-calorie" foods, such as candy, soft drinks, and sweet desserts. These foods have calories but few nutrients. They should not be eaten in place of foods that supply necessary nutrients.

Fats

Although some fat in the diet is necessary, eating extra fat is not recommended. Fats add calories, and many nutritionists agree that eating too many fatty foods may be harmful to the circulatory system. Fatty foods are also difficult to digest.

Fat is hidden in many foods, such as meat, poultry, eggs, dairy products, and baked goods. Butter, margarine, and oils are all fats.

A pregnant woman should likewise limit her intake of french fries, potato chips, donuts, and other fried foods as much as possible. Instead, she should choose foods that have been broiled, steamed, roasted, or baked.

◆ ◆ *Self-Esteem* ◆ ◆

Pregnancy is a time when parents-to-be may doubt their ability to nurture and care for their future child. By learning all they can about how children develop, they will be able to enjoy watching their own child grow. They will be better prepared to offer encouragement and support at each stage of the child's development.

Problem Solving. Have students list all the foods they have eaten in the last 24 hours. Then ask: Did you get the necessary servings of each food group? If not, what is lacking?
Activity. Ask students why carbohydrates found in breads, cereals, fruits, and vegetables are healthier than carbohydrates found in candy, soft drinks, and sweet desserts. Have students create a 3-D display of empty-calorie food wrappers, bags, boxes, and cans.

Food Guide Pyramid
A Guide to Daily Food Choices

Fats, Oils, & Sweets
Use sparingly

KEY: Symbols show fats, oils, and added sugars in foods.
○ Fat (naturally occurring and added)   ▽ Sugars (added)

Milk, Yogurt, & Cheese Group
2–3 servings

Meat, Poultry, Fish, Dry Beans, Eggs, & Nuts Group
2–3 servings

Vegetable Group
3–5 servings

Fruit Group
2–4 servings

Bread, Cereal, Rice, & Pasta Group
6–11 servings

What Counts as One Serving?

Bread, Cereals, Rice, and Pasta
- 1 slice of bread
- ½ cup cooked cereal, rice, or pasta
- 1 ounce ready-to-eat cereal

Vegetables
- ½ cup chopped raw or cooked vegetables
- 1 cup leafy raw vegetables
- ¾ cup vegetable juice

Fruits
- 1 medium whole fruit or melon wedge
- ½ cup chopped, cooked, or canned fruit
- ¼ cup dried fruit
- ¾ cup fruit juice

How Many Servings Do You Need Each Day?

Food Group	Women and some older adults	Children, teen girls, active women, most men	Teen boys and active men
Bread	6	9	11
Vegetable	3	4	5
Fruit	2	3	4
Milk	2–3*	2–3*	2–3*
Meat	2, for a total of 5 ounces	2, for a total of 6 ounces	3, for a total of 7 ounces

*Women who are pregnant or breastfeeding, teenagers, and young adults to age 24 need 3 servings of the milk group.

Milk, Yogurt, and Cheese
- 1 cup milk or yogurt
- 1½-ounces ripened cheese
- 2 ounces process cheese

Meat, Poultry, Fish, Dry Beans, Eggs, and Nuts
- 2½ to 3 ounces cooked lean meat, poultry, or fish (An average hamburger is about 3 ounces.)
- The following equal 1 ounce of lean meat:
  ½ cup cooked dry beans
  1 egg
  2 tablespoons peanut butter

Activity. Have students plan five days of healthy meals and snacks for a pregnant woman, using the Food Guide Pyramid. If possible, display a poster of the Food Guide Pyramid for students to observe and remember.

Discuss. What are some foods that are high in fat and calories? (Every gram of fat contains nine calories compared to only four calories per gram of the other nutrients.)

Vitamins

A well-balanced selection of foods from the Food Guide Pyramid is the best source of essential vitamins. They are needed to regulate body functions, to help protect against infection and disease, and to promote good health. Fresh fruits and vegetables, whole-grain breads and cereals, and milk are excellent sources of vitamins.

Most doctors also prescribe a prenatal vitamin supplement. This helps ensure that a pregnant woman receives the daily essential vitamins. However, she should take supplemental vitamins only as directed by a doctor. Large amounts of certain vitamins can be harmful.

Minerals

Minerals are required for developing strong bones and teeth, maintaining healthy blood, and regulating body fluids. Minerals are found in a variety of foods.

Calcium is the mineral needed for strong bones and teeth. Milk and milk products are excellent sources of calcium. Therefore, a high intake of foods from the milk group is essential during pregnancy. Skim milk is especially healthful because it has all the essential nutrients of whole milk but none of the fat. Even if a pregnant woman does not enjoy the flavor of milk, she should include a quart a day in her diet. She can use milk in soups, cereals, or milk shakes. Milk products such as low-fat yogurt and cheese can also make up part of the daily requirement.

During pregnancy, a woman's red blood cells increase in volume up to 45 percent. During the last trimester of pregnancy, the fetus stores enough iron in its body to last for the first six months after birth. Thus a woman needs a high level of iron during pregnancy. A woman who does not have enough iron in her blood has anemia, a condition that causes her to feel tired. Iron is found in red meats,

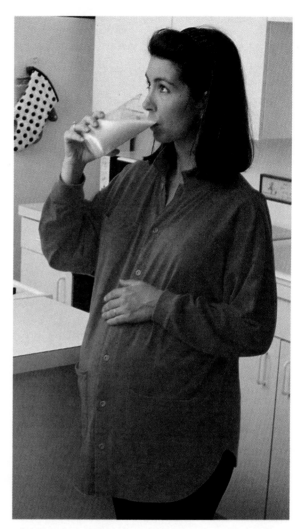

Low-fat milk, yogurt, and cheese are good sources of calcium. A pregnant woman needs three or more servings from this food group every day.

liver, eggs, whole-grain cereals, and some green vegetables. Many doctors prescribe iron supplements because a pregnant woman's iron requirement is so high.

Salt, or sodium chloride, is important to the diet in moderation. A doctor may recommend reducing salt intake if too much swelling occurs in the ankles, hands, or feet. If so, a pregnant woman should cook food without salt. She should also read labels carefully because canned, frozen, and processed foods are often high in salt.

Water

Water is especially important in a pregnant woman's diet because it helps remove wastes from her body and from the fetus. Drinking eight glasses of water, juice, and other liquids each day is essential to good health.

◆◆ Weight Gain

Because of social pressures to be thin, some women may feel or think of themselves as fat while they are pregnant. This is a false and unhealthy attitude toward pregnancy. Weight gain during pregnancy is a normal physical event that should not be confused with being overweight.

Recent studies show that babies who weigh at least 7 pounds at birth are healthier, stronger, and have a far better chance of survival than do smaller babies. The amount of weight a pregnant woman should gain varies according to her height and her weight before becoming pregnant. The average recommended weight gain is 25 to 35 pounds. However, most doctors agree that weight gains of as much as 40 pounds are not dangerous. On the other hand, these doctors stress that weight gain should come from eating healthful, nutritious foods. Weight gain should not come from eating foods that are high in sugar or fat and low in nutritional value.

Doctors recommend a slow, steady weight gain. During the first trimester, they suggest that pregnant women gain 2 to 4 pounds. After that, 1 pound per week is generally best. Gaining too fast or too slowly suggests a problem pregnancy.

A weight gain of 28 pounds may seem like a great deal. However, many tissues increase in size or amount to support the life of the fetus. The chart on the next page shows how an average weight gain is distributed during pregnancy.

Extremely large weight gains do not benefit either the pregnant woman or the fetus. Carrying too much weight can strain the woman's circulatory system, especially if she is overweight at the outset. In addition, a woman who is overweight after her baby is born may feel depressed because she has so much weight to lose.

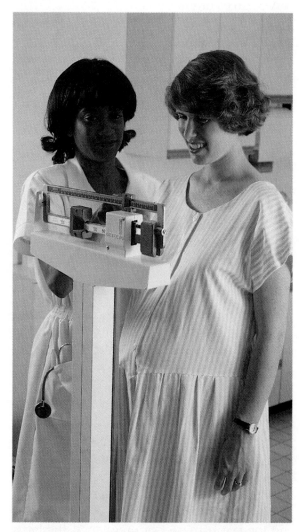

Pregnancy is not the time for a woman to avoid gaining weight. A weight gain of 25 to 35 pounds is considered healthy for most pregnant women.

Discuss. Why is it important for a woman to gain at least 25 pounds during pregnancy? Why is it not good for her to gain more than 40 pounds?

Activity. Have students compare the calories contained in various types of snack foods. Then have them suggest healthy, but low-calorie, snacks for a pregnant woman.

◆ ◆ Health & Safety ◆ ◆

Pregnancy Weight Gain and Loss

How much weight should a pregnant woman expect to gain? In a healthy pregnancy, the average mother-to-be gains 25 to 28 pounds. Here is how that weight breaks down:

	Weight in Pounds
Fetus	7.5
Uterus	2.0
Placenta	1.5
Amniotic fluid	2.0
Blood volume	3.0
Extracellular fluid	2.0
Breast tissue	1.0
Body fat	9.0
Total	**28.0**

During the first three months of pregnancy, a woman should gain about 2 to 4 pounds. After that, she should expect to gain about a pound a week for the remainder of the pregnancy.

At the birth, the baby's weight and the amount of fluid lost during delivery may add up to an immediate 10-pound loss. Generally, the mother loses another 5 pounds the first month after the baby is born. It takes most women about 6 to 12 months to lose the rest of the weight. After all, it takes 9 months to gain the weight needed for a healthy pregnancy. It can take just as long to lose it.

◆◆ Health Concerns and Food

In the early stages of pregnancy, a woman's body must adjust to many physical changes. As a result, she may experience nausea. As noted in Chapter 8, to control the problem, she might eat a cracker or dry toast to settle her stomach. Eating small meals throughout the day should also help. Above all, she should not stop eating. She should try to control her nausea by her choice of foods rather than by resorting to drugs that might harm the fetus.

Constipation is common toward the end of pregnancy. Exercise, rest, and a high-fiber diet with more fruit and plenty of fluids might relieve this problem. Laxatives should not be used without a doctor's guidance.

Also, toward the end of pregnancy, heartburn and indigestion may be common. The fetus is growing rapidly and tends to push on the surrounding digestive organs. It may help to eat smaller, more frequent meals and to eat slowly. Spicy foods, fatty foods, and foods that cause gas may cause discomfort. A pregnant woman can stop eating these foods one by one to find out which is causing the problem.

Some pregnant women have a strong desire for certain foods. If these women eat a balanced diet, this craving should pass.

Discuss. Using the pregnancy weight gain and loss chart, have students discuss the pros and cons of dieting during and following pregnancy. What would be a healthy weight loss per week after birth?

Activity. Ask students to interview pregnant women or women who have gone through pregnancy and ask if they had any food cravings or discomforts. Have students share their findings with the class.

Activity and Rest During Pregnancy

Most healthy women will be able to continue their normal activities for most of the pregnancy. Many women who work outside the home continue their jobs until the day their babies are born. Other women feel the need to begin their maternity leave earlier.

While a pregnant woman continues to be active, she may need to increase the amount of sleep and rest she gets. Fatigue is common in the early months of pregnancy as the body shifts into more complicated work. The amount of sleep needed varies. Some women require eight hours; others may need more. Many women find that a daytime nap—even if it is for only a half hour—refreshes them more than extra nighttime sleep.

◆◆ Exercise

Exercise of some type is recommended for almost all pregnant women. Walking, biking, swimming, playing tennis, and dancing are beneficial to women accustomed to these activities. However, many doctors recommend that women do not take up a new sport or vigorous activity during pregnancy.

A pregnant woman should pay attention to her body's signals during exercise. If she becomes very tired or feels any unusual pain, she should stop. Before resuming the exercise, she should seek the doctor's advice.

Physical activity has many benefits during pregnancy. It can strengthen muscles and

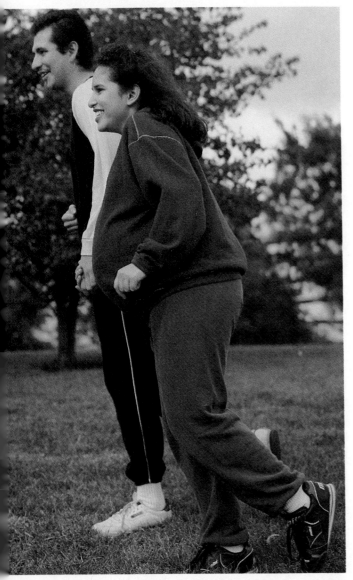

Healthy women can continue their normal activities during pregnancy. Doctors recommend moderate exercise, such as jogging or biking.

Emphasize. Pregnant women are in need of additional rest and sleep.

DECISIONS ◆
◆ DECISIONS

Charlene stopped exercising as soon as she learned she was pregnant. She feared that the activity would harm the fetus. Now she has read that moderate exercise is good for both the pregnant woman and her developing child. Should Charlene start exercising again—or is it too late? Why?

Discuss. Have students suggest ways that pregnant women can benefit from regular exercise. What types of exercise could they do with their partner or with friends?

improve circulation. Good muscle tone not only helps a woman during labor, it also helps her return to her original shape after the birth of the baby. Moreover, physical activity may prevent swelling of the legs and ankles and relieve heartburn and constipation. Specific exercises often relieve backaches caused by the increased weight and strain on a pregnant woman's body. Most of all, exercise makes a woman feel more energetic.

Some women participate in special exercise classes for pregnant women. Others enjoy joining their partner or friends in informal physical activities.

❖ Maternity Clothing

Around the fourth month of pregnancy, a woman may need to start wearing more comfortable, nonrestrictive clothing. Physical changes in a woman's body during pregnancy create the need for clothing with a different cut.

The first physical change the pregnant woman notices is that her breasts are getting larger and need extra support. Bras made of knitted fabric and spandex are useful because they stretch as the breasts enlarge. Bras that have special snap-down cups may be used later if the woman decides to breast-feed. Special girdles are helpful for women who have pain in the lower back due to the increasing size and weight of the fetus.

Swelling in the legs and feet calls for support stockings and larger shoes. Shoes should be comfortable and provide good support. They should help the woman maintain balance and prevent her from falling. She should avoid wearing high heels.

The expectant mother should buy maternity clothing that is the same size as her regular clothes. The designers add the fullness she needs for her changing weight and shape.

Costs for maternity clothes range from very expensive to reasonable. However, because this clothing is needed for only five months or so, many women do not want to invest much money in a maternity wardrobe. Some sew their own maternity clothes. Others exchange clothes with friends. Garage and rummage sales and thrift and consignment shops are inexpensive sources of good maternity clothing. Restyling maternity clothes after pregnancy allows women to get more wear per clothing dollar. For example, dresses that are worn loose during pregnancy can be belted afterward.

Many women borrow maternity clothes from friends. Garage sales and thrift shops are other sources of low-cost maternity outfits.

Emotions During Pregnancy

Women who are happy to be pregnant will usually feel positive most of the time. However, all women experience mixed feelings about the new role of becoming a mother. They wonder how much their lives will change after the baby is born. Sometimes they may feel they have made a mistake. Even when the fathers-to-be are happy and excited about the pregnancy, prospective mothers may feel lonely at times. Some may feel unattractive as they see themselves growing bigger. Others fear they will never lose all the weight they are gaining.

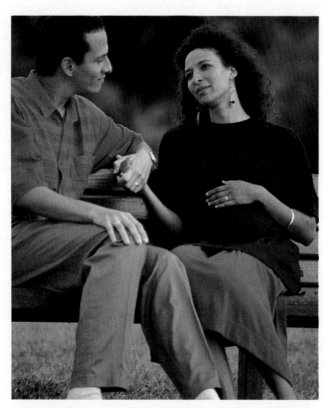

Both husband and wife may wonder how their future child will affect their lives. Pregnancy is a time for both partners to share their feelings and concerns about parenthood with each other.

Men wonder, too, about the changes that will soon be taking place in their lives. Some worry about finances and about their role as a father. They may feel inadequate and unprepared to assume responsibility for a child. Most men experience great curiosity about the physical sensations of pregnancy. Some may feel a little resentful of the special attention their partner is receiving. They are both fascinated by and afraid of the changes that are taking place in their relationship.

All these feelings are normal. Instead of feeling guilty about such thoughts, men and women should talk about them together. They should also feel free to talk with family, friends, doctors, and other prospective parents. Just learning that others have the same feelings often helps.

Dangers to the Fetus

Along with the joys and concerns of becoming parents, both partners share certain responsibilities. Some of these begin even before pregnancy. For example, the couple should decide how they will help ensure the health of their future baby.

A fetus is completely dependent on the woman who carries it. Substances and conditions that affect her affect the fetus. Less directly, the health of the fetus can also be influenced by the father-to-be. Tobacco, alcohol, caffeine, drugs, certain diseases and medical conditions, and extensive radiation can be hazardous to the proper development of the fetus.

◆ Tobacco

Research indicates that women who smoke during pregnancy increase their risk of having a premature baby. They also risk having a baby with a low birth weight. This

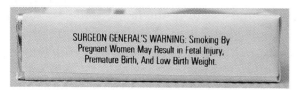

Women who smoke during pregnancy increase their risk of having a premature baby or a baby with a low birth weight. Women who drink alcohol while pregnant may have a baby with fetal alcohol syndrome.

may be because smoking deprives the fetus of vital oxygen. Babies who are small or premature do not have the same chances of survival that larger babies and full-term babies have. For this reason, women who wish to become pregnant should stop smoking before they conceive. If they are already pregnant, they should stop smoking immediately.

Growing evidence also indicates that individuals who breathe other people's smoke may suffer respiratory problems, too. If the prospective father or others in the home smoke, they are polluting the environment of the prospective mother and the developing fetus. In addition, once the baby is born, such smoke continues to affect his or her health and may cause pneumonia and other respiratory problems.

❖ Alcohol

Alcohol has a toxic effect on the fetus. Absorbed into the pregnant woman's bloodstream, it passes through the placenta into the fetus. A pregnant woman who regularly drinks alcohol, or who drinks heavily from time to time, runs a high risk of harming the fetus. Liquor, beer, and wine—as well as mixed drinks made with them—all contain alcohol.

Research has found that many infants born to mothers who drank large amounts of alcohol while pregnant have a very serious birth defect called **fetal alcohol syndrome (FAS).** Babies with this problem show many physi-

Around the World

Infant Mortality Rates

There are many reasons why babies die at birth or during infancy. Some die because they were exposed to hazards, such as drugs, during the prenatal period. Others die from childhood diseases that could be prevented by immunization programs. Still others die because their mother did not have adequate prenatal care during pregnancy. Even countries with a high per capita income, such as the United States, may not have a prenatal health care program that reaches everyone who needs it.

The infant mortality rate, or number of deaths per 1,000 live births, varies from country to country. The following rates were obtained from the Statistical Office of the United Nations.

Country	Infant Mortality Rate
Japan	5.0
Switzerland	6.8
Canada	7.3
France	7.7
United Kingdom	8.8
United States	10.0
Czechoslovakia	11.9
China	12.0
Nigeria	17.6

cal and mental defects. They may have a very small head, improperly formed nose and mouth, sight and hearing problems, heart and kidney defects, poor coordination, and mental retardation. Some may be overactive and have learning and behavior problems later in childhood. Babies born with FAS will suffer its effects throughout their lives.

Problem Solving. Ask students to discuss why "second-hand smoke" is harmful to the pregnant woman and to the fetus. How might a pregnant woman convince people around her to quit smoking?

Activity. Have students read magazine articles, watch a video, or listen to a speaker on fetal alcohol syndrome. Then have students create posters or write a pamphlet on the toxic effect of alcohol on the fetus.

Other babies may show some but not all of the problems of FAS. They may be small, restless, grow slowly, and have below normal intelligence.

Research indicates that even a small amount of alcohol may be too much. Many doctors recommend that a pregnant woman have *no* alcohol. It may be helpful to the pregnant woman for her partner also to avoid alcohol at this time.

❖ Caffeine

Caffeine is a drug suspected of being harmful to the fetus. Caffeine is present in coffee, tea, chocolate, and some cola drinks. Pregnant women may want to eliminate caffeine from their diet. At the least, they should reduce the amount they consume, especially during the first trimester. Many doctors recommend that pregnant women drink fewer than four cups of liquids containing caffeine per day. Many kinds of coffee, cola, and tea that contain no caffeine are now available.

❖ Medications and Drugs

Any medication or drug that a pregnant woman takes passes through the placenta into

DECISIONS ◆
◆ DECISIONS

Shanika loves going out for coffee with her friends. Now that she is pregnant, she worries that caffeine will hurt her developing child. Shanika doesn't want to give up her time with her friends, but she is afraid that watching them drink coffee will tempt her to have a cup. What would you recommend?

the bloodstream of the fetus. Some are dangerous when taken at any time during pregnancy. Others appear to be dangerous only when taken early in pregnancy, when the embryo is developing. Still other medications and drugs seem to be more harmful to the fetus when taken later in pregnancy.

Problems linked to medication and drug use include miscarriage, early labor and premature birth, low birth weight, infant addiction and withdrawal, and infant death. To be safe, an expectant mother should not use any medication or drug unless her doctor advises her to.

Over-the-Counter and Prescription Medications

Every year the list of over-the-counter, or nonprescription, medications (such as aspirin, antacids, and laxatives) that may be harmful to the fetus grows longer. About 62,000 nonprescription medications must carry the following warning label from the Food and Drug Administration (FDA): "As with any drug, if you are pregnant or nursing a baby, seek the advice of a health professional before using this product."

Doctors generally prescribe medications such as antibiotics only if they are absolutely necessary for the health of the pregnant woman. Some prescription drugs can cause severe damage to the fetus. Drugs such as amphetamines (speed) and barbiturates (downers) can be especially dangerous. No one, especially a pregnant woman, should ever use a medication that is prescribed for another person.

Illegal Drugs

Drugs such as marijuana, cocaine, crack (a very potent form of cocaine), and heroin are both illegal and dangerous. A mother-to-be who uses any of these drugs passes them along through the placenta to the fetus. Drugs

A pregnant woman should not take any medication or drug without the advice of her doctor. Both legal and illegal drugs can cause severe damage to the fetus.

can cut the flow of nutrients and oxygen to the fetus, causing permanent damage.

Research shows that infants exposed to drugs in the uterus are at risk of being physically deformed. They are also at risk for respiratory problems, fetal brain damage, premature birth, low birth weight, and even death. Crack and cocaine, in particular, can damage the infant's central nervous system. This can cause long-term physical, mental, and emotional problems. Because the chances of harm to the unborn vary, it is important to avoid all illegal drugs—before and during pregnancy. Responsible parents will also avoid all illegal drugs after their child is born.

Pregnant women who are addicted to drugs may pass the addiction on to their babies. After birth, these infants may have to go through withdrawal—suffering breathing difficulties, fevers, vomiting, tremors, and convulsions. Babies experiencing withdrawal

have a high-pitched, shrill cry and have difficulty sleeping. Many are jittery, irritable, and difficult to comfort. Some may cry at the gentlest touch or sound. Others may be withdrawn and unresponsive. These infants are usually premature and have a low birth weight. As a result, they are 40 times more likely to die in their first month than are babies of normal birth weight.

Survivors are likely to have lifelong problems, such as visual and hearing disabilities, emotional outbursts, or mental retardation. They are therefore at high risk for behavioral and educational problems during childhood. For example, they may be aggressive and hyperactive, unable to sit still for even a few minutes. They may have difficulty in expressing ideas or even learning simple information. In addition, babies born to women and men who use drugs are often victims of child abuse and neglect.

All the problems caused by illegal drug use are completely preventable. Women who use drugs should stop before they get pregnant or delay pregnancy until they can avoid drugs completely.

❖ Rubella (German Measles)

Rubella (ruh-BELL-uh), commonly known as German measles, is a disease caused by a virus. It can affect both the pregnant woman and her fetus. A woman who has rubella during the first trimester of pregnancy runs a very high risk of having a baby who is mentally retarded or physically impaired. Blindness and heart defects are common.

If a woman has not had rubella or cannot remember whether she has had it, she should have a blood test. This can indicate whether she is immune to the disease. If she is not immune to it, the doctor will usually give her a vaccination and advise her to wait at least three months before trying to become pregnant. It is important to take precautions in advance because the most damaging effects of rubella take place during the early weeks of pregnancy.

◆◆ Sexually Transmitted Diseases

Sexually transmitted diseases (STDs) are spread through sexual contact. They include chlamydia, syphilis, gonorrhea, genital herpes, and AIDS. These diseases can cause serious illness and deformities of the fetus if a pregnant woman contracts them.

If either partner has symptoms of an STD, he or she should be diagnosed and treated—preferably before conceiving a baby. The affected person's sexual partner should be treated at the same time. Otherwise the disease can be passed back and forth between the partners. The health departments of most counties and cities have programs to diagnose and treat STDs.

It is very important for a pregnant woman to tell her doctor early about the possible presence of an STD. By doing so, she may avoid risk to the fetus if the disease is treated quickly.

Chlamydia

Chlamydia (kluh-MID-ee-uh), the most common STD, is an infection caused by a bacteria-like organism. If untreated, the infection can lead to pelvic inflammatory disease in women. In men, chlamydia takes the form of an urethral infection. Women infected with chlamydia have no symptoms so the disease may go undiagnosed. However, laboratory tests can identify the infection. Once identified, it can be treated with antibiotics. If untreated, chlamydia can damage the reproductive organs of both men and women. This

can make it impossible for them to have children.

Babies born to women infected with chlamydia often develop eye infections. These are sometimes followed by ear and lung infections that can cause death.

Syphilis

Syphilis (SIF-uh-luhs) is a disease caused by bacteria that enter the blood and infect the entire body. If a pregnant woman has syphilis, she can pass it on to the fetus and cause a miscarriage. If the baby is born and lives, he or she may have problems of the nervous system, lungs, heart, or liver. Some infected infants may not show symptoms of syphilis

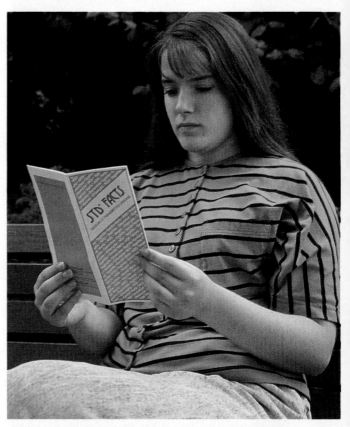

If a woman thinks she has been exposed to a sexually transmitted disease, she should tell her doctor. Then she can receive treatment for the disease. STDs can harm both the fetus and the pregnant woman.

More About. Chickenpox can be passed to a fetus while it is in the uterus. The greatest risk to an infant is being exposed to the virus just before delivery because it has not yet received the mother's antibodies.

Activity. Divide the class into groups and have each group research a STD. They should gather information about the infection, its effect on women and men, its effect on a fetus, and possible treatment. Have groups share their findings.

at birth. If the disease is not diagnosed and treated, it can lead to heart disease, blindness, paralysis, or insanity later in life.

A pregnant women may not know that she has syphilis. For that reason, a blood test is done early in pregnancy to test for the disease. The test is repeated later to be sure that the woman was not exposed to the disease after she became pregnant.

Gonorrhea

Another STD caused by bacteria is gonorrhea (gahn-uh-REE-uh). It attacks the mucous membranes of the body. If a pregnant woman has gonorrhea, her baby could eventually become blind. Doctors usually prevent this by routinely putting eye drops into the eyes of all infants right after birth.

Because a woman may have no symptoms, she may not know she has gonorrhea. However, the disease can be diagnosed and treated by a doctor or clinic. If left untreated, gonorrhea can cause pelvic inflammation, infertility, heart disease, arthritis, and blindness.

Genital Herpes

Genital herpes (HER-pees) is caused by a virus. Symptoms of this STD are painful, blisterlike sores in the genital area. The symptoms of this disease may go away temporarily even though the virus remains in the body.

A woman who has genital herpes requires close medical supervision during pregnancy. The same holds true for her partner. If the disease is not active at the time the woman gives birth, it is possible for the woman to have a normal delivery without infecting the baby. If the disease is active, it may be necessary for the baby to be delivered by cesarian section (Chapter 11) so that he or she will not pass through the infected birth canal. Newborns who are infected with the virus can suffer mental or physical defects or even die.

AIDS

Acquired immunodeficiency (im-YOO-noh-dih-FISH-uhn-see) **syndrome (AIDS)** can destroy the immune systems of a pregnant woman and the developing fetus. The virus that causes AIDS is called HIV. It is transmitted from person to person through sexual contact, shared drug needles, or transfusions of infected blood. An infected pregnant female can pass the virus on to her unborn baby.

People contract the HIV infection a long time before symptoms of AIDS appear. AIDS is difficult to treat because those who have it become sick with other infections. Today there is no known cure for AIDS.

About one-third of the babies born to mothers infected with HIV will also have the virus. There are three known ways that the virus can be passed to the fetus or infant:

- By the exchange of blood from the mother to the fetus through the umbilical cord.
- From infected blood entering a cut on the infant's body during childbirth.
- Through the mother's breast milk during nursing.

All individuals should learn the medical facts about AIDS. Only by staying informed can they take measures to protect themselves and their children.

❖ Radiation

X-rays generally are not used with pregnant women because radiation can cause birth defects. When possible, medical and dental treatment requiring x-rays should be postponed until after the birth. Women should always tell medical personnel if they are pregnant. Then if x-rays are essential, special precautions can be taken.

Discuss. What is the effect of HIV/AIDS on children? How are they infected? What problems are created if both parents and children are suffering from AIDS? Gather current statistics about the number of infected children and mothers in U.S.

Problem Solving. Women of childbearing age should be cautious about having x-rays. What precautions can doctors and dentists take if x-rays are absolutely necessary for a pregnant woman?

❖❖ Pregnancy Complications

Pregnancy induced hypertension (PIH) is a potentially serious condition that involves high blood pressure. PIH is easily detected during the routine blood pressure check that is part of each prenatal visit. In some women the blood pressure continues to increase, fluid accumulates in the body, and protein is detected in the urine. This condition is called toxemia, or preeclampsia. Symptoms include rapid weight gain, severe headaches, and blurred vision. PIH occurs most frequently in the last trimester of pregnancy. If untreated, it can lead to severe convulsions and coma. This is called eclampsia and can be fatal to both the mother and the baby.

Pregnant women who have diabetes have an increased risk of PIH. They may also have very large babies, making delivery difficult. Women who have diabetes require careful monitoring throughout pregnancy. Some pregnant women develop gestational diabetes. This form of diabetes must be monitored, but it usually goes away after the baby is born.

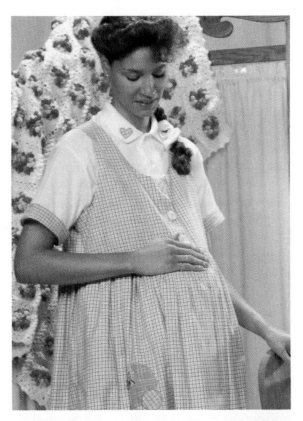

All pregnant women have emotional ups and downs during pregnancy. Being pregnant may be a time of stress for expectant mothers, but it can be a happy time as well.

❖❖ Emotional Hazards

There is some evidence that severe strain on a pregnant woman's emotional health can affect the fetus. A woman who is under constant stress from problems with her marriage, her job, or other personal relationships sometimes develops physical problems that do affect the fetus. For example, rage, anger, or anxiety can cause the pregnant woman's body to send chemicals into her bloodstream that pass through the placenta to the fetus. These chemicals can disrupt the flow of oxygen to the fetus. In the later stages of pregnancy, stress may cause increased movement or hiccuping by the fetus or even low birth weight.

It is very important to the health of the fetus for the woman to feel generally positive and calm during pregnancy. This does not mean that a woman must be constantly cheerful for nine months. All women have emotional ups and downs during pregnancy. Discussing their feelings and concerns with others can help minimize stress. Relaxation techniques and a regular exercise program can also help.

A woman who is constantly depressed, nervous, or upset, may need professional counseling to help her through pregnancy and the weeks following childbirth. Her partner, family, and friends should be especially supportive and help her get the professional assistance she needs.

Activity. Have students gather additional information about the affects of high blood pressure, PIH or toxemia, and eclampsia on a pregnant woman and the fetus. What precautions can women take to minimize the chances of developing these conditions?

Discuss. What are some emotional hazards that a woman might have to face during pregnancy? How could she work out these problems? What could she do to minimize various types of stress?

CHAPTER 9 REVIEW

Summary

- Women who have a well-balanced diet containing each of the essential nutrients help ensure their baby's health.
- The Food Guide Pyramid tells how many servings a person should eat from each of the food groups.
- The average recommended weight gain during pregnancy is 25 to 35 pounds.
- Exercise before, during, and after pregnancy is helpful to a woman's general health.
- Prospective fathers and mothers should share their thoughts and emotions during the pregnancy period.
- Tobacco, alcohol, medications, illegal drugs, and x-rays can have harmful and long-lasting effects on the developing fetus.
- Sexually transmitted diseases (STDs) and pregnancy induced hypertension (PIH) can seriously affect both the pregnant woman and the fetus.

Questions

p. 157 **1.** What are the six essential nutrients in a well-balanced diet?

p. 158 **2.** How many servings of the milk group do women who are pregnant or breast-feeding need each day?

p. 160 **3.** Ideally, how much weight should a pregnant woman gain in the first trimester? In the second and third trimesters?

p. 162 **4.** What are two benefits of physical activity during pregnancy?

5. How can a prospective father's smoking affect his partner and their developing fetus? p. 165

6. What is fetal alcohol syndrome? p. 165

7. What types of problems are linked to a woman's use of illegal drugs during pregnancy? p. 166

8. What is chlamydia? What effect does it have on a man, a woman, and a fetus? p. 168

9. List the three ways that the HIV virus can be passed to a fetus or infant. p. 169

10. What is pregnancy induced hypertension (PIH)? p. 170

Activities

1. Analyze your diet for three days. Keep a record of the number of servings you eat each day from each of the main food groups. If you were pregnant, would your diet be adequate? If it is not adequate, what changes would you make?

2. Plan a maternity wardrobe using clothing catalogs or original drawings. Calculate the cost of purchasing new items versus sewing or borrowing outfits.

3. Find out whether you have had rubella or have received immunizations for the disease.

Think About

1. Why is the health of the developing fetus directly affected by the health and life-style choices of the mother?

2. In addition to not smoking, what other steps can a pregnant woman's partner take to help ensure the health of their developing child?

Preparing for Baby's Arrival

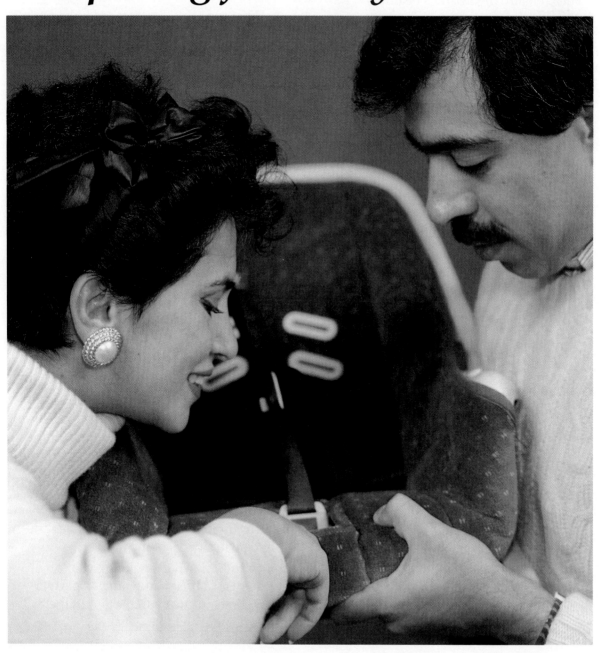

Objectives

This chapter will help you to:
- Describe prepared childbirth and the training involved.
- Compare the advantages of breast-feeding and bottle-feeding a baby.
- List essential clothing, equipment, and other supplies needed for a baby.
- Discuss parental leaves and child care options for working parents.

Vocabulary

prepared childbirth   parental leave
labor   sibling
delivery
Lamaze method
Bradley method
delivery room
birthing room
pediatrician
formula
layette

"I painted the baby's room yellow last night," announced Dwayne. "That way it will be fine for either a boy or a girl."

"We shopped for baby clothes," Luisa told her sister.

"We're teaching our older son how to go up the stairs quietly, so he'll know what we mean by 'quiet' when the baby comes," Josh said to his coworker.

"My bag is packed. It's right by the door," Tylette told her husband.

These comments indicate some of the preparations that parents-to-be must make before the baby's arrival.

Sharing Preparations for Childbirth

Fathers and mothers have equal rights to the hopes and joys that come with rearing a child. They also have equal obligations. As you learned earlier, they can begin sharing decisions in the prenatal period.

The parents-to-be can visit the doctor together. They can both ask questions, talk about their concerns, and get accurate medical information from the doctor. The couple can read books about what can help or harm the health of the expectant mother and fetus and about childbirth and child care. Talking to each other, to other couples who have had babies, or to parents and in-laws also helps expectant parents better understand the pregnancy and the birth process.

A prospective mother and father may find that they have different views on child rearing. There is no one right way to rear a child. Rather than thinking that they have to choose one best way, couples should explore how they feel about child care. They need to trust their own feelings. Parents who are confident will make a baby feel more secure than parents who do everything "by the book" but have not examined their own feelings and opinions.

Pregnancy is an easier and more enjoyable experience if expectant parents share in the preparations for childbirth and for the baby's care. A couple can do many things together,

Chapter Opener. Ask students to read the opening scenario to the chapter. Ask these questions: What preparations are each parents-to-be making? Why might these be important to do before the new baby arrives?

Discuss. Why should expectant parents talk to each other about their hopes and dreams for their child?

such as shopping for baby clothes or choosing a car seat.

Here are some other enjoyable activities that expectant parents can share:

- Making lists of names and choosing favorite ones they may use for the baby.
- Window shopping to get ideas for items to make, borrow, or purchase for the baby.
- Borrowing baby clothing and furnishings from friends and relatives.
- Painting or refinishing furniture for the baby.
- Making items such as toys, quilts, sweaters, or shelves.
- Rearranging or redecorating the home to make a special space for the baby.
- Shopping for essentials such as diapers, bibs, and bottles.
- Visiting with friends who enjoy their own children and sharing ideas about being parents.
- Talking about changes they will have to make to adapt to a new baby in the family.

Parents-to-be can share in the preparations for baby's arrival. Since some babies arrive early, essential baby items should be purchased or borrowed several weeks before the due date.

Prepared Childbirth Training

The idea of preparing parents for childbirth began with the book *Childbirth Without Fear* by Grantly Dick-Read. This British doctor believed that if women are prepared for childbirth, they will lose their fear and feel less pain.

Prepared childbirth means that the expectant parents understand the birth process, can control the pain through breathing and relaxation techniques, and take an active part in the birth process. Many hospitals, clinics, and community centers offer courses on prepared childbirth. Usually there are only six to twelve people in a class. Doctors' offices, health clinics, local hospitals, the Red Cross, the Mental Health Association, and public health offices have information about such classes.

Expectant parents who attend these classes hear health care professionals discuss childbirth and see them demonstrate specific techniques. Typically, these programs focus on giving instructions that will guide the expectant parents through the birth experience.

For example, the expectant parents learn about the various stages of **labor.** This is the contractions of the uterine muscles that gradually push the baby out of the mother's body. Expectant parents also learn exercises to help control the pain of labor. These exercises help the pregnant woman assist rather than struggle against the labor process. At the same time, the expectant father learns how to assist the mother in doing these exercises. He also learns how to give emotional and physical support as she nears the time for **delivery,** or the actual birth. Couples usually become much closer when they work as partners to get ready for the birth of their baby.

❧ Breathing and Relaxation Techniques

Many couples prepare for childbirth by attending Lamaze classes. The **Lamaze** (lah-MAHZ) **method** involves special breathing and relaxation techniques for women in labor. It was developed by Fernand Lamaze, a French obstetrician. By learning these techniques, the woman keeps from pushing the baby until the cervix opens wide enough for birth to occur. The rhythmic breathing and relaxation help her participate in the labor and delivery. The Lamaze method also stresses the helpful role that a prepared father, relative, or friend can play in the childbirth process.

A similar breathing and relaxation technique, the **Bradley method,** was developed by physician Robert Bradley. It, too, stresses the role of a coach during labor and delivery. The Bradley method emphasizes birth without medication.

Breathing and relaxation techniques decrease or eliminate the need for pain-relieving medication. This is desirable for at least two reasons. Without medication, the mother remains fully conscious and is thus able to participate actively in the birth. Second, by not using a painkiller, the mother eliminates the possibility of any medication reaching the baby through the placenta. However, couples must be realistic and flexible. Some women who receive childbirth preparation training still find medication necessary during labor and delivery. There should be no sense of failure if medication is needed.

❧ Childbirth Coaches

Childbirth can be difficult to face alone. The mother-to-be will be less fearful and happier having someone give her support at this time.

Most hospitals and alternative birth centers allow an expectant father who has had childbirth training to stay with the mother during labor and delivery. He helps her use breathing and relaxation techniques. He coaches her to push when the cervix finally opens and the baby is ready to be delivered. After all their work together, both parents see their baby born.

Sometimes the expectant father may be unable or unwilling to participate in prepared childbirth classes. If so, the woman can ask a friend or relative to be her coach during the training classes and labor and delivery.

Regardless of who the coach is, it is best to check in advance on whether the hospital allows a coach in the delivery room. If not, the pair may want to find another hospital or a birth center that allows this practice.

In courses on prepared childbirth, expectant parents learn about the various stages of labor. Women can practice breathing and relaxation techniques to aid them during childbirth, while their partners serve as coaches.

Activity. Invite a prepared childbirth instructor to talk to the class about breathing and relaxation techniques. Then have students practice the specific techniques shown by the instructor.

Activity. Have students find out more information about the Lamaze method, the Bradley method, and the Leboyer method and the doctors who developed each method. What are the advantages of each?

Location of Birth

The decision of where the baby will be born should be made well before the expected birth date. Location choices vary from community to community. Typically, they include one or more hospitals, an alternative birth center, or the mother's home. Sometimes couples have the choice of either a delivery room or birthing room at the same hospital. However, an expectant couple may want a specific doctor or nurse-midwife to deliver their baby. In this case, the choice is usually limited to the facilities in which that doctor or nurse-midwife practices.

❖ Delivery Room in Hospital

A **delivery room** is a sterile hospital area that is specifically used for delivering babies. It is equipped for surgery and emergency procedures. Thus a delivery room is recommended when birth complications may result from a high-risk pregnancy. Such potential

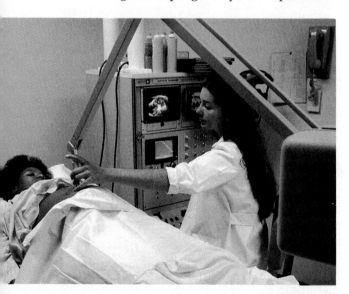

Hospital labor and delivery rooms are equipped for emergency procedures. Thus hospitals are recommended for women who might have problems during childbirth.

Activity. Arrange for students to tour the obstetrics unit of a hospital. Is the father or another person allowed in the labor room? Delivery room? Recovery room? Does the hospital have birthing rooms? How do they differ from other rooms?

complications include health risks for either the mother or the child.

The pregnant woman remains in a labor room until shortly before delivery. Then she is transferred to the delivery room for the actual birth. After delivery, she may be moved to a recovery room before going to a regular hospital room. The new mother and child are usually released from the hospital two or three days later.

❖ Birthing Room in Hospital or Birth Center

A **birthing room** is a specially designed labor and delivery room located in a hospital or an alternative birth center. The room has many of the comforts of home. The bed is a modified hospital bed that can be raised at one end to allow the woman to sit up. Home-like features may include easy chairs, wallpaper, pictures, music, and television. A relaxed atmosphere is encouraged.

The woman remains in the birthing room throughout labor and delivery. Family members are encouraged to stay with her during the entire childbirth procedure. Some birthing rooms even allow other children to remain with the mother. Most new mothers stay in a birthing room six to twelve hours after delivery. Then family members can accompany the new mother and baby home.

Birthing rooms located in an alternative birth center are usually staffed by nurse-midwives. Most centers are affiliated with a nearby hospital. If any sudden complications occur during labor or delivery, assistance can be obtained from the hospital.

❖ At-Home Birth

Births at home are usually attended by nurse-midwives. Although a small number of people prefer at-home births, they are not

Problem Solving. Have students discuss the birth location choices in your community. Where would they want their own baby to be born? Who would they want to be present or not present during labor and delivery? Why?

A birthing room in a hospital or birth center has many of the features of home. Family members are encouraged to stay with the woman during labor, childbirth, and recovery.

Choosing a Pediatrician

Parents need to choose a doctor to provide health and medical care for their baby. Many parents select a **pediatrician** (PEE-dee-uh-TRISH-un), a specialist in the treatment of infants and young children. Other families seek the services of a family doctor or a clinic.

It is wise to choose a pediatrician before the baby is born. One way to do this is to ask the obstetrician for recommendations. This helps promote a smooth transition between the obstetrician's focus on the health of the mother and fetus during prenatal development and the pediatrician's focus on the baby's health after birth. The two doctors can share medical information before and after the baby is born.

Parents-to-be should feel free to ask questions that will help them decide on a pediatrician. It is important that the expectant parents feel comfortable with the doctor. For example, they should find out how the pediatrician feels about issues such as feeding. A mother who wants to breast-feed her baby should have a pediatrician who supports this decision. A mother who wants both parents to bottle-feed their child should not be pushed into breast-feeding.

Expectant parents should ask about office hours and making appointments. Many pediatricians have special calling hours when parents can telephone for advice. This is very helpful when parents have special concerns about their child's health or development. The cost of office visits and additional treatment should also be discussed. Even billing procedures are important. Must the fee be paid when the service is provided or can it be paid later by mail? Some families have insurance or welfare benefits that cover certain medical procedures.

generally advised. In some states at-home births are illegal. Plans for having the baby at home must include provision for quick medical assistance in case an emergency arises.

Some births come close to occurring at home because the woman does not leave for the hospital or birth center early enough. Medical emergency teams are trained to assist a woman in advanced labor. In many communities, they can be reached by calling 911 or the local emergency number. Usually the woman will be transported by ambulance to the nearest hospital.

◆ ◆ Self-Esteem ◆ ◆

Some pregnant women have anxieties or fears about labor and delivery. By taking a course on prepared childbirth, pregnant women and their partners learn about the various stages of labor. This knowledge helps them understand their own roles in the birth process. Then they can look forward to the birth with added confidence.

Expectant parents should ask how the pediatrician handles emergencies. For example, must the baby be taken to the doctor's office or to a specific hospital or clinic? You will learn more about health care for infants in Chapter 15.

Deciding How to Feed the Baby

During pregnancy, the couple should start thinking about whether the baby will be breast-fed or bottle-fed. Breast-feeding means that the baby nurses, or takes milk from the mother's breast. Bottle-feeding means that the baby drinks from a bottle. Each method has certain advantages. The couple may want to discuss these advantages with the obstetrician or pediatrician.

For many centuries, mothers breast-fed their babies without question. Then from about 1920 to 1970, bottle-feeding became much more common than breast-feeding. Now more women are again choosing to breast-feed their infants.

❖ Breast-Feeding

Breast-feeding has definite advantages for both infants and mothers. Breast milk is a perfect food. It provides special health benefits for the baby and the mother. Breast-feeding also promotes a special emotional bond between mother and child.

Breast-feeding is convenient because it requires no prior preparation. The milk of breast-feeding mothers is ready at all times and at the right temperature. A large supply of bottles and nipples is not necessary. Furthermore, breast-fed babies can regulate the amount of milk they drink. They are less likely than bottle-fed babies to be overfed. In addition, breast-feeding is more economical than bottle-feeding.

The health benefits an infant receives from mother's milk are very important. This milk contains disease-fighting agents produced by the mother's body. These antibodies are especially helpful in protecting the baby during the first few months after birth. Studies have shown that breast-fed babies generally have fewer illnesses than bottle-fed babies. In addition, mother's milk is easier for babies to digest than cow's milk. Breast-fed babies are less likely to develop allergies to different foods as they grow older. They rarely suffer from constipation, as do many bottle-fed infants. A health benefit for the mother is that breast-feeding stimulates her body to produce a hormone that helps her uterus return to its normal, nonpregnant condition.

Mothers who breast-feed enjoy the special closeness with their infants. Women who are mothers for the first time find this especially encouraging. It gives them a sense of self-confidence and the infant a feeling of security and warmth.

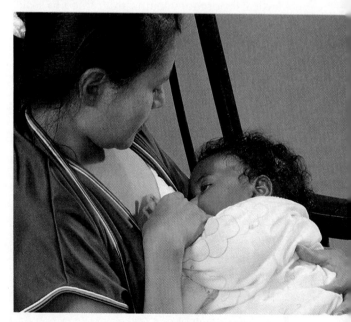

Breast-feeding offers many advantages for both mother and baby.

Discuss. Ask students to debate the advantages and disadvantages of breast-feeding versus bottle-feeding. Could parents do both methods? If the students were expectant parents, which method would they prefer? Why?

More About. Display a breast pump and explain when and why it might be used. Ask students why some mothers would want or need to pump breast milk for their babies.

DECISIONS ◆ ◆ DECISIONS

Suzanne is trying to decide whether to breast-feed or bottle-feed her baby. She has read articles about the many advantages of breast-feeding. Her doctor also recommends breast-feeding for most mothers. However, Suzanne worries that her baby might not get enough milk if breast-fed. Besides, the baby's father and other relatives would not be able to help with the feedings. Suzanne plans to take a six-week maternity leave after the birth and then return to work full-time. What recommendations would you make to Suzanne?

Expectant mothers sometimes fear that breast-feeding will tie them down or prevent them from going out when they need or want to. This does not have to be true. Many working mothers nurse their babies in the morning and evening and have caregivers bottle-feed the infants during the day. Some mothers even express, or pump out, their own milk into the bottles. This milk should be frozen if it is not to be used immediately.

Almost every woman can nurse her baby if she wants to. Occasionally, a woman will have some difficulty getting started with breast-feeding. If she has patience and keeps trying, she probably will be successful. Sometimes it takes a while for the milk supply to be established. A doctor, nurse, other health professional, or a more experienced mother can offer advice and encouragement.

The La Leche League is a support group of people who encourages mothers to nurse their babies. *Leche* (LAY-chay) is the Spanish word for *milk*. The organization provides emotional support and free advice about breast-feeding. The telephone numbers of the league's chapters are usually listed in local telephone directories.

◆◆ Bottle-Feeding

Some women do not want to or are unable to breast-feed. A woman who is uncomfortable with the idea should not force herself to breast-feed. If she does, the baby may sense her discomfort. Then neither mother nor baby will enjoy the experience. Even though breast-feeding offers many advantages, a mother should not feel inadequate for not breast-feeding.

Babies who are bottle-fed are given an infant formula. **Formula** is a commercially prepared mixture of milk or milk substitute, water, and added nutrients. Infant formulas are nutritious, and bottle-fed infants can be given just as much love and cuddling as breast-fed infants.

Bottle-feeding allows the mother to be away from the infant for many hours at a time. It also gives fathers, grandparents, and other relatives more opportunity to share in feeding the baby.

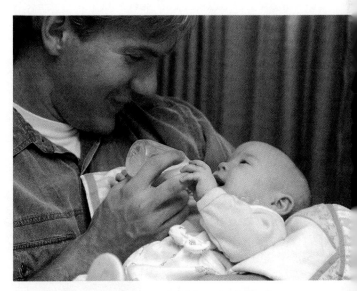

Bottle-feeding gives fathers, grandparents, and others the opportunity to feed the baby.

Activity. Invite a representative of the La Leche League to discuss breast-feeding with the students.
Reference. See pages 249-252 for a discussion of feeding, burping, and weaning a baby.
Activity. Have students compare the prices of various brands of formulas at local stores. How much would it cost for one month's supply of formula for a newborn? For a six-month-old?

Obtaining Essential Baby Items

The couple will want to gather some essential baby items before the newborn's arrival. Getting these things before the birth gives parents more time to devote to their new baby during the first few weeks after birth.

Even though babies are tiny, they require considerable space. The home needs to be organized and prepared to welcome the new family member. If possible, it is best to have a special area or room where the baby's bed and other belongings are kept. If the home has an extra bedroom, that can become the baby's room. If not, a simple room divider can be set up to screen off part of a room for the baby.

◆◆ Bedding

A bassinet (small baby bed), carriage, wicker basket, or even a dresser drawer can serve as a temporary bed. It should hold a firm mattress that can be covered with a pillowcase.

Eventually, the baby will need a crib with a firm mattress that meets recommended safety standards. A child can usually use a 54-inch crib until he or she is three years old.

Couples need not buy the most expensive crib available. In fact, some couples borrow a crib. Others enjoy finding an old crib and other baby items at a garage sale or used furniture store. They refinish or paint the furniture and save a lot of money. However, they should check old cribs carefully to see whether they meet current safety standards. Some are unsafe because the bars are far enough apart to allow a baby's head to get stuck between them. Older cribs may have been painted with lead paint. This is dangerous if the baby chews on a railing.

Several fitted sheets and a waterproof pad or mattress cover will be needed for the crib. A large towel placed on the mattress and under the sheet will absorb moisture. Special flannel-covered plastic or rubber sheets can also be used. A few lightweight blankets and a warm crib-sized blanket are good for cooler climates. Pillows are not recommended. Infants are not yet strong enough to move their head if a pillow should accidentally cover their face and prevent them from breathing.

Newborns can sleep in any small bed, such as a cradle, bassinet, or basket. However, older babies will need a sturdy crib.

Crib Safety

A secondhand crib can save parents money. An antique crib can be very charming. However, safety is the most important feature to look for in any crib, new or old.

When selecting a crib, parents should check for the following:

- **Bars or slats that are no more than 2⅜ inches apart.** Wider spaces make it possible for the baby's head to get stuck between the slats.
- **Corner posts that are no higher than ⅓ inch above the side or end panels.** Higher posts can be a safety hazard.
- **A mattress that fits snugly in the crib.** This prevents the baby from becoming wedged between the edge of the mattress and the crib slats.
- **At least 26 inches between the top of the rail and the top of the mattress when the mattress is set at its lowest level.** Otherwise, older babies may be able to climb out easily.
- **A secure locking mechanism on a crib with drop sides.** This prevents the sides from suddenly dropping and the baby tumbling out.
- **A plastic covering at the top of the crib rail.** This gives the baby a safe place to teethe.
- **No rough edges or exposed bolts.** These could injure the baby.

Finally, parents should never use an old crib that has been painted unless they are certain that the paint does not contain lead. Infants often chew on the bars and slats of their crib. Lead-based paints are a leading source of lead poisoning in young children.

Bumper pads can be used around the inside of a crib just above the mattress. These prevent the baby's arms and legs from poking through the bars.

◆ Clothing

A collection of baby clothing and equipment is called a **layette** (lay-ETT). The number of items of baby clothing is often determined by the availability of laundry facilities. Fewer clothes are needed if the family has a washing machine. More are needed if laundry is done at a laundromat. In addition, babies grow very rapidly the first year. Therefore, it is wise to buy only a few shirts and outfits in smaller sizes.

Criteria for judging clothing items for a baby are comfort, warmth, washability, ease of dressing, and size. For example, a baby born in spring or early summer will not need a winter snowsuit in an infant size. By the time a cold-weather garment is needed, the baby may weigh 15 to 20 pounds.

A useful layette consists of four to six undershirts, four to six gowns or one-piece sleeper suits, two sweater and cap sets, two to four waterproof pants (if cloth diapers are used), three to four cotton receiving blankets, and a warm blanket or sleeping bag. Many sleeper suits are so comfortable and so easily washed that parents prefer to keep babies in them instead of dressing them up for outings.

Emphasize. Be sure to check a used crib and other baby equipment for safety features.

Activity. Have students calculate the cost of a layette containing the above items. Then have students suggest ways that parents could reduce this cost.

Therefore, dress-up clothing is seldom needed before age one and buying clothing in sizes 12, 18, or 24 months is more practical. Shoes are not needed until the child walks.

Many couples borrow clothing from relatives and friends who have babies a few months to a year older in age. Since babies grow so quickly, borrowing is a good way to get the most wear out of baby clothes. Many good buys can be found at garage sales, rummage sales, and used clothing stores. A chest of drawers or open shelves can be used to store the baby's clothing.

Babies need lots of clothes, but they outgrow them quickly. Borrowing baby clothes from friends or buying used clothing makes more sense than buying all new clothes.

◆◆ Diapers

The most essential garment for a baby is a clean, dry diaper. Families can choose one or more of three options: home-laundered diapers, diaper-service diapers, or disposable diapers. Whatever the choice, diapers should be kept out in the open, close to the changing area, not in a drawer. This allows for easy access when both hands are busy holding and changing the baby.

Home-Laundered Diapers

Purchasing cloth diapers and laundering them at home is the least expensive option. However, this takes a good deal of time and effort because cloth diapers require careful laundering. They must be washed with a disinfectant, such as bleach, then dried and folded. The use of home-laundered diapers can save a lot of money when you consider the average diaper use for a newborn is 80 diapers a week. Usually two dozen cloth diapers will be needed if washing can be done three times a week. With cloth diapers, the baby will need plastic pants to cover the diapers and make them waterproof.

Even if parents choose another diaper option, they should buy about a dozen cloth diapers. These are useful in case of a shortage or if the baby develops an allergy to disposable diapers. Cloth diapers also can be used as burping pads.

Diaper-Service Diapers

Some communities have home delivery diaper services. They provide sterilized cloth diapers each week. These are less likely to cause diaper rash than home-laundered diapers. A special deodorized container for storing soiled and wet diapers must be kept in the home until the next pickup.

A diaper service costs more than buying and home laundering diapers and may not be available in every area. Again, plastic pants are needed to cover the diapers.

Disposable Diapers

Disposable diapers come with a special plastic liner that makes them waterproof. They are available in a variety of sizes ranging from newborn through toddler. Some disposables come in an overnight size, which is thicker and more absorbent than the daytime size. Disposable diapers are very convenient to use, but they sometimes cause diaper rash.

Although disposables generally cost about the same as using a diaper service, they must be disposed of properly. Parents and caregivers should dispose of them only in an appropriate trash can. Unlike cloth diapers, they are not reusable. Thus disposable diapers are creating an environmental waste-disposal problem.

❖ Feeding Equipment

If the parents choose to bottle-feed the baby, they will need several bottles and nipples. If the baby will be breast-fed, they will need two to three bottles for supplemental feeding. Several smaller 4-ounce bottles can be used for water and juice. Bottle caps, extra nipples, and a bottle brush will be needed for these.

Bottles with disposable liners are available, but they are more expensive than plain bottles. Prefilled bottles of formula are the most expensive choice. Parents should discuss the various options and costs before the baby arrives.

❖ Bathing Supplies

Special portable plastic bathtubs are available for bathing the baby. However, a large plastic dishpan placed in the kitchen sink can work just as well. The sink is at a good height for the adult giving the bath. Parents should be sure the plastic tub or dishpan is large enough for playful kicking.

Additional bathing supplies include several soft washcloths and bath towels; a mild, pure soap; and a gentle baby shampoo.

❖ Travel Equipment

All states require infants and young children to be buckled into a safety-approved car seat when riding in an automobile. Newborns are no exception. See "Safety in Cars" in Chapter 15.

An infant carrier and stroller or carriage are useful for outings. Often these can be borrowed from relatives and friends or purchased second-hand. A large totebag is handy for carrying baby supplies.

An infant car seat must meet current safety standards. The infant must ride in a reclining position, facing backward. The seat must be secured in the car, and the infant must be latched into the harness.

Family Considerations

Most couples look forward to returning home with their baby. One subject they need to discuss in advance is whether they will need or want extra help. For example, sometimes one or more of the baby's grandparents offer to help. What response will the couple give? Do they want to be independent? Do they want to rely on close friends if they need help? The couple should talk over such questions before they arise. Without hurting any feelings, they can then communicate their decisions to those who wish to help.

Other family considerations include possible job leaves, child care arrangements, and preparing other children for the baby's arrival.

Parental leaves allow parents to take time away from a job after the birth or adoption of a child. During this time new parents can adjust to the demands of parenthood without the pressures of work.

Discuss. Ask students whether they would want or need help after the birth of a baby. If so, who would they want to ask? For how long would they want or need help?

◆◆ Parental Leaves

Parental leave is time away from a job that a parent is allowed to take after the birth or adoption of a child. Parental leave also may be granted to care for a seriously ill child. If the parental leave is short, the employee may continue to receive all or some pay. The amount usually depends on the length of time that the parent has worked for the company. Longer leaves are usually unpaid. However, the employee's job is held secure until he or she returns to work.

Parental leave provides time for a parent to develop an emotional attachment with a new child. The baby develops a sense of love and security that is important for infant development. In turn, the parent learns to care for the new child without job pressures.

More and more companies are including parental leaves in their benefit packages. Small companies with few employees usually have the most difficulty in granting extended leaves. If a parental leave is not available from an employer, a father or mother might plan to take vacation days or personal days to care for a new child.

Parental leave is also known as maternity leave for the mother and paternity leave for the father.

Maternity Leave

Most women begin a maternity leave shortly before the baby is due. Some must return to work four to eight weeks after delivery. Others may be able to take an extended maternity leave—for six months or even a year—before returning to work. Some companies allow mothers to return to work on a part-time basis.

During a maternity leave, it is important for a new mother to recover physically from giving birth. She should get extra sleep to compensate for the time she spends feeding

Activity. Have each student choose a local business and survey their policy for maternity and paternity leaves. Ask students to share their findings with the class.

Around the World

Parental Leave

In February 1993, President Clinton signed the Family and Medical Leave Act. This law allows employees to take up to 12 weeks of unpaid leave for the birth or adoption of a child, for the care of a sick family member, or for the worker's own serious health condition. Employees must be returned to their former job or an equivalent position upon returning to work. The employer is required to provide health care benefits but not pay during the leave.

Companies with fewer than 50 employees are exempt. A company can deny leave to a salaried employee within the highest paid 10 percent of its workforce if the leave would create a substantial hardship for the business operations. Approximately 40 percent of U.S. workers will be covered by the act.

Many other countries have specific national policies for new parents.

- In Sweden, working parents have the right to a paid, job-protected leave from work for the first 12 months after the baby is born. In addition, Swedish parents have the right to take additional leave until their child is eighteen months

old. This leave is unpaid, but the job is protected. When the parents go back to work, they can decide to work a six-hour day until their child is eight years old. Although they will not make as much money as they would if they worked an eight-hour day, many parents prefer the extra time at home.

- In Greece, parents who have worked at least one year for a company with more than 100 employees are entitled to supplementary leave. This means that both fathers and mothers can take three months unpaid parental leave per year for each child under two and one-half years of age.

- In Israel and the Netherlands, the minimum paid maternity leave is 12 months. In Canada, the minimum is 16 weeks of paid leave.

- In France, women are guaranteed the right to a paid, 16-week maternity leave. Their job is protected. If the baby is a third child, if two children are born close together, or if it is a multiple birth, longer paid parental leave is granted.

the newborn during the night. A maternity leave is also a time for love and affection to develop between mother and child. Such an emotional tie will have a positive long-lasting effect on the parent-child relationship.

Paternity Leave

Paternity leaves are not yet as common as maternity leaves. However, more and more fathers are seeking time off from work to be with a new child. Some men may take off a few days or weeks to help care for the new

baby. This can be very important during the first hectic days of parenthood. Other fathers are able to take a paternity leave after the mother's maternity leave has ended. This enables the baby to be cared for by a parent for a longer time.

A paternity leave offers the opportunity for a father to spend valuable time with his new baby. It enables him to develop parenting skills and to establish emotional ties with his child. Babies will benefit from knowing their father as well as their mother.

More About. Until 1993, the United States did not have a national policy regarding parental leave.

Discuss. Why might other countries provide generous benefits for new parents? What are the advantages and disadvantages for the parents? For the employers? For their society?

❖ Child Care Options

If both parents either must work or want to work outside the home, they must look for suitable child care for the baby. If possible, this should be arranged before the baby is born.

Parents-to-be should carefully examine all the child care options available to them. Some arrange for their parents, brothers or sisters, or other relatives to care for the baby. Others pay a neighbor or friend for this service. Still others hire a professionally trained caregiver. In these cases, the baby is either cared for at home or in the caregiver's home. Another alternative is to take the baby to an infant or child care center. Here a trained staff will care for the baby along with other children. Infant care is usually more expensive than child care. Babies need a great deal of attention, and one caregiver can legally care for only four babies. You will learn more about selecting child care in Chapter 28.

Parents also should consider various work options. Some families decide that one parent will stay home to care for the child full-time. This means adjusting to a reduced income if that parent leaves a paying job. However, these families believe that it is important for a parent to care for the child, at least when the child is young. Often the parent returns to work full- or part-time when the child enters school. Although most stay-at-home parents are mothers, more and more fathers are choosing to be full-time caregivers for their children.

Other families arrange for flexible work schedules so that one parent is always at home with the baby. For example, the mother may work a day shift and the father a night shift. One disadvantage of this arrangement is that the parents have very little time to spend together.

Another alternative is for one or both parents to work part-time. This enables at least

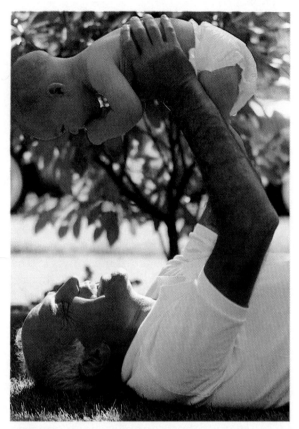

Sometimes grandparents can care for a child. However, new parents should not assume that their parents will want or be able to care for the baby.

one parent to be home with the infant part of the time. Then a caregiver can take care of the child when neither parent can be at home. Some employers permit two employees to share a job, each working part-time.

Yet another option for some parents is to work at home. Some employers allow a parent to work at home, at least for awhile. With computers, modems, and fax machines, at-home workers can stay in continuous communication with their company. Other parents start their own home business. A wide variety of services can now be provided from the home. However, many at-home workers discover that it is difficult to balance working and parenting at the same time. Some therefore choose to have a caregiver look after the

Discuss. What child care options are available in your community? What might be the advantages and disadvantages of each? If students were parents, which option would they prefer? See Chapter 28 for information about child care services.

Discuss. Ask students to brainstorm ideas for jobs or businesses that would enable parents to work at home.

DECISIONS ◆
◆ DECISIONS

John and Kimi are expecting their first child. They live near both sets of parents, who are eager to help with the baby. Kimi's mother and father want to help out because the baby will be their first grandchild. John's parents had four children and say they can offer plenty of experience in taking care of children. Kimi and John do want help, but they don't want to hurt anyone's feelings. Do they have a problem? If so, how do you think they might be able to solve it?

child, at least part-time, even though they are working at home.

Which option is best? Only by discussing all the different factors can a couple know what is best for them. Career goals, economic considerations, personal satisfaction, and child care needs all play an important part in the decision. Sometimes parents discover that the child care decision they make is not satisfactory. When this happens, it is important for the couple to reexamine all their choices. They may find that different options are suitable for various stages of parenthood.

❖ Preparing Other Children for the New Baby

If there are other children in the family, the couple should help prepare them for the baby's arrival. They should do this well in advance of the expected birth date. Then the children will have time to get used to the idea of having a new **sibling,** a brother or sister.

Young children may not understand pregnancy, but they know things are different.

They may be curious about the growing shape of the mother's body. Simple explanations will help them better understand what is happening. Many books are available in public libraries to help prepare children for a new baby in the family.

Siblings should be encouraged to participate in the plans for the baby. They can help choose clothing and supplies for the new arrival. If a child has to give up his or her crib or room for the new baby, this should be discussed and arranged well ahead of the birth. Parents should explain that the child is being asked to move because he or she is more grown-up, not because the new baby is more important.

Parents should emphasize that the baby who will soon be born is a member of the family. The baby will be as important to the other children in the family as to the parents. One way to make children feel comfortable about the new arrival is to have them visit other families with infants. This gives the children an opportunity to watch and touch a baby, something they may never have done before.

The couple also should decide where the siblings will stay when the mother is in the hospital or alternative birth center. Some parents arrange for a relative or friend to come and care for the children. Others plan for the children to go to the home of a relative or friend. If possible, the caregiver should be someone the children already know. Otherwise, young children may fear that something bad has happened to their mother or that she has abandoned them. Parents may also enroll their children in a children's preparation class offered by some hospitals and birth centers.

When the mother is away, phone calls can ease the separation. Some hospitals allow siblings to visit their mother and the baby. Most birth centers allow family members to visit the mother whenever they wish.

Activity. Have each student create an illustrated book that would help siblings adjust to the arrival of a new baby.

Problem Solving. Have students discuss how a young child might feel if asked to give up his or her crib or room for the new baby. What could parents do or say to make the adjustment easier for the older sibling?

Parents need to make sure their children do not feel left out when the family talks about the coming baby. All family members wonder how the baby will change their relationships.

Once the new baby is home, parents should make an effort to help siblings adjust to the new arrival. Toddlers may want to be held and cuddled along with the baby. Older children can help care for the baby. Even three- and four-year-olds can help by getting a diaper, holding the baby on their lap, and so on. Helping with the baby encourages siblings to regard the newcomer as a member of the family rather than an intruder.

Final Preparations

As the due date approaches, expectant parents should make final preparations for the coming birth. It is important that they not leave all arrangements for the last few weeks. Some babies arrive early.

❖ Prebirth Visit

If a couple is taking a childbirth preparation course, the instructor usually will take the class to various birthing places within the community. At that time, couples will find out about the appropriate entrance to use and the typical admission procedures at the site they have selected. They may even be allowed to preregister. If they are not taking a course, they can call their hospital or birth center and possibly arrange for a private visit.

❖ Packing a Bag

Two weeks before the due date, the expectant mother should pack a bag with a toothbrush, toothpaste, comb and brush, soap, cosmetics, and other personal care items. She should also pack sanitary napkins because some minor bleeding may continue for a week or more after the baby is born.

The bag should contain a change of clothes for the mother, one or two nursing bras, a bathrobe, a nightgown or two, and slippers. The change of clothes should be loose-fitting because the weight gained during pregnancy is not all lost at once. If the mother expects to breast-feed her baby, the nightgowns should button in front. Even if the mother chooses not to nurse, nursing bras provide needed support until the breasts return to their normal size.

Clothing for the baby's trip home should also be included. The current weather and temperature will determine what blankets are needed for taking the baby home.

CHAPTER 10 REVIEW

Summary

- Parents-to-be can share in the preparations for the baby's birth and care.
- In prepared childbirth classes, couples learn breathing and relaxation techniques and how to be active participants in the birth process.
- Births can take place in a hospital delivery room, a hospital or birth center birthing room, or at home.
- Parents should choose a pediatrician, family doctor, or clinic to provide health care for their baby.
- Couples should consider in advance whether they want to breast-feed or bottle-feed their baby.
- A baby will need bedding, clothing, diapers, feeding and bathing supplies, and travel equipment.
- Clothing items in a layette should be selected on the basis of comfort, warmth, washability, ease of dressing, and size.
- Parental leave is time away from a job that a parent is allowed to take because of the birth or adoption of a baby.
- Parents must arrange for child care if both parents work outside the home.
- Parents should prepare other children in the family for the new baby's arrival.

Questions

p. 174 1. What are the advantages of prepared childbirth?

p. 175 2. What should a woman do if the father-to-be is unable or unwilling to be her childbirth coach?

p. 176 3. How are a delivery room and a birthing room different?

4. What is a pediatrician? p. 177

5. What are the advantages of breast-feeding? p. 178

6. What should parents look for when selecting a crib? p. 181

7. Compare the pros and cons of using home-laundered, diaper-service, and disposable diapers. p. 182

8. Why are parental leaves important for both the parents and baby? p. 184

9. Give examples of various child care and work options that parents could consider. p. 186

10. How can parents prepare other children in the family for a new baby's arrival? p. 187

Activities

1. Design a nursery space for a baby that uses only part of a room. Consider cost, practicality, and convenience.

2. Use catalogs or visit stores to research the cost of baby items. Calculate the total cost of essential items needed for a newborn. How could this cost be decreased?

3. Gather information on the Family and Medical Leave Act of 1993. Report your findings to the class.

Think About

1. Would you prefer to have your baby born in a delivery room or a birthing room? Give at least two reasons for your choice.

2. When it is financially possible, do you think a parent should stay home to take care of the baby? Why or why not?

Reference. See the Teacher's Manual in the front of the Teacher's Annotated Edition for complete answers to the chapter review questions.

189

Birth

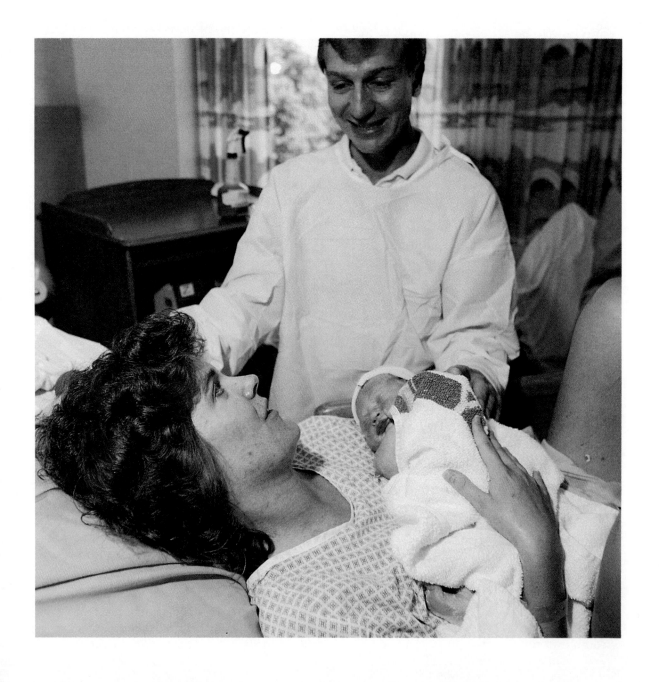

Objectives

This chapter will help you to:

- Summarize the three stages of labor.
- Identify problems that might occur during delivery.
- Describe the mother's recovery after labor.
- List important care procedures for the newborn.

Vocabulary

contractions
dilate
fetal monitor
episiotomy
anesthetic
forceps
breech delivery
cesarean section
colostrum
neonate
Apgar scale

bonding
circumcision

Tanisha and Michael are on their way to the hospital. It is 11:00 P.M. Tanisha has been timing her contractions for two hours, and they are now coming ten minutes apart. When she spoke to the nurse on the telephone, she advised Tanisha to head to the hospital.

Tanisha and Michael arrive at the hospital emergency door as directed. A wheelchair is available for Tanisha to ride in style to the admissions desk. Michael helps with the business matters, giving the admitting clerk needed information. The nurse takes Tanisha to an examining room.

Michael and Tanisha are both smiling. This is the moment they have looked forward to for a long time—the birth of their baby!

Labor

Labor begins with **contractions,** rhythmic tightening and relaxing motions of the muscles of the uterus. Eventually, these contractions help push the baby out of the uterus through the cervix and out through the vagina. As you learned in Chapter 8, the cervix is the narrow lower end of the uterus that leads to the vagina. Before labor starts, the diameter of the cervix is smaller than that of a nickel. During labor, the contractions help **dilate,** or widen, the cervix to about 4 inches (10 centimeters) in diameter.

At first the contractions are weak and last only for seconds. They may be spaced 20 or 30 minutes apart. As labor continues, the contractions become stronger and last longer. They also become more frequent, occurring every few minutes.

Chapter Opener. Ask students to read the opening scenario to the chapter. Ask these questions: What emotions might Tanisha and Michael be feeling? What preparations might they have made for this day?

Discuss. What myths have you heard about labor and childbirth?

Gradually, the cervix dilates as the shape of the uterus changes. When the cervix is completely dilated the woman can begin pushing with her abdominal muscles to help the baby to be born.

❖ First Signs of Labor

Several signs may signal the beginning of labor. Possible indications are a vague nagging backache, soft bowel movements, cramps, and an unusual burst of energy. However, these signs may be due to something besides labor, such as indigestion or fatigue.

Preliminary signs of labor include the appearance of a pinkish discharge or a few drops of blood from the vagina. This is sometimes called the *show*. It indicates that the mucous plug, which has sealed the cervix, has become loose. Continuing contractions which do not become longer, stronger, or closer together are another preliminary sign. These are sometimes called *false labor* or *prelabor*. Labor may still be hours or days away.

There are two important events that signal the beginning of labor. Whenever one of these events occurs, the woman should call the doctor or nurse-midwife. She will then be told when to go to the hospital or birth center.

These are the two signs of labor:

- *Progressing contractions.* These become longer, stronger, and closer together over time.
- *Spontaneous rupture of the amniotic sac.* Amniotic fluid begins to leak or gush out of the vagina. This indicates that the sac surrounding the fetus has broken. Some refer to this as "the water broke."

❖ Hospital/Birth Center Procedures

Once the expectant mother is admitted to the hospital, she changes into a hospital gown. Then an identification band is put on her wrist.

Next a nurse or doctor checks her blood pressure and may give her a pelvic examination. This examination is similar to the ones she had during her office or clinic visits. The nurse also determines the position of the fetus and the amount of dilation of the cervix.

Following the initial preparation, the woman is given a bed in the labor room. Here a nurse or nurses are available at all times. Many hospitals have private labor rooms, one for each woman. Most hospitals encourage the woman to move around as long as she can during labor.

A woman should call her doctor when the first signs of labor begin. Couples who prepare ahead of time know what to expect and what to do.

More About. Braxton Hicks contractions (false labor) occur throughout pregnancy. They usually do not cause discomfort until the last few weeks of pregnancy. Then many women confuse them with real labor pains.

More About. The amniotic sac is known as the "bag of waters." It contains about one quart of amniotic fluid.

More About. Many doctors advise a pregnant woman to go to the hospital when contractions are three to five minutes apart.

DECISIONS ◆
◆ DECISIONS

Colleen has been having contractions all morning. They are about ten minutes apart. Her baby was due three days ago, and Colleen is packed and ready for the hospital. Her husband, Patrick, wants to go to the hospital now. Colleen read that during labor, contractions come more often than every ten minutes. She does not want to get to the hospital too soon. What do you think Colleen and Patrick should do?

Expectant fathers no longer have to stay nervously alone in halls or waiting rooms. They can usually stay with their partner to help and support her during labor. If they are informed and prepared, expectant fathers want to be present during the delivery. Most hospitals will encourage a woman to have at least one person with her during labor and birth.

Many of the same procedures just outlined also take place at a birth center. Here a nurse-midwife may perform the same duties the doctor performs at a hospital.

At a birth center the woman is given a room in which to stay during labor and delivery. She may be encouraged to sit up or walk around as long as she is comfortable. A birth center allows the expectant father and other family members to stay with the woman during labor and delivery.

◆◆ Stages of Labor

Labor is well named. The woman uses a lot of energy in labor. She may feel tired for several days afterward. The average length of labor for a woman having a first baby is between 12 and 14 hours. For some women, labor resembles severe menstrual cramps.

Other women feel most of the pain in their lower back. Each woman is unique and will experience labor in a very individual way.

Labor varies from woman to woman in both time and intensity. Some normal labors last 24 hours or more. Others may last only 3 hours. Nevertheless, the sequence of stages is the same.

There are four stages of labor.

- During the first stage, contractions dilate the cervix.
- During the second stage, contractions push the baby through the birth canal.
- During the third stage, the placenta is expelled from the uterus.
- During the fourth stage, called recovery, the mother's condition is stabilized.

First Stage of Labor

The first stage of labor lasts an average of 10 to 12 hours, counting from the first contractions that come at regular intervals. Labor contractions soften, shorten, and open the cervix. This first stage of labor may go more quickly for a woman who has had a baby before.

During the early part of this stage, contractions are mild. They may come every 20 to 25 minutes and last between 35 and 45 seconds. By the time the first stage of labor is over, the contractions are extremely powerful. They come more frequently and last 60 to 90 seconds.

It is during the first stage that the value of prenatal exercises and training for delivery come into play. Those who have received training know what is happening. They know how to breathe and how to use relaxation techniques. Although these techniques do not guarantee a pain-free birth, they can make pain and stress more manageable. They also enhance the labor process. Additional comfort measures can be provided by the woman's partner and the medical staff.

More About. A pregnant woman in labor may be given an enema and have her public hair shaved. These procedures are up to the doctor and patient.

Emphasize. Being knowledgeable about what is happening during labor and using breathing and relaxation techniques can make labor much easier for an expectant mother.

During all stages of labor, the woman's blood pressure and other vital signs are closely watched. The medical staff also listens to the fetal heartbeat. Many hospitals routinely use a **fetal monitor.** This device, which looks somewhat like a fat belt, is wrapped around the woman's abdomen and connected by wires to a machine. The machine records the contractions and the fetal heartbeat.

Many hospitals give the woman intravenous feedings of sugar water, or glucose. This keeps her blood-sugar level high and gives her energy. If she has not eaten recently and her labor is fairly long, the glucose helps reduce fatigue. Clear fluids, such as fruit juice, or ice chips, may be offered.

During the first stage of labor, the expectant father can help his partner feel comfort-able. Some women lie on their side part of the time; others prefer a sitting position. Women who experience back labor may find that getting on their hands and knees relieves the pressure. The father-to-be can help his partner focus on breathing and relaxation techniques. He can massage her arms, legs, or back if they become tight. Walking also helps to make labor shorter and easier to manage.

Toward the end of the first stage of labor, usually when the woman's cervix is dilated to about 3 inches (8 centimeters), transition occurs. *Transition* means movement, passage, or change from one stage to another. This is usually a period of long, irregular contractions that come very close together.

Most women report that transition is the most difficult part of labor. Some women

An electronic monitor records the fetal heartbeat during labor. If any irregularities occur, the machine signals a warning.

More About. Some woman may have an internal fetal monitor. An electrode is inserted through the vagina onto the baby's scalp; another is attached to the woman's abdomen. They record the contractions and the response of the baby's heart to each contraction.

More About. It is very common to have an IV needle inserted into the woman's arm. This is a safety measure in case needed solutions or medications must be quickly administered during labor.

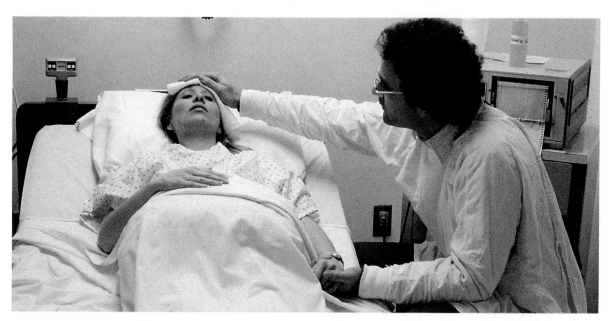

A woman's birthing partner can help her feel comfortable and concentrate on breathing and relaxation techniques.

become irritated and may speak sharply to those around them. Medical professionals know that this behavior is normal, and they try to be as comforting and supportive as possible.

Second Stage of Labor

The second stage of labor begins when the cervix is fully dilated. The contractions continue, making the woman want to bear down with her abdominal muscles to move the baby down the birth canal. This stage ends when the baby has been pushed down the birth canal and through the vaginal opening into waiting hands. This pushing stage lasts an average of 45 minutes for a woman having her first baby.

Women who have had training in childbirth classes know how and when to push and when to relax. Some women report that the pushing stage is more satisfying than it is painful. Most women experience more energy as the birth approaches.

A father-to-be trained through childbirth classes can participate actively in this stage. He can stand by the woman's bed, look into her eyes, and help her interpret the clues from her body and from the medical staff. The woman breathes, bears down, and relaxes in response to her body's cues. During this second stage of labor, contractions are very strong. They come every three to five minutes and last for more than one minute. Between contractions, the woman may feel completely relaxed and may even laugh and joke. Soon the medical attendant tells her that the baby's head can be seen. She knows it will not be long now before she holds her baby.

If the woman is in a labor room, she is moved to the delivery room when the baby is about to be born. If she is in a birthing room, it is readied for delivery. Her lower abdomen and vaginal area are scrubbed and painted with an antiseptic solution. Her legs may be covered with sterile cloth boots. Her heels may be placed in stirrups connected to the delivery table. Her body is covered with a

Discuss. How can a father-to-be provide support for his partner during labor? Why is this important for the mother-to-be? For the father-to-be?

More About. If at any time during labor the baby's heart rate indicates possible distress, the medical staff may decide to deliver the baby immediately by a cesarean section. See page 199.

sterile cloth. Some delivery tables have slanted backs so that the woman can deliver in a semi-sitting position. If the delivery table is flat, pillows may be used to prop her up.

Most hospitals encourage the father-to-be to stay for the delivery. First, the man must scrub well and put on a sterile gown and mask just as the medical personnel do. He may stand near the woman's head where he can see and talk to her. He may support her back during pushing contractions. By now several other people are also in the room: the doctor or nurse-midwife, one or more nurses, and possibly an intern or medical student. All of them will be encouraging the woman as she works to push the baby out.

An episiotomy may be performed just before the baby emerges. An **episiotomy** (ih-PIHZ-ee-OTT-uh-mee) is a small incision made at the back of the woman's vagina. This cut makes the opening of the vagina larger. It also prevents tearing of the vaginal opening during birth. The incision is repaired after birth. The stitches used are self-absorbing and will not have to be removed later on.

Finally, the baby's head emerges. After a few last contractions, the entire baby is released. A new child has been born. The baby's nose and mouth may be suctioned to clear the airway of mucous and amniotic fluid. The parents see their child. The baby may cry. The doctor or nurse-midwife then clamps, or ties, the umbilical cord and cuts it. The nurse gently holds the baby on the mother's stomach, where she can see and feel her child. Sometimes the father helps receive the baby as he or she is born. He may present the child to the mother to see and hold.

The newborn's body is covered with flecks of blood and a white, greasy material called *vernix* (VUR-niks). This keeps the skin from getting waterlogged in the amniotic fluid. It also helps the baby slide through the birth canal. Some newborns are covered with fine hair, called *lanugo* (luh-NOO-goh). This will disappear within a few weeks.

Both the mother and newborn are wrapped in warm blankets. Now the mother's attention is directed to the third stage of labor.

Third Stage of Labor

In the third stage of labor, the placenta and other membranes come out through the birth canal. The nurse massages the uterus as it contracts and expels its contents. This stage takes about ten minutes. If an episiotomy was performed, the doctor or nurse-midwife repairs it with absorbent stitches.

◆◆ Medication During Labor

Many different types of medication can relieve a woman's discomfort during labor. An **anesthetic** (an-ehs-THET-ik) is a medication used to eliminate pain. Most hospitals require that a specialist be present in the delivery room in case an anesthetic is needed. An *anesthetist* (an-NESS-thut-uhst) is a person trained to administer anesthetics. An *anesthesiologist* (an-ehs-THEE-zee-AHL-uh-juhst) is a medical doctor who specializes in administering anesthetics.

Some childbirth classes may lead women to believe that they will deliver their babies without medication. However, many women are given some type of medication during labor. Most types can help a woman relax without dulling her senses too much. She can remain fairly alert and be able to participate in her baby's birth.

No long-term effects of such medication on the baby have been proved. However, a baby whose mother was medicated is less responsive in the first hours after birth. All medications pass through the placenta and enter the fetal bloodstream.

Discuss. In many delivery rooms and birthing rooms, the new father (or coach) may cut the umbilical cord after it is clamped. What emotional benefits might this provide for the new father?

More About. The placenta is also called the "afterbirth." After it is delivered, the doctor or nurse-midwife will examine it to make sure it is intact and not torn. Massaging of the uterus also helps to make sure that all of the placenta is expelled.

Stages of Labor

Before labor begins, the fetus is head down in the uterus and the cervix is still narrow (1). During the first stage of labor, the cervix starts to dilate (2). The muscles of the uterus begin to force the head through the birth canal (3).

During the second stage of labor, the head emerges and turns upward (4). The next step is the birth of the shoulders which is helped by the turning of the baby's head (5). The baby's complete exit is rapid after the shoulders are out. The third stage of labor is the delivery of the placenta (6).

1
Pubic Bone
Bladder
Placenta
Cervix
Spine
Colon

2

3

4

5

6
Placenta

Activity. Show a film or video of the actual birth of a baby.

More About. In the usual birth position, the baby's nose is parallel to the mother's backbone. The emerging of the head is referred to as crowning. The rotation of the baby's body a quarter of a turn after the head emerges is a natural phenomenon.

No responsible person suggests that a woman should suffer severe pain during labor without medication. Still, many women can be helped through the more difficult periods of a normal labor if they have a supportive person to encourage them and if they follow the steps learned in childbirth classes.

Different types of medications may be used during labor.

- **Analgesics.** Analgesic medications change the sensaton of pain without relieving it altogether. An analgesic is administered intravenously or by injection.

- **Local anesthetic.** A local anesthetic numbs a small area. A woman may have an injection of a local anesthetic before an episiotomy. Often, however, the pressure of the baby's head causes numbness so no injection is needed. A local anesthetic is usually given before a new mother gets stitches to repair an episiotomy.

- **Regional anesthetic.** A regional anesthetic blocks sensation in nerves in a certain area. An *epidural* is the injection of an anesthetic between the vertebrae in the lower back. This causes the woman no longer to feel sensation in the pelvic region. A woman who has had a regional anesthetic may have difficulty pushing the baby out because she cannot feel her contractions. Sometimes instruments are used to help her. A regional anesthetic is often used for cesarean deliveries, which will be discussed shortly.

- **General anesthetic.** A general anesthetic is given to a woman to put her to sleep. It may be administered when the baby must be born quickly by cesarean section.

Types of Delivery

The usual type of delivery is through the birth canal and out of the vaginal opening. The baby is born head down, with the face toward the mother's backbone. The baby's skull is made up of plates of bone that are not yet firmly joined together. Thus the head may be temporarily molded into an odd shape as it passes through the narrow passageway. As the head comes down the birth canal, it causes the canal to expand so that the rest of the baby's body can easily pass through it. As

When the cervix is completely dilated, the woman is urged to push down with her abdominal muscles. This helps push the baby through the birth canal.

Activity. Invite an anesthetist or anesthesiologist to talk to the class about his or her career. Ask which types of medications are most commonly used during labor. Why?

Discuss. Ask students what type of medications, if needed, they would prefer during labor. Why?

the head emerges, it extends. The emerging of the head is referred to as *crowning.* Next, the baby's body rotates naturally to one side. This usually enables the shoulders to emerge. If they do not, the doctor or nurse-midwife will gently rotate the head to help the shoulders slip out one at a time. The baby's complete exit is rapid once the shoulders are out.

Sometimes a woman is not able to push the baby out by herself. Then the doctor must use **forceps,** an instrument for reaching into the birth canal and pulling the baby out. Babies delivered with forceps may have marks on the face and head. These marks usually disappear in a few days. A vacuum extractor may also be used.

Sometimes a baby is born with the feet or buttocks appearing first. This is called a **breech delivery** and requires more skill on the part of the doctor or nurse-midwife. Sometimes he or she will use forceps to aid the delivery.

◆ Cesarean Birth

Sometimes a surgical operation is performed to deliver the baby. A **cesarean (sih-ZAIR-ee-uhn) section** is an operation to deliver the baby through an opening cut in the mother's abdominal wall and the uterus. This procedure is done if complications occur for either the mother or child.

Sometimes the mother and doctor know ahead of time that a cesarean section will be performed. Perhaps the woman's pelvis is too small to allow the baby to pass through the birth canal. Surgery may be planned if the baby is very large or if there will be multiple births.

At other times, a cesarean section becomes necessary after labor has begun. If the cervix fails to dilate properly, labor may be very prolonged. If the baby is in a difficult breech position or shows signs of distress, such as a reduced fetal heartbeat, surgery may lessen

Breech Delivery

Most babies are born head first, with the face toward the mother's back. If the fetus is positioned with the buttocks near the cervix, it is in a breech presentation. Either the buttocks or the feet emerge first instead of the head. Breech deliveries are more common in premature infants. Many fetuses do not assume a head-down position until the last few weeks or even days of pregnancy.

the danger to the baby. Another condition requiring a cesarean section is placenta previa. Here the placenta is across the cervix, preventing the baby from passing through.

Whether the mother remains awake during the surgery depends on the type of anesthetic she receives. The father may also be present if the doctor approves. More time is needed for the mother's recovery when she has a cesarean section than when she has a vaginal delivery.

More About. A vacuum extractor may be used instead of forceps. A metal cup is fitted over the baby's scalp with the aid of a pump. Using the cup's handle, the doctor can rotate the head and pull the baby out of the birth canal. The method is considered gentler than forceps.

Activity. Have students research the cost of a cesarean birth versus a vaginal birth.

Around the World

Cesarean Section

A cesarean section is a surgical operation in which the baby is delivered through an incision in the mother's abdomen. Some people believe the procedure is named after Julius Caesar, a Roman emperor in the first century B.C., who may have been delivered by this method. However, historians cannot prove that the story is true.

Historical records indicate that cesarean sections were first performed in the fifteenth century A.D. The procedure was originally performed to try to save the baby after the mother's death.

In *Macbeth*, a famous play written by William Shakespeare sometime around A.D. 1600, a cesarean section is an important part of the plot. A ghost tells Macbeth that "none of woman born shall harm Macbeth." Macbeth believes that this means no harm will come to him in battle. Later in the play, he learns that an enemy named Macduff had been "from his mother's womb untimely ripp'd." This means Macduff was born by cesarean section after his mother died during labor. At the end of the play, Macduff kills Macbeth.

Anesthetics and germ-free surgery techniques were developed in the nineteenth century. Since then, a cesarean section has become a way to save both the baby and the mother in a difficult childbirth. Today, approximately 25 percent of the babies born in the United States are delivered by cesarean section. The procedure has saved many lives. However, some people believe it is performed more often than is necessary.

Approximately 25 percent of all births in the United States are cesarean births. However, some experts believe that many are performed unnecessarily. Although the operation can save lives when serious complications occur, it may be scheduled for those who are not at high risk. Parents-to-be should discuss the advantages and disadvantages of the procedure with the doctor.

A cesarean section should not be chosen to avoid labor or meet a particular due date. The procedure poses a risk for the mother. It also requires a longer recovery period and is more expensive than a vaginal delivery. A cesarean section is major surgery. It should therefore be performed only when the woman's or baby's health and life are in danger.

Most doctors allow parents to hold their baby immediately after birth. This is a special time for new parents to look at, touch, and talk to their baby.

More About. Most women who have a cesarean section can give birth vaginally in the future.

Discuss. When might it not be possible to allow parents to hold their baby immediately after birth?

The Mother's Recovery

The recovery period is often considered the fourth stage of labor. Hospitals generally keep the mother under strict observation for at least an hour after the delivery. Her pulse, breathing rate, and blood pressure are checked at least once every 15 minutes. A significant change in any of these signs could indicate a variety of complications.

During recovery, the mother may be extremely thirsty and need fluids. Since she has not eaten for several hours, the doctor or nurse-midwife may allow her to have a snack.

After delivery, the uterus shrinks like a balloon with the air let out. There may be after pains similar to strong menstrual cramps as the uterus continues to contract. A heavy, bloody discharge similar to a menstrual period may continue for a week or so.

If the woman has had an episiotomy, she may have some discomfort. A nurse will show her how to keep the episiotomy clean and prevent it from becoming infected.

Breast milk will become available naturally in two to three days. If the mother plans to breast-feed, the baby should nurse frequently for short periods to stimulate milk production. During this time the baby will get **colostrum** (kuh-LAHS-trum), a yellow fluid present in the breasts. Colostrum contains protein and substances that help protect the newborn from infections. In a few days the secretion will change to thin, bluish fluid, which is the normal appearance of human milk.

For the mother planning to bottle-feed her baby, some doctors will prescribe a hormone drug that prevents milk production. Other doctors have the mother bind her breasts. In place of the mother's milk, the baby will be given water at first and then formula.

The average hospital stay is one or two days following normal delivery. This time increases to four or five days if a cesarean section was performed. A mother may stay in a birth center for less than one day. You will learn more about the mother's recovery and adjustment in Chapter 12.

During the first few hours after delivery, a mother may be tired but eager to be with her baby.

◆ ◆ Self-Esteem ◆ ◆

One of the most important tasks of parenthood is to give the baby the emotional support that comes from genuine caring and love. This means holding and touching the baby just as much as meeting the baby's physical needs.

More About. After the placenta is delivered, the woman's body temperature and blood pressure go through an adjustment period. During this time her body shakes with chill-like shudders, even though she is not cold.

More About. The bloody show is called lochia.
More About. If the new mother chooses to breast-feed, she will usually be guided by a nurse or lactation specialist on the hospital staff.

Care of the Neonate

The newborn baby is called a **neonate** (NEE-oh-nate) during the first month. Neonates born in hospitals receive a medical checkup immediately after birth. The attending physician or nurse-midwife may also put eye drops into the neonate's eyes at this time. This prevents possible infection from sexually transmitted diseases. Then the doctor or nurse-midwife checks the baby to see that he

The newborn is examined immediately after birth for any medical problems. Various other procedures are also done before the neonate leaves the delivery room.

Discuss. Why is an identification band attached to the baby and footprints recorded? What other safety precautions do hospitals take to prevent mix-ups and kidnappings?

or she is properly developed. Next the infant is weighed, measured, and washed. Sometimes these procedures are delayed until the parents have a chance to hold their baby for the first time.

Before the baby leaves the delivery room, an identification band is attached to his or her wrist or ankle or both. The information on it matches that on the mother's identification band. In addition, the baby's footprints are recorded for the hospital records. Both of these procedures ensure that the mother and baby will be properly matched when leaving the hospital.

◆◆ Neonatal Checkup

The neonate's medical checkup includes the doctor's use of the **Apgar scale,** named for anesthesiologist Virginia Apgar. This is a quick evaluation of the neonate and calls attention to the need for any emergency steps. The letters in Dr. Apgar's name tell what the neonate is tested for:

Appearance or skin color.
Pulse or heart rate.
Grimace or reflex response.
Activity or muscle tone.
Respiration or breathing.

The test is first given immediately after birth. It is repeated five to ten minutes later. See the chart on the next page.

The Brazelton neonatal assessment scale (BNAS) may also be used. This scale was developed by T. Berry Brazelton, a pediatrician at Harvard University. The assessment takes about 20 minutes and requires a flashlight, a bell, a rattle, and a needle. The examiner records the following information:

- Whether the neonate is asleep, alert, or screaming. (These conditions are called states.)

- Whether the neonate changes from one state to another during the examination.

More About. Sometimes a newborn needs to be kept in a warming unit until his or her body temperature adjusts to the environment outside the womb.

The Apgar Scale

	Score		
	0	**1**	**2**
Appearance/skin color	Blue or pale	Pink body and blue limbs	Entirely pink
Pulse/heart rate	Absent	Slow (under 100)	Normal (100-140)
Grimace/responsiveness nasal tickle heel prick	No response No response	Grimace or frown Mild movement	Cough or sneeze Withdraws foot or cries
Activity/muscle tone	Limp	Weak	Strong, active motion
Respiration/breathing	Absent	Slow or irregular	Good, crying

- How much and what kind of stimulation—noise, light, or movement—upsets the baby.
- Whether the baby can quiet himself or herself when upset.
- Whether the neonate has strong reflexes, head control, and hand-to-mouth reactions.

Both of these scales produce reassuring results for most parents. However, they can show other parents that their baby has a birth defect or a birth injury. Fewer than 3 percent of all babies are born with birth defects. Many of these are minor and can be easily corrected. Birth injuries are the result of stress at birth. The use of forceps or a shortage of oxygen can cause injury to the neonate's brain. Cerebral palsy, a condition that affects muscular control and speech, is the result of brain injury before or during birth.

◆◆ Premature Infants

Infants born three or more weeks before their due date are considered premature. This means they are born before prenatal development is complete.

Many premature babies have a low birth weight. A baby of 5½ pounds or less is considered at risk and is treated as a premature infant. However, some babies weighing less than 2 pounds at birth have survived.

Premature infants often have a variety of health problems, such as undeveloped lungs and infections. They need the care of specialists and special hospital supports. Many must be placed in an *incubator*. This is a boxlike apparatus with a transparent cover that controls temperature, humidity, and oxygen level. Premature infants are sometimes connected to feeding tubes and monitors. They often stay in the hospital many days after the

More About. Most neonates have a score of 7-9 on the Apgar scale and only require having mucus suctioned from their airways. Coloring often is the lowest rating due to the normal bluish tinge of a newborn's hands and feet. Infants with a score of 4 or less require immediate assistance with breathing. The Apgar score does not predict the child's future growth and development. **Activity.** Have students find more information about Dr. Virginia Apgar and Dr. T. Barry Brazelton.

mother is released. See "Neonatal Intensive Care" below.

Premature infants have emotional needs, too. It is important that parents hold a premature baby when possible, or at least caress the tiny body with a warm hand. Although a premature baby may be too weak to suck, the mother may be able to pump milk from her breasts to give to the baby.

Premature babies are often slow in development. It is best to start from their expected birth date when making judgments about their development. They must mature outside the uterus, whereas full-term babies continue to develop within the uterus during their last prenatal weeks.

◆◆ Health & Safety ◆◆

Neonatal Intensive Care

Imagine a tiny, newborn baby hooked up to tubes, monitors, and other high-tech medical equipment. It may not be an easy way to begin life, but more and more premature infants are able to survive with neonatal intensive care.

Premature infants often have a very low birth weight and other serious health problems. Such problems include heart defects, infection, anemia, jaundice, pneumonia, and respiratory distress.

One of the biggest problems associated with premature birth is underdeveloped lungs. With this condition, newborns have difficulty breathing. It may result in hyaline membrane disease, which accounts for a significant percentage of all neonatal deaths. Newborns with this disease require constant monitoring and must be given oxygen until their lungs develop. In most cases, this occurs within ten days to two weeks.

Premature babies are taken to neonatal intensive care units. They are placed in individual incubators to conserve body heat and reduce the chance of infection from the environment. Monitors provide information about their heart rate, blood pressure, body temperature, and rate of respiration. Infants who have breathing problems may be attached to a ventilator by a tube inserted into their windpipe.

Many premature infants are too weak or immature to suck. These infants are given liquid nourishment through a tube inserted through their nose or mouth into their stomach. Some are unable to digest food and must be fed intravenously.

Doctors and nurses in neonatal intensive care units receive specialized training. They must handle all types of illnesses, birth defects, and emergencies. It is not uncommon to see two or more doctors and nurses caring for one tiny infant.

Today, parents are encouraged to spend time with their infant in a neonatal unit. They can touch and stroke the baby in spite of all the tubes, wires, and equipment. Sometimes they are even allowed to feed the baby and change a diaper.

Premature babies have to continue their development outside the womb. Neonatal intensive care units provide a protected environment to help even the smallest infants survive.

Activity. Have students research whether there is a neonatal intensive care unit in your local hospital. If not, to where might a premature infant requiring intensive care be transferred?

Activity. Ask students to research the cost of neonatal intensive care for premature infants.

Premature infants often have a low birth weight and health problems. They need special care to allow their body systems to further develop.

✦ Bonding

Many families and child psychologists question the old practice of taking the newborn away from the new parents for several hours or more. They believe that the family should be together for a long period following the baby's birth.

The closeness of the family at this time contributes to the bonding between the new parents and their baby. **Bonding** is the attachment between a parent and child that establishes the basis for their ongoing relationship. It is a part of the love that grows between parent and child.

Hospital and birth centers encourage bonding by allowing the newborn to lie on the mother's abdomen and feel her skin and heartbeat. The father is often encouraged to remain close to both of them at this time. After routine medical procedures are performed, the newborn is placed in the mother's arms. The parents can look at, talk to, and stroke the baby. In turn, the baby can see the parents' faces, hear their voices, and feel their warmth. This process also helps the parents to demonstrate their love for their baby.

Many hospitals have a rooming-in plan. This allows the mother to have her baby stay in the same room with her. That way she can learn to care for the baby and nurse whenever the baby appears hungry. Both breast-fed and bottle-fed babies need to be cuddled closely when fed. This is important for their development. In some hospitals, the baby will stay with the mother both day and night. In other hospitals, the baby will stay during the day and then be taken to a nursery for the night. The father can visit whenever he wishes. A nurse will stop by to see how the family is getting along. He or she will answer the parents' questions and show them how to care for the

DECISIONS ◆
◆ DECISIONS

Julia's baby was born six weeks prematurely. The little girl must stay in the hospital until she gains at least 2 pounds. Julia wants to spend as much time as possible at the hospital with the baby. Her husband, Eduardo, thinks Julia should rest at home and visit only occasionally. He says the baby doesn't even know they are visiting her because she sleeps all the time. Julia and Eduardo have asked your advice. What do you tell them?

Emphasize. If bonding cannot happen soon after birth, the infant will not suffer. Bonding will occur even if it is delayed a few hours or days after birth.

Discuss. What are the advantages and disadvantages of a rooming-in plan? Why should mothers not feel guilty if they choose to have their baby sleep the first night in the hospital nursery?

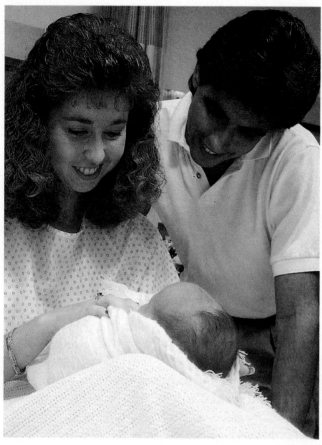

Bonding is important for both parents and baby. By spending time together, the family members develop a lasting emotional attachment to each other.

baby. By spending time together, parents and baby learn to interact with one another.

Although bonding usually occurs shortly after birth, sometimes parents and child must be separated. Health problems may occur or special medical procedures may have to be performed on either the mother or baby. If this happens, parents should not worry that bonding will be prevented. Bonding will still occur once the parents and child can be together.

◆ Circumcision

One of the first medical procedures some baby boys experience is **circumcision** (sur-kuhm-SIZH-uhn). This is a procedure in which the foreskin is cut away from the head of the penis. In hospitals, this is usually done the second day after birth.

There are differences of opinion about circumcision. Some think the procedure makes it easier to clean the penis and helps prevent infections that could occur under the foreskin. Others believe circumcision offers no cleanliness or health advantages. Therefore, the decision about whether to circumcise a baby boy should be left to the parents.

◆ Birth Certificate

Soon after the baby is born, parents should be sure the birth is recorded. Usually the hospital handles the paperwork. The office of vital statistics of the county, city, or town in which the baby is born then issues the birth certificate. This is the child's proof of identity.

A birth certificate is a very important document. It should be kept in a safe place along with other important records. It will be needed when the child goes to school or applies for a social security number. It serves as proof of age, relationships, and citizenship.

A birth certificate is essential in the following situations:

- To prove age in order to drive, to vote, to serve in the military, to get married, or to sign a contract.
- To prove citizenship in order to vote or to be issued a passport.
- To prove relationships in order to identify parents, guardians, and—for inheritance purposes—heirs.
- To qualify for social security, public assistance, special scholarships, and other benefits.
- To meet legal standards in terms of being a minor or an adult.

CHAPTER 11 REVIEW

Summary

- Two signs of beginning labor are pro-gressing contractions and the rupture of the amniotic sac.
- There are four stages of labor, which vary in time and intensity for different women.
- In most deliveries, the baby moves head first through the birth canal. Sometimes a baby is born feet or buttocks first, called a breech delivery. In a cesarean section, the baby is removed through an opening made in the abdominal wall and the uterus.
- During the recovery period, the mother is monitored for any signs of complica-tions.
- Immediately after birth, newborns re-ceive a medical checkup.
- Premature infants may have a low birth weight and other health problems.
- Bonding usually begins shortly after birth.

Questions

p. 192 **1.** What two signs indicate the beginning of labor?

p. 193 **2.** Name the four stages of labor. Briefly describe what takes place during each stage.

p. 194 **3.** How can the father-to-be help the expectant mother during labor?

p. 196 **4.** What is an episiotomy?

p. 199 **5.** What is a breech birth?

p. 199 **6.** When might a cesarean section be per-formed to deliver a baby?

7. What physical sensations may a mother experience during the recovery period? p. 201

8. What five characteristics of a neonate's physical condition does the Apgar scale rate? p. 202

9. Why do premature infants require spe-cial care? p. 203

10. Why is a birth certificate an important document? p. 206

Activities

1. Ask five fathers over the age of sixty whether they were present during the delivery of their children and why or why not. Then ask the same questions of five fathers under the age of thirty-five. What conclusions can you draw from their answers? Share your find-ings with the class.

2. Find out more about the Apgar and BNAS scales. What do the scores obtained from these scales indicate about a newborn's health?

3. Research the reasons why infants are born premature. Prepare an oral or written report on how some premature births can be prevented.

Think About

1. The number of cesarean births has in-creased in the United States over the last 15 years. What might be some rea-sons for this increase?

2. Should circumcision be performed rou-tinely on male babies? Why or why not?

Reference. See the Teacher's Manual in the front of the Teacher's Annotated Edition for complete answers to the chapter review questions.

207

Adjusting to Parenthood

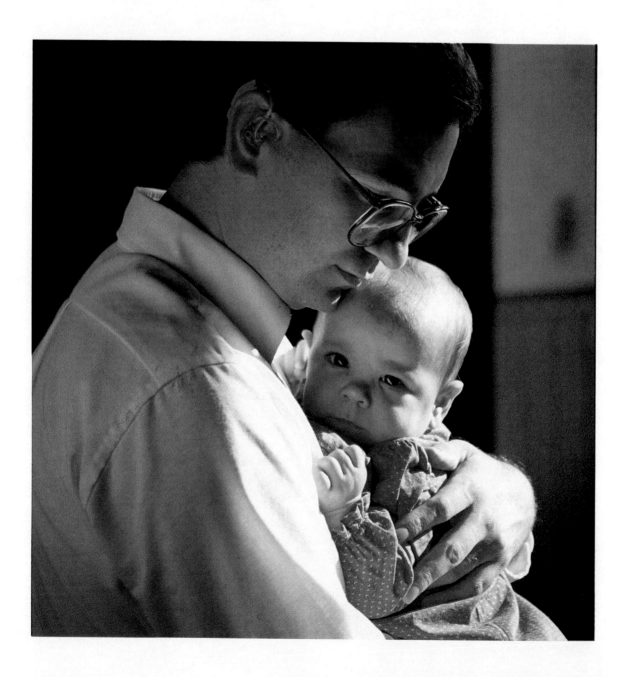

Objectives

This chapter will help you to:
- Explain the physical and emotional adjustments that take place after birth.
- Describe how a new baby can change the parents' life-style.
- Discuss how relationships can be affected by a new baby.
- Give examples of coping strategies that can help new parents.

Vocabulary

postnatal
postpartum blues
coping
stress
priorities
depression

After going home to shave, eat, and take a quick nap, Tom returns to the hospital. A few hours earlier his wife, Megan, gave birth to a healthy baby girl weighing 7½ pounds. Tom was with Megan throughout the labor and delivery. He feels it was one of the most fantastic experiences of his life.

Now, as Tom enters his wife's room, he sees his new daughter sleeping in the bassinet next to Megan. He feels a surge of love and pride as he looks at the two most important people in his life.

Megan opens her eyes and smiles warmly at Tom. He kisses her and asks, "How are things going?"

The birth is over. Now Tom and Megan are entering a new phase of life—parenthood. It will last them both a lifetime.

Home at Last

The first days of parenthood are filled with adjustments. There are adjustments for the baby, for the parents, and for other family members. The new family life the parents have planned for now becomes a reality.

After two or more days in the hospital, both mother and child come home. It is an exciting event. However, new parents may also feel anxious or scared. They realize that their baby is totally dependent on them for food, security, and love. They must manage frequent feedings and diaper changes. They must respond to their baby's cries. Yet newborns are more resilient than many parents realize. You will learn more about caring for a new baby in Unit 3.

New parents must make physical and emotional adjustments to their new roles as parents. Initially, they may have trouble adjusting to a daily routine that revolves

Chapter Opener. Ask students to read the opening scenario to the chapter. Ask these questions: What various emotions might Tom be feeling? What emotions might Megan be feeling? What adjustments await them when they return home with their daughter?

Activity. Have students role play the first night after new parents bring the baby home from the hospital. What situations might they encounter?

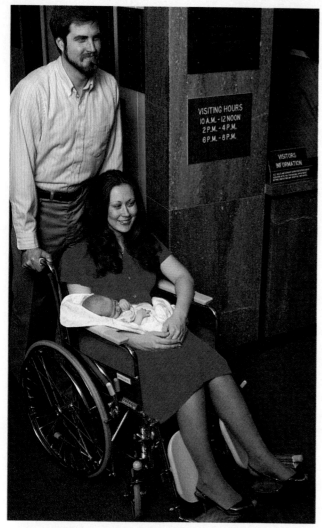

Bringing the new baby home is an exciting event.

around the baby. However, once they become comfortable responding to the baby's needs, they will gain confidence in their parenting skills. Then they can enjoy watching their new baby grow and develop into a unique little individual.

❖ Physical Adjustments

The mother's body begins returning to normal during the month after her baby's birth. The episiotomy heals and breast-feeding may be under way. If the baby is bottle-

fed, the woman's milk supply dries up. Any problems are usually resolved by a visit to the doctor.

It is also important for the new mother to get plenty of rest and to eat nutritious meals. Exercise will help her maintain her energy and return to her earlier shape.

Physical adjustments are also necessary for the father, though to a lesser degree. He may be getting little sleep as he tries to help with the new baby, manage household tasks, and maintain a full-time job. It is important that both mother and father communicate their needs to each other. It is a time for mutual understanding and support.

Medical Checkup

About four to six weeks after birth, the mother should have a **postnatal,** or after childbirth, physical examination. The obstetrician will check that her uterus is returning to normal. The doctor will also check the episiotomy, if one was made during delivery, and look for any problems.

During the postnatal checkup, the mother should ask questions about her own health and adjustment to parenthood. The doctor can also give her advice about feeding and caring for the baby.

Rest and Sleep

In the first few weeks of life, newborns spend much of their time sleeping. While the baby sleeps, parents often find themselves busier than ever with other tasks. Yet the mother's body also needs rest to return to its condition before pregnancy.

The mother needs to take regular rests along with the baby. For example, she might be able to nap in the morning or afternoon while the baby is sleeping. To prevent interruptions, she can turn off the telephone and put a "Do Not Disturb" sign on the door. Getting extra rest during the day will help a new mother better cope with nighttime feedings.

More About. At the postnatal checkup, the doctor will usually discuss methods of contraceptives or family planning. Most doctors recommend waiting three or four weeks before having intercourse after the birth of a baby.

Emphasize. It is essential for new mothers to get as much rest and sleep as possible during the day and night. Most have a feeling of general fatigue for weeks or months after the birth.

Around the World

Where Does the Baby Sleep?

In most Western societies, the ideal is for a baby to sleep alone in a specially decorated nursery. Many child care experts in our culture believe that a baby should always sleep in his or her own bed. They also believe that moving a fussing baby into bed with the parents will spoil the baby.

In many non-Western societies, these are very shocking ideas. Studies have shown that in almost half of the world's societies, mother and infant share a bed. In other societies, the infant sleeps in the same room with the parents. People in these cultures believe that parents cannot spoil an infant too much.

For example, mothers from the !Kung, a society of hunter-gatherers in Africa, believe babies cry only because they are babies. When children are old enough to understand what is going on, they will not cry anymore. These mothers also believe that children will become more independent as they grow up, no matter how much they are spoiled by parents and others.

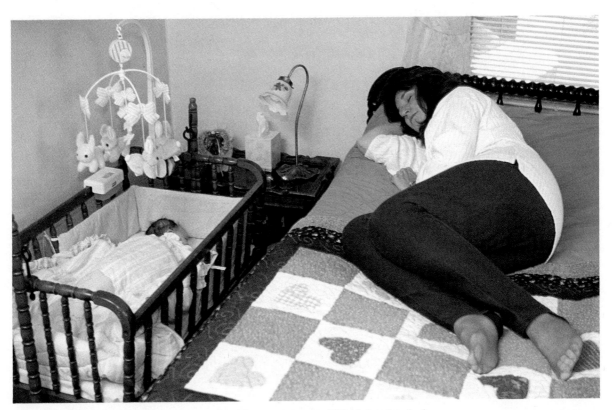

When the baby sleeps, a new mother should get some rest. This helps her body recover from childbirth and helps prevent fatigue. Caring for a newborn takes a lot of energy.

Problem Solving. If parents feel uneasy about having the baby sleep in another room, what would be the advantages of having a room monitoring device? (Sending unit is in newborn's room; receiving unit goes wherever parent is in the home.)

Reference. See page 259 for information about rest and sleep requirements of newborns.

Many parents prefer that the newborn sleep in the same room with them. This makes it easy to check on the baby. Breast-feeding mothers can nurse the baby and then return quickly to sleep. However, light sleepers may be disturbed by every movement the baby makes. If this happens, the parents may want to have the baby sleep in a different room at night.

Visits from relatives or friends should be brief. They should not overtire a new mother or baby. Often visitors want to waken the new baby. At such times, parents should ask the visitors to return again during a time when the baby will be awake.

Nutrition

Good nutrition is as important during the postnatal period as it was in the prenatal period. If a mother is breast-feeding, she needs the same number of servings from the various food groups as she did when she was pregnant. See the chart in Chapter 9. This will provide the essential nutrients and calories required for good milk production.

A mother who breast-feeds also needs plenty of fluids. Every day she should drink at least three quarts of liquids, such as water, milk, and juice. This will help with milk production. She should avoid alcohol and caffeine drinks—such as coffee, tea, and some sodas—while breast-feeding. Both alcohol and caffeine can be passed to the baby through breast milk.

Strict dieting is not recommended while a mother is breast-feeding. Food restrictions, especially during the early weeks of breast-feeding, can decrease the milk supply. After

Good nutrition is as important after childbirth as it was during pregnancy. A nursing mother needs at least three servings from the milk group every day.

Discuss. Using the Food Guide Pyramid on page 158, compare the nutritional requirements of a pregnant woman, a woman who is breast-feeding, and a woman who is bottle-feeding the baby. What are the requirements of teenagers?

Activity. Ask students to gather information about healthy ways to lose weight following pregnancy. Have them plan three meals and three snacks that are high in nutrients and low in calories. Have them demonstrate three appropriate types of exercise.

the milk supply is established, she can gradually lose weight without affecting the milk supply.

Mothers who are not breast-feeding should also eat nutritious meals and snacks. This will help provide the energy needed to care for the new baby.

To lose weight, a new mother should eat a variety of foods that provide important nutrients without extra fat and calories. Foods such as fruits and vegetables, low-fat milk and yogurt, lean meats, poultry, fish, and whole-grain breads and cereals supply the vitamins, minerals, and other nutrients needed for a healthy diet. She should avoid eating a lot of snack foods, such as french fries, chips, cakes, and candies. These foods are high in calories and low in nutrients.

A healthy diet combined with moderate physical activity will help a new mother lose weight. A safe weight loss is about 1 pound a week. By losing weight gradually, she will be more likely to maintain the weight loss. Her doctor or health clinic can give advice about food choices and weight loss. It is important to remember that it takes nine months to gain the weight for a healthy pregnancy. It probably will take another nine months to lose it.

Exercise

Physical activity can help a new mother feel more healthy and energetic. It can also help her lower her weight and regain her shape.

As soon as the doctor approves, she can begin some postnatal exercises. At first, the exercises should be gentle, such as stretching and relaxing. Gradually, she can build up to more strenuous exercises. Some floor exercises can actually be done with the baby lying on the mother's chest or abdomen. Even walking can be very beneficial.

❖ Emotional Adjustments

New parents experience many different emotions after the birth or adoption of a baby. They may be excited, happy, and proud. At the same time, they may be anxious or scared. Because it takes time for parents to adjust to their new roles, they need to understand that their conflicting emotions are normal.

Many parents expect to be overwhelmed by feelings of love as soon as they see their new baby. They may be disappointed if this does not happen exactly as they had imagined. The lifelong bond between parents and child develops gradually. It comes from spending time with each other.

Parents may be concerned about how to care for the baby. They may worry about the added responsibilities and financial costs. Some may feel frustrated about having to quit a job. Others may doubt whether they will be good parents.

It helps for parents to talk over these conflicting feelings and to talk with others. Knowing that other parents have these reactions may help them resolve their own feelings. Then they can start to enjoy the emotional rewards of parenthood.

The Mother's Emotions

Many mothers go through an emotional upheaval after the baby is born. They may feel

Self-Esteem

A new baby can create conflicting emotions in parents. Rather than ignoring these feelings, parents should talk about their self-doubts with others. This experience usually helps parents increase their understanding and acceptance of themselves.

Emphasize. To take care of your back, remember to pick up items by bending from your knees, not from your waist.

Emphasize. The love bond between parent and child is a life-long building endeavor.

overwhelmed with the responsibility of caring for the newborn. They may wonder how they will be able to manage their home, their family, and possibly a job. They may experience a letdown and feel frustrated.

These feelings after childbirth are called **postpartum blues.** They may occur as early as a few days after the baby is born or several weeks later. Even though postpartum blues are very common, doctors are not exactly sure what causes them. Here are some possible causes:

- Change in hormone levels.
- Body fatigue and soreness from the birth experience.
- Tiredness because of lack of rest and sleep.
- Discomfort from sore nipples or swollen breasts.
- Discomfort from the healing episiotomy.
- Anxiety about the responsibility of caring for the baby.
- Disappointment over the baby's appearance or condition.

- Adjustment problems of the father or older children.

Usually postpartum blues disappear within a few weeks without any treatment. It helps for the mother to talk about her feelings with her partner, doctor, or sympathetic friends and relatives.

In some cases, postpartum blues are so severe that the mother is not able to care for her infant adequately. The father or a close friend or relative who recognizes such symptoms should alert the woman's doctor so that she can get help immediately. It does little good to tell the woman she has everything to be happy about. She needs professional care.

The Father's Emotions

Fathers, too, have various emotions after the birth of their child. If they have supported the mother through the pregnancy, labor, and delivery, they may be exhilarated. One father said that observing his child's birth was "the most emotionally satisfying moment of my life."

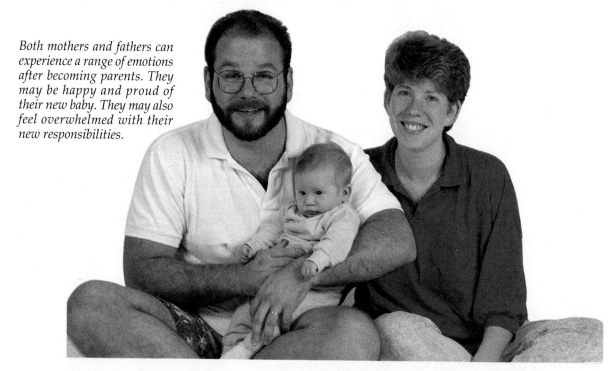

Both mothers and fathers can experience a range of emotions after becoming parents. They may be happy and proud of their new baby. They may also feel overwhelmed with their new responsibilities.

More About. A woman's body experiences an abrupt hormonal change after the birth of a baby. This has a physical and emotional effect and is an important factor in producing postpartum depression.

Problem Solving. Have students discuss how a new father might provide encouragement and support to a new mother experiencing postpartum blues.

DECISIONS ◆ ◆ DECISIONS

As Elvin enters the hospital room, his wife, Tina, is holding their newborn son. "Here" she says, holding the baby out to Elvin, "now it's your turn." Elvin draws back. "Me?" he asks. "No, I'm too clumsy. I'm afraid I might hurt him." How can Elvin overcome his anxiety. What might Tina do to help him? Who else might help?

Becoming a father often enhances a man's self-esteem. It provides evidence of his masculinity and his love. Yet a father may be jealous of the attention the baby receives from the mother and other relatives. He may feel his needs and interests are being overlooked. To get over these feelings, a father should participate more and more in the baby's care. This will help him recognize and identify with the baby's needs. It will also give him a greater appreciation of the time and effort needed to care for an infant.

Many fathers worry about the financial responsibilities of supporting a family. Some may be frustrated by their lack of experience in caring for children. Others may be upset because they are not able to spend much time alone with their partner. Both fathers and mothers need to share their feelings with each other. Through understanding and support they can gain confidence in their ability to be caring and loving parents.

◆ New Routines

A new baby will mean dramatic changes in the family's routines. Now time must be allowed to hold and comfort the baby as well as to feed, change, bathe, and dress the baby. At the same time, other daily tasks still need to be done.

At first, most newborns have irregular and unpredictable schedules. It may take several weeks for a new baby to establish a regular pattern of eating and sleeping. As a result, parents must adapt their lives to the baby's schedule. This means being available even during the middle of the night. It also means never leaving the baby completely alone, even for a short time.

Because each baby is different, each family's schedule will be different. Some babies sleep a great deal; others sleep less. Some parents prefer to bathe the baby at night when both parents are around to help. If parents are bottle-feeding, they may take turns at the morning, evening, and middle-of-the-night feedings. If both parents return to work outside the home soon after the birth of the baby, substitute caregivers are needed to care for the baby.

Years ago, many doctors recommended that babies be kept on strict schedules. Today, most experts believe it is better to have a flexible routine. This means that the baby should be fed when hungry, not at some specific hour. Baths can be given in the morning, afternoon, or evening. Playtime can be whenever parents and other family members are available.

Can you spoil newborn babies by giving them too much attention? No, say pediatricians. Infants need to be fed when hungry, kept warm and dry, and comforted when fussy. They need to be held, cuddled, and loved. When they are older, they can learn to wait a short time before being fed or comforted. Now it is important for their needs to be met as soon as possible. This helps babies develop a sense of security in their new surroundings.

Activity. On the chalkboard, write the students' list of all the responsibilities involved in caring for a newborn. Then discuss whether each responsibility should be that of the mother, the father, or both parents.

Discuss. Have students debate the issue: Can newborns be spoiled? Each side must defend their views.

Life-Style Changes

Certain adjustments and changes in the couple's life-style, or way of living, occur with the newborn's arrival. No longer can new parents make last-minute plans to go out. Their activities, such as shopping or visiting friends, must be planned in advance. They must schedule their activities around the infant's sleeping and feeding schedules. Every time they go somewhere with the baby, they must carry a supply of diapers, clothing changes, bottles, toys, and other items.

Especially during the first few months after birth, a baby's needs must come first. As a result, there is less time for social life. Both mothers and fathers should be involved in the infant's care. One parent should not go off frequently with friends, always leaving the other parent to care for the baby alone.

When going to the movies or a party without the baby, parents must arrange for someone to care for the child. In many cases, parents of newborns do not feel comfortable leaving infants in the care of someone else except for very short periods. In addition, hiring a babysitter may be too expensive for many family budgets. Some families are fortunate to have nearby grandparents or other relatives who volunteer to stay with the infant from time to time. Others exchange babysitting hours with friends or neighbors.

Many couples discover that some of their interests change once the baby is born. New friendships often develop as parents find themselves drawn to other new parents who share the same experiences. Friendships first formed in childbirth preparation classes may continue. Parents can continue to share information and provide support. Religious organizations, YMCA/YWCAs, community

A baby creates many changes in the parents' lives. Now parents must take the baby with them or arrange for others to provide the necessary care.

DECISIONS ◆
◆ DECISIONS

Phil and Stacy are enjoying their first days together with their new daughter, Gina. Relatives and friends have been stopping by the apartment each day to see the baby. Some have tried to wake Gina up when she was asleep. Others have stayed for several hours until the baby did awaken. Now another friend has called to ask when he may come to see the baby. Stacy and Phil were looking forward to a quiet evening alone. What should Phil say to his friend? What should the couple say to relatives and friends who stop by?

Activity. Have students make up a detailed list of all the supplies and equipment that parents of a newborn should take with them when going away for six hours. What would be needed for a weekend?

Discuss. How could parents locate a reliable babysitter? What qualities should they look for? What is the going hourly rate for a babysitter in your community? How much would it cost for an evening out? See page 576 for information about babysitting.

Many new parents enjoy spending time with other parents. They can talk about their children and share information about parenting and child care.

centers, and similar groups often offer programs for parents with infants. Members of the Mothers of Twins club support each other in adjusting to the extra challenges of a multiple birth.

New parents must also adjust to the new financial responsibilities that come with parenthood. Many families have a much tighter budget. This is especially true if one parent has taken an extended parental leave from work without pay. Couples who have been able to save some money before the baby's arrival will be in better shape than those who have not. Even so, most new parents have to forego expensive dinners or vacations after the baby is born. By carefully planning their family budget and adjusting their life-style, they can often avoid financial problems.

Most new parents are happy to make the necessary changes and adjustments in their life-style. They want to spend time together with their new baby. Caring for an infant can be an exciting achievement. Most of all, they enjoy their new roles as parents.

Activity. Have students create a monthly budget for a couple who have a new baby and live in your community. What extra expenses are created by the arrival of the baby?

Discuss. Ask students to brainstorm activities that parents could do with a baby. Which activities would involve little or no cost?

New Relationships

The birth or adoption of a baby creates new relationships within a family. First-time parents take on the roles of mother and father. If there are other children in the family, they have to adjust to a new sibling. Even grandparents, aunts, uncles, and cousins are affected by new relationships.

❖ The Couple's Relationship

Having a baby means change. There are changes in the way each parent thinks about herself or himself. There are changes in the couple's relationship with each other. For example, a mother and father will no longer have the exclusive companionship of each other. They must be willing to share a good part of their time with the baby.

This is a time that can strain a couple's relationship. New parents may feel physically exhausted. After all, child care requires a great deal of time and energy. They may feel frustrated or discouraged as they try to manage all their responsibilities. As a result, some new parents find themselves constantly arguing with each other. If there have been problems in the relationship before the birth, a new baby will probably add to the conflict. A couple should never expect a baby to improve a shaky relationship.

Good communication can help a couple resolve problems before they become major sources of conflict. It is important to communicate honestly with each other and to try to understand each other's feelings. Discussing problems in a calm manner is far more productive than getting angry or shouting at each other. It also helps to keep a sense of humor. When a couple can laugh at themselves and their mistakes, they can maintain a better balance in their lives.

New Roles

The first step a couple must take is to get used to their new roles as mother and father. They may be used to thinking of themselves as husband and wife or as people with a particular career or interest. Now they must learn to see themselves as parents as well.

New roles mean new opportunities and challenges. For example, a woman may have to balance the many responsibilities of being mother, wife, worker, and household manager. A man may have to assume new responsibilities for child care and household tasks, as well as for husband and worker.

If the new mother continues working, the couple must arrange for good child care,

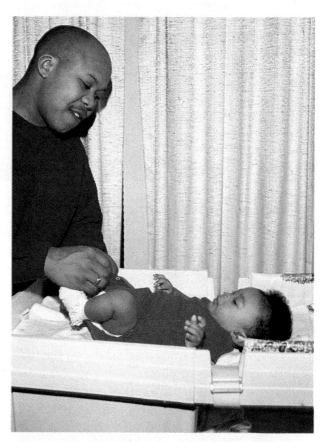

A new father can develop a closer bond with his baby by sharing in the baby's care.

Discuss. Ask students to think about what it means to be a parent. In what ways does parenthood affect or change a parent's life? What changes might be positive? Negative?

Problem Solving. Have students suggest ways that new fathers and mothers can communicate their needs to each other. See pages 501-505 for information on communication skills.

which often is expensive. She must handle the special challenge of balancing work and family responsibilities. If she decides not to work—either for a few months or for several years—she may have mixed feelings about leaving her job. She may miss her coworkers and salary, as well as the personal satisfaction and independence her job provided. The roles of worker and mother offer different rewards and challenges.

A woman who did not work outside the home before the birth will have to adjust to all the demands a baby will make on her time. As a mother she must reorganize her activities around the baby's needs. She will no longer have as much time to devote to herself, her partner, and friends.

A new father also has to assume new roles. He needs to learn how to care for the baby. Changing diapers, giving a bottle, or comforting a crying baby are tasks that both fathers and mothers can share. They provide opportunities for the new baby to bond with both parents.

A new father should take responsibility for various household tasks. For example, he can shop for groceries, baby supplies, and other household products. He can help prepare nutritious meals and snacks for the family. He can be responsible for doing the laundry or cleaning the home. When both parents share in the household tasks, adjustments to parenthood can be made more easily.

Because many fathers take only a short parental leave from work, they may need to find other ways to help their family during early parenthood. Some fathers are able to telephone or stop by the home during the day. Others can ask relatives, friends, or neighbors to help with the baby or other tasks when needed.

Spending Time Together

New parents should find ways to spend time together as a couple. This is easy when both parents are involved in caring for their baby and for their home. By doing tasks together, they can strengthen their relationship as a couple and their roles as parents.

Parents also need to spend time having fun as a family. Playing with the baby, going for walks, and visiting a park are relaxing

New parents need some time to be alone together. This helps them strengthen their own relationship. However, they must always arrange for reliable child care when they are away.

Discuss. Do you think more fathers are taking an active role in caring for their children? If so, how are they helping? If not, why?

Reference. See pages 514–517 for ways to successfully balance work and family life.

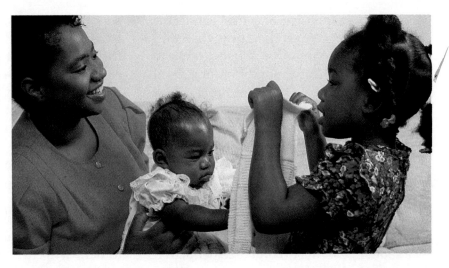

Older siblings feel important when they can help with the baby's care. They also need reassurance of their parents' love.

activities that parents and child can enjoy together.

Occasionally parents need to escape from the responsibilities of child care and household tasks. Often relatives or friends can help out with the baby and do other chores. Whether going out for dinner or spending a quiet afternoon at home, a couple need time to be alone together. This helps them to nurture their own love and relationship.

◆◆ Sibling Relationships

Siblings, as well as parents, can bond with the new baby. This relationship can be nurtured by having the siblings help care for the baby.

Even young children can do little things that will make them feel important to the family. They can bring the parent a diaper. They can talk to the baby or show the baby a toy. They can sit on the floor and gently hold the baby. Older siblings can be more involved in the baby's care by rocking or carrying the baby. As the baby gets bigger, siblings can laugh and play with her or him. All these activities will help siblings feel like big and important brothers or sisters.

Siblings around four or five years of age may at first be disappointed in the long-awaited baby. People may have told them that they will have lots of fun playing with the baby. Then the newborn turns out to be very small and not playful at all. Parents need to explain when the baby will be able to do different things, such as smile, sit up, and crawl.

Sometimes a sibling will show signs of jealousy toward the new baby. Parents should accept these feelings but make sure that the child never hurts the baby. Sometimes young siblings will want to be held and cuddled just like the baby. They may even want to drink from a bottle or sleep in the crib. These actions show that they need reassurance of their place in the family. The more a child can feel helpful and needed, the less jealousy he or she will feel toward the new baby.

All children who have a new sibling need continual reminders that they are loved by their parents. It is important for each child to have some special time alone with a parent. For example, a parent can read a story or play a game with an older sibling while the newborn sleeps. This provides an opportunity for the parent to focus attention on each child.

Discuss. Why do you think young siblings may want to be held, rocked, and fed after a new baby arrives in the family? How should parents respond to these requests?

Reference. See pages 481-484 for information about handling jealousy and sibling rivalry.

❖ Relationships with Relatives

Grandparents, aunts and uncles, and cousins will be eager to meet the new baby. Some may help the new parents care for the baby during the first few days or weeks after the birth.

It is important for new parents to feel confident in their own decisions about caring for their child. Otherwise, they may be hurt if a relative suggests different ways of doing different tasks. Many relatives offer well-meaning advice that is not meant as criticism. Sometimes the advice is helpful because it comes from years of experience. At other times it may be the opposite of what the pediatrician recommends. New parents should let relatives know that they will appreciate any advice but that the final decisions must be their own.

Grandparents often have a special role in the new baby's life. If they live nearby, they can give the child attention and love. Some are even able to provide regular child care. As the child grows older, grandparents can tell stories about the child's parents when they were young. However, new parents should not assume that their parents will always want or be able to care for the baby.

Relatives can also provide a family and cultural heritage for the new family unit. Special traditions and celebrations can enrich the lives of all members of the extended family.

Relatives will be anxious to meet the new baby. Grandparents, especially, can play an important role in the child's life.

Coping Strategies

Coping (KOHP-ing) is being able to deal with responsibilities and problems with some degree of success. New parents often are challenged by the question of what to do next or what to do instead. Since the baby cannot talk, they do not always know how to interpret his or her signals. For example, when the baby cries, is it because of hunger, soiled diapers, a need for cuddling, illness, or something else?

Parents can do several things to help themselves cope with the new responsibilities of parenthood. These include sharing responsibilities, managing stress, and getting support from others.

◆ Sharing Responsibilities

Taking care of a baby is a twenty-four-hours-a-day job. An infant needs lots of physical care, love, and attention. Parents can feel overwhelmed by the many responsibilities involved in child care. When both parents share the responsibilities, one parent does not feel overburdened.

At first, some parents feel awkward and clumsy trying to help the tiny, fragile baby. Others, especially fathers, feel embarrassed around relatives or friends as they try, for example, to change the baby's diapers. Patience and encouragement can help both parents as they learn the skills of infant care.

The same is true of sharing household responsibilities. Some couples prefer to divide up the chores. One parent may scrub the bathroom, while the other does the laundry. Other couples prefer to alternate tasks. For example, one day the man prepares dinner, and the next day the woman prepares it.

Even the responsibilities of taking care of the family finances can be shared. One partner can write all the checks. The other part-

New parents need to share household and child care responsibilities. Then neither parent feels overwhelmed with the many tasks involved in caring for the baby and the home.

ner can see that the check register balances with bank statements.

For sharing of responsibilities to work best, the couple should maintain some flexibility. Perhaps one person has to work late or feels ill or is unusually tired. Then the other person needs to step in and relieve the pressures on the partner. Being part of a team means helping out the other person because that other person will do the same for you.

Discuss. How can new parents share responsibilities for child care? For household chores? Why is flexibility so important?

Reference. See pages 516-517 for information about ways to manage more successfully.

❖ Managing Stress

New parents need to learn how to handle **stress.** This is tension caused by important events or changes in one's life. Stress can affect all of us both physically and emotionally.

Some degree of stress is positive. It gives us the energy to accomplish a task. Too much stress, however, can cause headaches, sleeplessness, and loss of appetite. This is called negative stress and it can make us feel emotionally drained.

It is important to recognize the signs of negative stress as soon as possible. Then it is easier to deal positively with it. Here are some ways that new parents—and all of us—can manage stress:

- *Try to relax.* Rather than always doing chores when the baby is sleeping, new parents need to take some time to relax. This may mean reading, listening to music, or taking a short nap.

- *Get some exercise.* Whether the exercise is doing aerobics or going for a walk, it helps relieve tension. Many couples enjoy exercising together.

- *Plan ahead.* Parents should make a list of things they need to do or buy. This helps them remember a doctor's appointment or the need for clean diapers. It also makes better use of parents' time. When shopping they can check the list to be sure they get everything they need in one trip.

- *Set priorities.* Setting **priorities** means deciding which tasks are most urgent— which should be done first and which ones can wait. The baby's needs must be a first priority. However, many household tasks can be postponed until a parent has more time or energy.

- *Remember that no parent is perfect.* Even though parents may try hard, they still will make mistakes. Caring for children is both

◆ *Health & Safety* ◆

Managing Stress

Every parent has days when he or she is overwhelmed with the responsibility of caring for a baby. Feelings of frustration are normal. Here are some ways that parents can relieve the tension and stress in their lives:

- Try to sleep when the baby sleeps. It is difficult to be cheerful when you are overtired. Even a short nap can be wonderfully refreshing.

- Phone an understanding friend.

- Get a pencil and notebook. Write down your thoughts and feelings.

- Listen to quiet music. If you want the music to calm the baby too, try different styles. You and the baby might not have the same musical taste.

- Take a hot shower or a warm bubble bath.

- Lie down on the floor and concentrate on a spot on the ceiling. Keep concentrating until you feel some of the tension start to slip away.

- Do sit-ups or aerobic exercises. Ask someone to watch the baby while you go for a jog or bike ride. Take the baby for a walk. Both of you will benefit from the fresh air and change of scenery.

challenging and rewarding. Many parents are successful at the tasks—but there is no such thing as a perfect parent.

Single parents may experience greater stress than two-parent families. Single parents should not hesitate to ask relatives or friends to take care of the baby from time to time.

It is important to recognize the signs of stress early and reduce the tension. If left untreated, stress can result in physical health problems or **depression.** This is a prolonged feeling of sadness marked by helplessness and an inability to enjoy life. It can even lead to suicide. If a person suffers from depression, it is important to get professional help.

◆ Getting Support

New parents need sources of support. Among the best of these may be their own parents and other relatives who understand the responsibilities that new parents have. Even if they live far away, these people can provide advice and encouragement through telephone calls and letters.

It is also helpful for new parents to talk with other new parents. They may be friends, siblings, neighbors, or members of the prepared childbirth class. All new parents go through many of the same experiences. Often they can share their solutions to particular problems with each other.

New parents can get advice about the baby or themselves from a family doctor, pediatrician, nurse, or health clinic staff member. These professionals are used to answering all kinds of questions from new parents. Many have special leaflets on topics such as feeding a baby, bathing a baby, and recognizing signs of illness.

Many resources are available to new parents within most communities. Libraries have many books on parenting and child care. Various organizations sponsor support groups and programs and provide information for parents. You will learn more about community resources in Chapter 26.

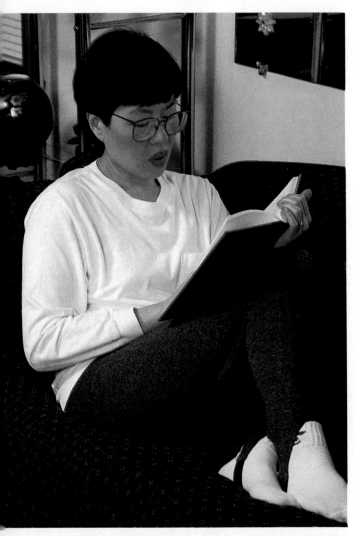

New parents need to take time to read a book, listen to music, or exercise. These activities help relieve the tension caused by stress.

Activity. Have students role play various stressful situations and work out the problems using the suggestions on page 223.

Reference. See pages 505-510 for information about community resources and support groups.

CHAPTER 12 REVIEW

Summary

- The first days of parenthood are filled with physical and emotional adjustments.
- A new mother should have a postnatal medical checkup four to six weeks after birth. She should get plenty of rest, eat nutritious meals, and exercise.
- Both mother and father often experience conflicting emotions after the baby is born. Many new mothers have postpartum blues.
- The newborn's arrival usually causes significant changes in a couple's life-style. They must adjust to new schedules and responsibilities.
- A couple's relationship changes as they assume the roles of mother and father.
- Siblings usually feel less jealousy toward a new baby when they can assist with the baby's care.
- Parents can help themselves cope with the new responsibilities of parenthood by sharing those responsibilities, managing stress, and getting support from others.

Questions

p. 210 1. What physical adjustments must both the mother and father make during the weeks after their baby's birth?

p. 212 2. Why is good nutrition still important for a woman during the postnatal period?

p. 213 3. How should a new mother lose weight safely?

p. 214 4. What are four possible causes of postpartum blues?

5. Why may a father feel jealous of the attention the baby receives from the mother and other relatives? What can he do to get over these feelings? p. 215

6. What specific changes in a couple's life-style occur with the newborn's arrival? p. 216

7. Why is it important for new parents to discuss their problems and feelings with each other? p. 218

8. How can parents help other children in the family bond with the new baby? p. 220

9. What is stress? List four ways that parents can help manage stress? p. 223

10. To whom might new parents turn for support? p. 224

Activities

1. Ask five parents of young children how their lives changed after becoming parents. What was the most difficult adjustment they had to make? Share your findings with the class.

2. Write about the world from a one-week-old baby's point of view.

3. Find out what organizations in your community offer programs for parents with infants. Prepare a fact sheet listing the name and telephone number of each organization, the name of the program, and a brief description.

Think About

1. Why do most experts now recommend a flexible routine for babies rather than a strict schedule?

2. Why should a couple never expect a baby to improve a shaky relationship?

Reference. See the Teacher's Manual in the front of the Teacher's Annotated Edition for complete answers to the chapter review questions.

225

A New Baby

CHAPTERS

Understanding Infants

Objectives

This chapter will help you to:
- Summarize the physical development of infants.
- Identify important goals for emotional and social development during infancy.
- Explain how infants use their senses to learn.
- Describe how language develops in infants.

Vocabulary

maturation
physical development
reflexes
fontanels
motor skills
emotional development
social development
stranger anxiety
separation anxiety
temperament
attachment
 behavior

cognitive
 development
sensorimotor
 stage

A muffled little cry accompanied by a slight shudder signals that baby Timmy, age two weeks, is waking up. Timmy's parents, Melody and Arnie, turn away from the TV program and peek in the bassinet. They smile at each other and realize that at any moment the action will start. Arnie squeezes Melody's hand. They both like anticipating what Timmy will do.

In a few minutes the little cry becomes more pronounced. Arnie gets up and brings Timmy to the couch. Both parents look lovingly at the baby and touch his little hands. They both start talking to him—almost in unison. They laugh together, amused.

The baby is uniting Melody and Arnie as they had never imagined. They agree that this new stage of life is very satisfying.

Growth and Development

Infants experience many stages of growth and development. *Growth*, you recall, refers to an increase in size or weight. Friends and family members often talk about children's growth. You probably remember someone saying to you, "I can't believe how much you've grown!"

Development refers to an increasing skill in physical, emotional, social, or cognitive abilities. In this chapter you will learn about the growth and development that occurs during a baby's first year.

Maturation is the process of reaching full growth and development. It is an internal process controlled by age and genetics. You have probably heard people say, "She's short for a five-year-old" or "He's immature." Usually, this means that some part of a person's

Chapter Opener. Ask students to read the opening scenario to this chapter. Ask the following questions: Why do you think Melody and Arnie enjoy watching their new child? In what ways will Timmy change from now until his first birthday?

Activity. Ask students to bring in their baby pictures. Assemble a "Who's Who?" with pictures labeled by numbers. Have students try to identify each baby. Have students compare their own changes and similarities since they were a baby.

growth or development is not up to the typical level for a person of his or her age.

By studying children around the world, researchers have found that there are typical ages at which various changes usually occur. *Typical*, *normal*, and *average* are terms that mean a baby grows or responds like the largest percentage of babies of a given age. For example, if a chart says a typical baby walks a few steps alone at age twelve months, it means that more than 50 percent have begun to walk at about that age. Some babies have walked earlier, at ten or eleven months, while others have walked at thirteen or fourteen months. If a child reaches eighteen to twenty months of age without walking, parents would ask the doctor why the child is not achieving that skill. There could be a problem that needs to be corrected.

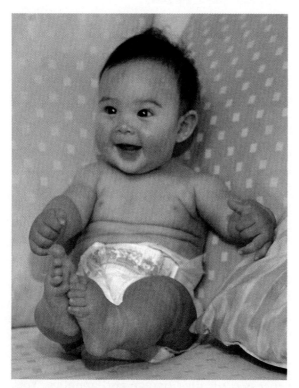

Physical growth and development is very dramatic during the baby's first year. During this time, the average baby triples his or her birth weight and learns to sit, crawl, stand, and eventually walk.

Physical Growth and Development

Leslie's father is encouraging his six-month-old daughter to sit, reach, and smile back at him. Her grandmother exclaims, "Look how Leslie is sitting up! I had forgotten how soon a baby learns to sit." Leslie's grandmother is noticing the baby's **physical development.** This refers to a child's increasing ability to control and coordinate body movements. Physical development involves much more than just growing in height and weight.

By six months of age, many babies can sit alone for short periods of time. They also can reach for an object and laugh out loud. However, babies cannot be taught these skills. They can come only after the babies' muscles mature. The biological clock seems to set the time for each child's muscles to mature, making it possible for that child to accomplish a skill. Each person's clock is different.

Growth in infancy, like prenatal growth, follows a predictable pattern. This pattern is very similar in all children around the world. By observing an infant's size, weight, proportion, and body movements, one gains clues about the child's physical growth and development.

◆◆ Size and Weight

The average baby is 20 inches long at birth. Of course, not all babies are that long. Some are shorter, and some are longer. They typically range from 18 to 21½ inches.

An average newborn weighs 7½ pounds. The typical range is between 5½ and 10 pounds. A newborn will lose weight during the first few days after birth. This is due to fluid loss and lack of appetite. This weight will be regained in about ten days. By the end of the first month, the average baby will have gained 2 pounds since birth.

As a general rule, a baby increases in height by 50 percent and triples the birth weight by the end of the first year. That is, a baby 20 inches long at birth will grow 10 more inches during the first year. A baby who weighs 7 pounds at birth will weigh about 14 pounds at six months and 21 pounds at one year. This is a very fast rate of growth. Clearly, the rate of growth slows down after infancy.

❖ Reflex Behavior

A newborn has little control over his or her body. However, the body will respond in predictable ways when the reflexes are stimulated. **Reflexes** are automatic, or involuntary, responses to stimulation of some kind. They help the infant deal with the world.

The grasping reflex is one example of such an automatic response. Newborns automatically grasp whatever touches their palm. This

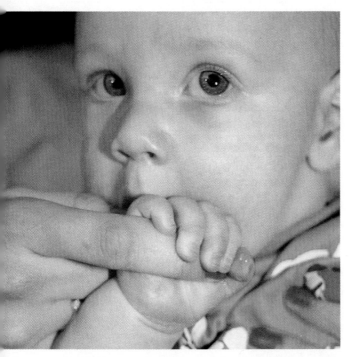

Young babies will automatically grasp anything that touches their palm. This grasping reflex disappears entirely when infants learn to control their hands at two or three months of age.

Witney is ten weeks old. Her four-year-old brother, Clinton, is watching her as she lies on a blanket. When Clinton places his fingers near hers, she grasps them with both hands. He starts to pull her up saying, "Look! Witney is so strong. I can pull her up!" Their mother immediately grabs hold of Witney and gently places her back on the blanket. She wants to explain to Clinton why it is dangerous for him to lift the baby in that manner. What should she say to her son?

reflex should never be used to lift babies up because they let go without warning. When infants learn to control their hands at three months, the reflex disappears entirely.

The chart on the next page describes the reflexes a baby is born with. As you read about the infant's body, notice how many parts are involved in a newborn's reflexes.

❖ Observing the Infant's Body

"Look how tiny his toes are! Will it take a long time for them to be as big as mine?" asks five-year-old Shelly. She is admiring her baby brother while her mother bathes him.

An infant's body proportions, or size relationships between parts, are different from an adult's. The head of a newborn baby is very large. Compared to the baby's total length of about 20 inches, the length of the head measures 5 inches, or one-fourth of the total length. In contrast, the head of an adult is about one-eighth of his or her total height. An infant's abdomen is large in comparison to adult proportions, while the infant's arms and legs are short and small.

The Head

A newborn's head usually looks elongated, or peaked. It becomes more rounded several days after birth. As you learned in Chapter 11, the skull is actually made up of plates of bone. These plates are loosely held together by tough, canvaslike tissue. Thus they move slightly as the baby is forced head first down through the birth canal. As this happens, the head is temporarily misshapen. The plates of bone will not grow firmly together until the baby is about eighteen months old.

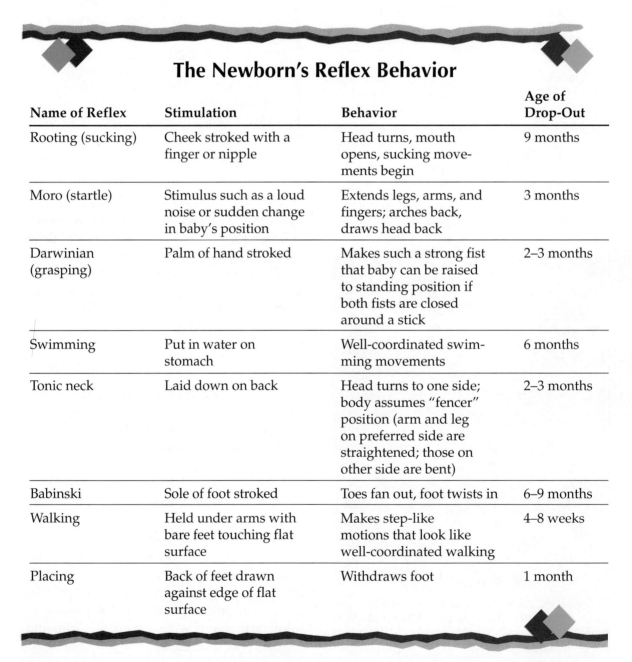

The Newborn's Reflex Behavior

Name of Reflex	Stimulation	Behavior	Age of Drop-Out
Rooting (sucking)	Cheek stroked with a finger or nipple	Head turns, mouth opens, sucking movements begin	9 months
Moro (startle)	Stimulus such as a loud noise or sudden change in baby's position	Extends legs, arms, and fingers; arches back, draws head back	3 months
Darwinian (grasping)	Palm of hand stroked	Makes such a strong fist that baby can be raised to standing position if both fists are closed around a stick	2–3 months
Swimming	Put in water on stomach	Well-coordinated swimming movements	6 months
Tonic neck	Laid down on back	Head turns to one side; body assumes "fencer" position (arm and leg on preferred side are straightened; those on other side are bent)	2–3 months
Babinski	Sole of foot stroked	Toes fan out, foot twists in	6–9 months
Walking	Held under arms with bare feet touching flat surface	Makes step-like motions that look like well-coordinated walking	4–8 weeks
Placing	Back of feet drawn against edge of flat surface	Withdraws foot	1 month

Discuss. Ask students: How could a parent possibly teach a newborn infant to suck if there was no rooting reflex?

More About. Another way to describe the newborn's head is cone shaped.

The areas between these bone plates at the top, back, and sides of the baby's head are called **fontanels** (fahn-tuh-NELZ), or soft spots. You can see the fontanels at the top and back of a newborn's head. You may have been warned not to touch a baby's soft spots. In fact, these areas are very strong because of the tough tissue beneath the skin and can be gently touched. Because the skull is still flexible, a baby rarely gets a concussion from bumps or falls.

Some babies have lots of hair on their head at birth. Others are nearly bald. Some lose their first hair. The hair that grows in later is sometimes a different color than the first hair.

Because the head is very wobbly, parents and other caregivers must put a supporting hand behind the head and neck whenever they hold very young babies. When newborns are lying on their abdomen, they can turn their heads from side to side. This helps strengthen the muscles that support the head. Parents and caregivers can encourage this exercise by letting babies lie on their stomach often. This also gives infants a chance to practice *head rearing,* the raising and lowering of the head.

By the age of three months, most infants can hold their head erect for a short time. By six months of age, infants' neck muscles can support the head for continuous periods of time. At this stage, babies can sit upright in a high chair or infant seat.

Eyes

Babies can see at birth. At first they focus only on single features, such as another person's eyes. They will stare intently at an object within their visual range. If the object moves, they soon follow it with their eyes. By the age of three months, babies can see as well as adults can.

Infants like bright objects and prefer colored objects to gray ones. If shown drawings, they prefer a human face to a geometric figure. Burton L. White has done extensive research on children from birth to three years. He has found that newborn infants can best see an object that is between 5 and 18 inches away. Dr. White has also found that until infants are six weeks old, they are extremely sensitive to bright lights. Newborns may open their eyes more in a dimly lighted room than in a brightly lighted one.

Ears

Babies have very good hearing. They hear single sounds and rapidly recognize patterns of sound. They often turn their head in the direction of sounds when they are only three days old. Babies prefer the sound of the human voice. They especially respond to the

Parents should teach older children to support the baby's head and neck while holding the baby.

sound of their mother's voice when compared to a strange female's voice.

Newborns startle easily and will often cry when they hear loud noises. This is called the startle reflex. When startled, babies jump, extending their legs. Their arms also wave jerkily, their back arches, and they throw back their head. Then they usually start to cry. The startle reflex may alarm new parents if they do not know it is a normal response.

If loud noises never startle a baby, he or she may have a hearing problem and should be checked by a doctor. Sometimes even a tiny infant can wear hearing aids to be able to hear.

Mouth

Infants' automatic sucking action is important at birth. This is called a rooting reflex. When the cheek is touched, infants turn toward the touch and start sucking automatically. This reflex helps them nurse instinctively from birth. Without it, they might not survive.

The taste buds on the tongue and roof of the mouth are very sensitive. New babies show their preference for certain tastes—especially sweets—by sucking continuously on sugar water but only briefly on salty water. If given something sour, they pucker up just as you do.

Teeth

Because tooth buds are formed during prenatal development, it is important for a pregnant woman to drink lots of milk. Milk contains calcium and phosphorus, which help build strong teeth.

The first set of teeth are called primary or baby teeth. They are largely composed of calcium that comes from the milk the baby drinks. On rare occasion, a baby is born with a tooth. Usually, however, the first teeth come in, or erupt through the gums, when a baby is between six and ten months old. Most often, the first teeth to appear are the two lower

front teeth, called *incisors* (in-SY-zuhrs). Next to come in are the four upper front teeth, also called incisors. These appear when the baby is between the ages of eight and thirteen months. By the time the baby is a year old, he or she will usually have six to eight teeth.

As the teeth come in, babies often feel some discomfort. Most babies also drool increasingly and have a continuing need to chew on things at this time. Some babies become restless and cranky, rub their gums, or lose their appetite. "He's cutting teeth" and "She's teething" are frequent explanations of babies' fussiness.

To help relieve the discomfort, parents and caregivers can massage the swollen gum for a couple of minutes, with or without a piece of ice. Some babies like to chew on a cold teething ring. However, a person should

As the primary teeth come in, infants may be fussy because their gums are irritated.

never tie a teething ring around a child's neck because the string could cause strangulation.

When a baby is teething, parents and care-givers need more patience then usual. Parents should consult a doctor if the child has a fever, digestive disturbance, or other ailments. These may or may not be caused by teething.

Although baby teeth are temporary, they serve important functions:

- Baby teeth promote good nutrition. Once infants can bite and chew, they can move from a liquid to a solid diet.
- Baby teeth help shape the jaw as they come in. Children need matching upper and lower teeth not only for the best chewing but for a normally shaped jaw.
- Baby teeth, if properly placed, help children pronounce words correctly.

Baby teeth last until children are about six or seven years old. Then, one by one, these teeth fall out and are replaced by permanent teeth. Baby teeth usually fall out in the same order in which they came in.

Arms and Hands

At birth, babies have no control of their arms and hands. Their hands are usually closed in tight fists, but they also have the grasping reflex. They will automatically grip tightly any object, such as a finger or pencil, that touches their palm. They will grasp the object in the palm of their hand, using the whole hand.

Babies cannot open their hands freely until they are about three months old. It will still be many months before they develop the ability to pick up an object with the thumb and forefinger.

Torso

The main part of the body is called the *torso*, or trunk. The torso will double and redouble in size several times before the baby reaches adulthood.

In newborns, control of the torso must wait until the brain matures. After about three months, control of the head and spine begins. At five months of age, babies can usually sit up with help. By fourteen months of age, most babies are walking.

Legs and Feet

Legs and feet are the most helpless parts of a baby's body. A newborn's legs are drawn up in the *fetal position*. This is the same position they were in inside the mother's uterus. Some newborns make automatic creeping or swimming motions with their legs.

The legs of most infants are slightly bowed, or curved. Normally, they will straighten by age two or three.

The first rule of development is that the baby develops in a head-to-toe direction. During infancy, the brain is the control center and is developing rapidly. Legs and feet are the last parts of the body to be controlled at will. Babies sit unsupported and grasp objects with their hands long before they learn to walk.

❖ Motor Skills

Motor skills are the ability to use and control the muscles of the body. These skills develop as the muscles mature.

Newborn babies have uncoordinated movements. They may grasp an object, such as a rattle, but let go quickly. By three months of age, babies can sit if supported and hold their head fairly steady. They may begin to swipe at objects but often miss.

During the next months of growth and development, babies are able to turn over, crawl, stand up, and eventually walk. As their muscles develop, they can put their toes in their mouth, take lids off containers, and make marks with a crayon. See "The First Year of Growth and Development" on the next page.

Discuss. What are some signs that a baby might be teething? What can parents due to help relieve the discomfort?

Activity. Ask students to design a toy that would help babies develop their motor skills and would appeal to their sense of sight, hearing, or touch. Refer students to page 386 for guidelines in selecting toys.

The First Year of Growth and Development

Each baby grows and develops at an individual rate. This chart shows what a typical baby might do at various times during the first year. Since few babies are completely typical, expect in real life to see a baby's size vary slightly or activity appear somewhat earlier or later than the chart indicates.

What can a three-month-old baby do?

At three months, a baby is alert and responding to the world. A typical three-month-old

- Can hold chest and head up for ten seconds when lying on stomach.
- Tries to swipe at objects.
- Cries less than a newborn.
- Smiles (at six weeks).
- Turns head toward an interesting sound or listens to voices.
- Stares at people's faces and begins to recognize family members.
- Coos and gurgles.

Height: about 23½ inches
Weight: about 12¼ pounds

What can a six-month-old baby do?

At six months, a baby is developing body control. A typical six-month-old

- Can sit with support and perhaps sit alone for short periods.
- Can roll over from front to back and from back to front.
- Explores objects by putting them in the mouth.
- Can reach for objects with accuracy.
- Can hold a bottle and switch objects from hand to hand.
- Will hold out arms to be lifted up.
- Laughs out loud, babbles, calls for help, and screams when annoyed.

Height: about 26 inches
Weight: about 14 pounds

What can a twelve-month-old baby do?

What can a nine-month-old baby do?

At nine months, a baby explores the environment. A typical nine-month-old

- Can sit unassisted.
- Can crawl, pull up to a standing position, and sidestep holding on to furniture.
- Can use fingers to point, poke, and grasp small objects.
- Eats finger foods.
- Imitates simple actions and plays games such as peekaboo and pat-a-cake.
- Knows own name and responds to simple commands, such as, "Wave bye-bye."
- Produces babbling that sounds almost like a foreign language.

At twelve months, a baby is striving for independence. A typical 12-month-old

- Stands and perhaps walks without help.
- Climbs up and down stairs and out of the crib or playpen.
- Drops and throws toys.
- Prefers using one hand over the other.
- Fears strange people and places.
- Expresses affection.
- Remembers events and uses trial and error to solve problems.
- Says, "mama," "dada," "hi," and "bye-bye."

Height: about 27½ inches
Weight: about 19 pounds

Height: about 30 inches
Weight: about 22 pounds

Emotional and Social Development

At birth, infants show the beginning of a personality all their own. Some babies cry a lot; others seldom do. Some may be tense; others are more relaxed. An infant's emotions in the first days after birth are probably related to several events. These include the birth itself, how well the baby adapts to life outside the womb, and how well his or her body systems are operating. If all goes well, the baby may be relaxed and happy. If a problem arises, the baby may seem tense and fretful.

Emotional development refers to a child's growing ability to express feelings. Among these feelings are love, trust, frustration, anger, and fear. According to psychologist Erik Erikson, a baby must develop a sense of trust during infancy. This means that the baby must feel safe and content in his or her world and with the other people in it.

Social development refers to a child's growing ability to relate to other people. Infants quickly start learning how to get along with others, how to behave as others expect them to, and how to communicate. Much social development is closely related to emotional development.

❖ How Emotions Develop

Every child is born with the capacity to express emotions. Infants communicate emotions through crying and body movements. Newborns start by making cooing sounds, waving their arms, or crying to show happy or unhappy emotions.

During their first year, babies develop more complex emotions. These come partly from maturing but mostly through learning. By age one, infants experience emotions such

as joy, curiosity, jealousy, and affection. They can also feel anger and fear.

Anger

Babies can be angry. This is a way of expressing the urgency of certain needs. For example, hungry babies may show anger when a feeding is delayed. They do this by crying, screaming, waving their arms and legs, and tensing their body.

Until babies are a year old, their outbursts of anger are spontaneous. They are simply

Infants are able to express a range of emotions. By age one, children can show feelings such as joy, affection, anger, and fear.

Activity. Invite parents to bring infants of different ages to class. For example, a three-month-old, a six-month-old, and a one-year-old child. Students should observe and compare the emotional and social development of the babies.

Problem Solving. Since young children model the behavior they observe, should parents and caregivers modify extreme emotions in the presence of a baby or young child? Why or why not?

reacting to the stress they feel in the only way they know.

Fear

Fear is another emotion that babies develop at an early age. They may be frightened by a loud noise, an abrupt change in temperature, or a sudden movement. They may fear people who speak loudly or pick them up roughly. As babies become aware of their environment, they begin to realize that they are small and vulnerable. Their fears are a form of protection against anything that seems threatening, even if it is not.

Between six and ten months of age, babies become afraid of people they do not know. This is called **stranger anxiety**. Babies will become anxious or start to cry.

By this age, babies know their mother and do not want her to leave them. They fear they will be left alone or abandoned. This is called **separation anxiety,** or the fear of being away from familiar people or a familiar environment. You will learn about how to handle children's fears in Chapters 14 and 17.

◆ Temperament

Temperament refers to the intensity and duration of a person's emotional response. It influences personality development and social relations. Even in the hospital nursery, one can see that different babies have different temperaments.

According to one study, babies can be classified as easy, difficult, or slow-to-warm-up.

- Most babies are *easy*. That is, they are playful, interested, and moderately responsive. They sleep soundly and can be easily soothed.
- Ten percent of babies are *difficult*. They are negative, unpredictable, and slow to adapt to new situations. These babies cry easily and are not quickly comforted. They may be cranky and not sleep soundly.

- Fifteen percent of babies are *slow-to-warm-up*. They have mild responses of low intensity. They adapt slowly and withdraw from new situations. These babies are quiet and passive.

Parents, too, can be classified by temperament. Parents who are active and energetic appreciate a baby who is like themselves. They may be disappointed if the baby is not. On the other hand, parents who like to take things more slowly may feel overwhelmed by a very active baby who is interested in everything. Obviously, a match between the temperament of a parent and that of a child can make parenting easier, while a mismatch can cause difficulties.

Psychologists believe that an infant's temperament affects how others care for him or her. An easy baby tends to shape the family environment in one way, a difficult baby in another way, and a slow-to-warm-up baby in yet another way. However, children in the same family may have different temperaments. In this case, parents have to learn different ways of responding to their different children.

DECISIONS ◆ ◆ DECISIONS

Bradley, age eleven months, has always liked his caregiver, Anne. Lately, however, Bradley cries whenever his father, Wes, drops him off at Anne's home. Wes has talked with the parents of the other children Anne cares for. None of the other infants has shown any distress. Wes has also learned from Anne that Bradley stops crying within five minutes after Wes has gone. Still, Wes hates to leave his son sobbing. He has mentioned his concern to you. What will you tell him?

Reference. See page 263 for information about how to handle stranger anxiety.
More About. The temperament classifications are also known as placid, aggressive, and sensitive.

Problem Solving. How should parents respond to an easy, a difficult, and a slow-to-warm-up baby? What problems might parents encounter with children who have a different temperament than their own?

How Sociability Develops

The family is the baby's first social group. Babies learn how to respond and relate to people by interacting with their parents, siblings, and other relatives. Babies' faces light up when they see a person's face. They smile and laugh with others, and they may cry when left alone. By the age of five or six months, babies can distinguish between themselves and other people in a mirror. They will pat their own mirror image and smile.

This growing sense of self and others also causes babies some distress. While very young babies react in almost the same way to all people, older babies develop stranger anxiety and separation anxiety.

The Family's Role

Parents and other caregivers can build a sense of trust by responding warmly to the

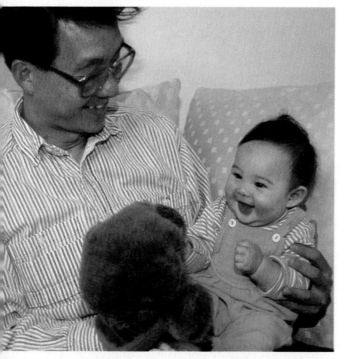

Babies learn how to respond and relate to others by interacting with family members. Social development is closely related to emotional development.

Activity. Have students suggest ways that parents and other caregivers can help babies develop a sense of trust.

baby's physical, emotional, and social needs. The infant needs to be fed when hungry, kept dry and warm, and soothed when fussy. He or she also needs to be cuddled and loved.

The emotional tone, or quality of the relationships among the family members, will be communicated to the baby. Babies are sensitive to tension. They often cry if a conversation gets loud and harsh, even when they do not understand the words. In a family with a happy, stable emotional tone, a baby develops a sense of emotional security.

"Elijah always seems to know the mood I'm in," says Ellen as she cuddles her four-month-old son. "When I'm happy and relaxed, he smiles and coos. When I'm tired or in a hurry, he becomes cranky. It's amazing how he knows my feelings when I don't say a word."

When babies are in child care centers, they should be in small groups, somewhat like a family. The same caregiver should be assigned to the same babies each day. This encourages them to develop an attachment to this person and gain a sense of security.

Babies need many things, as we have seen, but most of all they need love. They feel loved when they are held and touched and spoken to gently. When they experience these things consistently, babies develop a sense of trust.

Goals for Emotional and Social Development

Parents and other caregivers should work toward five important goals during infants' early months.

1. *To develop an attachment, or bond.* Bonding begins even before birth. As you learned in Chapter 11, bonding is the strong attachment, based on love, between parent and child. Babies between three and six months of age begin to recognize

Discuss. Compare the definitions of love and bonding. How are they alike? How are they different?

Babies develop a sense of trust when they are cared for and loved by their family.

the people who most frequently attend to their needs. They become excited when those people appear and show distress when they leave. This is called **attachment behavior.** This attachment gives babies a secure base from which to reach out and explore the surrounding environment. Research indicates that children who explore most are those who have had a firm attachment to a caring person during infancy. Therefore, it is important that there be at least one caring person who remains constant during an infant's first year.

2. ***To develop a strong ability to give affection as well as to receive it.*** During their first months, infants receive affection from parents and other family members and caregivers. Later, babies learn to give affection in return.

3. ***To develop a positive self-concept.*** Parents and other caregivers want babies to feel good about themselves. They want babies to feel that people love them. They want babies to grow into capable individuals who can eventually take responsibility for

◆ ◆ *Self-Esteem* ◆ ◆

Self-esteem has its beginning during infancy. One mother made up songs to sing to her newborn baby during feeding and bathing. Among the words were, "I'm so glad you're my baby. You are so very special." Even though the baby could not understand the words, the feelings of love were communicated to the infant.

Problem Solving. What could a mother do if her baby develops a stronger attachment for the child care worker than the baby does for the mother?

Reference. See pages 324-328 for information about self-concept and self-esteem, along with specific ways to help children develop high self-esteem.

shaping their own environment. Babies should feel, "I am wanted"; "I like myself"; "I am in control of my world." Such a positive self-concept usually brings more laughter than tears, more confidence than fear, and more joy than anger.

4. ***To develop an interest in other people.*** Being with people is important for young babies. They need enough experience with people to feel comfortable and unafraid in family gatherings and public places. Positive feelings toward others grow out of positive experiences. Families help their babies when they expose them to pleasant social experiences.

5. ***To learn to communicate with others.*** Communication is a two-way street. It means letting someone know what you think or feel and understanding what the other person thinks or feels. Long before verbal language develops, a baby learns to understand parents and others by interpreting their body language. For instance, you may have seen a parent put on a coat while a baby in the family watched. The baby may have immediately wanted to put on a coat so he or she could go outside, too. People communicate their intentions through actions, and infants quickly learn to understand those actions.

◆◆ *Health & Safety* ◆◆

Failure to Thrive

Failure-to-thrive syndrome is a condition in which babies have a difficult time getting started in life. Such babies do not grow or gain weight at a normal rate. They are usually listless and inactive. Physical milestones, such as holding up their head easily and sitting up alone, happen much later than they do for other babies.

A baby who fails to thrive does not relate well to parents or other caregivers. The baby will not respond to holding, cuddling, or other attempts at affection. Sometimes, the parents lose interest and neglect the baby's physical and emotional needs. This makes the baby's problems worse.

Failure to thrive can be caused by poor nutrition, an infection, or some other medical problem. Sometimes, the baby fails to thrive for psychological reasons, such as the lack of bonding with the parent.

There are many ways to help such a baby. Often, a change in the baby's diet is all that is needed. Concentrated formula or nutrient-dense foods can supply added calories and nutrients. Sometimes, the baby will be hospitalized so a medical problem can be diagnosed. If the problem is behavioral, a health care professional with training in family relationships can help the parents learn how to care for the baby in a warm, loving way.

Doctors, nurses, and other health care professionals are trained to recognize the symptoms of the failure-to-thrive syndrome. However, parents and caregivers are often the first to notice the signs in a baby. It is important for parents to discuss their concerns about health and behavior with the doctor or nurse during the baby's regular checkups.

Activity. Have students work in groups to create posters that illustrate the five important goals for emotional and social development.

Reference. See pages 426-433 for effective ways to communicate with children.

Cognitive Development

Cognitive development refers to a child's growing ability to perceive, remember, think, reason, and solve problems. Sometimes cognitive development is called mental development or intellectual development.

Through cognitive development, an infant comes to know about the world. An infant's mind cannot be tested in the same ways that older children's mental abilities are tested. Infants cannot complete paper-and-pencil tests or give oral answers to questions. However, experts in cognitive development can estimate how an infant's mind is working by watching his or her actions and movements.

Cognitive development takes place gradually as the brain develops. The parts of the brain that develop earliest are those controlling the spine, arms, and legs. That is why experts can determine a young infant's level of cognitive development by observing the infant's motor development.

❖ Early Clues to Cognitive Development

Nancy Bayley is a well-known psychologist who has studied infants and watched them grow and develop over many years and into adulthood. In her book *Studies in the Development of Young Children*, Dr. Bayley lists typical indications of growth in the mental ability of infants.

- At 6 months, the baby turns in the direction of a spoon that drops out of the baby's sight to the floor.
- At 6.5 months, the baby makes sounds of satisfaction after getting something that was wanted.
- At 7.2 months, the baby smiles at his or her image in the mirror.
- At 7.3 months, the baby looks for the fallen spoon.
- At 8.5 months, the baby cooperates in a game of peekaboo or pat-a-cake.
- At 8.5 months, the baby listens to familiar words.
- At 9.5 months, the baby pulls a string attached to a ring to bring the ring closer.
- At 9.8 months, the baby understands the meanings of several words.
- At 10.4 months, the baby puts a block in a cup when shown how.
- At 10.6 months, the baby unwraps a toy after seeing it being wrapped.
- At 11.7 months, the baby imitates words.
- At 12.9 months, the baby says two words.

Dr. Bayley has found that infants who do very well on tests such as those just listed do not always do as well on mental-ability tests once they reach kindergarten or elementary school. Slower infants often catch up with and pass their faster friends. Therefore, in your own observations, avoid making long-range predictions about cognitive development.

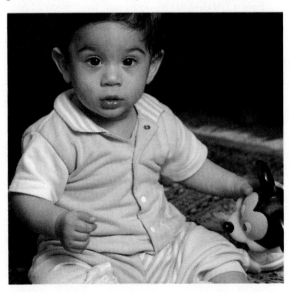

Infants use their five senses to learn about their world. They like to look at, listen to, smell, taste, and touch everything around them.

❖ Using the Senses to Learn

Healthy people have five senses that help them learn: sight, hearing, taste, smell, and touch. Babies begin to learn about the world by using these five senses.

Babies learn through their senses while they are playing, looking, listening, eating, bathing—in fact, while doing everything they do. They listen to the sound of a voice, music, or a bell. They look at a pretty picture, a twirling toy, or themselves in a mirror. They touch a fuzzy blanket, a smooth rattle, or cool water. They taste their fingers, toes, clothes, and toys. Everything seems to go into their mouth. If an odor is strong and unpleasant, they turn their head away from it. See the chart below.

All this sensory exploration aids learning. Not until children are older can they learn about the world by having someone tell them about it.

❖ Piaget's Stages of Cognitive Development

Many leading educators and doctors have spent their career studying how children develop mentally and physically. Their work has helped parents and teachers observe and understand children's behavior. One of the most respected of these researchers was Jean Piaget. His theories about the ages and stages of children's development are widely accepted today.

Dr. Piaget was a Swiss psychologist who watched children of different ages as they thought and solved problems. He did not especially care what children knew or whether they solved the problems correctly.

The Newborn's Senses

From birth, infants can see and hear. They are sensitive to tastes, smells, and touch. Through their five senses they learn about their world and respond to it.

- **Sight.** If a brightly colored object is held in front of newborns, they become alert and try to focus their eyes on it. They can distinguish some patterns and shapes. In very bright light, they shut their eyes and keep them closed until the light is gone.

- **Hearing.** Fetuses respond to loud noises while in the uterus. Newborns prefer certain sounds: human voices, music, soft rhythmic drumming. They respond most readily to high-pitched and longer-lasting tones. They are startled by loud noises. When one baby starts to cry in a nursery, others are likely to start crying, too.

- **Taste.** Newborns can tell the difference between a sweet flavor and a bitter one. As early as two or three days of age, they reject the bitter and accept the sweet.

- **Smell.** Newborns can tell the difference between two smells presented at the same time. As early as six days of age, newborns can recognize the odor of their own mother's milk. They cry and turn away from an unpleasant odor.

- **Touch.** Newborns are sensitive to touch. They respond quickly to a light touch on the skin. They usually stop crying when gently rubbed or held. They can feel pain.

Discuss. Because babies learn by doing, it is important to allow them freedom to explore. Should parents limit the use of playpens and walkers? Why or why not?

Emphasize. Since babies learn through touching and tasting, it is very important that parents childproof their home and closely supervise babies' activities. See pages 276-283 for safety precautions.

Instead, he wanted to know how they reasoned things through. Piaget studied cognitive development. Through his studies, he found that thinking processes change in many ways as a child grows older.

By watching his own children and many others, Piaget found that children gradually go through a series of cognitive stages. In each stage, children use different kinds of thought processes to solve problems. These stages do not start and stop at precise ages. In different children they happen at different ages. Sometimes the stages even overlap slightly. However, the stages always occur in the same fixed order. That is, the more complex stages always follow less complex ones.

According to Piaget, the first major period in a child's cognitive development is the **sensorimotor stage.** *Sensori* refers to the five senses; *motor* refers to movement. During this period, infants learn to use the things they see, hear, feel, taste, and smell from their outside world and to manipulate and control their muscles. This stage begins at birth and ends when a baby is about two years of age. It includes three substages.

- In the early *reflexive substage,* from birth to one month, the baby's inborn reflexes, such as sucking and grasping, become active.

- In the *circular-reaction substage,* from ages one to eighteen months, the baby combines reflex actions and begins to develop coordination. He or she also shows an increasing interest in the surrounding world. As this substage progresses, the baby repeats acts over and over. For example, the baby will throw a toy out of the crib repeatedly to watch the results.

- The *substage of mental combinations* begins when the child is about eighteen months old and ends when he or she is about two years old. During this time, the child begins to think about the effects of an action before acting. For example, the child will think, "If I want my talking toy to say something, I must pull its string."

You will read more about Piaget's stages of cognitive development in Chapter 19.

❖ Language

Language and intellectual development appear to be closely related. Thus observations of how children develop language also provide information on their cognitive development. Babies around the world acquire language in similar ways. This is true even though the specific words may be in Chinese,

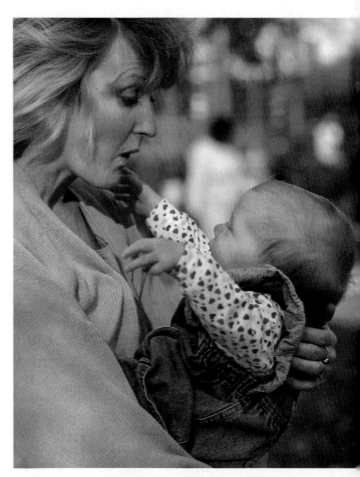

Parents can encourage language development by imitating a baby's sounds.

Swahili, English, or one of thousands of other dialects and languages.

During infancy, babies hear language spoken around them. After first making noises

Around the World

Mama

A North American baby's first word is often *mama*. It is also a Chinese baby's and an East African baby's first word. All over the world, *mama* is one of the first words that infants babble, long before they actually learn to speak the language of their own culture.

How is it that babies born into totally different language groups say the same word? Babies playfully experiment with sounds. Toward the end of the first year, they begin to repeat syllables such as *ma-ma, na-na,* and *ba-ba* over and over. Mothers, by responding to what sounds like *mama* with smiles and attention, teach their babies that this sound means mother. Thus cultures may have originally assigned the meaning of mother to the sound of *mama*.

Similarly, the sound of *nana* has come to be associated with grandmother or nurse. *Dada* or *papa*—or *baba* in some parts of the world—has come to mean father.

Notice the similarities in the following words for the English word *mother*. For example, all but one begin with the *m* (just as *mama* does).

German:	Mutter
Spanish and Italian:	madre
Polish:	matka
Swahili:	mama
Hebrew:	ima
Chinese:	mu-ch'in
French:	mère
Swedish:	moder
Hindi:	mata

called cooing, they begin making sounds that are like the vowels and consonants of that language. This vocalizing is called *babbling*. It is a playful use of the lips and vocal cords that all babies seem to enjoy. They repeat sounds over and over. They may babble, "boo-boo-boo" or "ma-ma-ma-ma" or "da-da-da," sometimes loudly and clearly. It is not known whether there is any purpose to these babblings. Babies probably enjoy babbling because it feels good to the mouth and sounds good to the ears. Deaf children often start to babble but soon stop. Because they cannot hear, they are not stimulated by the sound of their own voice.

Sometime after the age of six months, babies begin to imitate individual sounds that they hear. Around the age of nine or ten months, babies will consciously imitate the spoken sounds other people make. They may understand only a few words—such as their own name and *bye-bye.* Yet they take delight in imitating speech through babbling.

When parents and caregivers regularly talk to babies, the amount and volume of the babies' vocalization greatly increase. Sometimes babies start social babbling conversations. These grow increasingly lively if adults respond with smiles, nods, or verbal replies. Studies indicate that if the adults do not respond, babies show obvious sadness and disappointment.

Babbling is an important first step in the development of language. Babies learn to understand the speech of others before they are able to produce words themselves. By the age of one, children usually understand such phrases as "eat your cracker" and "clap hands."

A baby's first year is a period of rapid change. In no other period of life will the child grow so rapidly, learn so much so fast, and form such strong bonds to other human beings.

Summary

- During their first year, babies grow and develop at a rapid rate unmatched in any other period of life.
- An infant's physical growth and development are measured in terms of size, weight, proportions, and motor skills.
- Newborns have a variety of reflexes that help them respond to stimulation.
- Emotional and social development are closely related.
- The five goals of emotional and social development are: to develop an attachment to parents and other caregivers, to develop the ability to give and receive affection, to develop a positive self-concept, to develop an interest in others, and to learn to communicate with others.
- Cognitive development progresses gradually as the brain develops.
- Babies use their five senses to help them learn.
- Language development begins with cooing and babbling.

Questions

p. 230 **1.** What does a typical newborn look like?

p. 231 **2.** Why are reflexes important to an infant?

p. 235 **3.** What are motor skills?

p. 238 **4.** How do babies show their emotions?

p. 239 **5.** What is the difference between stranger anxiety and separation anxiety?

p. 240 **6.** How can parents and other caregivers build a child's sense of trust?

7. How do babies use their five senses to help them learn? p. 244

8. What is the sensorimotor stage of cognitive development? p. 245

9. How can parents and other caregivers encourage a baby's language development? p. 246

10. What can six-month-old babies do that three-month-olds cannot do? p. 236

11. What can twelve-month-old babies do that nine-month-olds cannot do? p. 237

Activities

1. For several hours observe a baby who is between eight and twelve months of age. Jot down specific examples of how the baby is progressing toward the five goals for emotional and social development. Share these with the class.

2. Almost all babies experience fear at some time. Ask your parents about any fears that you might have had when you were a baby. How did your parents help you deal with these fears?

3. Create an activity, game, or toy that would help stimulate a baby's cognitive development.

Think About

1. Why should parents avoid comparing one child's rate of development to that of another child?

2. Some people say, "Baby teeth are not very important because they are only temporary." Do you agree or disagree? Why?

Reference. See the Teacher's Manual in the front of the Teacher's Annotated Edition for complete answers to the chapter review questions.

247

Parenting Infants

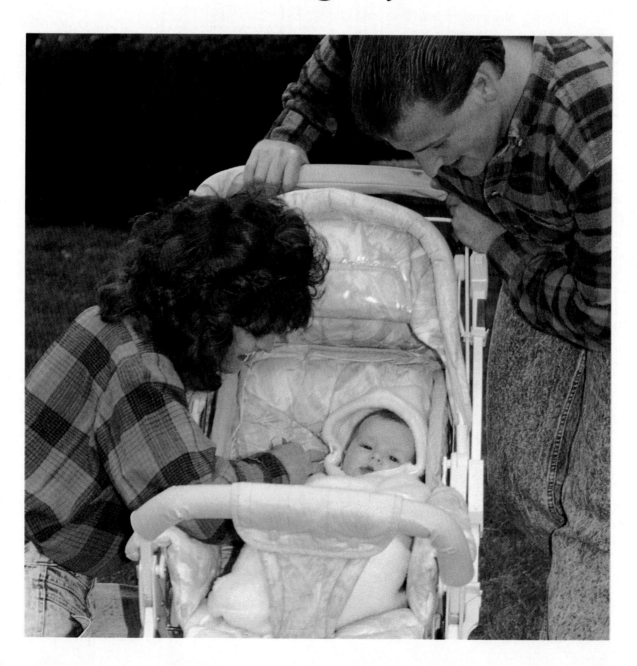

Objectives

This chapter will help you to:
- Suggest ways to meet infants' physical needs.
- Explain how to deal with babies' emotions.
- Describe how to encourage sociability.
- List ways to provide a stimulating environment.

Vocabulary

self-demand feeding
sterilizing
weaning
pacifier
diarrhea
cradle cap
colic

"I'll help with the baby's bath if you want me to," volunteers Tricia. She is a nurse who lives next door to the Barners, who have a new baby.

"Thanks, Tricia," replies Beth, "but Peter and I already bathed him this morning. Peter wanted to help with the baby's first bath. He called it Jonathan's launching!"

As they walk to the door, Beth tells Tricia, "I really appreciate your offer to help because I'm sure your nursing experience will come in handy sometime. I hope I can call on you then."

"Of course, anytime," replies Tricia.

Parenting involves taking care of infants so that all their many needs are met. It means providing for their physical, emotional, social, and cognitive needs. Parenting is also demanding work. It includes physical care, nurturance, and guidance. However, relatives, friends, and neighbors like Tricia can help new parents by providing information and support.

Meeting the Baby's Needs

Newborn babies need food and sleep. They need to be clean and warm. They also need love and security. Parenting begins with planning for the baby's arrival. It expands with loving and caring for the baby. Through their early acts of caring, parents ensure that their infant's needs will be met. A sense of trust begins to develop.

The newborn's caregivers may be the biological parents, foster parents, or adoptive parents. They may be relatives caring for the child at home or professionals in a child care center. No matter who is caring for the baby, the infant's needs are the same.

◆◆ Food

A baby's need for food is usually irregular at first. For this reason, most pediatricians advise **self-demand feeding.** This means feeding babies when they seem to be hungry rather than according to a fixed schedule.

Typically, a newborn's stomach will hold only 2 ounces (4 tablespoons) of breast milk or formula. This is why an infant may take only a little milk from the breast or bottle, fall asleep, then awaken crying with hunger in two hours or even earlier.

Newborn babies need to be fed at least six to eight times a day. Frequent feedings can be exhausting to new parents. However, this stage does not last long. Babies soon begin taking larger amounts of milk or formula and going longer between feedings. They set their own schedule eventually, even though it might not be just what the parents would have planned. By age seven months, most babies are on a schedule of three or four meals a day.

Cuddling and feeding go together. That is obvious with breast-feeding, but parents should also hold a bottle-fed baby in their arms during feeding. They should smile and talk to the newborn while the formula disappears. Some busy parents and caregivers may be tempted to prop up the baby's bottle. This should not be done. An important part of the baby's sense of trust and security begins to develop during feeding. Even parents with twins and triplets should take time to hold each baby during the feeding. If necessary, relatives or neighbors can help.

Breast-Feeding

As you learned in Chapter 10, breast-feeding has many advantages. It is convenient. It offers health benefits for both the baby and the mother. It helps establish a strong bond between the baby and the mother.

A nursing mother's milk supply is not established until about three days after birth. At first the baby gets colostrum, the fluid present in the breasts before the milk becomes available.

The baby's sucking stimulates regular milk production. Usually, the more a baby nurses, the more milk the mother's milk glands will produce. A baby can be nursed for as long as the mother wishes. This may be for a few months or as long as one year or more.

To maintain her milk supply, the nursing mother needs plenty of rest, nutritious meals, and as little stress as possible. She should also drink plenty of liquids and not use alcohol, tobacco, or drugs. Sometimes chocolate and spicy foods make the breast milk taste strange to the baby. When this happens, the breast-feeding mother may want to cut back on these foods.

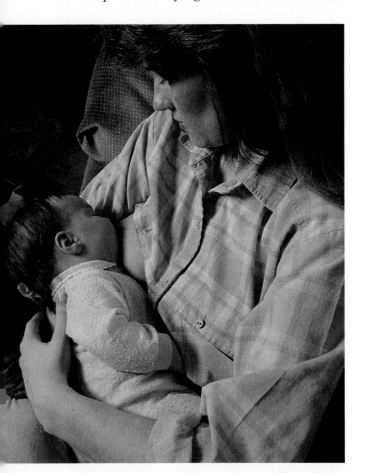

Breast milk is very nutritious and easy to digest. It contains antibodies that help protect the baby against diseases. Breast-feeding encourages bonding between the mother and child.

More About. The larger the baby at birth, the more milk he or she will take at a feeding and the longer the baby can go between feedings. With smaller babies, the reverse is true.

Reference. See pages 178-179 for a discussion of the advantages and disadvantages of breast-feeding and bottle-feeding.

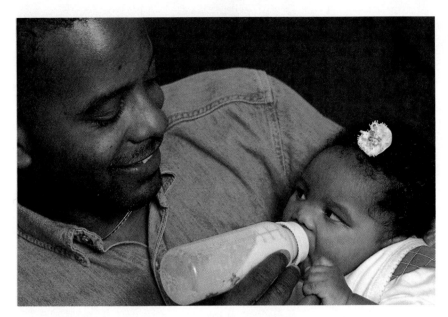

If parents decide to bottle-feed their baby, the doctor will recommend a formula that provides essential nutrients. Then the father can share in feeding the baby.

Some mothers who breast-feed their babies also give them an occasional bottle. This gives the mothers some time to be away from the babies and allows other family members to share in feedings.

Bottle-Feeding

When parents decide to bottle-feed their baby, the doctor usually recommends which of the many prepared formulas to use. Prepared formulas are available in different forms. These include dry milk powders and condensed liquids to which water must be added and ready-to-use liquids that come in cans or baby bottles.

Formulas are expensive, so some parents consider switching to cow's milk after a few months. Most pediatricians, however, recommend that babies stay on formula or breast milk for most of the first year.

Some babies are allergic to formula made from cow's milk. For these babies, formula made mostly of soybean powder is available. Parents of allergic babies should ask their pediatrician about substitute formulas.

During the first weeks after birth, an infant's digestive system is just beginning to function. Germs that might not affect an adult can make the baby sick. Although a bottle may look clean, any germs present in the bottle will grow in milk. Many doctors recommend **sterilizing** the bottles and nipples for newborns. This means bringing the items to a high temperature, usually by boiling, to destroy any germs.

Some parents prefer to use presterilized plastic liner bags that are filled and placed inside special bottles. Once used, the bags can be thrown away. Even more convenient are the ready-to-use bottles of formula. However, these items are expensive to use daily.

Bottles of formula should be stored in the refrigerator. A bottle can be warmed by setting it in a pan of warm tap water. Parents should check the temperature by dropping a bit of milk on the palm side of the wrist. If it feels neither cold nor hot, it should be just right for the baby. Heating the bottle in a microwave oven must be done with extreme caution. The bottle may feel only warm even when the milk is too hot in the center.

More About. An occasional bottle for a breast-fed baby can be formula or expressed breast milk, which can be frozen for future use.
Emphasize. Bottle-fed babies should be held in a manner sim-

ilar to the way you would hold a baby for breast-feeding. This enhances the bonding between parent and baby.
More About. Many babies do not mind cold bottles straight from the refrigerator. Cold milk will not cause a stomachache.

DECISIONS ◆ ◆ DECISIONS

Amy decided to bottle-feed her baby. However, she has read that breast milk contains more nutrients than formula does. Now she is concerned about her baby's health, so she has been trying to give her daughter more formula than babies usually drink. Amy hopes this will make up the difference in nutritional value. Do you agree with Amy's solution? What would you suggest?

Most infants need to be burped at the end of each feeding; some need to be burped during the feeding as well. Hold the baby against your shoulder and gently pat or rub the baby's back. Another method is to hold the baby upright on your lap and pat the baby's back or rub the stomach.

When bottling the formula for a newborn, parents should fill each bottle with a maximum of three ounces. As the baby grows and wants more at each feeding, the amount per bottle can be increased to four or five ounces. Later it should be increased to six to eight ounces.

It is important not to force babies to drink more formula or juice than they want. Babies who are full will turn their head or push the nipple out of their mouth. Overfeeding may give babies a stomachache or cause them to spit up. Overfeeding can also cause babies to become overweight. There is some evidence that overweight infants become overweight children and adults.

When the baby is through drinking, parents should take the bottle out of the baby's mouth. Letting the baby suck on formula or juice for long periods of time can contribute to tooth decay. Any formula or juice remaining in the bottle should be discarded.

Burping

Because all babies swallow some air when they are drinking breast milk, formula, juice, or water, they need to be burped during or after feedings. To do this, parents should hold the baby upright, either sitting on their lap or against one shoulder. Then they should rub or pat the baby's lower back opposite the stomach until they hear the baby let the air out.

Weaning

Weaning means getting the baby used to drinking milk from a cup rather than from a bottle or breast. Sometimes babies between nine and fifteen months of age give clues that they are ready to be weaned. They show an interest in feeding themselves or become bored with the bottle or breast. When this happens, parents can offer them milk or juice in a cup. It may take a few weeks to wean a baby completely.

Problem Solving. Have students find information about "nursing bottle syndrome." What is it? How is it caused? How can it be prevented?

Problem Solving. How will a mother know when her baby no longer needs to be breast-fed? What are the advantages and disadvantages of breast-feeding past this time?

Solid Foods

In the past, parents were encouraged to give solid foods to babies as early as possible. However, experts have found that the digestive system of young babies is too immature for solid foods. Breast milk or formula is the only food most healthy babies need for their first six to twelve months.

Once babies begin eating solids, they usually start with cereal mixed with formula. Soon after, they may be given strained fruits, such as bananas and applesauce. Although these foods are called solids, they are actually thinned and strained so that babies will not gag. Baby foods can be made at home with a blender, food processor, or strainer. Parents can also use special baby-food grinders to prepare small amounts of food right at the table.

Many parents feel homemade baby foods are healthier than those commercially prepared because they are fresh and have no additives. Responding to this, some baby-food manufacturers now make baby foods with no salt, sugar, or preservatives.

"The first time I gave Kimberly solid food she got a funny, puzzled look on her face," said Kimberly's mother. "The food seemed to roll back out of her mouth as fast as I spooned it in."

Babies need plenty of time to explore a new taste and feeling in their mouth. If they fret and spit out the food, they should not be forced to eat it. Children who are forced to eat may grow to dislike the food and to dread mealtime. Parents should wait a few days and then try the food again. They might do this at a different time of day, before the baby has had breast milk or formula, or when the baby seems especially hungry. A small amount of the new food should be offered to the baby on the rounded end of a small spoon.

Even if it looks as though the baby is spitting out most of the food, he or she is still tasting and swallowing some of it. Soon the baby will learn to like new foods.

It is a good idea to offer the baby only one new food at a time every five to seven days. This way if a certain food causes a problem, such as a rash or an upset stomach, parents will know which food to eliminate.

Once the baby is eating cereal and likes a variety of fruits, it is time to offer strained vegetables. A little later, the baby can be given strained meats.

Babies who are old enough to sit up (usually when they are six to eight months old) enjoy eating with the family at mealtime. They can have a taste of suitable family food from the table. Mashed potatoes, cottage cheese, and applesauce are family foods that many babies like. By the time they are a year old, babies can eat most of the foods the rest of the family eats.

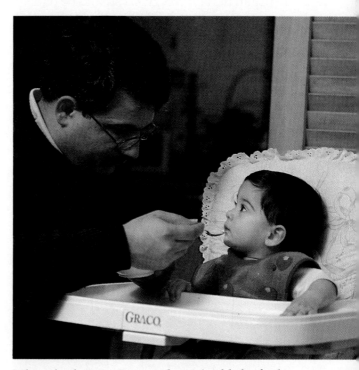

When the doctor recommends strained baby foods, parents should offer only one new food at a time. Babies may spit food out until they get used to the new taste and texture.

Self-Feeding

Babies' efforts to feed themselves should be encouraged. This is true even if the feeding takes longer and results in drips and spills. Older babies can be given finger foods, such as fruit, cheese, cooked vegetables, hard-cooked egg, crumbled cooked meat or poultry, and bits of soft toast. They can pick up and put these foods into their mouth. Although this can get rather messy at times, it helps babies learn important steps toward independence.

Babies can also eat some of their food with a spoon. When they try to feed themselves with a spoon, they often turn the spoon over just when the food gets near their mouth. This, too, is messy, but it is also a valuable learning experience. Babies have to practice, just as a basketball player practices hitting the basket. Skill in eating will come in time. Until then, parents and caregivers should be patient

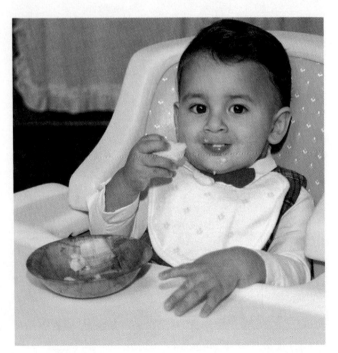

When babies show an interest in picking up foods with their fingers, they can be encouraged to feed themselves.

and encourage babies' attempts to feed themselves. Most children will be able to do this successfully by the time they are two or three years old.

Nutritious Meals

A parent's most important job in meeting the baby's food needs is to make sure the baby eats nutritious meals. Babies' tastes vary just as other people's do. One baby likes spinach, while another likes green beans. When offered a variety of foods, most babies learn to eat many different foods. In this way they are likely to get all the nutrients they need to grow and develop normally. As you learned earlier, the important nutrients include minerals, proteins, vitamins, carbohydrates, and water.

Minerals. Calcium and phosphorus are minerals that are needed to build strong bones and teeth. Milk is very rich in these minerals. Therefore, it is extremely important for a baby to get enough breast milk or formula.

Proteins. Proteins are needed to build body tissues. They form the major part of cells throughout the body. Milk provides much of the required protein supply. Some cereals are also rich in proteins. Later on, the baby can get additional proteins from meat, poultry, fish, and eggs.

Vitamins. Babies need a number of vitamins for healthy growth. One of these is vitamin C, which is found in citrus fruits. If a mother is breast-feeding and eats citrus fruits and other foods containing vitamin C, the baby will get vitamin C. Otherwise, the pediatrician may recommend that the baby be given vitamin drops as a supplement. These should be given exactly as directed. Overdosing with vitamins can be dangerous.

Another important vitamin is vitamin D. It is essential for the effective use of calcium and phosphorus in building bones and teeth. Cow's milk usually has enough vitamin D for a baby's needs because milk-processing companies add it to milk. The doctor may suggest vitamin drops for breast-fed babies.

Carbohydrates. Carbohydrates are the sugars and starches found in many foods, such as cereals, breads, and fruits. Carbohydrates are essential sources of energy for the baby.

Nutrition experts caution parents not to give a baby foods sweetened with extra sugar or artificial sweeteners. These sweetened foods tend to satisfy the appetite quickly. As a result the baby may not eat other foods containing important nutrients. By eating or drinking too many sweetened foods, the baby also may develop a taste for sugar that will last into adulthood.

Water. Babies need water to keep their digestive and elimination systems working properly. Milk and formula contain a large amount of water. They also provide all the water a baby needs in the early months. However, a baby may like a sip of water from a bottle or spoon occasionally, especially in warm weather. Extra water may also be given to prevent dehydration if the baby has a fever.

❖ Sucking

Babies have a need to suck. For some, breast-feeding is enough to satisfy that need. Bottle-fed babies may need to have a nipple with only a very small hole in it so that the bottle lasts longer.

Many babies, both breast-fed and bottle-fed, need more sucking time. For these babies, parents may wish to use a **pacifier,** a nipple-shaped device for babies to suck. The disk that rests against the baby's lips should be large enough so that the baby cannot get the entire pacifier in the mouth and choke. The pacifier must be kept clean and handled with

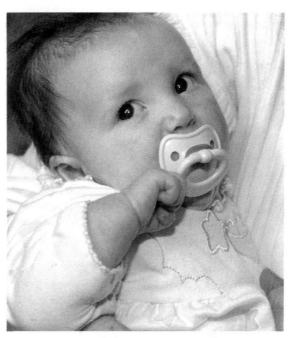

Sucking on a pacifier calms many babies and makes them feel more contented. Many babies who use a pacifier reject it at five or six months of age.

clean hands. It should not be tied on a string and put around the baby's neck because the baby might strangle.

Some babies learn how to get their thumbs or fingers in their mouth, even at a very young age. In fact, babies are known to suck their thumbs or fingers while they are still in the womb. Many child care experts feel that thumb sucking is normal and healthy. Some physicians have observed that thumb-sucking babies are usually very secure.

Despite these experts' opinions, some adults feel uncomfortable about allowing a baby to suck a thumb, fingers, or a pacifier. They think a crying baby is preferable to one who needs to suck on something. However, if this sucking helps an infant feel more contented, there is no reason why the baby should not do so. Eventually, the need is satisfied, and the baby stops sucking either the thumb or pacifier.

❖ Elimination

Elimination, especially the bowel movement, is related to the baby's diet. Parents and caregivers will become experienced in noting any unusual changes in the bowel movement. Some foods cause the baby to have **diarrhea** (dy-ah-REE-ah), or extremely loose bowel movements. Babies who take only breast milk normally have loose bowel movements. However, this is different from diarrhea, which is more severe. If a food seems to be causing diarrhea, parents should immediately stop giving it to the baby. The child should continue to get water and milk, however, to prevent dehydration.

Diarrhea can also be caused by an infection. If diarrhea persists, parents should contact the baby's doctor. The physician may recommend water with a little sugar and salt added to treat the condition.

Certain foods cause changes in the color of bowel movements. For example, a baby who eats beets may have bright red bowel movements. Parents who do not know this may become alarmed, thinking that there is blood in the bowel movements. Parents should also know that the baby's digestive system is still developing. Bowel movements may therefore contain bits of carrot or other foods that the baby has swallowed whole. Again, this is no cause for alarm.

❖ Cleanliness

Babies should always be kept very clean. They need frequent diaper changes. Cornstarch or baby powder may be used on the baby's bottom after a wet diaper is removed. However, this is not necessary. Parents who use baby powder should be sure to shake it into their hand first, away from the baby's face. Then they should gently pat it on the baby. Baby powder contains talc, which can harm the baby's lungs if the baby breathes in powder from the air.

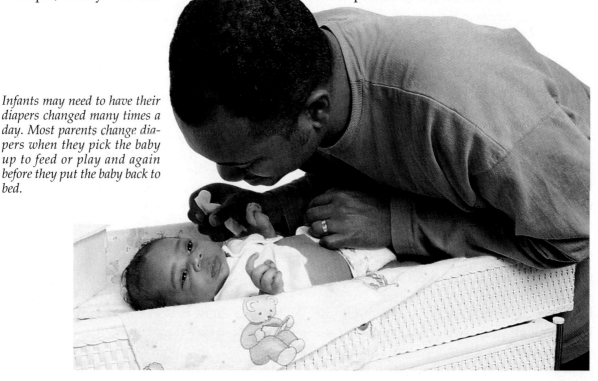

Infants may need to have their diapers changed many times a day. Most parents change diapers when they pick the baby up to feed or play and again before they put the baby back to bed.

Activity. Demonstrate how to change diapers, using a baby or a demonstration doll.
Problem Solving. Have students find information about how to cure diaper rash.

More About. Bowel movements from breast-fed babies are usually yellowish in color, have no odor, and may occur after every feeding. Most babies' bowel movements do not have much odor until the toddler starts digesting cow's milk.

◆◆ Health & Safety ◆◆

Safety in the Bath

Babies usually need a bath every day. Because most babies love to wiggle and squirm and play in the water, bath time can be fun. However, soap and water can make a baby's body slippery. Here are some ways to make bath time both happy and safe.

- Bathtubs are slippery. Use a nonskid tub mat, or line the basin with a towel before filling with water.

- Fill the tub or basin with only 3 or 4 inches of water. Test the water temperature before putting the baby in the water.

- The water faucet may remain hot after the tub is filled. If so, wrap it with a washcloth before putting the baby in the tub.

- Put everything needed for the bath within hand's reach. This includes soap, shampoo, bath toys, a washcloth, and a towel.

- Never turn around or leave the room while the baby is in the bath. It only takes a second for an infant to slide under the water.

- Keep one arm around the baby at all times. Use the other hand for washing and playing.

- Never let a baby practice sitting without support in the bath. If the baby falls over, he or she could be hurt. Even if the baby is not hurt, a fall could scare the baby, making him or her afraid of baths and water.

After a bowel movement, the baby should be cleaned with baby lotion and a facial tissue or damp washcloth. Special premoistened towelettes are also available for this purpose. Soiled cloth diapers should be rinsed in the toilet and soaked with other diapers in a soapy solution in a covered diaper pail.

Most pediatricians recommend bathing babies every day. A sponge bath should be given until the navel heals. This may take two weeks. Then the baby can be bathed in a basin of water. Special portable plastic bathtubs are also available. Later, when the baby can sit steadily, the regular bathtub can be used.

Bath time should be quiet, gentle, and pleasurable for the baby. Some babies enjoy their bath right from the start. Others need a few weeks or months before they relax and enjoy it. Many newborns cry when their clothes are removed for a bath. Parents should

be sure that the baby is not hungry at bath time. If hungry, the newborn may cry with dissatisfaction and associate bathing with unpleasantness.

Doctors also recommend washing the baby's scalp daily to prevent **cradle cap.** This is a dirty-looking, patchy scalp condition. A firm but gentle massage with a soft hairbrush or toothbrush will not hurt the baby's head. If cradle cap does develop, parents should consult their pediatrician or clinic.

◆◆ Clothing

A baby's primary clothing need is for plenty of clean, dry diapers. See Chapter 10 for a discussion of cloth and disposable diapers.

Other clothing needs depend on the weather. Newborns seem to like being wrapped up tightly. Perhaps this gives them

Emphasize. When changing a baby's diaper after a bowel movement, double check all creases and folds for fecal material.

Activity. Invite a parent to demonstrate the proper techniques of bathing his or her infant. Why is it important to have all bathing supplies gathered near-by before starting to bathe the baby?

the kind of security they felt in the womb. If the weather is warm, they can be dressed in just an undershirt and a diaper and wrapped in a lightweight blanket. In cooler weather, stretch suits and warmer blankets are useful. A sweater and hat are needed for outings.

Many adults believe that babies need heavier clothing than adults do. According to most experts, this is not true. Overdressing

Swaddling

Swaddling is the ancient practice of tightly wrapping an infant with long bands of cloth. It is mentioned in the Bible and in European poems of the Middle Ages.

Members of some cultures, such as the Sioux Indians, still wrap the baby tightly. The swaddled baby is then attached to a cradleboard. The mother carries the board on her back. This is done to keep the infant warm and to prevent him or her from scratching. It also allows the mother to go about her work in the home or field without worrying about the child's safety.

The practice of lightly wrapping an infant in a light cotton blanket is also called swaddling. Hospitals often provide light blankets, called receiving blankets, for this purpose. The infant is placed diagonally on the blanket with his or her head at one corner. The body is in a naturally relaxed position: arms bent at the elbow, legs flexed. The bottom corner of the blanket is pulled up, over the baby's feet and stomach. Then each side is folded in, across the baby's body. Thus the infant's limbs are gently held against the body, imitating the position of the fetus in the uterus. This helps the baby feel warm, secure, and comfortable.

babies can make them perspire and increase the chance that they will get chilled. Most doctors recommend that parents dress a baby only as warmly as they dress themselves.

Once a baby is able to kick off blankets, footed sleepers can be purchased. These sleepers keep the baby warm without restricting movement. When the baby starts to crawl, sturdier clothes—one-piece outfits or T-shirts and overalls—are needed. Shoes are unnecessary until the baby starts to walk.

Many parents and grandparents love to dress babies up in fancy outfits for special occasions. However, most of the time babies should be dressed for comfort, warmth, and protection. Clothes should fit loosely, especially around the arms and legs. It is best to buy clothing one size too big because babies grow very quickly. To help make dressing easier, clothes should have snaps or a wide opening for the head. All clothing should be washable because babies wet, soil, and spit up on their clothes.

An infant's clothing should be comfortable and easy to wash. Clothes with snaps or a wide opening for the head make dressing easier.

Activity. Demonstrate how to swaddle a baby in a light cotton blanket.

Activity. Bring a variety of baby clothes borrowed from parents or a local store to class. Have students compare styles, fabrics, care labels, sizes, and prices. Why is it better to buy baby clothes according to weight, rather than by age?

No matter how many clothes a baby has, it may not seem like enough. Some parents feel that they are constantly doing laundry. However, by washing several times a week, parents need only a few changes of clothing for the baby.

❖ Rest and Sleep

Most newborn babies sleep a great deal—from 14 to 20 hours a day. They are growing very fast and need this amount of rest. Where they sleep is less important than how long they sleep. They may sleep in a crib, a bassinet, a carriage, an infant seat, or a dresser drawer. Some parents like to put their babies in special infant carriers that strap onto a parent's chest or back. Then the parent can carry the baby around while running errands and doing other tasks. The warmth and closeness of this arrangement may help give the infant a sense of security.

Most babies prefer to sleep on their stomach. Some like to curl up in the fetal position; others sleep in a froglike position. Many newborns seem more comfortable when placed crosswise at one end of the crib with their head tucked up against the crib bumper. This contact seems to give them a feeling of security.

Most experts agree that parents need not sacrifice all their plans for the baby's sleep schedule. Babies can sleep while riding in cars or grocery carts and when they are in rooms full of people. In fact, some pediatricians believe that it is better not to be extremely quiet around a sleeping baby. That way, the baby becomes used to sleeping in all kinds of circumstances. Some babies actually seem to enjoy the sound of a vacuum cleaner. Many will sleep peacefully while a parent vacuums in the same room.

Parents are thankful when the baby sleeps through the night. Although some babies do

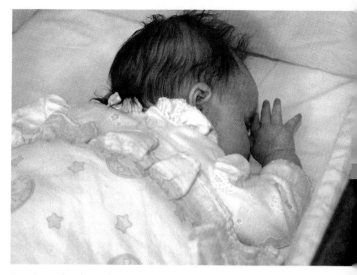

During the first few months of life, babies usually sleep between meals.

so by the time they are three months old, many awaken during the night for several months longer. Parents do not have to jump up at the first whimper they hear. However, they should check on a baby who cries in the night. A fussy baby can be comforted by rocking, cuddling, or soft music. Lullabies are an age-old remedy because they do help to soothe babies.

As babies grow older, they sleep less. By five months of age, most babies are taking two or three naps a day and sleeping through the night. Of course, sleep habits vary among babies just as they do among adults. Some babies fall asleep instantly and sleep soundly for long periods. Others take brief naps and are easily awakened.

A difficult period for both baby and parents may occur at the end of the baby's first year. The baby may be too old for both a morning and an afternoon nap but too young for just one nap. One way to avoid this problem is to delay the morning nap until right after lunch. Then the baby will be refreshed for the rest of the afternoon and will probably fall asleep right after an early supper.

More About. Newborn babies spend approximately 80% of the time sleeping. By age one, about 50% of the time will be spent sleeping.

Discuss. Why might babies feel more secure when they are swaddled or when their head is wedged in the corner of the bumper pads?

Encouraging Motor Skill Development

Parents and caregivers can encourage babies to practice motor skills as soon as their muscles are mature enough. Adults should watch for signs of increased body control. They also can prepare for babies' motor skill development by knowing what babies generally can do at each age level.

Play activities provide many opportunities for infants to practice new motor skills. Babies like to examine and handle new objects. They will take a new toy and squeeze it, shake it, and put part of it in their mouth. They like to examine objects with different textures—furry, smooth, bumpy.

Some toys have knobs to pull, buttons to press, and handles to turn. Each time the baby pulls, presses, or turns, the toy makes a different sound. Other toys give babies a chance to exercise their arms and legs by pulling on rings and bars. Once babies are able to crawl, they like to follow objects such as balls and pull toys. You will learn more about the value of play and the selection of appropriate toys in Chapter 20.

When babies fail to develop motor skills according to the usual timetable, parents should seek medical advice. For example, one doctor discovered that a nonwalking eighteen-month-old had fluid in her inner ear. This prevented proper balance when she tried to walk. A minor operation drained the fluid, and soon the child was walking.

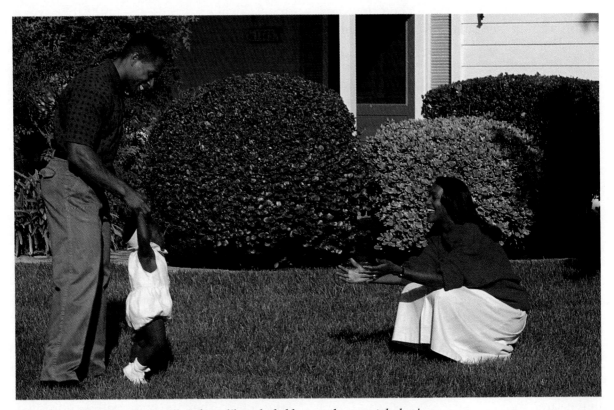

For some weeks before they walk, infants like to be held up so they can take beginning steps. This encourages their motor skill development. However, no amount of urging will make children walk until they are physically ready.

Reference. See Chapter 20, beginning on page 378, for information about toys and the value of play.

Emphasize. When infants are outside in the sun, they should be guarded against ultraviolet rays from the sun. See page 382.

Dealing with the Baby's Emotions

Parents and other caregivers can encourage emotions such as joy, happiness, and love by responding positively when the baby expresses these feelings. For example, speaking to, cuddling and kissing, or playing with the baby rewards happy behavior.

Within a few weeks after birth, babies recognize their mother's face and respond by cooing. This indicates delight and satisfaction with life. By the time babies are three months old, they smile at other people. They respond by reaching out their arms and kicking their legs. At about four months of age, they start to laugh. Talking to babies and maintaining eye contact with them encourage these positive emotional responses.

Parents and caregivers must also deal with a variety of other emotions. Some of these emotions are expressed through crying. Others include anger and fear.

◆ Crying

All babies cry—some more than others. Responding to a baby's cries is positive and essential. Babies whose needs are met promptly when they cry will develop a strong sense of trust and security. However, if parents or caregivers pay attention to babies only when they are crying, babies will learn to use crying to get attention.

Sometimes it is difficult to know why a baby is crying. At first all cries sound pretty much the same. Parents must try to discover what need the newborn is communicating. Is it time for a feeding? Is the baby uncomfortable or in pain? Does the diaper need changing?

By the time babies are a month old, they seem to cry in several different ways. Their cries vary in pitch, intensity, and pattern. A cry of hunger, for example, differs from a cry of pain. Parents soon learn to interpret these cries and try to respond accordingly. If they are successful in comforting the baby, they have probably understood the meaning of the cry. If the cry is caused by hunger, the baby can be fed. If it is caused by being too cold, the baby can be dressed more warmly. These are the easy-to-understand cries of distress.

Sometimes babies cry simply because they are annoyed, frustrated, or bored. The reasons for these emotions are usually harder to identify. Some babies have a fussy spell at the same time each day. There may be no particular reason—they just feel fretful. Other babies develop **colic,** (KAHL-ik), or pain in the abdomen for which no cause can be found. Their loud and prolonged crying occurs about the same time each day, usually in the evening. Colic usually begins about the second or third week after birth and disappears by itself within a month or two.

What can be done to comfort a crying baby? Some babies can be soothed by being held and comforted. Talking softly or singing to the baby may provide the needed comfort. Other babies feel better when they are carried around for a while, rocked in a rocking chair, or pushed in a carriage or stroller. For some

◆ ◆ Self-Esteem ◆ ◆

From the moment babies are born, they show their uniqueness. They have different temperaments and respond to people in different ways. Yet all babies demonstrate their needs by crying—their main method of communication. When parents answer babies' cries by picking them up, cuddling them, and speaking in gentle tones, babies learn that they are loved and valued.

Discuss. How can parents and caregivers encourage a baby to express feelings of joy, happiness, and love? Why is this important?

Problem Solving. Play a tape of a crying baby for five minutes or longer. Ask students what they could do to comfort the baby? What should parents or caregivers do when they can no longer tolerate the prolonged crying?

babies, a pacifier may help. Many babies develop an attachment to a favorite object, such as a soft blanket or toy. They are comforted by holding or stroking the treasured item. In general, rhythmic movement and soothing sounds seem most effective in calming babies.

Perhaps more important than the particular method chosen to soothe the baby is the mere fact of responding to the cries. Even if the baby does not stop crying, the comforting should continue. Though the response may appear ineffective, it reassures the baby that someone cares.

Some parents are wary of responding too quickly or too often to a baby's cries for fear of spoiling the baby. Most experts believe it is much better to try to soothe young babies than to ignore their cries. Babies are not con-

sciously trying to monopolize their parents' time. They are simply expressing their needs in the only way they can. Of course, there is a difference between a crying three-month-old and an older baby. One-year-olds have probably learned that they can attract parents' attention by crying. There are certain occasions when it is not wise to give babies of that age everything they want simply because they cry. For young babies, however, the best response to crying is prompt attention.

Prolonged crying is hard to tolerate, and parents often feel it will last forever. They should try to keep calm and help each other. Becoming frustrated will only make the baby more irritable. A doctor or nurse may suggest remedies for helping a baby stop crying. Parents may also be able to get useful advice or help from friends, family, or neighbors.

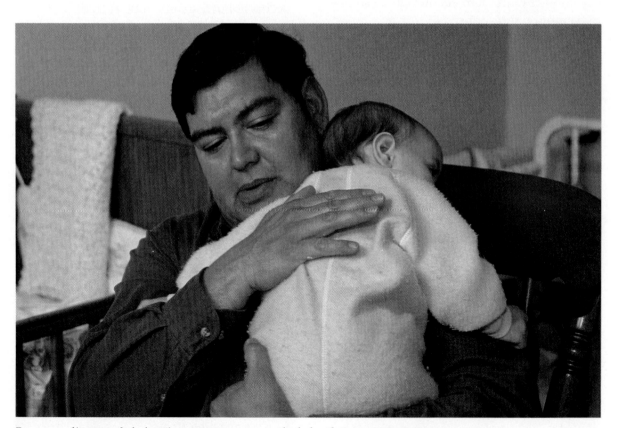

By responding to a baby's cries, parents reassure the baby that someone cares. This helps the baby develop a sense of trust.

DECISIONS ◆ ◆ DECISIONS

Aaron is two weeks old. Suddenly, he has crying spells that begin around suppertime and last for several hours. His parents, Ginny and Victor, have tried feeding him, burping him, and changing his diaper. Aaron continues to cry regardless of whether he is held or lies in his crib. He cries so hard that his face becomes red. Nothing his parents do seems to help. Ginny is becoming very frustrated in her ability to care for the infant. The pediatrician has told the parents that Aaron has colic and is not seriously ill. Still, Victor fears that something is terribly wrong with their son. They have mentioned their worries to you. What will you tell them?

◆◆ Anger

Anger usually occurs when babies do not get what they want. The most common reason for an angry outburst is a delay in being fed. Fortunately, such outbursts usually last for only a short time.

Parents are often troubled by angry outbursts and may become angry themselves. This only adds to the baby's rage, however. At times the angry baby may have a real need—such as the need for food—and this need must be met. At other times, the best reaction is simply to be calm and patient.

Often, an infant wants to play with an object that could be dangerous. Usually this problem can be overcome by directing the baby's attention toward another object or toy. This will protect the child without causing anger. Obviously, babies cannot be allowed to hurt themselves or to have everything they want. However, their feelings should always be acknowledged with understanding.

Adults should never deliberately make a baby angry. They should not give in to a baby's wishes simply to stop the angry outburst. This behavior teaches the child to use anger to get whatever he or she wants.

Adults must remember that babies have no sense of appropriate behavior. Only when children are older can they learn how to control their emotional responses.

◆◆ Fear

Parents and other caregivers can help the baby avoid fear by recognizing those situations that usually frighten the baby. For example, sudden actions can cause fear. The newborn should always be lifted slowly and gently and held securely. The infant should never be bounced or tossed up in the air. Not only is this dangerous, but the infant will be startled and begin to cry.

Babies between the ages of six and ten months develop stranger anxiety and may start to cry when they see someone they do not know. Newcomers should approach a baby slowly or, better yet, let the baby approach them. Babies need time to adjust to strangers before being talked to or held.

Encouraging Social Development

Newborn babies are not sociable. They eat, sleep, and cry without paying much attention to the people caring for them.

Between the ages of six weeks and three months, babies begin to smile in response to another person; some babies smile at a parent even earlier than this. They love to have people talk to them, sing to them, and hold them. Games such as peekaboo and "This little pig went to market" amuse babies and encourage social development.

Discuss. Do you agree with the statement, "Fear is nature's way of alerting to danger"?
Emphasize. Infants should always be held gently and securely. "Shaken child syndrome" can occur in rough play (throwing child in the air), as well as during child abuse. The brain slams against the skull or the spine snaps at the neck, causing serious injury or death.

Babies cannot be forced to be sociable or friendly. It is better to let them see other people and decide how to respond to them. Parents and caregivers can encourage babies' responsiveness by smiling and making frequent eye contact with them. Once babies can crawl, they may move toward a stranger. They may poke an inquiring finger into a neighbor's open-toed sandal. They may pull themselves up to stand at a person's knee. Then is the time for the person to say hello.

By nine months of age, babies like to imitate what parents do when they play with them. Babies enjoy performing action games such as pat-a-cake and "so-big"—and then wait in anticipation for the approval they expect. Through this kind of play they learn that relating to other human beings is a rewarding source of enjoyment.

Babies often respond more readily to children than to adults. They may play games, such as dropping a toy out of the playpen to an older child who will pick it up for them. Sociability begins in this way.

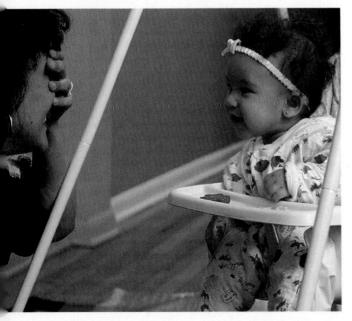

Parents can encourage a baby's sociability by playing games such as peekaboo.

Discuss. What types of activities can encourage a baby's social development?

Encouraging Cognitive Development

Recent studies have shown that cognitive development increases if children live in a stimulating environment during their early years. Such an environment is one that allows them to use their five senses. It contains colorful objects to look at, interesting sounds to hear, and a variety of things to touch.

❖ Providing a Stimulating Environment

When they are just a few months old, babies are most attracted to things they can watch and listen to: mobiles, colorful posters, hanging disks, ticking clocks, and music boxes. Between the ages of four and six months, they like things they can grasp and manipulate: rattles, squeeze toys, and stuffed animals. At seven to nine months of age, they enjoy toys they can pound, bang, throw, and shake: blocks, balls, and rattles. From ten to twelve months of age, actively crawling babies like to follow objects such as balls and pull toys.

Of course, much learning takes place without toys. Infants should not be kept in one room but be moved about to see new sights and be with other family members. Older babies need to be able to crawl and explore and not be confined to a playpen at all times. Children gain stimulation by being taken to the park, to the store, or for a ride in a stroller or car. All these activities provide new learning experiences.

A stimulating environment includes a great deal of interaction between infants and other people. Babies want to learn. Learning comes naturally to them. Adult encouragement helps promote their cognitive develop-

Problem Solving. On the chalkboard, list all the students' suggestions, other than toys, for creating a stimulating environment for a baby. Which suggestions involve little or no cost?

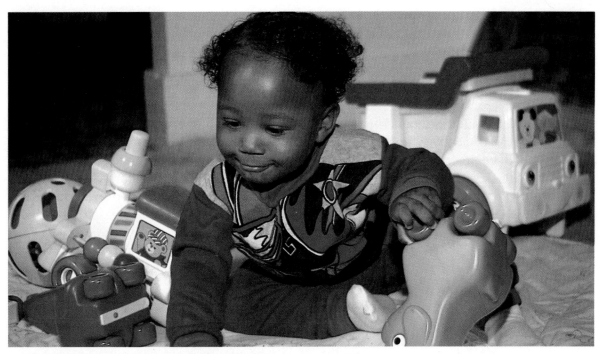

A stimulating environment provides lots of learning experiences for infants. They can play with objects, interact with other people, and see new sights.

ment. Let's look at an example of how this works.

Ten-month-old Becky is getting ready for a bath. Her father, Reuben, slips her socks partway off. Becky pulls them completely off and holds them up.

"Good!" exclaims Reuben.

While Becky watches, Reuben hides the socks under a nearby toss pillow on the sofa. "Where did your socks go, Becky?" asks Reuben.

Becky looks at her feet, looks up at her father's face, and then looks at the pillow. She laughs with delight as she lifts up the pillow and reveals the socks.

Becky's ability to remember for a brief moment where her socks were hidden is evidence of her developing mental ability. A few weeks earlier, she only looked confused and did not watch as her father hid her socks. Every night since then, he looked under several objects before showing her the socks

under the same pillow. He would say, "Are they here? No. Are they here? No. Here they are! Here are Becky's socks!" It was a game they both enjoyed. Now Becky has learned that objects still exist even when they are out of sight. This game gives Becky's parents evidence of her developing cognitive ability.

◆◆ Encouraging Language Development

Communicating with others is one of the most important skills human beings acquire. During their first year, babies are mastering the beginning stages of language development. This development takes place almost exclusively through the interchange of human voices. It is important that parents and caregivers talk and sing to babies even while doing routine tasks, such as feeding, bathing, and changing diapers. They should speak

More About. Learning that objects still exist when they are out of sight is called object permanence. See page 359 for more information.

Discuss. Since infants like to examine objects with different textures, what items can a parent make or find around the home that have a variety of textures? Show or explain a "touch ball" or a blanket of different textures.

clearly and slowly in a soothing tone and name objects as they give them to babies. Parents and older siblings can look at picture books with babies and point out different objects, sing songs, and repeat rhythmic verses.

Babies can communicate, too. When someone talks directly to a baby, whether the topic is love or a ball game, the baby will begin to watch that person's face. Then the baby will lean forward, gurgling and making imitative sounds. When tired or overstimulated, the baby communicates this feeling by turning his or her head aside for a moment. The other person can rest a moment, too, then talk again when the baby turns back and leans forward as though to say, "Now let's talk some more."

When babies are between the ages of eight and twelve months, their first words usually become understandable. Caregivers can encourage language development by giving positive responses to these words. For example, babies all over the world make sounds resembling the word *mama*. See page 246. A mother enjoys hearing her baby say the word and may respond with smiles, hugs, or kisses. In this way, the baby learns to repeat the word. With positive responses from the father, *dada* or *papa* becomes part of the child's vocabulary.

Babies love to hear parents and others speaking to them. In addition to helping babies develop their language skills, this gives them a sense of being cared for and loved.

Parents should encourage language development by talking and singing to infants. By responding to babies' babbling, parents help children associate certain sounds with people and objects.

Activity. Have students share various songs and lullabies that parents can sing to infants.

Activity. Bring to class a variety of books that are suitable for infants, such as board books, touch and feel books, and books with large colorful pictures and few or no words. Then have students create their own infant book.

CHAPTER 14 REVIEW

Summary

- Babies need food, sleep, and to be kept clean and warm. They also need security and love.

- During the first months, babies are able to get the important nutrients from breast milk or formula. Solid foods should be introduced gradually to older babies.

- Babies need frequent diaper changes and daily bathing.

- By five months of age, most babies sleep through the night.

- Babies should be encouraged to practice motor skills as soon as their muscles are mature enough.

- Parents and other caregivers should always respond to a baby's crying and be alert to the possible causes of crying.

- Social development increases when babies are allowed to see and respond to a variety of people in their own way.

- Cognitive development increases when children live in a stimulating environment that encourages the use of the five senses.

- By talking and singing to babies, parents and others help them develop language skills, as well as feel important and loved.

Questions

p. 249   **1.** What is self-demand feeding?

p. 250   **2.** Why should parents and caregivers not prop up a baby's bottle during feedings?

p. 251   **3.** How should the temperature of formula be checked after warming? Why?

p. 253   **4.** Why should new solid foods be offered only one at a time?

5. What is cradle cap? How may it be prevented and treated?   p. 257

6. Describe the kinds of toys that allow babies to practice new motor skills?   p. 260

7. How can a fussy baby be comforted?   p. 261

8. What signs indicate that a baby may have colic?   p. 261

9. How can playing games such as peek-aboo with a baby encourage social development?   p. 263

10. How can parents provide a stimulating environment for their baby?   p. 264

11. How do babies communicate with others?   p. 266

Activities

1. Using a life-size baby doll, demonstrate how to hold, burp, diaper, or bathe a baby.

2. Design a toy for a six-month-old. Write an advertisement for your toy, explaining how it encourages at least two kinds of development.

3. Demonstrate various rhymes, finger play, and action games that parents and caregivers do with babies. Then create an original rhyme, activity, or game to play with babies.

Think About

1. Why do most pediatricians recommend that babies stay on breast milk or formula for the first year?

2. Do you think babies should be allowed to suck their thumb or fingers? Why or why not? Would you give your baby a pacifier? Why or why not?

Reference. See the Teacher's Manual in the front of the Teacher's Annotated Edition for complete answers to the chapter review questions.

267

Health and Safety

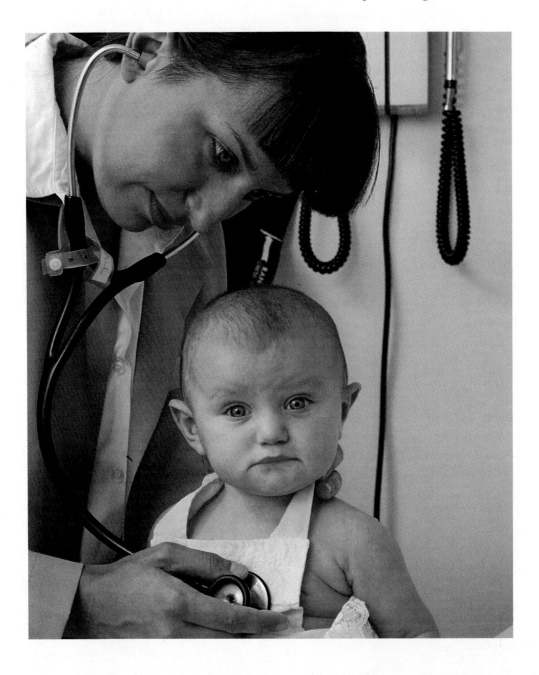

Objectives

This chapter will help you to:
- Describe ways to maintain a child's good health.
- Explain procedures to follow when a child becomes ill.
- Identify safety precautions to protect children.
- Demonstrate the steps to follow in an emergency situation.

Vocabulary

wellness
immunizations
croup
allergy
sudden infant death
 syndrome (SIDS)
first aid
cardiopulmonary
 resuscitation (CPR)

artificial respiration
convulsion
fracture

Andrea Cohen is speaking on the phone to her health care provider at the health maintenance organization (HMO). The HMO provides telephone consultations and routine health care for insured families.

"My six-month-old daughter woke up this morning with a stuffy nose," Andrea tells the health care provider. "I'm wondering whether I should bring her in for a checkup."

"Does she have a fever?" the health care provider asks.

"No," responds Andrea. She has learned that before calling the HMO she should take the baby's temperature and write it down, along with any symptoms of illness. This way she is prepared to describe the baby's condition and discuss her concerns.

It is reassuring to talk to a specialist about her child's health. Being a first-time parent, Andrea is still learning about common childhood illnesses. She is getting advice on what the symptoms mean and what procedures she should follow in caring for her child.

Health Protection

Health protection for the baby begins at birth with a checkup by the baby's doctor or the hospital pediatrician. As you learned in Chapter 10, it is a good idea for parents to decide in advance whom they would like for their baby's doctor. Parents should find a pediatrician with whom they feel comfortable. They should feel free to ask questions, even if they think their questions might sound silly. An understanding doctor knows that many parents feel unsure of themselves.

Parents will also want to find out how a doctor feels about such issues as feeding and the use of pacifiers. However, the doctor should not insist that parents accept his or her suggestions on such matters. After the doctor has stated a position, the final decision must be made by the parents.

Well-baby clinics are becoming more and more popular. These clinics are usually less expensive than private doctors. They can be used in the same way for routine checkups and medical advice.

Whether through a private physician or a clinic, parents should have a regular, reliable source of medical care for their baby. Then, if emergencies arise, they can telephone for assistance. The doctor's or clinic's phone number should be kept handy and should be left with babysitters.

❖ Wellness

Being healthy means much more than not being ill. Parents and children should focus on achieving and maintaining a state of good health. This concept of health is called **wellness.** It involves four main aspects of health: physical, emotional, social, and mental. All four components are interrelated.

Practicing good health habits lessens people's chance of illness and helps them stay well. It involves being alert to ways to protect health and safety. When people practice wellness behavior, they actively make choices and decisions that promote good health.

Today doctors and clinics do not see children only when they are sick. They want to see children on a regular basis to observe their development. During scheduled checkups, the doctor looks for evidence of physical, emotional, social, and mental well-being. The doctor observes, asks questions, and conducts tests. The health of the whole child is important.

❖ Regular Checkups

Most pediatricians like to see the newborn immediately after birth, then again in about three weeks. After that, the baby usually has routine examinations every one or two months. These checkups continue until the baby is a year old.

A good pediatrician takes plenty of time with a baby and tries to develop a relation-

ship with the infant. At least one parent should always be present during the checkup. The parent should be allowed to hold and comfort the baby if necessary.

Examination

During a regular checkup, the doctor or health care assistant examines the baby's body systems and records the findings. The baby's general appearance and alertness are also observed. Often the doctor asks questions regarding the baby's eating, sleeping, and elimination. This information gives the doctor some guidelines about how the baby is progressing.

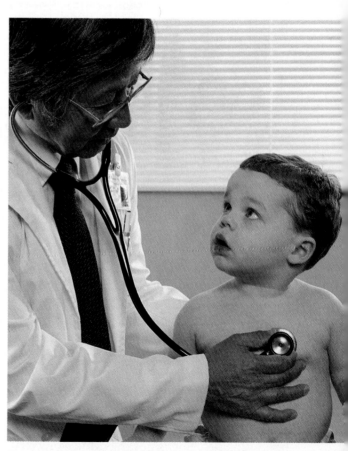

Regular checkups enable the doctor to monitor the infant's growth and development. Many doctors will talk or play with the baby during the examination. Then the baby may be less fearful and more at ease.

DECISIONS ◆ ◆ DECISIONS

Brooks, age four, hates to go to the doctor. He whimpers in fear whenever he goes for checkups, immunizations, and treatment for earaches and other minor ailments. Because he gets so upset, his parents are considering letting him skip this year's checkup. They have not yet made up their mind. What do you think they should do? Why?

The baby's weight and length are recorded. These measurements are compared with the records from the previous visit and with the average size of other children at the same age. These serve as a guideline for growth. The baby's temperature may be taken. Since every baby does not have exactly the same normal temperature, this serves as a baseline for comparison when the baby has a fever.

The baby's eyes, ears, and throat are examined with a special flashlight. A stethoscope is used to listen to the heart and lungs. These instruments are fascinating to children as they grow older. The doctor may let them examine the tools when they show interest.

The doctor presses on the baby's glands, stomach, and groin areas and examines the genitals. The doctor actually goes over the baby from head to toe—from checking for cradle cap to toeing in of the feet. Because growth and development proceed at varying rates, checkups may differ according to the baby's age. Later, when the baby is older, vision and hearing tests will be given.

Following the examination, the doctor discusses the findings with the parent. This is the time to talk about special concerns, ask questions, and get feedback. Many parents write down their questions prior to the scheduled visit. It is easy to get involved with the baby during the examination and forget to ask important questions.

The doctor's office or clinic keeps detailed records of each examination. These are used as a reference for future visits or calls if the parent telephones for advice.

Immunizations

Children need to be protected against a number of childhood diseases through **immunizations** (im-yoo-nih-ZAY-shuhns). These are vaccines that are given in shots or taken by mouth to protect children from certain diseases. Years ago, children were disabled or killed by diseases such as polio,

Immunizations are a series of vaccines that help protect children against certain childhood diseases. Some vaccines can be given orally; others are given by injection.

More About. Many parents write information from checkups in a baby book or calendar. Years later the child may enjoy learning this information about his or her early years.
Emphasize. When parents move to a new community, they need to arrange for their child's medical records to be sent to the new doctor.
More About. A vaccine is a form of the disease that causes the body to develop an immunity to the disease.

Immunization Schedule

AGE	2 months	4 months	6 months	15 months	4–6 years	7–12 years
IMMUNIZATIONS	DTP–1 OPV–1 HIB–1	DTP–2 OPV–2 HIB–2	DTP–3 HIB–3	DTP–4 OPV–3 HIB–4 MMR-1	DTP–5 OPV–4	MMR–2

American Medical Association 1992

diphtheria, and whooping cough. However, because these diseases are now so rare, parents may not realize the importance of immunizing babies against them. Unless babies receive immunizations, they are just as vulnerable to these diseases as children were a hundred years ago.

Most immunizations start when the baby is two months old. Then additional ones are given on a regular schedule until he or she is fifteen months of age. During the preschool and school years, booster shots and oral vaccines are given. The doctor or clinic advises parents of the specific timing and frequency of each immunization. See the sample immunization schedule shown above. Parents should keep a careful record of all the immunizations their baby receives.

The following immunizations are recommended for all children.

- **DPT:** diphtheria, pertussis (whooping cough), and tetanus vaccine; given five times.
- **OPV:** oral polio vaccine; given four times.
- **HIB:** hemophilus influenza type b (causes meningitis, pneumonia, and infections) vaccine; given four times.
- **MMR:** measles, mumps, and rubella virus vaccine; given two times.

Some babies have reactions to these immunizations. They may be unusually cranky or even run a slight fever. Doctors can advise parents about what to do if such reactions occur.

Calling the Doctor

Parents should feel free to call the doctor or clinic any time they have a question about their baby's health. Often, the first sign of illness is the baby's behavior. The baby may be cranky, listless, or irritable. He or she may refuse to eat or may sleep restlessly. The baby's crying may sound different from the usual cries of hunger or frustration.

Other signs of illness are more direct. Here are some of them and the actions parents should take.

- If the baby has a high fever, several degrees above normal temperature, parents should contact the doctor. Fever usually means there is an infection somewhere in the body. All parents should keep a rectal thermometer on hand and learn to take the baby's temperature.
- If the baby is screaming and pulling at an ear, parents should take the baby's temperature and call the doctor. The baby may have an ear infection.

Activity. Ask students to research diseases, such as smallpox or polio, that were common years ago. Have them ask their parents and grandparents if any relatives had one of these diseases. Have them share their findings.

Emphasize. Children must be immunized before starting school. Parents who put off having their child immunized until entering school place the child in needless risk of contracting a serious disease.

- If the baby has diarrhea, parents should give the baby liquids and consult the doctor. Allowing a baby to get severely dehydrated—as can happen when diarrhea occurs—is extremely dangerous.
- If the baby has any unusual skin rash, loss of appetite, or vomiting, parents should contact the doctor.

Many doctors and clinics have calling hours when parents can telephone for advice. Sometimes the doctor suggests watching the baby to see how the illness progresses. At other times the doctor may ask a parent to bring the baby to the office or clinic for an examination. Babies cannot tell their parents what hurts. They sometimes have sore throats

DECISIONS ◆ ◆ DECISIONS

Dawn and Alex are first-time parents. Dawn has been home with their baby boy, Christopher, for two weeks. During that time, she has made three phone calls to the doctor. She called once when the baby spit up, once when he cried for quite a long time, and once when his bowel movement seemed a strange color. In each case, the doctor told her not to worry; the baby was fine. Now Christopher is running a slight fever. Dawn does not want to be a pest, but she is concerned about the baby. What do you think she should do?

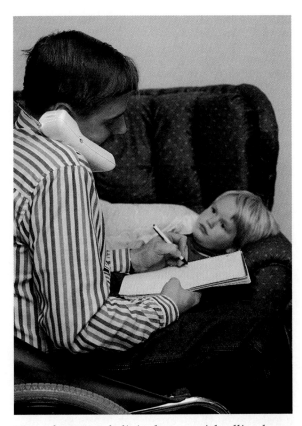

Many doctors and clinics have special calling hours when parents can telephone for advice about an ill child. Parents should write down the doctor's instructions to avoid any confusion.

or other problems that parents cannot determine. Minor illnesses may develop into serious ones if left untreated. That is why a physician should be consulted whenever a baby appears to be ill.

❖ Common Childhood Illnesses

All children get illnesses, especially colds and coughs. During some illnesses, they may be less active and sleep more frequently than usual. During other illnesses, they may lose interest in eating food. Whatever the reactions, parents must encourage ill children to drink plenty of liquids to prevent dehydration. If medication is prescribed, it is important to follow the directions exactly and give the prescribed dose for as long as indicated. Sometimes parents stop medications when the baby starts to feel better, and then the illness returns.

During an illness, children usually require extra attention. They may enjoy playing quiet games, looking at books, or being comforted. They need reassurance that they will soon be feeling better.

Colds and Coughs

Both colds and coughs are common in childhood. A runny nose, sneezing, and coughing are the usual symptoms. Most colds are not serious unless the child runs a high fever. Parents should call the doctor, describe the symptoms, and ask for advice.

People around the baby—even little children—should cover their nose and mouth when they sneeze or cough. They should also wash their hands with soap frequently to prevent the spread of germs.

People should not smoke around children. Exposure to passive cigarette smoke increases children's risk of developing bronchitis, pneumonia, and asthma.

Croup

Croup (KROOP) is a condition marked by a loud, barking cough and difficult breathing. If parents suspect their baby has croup, they should call the doctor for advice. Some doc-

◆ ◆ *Self-Esteem* ◆ ◆

When children are sick, they often need extra reassurance and love. Children feel valued when parents and caregivers pay attention to them. Reading to children, playing with them, and listening to them talk or tell stories are ways to assure children that they are important.

tors recommend placing the baby in a steamy room for quick relief. Parents can take the baby into the bathroom and run hot water in the shower for several minutes. This should help the baby's breathing improve. As an alternative, a cool mist humidifier or vaporizer can be used to moisten the air in the baby's room.

Ear Infections

Middle ear infections are common in young children. The ear canals may not be sloped enough to permit proper drainage. Thus, infection may develop. Babies often cry and pull at their ears when they ache. Parents must contact the doctor for an accurate diagnosis and proper treatment.

Sore Throats

A child who has a very red throat and cannot swallow easily may have an infection that could lead to serious complications. Parents should contact the doctor. He or she may want the child tested for bacteria that cause strep throat and scarlet fever.

Allergies

A child who has an **allergy** is sensitive to a substance that causes reactions such as a skin rash, itching, sneezing, or coughing. Allergies can be caused by foods, feathers, animal hair, pollen, and dust.

When children are ill, they need extra attention and reassurance. They can be kept occupied with a variety of quiet activities.

Problem Solving. Have students suggest specific activities that can keep children occupied when they are ill and need to rest.

Emphasize. Ear infections can seldom be cured with home remedies. It is important to get medical assistance early.

The doctor can help parents try to discover what substance is causing a child's allergic reactions. The child must then avoid the identified substance if possible. The doctor can also prescribe medication for various reactions. Fortunately, children often outgrow allergies.

◆ Crib Death

Occasionally, a seemingly healthy baby is put to bed and later is found dead. This tragic event is called **sudden infant death syndrome (SIDS)** or crib death. No illness or accident can account for the death.

Fortunately, SIDS happens only rarely. When it does occur, it strikes babies older than three weeks and younger than seven months. Babies of the rich and poor alike have died from SIDS. The baby of a careless parent is no more likely to be a victim than the baby of a careful parent. SIDS occurs in all parts of the world and has been recorded since ancient times. It was as common in the 1700s as it is today.

Scientists have studied SIDS at great length. As yet, they have no explanation for it. SIDS is not caused by suffocation, choking, bottle-feeding, drugs, or cigarettes. It is not inherited.

Some parents use an electronic monitor that transmits sounds from the baby to the parents' room. This equipment helps relieve parental anxiety over sudden infant death syndrome.

When SIDS does occur, it is shocking and heartbreaking for the parents. They often blame themselves or each other for things they did or did not do. Couples may be helped to deal with their reactions and grief by talking with a member of the clergy or a psychiatrist. A counselor at a mental health agency or a support group may also be of help.

Activity. Have students gather information about electronic monitors, including their cost.

Around the World

The High Risk of Childhood Diseases

Approximately 4 million African children under the age of five die every year. More than half of them die from childhood diseases that could be prevented. Illnesses such as diarrhea, malaria, and acute lower respiratory tract infections can be cured with proper treatment. Diseases such as measles, pertussis (whooping cough), and polio can be prevented with proper immunization.

The Combating Childhood Communicable Diseases (CCCD) project is part of the United States Agency for International Development. CCCD is working with ten countries in Africa to help lower the rates of childhood illness and death.

In these countries there are not enough doctors to go around. Thus medical care is usually provided by nurses and health care workers. Even serious childhood illnesses are treated at home because most families cannot afford the high cost of hospital care. Programs have been developed to train young Africans in health care work and to teach parents about the importance of immunizations. Other programs train parents to take care of their sick children at home.

Progress is steady but very slow. For example, the number of children receiving measles vaccine has increased in nine of the ten countries. Health experts estimate that this has prevented 3.5 million cases of measles and 100,000 measles-related deaths per year. However, many children in these countries still have not received immunizations.

More About. Many states require a full criminal investigation of SIDS to be sure that abuse was not involved in the death. This adds an even greater emotional stress on the parents.

Safety Precautions

Many safety precautions must be taken in the home to protect babies. These include making rooms safe for babies and generally protecting them against accidents throughout the home.

❖❖ Childproofing Rooms

Taking safety measures in the home and in other places where babies and young children spend a great deal of time is called childproofing. This means planning ahead to ensure the safety of the child. See pages 278-279 for a checklist and diagram for childproofing a home.

As babies develop and move about on their own, more and more places become dangerous. Babies cannot recognize when serious dangers are present. Parents and caregivers must be alert to potential hazards in the environment. They need to get down to the baby's level—sit on the floor—and look around. Where are the dangers? How can the baby be protected? Accidents are the most common cause of death among babies and young children.

Many psychologists are opposed to the use of playpens. They feel that keeping babies in these pens can slow their development by preventing them from exploring the environment. However, there are times when parents and caregivers must turn their attention to other tasks. At such times, a playpen can be very useful.

A playpen that folds or is narrow enough to fit through a door is most convenient. Such a playpen can easily be moved from room to room or outside. A folding playpen can also be taken on trips to provide a safe sleeping

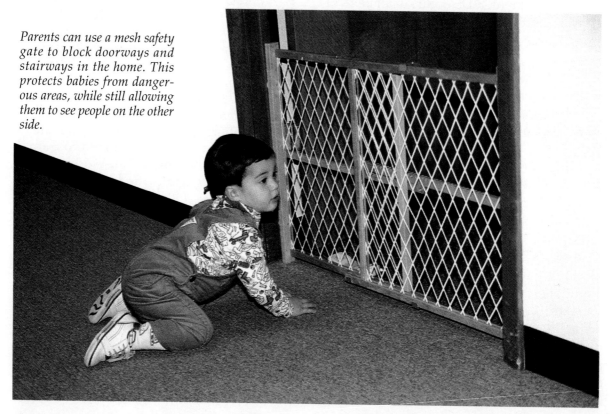

Parents can use a mesh safety gate to block doorways and stairways in the home. This protects babies from dangerous areas, while still allowing them to see people on the other side.

Activity. Set up a variety of hazardous situations in the classroom, department living room, or foods lab. Give a prize or extra points to the student who identifies the most hazards in a given length of time.

Discuss. Why are many psychologists opposed to the use of playpens? What are the advantages and disadvantages for the infant and for the parent? When might a playpen be very useful?

and playing space for the baby. Parents should never leave the baby in a playpen with one side folded down. The baby could get caught in the mesh.

A plastic mesh gate can be used to close off doorways or to keep a baby away from stairs. It can also keep a baby out of the kitchen when parents are preparing hot foods that might accidentally spill on the baby. A gate has the advantage of allowing the baby to see people on the other side. It also leaves the baby free to move about in a safe room.

◆◆ *Health & Safety* ◆◆

Lead Poisoning

Did you know that lead poisoning is placing millions of young children at risk? Even relatively low levels of lead in the blood can impair a child's learning skills and cause behavioral problems. Because low-level lead poisoning has no easily identifiable symptoms, children should have a blood test by the time they are one year old. High-risk children need to be screened every six months until they are three years old.

What are some common sources of lead around the home?

- **Lead-based paints.** Many apartments and houses built before 1960 contain lead-based paints. Peeling or chipping paint is particularly risky because young children may breathe in or swallow tiny chips of paint. Even windows sliding up and down can produce paint chips and release lead dust into the air.
- **Food containers.** Lead from open cans, certain types of pottery, and lead crystal can leach into food.
- **Water pipes.** Many old water pipes contain lead.
- **Soil.** Backyard soil in urban areas, near factories or highways, or near lead-based exterior paint can contain lead.

What can parents do to protect their children from lead poisoning?

- Check the home for sources of lead. Call the local health department or cooperative extension service for information. If peeling paint must be removed, hire a specialist in lead removal. Small children and pregnant women must not remain in the home while the paint is being removed.
- Do not let children chew on woodwork.
- Wash children's hands frequently—especially before they eat and go to sleep.
- Wash pacifiers regularly.
- Make sure children get enough calcium and iron. These minerals decrease the absorption of lead.
- Damp-mop floors and clean windowsills and other dusty areas regularly.
- Flush any lead out of the water pipes by running the water for a few minutes before drinking.
- Do not serve or store food or beverages in open cans, lead crystal, or certain types of pottery.
- Check other places where children spend a good deal of time—at the home of grandparents, at a child care center, or at school.
- See that children get blood tests for lead.
- Help clean up the environment.

Emphasize. Parents should avoid using expandable wooden gates with crisscrossed slats. A child's head or neck can become caught between the slats, causing serious injury or death.

Problem Solving. Have students gather more information about the risk of lead poisoning. Ask them to evaluate their home and community for possible sources. Discuss risks, screening and treatment procedures, and ways to avoid exposure.

How to Childproof a Home

1. Use a mesh gate, securely placed, to keep children from stairways and dangerous areas.

2. Cover electric outlets with special caps. Tape electric cords to the floor or wall molding.

3. Keep fans and space heaters out of reach.

4. Turn pot handles toward rear of cooktop.

5. Use cribs or playpens with slats no farther apart than 2 ⅜ inches. Keep crib sides at highest level for toddlers.

6. Lower hot water temperature to 120° F. to prevent scalding.

7. Put all dangerous household products in securely latched cabinets.

8. Lock medicine cabinet. Buy only those medicines with childproof caps.

9. List phone numbers of child's doctor, police and fire departments, nearest hospital, and Poison Control Center next to telephone.

10. Fasten seat belts in high chairs, strollers, shopping carts, and cars.

11. Stick rubber appliques on bottom of bathtub, or use nonslip tub mat.

12. Install smoke detectors on every floor of home. Have a family plan of action in case of fire.

13. Use placemats or short tablecloths that do not hang down over edge of table.

14. Unplug cords from irons, coffee pots, blenders, hair dryers and other appliances that can be pulled over.

15. Buy flame-retardant sleepwear for children. Follow the washing instructions that come with them.

16. Protect valuables by putting them out of reach or packing them away until the child is older.

17. Use paper or plastic cups instead of glass or china ones.

18. Lock up power tools and hobby supplies.

Lamps and appliance cords should be hidden from view as much as possible. Some cords can be attached to a floorboard or wall molding. This gets them out of the way and makes them less interesting to a crawling baby. Electrical outlets should be covered with special plastic covers.

Medicines, harmful cleaning supplies, and tools should all be removed from low cupboards and shelves. Small objects that a baby could place in the mouth and swallow should be removed from any area the baby can reach.

As children grow older, they may be fascinated by fire. It is important to keep all matches and lighters out of their reach and to explain the dangers of playing with matches and fire. Children should also be taught what to do in case there is a fire in the home. They should practice using escape routes from various rooms if the smoke alarm sounds.

◆ Protection Against Accidents

The old adage "An ounce of prevention is worth a pound of cure" is especially true for babies. Parents and caregivers who think babies will stay safely in one place are sadly mistaken.

In addition to childproofing rooms, parents and caregivers need to supervise babies and young children closely. Most accidents can be prevented.

Preventing Falls

Babies can fall off beds and changing tables, down stairs, and out of cribs. They can dig their tiny toes into bed covers and inch along to an edge. They soon learn to roll over and can fall if left alone for only a moment. Many are badly hurt—even killed—from falls every year.

Babies should never be left alone on a bed, sofa, or changing table. They are much safer in a crib or playpen. Crib and playpen sides should be kept up for protection.

Once they can crawl, some babies are attracted to windows. Parents and caregivers should make sure that there is nothing for a child to climb up on to reach a window. If windows are open, they should be covered with secure screens or safety gates.

Babies often fall down stairs because parents do not realize how far their babies can crawl. Most babies survive such falls. Their bones are still soft and flexible, and their soft spots usually protect them from concussions. However, such falls can be very dangerous, and they are frightening for both babies and parents. Responsible parents and caregivers anticipate babies' crawling before it happens. They latch doors that open onto stairways or put gates in front of them. Most important, responsible adults stay with babies while they are crawling.

Safety in Baths

Babies are easily scalded when their bathwater is too hot. This is a needless danger. A parent or caregiver must test the water temperature before putting the baby into the water. No hot water should be turned on in the tub or sink while the baby is in it.

The baby must be held securely during the entire bath. If the phone or doorbell rings, the person bathing the baby should either ignore the ring or wrap the baby in a towel and carry the child along to answer the ring.

All hair dryers and other electrical appliances should be removed from the bathing area so the baby cannot pull them into the water. Electricity from an electrical device can electrocute anyone in the water.

Most parents know they should never leave a baby or young child alone in the bath. Equally important, however, is never leaving a baby and young child together in a bath. A recent study revealed that many infant deaths took place when another child between the ages of two and five was also in the bathtub. Parents had left the room assuming that the

Emphasize. "Head rearing" typically begins at one month. Then a baby may accidentally turn over and fall off a bed, couch, or changing table.
Emphasize. If there are stairs in the home, parents should

teach a baby as soon as possible to crawl down backwards.
More About. Set temperature of hot water heater no higher than 120° F. to prevent accidental scalding. Test baby's bath water with your elbow—it is more sensitive than the hand.

Babies should be held securely at all times during a bath. They should never be left alone—even for a moment.

older child would know when the baby was in danger. The study also found that the average age of babies who had died of bath accidents was nine months. Babies of nine months can sit unassisted and have good muscle control. Even so, babies of this age were still not able to save themselves from drowning in only a few inches of water.

Safety in Beds

The baby should have a firm mattress but no pillow. Overly soft mattresses or pillows can smother babies if their nose becomes buried in them. The mattress should also fit the crib, leaving no room for the baby to roll into a space along the side of the crib. Padded crib bumpers keep the baby from hitting

against the crib bars and arms and legs from getting stuck between the bars. Newer cribs are required by law to have bars no more than 2 ⅜ inches apart so babies cannot poke their head between the bars. Parents with older cribs should check the width between bars and may need to insert extra bars.

Toys left in the crib should be free of sharp edges. There should be no small pieces that the baby could pull off and swallow. Plastic eyes on stuffed toys are a particular danger in this regard.

Safety in Kitchens

A high chair may be dangerous when a baby becomes active enough to stand up in it. Many parents prefer lower feeding tables. Seats should have safety straps that hold a

Reference. See page 257 for more information about safety in baths.

More About. Bumper pads should be removed from the crib when the infant is able to stand in the crib. This will prevent the baby from climbing up on the pads and falling out of the crib.

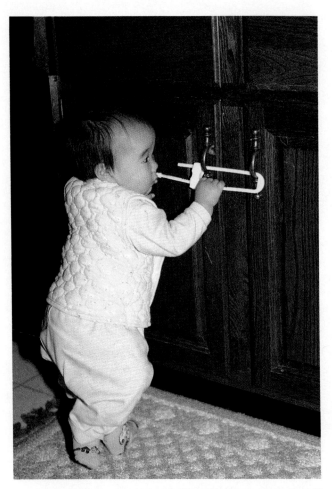

The kitchen contains many hazards. Safety locks should be attached to cabinets containing breakable dishes, sharp utensils, and cleaning agents.

baby securely. The high chair or feeding table should be kept away from the range. A baby who can reach high or far enough might grab a pot handle, overturn the contents, and get burned. An adult must always keep an eye on a baby in a high chair or at a feeding table.

Tablecloths invite creeping babies to tug on them, bringing down dishes, knives and forks, and hot food. Placemats can be used until children are old enough to understand that they may not pull on tablecloths.

An ironing board may come crashing down if a baby pulls up while holding onto it. The cord on an iron is inviting to a curious

baby, as are the dangling pieces of clothing that are being ironed. While ironing, adults should keep the baby away from the ironing board. When they are finished, they should immediately put the board away.

Safety Around Heaters

To protect against burns, parents should keep babies away from radiators, floor furnaces, and space heaters. An unvented gas heater should never be used anywhere in the home. Vented gas heaters should have a valve that shuts off the gas if the pilot light goes out. Without this protective device, there is danger of death from lack of oxygen and from explosions. Because of the same dangers, a gas oven should never be used to heat a room.

Protection from Suffocation

For babies, one of the most dangerous household items is a thin plastic bag from a dry cleaner. Babies enjoy pulling small blankets over their face to play peekaboo. Infants cannot tell the difference between blankets and plastic bags. In addition, the bags make attractive rustling noises. Babies who pull bags over their face can suffocate within minutes. The best prevention is for parents to tie knots in plastic bags from the dry cleaner and discard them immediately. Other plastic bags, such as food and garbage bags, should be stored out of the baby's reach.

Safety in Cars

From birth, babies riding in cars or trucks are legally required to be strapped into infant safety seats. Young infants must ride in a reclining position, facing backward. Once children reach 20 pounds or age one, they can ride sitting up and facing forward in a child's safety seat. Some safety seats convert from a reclining position to an upright position. The shoulder straps of the safety seat must be fastened snugly over the child's shoulders.

Infants and young children must be securely restrained in a safety seat whenever they ride in a car. Infants must ride in a reclining position, facing backward. Older children can sit up and face forward. For best protection, the safety seat should be used in the back seat of the car.

Infant and child safety seats must meet federal safety standards and be so labeled. Parents should choose a system that is easy to anchor with the car's seat belts. The buckles should fasten and unfasten easily. Before purchasing a used safety seat at a garage sale, parents will want to be sure it meets current federal crash standards. Some car manufacturers offer fold-down safety seats built into the seat backs of their cars and vans. Until all vehicles have such devices, however, parents must rely on separate car-restraint systems.

Parents and other caregivers should never hold a baby or young child while riding in a car. This is dangerous to the child and to the adult. Even in a 30-miles-per-hour crash, an unrestrained child sitting on an adult's lap will be hurled out of the adult's arms.

When children weigh more than 40 pounds, they can use the car's seat belts. The lap belt should be low and snug over the hip bones. The shoulder strap should fit across the child's chest, not the neck. Two children should never be buckled into the same safety belt.

Adults must also buckle their own seat belt. When children see adults buckle up, they will do so too.

Discuss. Why should a regular baby seat or carrier not be used as a car safety seat? If possible, bring a regular baby seat/carrier and a car safety seat to class for students to examine and compare.

Activity. Have students research the federal safety standards for infant and child safety seats. Then have them create posters that promote the use of safety seats that meet federal standards.

First Aid

Parents and caregivers will have many occasions to deliver first aid to infants and children. **First aid** is emergency treatment given to a person who is injured or ill. An emergency is a situation that requires very fast action.

Taking first-aid and CPR courses is highly recommended for all parents and caregivers. **Cardiopulmonary resuscitation** (kard-ee-oh-PUL-muh-nehr-ee reh-suhs-uh-TAY-shuhn), or **CPR,** is a technique for reviving a person or keeping that person alive until an emergency team can take over. People trained in CPR give the victim oxygen by breathing into his or her lungs. They also apply pressure to the victim's chest to force the heart to pump blood.

Communities frequently offer first-aid and CPR courses. These courses are taught by specialists who help individuals learn the appropriate actions to take in an emergency. Such classes are sometimes free of charge.

❖ Following General First-Aid Procedures

It is not always possible to tell which emergencies are serious and which are not. However, certain conditions such as failure to breathe, severe bleeding, and poisoning must be attended to at once. The following general rules apply for both children and adults.

- *Keep calm and act quickly and quietly.* Speak in a normal tone of voice. Try not to worry the injured or ill person.

- *Check for breathing.* Make sure that the ill or injured person has an open air passage. If the person is not breathing, start artificial respiration at once. **Artificial respiration** is a way of forcing air into and out of the lungs of someone who is not breathing. This is done through mouth-to-mouth or mouth-to-nose rescue breathing.

- *Check the pulse.* If there is no pulse, send for help immediately. If you have been trained and certified, begin CPR.

- *Check for bleeding.* Get serious bleeding stopped as quickly as possible.

- *Do not move an injured person unless it is necessary for safety reasons.* Moving an injured person the wrong way can cause even more harm.

- *Get medical help from trained personnel quickly.* However, do not leave the injured or ill person to get help unless there is no other choice.

All adults and older children should learn how to call for emergency help in their own community. Typically, telephone numbers for the local police or sheriff's office, the fire department, and the national Poison Control Center are listed in the front of the local telephone directory. The number of the first-aid or rescue squad may be listed separately. Some communities have a 911 emergency number. These numbers should be taped to the telephone. Most hospitals have an emergency room where ill or injured people can be taken for treatment.

❖ Handling Specific Emergencies

You have just learned the general procedures to follow in a medical emergency. It is also important to know how to deal with specific emergencies that may involve anyone but particularly children. For example, if a child seems to have swallowed aspirin, drugs, or poison, call the doctor or the Poison Control Center immediately. Time may be critical. See the next page.

Activity. Invite a member of a local ambulance service to demonstrate first aid and CPR procedures for the students.

Problem Solving. Have students create a list of emergency telephone numbers and post them by every telephone in their home. They should also memorize the most important ones.

First Aid for Choking

To help a choking infant:

1 Lay the infant face down on your forearm so that the head is lower than the rest of the child's body. With the heel of your hand, give four quick blows to the infant's back between the shoulder blades. The blows should be forceful, but not as hard as for an older child or an adult.

2 If the infant continues to choke, turn the child onto the back. Keep the head lower than the rest of the body, but support the infant's head and back. Put two fingertips on the infant's chest between the nipples. Press quickly and fairly hard four times.

3 If the infant continues to choke, have someone get medical assistance while you keep repeating steps 1 and 2. Alternate them quickly until medical assistance arrives.

If the child is more than one year old, perform the Heimlich maneuver.

1 Wrap your arms around the child's waist and make a fist with one hand. Press the thumb-side of your fist against the child's abdomen above the navel and below the ribs. Grasp your fist with your other hand.

2 Give four quick, hard, inward and upward thrusts, pulling your fist into the child's abdomen. Do not squeeze with your arms.

3 Continue the thrusts until the object is dislodged, the child begins coughing forcefully, or medical assistance arrives.

Choking

Choking is a leading cause of infant death. Small children and infants can choke on food or other small objects they put into their mouths.

A choking child cannot speak or breathe and starts to turn blue. If a child is choking but coughs forcefully, do not give first aid. Forceful coughing is more effective than first aid. If the child coughs faintly and breathes with great difficulty or does not cough or breathe at all, give first aid immediately. The child has only a few minutes to live if the object is not removed. Follow the steps in the chart on the previous page. This action will force a burst of air from the lungs and dislodge the object. If a sharp object is lodged in the throat, get medical assistance quickly.

Convulsions

A **convulsion** is a series of strong, involuntary contractions of muscles. Convulsions may be caused by head injuries, poisoning, epilepsy, and various illnesses.

First-aid treatment includes protecting the child with convulsions from getting hurt. Do not try to restrain the child's movements. If possible, put a folded blanket under the head. When movement has stopped, place the child on his or her side and be sure that breathing is normal. Then call the doctor at once. Convulsions sometimes accompany high fevers and the start of a serious illness.

Fractures

A break in a bone is called a **fracture.** If you suspect a child has a broken bone, keep him or her quiet. Avoid moving the child if possible, and call the doctor for advice.

In case of injury to the back or neck, do not move the child until professional help arrives. Picking the child up suddenly could further damage the bone or cause injury to the spinal cord.

Cuts and Puncture Wounds

Bleeding from small cuts stops naturally as the air helps the blood clot. For large cuts or gashes, apply direct pressure to the wound. First, place a clean cloth over the wound. Then place the palm of your hand over the cloth and press firmly. While still pressing on the area, call for medical help.

Punctures may require a tetanus shot or booster. Cleanse the wound with fresh water, and consult a doctor.

Bruises

If the skin is bruised but not broken, apply cold, wet cloths or ice to the area for 30 minutes or longer. This relieves pain and helps reduce swelling. If the pain does not go away or the child has great difficulty moving the bruised body part, consult a doctor.

For minor cuts and scrapes, clean the wound and apply a bandage to keep out dirt.

Activity. Invite the school nurse or other health professional to demonstrate the procedures to follow if an infant or child is choking.

Problem Solving. Ask students to demonstrate what to do in each emergency situation given in the chapter.

Nosebleeds

A child with a nosebleed should sit still with the head tilted slightly forward. Hold the bleeding nostril closed with slight pressure on that side of the nose. Apply continuous pressure for five to ten minutes. Also apply a cold towel to the child's nose and face. Most nosebleeds can be stopped this way. If bleeding continues, get medical attention for the child.

Splinters

Splinters that have an open path to the surface of the skin work their way out. Soaking the area in warm water softens the skin and speeds the process. However, if a splinter has not worked itself out after a few days or the skin around it is red, remove the splinter. Use a sterilized needle, tweezers, or knife point to pluck it out. To make instruments sterile, cover them with alcohol or pass them through a flame. If a splinter is not removed, the surrounding area may become infected. Cleanse the wound with a mild antiseptic.

Animal Bites

Animal bites have the potential for infection from rabies. This is an infection of the brain and spinal cord transmitted to humans through the bite of an infected, or rabid, animal. Local health authorities can run a test on the animal to determine whether it is rabid.

A bite from a rabid animal can be fatal if untreated. If the animal is not rabid, the physician will probably not advise rabies shots for the child. The doctor will want to see that the wound has been cleaned and may give the child a tetanus shot.

Insect Bites

If a child is bitten by an insect, check the affected area. If necessary, remove the stinger by scraping it with the blunt side of a knife or another flat object. Do not use tweezers because they may squeeze more venom into the sting area.

Get medical assistance if the child shows an unusual reaction or has a large number of bites. If the child has had an allergic reaction to an insect bite in the past, the doctor may want to see the child.

Ticks can get into children's hair in tick-infested areas. Remove the tick's head as well as its body by pulling slowly and firmly with tweezers. Then cleanse the wound with a mild antiseptic. Some ticks carry bacteria that cause Lyme disease. The symptoms include a circle of reddened skin around a pale area where the tick attached itself. After a few days, similar rashes appear elsewhere on the body, along with fever and flulike symptoms. Contact the doctor immediately. Antibiotics can be given to prevent more severe stages of Lyme disease.

Burns

Treat small burns where the skin is not broken with an ice pack or by soaking the skin in cool water. Apply a clean, dry dressing. If the burn is deep and the skin is charred or destroyed, get medical assistance immediately. Do not apply ice or water, and do not attempt to remove charred clothing. To provide temporary protection, cover the burn area loosely with only a sterile dressing.

When a burn is caused by a chemical, quickly flood the area with a large amount of cold water. Then lightly cover it with gauze and get medical help.

Fast action may keep a child whose clothing is on fire from being badly burned. Place the child on the floor or ground, and smother the flames by rolling the child over. If possible, wrap the child in a heavy material, such as a rug, coat, or blanket to smother the flames.

Activity. Have students research the current method of treating rabies. How does the treatment differ from earlier types of treatments?

Discuss. Ask students what they do to prevent insect bites. What do they apply to an insect bite to reduce itching?

Electrical Shock

It is dangerous to rescue an unconscious child from a live electrical wire. You could be electrocuted by touching the child. If possible, turn off the current. Otherwise, use a dry stick or some other dry material that will not conduct electricity to remove the wire from the child's body. Send for help immediately.

Poisoning

If a child has swallowed a poisonous substance, call the Poison Control Center or local hospital emergency service immediately. Quick action is very important. Be sure to save the bottle or container the poison came from so the contents can be identified. It is a good idea to have syrup of ipecac in the medicine cabinet in case vomiting needs to be induced. Give this syrup to the child only when so instructed by a physician or someone from the Poison Control Center. Some poisons should not be vomited because they would cause as much damage coming up as they did going down.

Drowning

If drowning occurs, remove the child from the water and begin artificial respiration. Send for help immediately. If the child has no pulse, begin CPR if you have been trained and certified. Continue first aid until breathing and pulse are restored and help arrives.

Personal Safety

Unfortunately, parents must also be concerned about keeping their children safe from crime. Babies and young children should never be left unattended in a public area. This includes a store, shopping mall, or park. They also should never be left alone in a car. As children grow older, they must be taught rules concerning their safety when they are away from home. For example, children must learn to tell caregivers where they are at all times. Children must learn never to accept gifts or rides from strangers. They should always be able to tell their parents if someone touches them in an inappropriate way.

It is important not to frighten children unnecessarily about other people and other places. However, parents need to talk openly and honestly with children about crime prevention and safety.

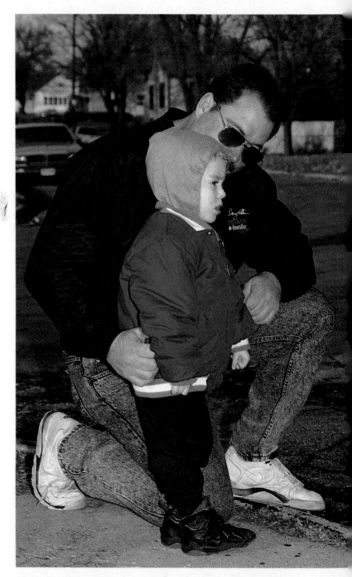

Parents must teach children about personal safety. Rules about crossing streets and talking to strangers can help prevent accidents and crimes.

Problem Solving. Have students locate the telephone number of the Poison Control Center. Then have them make a list of items commonly found in a home that could be poisonous if swallowed by a child.

Activity. Ask students to create a booklet for children on the topic of personal safety.

Summary

- Parents should have a regular, reliable source of medical care for their baby, whether through a private doctor or a clinic.
- Babies should have regular checkups every one or two months.
- Children need to be protected against certain childhood diseases through immunizations.
- Parents should contact a doctor or clinic any time they are concerned about their baby's health.
- Childproofing the home helps prevent injuries and accidents.
- Parents and caregivers should supervise babies and young children closely to prevent falls, burns, suffocation, poisoning, and drowning.
- Parents and caregivers should learn first aid procedures and how to handle specific emergencies.

Questions

p. 270 **1.** What is wellness?

p. 270 **2.** How often should babies have medical checkups?

p. 272 **3.** Name the four types of immunizations that are recommended for all children.

p. 272 **4.** What physical signs may indicate that a baby is ill?

p. 274 **5.** What is croup? How is it usually treated?

p. 275 **6.** What is SIDS?

p. 276 **7.** Why is it important for parents and caregivers to childproof rooms in the home?

8. If the telephone or doorbell rings when a parent is bathing a baby or young child, what should he or she do? p. 280

9. Describe how infants and children should be secured when traveling in a car or truck. p. 282

10. What should a parent or caregiver do if an infant or young child is choking? p. 285

11. If a child has swallowed a poisonous substance, what should a parent or caregiver do? p. 288

Activities

1. Research your own immunization history.

2. On your hands and knees, check your home for infant safety. (That is the way the baby checks it.) List the things that could be dangerous to a crawling baby. Write a description of how you could make your home safe for a baby.

3. Research car safety seats for infants and children and answer the following questions. Why is it important for children to always ride in a safety seat that meets federal safety standards? Which brands and models are most highly recommended? What do the recommended safety seats cost?

4. Demonstrate the Heimlich maneuver.

Think About

1. What items should be included in a first-aid kit in your home?

2. How can parents teach young children about personal safety without frightening them about meeting other people and visiting new places?

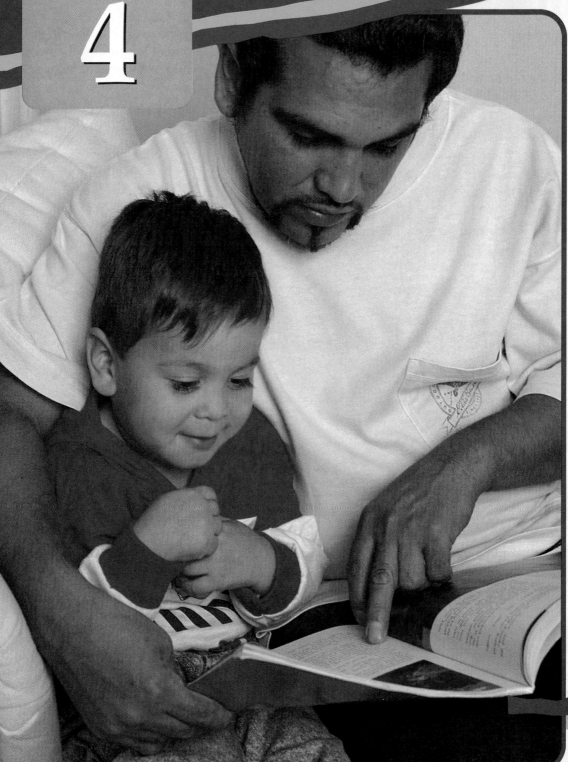

UNIT
4

Nurturing Children

CHAPTERS

Helping Children Grow and Develop Physically

Objectives

This chapter will help you to:
- Describe how a child's body grows and changes.
- Give examples of activities that help the development of large and small motor skills.
- Explain how parents and caregivers can influence a child's physical development.
- Identify the daily food, clothing, and personal hygiene needs of a child.

Vocabulary

growth spurt
large motor skills
small motor skills
eye-hand coordination
dexterity
ambidextrous
malnutrition
flame retardant
sphincter muscles
fluoride
orthodontist

"Mommy, do we have any relatives who are very short?" asked seven-year-old Jessica, as she ate an apple and drank a glass of milk after school.

"Not very short," said Jessica's mother, puzzled by the question. "Why do you ask, Jessica?"

"Today my teacher told me that I'm the shortest kid in my class. I don't think I'll ever grow bigger," sighed Jessica.

As babies gradually emerge from infancy, their physical growth slows down. During the toddler and preschool years, motor skills develop rapidly. With greater physical mastery comes a greater feeling of independence.

However, physical growth and development are marked by sharp differences in individual children. These differences become even more marked in the adolescent years. It is not until the later teens that most children catch up with one another in physical development.

Physical Growth

Earlier in this book, we defined physical growth as an increase in size and height. It occurs in an orderly sequence until an individual reaches adulthood. Heredity, nutrition, and health influence a person's final height and size.

Doctors and clinics have charts that show the usual height and weight ranges for children of various ages. By referring to such a chart, parents can tell whether their child is within a normal range.

◆ Height

By the time a baby is one year old, he or she has grown from a birth height of about 20 inches to a height of about 30 inches. At age two, the toddler is about 36 inches tall. At age three, he or she is about 39 inches tall. During the child's third year, the growth rate slows dramatically to about 10 percent. This is in comparison to the 50 percent growth rate during the first year of life.

During the preschool and school-age years, the child continues to grow steadily. The average height gain is about 2 or 3 inches a year. From age ten on, however, the child's slow, steady rate of physical growth changes. Growth begins to take place in spurts and stops, with many individual variations. Next to infancy, the second fastest period of growth is adolescence.

A child who is in the midst of a **growth spurt** may find that parts of the body are growing at different rates. The legs, arms, hands, and feet usually grow at a faster rate than the body trunk. The child may feel—and actually look—gangly, awkward, and bony. Then the trunk grows longer, making the adolescent taller. Girls, on the average, go through this process about two years before boys do.

Average Height and Weight for Boys and Girls

Age	Height in Inches		Weight in Pounds	
	Boys	Girls	Boys	Girls
1	30.2	29.5	22.7	21.3
2	35.9	35.3	29.9	28.6
3	39.1	38.4	34.5	32.8
4	41.7	41.2	39.2	37.4
5	44.3	43.9	43.7	43.2
6	47.0	46.6	50.6	48.8

At times, children are unnecessarily worried about their height, especially if they are taller or shorter than their friends. It is important to remember that each child develops according to an individual growth pattern.

◆ Weight

Weight is another measure of physical growth. At one year of age, a toddler has usually tripled his or her birth weight of about 7 pounds to approximately 21 pounds. During the toddler years, a child gains about a half a pound a month. By the end of the fifth year, the average child will weigh about 45 pounds. During the early school-age years, the child gains about 4 to 5 pounds per year.

◆ Proportions

The proportions of a child's body also change. During infancy, a baby's arms and legs are short in comparison to the head and trunk. If you hold an infant up in a standing position, the legs are so short that the baby seems scarcely higher off the ground than when he or she is sitting down. During the toddler years, there is rapid growth of the

Each child develops according to his or her own individual growth pattern. Parents should avoiding comparing the height of one child with another child.

arms, legs, and lower body. This changes the body's proportions and redistributes the weight. The toddler becomes less top-heavy and has better balance than before.

During the preschool and school-age years, the body becomes straighter and slimmer. The abdomen flattens, the shoulders widen, and the legs lengthen. The muscles and skeletal system become more developed.

❖ Teeth

Teeth are another measure of physical development. By age one, a baby usually has 6 teeth. During the toddler period, 14 of the entire set of 20 baby teeth usually come in.

Most children are eager to have their baby teeth start falling out. They consider it an important event when the first one becomes loose. Then they enjoy wiggling the loose tooth. For many children, the first tooth comes out during kindergarten or first grade. For some children, this does not happen until later.

Most children lose their first tooth around six or seven years of age. Permanent teeth eventually replace the 20 baby, or primary, teeth.

Activity. Ask students to share their family's tradition regarding the "tooth fairy."

When a baby tooth becomes loose naturally, the permanent tooth is usually close behind. When children are between seven and twelve years old, permanent teeth usually replace their 20 temporary teeth. More molars are added during the teen years until there are 32 permanent teeth. This is 12 more than were in the temporary set.

❖ Puberty

Most of the dramatic physical changes associated with adolescence take place around the time of puberty. A girl develops breasts, and her pelvis and hips broaden. A boy's penis and testes grow larger, and his shoulders broaden. Body hair develops under the arms, in the pubic region, and on the legs. All of these growth activities are triggered by hormones, chemical substances that are produced in glands and regulate many body functions. These physical changes are preparing the child for adulthood.

Motor Skill Development

During the toddler years, the greatest growth and development occur in the muscles. The large muscles of the arms and legs grow stronger with activity, and children can control them better. Perhaps the most exciting achievement in motor skill development for toddlers is walking. Once children are steady on their feet, they begin to run, jump, and climb up and down stairs. Toddlers are constantly on the move. The more they move, the better coordination and balance they achieve.

Motor skill development in early childhood follows a definite sequence. Children must learn certain motor skills before they can go on to master others. In general, large motor skills develop before small motor skills.

Discuss. As you were growing up, what physical changes were most difficult to accept or adjust to? Why?

◆ Large Motor Skills

Large motor skills are those involving the control and use of large muscles, especially those in the arms and legs. These skills include walking, climbing, jumping, throwing, and catching.

Generally, three-year-olds walk well and can run and climb. By age four, most children are full of self-confidence on a jungle gym or tricycle. They move fast, making a parent or caregiver fear that they will fall. They seldom do. They know their own limitations.

Preschoolers can imitate dance steps to music and walk a balance board with confidence. They may also learn to throw and catch a ball. School-age children seem to be constantly in motion. Their large muscles get plenty of exercise as they run, skip, climb, slide, and join in active games.

Walking

As you learned earlier, babies develop in a head-to-toe direction. They must gain control of their head and trunk before they can gain control of their feet. A newborn's head is large in relation to the size of the trunk, legs, and feet. It takes a year for control of the legs and feet to develop. Babies are considered to be toddlers when they begin walking.

Learning to walk means learning a series of skills. Infants begin by crawling around on their hands and knees. Then they pull themselves up and stand, supporting themselves by holding on to a chair or the side of the crib. They may try taking a few steps, still holding on. Babies next learn to stand alone and try walking while holding on to someone else's hand. Finally, they walk unassisted.

Putting one foot in front of the other may seem simple. However, it is a complicated skill that requires the coordination of the nerves, muscles, and senses. Most babies begin walking alone when they are between eleven and fifteen months of age. Some children walk when they are only nine or ten months old. Others do not walk until they are eighteen months old.

For some weeks before they walk, babies like to be held up so that they can put their weight on the floor. If they are sitting in a stroller, they may try to stand up in it. Holding on to the side of the crib or playpen, they will cruise around the edge. Usually, if they let go, they simply plop down and do not hurt themselves because of diaper padding. Parents and caregivers can help babies by laughing with them about these little falls rather than telling them to be careful. On the other hand, no amount of urging will make children walk alone until they are ready. Their body must be mature enough to be able to walk, and they must have enough self-confidence to try to walk.

Learning to walk changes toddlers' whole world. Now they are free to explore and to play at a wide variety of new activities. Once they have learned to walk, they can learn to run, hop, skip, jump, and so on.

◆ ◆ *Self-Esteem* ◆ ◆

Children's level of motor skill development can affect their self-esteem. If children believe they have good motor skills, they usually join group play with confidence. They feel capable of trying new skills, such as climbing a jungle gym. In contrast, children who believe they have poor motor skills may not feel capable. They may avoid situations in which they do not perform well. Thus encouraging motor skill development should be a high priority for parents and other caregivers.

More About. Large motor skills are also known as gross motor skills.
Discuss. How does walking change a toddler's world? What advantages and disadvantages are there for the parent?

Activity. Have students make a poster illustrating the series of skills needed to learn to walk.
Activity. Have students find out when they started walking. What is the average age and the mean age for the class?

Children need to practice motor skills such as bouncing a ball. Such activities help improve the control and use of large muscles.

Catching and Throwing

Young children can catch a large ball by scooping it into their arms and holding it against their chest in a bear hug. They keep their feet squarely planted in one spot. At this stage, they need someone who can toss the ball right into their arms. Three- or four-year-olds can catch a tennis ball or one a little smaller that will fit into their small hands. It will be a long time—into elementary school—before children are ready for a real softball and glove. It will be even longer before they are coordinated enough to run and catch a ball at the same time.

During an early stage of learning to throw a ball, a child tosses the ball and steps off with the foot on the same side as the throwing arm. By age six, a child who has been helped a little can remember to step off with the foot opposite the throwing arm. For right-handed throwers, this means stepping off with the left foot. This stance gives the ball much more momentum and eventually more accuracy.

Combining skills comes naturally after children are able to catch, throw, run, and jump. They can learn to dodge a ball being rolled on the floor. They can learn to dribble a ball—first dribbling while standing still and, much later, while running.

DECISIONS ◆ ◆ DECISIONS

Jim and Patti are teaching their four-year-old son, Benjamin, to toss and catch a ball. Benjamin likes to play catch with his parents, but he shies away from the ball when it is thrown toward him. How do you think Jim and Patti should respond to their son's nervousness?

Activity. Using a variety of balls of different sizes (ping-pong ball to beach ball), have students observe a group of young children playing with the balls. Ask them to note the differences in the children's abilities to throw and catch. How did they stand? What were their arm movements? When throwing, did the ball go high into the air or project forward? What arm did they use? Which balls were the easiest to throw and catch? The most difficult? Why?

Riding a Tricycle and Bicycle

During their third year, many children begin to learn to ride a tricycle. At first, they may straddle the tricycle and walk. They do not understand that when they sit on it, they must push the pedals to make it go. Some instruction and a gentle shove from the back usually help them get the idea. A tricycle needs to be small enough so that a child's legs can easily reach the pedals.

By five years of age, many children want to ride a two-wheeled bicycle. Training wheels—two small wheels attached to the back bicycle wheel—can help children combine the skills of steering, pedaling, and bal-

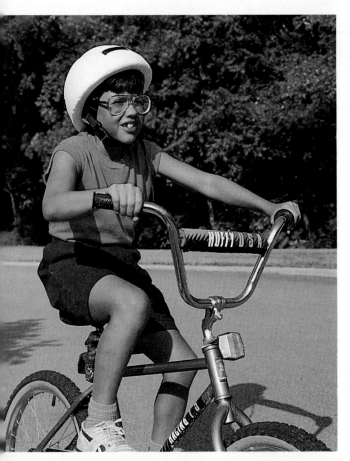

Learning to ride a two-wheeled bicycle takes concentration. The child must learn to coordinate steering, pedaling, and balancing.

ancing. Some children refuse to use training wheels because other children call them baby wheels. Skillfully riding a bicycle without training wheels is a status symbol for many kindergartners.

When buying a bicycle, parents should choose a size that is appropriate for the child's size. The child should be able to sit on the seat and reach the pedals. Some children may need extra encouragement when learning to ride a bicycle. Criticizing children who fall will only discourage them from trying.

◆◆ Small Motor Skills

Small motor skills are those involving the control and use of small muscles, especially those in the fingers and hands. Small motor skills include holding a spoon, writing, and dressing. Children must coordinate their vision and small motor skills. This is called **eye-hand coordination.**

Toddlers begin using their hands with a full-fist grasp. Later, they learn to pick up objects with the thumb and fingers.

By age three, most children can build a tower of blocks and manipulate puzzles with large pieces. They can unbutton their coat and put on their shoes. They love to draw with large crayons and markers. They can handle a spoon or fork better than they could earlier, so mealtimes are less messy. Five-year-olds can turn knobs, fasten buttons, and pour liquid from a small pitcher into a glass. They can draw circles, squares, and triangles. Some may be able to tie shoelaces.

During the school-age years, children are involved in writing, drawing, and cutting with scissors. They use computer keyboards and electronic games. Many show a strong interest in model building and handicrafts. All these activities help children improve their **dexterity** (dek-STER-ih-tee), or skilled use of their hands.

Hand Preference

At about age two, children's hand preference begins to develop. This means that children consistently use one hand rather than the other for activities such as drawing, eating, and throwing a ball. By age three or four, 85 percent of all children use their right hand for most activities. About 95 percent of all adults are right-handed. A few people are considered **ambidextrous** (am-beh-DEK-struhs) because they are able to use both hands equally well.

Whatever the hand preference, parents and teachers should encourage children to practice their small motor skills. If a child is left-handed, adults should show the child how to hold a pencil in the correct position for the left hand. This encouragement helps build the child's self-esteem and fosters writing skill.

❖ Influencing Motor Skill Development

Parents and caregivers have many opportunities to guide a child's motor skill development. Exercise is necessary for bones, muscles, and tissues to grow and develop properly.

Unfortunately, many children do not get as much exercise as they should. Television encourages them to sit passively for many hours instead of playing actively. Older children are often driven from place to place instead of encouraged to walk or ride a bicycle. Children will exercise more vigorously if parents or caregivers accompany them and offer encouragement.

Children can practice large motor skills at home, on the sidewalk, or at the park. Activities such as walking, running, pedaling, and skating help develop the leg muscles. The arm muscles are involved in activities such as catching, throwing, and batting. Many activities, such as climbing, dancing, and swimming, involve all the large muscles.

Parents should also provide children with toys and equipment that encourage the use of their hands and fingers. Large crayons, puzzles, blocks, building sets, lacing kits, small cars, and dolls help children develop small motor skills.

Mastering motor skills requires much practice and patience for youngsters. Parents, caregivers, and teachers can help by praising children as they attempt new and more complex skills. Chapter 20 describes additional activities that help in the development of motor skills.

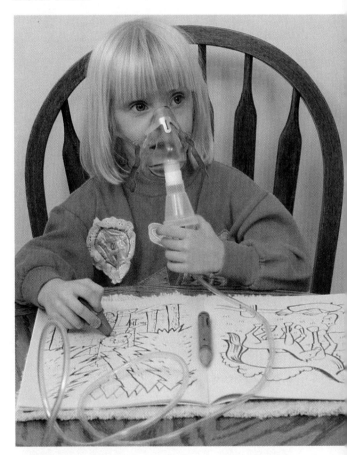

Children are constantly working on increasing their skills and abilities. Drawing with large crayons or markers helps develop small motor skills and eye-hand coordination.

Physical-Motor Development Age 1 to 6

One-Year-Old

Walks haltingly.

Walks up stairs but may fear walking down.

Can slide down stairs on tummy.

Holds crayon and other objects in a fist grasp.

Scribbles with crayons and pencils.

Can pick up pieces of food and feed self.

Two-Year-Old

Walks with good coordination.

Runs with confidence.

Wobbles unsteadily when carrying an object.

Straddles tricycle and walks it.

Uses pincer grasp (thumb and finger) to pick up objects.

Scribbles in deliberate directions.

Can remove slip-on clothes.

Can feed self with spoon.

May show interest in using toilet.

Three-Year-Old

Walks with easy stride.

Walks upstairs using alternate feet.

Stands briefly on one foot.

Rides tricycle using pedals.

May try to climb jungle gym or pump self while swinging.

Draws simple pictures with crayons and pencils.

Puts together simple puzzles.

Builds towers with blocks.

Can nest smaller containers inside larger ones.

Feeds self with little spilling.

Pours from pitcher.

Puts on own shoes.

Verbalizes toilet needs.

Four-Year-Old

Hops in place; spins like a top.

Skips on one foot.

Throws ball over head.

Catches bounced ball.

Copies circle shape in drawing or coloring.

Imitates drawing of square.

Draws person with head, arms, and legs.

Builds more complex structures with blocks.

Points to objects and counts.

Washes and dries face and hands.

Brushes teeth.

Dresses and undresses self with supervision.

Five-Year-Old

Walks backward, heel to toe; runs on tiptoe; climbs well.

Skips using alternate feet.

Sits cross-legged.

Imitates dance steps that others perform.

May master skating and swimming.

Has stamina to take long walk with adults.

Prints a few letters.

Prints first name; recognizes own printed name.

Writes numbers 1 to 5.

Cuts food with knife.

Dresses and undresses self without help.

Laces shoes and ties them.

Six-Year-Old

Likes running, jumping, climbing.

Is very active and in constant motion; even wiggles while sitting.

Is sometimes clumsy.

Throws ball; steps off with foot opposite to throwing hand.

Gets first permanent molars.

Helping Children's Physical Development

Parents and other caregivers have many opportunities to influence young children's physical development. Parents, especially, are responsible for children's nutrition and health.

During the toddler and preschool years, children ask many questions. "Why do I have to wash my hands?" "Why do I have to wear a jacket?" "Why can't I have a cookie now?" Parents and caregivers should try to answer these questions in an honest, relaxed way. By encouraging children to begin to take responsibility for their food, clothing, and personal hygiene needs, adults help children develop independence.

Good nutrition is essential to a child's health. Nutrients in food build and repair the body and provide it with energy. For proper nutrition, children need food from each of the food groups daily.

❖ Nutrition and Food Choices

A parent's or caregiver's influence on a child's physical development begins with proper nutrition. The food a child eats has profound effects on his or her physical development. It also provides energy for exercising and developing motor skills.

During children's early years, the responsibility for adequate nutrition rests largely with parents and caregivers. These adults buy, prepare, and serve the foods children eat. It is important to provide foods from each of the food groups in the Food Guide Pyramid (see page 158). The exact amounts consumed are less important than maintaining a daily balance of different kinds of nutrients: proteins, fats, carbohydrates, vitamins, and minerals.

Children with a poor or inadequate diet can develop a physical condition called **malnutrition.** Such children usually tire easily and have less resistance to disease than do children with an adequate diet. Prolonged malnutrition can interfere with physical and mental development. Most communities have clinics or other health centers that can give parents advice about good nutrition and healthy food choices.

Food Needs of Young Children

Growth occurs at a slower rate for toddlers than for infants. This means that the amount of food a toddler eats does not increase as quickly as it did during infancy. This period of slower growth may be confusing for parents and other caregivers. They may play games to encourage a toddler to eat more. Some insist that a child clean the plate, even though he or she is no longer hungry. An important rule for parents and caregivers is to let the toddler decide how much to eat.

Serving Sizes. It is best to put only teaspoon-size servings of various foods on the

Food Needs of Children

Food Group	Servings per Day	Size of Serving*
Fruits	2 or more servings, including at least one vitamin C source	1 medium apple, orange, or banana 3/4 cup juice 1/2 cup cooked fruit
Vegetables	3 or more servings	1 cup leafy salad greens 1/2 cup cooked vegetables
Grains	6 or more servings	1 slice whole-grain bread 1/2 cup cooked rice, pasta, or cereal 1 ounce ready-to-eat breakfast cereal 1 tortilla, muffin, or dinner roll 1/2 bagel or hamburger bun 4 to 6 crackers
Milk, Cheese, Yogurt	4 servings	1 cup low-fat or non-fat milk (Children under 2 years of age should drink whole milk.) 1 cup yogurt 1 1/2 ounces cheese
Meat, Poultry, Fish, Beans	2 to 3 servings	2 to 4 ounces cooked, lean meat, chicken, or fish Substitute the following for 1 ounce of meat: 1 egg 2 tablespoons peanut butter 1/2 cup cooked peas or beans
Fats and Sweets	Go easy on these foods and beverages.	

*Younger children may eat smaller serving sizes.

National Center for Nutrition and Dietetics, 1992.

child's plate. This encourages the child to taste everything. Toddlers also enjoy asking for more.

The amount toddlers eat at each meal may vary from day to day. At times, they may be too busy learning about the world to care about stopping for lunch. When they are hungry, they will eat. At other times, toddlers may take only a few bites. After 10 or 15 minutes, an adult should take away the uneaten food. Insisting that children eat more than they need can lead to overeating and obesity later in life.

Eating Problems. Toddlers are in a negative stage and often say no to any question. For example, if you ask, "Do you want some carrots?" they will probably answer "No." Say instead, "Here are your carrots. See if your spoon can pick them up." Caregivers

More About. A guideline for serving sizes of fruits and vegetables is one tablespoon for each year of age up to age eight. **Discuss.** What developmental characteristics of toddlers (growth, coordination, independence) affect their eating habits?

Activity. Have students plan three days of nutritious meals suitable for a toddler.

should avoid giving toddlers a choice unless they are willing to accept a negative reply.

By age three or four, children typically outgrow most eating problems that were troublesome in earlier years. Sometimes they have to be reminded or coaxed to stop other activities to eat a meal. They continue to find running, playing, and almost everything else more interesting than eating.

Snacks. Many young children become hungry between meals. Parents and caregivers should provide nutritious snacks, such as whole-grain crackers, low-fat cheese, fruit, and fruit juices. Some children enjoy a cup of soup, a peanut butter sandwich, or yogurt. Most commercial snack foods, such as chips and candy, are high in fats and/or sugar. These provide few nutrients needed for growth and health.

At first, children take a lot of time and effort to feed themselves. Gradually their skills improve with practice.

Children should not be given snacks right before a meal. This will reduce their appetite for milk and a variety of foods. Children should not be given snacks shortly after refusing to eat a meal either. Otherwise, they will learn that if they do not eat at mealtime there will be a snack to eat soon. These habits are difficult to break once they get started.

Self-Feeding

A major advance for children is learning to feed themselves. By the age of twelve months, many toddlers can hold a spoon. Most are eager to try. Although they may still want a bottle occasionally, toddlers usually drink milk from a cup.

The first few months of self-feeding are a messy time. Cereal gets all over the child's face and hands. Milk frequently spills. Here are some tips to make mealtime more enjoyable:

- Set the toddler's high chair or feeding table next to the family's dining table. Place a plastic cloth or newspaper under the chair or feeding table to catch spills.

- Have the child wear a plastic feeding apron with a pocket along the bottom for catching food.

- Fill the child's cup only one-quarter full at a time. Then, when a spill occurs, there is less to clean up.

- Give the child only small amounts of food. If a toddler wants more, he or she will ask for it.

- After the meal, use a damp washcloth to wipe the child's face and fingers. Some toddlers accept the face washing better if they are handed the washcloth and told, "Wash your face, please."

- Plan bathtime for after the meal. Toddlers who are just learning to manage a spoon and a cup can be very messy.

By fifteen or sixteen months of age, toddlers who have had practice feeding themselves are usually quite capable. At around age two, they begin to use a fork to pick up pieces of fruit, vegetables, or meat. Children should not be allowed to use a knife until they are three years of age or older.

Food Preferences

Children vary in their food preferences and eating habits. One may be a picky eater, another may be on a mashed potato binge, while a third may enjoy a little of everything and ask for seconds.

Parents and caregivers should introduce a new food by placing a tiny piece of it on the child's plate. If the child likes it, a little more may be put on the plate. If the child does not seem to like it, parents should wait and try it again in a few days. Children usually will try a new food if they see others eating it and if they are allowed to decide how much to eat after tasting it.

According to several studies, children have certain food preferences.

- Children like foods separated, rather than mixed together in casseroles or salads.
- Children like mildly flavored foods and mildly spiced foods. They have far more taste buds than do adults.
- Children like meals with a variety of textures—some soft, some crisp, some chewy foods.
- Children like food at room temperature.
- Children usually like any food they help prepare.

These are general characteristics, and individual children differ. For example, some children prefer spicy foods because these are the types of food they have always eaten. Others may have preferences based on their cultural background or the region where they live.

Adults should respect individual preferences and never force any food on a child. Trying to force-feed a child turns mealtime

Around the World

A Good Breakfast

Breakfast is a very important meal. After a long night's sleep, it refuels the body and provides the energy one needs to start the day.

At breakfast tables around the world, parents urge their children to eat a good breakfast. In the United States, this might consist of cereal topped with a sliced banana and milk, orange juice with a muffin or bagel, or scrambled eggs and whole wheat toast.

In other cultures, the first meal of the day may be very different from ours. Here are some typical breakfasts around the world:

Argentina:	Steak, eggs, and milk.
China:	Dried pork, rice or porridge, and soybean juice or milk.
England:	Boiled eggs, sausage, toast, and tea.
France:	French bread with butter and jam and hot chocolate.
Israel:	Sliced cucumbers, sliced tomatoes, juice, and bread with butter and honey.
Sudan:	A mixture of warm fava beans, tomatoes, onions, and goat cheese topped with a lemon and oil dressing, and hot tea with milk.
Turkey:	Bread with butter and jam, cured olives, goat cheese, and hot milk.

into an unpleasant battle. Some children use their food dislikes to get the attention of parents and caregivers. Therefore, adults should avoid making a big issue over what a child eats or does not eat.

Discuss. What foods did you dislike as a child? How did your parents handle the situation when those foods were served? What are your feelings now toward these foods? How would you handle your children's food preferences?

Problem Solving. Have students identify alternative foods from each of the food groups. For example, if a child refuses to drink milk, how can parents provide foods rich in calcium that the child will eat?

DECISIONS ◆
◆ DECISIONS

On their birthday, the children at Kaitlin's school bring in snacks to share with their classmates. Kaitlin had a birthday early in the school year. She brought raisins and apple juice for the children in her class. Other children, however, have brought snacks that are high in sugar and fat. Kaitlin's parents do not want their daughter to eat a lot of junk food. What do you think they should do?

Food Needs of Older Children

During the early school years, children may be picky eaters one year and hearty eaters the next. Seven-year-olds may not want to try unfamiliar foods. Given their choice, many would prefer hamburgers as the main course at every meal. By age nine, children are often more willing to try new foods. At age eleven or twelve, their appetite often increases dramatically. If children are in a growth spurt, their capacity for food seems endless.

School-age children become increasingly able to understand the nutritional facts that parents and teachers present. Parents should talk about the importance of a balanced diet and explain why some foods are more nutritious than others. They can encourage children to eat foods from each of the food groups every day.

Adolescence is a time of rapid growth and great activity. Teenagers at the peak of their growth spurt may gain 20 pounds in one year without becoming overweight. Good nutrition continues to be important. Both males and females need extra servings of foods high in calcium, such as milk. Females may need

extra iron to prevent anemia because the body loses iron during menstruation.

This is the time when teenagers assume responsibility for their own food choices. They may purchase or prepare many of their own meals and snacks. Unfortunately, many teens choose high-fat and high-sugar foods and snacks instead of more nutritious ones. Poor eating habits can create health problems such as always feeling tired or gaining too much weight.

Parents and caregivers need to lay the foundation for healthy eating habits when children are young. Children need to learn about nutrition. They should enjoy eating a wide variety of foods. Then they will have a better chance of making healthy food choices as they grow older.

◆◆ Clothing

Children's clothing should provide protection and comfort. Childhood is a time of energetic physical activity. Children need to be able to move freely and safely. Their clothing should be loose-fitting and durable. However, children often have definite tastes in clothing just as they do in foods.

Selecting Children's Clothing

Here are some guidelines for selecting children's clothing.

- **Appropriate for the child.** Clothing should fit the child's body. It should be loose enough to feel comfortable but not so large as to be hazardous. Toddlers who are being toilet trained need pants with elastic waistbands. Active preschoolers need wide straps that stay on the shoulders. Young children enjoy wearing their favorite colors and expressing their individuality. Yet school-age children are often happiest when they can wear styles that are similar to their friends'.

Activity. Have students plan one week of nutritious school lunches for school-age children. Lunches can either be purchased at school or prepared at home. Discuss factors such as appeal, cost, and preparation time.

Problem Solving. Have students identify and discuss ways of handling mealtime dilemmas such as burping, talking with food in the mouth, and arguing at the table.

- **Appropriate for the occasion.** Casual styles are appropriate for play, school, and most events that children attend. Some children enjoy wearing a fancy outfit for a special occasion. However, dressy clothes get in the way of active play when worn to a child care program or school.
- **Durable.** Because children are very active, they need clothing made of sturdy woven or knitted fabrics. Reinforced seams and knees can help clothes last longer. Adjustable straps provide some room for growth.
- **Easy care.** Children's clothing should be easy to wash and dry and require no ironing. Before making a purchase, parents should carefully read the care labels and hangtags on children's clothing. These give information about the fabrics and type of care recommended.
- **Safety.** Safety laws require children's sleepwear to be made of **flame retardant** fabrics. Such fabrics are not easily set on fire and do not burn quickly. Parents may want to avoid children's clothing with decorative trims and buttons. If these items become loose, a young child can pull them off and swallow them. Long strings, dangling scarves, and long skirts can also be dangerous. They can get caught on play equipment and cause serious injury to a child. Parents will also want to make sure a hood on a jacket does not obscure the child's vision. Similarly, they should see that their child's shoes have nonslip soles.
- **Ease of dressing.** It is wise to buy clothing that children can put on by themselves. Pants and skirts with elastic waistbands are easier to pull on and off than those with belts. Large buttons, snaps, and zippers with big tabs are easier for little fingers to manage than are tiny buttons and ties. Clothes that fasten in the front are easier to open and close than those that fas-

Children need play clothes that are comfortable and durable. They also want to wear clothes that are similar in style to those worn by their friends.

ten at the shoulder or in the back.

Shoes with Velcro® closings or buckles eliminate the challenge of tying shoelaces. Rain or snow boots slide on easily if a plastic bag is first placed over each shoe. Mittens are hard to lose if attached to coat sleeves with grippers.

- **Affordable.** Clothing is a major expense in a family's budget. Because of children's rapid growth, they can quickly outgrow their clothes and shoes. Parents can look for clothing on sale or at special discount prices. Secondhand clothing stores and garage sales are good sources of inexpensive used clothing. Many families recycle clothes among relatives, friends, and neighbors.

Self-Dressing

"I can do it. I can do it," said three-year-old Juanita with strong emphasis on the *I*. She took her blue sneakers from her grandfather, sat down, put them on, and closed them securely with the tab. She smiled triumphantly as she reached for her grandfather's hand.

Children are eager to learn how to dress themselves. One-year-olds can take off a hat, a shoe, or a sock. Two-year-olds try to put their legs into pants and their arms into a shirt. Often the clothes are put on backwards or inside out. By the age of three, most children can both dress and undress without

Children experience feelings of pride and independence when they finally learn to tie their own shoelaces.

much assistance. However, they still need help starting a zipper, tying shoelaces, or pulling on boots. To encourage self-dressing, parents should buy children's clothes that are easy to put on and take off.

Sometimes children mix colors, patterns, and styles to a parent's dismay. Despite this, children should be allowed to make some choices about which clothes to wear. To avoid inappropriate choices, it is best to offer the child a choice between two suitable garments. For example, "Do you want to wear your sweater or your jacket?" asks Anna's father. Children should also have some choice when shopping for clothes with a parent. They will be more enthusiastic about wearing a shirt if they are allowed to choose between the blue stripe and the red plaid.

❖ Personal Hygiene

Parents and caregivers are responsible for teaching children good health habits, or personal hygiene. For example, children must be encouraged to wash their hands with soap before eating and after using the toilet. Cleanliness can help prevent the spread of many illnesses.

For the most part, four-year-olds are competent in the bathroom. However, young children still need help and supervision when bathing and brushing their teeth.

Toilet Training

Learning to use the toilet is another great achievement for toddlers. Successful toilet training depends on the physical and emotional development of the individual child. The **sphincter** (SFINK-tuhr) **muscles** in the bowel and bladder regions control elimination. They must be mature enough for the child to close and release them at will. This control does not come until after the child is able to sit, stand, and walk well. The child

Discuss. Why is it important to let children make choices about which clothes to wear? How can parents help children with styles and color coordination and still allow independence?

Activity. Have students observe each other tying shoes. Are there different methods used? Can students remember learning to tie their shoes?

must be able to recognize the need to use the toilet ahead of time. Also, the child must be able to get to the bathroom or signal to an adult the need to be taken there. Trying to toilet train toddlers before they are mature enough causes stress to both children and parents.

Toilet training should start when the child begins to show an interest in using the toilet and in being dry. This usually occurs when the child is about two years of age or a little older. Some toddlers are happy to use a small seat attached to an adult toilet because it makes them feel grown-up. Others prefer a small children's toilet set directly on the floor.

Some children may be afraid of falling into the adult toilet and never should be forced screaming onto one. Others may be frightened by seeing a bowel movement disappear when the toilet is flushed or simply by hearing the sound of the flushing. If these things

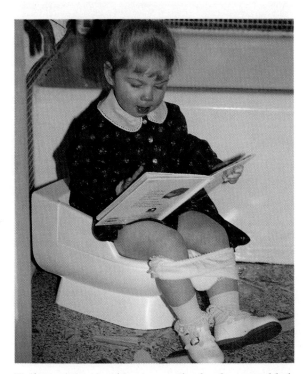

Toilet training is a big step up the developmental ladder. Parents and caregivers should make toilet training a positive experience for children.

More About. A "teachable moment" for toilet training is when the older toddler brings a clean diaper, indicating he or she is ready to be changed.

bother the child, a wise parent or caregiver will flush the toilet later, when the child is busy elsewhere.

Adults should never scold, embarrass, or punish a child for having an accident during the course of toilet training. Bladder control usually takes longer than bowel control. It may take a year or more—until age three or later—before the child has full daytime control over both bladder and bowel. Nighttime control is usually achieved later. Thus, a toddler who uses the toilet during the day may still need a diaper at bedtime and naptime.

During toilet training, adults should offer encouragement and praise as the child works on this new set of skills. Sometimes a child suddenly refuses to use the toilet. If this happens, it is better to postpone training for a while than to get into a power struggle with the child. When the child is both ready and willing, toilet training will be successful.

Most four-year-olds are dry during the day and night. They go to the toilet without any help and often insist on privacy. Some young children may have to get up to go to the bathroom during the night. (See Chapter 25 for information about bedwetting.) By age five, most children are capable of attending to their own needs.

Bathing

Bathing is fun for children. Many families develop relaxing evening rituals around the sequence of taking a warm bath, reading a story, and saying good night. Children need baths to feel clean. Toddlers and preschoolers usually want to participate by handling the soap and washcloth. They especially enjoy playing with water toys or pouring water from one container to another. However, young children should never be left alone in a tub—even for a few moments. They can turn on the hot water and burn themselves or slip under the water and drown.

Problem Solving. Why do some parents try to toilet train their toddler too soon? What types of encouragement can be given young children to become toilet trained? How should parents handle accidents?

Washing children's hair can be combined with bathing. Children particularly dislike having soap get in their eyes. Special shampoos are recommended for children because they are less irritating than adult shampoos. Children with long hair may need a special rinsing solution to prevent tangling.

When using a shower, many young children like to be held by a parent until they become used to the water falling over their face. A special hand-held attachment can be installed in the shower to make bathing easier and more pleasant for children.

School-age children often show little concern for personal cleanliness. They may need constant reminders to wash their hands or take a bath. Once in the tub, however, older children seldom need help in bathing and shampooing, unless they have long hair.

As children approach adolescence, they become more concerned with their body and their appearance. They may prefer showers to baths, especially if they take showers at school after sports activities. Teenagers need daily showers or baths because of the increased perspiration that comes with adolescence.

Care of Teeth

Teeth play an important part in a person's appearance. They are also important for proper speech development and eating. For these reasons, both temporary and permanent teeth are well worth protecting. Proper dental care is essential to that protection.

Dentists suggest that brushing should begin by age two. Parents can gently brush children's teeth until they are old enough to do it themselves. This early beginning helps establish the habit as an important one. Both brushing and flossing should be done in the morning, after meals, and at bedtime.

Fluoride (FLUR-eyed) is a mineral that makes tooth enamel resistant to cavities. In some communities fluoride is added to the water supply to help prevent tooth decay. Doctors and dentists can prescribe fluoride in a vitamin supplement for children. Fluoride can also be applied to the surface of teeth.

Regular dental examinations are important for children, as well as adults. Children should have their first dental examination by age five or even earlier. Baby teeth can develop cavities that need to be filled. A tooth knocked out in an accident can be reset. Retaining the baby teeth until the permanent teeth come in is important for proper spacing of the permanent teeth and for speech development.

By age twelve, most children have lost all their baby teeth and have most of their permanent teeth. Regular dental checkups can detect tooth decay or improper alignment before serious dental problems develop. Some

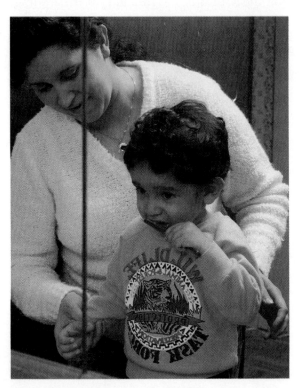

Parents can encourage young children to brush their teeth. This helps establish an important habit that is essential for good dental care.

children may be referred to an **orthodontist** (OR-thuh-DON-tist), a specialist in straightening and realigning teeth. Although these children may need to wear braces for two years or longer, they can make a dramatic change in an individual's appearance and self-image.

❖ Health Care

Health care also affects children's physical growth and development. Healthy children have lots of energy and usually eat and sleep well. After the first year, toddlers should have medical checkups at ages fifteen months and eighteen months. During these visits, children are examined to see that their growth and health are normal. They also receive immunizations to protect them from diseases such as polio, tetanus, measles, and mumps. See the immunization chart on page 272. Parents should keep a careful record of their children's immunizations. These records are required when children enter school or child care centers.

Three- and four-year-olds need a medical checkup twice a year. At this age, most children are cooperative enough to be given an eye examination. It is important to discover any visual problems early so they can be corrected before children enter school.

School-age children should visit a doctor or clinic yearly. They need booster immunizations from time to time to be fully protected against certain diseases. Some children who are having difficulty in school—in reading, for example—may have a visual or hearing disability. Eyeglasses, contact lenses, or hearing aids can often correct such a problem.

Illness

Parents learn to recognize common signs of physical illness. Among these are loss of appetite, sudden irritability, restless sleep, extreme fatigue, a rise in temperature, pain, vomiting, or diarrhea. When these signs appear, parents should call the doctor or clinic and describe the child's symptoms.

When children have a high fever, they usually sleep most of the time. However, once

◆ *Health & Safety* ◆

Chicken Pox

Chicken pox is a common childhood disease. There is no immunization for chicken pox, which is highly contagious. If one child in a child care center or school gets the disease, it often strikes most of the other children in the group.

Many children with chicken pox feel well until they begin to break out in a rash. This is why they expose so many of their friends or classmates to the disease. About 11 to 19 days after exposure, a number of red pimples first appear on the chest and face. Then tiny blisters, or pustules, form on top of the pimples. The blisters may spread until they cover the entire body. The itchy blisters can be very uncomfortable, but they should not be scratched. Scratching can spread the blisters and cause permanent scarring of the skin. A cool bath or calamine lotion can help relieve the itching.

Once children have had chicken pox, they usually become immune to it for life. Some children have natural immunity and never contract the disease.

their temperature comes down, it is difficult to keep them in bed. Parents and caregivers can read to or play with them to help pass the time. Quiet activities, such as drawing and coloring, may keep them occupied. Older children may enjoy telephoning friends and relatives. Allowing a bit more television watching than usual also helps.

Children should not go to school if they have a fever or a bad cough. They need to rest and avoid exposing other children to their illness. After children have been fever-free for 24 hours, they can return to school.

Hospitalization

Hospitalization can be a very frightening experience for a young child. Many hospitals recognize this and encourage parents to stay with their child. Hospitals sometimes even provide a bed for a parent in the child's room.

If parents know in advance that their child will be hospitalized, they can prepare the child. Sean, age five, was scheduled for a tonsillectomy. Several days before the operation, his mother told him exactly what was going to happen and why. "The doctor is going to take your tonsils out so that you won't get so many sore throats. Someone will give you a special shot to make you sleep while the doctor takes your tonsils out. When you wake up, I'll be with you. Your throat may be a little sore for a few days, but soon you'll be feeling fine." Whenever Sean asked questions about the operation, his parents answered them honestly and gave him reassurance.

Children are perfectly capable of understanding the truth. They are less afraid of hospitalization when they know what to expect. They need to feel that they can trust the adults who take care of them.

Hospital stays can be frightening for children. Most hospitals encourage parents and other family members to stay with the child as much as possible.

Problem Solving. Suggest bedtime activites for a child recovering from an illness.

Discuss. Have any of you been hospitalized? If so, what do you remember about the experience?

CHAPTER 16 REVIEW

Summary

- A child's physical growth and motor skill development follow a predictable path.
- Height, weight, body proportions, and teeth are measures of physical development.
- Large motor skills involve the use of large muscles in the arms and legs. Small motor skills involve the use of small muscles in the hands and fingers.
- Parents should encourage children to exercise and develop their large and small motor skills.
- Parents and other caregivers should provide nutritious meals and snacks for children.
- Children's clothing should be appropriate for the child and the occasion. Other criteria include: durable, easy care, safety, easy dressing, and affordable.
- Parents and caregivers must teach children about personal hygiene.
- Children should receive regular health care throughout childhood.

Questions

p. 293 **1.** What is the purpose of height and weight charts?

p. 294 **2.** Describe how a child's body changes proportions from infancy to the school-age years.

p. 295 **3.** How are large and small motor skills different? Which develop first?

p. 296 **4.** Name three activities that help develop large motor skills and three activities that help develop small motor skills.

p. 298 **5.** What is dexterity?

p. 304 **6.** How can parents make mealtime easier and more pleasant when children are learning to feed themselves?

p. 307 **7.** What type of clothing makes it easy for children to dress themselves?

p. 308 **8.** When are children mature enough to begin toilet training?

p. 310 **9.** Since baby teeth are only temporary, why should young children brush their teeth and receive dental checkups?

p. 311 **10.** How often should three- and four-year-olds have a medical checkup? How often should school-age children?

Activities

1. Observe preschool children practicing small motor skills. When coloring, do they use a fist or forefinger grasp? When cutting out shapes with safety scissors, what are the results? Are the children right- or left-handed? Share your findings with the class.

2. Plan three nutritious snacks for young children.

3. Examine children's clothing in a store. Evaluate items for durability, safety, ease of dressing, and ease of care. What growth features are included? Summarize your observations in a report.

Think About

1. What were your reactions to the changes that took place in your body during puberty? How might parents prepare children for such changes?

2. If your child showed a preference for using the left hand, would you encourage him or her to use the right hand? Why or why not?

CHAPTER 17

Helping Children Develop Emotionally

Objectives

This chapter will help you to:
- Describe the emotional characteristics of children at different ages.
- Explain how parents and caregivers influence children's self-esteem.
- List ways to help children develop independence.
- Discuss how children can cope with stress.

Vocabulary

egocentric
empathy
negativism
temper tantrum
sibling rivalry
personality
autonomy
initiative

identity
birth order

"Good morning, Corey," says Mr. Davis as Corey's mother brings him into the child care center. Corey, two-years-old, smiles at Mr. Davis but does not answer.

"Okay, Corey," says his mother, taking off her son's coat. "I'm going to leave now. You play with the other children until I come back."

Although Corey has been coming to the center for several weeks, he bursts into tears. "Don't go, Mommy," he cries. Corey's mother kisses him and leaves him with Mr. Davis.

Thirty seconds later, Corey is smiling and chattering with Mr. Davis. Then Corey races for the sandbox.

Later, when his mother returns, Corey is busily pushing a truck around the room. He protests loudly when told it is time to go home. However, when he sees other parents picking up their children, Corey lets his mother help him with his coat. Then he waves good-bye and trots happily out the door.

Corey's emotional behavior is typical of many toddlers. Although he does not want his mother to leave, he is obviously happy and comfortable at the child care center.

Emotional Development

All children have many emotions, including feelings of happiness, love, fear, sadness, anger, and jealousy. Emotions should never be categorized as good or bad. Instead, they need to be accepted as an expression of the feelings that a child is experiencing. By understanding emotional development, parents, caregivers, and teachers are better able to nurture and guide children.

❖ Emotional Patterns

Early childhood is an emotional stage. Children's feelings are intense and changeable. Toddlers express their feelings openly and often have strong emotional outbursts. Fortunately for caregivers, toddlers can be easily distracted. Rosa protests angrily when she has to put on her pajamas for the night. However, she instantly giggles with pleasure when she is handed a clown doll.

Toddlers are very **egocentric,** or self-centered. That is, they can view things only in relation to themselves. They demand

Young children show their emotions freely and without embarrassment. Their moods may change quickly and frequently.

immediate fulfillment of their desires and often become furious when they cannot get what they want. Eager to try out their new-found powers, young children squeal with triumph when they succeed in fitting together a puzzle. Yet a moment later, the same children cry with frustration when they cannot reach a toy on a high shelf. Sometimes toddlers feel ready to tackle the world and then suddenly become shy and frightened, perhaps realizing they are not so ready after all.

During the preschool years, children shift quickly from one intense emotion to another and back again. Moreover, preschoolers have not learned to modify their reactions according to the situation. They will cry as hard when their block construction collapses as when a pet rabbit dies.

During the school-age years, emotional growth tends to follow a pattern. Longer periods of emotional calm alternate with shorter periods of emotional swings. By age nine or ten, most children are learning to control their emotions. They may still get angry, particularly if they feel someone is being unfair. However, their anger is less likely to result in physical outbursts than it did in earlier years.

Adolescence can be a time of excitement and discovery, as well as confusion and doubt. Therefore, adolescents' emotions may change from day to day or even from hour to hour. At this age, individuals are often surprised by their own mood swings. Despite all the interaction with others, adolescents may still feel very lonely. They are learning who they are and trying to gain independence.

❖ Emotions and Behavior

Emotions reflect a person's innermost thoughts and feelings. They may be revealed in sudden outbursts, or they may be subtle and hardly noticed. Emotions cause people to behave in certain ways, such as laughing, crying, being angry, or remaining calm.

Affection

Toddlers begin giving as well as receiving love and affection. Parents demonstrate ways to express love when they hug, kiss, and speak softly to their children. The way that parents show affection varies from family to

Children who receive love and affection from parents will learn how to share their affection with others.

family and can be influenced by cultural heritage. Some men who once thought it was unmanly to show affection are now feeling more and more comfortable expressing their love to their children.

Young children clearly respond to love and affection from their parents, relatives, and important caregivers. Parents can encourage children to show affection by saying, "Kiss Daddy" or "Give Grandma a big hug."

Although toddlers are basically self-centered, they are capable of comforting another person who is experiencing sadness or discomfort. They may give a touch, a hug, or a pat on the back. They may offer to share a toy, a cracker, or a favorite blanket with the other person. For example, fifteen-month-old Jason gently touched the chin of his crying brother as if to say, "Can I help you?" Three-year-old Laura brought her favorite doll to cheer her mother, who was not feeling well. This ability to understand and share another person's feelings is called **empathy.**

Children should be encouraged to show empathy toward others. An older child may help a younger child who has fallen or hug a friend who is teased by others. By responding to someone else's suffering, children develop a concern for the welfare of others.

Negativism

At about age two, children have a tendency to say no to everything—or so it seems to parents. This is a stage of **negativism,** or a tendency to resist suggestions and commands. At this stage, toddlers are beginning to seek independence. They enjoy their budding sense of power—the ability to choose to do something or not to do it. However, toddlers often feel frustrated because they are unable to express their feelings in words. As a result, they may say no to things they really want to do. Two-year-old Tyler enjoys eating a variety of foods. Yet when his mother tells

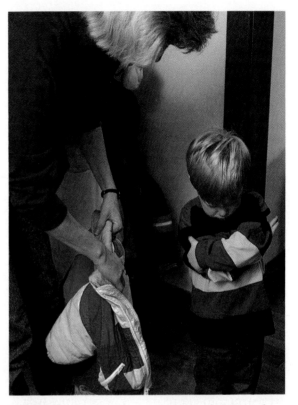

Toddlers begin to resist suggestions and commands as they develop independence. Parents should offer a child choices rather than ask questions that can be answered no.

him that it is time for lunch, Tyler shouts, "No! No!" As his mother takes the food away from the table, Tyler begins to scream: "Want lunch!" When the food is brought back, he sits down and calmly begins to eat.

Because of such behavior, people sometimes refer to this stage as the "terrible twos." Yet it is a normal part of development for toddlers. They are showing that they are individuals and can make their own decisions. Gradually, as they gain a more secure sense of themselves, the decisions they make and the way they express them will change.

Fortunately, toddlers can be easily distracted. If a child wants something that is prohibited, the parent can point to a bird outside the window and tell the child, "Oh! See the robin!" While the child looks, the item can be

Problem Solving. Discuss what serious effects might result if a child is deprived of learning to express love and affection. **Discuss.** Why has the "terrible twos" label been linked with two-year-olds rather than with three- or four-year olds?

Problem Solving. Ask students to describe various ways that a parent can deal with specific examples of a toddler's negativism. How can parents help toddlers deal with frustrations, such as trying to put on a coat?

whisked away, and the toddler will simply forget about it.

When an older child is consistently negative, parents need to evaluate the situation. Perhaps the child really needs to go outdoors for some exercise, but one parent insists on indoor chores or homework. Some children learn that by pouting or arguing they eventually get their way. To help avoid such conflicts, parents and children should talk over their feelings and expectations. Afterward, they can usually settle their differences through negotiation.

Anger

Anger is a strong feeling of displeasure. Sometimes during play, one toddler tries to grab a toy from another toddler. The anger that results may be revealed by crying, shouting, or hitting. At this age, children have not yet learned to express their anger in words.

A **temper tantrum** is a fit of anger that may be expressed through screaming, hitting, and kicking. Almost all toddlers have occasional temper tantrums, usually when they are tired, frustrated, impatient, or angry. Often, like adults, they are not really sure what is bothering them; they just know that they are very upset.

Jeb Larson took his son Brian with him to the supermarket. Seeing a brightly colored cereal box, Brian pointed to it and told his father that he wanted it. Jeb did not want Brian to eat that brand of cereal because it contained a lot of sugar. He explained that the cereal was not on their shopping list and they were not going to buy it. To Jeb's dismay, Brian threw himself down on the floor, kicked his feet, waved his arms, and screamed at the top of his lungs. Such a temper tantrum can best be understood as a combination of the child's need to assert himself and his inability to express his emotions in words.

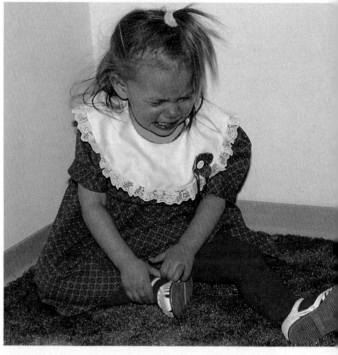

When children have temper tantrums, parents should avoid shouting and losing their own temper. This only makes the tantrum worse.

How should parents and caregivers respond when a child has a temper tantrum? The best response is to ignore the behavior and not give in to the child's demands. It is important to remain calm and objective and not join the child in being angry. At home, parents can ignore a temper tantrum by going into another room. They should not reward the child later with extra hugs or cookies. Such rewards only help reinforce the negative behavior. In general, the less attention given to temper tantrums, the less they will occur.

When tantrums occur in a public place, parents and caregivers may be embarrassed by the child's behavior. This usually makes the situation even more frustrating and harder to handle calmly. If necessary, the adult may have to pick the child up and carry him or her to another location.

As children grow older, their anger usually becomes less explosive. Instead of hitting

Problem Solving. Discuss ways that parents can avoid problems when shopping with a small child in a supermarket.
Reference. See page 478 for more information on handling temper tantrums.

Problem Solving. Have students describe how they have seen adults react to children's temper tantrums. Which methods seemed to be the most effective? Least effective? Why?

and kicking, they show anger in a variety of other ways. Some children are impulsive and react by threatening and name-calling. Other children are more passive and pout and feel sorry for themselves. Still others learn to hide their angry feelings.

Parents and caregivers can help children learn to express angry feelings in acceptable words and actions. They need to learn to avoid hurting others or themselves. When Belle tried to strike her father in a fit of anger, he said to her, "I understand why you're angry. I won't let you hit me, but you may stamp your foot if you like."

Parents and caregivers should always demonstrate acceptable ways of dealing with anger. Children learn to express their emotions by what they see adults do, not by what adults tell them to do. When Annette is angry, she slaps her favorite doll. Emil repeats vulgar words that he has heard an adult use, even though he does not understand their meaning. Both children are reflecting the way they have seen adults express anger. By hitting or swearing at children during spurts of anger, adults set examples for children to hit or swear at others when they become angry. On the other hand, parents who talk about how they feel when they are angry help children learn to express such feelings in constructive ways.

DECISIONS ◆
◆ DECISIONS

Margarita, two years old, is afraid of the sounds of the vacuum cleaner and other household appliances. She screams and cries until they are turned off. Margarita is not a fearful child in other respects, but she is terrified of these noises. What can her parents do to help her?

Fear

As toddlers move into the world, they meet people, animals, and things that frighten them. Fear is a protective emotion. It keeps children from dangerous situations, such as high places or wild animals. In fearful situations, children quickly seek their parents or caregivers.

Parents and caregivers should understand that feeling fear is normal for children. Knowing this, adults can comfort children and help them overcome their fear. For example, if a toddler is afraid of cats, the parents can give the child some pleasant experiences with cats.

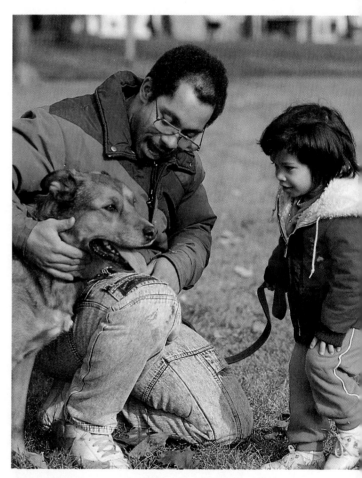

Most children have fears. Parents should always reassure and comfort a child who is fearful. This will help the child to overcome or cope with the fear.

Problem Solving. How can parents help children deal appropriately with their anger?
Discuss. When might fear be beneficial to young children?

Problem Solving. Have students discuss how certain fears might be learned. What can parents and caregivers do to avoid "teaching" a fear to children?

Around the World

Happy Birthday!

The song "Happy Birthday" was written in 1935 by two American women, Mildred and Patty Hill. Today, it is sung all over the world. However, the way people celebrate birthdays is not always the same.

In Japan, boys and girls have a special birthday celebration known as the "seven, five, three." Girls who have had their third or seventh birthday and boys who have had their fifth birthday celebrate on November 15. This tradition started long ago, when many children died before reaching their third, fifth, or seventh birthday.

Even today, many Japanese children go to a shrine to give thanks for their good health and strength. They also pray for a long life. Both boys and girls wear their best kimono, and girls put a ribbon in their hair. After the visit to the shrine, there is a family feast at home. Sometimes the children receive special bags of candy with the message "Sweets for 1,000 years of life" written on them.

In Mexico, a piñata is more exciting than a birthday cake. A piñata is a pottery or paper-mache figure filled with treats. It is decorated with colored paper to look like just about anything from an elephant to an airplane. It is hung on a long rope, which is usually held by two people. If the birthday party takes place outdoors, the two may stand on a low wall or a flat roof. If it is indoors, they stand on chairs. Each child is blindfolded and given a turn to break the piñata by hitting it with a pole. As the child attempts to do this, the people holding the rope raise and lower the piñata to keep it from getting broken. When someone finally shatters it, everyone scrambles for the candies or toys that fall out.

They might point out cats at a distance and let the child see other people petting cats. As the toddler realizes that most cats are harmless, he or she may agree to pet a little kitten. Liking cats is not the important goal here. It is overcoming an unnecessary fear of animals that is important.

Some fears seem totally unreasonable to adults who do not understand children's mental processes. Many toddlers, for example, develop a fear of the bathtub. One night they play happily in the bath, the next night they scream and stiffen when parents try to bathe them. At a certain point in the toddler stage, children do not understand relative size. That is, they truly believe they can go down the bathtub drain and disappear, just as the water does.

When Sam was eighteen months old, he demonstrated such a fear. He suddenly became terrified of the bathtub. For several weeks, his parents gave him sponge baths. One night, he finally agreed to being put in the bathtub. He seemed to enjoy his bath. Yet when his father said, "It's time to get out now," Sam jumped out as fast as he could. He was taking no chances.

Children are often frightened by the dark, storms, or loud noises because they imagine various dangers. They need to be reassured and comforted, not ridiculed or punished for their fears. Sometimes explanations help. Lu-yin was frightened by the siren of the fire engine. Her mother reassured her that the siren warns cars to move over and let the engine hurry by to its important job of putting out a fire. Mrs. Chen later read a story about fire engines to Lu-yin.

As children grow older, they learn to cope on their own with their fears. An occasional sympathetic comment from parents to the effect that everybody is afraid sometimes usually helps. It reassures children that their fears are normal and manageable.

Activity. Ask students to list common fears of children and suggest ways that parents can help reduce these fears.
Reference. See pages 479-481 for more information on handling fears.

Discuss. What fears did you have as a child? How did your parents help you deal with these fears? How have you learned to manage fears that you might still have?

A certain amount of sibling rivalry is normal in a family. However, parents should avoid comparing children with each other or encouraging competition as this will only foster more jealousy.

Jealousy

Jealousy is an emotion that combines anger, fear, insecurity, and anxiety. It stems from a real or imagined loss of love. Children are sometimes jealous of a parent, a sister or brother, or a close friend.

Sibling rivalry, or competition among brothers and sisters for parents' attention, is a form of jealousy. Parents almost always observe some jealousy when there is a new baby in the family. From the child's point of view, the new sister or brother is a rival. Smaller and more helpless, the baby seems to claim everyone's attention, making the older child feel left out.

Children find it easier to overcome the feeling of jealousy toward a new baby if they are given a sense of being responsibly involved in caring for the newborn. Three-year-old Andrew feels very grown-up when his mother asks him to help by getting a clean diaper, a sweater, or a favorite toy for his baby sister. Toddlers also feel important when they are reminded of all the things that they can do but the baby cannot do.

Sometimes brothers and sisters get into explosive quarrels and arguments. When this happens, parents can help the children learn to resolve their conflicts in more positive ways. Chapter 25 gives additional information on dealing with sibling rivalry.

DECISIONS ◆ ◆ DECISIONS

Brennan, five years old, has a good relationship with his two-year-old sister, Lindsay. He helps his mother and father take care of her, and he rarely seems jealous. Recently, however, Brennan's parents have noticed that he has started a new playtime activity. He lines up his stuffed animals in a row and lectures them. He has named one of them Lindsay and scolds her vigorously, then throws her out of the room. Brennan's parents are worried about the negative feelings they are witnessing. What would you tell them?

Discuss. Why do some people feel that sibling rivalry is healthy?
Reference. See pages 481-484 for ways to handle jealousy and sibling conflicts.

Problem Solving. Ask students to suggest ways that parents can reduce sibling rivalry among young children, school-age children, and adolescents. When should parents intervene in a conflict rather than let siblings resolve the conflict?

Personality Development

Have you ever heard someone say, "She has such a pleasing personality"? **Personality** is the sum total of a person's emotional, social, cognitive, and physical characteristics as seen by others. It is demonstrated by patterns of behavior.

Many people have tried to explain why children grow up to be so different from each other. One theory was developed by psychologist Erik Erikson. He believes that cultural and social influences are an important part of personality development. According to Erikson, children form lasting personality characteristics at each stage of life.

◆◆ Erikson's Theory of Personality Development

Erikson describes the important stages of personality development from birth to old age. Each stage is characterized by a central emotional task that a person must master. There are two possible outcomes—one favorable and the other unfavorable. According to Erikson, the successful or unsuccessful mastery of those tasks can determine a child's emotional health as the child grows older.

Erikson has identified the following stages of personality development.

1. **Trust versus mistrust.** The first stage, from birth to eighteen months, lays the foundation for later emotional growth. Trust is established through consistent attention to infants' needs. This makes babies feel that the world is a safe place. They are able to develop a secure sense of their own value as a person. Babies who have been mistreated or neglected feel frightened and insecure. They are likely to have emotional or behavioral problems later on.

2. **Autonomy versus doubt.** The second stage builds on the level of trust. From eighteen months to about three years of age, children develop **autonomy,** or independence. During this stage, toddlers strive to act freely and independently. They delight in the emotional satisfaction that comes with self-sufficiency. However, when they are unable to master their own free will, they come to doubt their ability to do anything.

3. **Initiative versus guilt.** The third stage occurs during the preschool years. **Initiative** (in-NISH-ee-eh-tiv) is the readiness and ability to start something on one's own. As children initiate activities, they enjoy the feeling of achievement and competence. They also begin to learn what they should not do. They feel guilty about behavior that parents or caregivers may disapprove of.

4. **Industry versus inferiority.** The fourth stage takes place during the school-age years prior to puberty. Children enthusiastically explore the world. They like to work hard and try to do well. They feel inferior when they fail to meet their own standards or the standards of their parents or teachers.

5. **Identity versus identity diffusion.** During the adolescent years, teenagers focus on developing an **identity,** or a sense of who they really are. They think seriously about what they believe and what they want to accomplish in life. During this stage, teenagers may feel very uncertain about their inner self. Their sense of identity may be spread out and unfocused. For many people this search for identity continues into adulthood.

Everyone has both positive and negative experiences during each stage of personality development. No one grows up in an environment that provides only one kind of experience.

◆◆ Influences on Personality Development

Each child's personality is the product of many intertwined sets of influences. Some are inherited, and others are environmental. Some are relatively fixed, and others are changeable.

- **Temperament.** Children are born with different temperaments. Although each child's personality does change somewhat as he or she matures, a very active child will not become a quiet and passive adult.

- **Birth order.** A child's **birth order,** or relationship to other siblings in terms of time of birth, affects personality. A firstborn child is likely to be given more attention as a baby than are later arrivals to the family. That is, parents may be more involved with their first child than with later children. However, most parents are also more anxious and less sure of themselves when dealing with a firstborn.

- **Family structure.** An only child living with a single parent will have different experiences than a child who has siblings and lives with both parents.

- **Relationships.** Of greatest influence during the early stages of personality development are the child's relationships with others. The most important are relationships with parents, other family members, and caregivers. It is the quality of the parents' care that establishes basic trust in the infant. Toddlers develop autonomy when parents and caregivers allow them to explore their world. Preschoolers develop initiative when family members concentrate on their successes rather than their failures. School-age children can be very industrious when they are not made to feel inferior by family members, teachers, and schoolmates. Adolescents can begin to take responsibility for their own identity.

Six- and seven-year-old children like to work hard and do well. These ballet students are trying to meet the standards of their teacher.

Reference. See pages 340-341 for more information about birth order.

Discuss. What influences on personality development do you think are most important? Why?

The Importance of Self-Concept and Self-Esteem

All children develop a unique and distinctive way of behaving. Their behavior is strongly influenced by the image they hold of themselves. This image of oneself is one's self-concept.

Self-esteem differs somewhat from self-concept because it involves feelings. Self-esteem is a person's opinion, belief, or judgment about his or her worthiness as a person. Each person's self-concept and self-esteem begin to develop in infancy and have lifelong effects on that individual.

◆ Self-Concept

How does your self-concept develop? It begins when you start knowing about yourself from how others respond to and act toward you. They may praise you, scold you, tease you, or comfort you. You start building a picture of yourself based upon what you learn from others. Are you tall or short? Are you graceful or clumsy? Are you shy or outgoing?

Perhaps your mother praised you because you were always happy. Maybe your uncle told you that you were tall for your age. Your teachers may have criticized your handwriting, or a friend may have teased you about your freckles. All of these comments helped you create an image of yourself. That image can be positive or negative, depending on whether you focus more on what you consider your positive or negative characteristics.

◆ Self-Esteem

Children who have high self-esteem feel they are worthwhile. They like themselves and believe they can do certain things well. They can make choices for themselves. Such children are not overwhelmed by their feelings. They can both give and accept affection. Children who think of themselves as lovable and capable have a head start in life. They can accept themselves for who they are, with both strengths and shortcomings. They can forgive themselves when they make mistakes.

Children with high self-esteem have the confidence to try new or difficult things. They are usually comfortable and confident in their interactions with others. They can make the most of the experiences that come their way because they are secure from within.

In contrast, children with low self-esteem do not like themselves. They have trouble making choices and believe they do things poorly. They minimize their accomplishments and dwell on their mistakes. Such children develop a sense of failure and inferiority. They have difficulty making friends and getting along with others. They may show off or boss other children to prove themselves. These children may have the feeling that they are worthless.

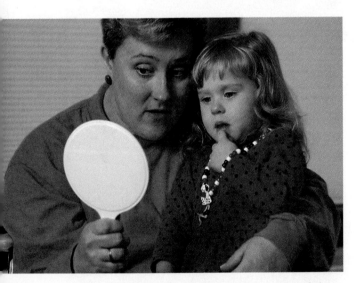

Young children begin developing an image of themselves. This self-image includes how they feel about their physical characteristics as well as how they feel about their emotions, thoughts, and social interactions.

Discuss. What are the long-term implications of a child's low self-esteem?

Activity. Have students list negative comments that are damaging to a child's self-esteem. Then ask students to rephrase each negative comment into a positive comment.

❖ Influencing Children's Self-Esteem

As children grow older, their self-esteem is influenced by friends, teachers, classmates, and others. They also begin to judge their own characteristics and abilities. However, young children form the foundation for self-esteem primarily from the words and actions of parents and caregivers.

Most young children accept as fact what others seem to think of them. They usually think that others see them as either good or bad. Then they tend to live up to that image. For example, parents who comment positively on their children's behavior and activ-

◆ ◆ *Self-Esteem* ◆ ◆

Children express their emotions differently according to their individual personality. When opening a birthday present, one child may show pleasure with a loud whoop. Another child may simply smile and murmur a quiet thank-you. Both children are equally delighted with their presents but express their emotions in different ways. When parents accept their child's individuality, they help promote the child's self-esteem.

Parents play an important role in helping a child develop high self-esteem. They do this best by providing attention, acceptance, and love.

ities usually find that their children are developing high self-esteem. These parents might say: "You did a great job of putting your toys away." "I like to watch you when you play with your baby sister. You seem to be having lots of fun." "You really look good in that blue shirt."

On the other hand, children whose parents continually tell them they are clumsy or slow or do not pay attention to what they are told often develop low self-esteem. Children who are constantly told about their mistakes and ridiculed or scolded generally behave in negative ways. They think others expect them to be inadequate or inferior, so they begin to behave according to that image of themselves.

The most important contributions to the development of self-esteem are the three A's: attention, acceptance, and active parenting.

Attention

Parents who give a child the attention needed, contribute to his or her high self-esteem. During infancy, a child needs to develop an attachment or bond with the parents. The warmth of the parents' love for the child contributes to the security and sense of trust that the child feels.

Activity. Distribute plain paper or pictures from coloring books, along with colored markers or crayons. Ask students to do their best job of coloring a picture. When completed, ask 2 or 3 students with *very high self-esteem* to leave the room. Have them return one at a time to show their picture. Immediately crush the picture and throw it away. Have class observe the facial expressions and body language as students react. Ask students to write the insights they gained from the experience.

Helping Children Develop Self-Esteem

Here are six ways to help a child develop high self-esteem.

1 **Praise the child for achievements, even small ones.** Praise good attempts, too. A quick hug, a smile, or a word is all that it takes.
Say: "You did a good job folding these socks and washcloths. I appreciate your help."

2 **When you need to correct a child's behavior, object to the behavior and not to the child.** Children can translate angry messages into rejection messages.
Say: "It makes me angry when you walk on the flowers. They won't grow if you keep on stepping on them."
Not this: "Get out of that flower garden! How many times have I told you to walk around it!"

3 **Give a child choices whenever possible.** Encourage decision making when a child does have a choice about something. Then praise the child's successful choice.
Say: "Would you like a banana or an orange for a snack?"
Not this: "How about some fruit this morning?"

4 **Give a child room to achieve and explore.** Let a child initiate some activities and be responsible for simple tasks.
Say: "You try it."
Not this: "Here, let me do that."

5 **Keep competition to a minimum.** Never compare children. Instead, set individual goals for each child. Remind the child of what he or she does well.
Say: "Before long, you'll be able to write your name."
Not this: "Scott can write his name. Why don't you try it?"

6 **Talk about the feeling the child is expressing and give it a name.** This helps children understand their feelings. It also helps them learn how to react to disappointments.
Say: "I know how sad you feel. You really wanted to stay outside and play."

As children grow older, parents provide attention by watching them turn a somersault, throw a ball, or climb a jungle gym. Children seek this attention by yelling, "Watch me! Watch me!"

Preschoolers feel proud when they see their drawings displayed where everybody can admire them. School-age children gain a sense of achievement when parents take time to look at their schoolwork and talk about their activities. Although adolescents may want independence and freedom, they still seek the attention of their parents and family.

Acceptance

Parents who accept their child—in appearance, gender, personality, and abilities—contribute strongly to the child's high self-esteem. Such parents believe and tell the child that he or she can do many things. Through encouragement and praise, they help the child discover his or her own skills, talents, and accomplishments. These can range from the ability to make people laugh to the ability to turn cartwheels to skill with numbers, words, or music.

Not all children can be the team captain, the star performer, or the class president. However, each child is a special and unique person. By accepting children on this basis, parents provide the support children need to reach their fullest potential in life.

Active parenting

Parents who are actively involved with their children are likely to have children with high self-esteem. These parents spend time with their children and do things together as a family. They play games, go for walks, and visit the zoo together. They attend music or dance recitals, watch athletic events, and meet teachers at back-to-school night. They nurture and guide their children through each stage of development.

Encouraging Independence

Independence comes from a sense of security and from opportunities for freedom. Parents and caregivers need to provide both for children. In turn, children develop independence slowly and unevenly. One day they are eager to try new things; the next day they want to be dependent.

Parents and caregivers should always encourage children to do for themselves whatever they can or want to try. New experiences help children learn and grow. However, adults need to let children know that they can slip back briefly whenever they have doubts or fears about being grown-up. Otherwise, children may lose interest in exploring new opportunities and skills.

❖ Stages of Independence

Growing from dependence toward independence is an important developmental task of children. However, children differ widely in how they adjust to new situations and responsibilities. This kind of development depends on each child's personality, experiences, and family life.

Toddler Stage

As toddlers, children begin the journey toward autonomy. They experiment with new activities and discover that they can do many things by themselves. In learning to walk, they eventually let go of a parent's hand—an expression of trust—and take steps by themselves. A stronger display of independence comes when toddlers no longer need to stay near parents and decide to walk farther away. They delight in the emotional satisfaction that comes with this sign of independence.

On the other hand, toddlers are still babies in many ways, dependent on their parents or caregivers. Although children at this age want

Discuss. In what other ways can parents contribute to the development of self-esteem?
Discuss. How does self-reliance and self-responsibility contribute to a child's self-concept?

Problem Solving. Discuss the use of "child leashes" for toddlers. What are the advantages and disadvantages for the parent and the child?

to be grown-up, they are fearful and unsure of themselves at the same time. One day a child will shout, "Me do!" The next day the child will demand, "You do it." This is true for activities ranging from getting dressed to digging a hole in the sandbox.

Lateesha and her father leave their apartment every Saturday morning to go to the supermarket. Each time they do this, Lateesha insists on going down the front steps by herself. She refuses to hold her father's hand. Once safely down, she proudly scampers back up and repeats the process. When father and child return from the store, Lateesha refuses to climb the stairs. She cries for her daddy, who is now loaded down with groceries, to carry her up.

Lateesha is not deliberately trying to make life difficult for her father. For one thing, she is tired. During the last hour, she has been obeying his request that she "be a big girl." Now she wants reassurance that she does not have to be grown-up all the time.

Preschool Stage

Preschoolers are very active explorers and adventurers. They are learning to do many more things for themselves. For example, they may want to fix their own peanut butter and jelly sandwich. Even though they work slowly and make a mess,

they have a sense of achievement. Wise parents and caregivers praise a preschooler for attempting such activities so that the child wants to learn. Other parents may be impatient and criticize a child for not doing things properly. In this case, the child may not want to try again.

Preschoolers, too, sometimes want to slip back into less mature behavior. Barry had been tying his own shoelaces for weeks. Yet one day he suddenly asked somebody else to tie them for him.

School-Age Stage

School-age children need little or no help fulfilling personal needs, such as dressing, bathing, and grooming. At this age, they delight in mastering new skills during school and after-school activities. They are proud of being moved to a more advanced reading group or finishing a difficult math problem before anyone else does. School-age children gain a sense of accomplishment by joining a team, a club, or an organization. They feel independent when they can walk or ride a bicycle around the neighborhood on their own. These experiences enhance their image of themselves as capable individuals.

However, some children may be doing poorly in school. Such children need extra help from teachers and parents or they may lose interest in school and develop a feeling of failure and inferiority. Perhaps they need extra tutoring or help in devel-

As children develop independence, they gain delight in achieving certain accomplishments.

Discuss. How might overprotective parents hinder a child's development?

Emphasize. When parents sneak out of the home while the babysitter distracts the child, the child develops feelings of mistrust rather than trust in the parents.

oping better study skills. Parents can encourage children to spend time doing homework and provide a special area where they can work. Although parents may check a child's homework after it is completed, they should not do the actual work. Doing so would rob the child of the opportunity to develop a sense of accomplishment and to learn from the assignment.

Some school-age children may need help in discovering and developing the things they are good at doing. Josiah enjoyed playing chess, so his parents encouraged him to join the chess club at school. Maria's art teacher saw that she was good at drawing, so he asked her to make posters for school events. Both children gained a sense of their own worth and capabilities.

Adolescent Stage

During adolescence, individual behavior varies just as physical development does. Some fifteen-year-olds are ready to take on increasing freedom and responsibility. Others have barely worked out the problems of childhood. Each adolescent deserves individual consideration.

Parents should provide opportunities for adolescents to gain independence gradually. Full independence cannot be won overnight. Instead, parents can begin to relinquish more control and allow teenagers to make many of their own decisions. These might be decisions about hair style, clothing, after-school activities, and part-time jobs. By creating a balance between freedom and control, parents foster children's self-confidence.

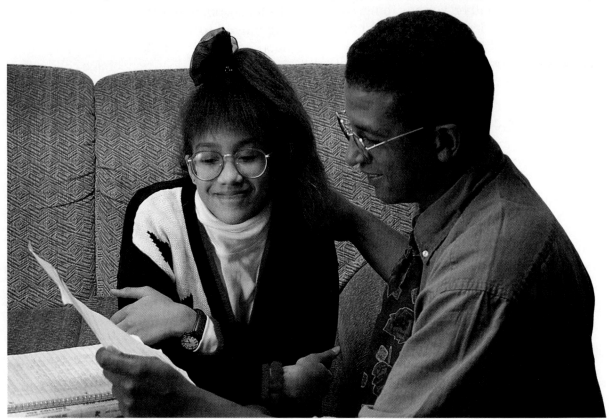

As children develop new skills and gain confidence in their abilities, they become more independent.

Activity. Ask students to describe situations that they have observed when children were treated differently because of being a boy or a girl.

Activity. Have students read current magazine articles on ways that parents and caregivers can encourage independence in children.

❖ Helping Children Become Independent

Parents and caregivers must provide both freedom and security for children. They must balance the needs of children with the responsibilities of parenting. There are a number of ways in which parents and caregivers can ensure their success in this important task.

Being Patient

Adults must be patient with children who are developing independence. A two-year-old may take a long time to zip up a jacket or put on shoes. If you are in a hurry to get somewhere, they may have to step in and complete the task quickly. At such times they might say, "I know you can do this yourself, but we have to hurry, so I'll help." If this occurs frequently, however, the child may give up trying to master a task and expect others to help.

Adults should give children enough advance notice to get ready. Young children may need at least 15 minutes to get dressed and additional time to put on a jacket.

Offering Encouragement

Children need lots of encouragement and praise as they try new skills. To criticize them for slowness or clumsiness would only be discouraging. Imagine how you would feel if your parents or caregivers ridiculed you for not being able to balance yourself the first time you ever got on a bicycle.

Both boys and girls should receive the same kind of encouragement to be independent. Studies have shown that some parents tend, without realizing it, to encourage boys to become more independent than girls. They may give girls more warnings to slow down, be careful, or "Don't do that—you might hurt yourself." When toddlers fall, boys may receive a few comforting words from a distance, while girls may be picked up and held.

Providing Reassurance

Sometimes young children cling to adults for reassurance. They may demand to be cuddled or object to letting their parents out of sight. Such behavior may come about from too many changes in a child's life—an illness, new child care arrangements, a move to a new home. In these cases, children need special reassurance that they are securely loved and in no danger of being abandoned, even briefly. Teasing children for "acting like a baby," punishing them, or threatening to leave them will only make matters worse. Instead, parents and caregivers should explain the changes. Above all, they should

Parents and other caregivers should reassure children that they are loved. This reassurance provides security for children as they gradually seek independence.

Activity. Have students write various statements of encouragement that parents and caregivers can tell children.

Reference. See pages 419-422 for additional information on providing encouragement for children.

give children opportunities to gain confidence in their own abilities. Gradually, the children will become more secure and independent.

Setting Limits

During the school-age years, children become increasingly able to travel around the community on their own. They need to be permitted only as much freedom as they can safely handle. Sometimes children will argue about this. For example, they may say, "Everybody else is allowed to walk to the park alone." Parents need to find out whether this is true. If so, they should ask themselves why their child cannot be allowed to do this or that. Are they being too protective? Have they failed to train their child to handle a particular challenge? It may be necessary for them to demonstrate how to follow safety rules, such as waiting for a green light and checking for cars.

School-age children often press parents to grant them more independence. At the same time, however, they tend to abide by the limits parents and caregivers set on their behavior. Children seem to know that such limits are a sign of parental love. At times, they are grateful to have a parental prohibition to use as an excuse for not undertaking activities that they know are not in their best interest. You will learn more about setting limits in Chapter 24.

Relinquishing Control

It is important that parents maintain a balance between giving advice and showing acceptance when their children reach adolescence. How do parents know what to do? Sometimes they must act on instinct and take small risks. Young people must be given the chance to prove themselves.

What happens if an adolescent fails? Adults should be there to listen and offer support. Most important, they should not make the adolescent feel like a failure by insulting, harshly criticizing, or saying, "I told you so." Parents may find that looking back to their own struggle for independence helps them understand what adolescents are going through.

It is difficult for parents to stand by and watch their teenage children make mistakes. However, such experiences often teach adolescents an important lesson in dependability or responsibility. Of course, adults cannot always stand by and watch. When children of any age are involved in activities that endanger their health or safety or are against the law, adults must draw the line.

Relinquishing control is hard for some parents. It seems to indicate that maybe they are not needed anymore. Yet children gain freedom and independence only one step at a time. Throughout the years, they continue to need their parents' encouragement, support, and guidance.

As children grow older, parents must maintain a balance between setting limits and relinquishing control. By talking about their feelings, parents and children have a better understanding of each other's needs and responsibilities.

Reference. See page 460-462 for additional information on setting, explaining, changing, and enforcing limits and rules.
Activity. Have students make a list of decisions that they believe adolescents should make on their own. Then have them make a second list of decisions in which parents should be involved or retain control. Ask students to give reasons for their choices.

Children and Stress

Stress is tension that usually results from changes in one's life. Stress upsets people and often causes a physical reaction. No child grows up today without experiencing stress. However, children are less able than adults to understand stress. Children are more likely to feel insecure and helpless. Yet they can learn to manage stress gradually over time.

❖ Signs of Stress in Children

Stress can be either good or bad. Uncontrolled bad stress (such as that triggered by the divorce of parents or the death of a family member) can lead to problems such as bedwetting, nail biting, or stuttering. Good stress (such as that resulting from a birthday party or having the lead in the school play) has a very different effect. It can give a child the extra positive energy to get through the situation with great success.

Children who are under a lot of stress may exhibit any of the following warning signals:

- Boasts of being first or best or perfect.
- Complaints of being afraid without knowing why.

Parents need to provide comfort and support when children show signs of worry, nervousness, or anxiety.

- Complaints of a pounding heart, an upset stomach, or neck pain.
- An uncontrollable urge to be clean.
- Ear tugging or hair twisting.
- Cruelty to pets or people.
- Downgrading of self.
- Jumpiness or fear of sudden sounds.
- Extreme worry or nervousness.
- Headaches.
- Lying or stealing.
- Nightmares.
- Teeth grinding (sometimes in sleep).
- Thumb sucking.
- Unusual shyness.
- Poor eating or sleeping habits.
- Explosive crying or screaming.

❖ Coping with Stress

Parents and caregivers should protect young children from stressful situations. Then as they grow older, children can gradually learn to cope with stress. As they do this, adults should watch for the warning signals that tell when children are beyond their coping ability.

To help a child under stress, adults should ask the child to describe what is happening. They must listen to what the child says and work together to find a way to lessen the pressure on the child. If the child is needlessly worrying too much, perhaps the adults can help the child look at the situation differently. However, if too much is being expected of the child, adult's should cut back some of the youngster's responsibilities.

Older children also experience stress in their lives. They may become anxious before taking a test or trying out for a team. They may be upset after an argument with a friend

Discuss. What are some positive benefits of stress?

Problem Solving. Have students find out where parents can obtain advice and help in your community for a child who exhibits the warning signs of stress.

◆◆ Health & Safety ◆◆

Depression and Suicide

Suicide is now the second leading cause of death for people between the ages of fifteen and nineteen. Many teenagers who commit suicide feel unable to cope with the stress in their lives. Problems in the family, with friends, at school, or on a job can overwhelm a teenager. Alcohol and drug abuse, pregnancy, or trouble with the law can create additional pressures.

Although a significant number of teenagers become depressed and suicidal, depression may also occur in young children. Most people who attempt suicide do not want to die but are making a plea for help. Usually they show some warning signs by their words or behavior.

If you know someone who is exhibiting several of the following signs, seek help from a teacher, counselor, member of the clergy, or other caring adult. Many communities have a suicide prevention center where counseling is available. Convincing someone to seek professional help for depression or thoughts of suicide could save a life.

Here are 12 clues that indicate someone may be considering suicide. The first letters spell SUICIDE SIGNS.

Social withdrawal and dropping out of activities.

Unusual preoccupation with songs, poems, or movies dealing with death.

Irritability or sudden change in behavior.

Crying for no apparent reason.

Investing in a means of suicide, such as a weapon, rope, or pills.

Disinterest in personal grooming.

Eating and/or sleeping too much or too little.

Suicide threats such as: "I can't take this anymore."

Increased use or abuse of alcohol or other drugs.

Giving away personal possessions.

Negative sense of self or a feeling of failure, shame, or guilt.

Sudden drop in grades or performance.

or a parent. Serious events, such as a major illness, a divorce, or a death in the family, can result in severe stress.

Parents can encourage children to develop techniques that help them deal with stress. Some like to exercise—jog, shoot baskets, or kick a soccer ball around—to release some of the tension. Others can relax by listening to music or writing in a journal. It also helps to think of possible solutions to problems. What can the child do to prepare for an exam? Does the child need to rehearse a speech one more

time? How can the child apologize to a friend?

If the feeling of stress continues, parents should get professional help for the child. Even young children can suffer from depression. This is a prolonged feeling of sadness characterized by hopelessness and an inability to enjoy life. Although children may not be able to control the events that cause stress, they can learn how to manage stress. Then they are better prepared to cope with the ups and downs of life.

Reference. See pages 223-224 for ways that parents can manage stress.
Emphasize. Never ignore the warning signs that a friend might be considering suicide. Seek help from qualified adults.

Activity. Have students gather additional information about teenage depression and suicide. What might be some of the causes why the rate of teenage suicide has been increasing?

CHAPTER 17 REVIEW

Summary

- Toddlers are very egocentric and go through a stage of negativism.
- Parents and caregivers can help children deal with feelings of anger, fear, and jealousy.
- The stages outlined by Erikson help us understand personality development.
- Personality is influenced by temperament, birth order, family structure, and relationships.
- A child's self-concept and self-esteem begin to develop in infancy and have life-long effects.
- Parents encourage high self-esteem by giving children attention and acceptance and being actively involved with them.
- To help children become independent, parents should be patient, offer encouragement, provide reassurance, set limits, and gradually relinquish control.
- All children experience stress, and most eventually learn how to manage it.

Questions

p. 315 1. Define the term *egocentric*. Give an example of a toddler's egocentric behavior.

p. 318 2. How should parents and caregivers respond to a child's temper tantrum?

p. 321 3. What is sibling rivalry?

p. 322 4. Name the positive outcome of each of Erickson's five stages of personality development.

p. 323 5. How do relationships influence personality development?

6. What is the difference between self-concept and self-esteem? p. 324

7. How can you tell if a child has high self-esteem? p. 324

8. How do parents and other caregivers influence a child's self-esteem? p. 325

9. How can parents and caregivers encourage a child's independence? p. 331

10. List eight signs of stress in children. p. 333

Activities

1. Interview the parents of at least three toddlers. Ask them how they deal with their child's negativism, fears, temper tantrums, and stress. Draw some conclusions from the parents' answers and the children's ages. Report your findings to the class.

2. Research Sigmund Freud's ideas on personality development. Write a report on how his ideas differ from Erikson's.

3. Write down the comments you remember hearing family and friends say about you as a child. Put a plus (+) sign by the positive statements and a minus (–) sign by the negative statements. Place a check beside each statement you believe is true about you. What does this say about your self-esteem?

Think About

1. Many young children have a security item, such as a favorite stuffed animal or soft blanket. How might a child feel if the item was lost or thrown away?

2. How can the parent of a ten- or twelve-year old determine how much freedom the child can safely handle?

Reference. See the Teacher's Manual in the front of the Teacher's Annotated Edition for complete answers to the chapter review questions.

335

Helping Children Get Along with Others

Objectives

This chapter will help you to:
- Define the socialization process.
- Discuss how family members influence a child's social development.
- Explain how children learn to share and cooperate with other children.
- Describe how children become aware of gender and ethnic differences.

Vocabulary

socialization
peers
peer pressure
stereotype
prejudice

Midori is playing with a doll in one corner of the kindergarten room. Marty, a boy in her class, asks to see the doll. He sits down beside Midori and gently holds the doll. The two children play happily together for 20 minutes.

Later, on the playground, Marty suddenly grabs the cap off a classmate's head. Roberto shouts, "Give it back! That's mine!"

Marty starts hitting and kicking Roberto. The teacher quickly intervenes. "Marty, you'll hurt Roberto. What's the problem here?" she asks. Without a word, Marty stops. His sudden outburst is over.

Marty is a five-year-old kindergartner. His interactions with Midori and Roberto occurred on the same afternoon. He was friendly and helpful to one classmate and hostile to another.

Children's behavior can go through many changes daily. Childhood is a time for learning how to cope with different situations and get along with different people. Relationships with other people have a strong impact on children's lives.

Social Development

Learning how to get along with others is an important skill for children to learn. Most parents want their children to interact happily with others.

Relationships are important because they help satisfy many emotional needs. Parents and relatives help fulfill children's needs for love, affection, and a sense of belonging. Family, friends, teachers, and coaches can provide acceptance and approval with a word of praise or a pat on the back. Spending time with family and friends provides an opportunity for children to share ideas, feelings, and experiences with others. In turn, children develop self-esteem by the way people respond to them and treat them.

You will notice that there is a very strong link between social and emotional development. It is difficult to separate the two because they are so integrated. Although each area of development is discussed separately, in reality they occur simultaneously within each child.

❖ Relationships with Others

Infants first learn to relate to their parents and other family members. Contact with other people increases as infants become toddlers. Parents help toddlers learn more about people by taking them to homes of relatives, to a shopping mall, and perhaps to a child care center. All these places have people—familiar faces and unknown faces. The social goal for toddlers is to like and trust people and for people to like them.

As children move from the self-centeredness of toddlers to the greater independence of preschoolers, they experience rapid social development. Their interests expand beyond home and parents. They increasingly seek out other children as playmates. They may prefer some companions over others.

School-age children spend more and more time away from their family, whether in class or playing with their friends. They begin to see themselves as members of a group of friends as well as members of the third grade or students at their school. They may develop a special relationship with their teachers. Many school-age children join organizations such as the 4-H Club, Little League, and the Girl Scouts or Boy Scouts. Membership in a formal organization offers new opportunities for social relationships with other children and with adult leaders and coaches.

Adolescents interact with many people other than family and friends. These may include teachers, counselors, religious leaders, employers, neighbors, and community leaders. Their influence will depend on the circumstances of each interaction. Some may be brief; others may last a lifetime. By the time adolescents enter adulthood, their relationships with many people will have had an impact on their lives.

Children first learn how to get along with other people from interactions within the family.

Discuss. How is social development closely related to emotional development?
Reference. See page 242 for information on the failure-to-thrive syndrome.

Activity. Ask students to write about one person who has had a great influence on them. They should explain how the person influenced them and why this was important to them.

❖ The Socialization Process

Socialization is the process by which people acquire the attitudes, beliefs, and behavior patterns of a society. Parents and family members are the strongest force in socializing children, even into adulthood. The cultural background of the family helps determine many of the specific habits and behaviors that children learn. Socialization is also carried out by neighbors, friends, teachers, religious leaders, and others in the community.

Socialization begins in infancy, when babies learn what their family expects of them. Some kinds of behavior are learned by imitating the actions of family members or by observing how they respond to the babies' own actions. Children quickly discover which actions please their parents and which are unacceptable. Socialization also takes place through direct teaching. For example, parents may explain to their toddler that people should not undress in public.

Children are being socialized when they learn to greet people when they arrive and to say good-bye when they leave. Children may be scolded for poking another child in the face or for eating with their hands instead of a fork or spoon. These lessons help teach the general rules of conduct in our society. The rules are not the same in all cultures.

Gradually, children become less self-centered. They learn that other people have their own needs and rights. They begin to understand what is fair and what is not fair. They learn to respect the rules and limits that protect themselves, others, property, and the environment. By the time children enter school, the socialization process is well underway.

Learning to handle conflicts and learning to control angry emotions are also important in the socialization process. School-age children learn how to settle their differences verbally, without resorting to physical violence.

However, they still may need help with understanding how their behavior affects other children or adults. Teachers help children learn about the rights of individuals, equality, and freedom of speech. These rights are outlined in the Constitution of the United States.

Many beliefs and behaviors are so much a part of our society that parents may not realize that children have to learn them. Before criticizing a child's behavior, adults should consider whether or not the child understands what behavior is expected. The socialization process helps children get along with others in our society.

The ideals, history, and traditions of a culture influence all members of a society. These influences are passed on from one generation to another.

Discuss. What family tradition or teaching has been significant to you in the socialization process?

Discuss. Why is it important for a child to learn to respect the rights of others? How do you feel about being around someone who has not learned this concept?

Interaction with Other Family Members

The family is the main social influence for young children. The larger the family, the more social interactions children experience. They may spend much of their time with their siblings, grandparents, uncles, aunts, or cousins. On the other hand, children in a small family may develop a close relationship with their parents. They do not have to compete with relatives for parental attention and affection.

Interaction with other family members helps shape a child's personality. The family also determines the various roles of its members.

Reference. See page 322 for Erikson's theory of personality development.

The family plays an important part in shaping a child's personality. Parents and other family members can help the child successfully master each of the stages of personality development outlined in Chapter 17.

As children grow older, their relationships with family members change. They also develop relationships with people outside the home, including friends and teachers. Yet even though a child's personality is not completely determined by others, the family unit remains an important influence throughout adolescence and into adulthood.

❖ Roles of Family Members

Each member of a family has certain roles, or parts one plays when interacting with others. For example, a female can be a daughter, granddaughter, sister, wife, mother, grandmother, aunt, niece, or cousin. A male can be a son, grandson, brother, husband, father, grandfather, uncle, nephew, or cousin. When relatives live nearby, children may be able to observe many roles and several generations of family members.

Roles are defined within the family and the society where each child is born. Children first observe the power status of men and women in their family. In some cultural groups, the elderly have a very powerful position. For instance, when a Chinese grandmother speaks, all eyes turn to her. Children are taught to respect the authority of their elders. In traditional Chinese families, the elderly are cared for by their children. These roles are expected of all members of the family.

❖ Influence of Birth Order

A child's birth order has an influence on family relationships. Whether the child is born first, last, or in the middle or is the only child in the family can affect how the family treats the child.

Activity. Ask students to list the roles they play in their family and in their community. Are some roles more difficult to play than others? What roles do you enjoy? Are there roles you wish you did not have to play?

The birth order of children with-in the family influences their personality. It also influences how parents and siblings interact with each other.

- **Oldest children.** The oldest child in a family may receive more attention as a baby than do children born later. As the "only child" for awhile, he or she has the parents' undivided attention. The oldest child is likely to become more independent and competitive than subsequent siblings. However, parents may tend to worry more about their first child and be overprotective. If firstborn children are not allowed to do things on their own, they may have less self-confidence as they grow older. At the same time, they may have a need to keep proving themselves to their parents. Firstborns tend to be high achievers.

- **Middle children.** Being neither the oldest nor the youngest, middle children may feel they have no status in the family. Yet they may be able to share something of both worlds—joining in activities with an older sibling and helping with the baby. Middle children may feel less pressure than a firstborn to be perfect. They may also receive less attention than the youngest child. It is especially important for middle children to discover special interests and abilities.

- **Youngest children.** Older siblings pave the way for the youngest child. Parents now feel more capable and experienced than they did when they had their first child. As a result, the youngest child in a family may be given privileges at an earlier age than older children were. The youngest child is often more sociable and self-confident than older siblings. However, he or she may object to being treated as the baby or having to follow in the footsteps of older siblings.

- **Only children.** An only child usually receives a great deal of attention and support from parents. The child may also be given more responsibilities than other children. This helps develop the only child's self-confidence. However, some only children may feel pressured by parents who place all their expectations on one child. Although an only child does not have to share possessions with siblings, he or she lacks the companionship that siblings provide. To overcome this, the only child can be encouraged to develop close relationships with friends. Many only children assume leadership roles as adults.

Activity. Divide students into groups according to birth order. What percentage of students are in each category? Have each group list the advantages and disadvantages of their birth order on large sheets of paper to share.

Activity. Have students research the birth order of famous people and prepare a report.

❖ Parents

Throughout this text, you have been reading about the importance of children's relationships with parents. These relationships are influenced by many factors, including family size and structure, birth order, personalities, communication, and parenting skills.

For example, children in small families may develop closer relationships with parents than do children in large families. In single-parent families, children may primarily depend on only one parent for love and support. In contrast, children in extended families are often cared for by several adult relatives. If parents work outside the home, children sometimes have strong relationships with caregivers, as well as with parents.

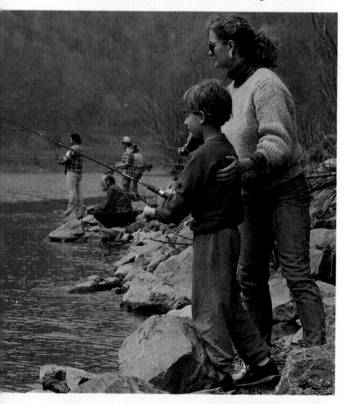

A single parent may have to provide all the care and guidance for a child. As a result, the parent and child may depend more on each other than parents and children do in large families.

Communicating effectively, showing respect and trust, providing love and support, and spending time together strengthen parent-child relationships.

❖ Siblings

Siblings provide early social relationships for each other. As they interact with each other, siblings learn how to communicate, share, cooperate, and compete. However, the closeness of sibling relationships varies from one family to another and even between different siblings in the same family.

Siblings who are close in age usually have far different relationships than siblings who are several years apart. For example, children close in age are often playmates during their early years. In contrast, a much older sibling may interact more as a caregiver with a younger sibling.

How siblings relate to one another often depends on their personalities. Some siblings have similar personalities, while others have very different ones. Because each child in the family has a certain temperament, siblings may respond in different ways to the same environment. In addition, the environment is slightly different for each child, depending upon birth order and how the child is treated by various family members.

Wise parents will expect a certain amount of competition and jealousy among siblings. To help minimize sibling rivalry, parents should be sure that each child is treated fairly and respected for his or her own individuality. At the same time, siblings may be extremely loyal to each other. One may strongly defend the other to parents or friends, especially during the school-age years.

Many parents hope their adult children will enjoy returning to the family home for special occasions. If that is the goal, parents should help their children develop close friendships with each other. The feelings that develop between siblings during their growing-up years usually last throughout their lives.

Twins

Twins usually grow up doing many things together. They may be considered "the twins" by friends and relatives. Even though identical twins are alike in many ways, they are still individuals and can have different rates of development. For example, one twin may crawl and walk earlier. The other twin may start talking sooner.

This is also true of fraternal twins. Unlike identical twins, fraternal twins can be of different genders. Since girls generally develop more rapidly than boys, a female twin often develops ahead of her brother in some ways.

Many twins are very close and enjoy a special emotional bond. Others show strong sibling rivalry, especially if they are competing with each other for their parents' attention.

DECISIONS ◆ ◆ DECISIONS

Allison and Ben have four-month-old identical twin girls. Sometimes people ask the parents questions such as "Which twin is smarter?" "Why aren't they dressed alike?" "Which one do you like better?" Allison and Ben want their daughters to develop a sense of individuality. What should they say to people who ask these questions?

Parents of twins should emphasize the uniqueness of each twin. They should avoid dressing twins alike and expecting them always to play together instead of with other children. By spending some time alone with each twin, parents help strengthen each one's sense of individuality.

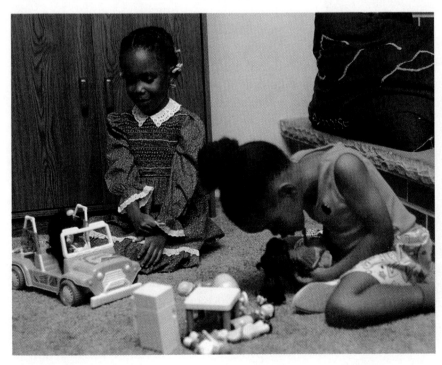

Parents of twins should encourage their individuality by dressing them differently and praising their own interests and abilities.

Discuss. What twin relationships have you observed? What behaviors support or refute the statement that sibling rivalry can be intense between twins?

Problem Solving. If you were the parent of twins, how would you try to promote each twin's individuality?

◆ Other Relatives

Some children become accustomed to having warm relationships with many relatives besides their parents and siblings. These may include grandparents, uncles and aunts, and cousins. These relatives may help care for the children when the parents are at work or away from home. Other children may see such relatives only occasionally.

Grandparents, especially, have much to offer children. They can share stories about family events and traditions. They may have extra time to spend with grandchildren, reading to them, taking them fishing, or working together in the garden. All these experiences help children develop affection, understanding, and respect for older family members.

When grandparents and other relatives live far away, relationships can be strengthened through frequent communications. The exchange of letters, cards, telephone calls, and videotapes helps build family ties.

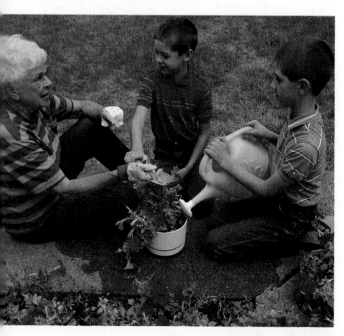

Grandparents can play an important role in children's lives. They can tell stories, teach skills, offer advice, and provide love.

Interaction with Other Children

Children enjoy being around other children. While toddlers tend to play beside each other, preschoolers actually play together. As they play and argue—over who gets the best crayons, for example—they learn how to adjust to each other's needs and personality. Certain skills, such as pumping on a swing, are almost always learned from watching another child.

Peers, or children of the same age, play an important part in the social development of children. Most children seek acceptance from others their age. Parents can help their children develop social skills by providing opportunities for them to get together with other children. If children are in a child care or preschool program, they are able to interact with other children on a regular basis. If not, parents should make special efforts to have their children spend some time each day with at least one other child of about the same age. For example, a mother might take her child to a neighborhood playground, invite a parent and child over to visit, or set up an informal play group with neighbors and friends.

During the school-age years and adolescence, friends play an increasingly important role in children's lives. They provide companionship, reassurance, and a sense of belonging.

From clothing styles and eating habits to favorite music and movies, friends enjoy many of the same things. However, during adolescence **peer pressure** is especially widespread. This is the strong influence of friends or others of the same age to make someone do whatever the group does. Peer pressure can be positive, as when it encourages one to join others in a school or community project. It can be negative, as when it

◆◆ Health & Safety ◆◆

Contagious Infections

Young children do not understand the importance of good health practices, such as washing one's hands before eating. Depending on their mood, they happily share or fight over personal items such as combs and facial tissues. Hands go easily from eyes to mouth and back again. As a result, children are prone to a variety of contagious infections.

Pink eye is a highly contagious form of conjuctivitis, an inflammation of the eye. When the eye is infected, it itches, burns, tears, and turns red. In addition, there is a slight discharge of pus. Fortunately, pink eye is very easy to cure. The doctor will prescribe antibiotic eye drops. These will clear up the infection in a few days.

Head lice are nits, or tiny insects, that can nest in the hair and scalp. The eggs cling to the hair and sometimes look like dandruff. However, if a person tries to brush them away, they will not budge. Sometimes the lice can be seen on the scalp, particularly along the part line and around the ears. Itching red pimples may also develop. Years ago, treatments for head lice included shaving the head or soaking the scalp with foul-smelling preparations. Today, doctors recommend the use of a special medicated shampoo. Combing the hair with a fine-tooth comb will also help dislodge the eggs. There is no guaranteed way to prevent head lice. However, keeping one's hair clean and never borrowing another person's brush or comb greatly reduce the risk of infection.

Impetigo is a contagious skin infection that is more common in children than adults. It begins with small red spots. They develop into small blisters, then change rapidly into large brownish crusts. These inflammations usually start on the face, but they can quickly spread to any part of the body that the hands touch. An antibiotic ointment prescribed by a doctor usually clears up the infection in a few days.

urges one to join others in experimenting with alcohol or drugs.

◆ Playmates

Toddlers enjoy being around other toddlers. Their eyes light up when they see a friend. When children of several ages are together, a toddler usually watches another toddler. Even though both obviously like to have other toddlers around, they still play independently of each other. They may exchange toys and quarrel over a single toy. At this stage, their play is not planned, and one play episode does not last very long.

Toddlers are often overwhelmed by large numbers of people. One or two other toddlers are usually enough for a play group or birthday party.

At age three, children usually play next to each other rather than with each other. There is little or no interaction or cooperation. The following conversation is typical of two three-year-olds. In this case, each one is pushing a toy vehicle along the sidewalk.

Elena: I have a great big truck, and I'm taking it to the dump.

Jose: I'm a fire fighter, and I'm in a hurry to put out a fire.

Elena: My mommy made me spaghetti for dinner.

Jose: I have a baby brother, and he can walk now.

Activity. Have students observe a group of preschoolers at play and describe what they see and hear. How do young children try to gain attention and approval from others?

Reference. See page 383 for information about solitary play, parallel play, and cooperative play.

Although these two children enjoy each other's company, they are not really playing together. They are talking but not listening to each other. Parents and caregivers should keep this in mind and not try to force children at this age to play directly with each other.

Four-year-olds' language and social skills have developed to the point where children of this age begin playing with each other. They may work together to build a garage for their vehicles or perhaps race them down a ramp. This stage of play requires the use of words to exchange ideas and the ability to plan activities.

At about the age of nine, playmates tend to separate themselves by gender. Boys play mainly with boys and girls with girls. Children of the same gender sit together during school activities unless a teacher assigns the seating. After school, they usually go off together in groups of the same gender. The groups may become organized into formal clubs, with secret code words and special signals. The clubs may even have officers, written rules, and regular meetings.

❖ Making Friends

Friendship is a new and important experience for many four- and five-year-olds. Three-year-olds talk a lot about friends. They may even make up imaginary ones. By age four or five, children tend to single out one or two of their peers as "best friends." Usually these are children who happen to live nearby or are brought together by their parents.

By age eight, most children deliberately select their own friends. Children choose other children as friends because they like them. Of all the children in second grade, Eric likes Glenn, Pam, and Angela best. They feel the same about him and each other. Gradually, as they play together, these four begin to think of themselves as a group of friends. They do have individual rivalries, however. Eric and Pam compete to see who is the fastest runner. Glenn sometimes complains that Angela is too bossy. Yet they all count on each other for approval and encouragement. Friendship may be short-lived at this age, but for now the four children enjoy their special relationship.

During high school, most teenagers have a small group of close friends. The group often serves as a miniature society, with leaders and followers, power struggles, and checks and balances. Many adolescents tend to conform to the styles, behavior, and expressed opinions of their friends. This conformity peaks around the ages of thirteen to fifteen. Although it continues throughout high school, older teenagers begin to develop their own individuality and sense of identity.

Friendships generally occur between children who have something in common. Parents of children who have trouble making

School-age children often play with children of the same gender. They form groups and may ignore others.

Discuss. What organizations in the community segregate boys and girls by gender during the school-age years? What might be possible advantages and disadvantages?

Problem Solving. Have students identify ways that children may be cruel to playmates, such as name-calling and choosing a child last for the team. How can parents, teachers, and other caregivers help in these situations?

DECISIONS ◆
◆ DECISIONS

Mario is four years old. When he is at a playground with children he does not know, he is very shy. Rather than joining in their play, he prefers to play alone. However, Mario enjoys playing with two friends whom he has known since infancy. Mario's father is very friendly and outgoing. He is concerned about his son's social development and has asked your advice. What will you tell him?

friends can encourage them to join a group such as a soccer team or science club. Many community and religious organizations have special youth groups. Sharing the same activities often leads to new friendships.

◆◆ Taking Turns and Sharing

Playing with others encourages the development of two important social skills: taking turns and sharing. Taking turns refers to getting equal chances to do something. For example, waiting in line at the slide is waiting to take a turn.

Sharing is a more complex social skill. The idea of sharing encourages generosity as

As children play together, they learn how to share and cooperate with one another. These are important skills that they will use throughout their lives.

Discuss. Who was your best friend when you were in kindergarten? Do you still have the same friend? Did you have a doll, animal, or "imaginary friend" as a best friend?

Problem Solving. Have students who have moved describe the adjustments they had to make to a new school and new friends. What was easy and difficult about the move? What can parents do to help children adjust to moving? See page 518.

opposed to selfishness. It includes a feeling of concern and respect for another person. This feeling makes one child care about letting another child have or use something they both want. Sharing is harder than taking turns. Children who feel secure and satisfied share voluntarily.

Learning to Share

To teach children to share, adults must help children feel good about themselves. Then they can take pleasure in seeing another child feel pleased. At home, parents should let children make decisions about what toys they want to share and which ones they would rather not share. For example, if a child invites a friend over, a parent might say, "You know, Josh will want to play with your toys when he comes." If the child says, "He can play with my blocks, but not with my teddy bear," the parent might respond, "All right, then we'll put the teddy bear away until Josh goes home."

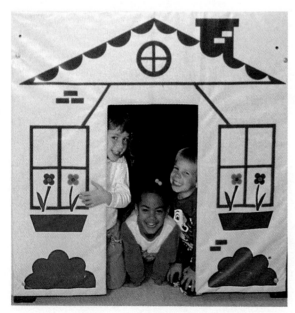

Learning to share involves a feeling of concern and respect for others. As children learn how to share, they develop empathy for other people's feelings.

When parents and caregivers see children sharing, they can say, "Bobby, I like the way you share your ball with Jennifer. She wanted to play ball, too." This gives Bobby a label for his act and empathy with Jennifer's feelings. The adult encouragement also makes him feel proud of himself. Children learn to share more easily if they play in small groups and get to know each other.

Sharing Possessions

Before children can share, they need to learn that their possessions really are theirs. To toddlers, ownership is often a matter of who has possession of an object at the moment. For example, Leroy's cup, plate, or chair may be his only for the duration of a meal. Thus he may think that "his" toys belong to him only for as long as he hangs onto them. When Carrie resists her father's efforts to talk her into giving Keiko a turn on her tricycle, he realizes it is best to accept Carrie's refusal. He also apologizes to Keiko and her mother, saying, "I'm sorry but Carrie just isn't able to share her tricycle yet."

To help toddlers learn that their possessions are indeed theirs, parents can provide each child with a place to store his or her own clothes and toys. This can be a few hooks for hanging jackets, special drawers for other clothes, and some shelves for toys. It may help to put labels with the child's name on the toys and clothes. Sometimes a child objects when parents want to pass certain toys down to a younger child. They should respect such feelings and allow the child to make the decision about giving up a toy.

In the classroom, toys and equipment are for all children to use. Teachers often say, "It's yours while you're using it." This means that when one child is through using the equipment, it is available for someone else. This concept of community property is new for most children when they enter school.

Problem Solving. Have students identify ways that parents can help a child learn to share. Why is it important for a child to learn this skill?

Discuss. Why would a child be willing to share some toys with a friend and refuse to share others? Are there times when children should not be made to share?

⸭ Cooperation and Competition

Four-year-olds begin to cooperate with each other as they play. Their developing language skills allow them to negotiate with each other about toys and types of games to play. They are learning to share and not to hurt each other's feelings. By cooperating children learn to play and work together.

Cooperative games, in which everyone has a chance to succeed, provide opportunities to learn and excel. Everyone can join in a game like balloon toss, in which a group of children try to keep a large balloon up in the air. They use their heads, not their hands. Nobody wins or loses, and the game continues as long as everybody is interested in playing. Cooperative games help develop children's physical and social skills. They give young children a chance to play with a minimum of competitive pressure.

By the end of the fifth year, children often become more competitive. Their games change to ones in which there are clear winners and losers. Many children become interested in simple competitive games, such as cards or board games.

Advantages and Disadvantages of Competition

Is competition good or bad for children? On one hand, competition encourages children to do their best. Those who try hard and take risks may find themselves rewarded. They have a good feeling about being the best at something. On the other hand, for every winner there has to be at least one loser. Young children are still developing their skills and abilities. To be labeled a loser can damage a child's self-esteem. Some children are able to handle competition at a young age; others are not.

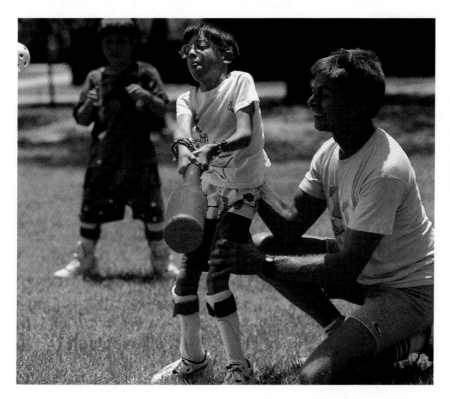

Games should help children develop physical and social skills, rather than create winners and losers. By encouraging everyone to succeed, parents help children learn to cooperate with each other.

Activity. Have students debate the pros and cons of competition. Each side must defend their viewpoints.

Activity. Have students describe a time when they won at competition and when they lost at competition. Ask them to describe their feelings after each experience.

Around the World

Rites of Passage

A rite of passage is a special event that marks the change in a young person's social status from child to adult. In times past, these events were formal ceremonies. For example, when a boy reached puberty in ancient Rome, he put on the toga virilis or "toga of manhood." This happened on March 17, during the Liberalia, a public festival honoring the Roman deities Liber and Libera.

Today, in some cultures a young person will be addressed differently when reaching adulthood. In England, a young boy is addressed as master. After puberty, he is addressed as mister. In Mexican villages, a niño (young boy) becomes a joven, and a niña (young girl) becomes a senorita.

In our culture, no one special celebration marks the change from child to adult. However, certain religious events do mark the passage into adulthood. These occasions include the Jewish bar or bat mitzvah, the Christian confirmation, and the Unyago, a ceremony based on African traditions and observed by some African-American church groups.

Other occasions are socially significant events. These include the quinceañera which celebrates a Latino girl's fifteenth birthday, the "sweet sixteen" party, and the "coming out" party that is popular in international circles. Graduation and commencement exercises are formal celebrations of educational achievements. Even informal occasions such as getting one's driver's license and reaching voting age are often times of celebration.

During elementary and high school, competition becomes more common. Most children know where they rank in various skills they are learning. They do well or poorly on a test; they are picked first or last for a softball team. Competition exists in athletics and other activities. The sprinter trains to come in first. The second chair violinist challenges the first chair. By developing their special talents and abilities, older children are preparing for the competition in the adult world. Competition can be a healthy part of growing up when the rewards are based on actual performance. Competition also helps many children develop leadership skills.

Managing Competition

Parents and caregivers can help children manage competition. Children should not be made to feel that they must always win. They need to learn how to lose comfortably and graciously. Parents can repeatedly point out that nobody wins all the time. Everyone is good at something. On the other hand, when children do win, parents may have to remind them not to gloat or boast about their success.

Competition often develops between siblings. Parents should avoid comparing siblings with each other. Asking Beth, "Why can't you get better grades like your brother does?" is no way to encourage her success in school. Neither is it a way to foster good relations between the children.

Many teachers use cooperative learning activities in the classroom. Instead of always competing with classmates, students learn to work together in small groups. They discuss information with each other, help each other understand it, and encourage each other to achieve. Social skills such as listening, sharing, encouraging, and resolving conflict are necessary for the group work to succeed. As adults, children will use these skills as they cooperate with others on the job or in the family.

Activity. Have students demonstrate a game for young children that promotes cooperation rather than competition.

Problem Solving. Ask students to discuss ways that children with disabilities can be helped to develop friendships and be involved in activities with other children. See Chapter 21 for information regarding children with special needs.

Awareness of Self and Others

Awareness of self emerges at about the age of two, when children first recognize themselves in the mirror. At this time, they start to refer to themselves as "me" in conversations. They also begin to learn whether they are girls or boys.

At the same time, children start to compare themselves to others of their own age. Preschoolers notice that some children are bigger and some are smaller than they are. Some have different colored hair or different colored skin. Such differences are usually accepted matter-of-factly. Unless cued by

Children gradually become aware of the similarities and differences among people. They accept these comparisons without judgment—unless they are taught differently by adults.

adults, young children do not feel one physical quality is better than another. Physical differences are interesting to children because they help children define themselves.

Preschoolers also notice ability differences among their peers. Joel is the best climber. Rose can print her own name, while Anita just makes scribbles. However, Anita is a fast runner—faster than Joel. In play groups, child care centers, and preschool programs, children learn what they can do compared to others.

Different personalities also show up in group play: "Shireen talks the most." "Carlos says funny things all the time." "Ray is mean." Group leaders soon emerge, and followers find their individual places in the group.

By the time children become adolescents, they have compared themselves with many peers. In the process, they come to realize the ways in which they are unique as well as the ways in which they are the same.

◆◆ Gender Awareness

Family and friends help children learn whether they are girls or boys. By age three, children know their own gender. They use clothing and hairstyles that help designate their gender. They also like to imitate parents and caregivers. Alicia, for example, clumps around the house in her mother's shoes. Billy likes to wear his father's caps. Sometimes young children imitate the behavior of the opposite gender. For example, Libby pretends to shave like her father. Mark imitates his mother putting on lipstick. Such play is normal as children learn about adult behavior.

During the preschool years, children learn to identify with adults of their own gender. Sometimes they may even show romantic feelings for a parent of the opposite gender. A boy may state, for example, that he intends to marry his mother. This may be his way of identifying with his father. Similarly, a little girl may form a special attachment to her father as a way of identifying with her mother.

When children are between four and six years old, they finally understand that girls grow up to be women who may become mothers and that boys grow into men who may become fathers. However they are often confused about husbands and wives. Their immature reasoning prevents them from thinking of people in more than one role.

Gender Roles

Young children learn their male or female roles from family members, friends, neighbors, and teachers. Watching family members who are the same or the opposite gender helps boys learn about being a boy, a son, and a brother. Girls learn about being a girl, a daughter, and a sister. Children also learn how both genders usually react to certain situations.

Children in single-parent families should be given the opportunity to interact regularly with relatives or friends of the opposite gender than the parent. This enables the children to learn certain aspects of that gender role. Without this natural experience, children may grow up to become uncomfortable with the opposite gender during adolescence, marriage, or parenthood.

Socially, gender roles have changed considerably over the past several years. In many families, all adult members have jobs outside the home. They often share the housework without regard to traditional gender roles. Both males and females care for the children. For such people, there is no such thing as women's work or men's work. There are only jobs to be done. In the workplace, many of the same kinds of jobs are held by both men and women. There are male nurses and secretaries as well as female ones. There are female and male doctors and executives.

Parents and caregivers should encourage children to develop their interests and abilities without regard to gender. Both boys and girls should develop physical skills of strength, agility, speed, and stamina. Both should learn to express emotions and to give and receive love. Both should learn to compete with others. These skills can help everyone live a happy and successful life.

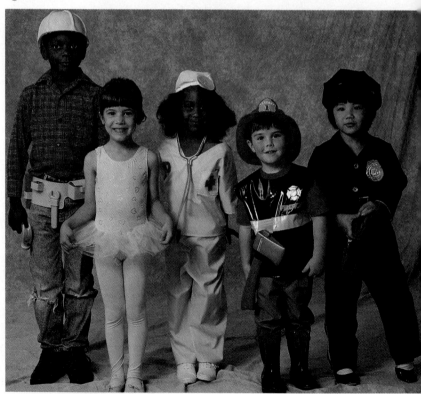

Children should learn about roles and jobs without regard to gender. Then they will be able to develop their own interests and abilities without limitations.

Discuss. How does the media influence gender roles? How has a movie or television show influenced your own awareness of gender roles?

Problem Solving. Ask students to describe ways that a single parent can provide role models of the opposite gender.
Activity. Have students identify fairy tales that reinforce traditional gender roles.

❖ Racial and Ethnic Awareness

Children become aware of racial groups and ethnic backgrounds as they compare likenesses and differences. People from many nations and racial groups exist together in neighborhoods, schools, churches, and shopping malls. Television and movies show people from around the world.

Today, many people want to be Americans and still maintain part of their cultural heritage. Instead of being viewed as a "melting pot," America is coming to be seen as a "salad bowl," where each ingredient maintains its separate character. As a result, many people describe themselves as African-Americans, Mexican-Americans, or Japanese-Americans.

In a kindergarten discussion about being Americans, a Chinese-American boy said, "I'm not American. I'm Chinese." The teacher attempted to help him understand that he could be both. "You are a Chinese-American, Derek. I think your grandparents lived in China and were Chinese, but you and your parents live in America. That makes you both Chinese and American. Derek disagreed. "No, I'm Chinese. My Daddy told me so."

Children at this age cannot hold two characteristics for one person or object in their mind at once. Not until Derek grows older will he be able to understand fully his heritage.

◆ ◆ *Self-Esteem* ◆ ◆

Children who are shy sometimes have difficulty joining in group activities. Other children may be rejected by a group they want to join. These social situations can be difficult for children. Parents and caregivers usually cannot change group behavior, but they can help a shy or rejected child develop his or her own interests. This, in turn, will give the child a sense of self-worth.

The United States Constitution calls for equal rights for all, regardless of race, religion, or national origin. Our laws protect each individual's rights. As people of different backgrounds live together in neighborhoods and communities, social skills are increasingly necessary to maintain good relations, peace, and order. Recognizing the rights of each individual and protecting those rights are obligations of everyone.

❖ Stereotypes

A **stereotype** is a standardized mental picture of a person or group held by many people. Most stereotypes are unfair. They classify people according to only their skin color or age or gender or even the way they speak or where they live. Stereotypes cause some people to think that those with a certain characteristic, such as red hair or athletic ability, are the same in all other ways. Because a few athletes act like bullies, some people incorrectly assume all athletes are bullies. As a result, these people act differently toward a person with athletic ability than they would if they were not influenced by that image.

What stereotypes have you heard? Maybe you have been told that all old people are absentminded or all teenagers are irresponsible. Perhaps you have heard that all blondes are dumb and all doctors are rich. There are other common stereotypes about men, women, racial groups, people from different regions, and people with disabilities.

Parents and caregivers should avoid making statements that reflect stereotypes. When they hear a child make such statements, parents need to point out why they are not true. It helps to talk about a person the child knows personally and to explain why this person does not reflect the stereotype.

Adults may overhear children playing in a very stereotyped way. For example, a boy might say to a girl, "You can't be the doctor.

Activity. Have students ask their parents or grandparents about their ethnic heritage. Then have students share information about their heritage with the class.

Activity. Ask students to observe and evaluate television shows which might be watched by young children. What stereotypes, if any, do they portray?

Only boys can be doctors." The boy's own pediatrician may be a male, and he may have seen only male doctors on television. Adults should say, "Of course women can be doctors" and explain why.

A more effective approach is to read children books that have pictures showing men and women in a variety of professions and activities. These might show fathers and mothers holding babies, male and female police officers, men and women driving trucks, and so forth. Such pictures teach children more effectively than do lectures from adults.

◆◆ Prejudice

The word *prejudice* comes from the word *prejudge,* meaning to make a decision about someone or something before having all the facts. **Prejudice** (PREJ-uh-dis) is an opinion or feeling formed without knowledge.

All people have prejudices of some sort. For example, some people think they do not like a certain food even though they have not tried it. Some people dislike other people of a certain color or religion—yet have never met any of those people. People with prejudices who gain additional information and experi-

ence often change their mind. They may discover they like broccoli or become friends with a person from a different ethnic group.

As children meet a wide variety of people, they learn that humans are alike in many ways. They play happily with children of various racial and ethnic backgrounds until someone tells them they should not.

Prejudice can hurt the self-esteem of both children and adults. This is especially true if they are judged on the basis of something they could not change even if they wanted to, such as gender or skin color. People prefer to be judged on skills, performance, knowledge, or behavior—characteristics over which they hold control.

Can new generations of children accept their classmates of various racial, ethnic, and religious backgrounds as equals in their social groups? At the very least, adults can help and encourage children to examine all the evidence before they decide to dislike a certain object or person. Children can learn that there are similarities and there are differences between people. However, the differences need not influence the way that people are treated. The world is much richer and more interesting with our wide variety of people than it would be if all people were alike.

Parents should help children learn to judge others according to their own experiences. This helps prevent the formation of stereotypes and prejudice.

Problem Solving. How do children learn stereotypes and prejudice? What should parents do when they hear their child mention a stereotype or a prejudice?

Activity. Invite a person born in another country to talk to students about his or her life as a child, including activities, games, and family life. Encourage students to identify the similarities between children throughout the world.

CHAPTER 18 REVIEW

Summary

- Acquiring the attitudes, beliefs, and behavior patterns of a society is known as socialization.
- The family is the main social influence of young children.
- Being the oldest, youngest, middle, or only child in a family affects the child's relationships with other family members.
- Most children seek acceptance from their peers, who play an important role in social development.
- Playing with others helps children learn to take turns, share, and cooperate and compete with others.
- All children should be encouraged to develop their interests and abilities regardless of whether they are male or female.
- Parents should avoid making statements that reflect stereotypes and prejudice.

Questions

p. 337 1. How do relationships help satisfy children's emotional needs?

p. 339 2. What is socialization? Why is it important?

p. 341 3. How does the birth order of children within the family influence their personality and relationships with family members?

p. 344 4. How can children maintain close relationships with grandparents and other relatives who do not live near them?

p. 344 5. What can parents do to make sure a child has opportunities to interact with other children?

6. What is peer pressure? p. 344

7. How can parents help children learn to share? p. 347

8. List at least one advantage and one disadvantage of competition. p. 349

9. How have gender roles changed over the past several years? p. 352

10. Why are stereotypes and prejudice so harmful to people? p. 353

Activities

1. As a class, list the socialization skills you have learned from your family, school, and community. Identify which ones children are usually taught and which ones they usually learn by observation.

2. What is your birth order in your family? Write a short description of how your experiences are similiar to and different from the description of your birth order in the chapter.

3. Observe a group of preschoolers at a park or playground. How do they interact with each other? What social skills do they display? What do they do to gain approval from others? Report your findings to the class.

4. Analyze four or five children's books. Find examples of stereotyped and non-stereotyped gender roles. Describe each.

Think About

1. Why does peer pressure seem to be stronger during adolescence than at any other period of life?

2. Why are many teachers emphasizing cooperative learning in their classes?

CHAPTER 19

Helping Children Learn

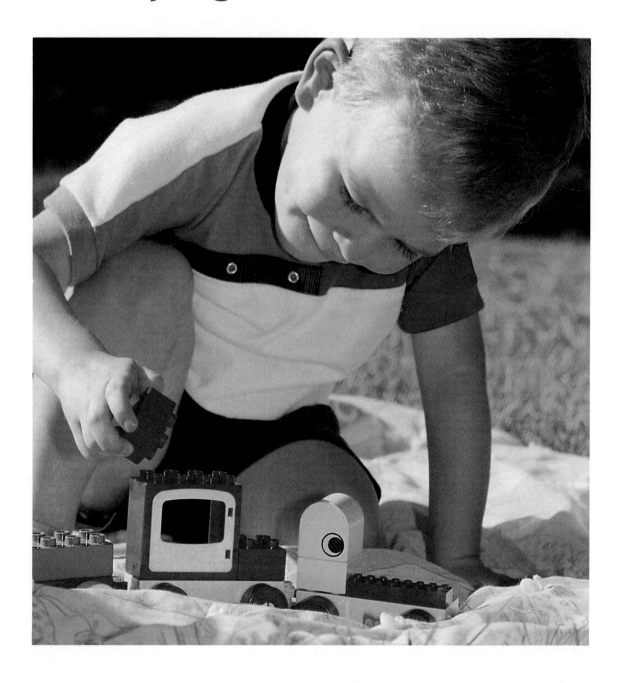

Objectives

This chapter will help you to:

- List and describe Piaget's stages of cognitive development.
- Explain various ways that children learn.
- Describe how children develop language skills.
- Give examples of ways that parents and caregivers can stimulate a child's cognitive development.

Vocabulary

stimuli
object permanence
preoperational stage
irreversible thinking
classification
seriation
concrete operations
conservation
reversibility
formal operations

concepts
creativity
reasoning
bilingual

"Spoon. Ball. Milk. Shoes," says two-year-old Nina, pointing to pictures in a book with cardboard pages. She cuddles against her father's arm as they hold the picture book in front of them.

"That's right," says Richard, Nina's father. "Good, Nina," he continues, as they turn the pages and Nina names each object. When a lamb appears, Nina does not seem to recognize it, so Richard says, "It's a lamb. It says, 'Baa, baa.'" Nina looks up at her father and repeats, "Baa." Richard realizes that Nina does not remember seeing a lamb. He decides to take her to the zoo sometime soon.

Parents and caregivers can have a major impact on children's lives by taking an interest in the children's cognitive development. This can make the critical difference that helps children succeed in school and achieve their goals.

Brain Development

Before birth and for two years afterward, the brain grows very rapidly. By the time a child is six years old, the brain is 90 percent of adult size. The portion of the brain that controls motor coordination and balance develops earlier and faster than other sections of the brain.

From early infancy, a child's brain is constantly being bombarded by **stimuli.** These are any things that arouse thoughts, feelings, or actions. Stimuli are received by one or more of five sensory areas: eyes, ears, skin, tongue, and nose. The information received by the senses is then transmitted to the brain, where it is recorded and stored. For example, a person remembers the perception hot. Then he or she learns to avoid touching something hot. In its ability to record, store, and manipulate information, the brain is far more complex than the computers we have today.

Chapter Opener. Ask students to read the opening scenario to the chapter. Ask these questions: How is Nina's father helping her cognitive development? What else can Robert do to help her learn about animals?

Activity. Ask students to develop a "senses game" in which children could close their eyes and identify sounds and smells. What could be included for toddlers and for preschoolers?

❖ Hemispheres of the Brain

The brain has two hemispheres, or halves—the right hemisphere and the left hemisphere.

- The right hemisphere specializes in spatial relationships, color, designs, and musical skills. It controls motor functions on the left side of the body.

- The left hemisphere specializes in language functions, such as speaking, hearing, reading, and counting. It controls motor functions on the right side of the body.

Most people use both hemispheres as they learn, but each person develops an individual learning style. Some people learn best by seeing an object and watching it work. These people are primarily using the right hemisphere of their brain. Other people understand something more easily if they are given a verbal description of it. They are primarily using the left hemisphere. One reason teachers give students both hands-on experiences and verbal or written explanations is that some students are left-brain oriented, while others are more right-brain oriented. For young children, whose brain is still developing, both hands-on activity and verbal explanation are crucial.

Children need a variety of stimulation and experiences for cognitive development. They learn from hands-on experiences, as well as from verbal explanations.

❖ Measuring Intelligence

For years, researchers have worked to devise methods of measuring intellectual capacity through IQ tests. A person's intelligence quotient, or IQ, is measured by relating that person's chronological age to his or her mental age, or score on the test. Different tests are written for people of different ages. On each test, a score of 100 is considered average because 50 percent of those taking the test score 100.

It has now been proved that IQ tests do not always tell us much about how intelligent an individual is. Such tests measure only language and logical-mathematical skills.

Today schools generally use achievement tests that measure knowledge in content areas. To be meaningful, these tests must be given by qualified testers and interpreted properly. However, achievement tests do not necessarily predict a child's future performance.

More About. Experts say that people retain 10% of what they hear; 30% of what they hear and see; 50% of what they hear, see, and read; 90% of what they hear, see, read, and do. The more senses a child uses, the greater the assimilation of knowledge.

Emphasize. Good nutrition is very important for young children because of the rapid growth of their brain. Malnourished children can suffer from permanent brain damage.

Cognitive Development

Learning is a complex process, and no single theory can fully explain how people learn. However, the work of Piaget has provided valuable information about how cognitive skills develop from infancy to adulthood. This information can help parents, caregivers, and teachers better understand how to stimulate the cognitive development of children at various ages.

❖ Piaget's Stages of Cognitive Development

In his studies of children, Piaget researched and defined the cognitive skills that children develop. From his observations, he formulated a sequence of four stages that describe how thought develops from infancy through adolescence. He theorized that these stages occur in the same fixed order, even though they vary in length and sometimes overlap.

Sensorimotor Stage

As you learned in Chapter 13, Piaget called children's way of thinking during their first two years the sensorimotor stage of cognitive development. In this stage, children move objects to their mouths, throw them, drop them, and so forth. Through this activity, children use all their senses to investigate their environment. What looks like only a physical activity has an important mental component. That is, children are figuring out new things to do with objects and new ways to think about them.

Toward the end of this stage, children learn that objects continue to exist even when they are out of sight. This is called **object permanence.** For example, toddlers will actively look for a ball that rolls out of sight.

If they feel lonely, they will search for a favorite toy.

Preoperational Stage

According to Piaget, the **preoperational stage** usually lasts from age two to age seven. In this stage, children begin to take more interest in the people and things around them. However, each child still sees these things only from an egocentric point of view.

Once children in this stage have made a decision about something, they have difficulty putting evidence together to form new conclusions. This is called **irreversible thinking.** That is, the child cannot go back in the thought process and think about things as they were. For example, a four-year-old can give a cracker to every child in the child care center. If the crackers are then taken away and put back on a tray, the child will probably be

During the preoperational stage, children learn seriation, or arranging items in order. They also begin to think in symbols. This is called symbolic thinking.

confused and think there are not enough for the children. The preschooler thinks there are more children because they are spread out over a larger area than the crackers are. The child cannot reason that only moments before, the crackers were matched up with the children.

During the preoperational stage, children learn to classify objects. **Classification** is the result of sorting or arranging items by common qualities or traits. For example, children can learn to sort out buttons according to shape. When someone asks whether there is another way to group the buttons, the children cannot see that they could group them by color or by material. Once children decide on a way to classify objects at this stage, they focus only on one characteristic.

Another skill is the ability to arrange items in order—according to size, number, or date. This is called **seriation** (SEER-ee-AY-shun). Children can learn to line up a set of plastic measuring cups in order of size, as well as nest them. They learn to arrange pennies according to date, putting a 1989 penny before one dated 1993 but after a 1986 coin. This is a skill that most children do not master until age five.

Children in the preoperational stage can also pretend and fantasize. When they push a toy truck, they imagine where it might be going. When they play with blocks, they have a definite goal in mind, such as building a house. They no longer just scribble but try to draw a picture of something. They have gone far beyond thinking only in terms of what they can see, hear, taste, smell, and touch.

Children in this stage also have the ability to think symbolically. That is, they can see an object not only for what it is but for what it represents. Mommy's coat is a coat, but it also symbolizes *going out*. A box wrapped in colorful paper and tied with ribbon represents a present. During play, an ordinary box can be

Self-Esteem

Children have their own individual way of acquiring new skills—their personal learning style. For example, one child learns skills quickly but often hurries and does a careless job. As a result, her parents have found that supervision during a task is more beneficial than criticism afterward. Another child masters new skills slowly but takes pride in doing each task well. This child resents supervision but welcomes comments on his performance. Parents need to respect these individual learning styles. This helps children develop self-confidence in their abilities.

turned into a boat, a plane, or a castle. A plastic cup may become a telephone receiver. Language skills, which involve the use of words as symbols, develop dramatically during these years.

Stage of Concrete Operations

The third stage of cognitive development, that of **concrete operations,** occurs when children are between ages seven and eleven. Piaget used the term *operations* to describe actions performed in the mind rather than physically. In other words, children in this stage can think about actions without physically doing them. Piaget used the term *concrete* because at this stage children can think only about real objects or experiences, not about abstract ideas or theories.

During this stage, children do mental operations such as relating things to each other in different ways. For example, two brothers are watching cars go by on the street where they live. Doug, who is four, notices that the cars are different colors. He is still in the preoperational stage of cognitive development. His brother, Kevin, is nine. When he looks at the cars, he sees small compacts, big station wagons, and sleek sports cars. He can identify the cars by brand name: Chevrolets, Fords, Chryslers. Kevin is in the concrete operational stage of cognitive development.

Children in this stage learn that objects keep the same weight, area, and number or amount when they are moved or rearranged. These properties remain the same, even though other characteristics—such as shape—may change. Piaget called this **conservation.** For example, if you pour liquid from a tall, narrow glass into a short, wide glass, a child under the age of seven will think there is less liquid in the short glass. However, a child who is able to understand conservation knows that the amount of liquid did not change. Piaget explained that by this stage, the child's rea-

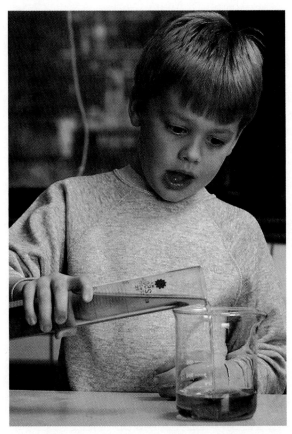

During the stage of concrete operations, children begin to understand the concept called conservation. They enjoy experimenting with amounts and volume.

soning has become more flexible, enabling backward and forward thinking.

Another example of this mental flexibility is **reversibility.** This is the ability to think about an object and change one's mind about it without having to manipulate it physically. For example, children in this stage can remember how the kitchen floor looked before they walked across it with muddy shoes.

During this stage, children also become able to take another person's point of view. Their thinking is more socialized and less egocentric than it was earlier. For example, children can now understand a friend's sadness or happiness or how another person views an object or experience. Children are also now able to understand rules.

Stage of Formal Operations

Piaget's fourth stage of cognitive development is called the stage of **formal operations.** It usually begins with adolescence and continues throughout adulthood. In this stage, individuals can perform mental operations that involve abstract or hypothetical objects or experiences without the help of real objects. Adolescents, for example, can think about prices without the aid of real money or even price tags. At age ten, these items were necessary.

Abstract thinking enables individuals to understand such concepts as right and wrong, legal and illegal. They can understand and discuss abstract questions: What is guilt? What is love? Adolescents and older individuals can consider complex ideas and relationships in order to arrive at a new awareness of issues, people, and objects.

At this level, adolescents can think about what might happen or what might have been the cause of something without really experiencing it. They are able to solve problems by just thinking. They can make plans and set

Activity. Have students demonstrate the concept of conservation through various activities. What game would help children learn this concept?
More About. Before the concrete operational stage, children

feel no need to explain how they arrived at a conclusion.
Discuss. What is *guilt* and *love*? What other abstract concepts are people in the formal operations stage able to understand and discuss?

goals for the future. They think not only in terms of realities but in terms of possibilities as well. "What might happen? What do I want to happen? What does the future hold?"

Progressing from Stage to Stage

The chart of Piaget's stages of cognitive development below shows how each stage builds on the previous one. Piaget cautioned that the average ages indicated are only approximations.

Studies have shown that education affects an individual's progress through the stages of cognitive development. Yet Piaget considered it wrong to try to push children ahead by teaching them about conservation, reversibility, and so on. Rather, he felt that children should be given a variety of life experiences. Through these experiences, children will learn to act on their environment in their own individual ways. They will discover and construct knowledge for themselves.

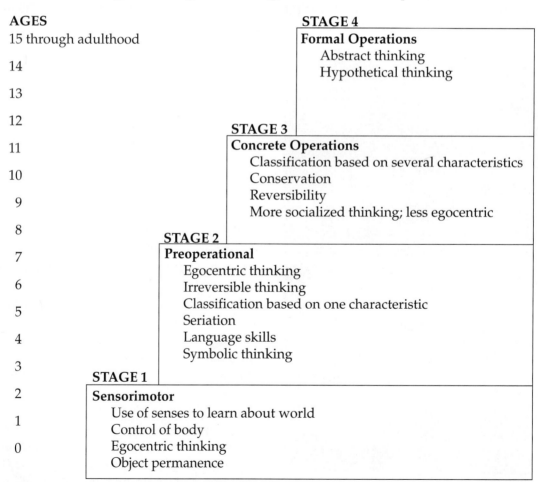

Piaget's Stages of Cognitive Development

AGES

15 through adulthood

14

13

12

11

10

9

8

7

6

5

4

3

2

1

0

STAGE 4
Formal Operations
   Abstract thinking
   Hypothetical thinking

STAGE 3
Concrete Operations
   Classification based on several characteristics
   Conservation
   Reversibility
   More socialized thinking; less egocentric

STAGE 2
Preoperational
   Egocentric thinking
   Irreversible thinking
   Classification based on one characteristic
   Seriation
   Language skills
   Symbolic thinking

STAGE 1
Sensorimotor
   Use of senses to learn about world
   Control of body
   Egocentric thinking
   Object permanence

Activity. Ask students to find out more information about Piaget. **More About.** J. P. Guilford, a psychologist, developed the theory that answering questions or solving problems requires five types of intellectual operations: cognition (recognizing a problem), memory (recall), convergent thinking (using information to find right answer), divergent thinking (using information to seek a novel solution), and evaluative thinking (thinking critically and making comparisons).

❖ Concept Development

Children are continually learning about their world. By learning to organize the information they receive from their senses, they are able to form **concepts.** These are general categories of objects and ideas formed by mentally combining their characteristics. Some concepts divide objects into classes, such as dogs, chairs, and toys. Others are concerned with qualities, such as size, shape, and quantity. The idea of time is an abstract concept.

Concept development begins in early childhood. It progresses from the ability to form simple concepts to an ability to form more complex concepts. Piaget's stages of cognitive development help explain concept development.

Children enjoy being able to identify objects by a specific characteristic. They usually learn to classify objects by color before they learn to classify by shape.

Activity. Ask students to create learning games that parents could use on a grocery shopping trip with two children, ages four and six.

Classification

Toddlers are able to make only general classifications. They often identify a wide variety of four-legged animals as "doggies." All different types of wheeled vehicles are "cars." Toddlers may link two unrelated events simply because they happen at the same time. Sara's birthday is July 4. It was several years before she realized that fireworks are not part of her own birthday celebration.

Preschoolers have trouble grouping objects if they have to consider more than one characteristic or feature. If shown a variety of wooden beads, for example, they will focus only on the beads' color. In contrast, school-age children can see that all the beads are wooden and most of them are white. They can put both perceptions together to see a relationship: "Most of the beads in this group of wooden beads are white."

School-age children can also classify different objects according to a single function. For example, they can group together a lamp, a flashlight, and a candle because all of these provide light. Moreover, school-age children usually understand the complex categories of relationships within a family. They know that their mother can be a sister, a daughter, an aunt, or a cousin to other people in the family.

Shape and Size

When toddlers match pegs to holes and fit smaller boxes into larger ones, they are learning concepts of shape, size, and spatial relationships. However, they cannot judge the size of an object that is far away because objects seem to be smaller when seen from a distance.

Toddlers can be taught to identify certain shapes, such as a circle, a square, a triangle. This is an early step toward reading because children must eventually be able to recognize the different shapes of the letters of the alphabet.

Activity. Have students assemble a group of objects with some similar characteristics. Then have students observe a group of preschoolers sort the objects into various categories.

By about age three, children can begin to learn the concept of size. Three-year-olds enjoy playing with empty cardboard boxes and plastic containers. Through trial and error, they learn that the smallest container fits into the middle-sized container which fits into the largest one.

Most preschoolers recognize the difference between a circle and an oval, between a triangle and diamond, between a rectangle and a square. Altogether, the average four-year-old recognizes eight different geometric forms. By age five, most children classify objects by shape rather than color.

Preschoolers are also learning about space. They begin to understand position words such as *above, below, inside, outside, in front of,* and *behind.* They can be helped by suggestions such as "Look behind the door" or "Put it on the table."

School-age children are aware of space relationships between their home, school, and neighborhood. Six-year-olds can follow a well-known route and point out particular landmarks along the way. They can name streets near their home and know where they are located.

Number and Quantity

A child's concept of number is based on personal experience with real objects. Children may be able to count by 10, 20, or even 100 and still not be able to count how many crackers are on a plate. Eventually, children begin applying the names of numbers to various objects, such as how many crackers are needed for their three friends.

By age six, most children can count to 20 or over. They may be able to add up to 10, with the help of their fingers. By this age, they can tell the value of certain coins, especially, pennies, nickels, and dimes.

Children enjoy manipulating numbers. First, they put them in strict sequence. Later they can skip-count by tens, then by fives, and eventually by even or odd numbers. These counting skills are useful in preparation for working with numbers later on.

However, counting skills and number concepts are not the same. Three-year-olds may be able to point out and count objects, but they do not understand the difference between "less" and "more." Four-year-olds understand the difference, but they still judge quantity by size. For example, "a lot of blocks" means a big pile of blocks, not a number such as 10 or 20. Not until age six or seven do children begin to think in terms of a certain number of units when judging quantity.

In many schools, children in the primary grades are introduced to mathematics through manipulating rods or shapes. They are able to see the effect of their actions. They realize that numbers stand for actual things that can be added to or taken away from a group. Outside of school, children practice their math skills through such activities as trading baseball cards and dividing candy among friends.

DECISIONS ◆ ◆ DECISIONS

Four-year-old Kari is proud that she can count from one to ten. She will repeat the sequence over and over. However, when her seven-year-old brother asks her how many plates are on the table, she gives the wrong answer. He laughs at her and says that she does not know how to count. Kari runs crying to her mother. What should her mother say to her daughter? What should she say to her son?

Problem Solving. Have students describe household activities that would help young children identify colors, shapes, size, number, and quantity.

Discuss. Why are teachers introducing mathematics to school-age children through manipulating rods or shapes? When does abstract thinking begin to occur?

Time

With television programs that come on the hour and half-hour and digital clocks that are easier to read than other clocks, it may seem as though children have a good sense of time. However, young children have very little real understanding of time.

Children's early concept of time is connected to their body rhythms and their family's schedule. For children under five years of age, time is often confusing. They think "a long time ago" means last week. According to research, a child of two understands the meaning of "now." At age three, the child understands "wait a minute," "today," "tomorrow," and "last night." At age four, the child understands the concept of "future" and can make plans for "next summer" or "next week." However, that same four-year-old may also ask, "When is summer?"

By age five, children can generally understand and use most ordinary time words. They know the days of the week, and they know them in the right order. They know how old they were on their last birthday—and how old they will be on their next birthday. They like to mark off the days on a calendar.

During the early school years, the concept of time is best taught when it can be related to something tangible or personal. A tadpole growing into a frog and a plant developing from a seed show one aspect of time. Children like to compare pictures of themselves at last year's birthday party with pictures taken this year. Eventually, they will be able to comprehend the idea of historical time so that dates farther back than a year will have meaning.

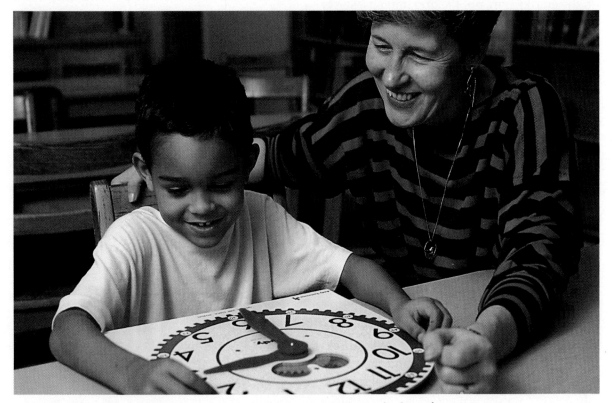

Around the age of five, children learn to tell time. They may also know the days of the week in the right order.

Activity. Have each student ask a preschooler to count as high as possible and then share the findings with the class.
Activity. Have students prepare questions about concepts of time, such as What did you do today? Yesterday? Last summer? Then have students present the questions to three-, four-, and five-year-olds and record responses. Compare the results.

Cognitive Activities

The learning process is very complex. Infants learn about the world by what they see, hear, smell, taste, and touch. As they mature, they are able to interpret the information they receive from their senses. Toddlers can name colors, repeat favorite sayings, and remember grandparents whom they see only once a month. They gather information by asking endless questions: "Why?" "What is this?" "How does it work?"

One type of learning is imitative. Babies watch other people and try to imitate what they do, such as waving and clapping hands. Another type of learning is cause-and-effect learning, or understanding that certain actions cause certain results. Gradually, four-month-old Vicky learns that pulling the ring on the cradle gym, not kicking her legs, starts the music. When four-year-old Kyle sees a meal being prepared, he understands something of how it is being prepared: "If you do this, then that will happen."

All the while, children are stretching their cognitive abilities. They continually add new information to their mental framework. With each new bit of information, the mental framework itself changes, adapting to the new information. Thus children are constantly building their ability to handle more complex ideas. At age six, Hannah can add numbers up to 20, and she can subtract numbers up to 10 from each other. As she goes on in school, she will learn how multiplication is related to addition. Still later, she will be ready for algebra and geometry. Eventually, she will develop higher-level thinking skills such as analysis, synthesis, and evaluation. *Analysis* is identifying elements and their relationships. *Synthesis* is combining elements into a single entity. *Evaluation* is determining the significance or quality of something.

Activity. Ask students to recall their earliest memories and then ask their parents at what age these incidents occurred.

◆◆ Memory

The use of memory—remembering people, objects, ideas, and events—is very important to the learning process. Two types of memory skills are recognition and recall. Babies first develop *recognition,* or the ability to realize that one has seen (or heard, smelled, tasted, or touched) something before. *Recall* is the ability to remember something that one has experienced or learned before—for example, where something has been placed.

One of the earliest indications of recall occurs when a toddler, after observing a toy being placed under a pillow, removes the pillow in order to find the toy. This is also an example of what Piaget called object permanence, as you will remember.

Techniques, called *mnemonic strategies,* can be used to help one's memory. For example, if you need to remember a list of items for a test, you might use the first letter of each item to spell a catchy word. Then, remembering the catchy word, you can recall the list for the test. To spell the word *arithmetic,* remember the sentence "*A rat in Tom's house may eat Tom's ice cream.*"

Most three-year-olds can remember their age. They may be able to recognize some letters and numbers.

Discuss. What mnemonic strategies have you learned to remember information? For example, use HOMES to remember the names of the Great Lakes: Huron, Ontario, Michigan, Erie, Superior.

❖ Curiosity

Around their third birthday, many children suddenly begin asking, "Why?" They ask this about almost everything. Every answer they get can lead them to another question. "Why don't the trees have any leaves? Why do leaves come out in the spring? Why isn't it spring now? Why is it winter?" All these questions help children learn how and why things happen as they do.

Parents, caregivers, and teachers must make every effort to listen to children's questions and answer them. Although these questions can test an adult's patience at times, they are essential to a child's early learning. Adults should try to answer the questions as clearly and as truthfully as possible. If adults do not know the answer to a question, they can ask the child what he or she thinks or simply tell the child they do not know.

Children whose questions are met with annoyance will eventually stop asking them. If their curiosity is dampened, children will become less enthusiastic about learning.

❖ Imagination

The imagination that children show in their play—alone or in groups—is evidence of their increasing cognitive development. Parents and caregivers may find that children are able to turn toys and objects into many different things. For example, Mary Beth had a set of plastic nuts and bolts that she used as "dirt" in her dump truck. The nuts and bolts became "corn" when she put them in the wagon attached to her tractor. When she put them in her "pocketbook"—an empty plastic bandage can—they were "money." While she played, she talked or sang songs to describe what she was acting out. All these activities show imagination, resourcefulness, and memory development.

As adults listen to children's conversations, they should be careful to distinguish between children's imagination and lying. The child who says, "There's a lion in my room" or who talks about make-believe playmates is using imagination. Such stories are not lies; they are signs of mental development

Playing dress-up gives children an opportunity to use their imagination and language skills creatively.

Problem Solving. A three-year-old has asked the same question repeatedly in the last five minutes. How should parents or caregivers respond? What are some common questions that children ask? How can parents answer these questions?

Discuss. What is the difference between imagination and lying? How can parents help children differentiate between reality and fantasy?

and should be encouraged. Adults should not worry that children will be unable to tell the difference between fantasy and reality. Children learn to make this distinction with the help of parents and teachers.

❖ Creativity

Creativity is the ability to produce something original and unique. It is closely related to imagination. To be creative, children use their imagination to make or invent new objects, ideas, or processes.

Creativity is often associated with artistic expression—music, art, drama, and dance. However, creativity takes place in homes, schools, offices, factories, and research laboratories and on farms. Language is a daily creative expression because individuals continuously pull words from their memory to create new sentences.

In school, children use creativity for new thoughts, ideas, and projects. If their only educational task were to recall what others tell them or to imitate what others do, then new ideas would never be generated. Creative ideas are needed to develop new products and new approaches that will benefit society. Creativity promotes progress.

Children should begin early to practice the creative process that they will apply throughout their lives. Parents and caregivers should encourage children to draw, tell stories, build objects, write poems, play a musical instrument, dance, and even daydream.

❖ Reasoning and Problem Solving

Reasoning is the ability to think logically, to make judgments, and to form conclusions. It is basic to making decisions and solving problems. The process involves several steps:

- Making a careful analysis of a situation.
- Thinking through possible solutions.
- Choosing a solution.
- Evaluating that solution.

Children begin by solving problems early. They figure out that by getting up on a chair they can reach the kitchen cabinet to get a cookie. At first, their reasoning is very egocentric, or focused on their own self-interest, in this case, getting a cookie. Later on, children are able to understand concepts such as conservation and reversibility.

Children need opportunities to develop their reasoning and problem-solving skills. Parents and caregivers can ask: "How could you solve this problem?" "Which is the best solution?" "Did you make the right choice?" These questions help children learn to think through problems and avoid snap judgments.

Parents can encourage children's cognitive abilities by talking to them. Children learn by asking questions and expressing their own thoughts and ideas. They also learn to connect new information with the knowledge they already have.

Activity. Have students observe a group of preschoolers during dramatic play. (See pages 388-389). Ask students to record the different roles that the children pretend to be and the various items that the children use as props during their play.

Problem Solving. Ask students to list specific ways that parents and caregivers can help children develop problem-solving skills.

Language Development

A child's gradual mastery of language is perhaps the most striking cognitive change. It is also the one most easily observed.

Language has two aspects. One is *productive language,* or the ability to speak. The second is *receptive language,* or the ability to understand words spoken and written by others.

◆◆ Productive Language

Once children begin saying words, they make very fast progress. The average twenty-month-old can say 50 different words and ten different phrases.

Productive language greatly increases communication between toddlers and other family members. It also makes toddlers better able to control their world. They may say, "No" or "Go out," for example.

Children develop productive language by imitating the speech of family members and others around them. Yet children also create their own grammatical forms. A child who says, "I get down" may never have heard parents or siblings say the sentence. The child alone has arranged the words, drawn from his or her own storehouse of words.

◆◆ Trial and Error in Early Speech

Observers sometimes describe the speech of young children as having a telegraphic quality. This means that each statement contains just enough words to get the message across. When a toddler says, "I get down," it means the child is through eating and wants to get out of the high chair.

Young children differ in their ability to use pronouns. A two-year-old may refer to herself by her given name, saying, "Susie wants a cookie." Another child will use the pronoun *I* much earlier.

Children practice grammar by trial and error. Of course, in the early stages of speaking, they make many mistakes. Those mistakes are often humorous, but family members should try to avoid laughing. Laughter can make children feel they are being ridiculed and inhibit them from practicing speaking.

Around the World

Nonverbal Communication

Children around the world learn to communicate nonverbally as well as verbally. They do this by observing the people around them. This is important because different cultures use different nonverbal signals.

For example, the way North American children wave "bye-bye" is the signal for "come here" in India. When North American children learn to count on their fingers, they start with a fist and release one finger at a time. When Japanese children do it, they start with an open hand and bring the fingers toward the palm, one at a time.

Children also learn how far apart people stand when talking to each other. This distance is called *personal space.* In some cultures, good communication cannot take place unless both people stand close enough to feel each other's breath. In other cultures, this type of closeness makes people feel uncomfortable. In North America, strangers stand farther apart than do close friends. However, they may slowly move together to show friendliness. Invading another person's personal space is considered very rude in many cultures.

Interestingly, many of the language mistakes children make have a certain logic to them. For example, five-year-old Joseph ran into the house and exclaimed, "My cat eated a big mouse!" His mother corrected him: "You mean *ate.*" "Yes," Joseph replied, jumping up and down, "My cat ated a big mouse, every bit of it!" Joseph was using a rule of grammar he had unconsciously learned—that we form the past tense of verbs by adding *ed* to them. In this sense, his choice of words was logical. All children will need to spend time learning the irregular rules of the language.

◆◆ Enjoying the Fun of Language

By age four, children enjoy coining new words, rhyming words, and experimenting with words. Five-year-olds begin to show a blossoming sense of humor. Most six-year-olds have a large enough vocabulary to understand the humor of simple puns or plays on words. They may appreciate two meanings of a word, or two words that sound the same but mean different things. They will laugh about a bare bear or a hoarse horse. Poems, riddles, songs, and humorous stories that use such wordplay are a delight to this age group.

School-age children take pride in saying long words such as *antidisestablishmentarianism.* They may not know what it means, but they have fun showing others that they know how to pronounce it. They are also beginning to use codes, passwords, and secret languages in group play with their friends. Their vocabulary is growing fast. By the age of ten, the average child understands more than 5,000 words and by the age of twelve, more than 7,000 words. New words are acquired in all sorts of ways: from television, books, conversations, and school lessons and trips.

School-age children have fun with language. They enjoy puns, wordplays, rhymes, riddles, and secret codes.

Activity. Write one or more riddles on the chalkboard and have students guess the answers in writing. Award points or prizes for correct answers.

Activity. Have students listen to a group of preschoolers or school-age children at play. Ask them to write down remarks the children make which evoke laughter.

◆ Health & Safety ◆

Speech Problems

Speech problems are the most common physical disability in children. These problems include stuttering, stammering, garbled speech, repetition of words, and muddled sentences. The cause may be physical or emotional.

Some speech problems stem from hearing difficulties. Most children learn to speak by listening to others. If children do not hear well, they may not learn to speak properly.

Sometimes physical deformities can interfere with the way a child speaks. These include problems with the shape of the child's jaw, lips, palate, or teeth. After corrective surgery, the child's speech usually improves.

Some speech problems are caused by an injury to the brain. Others are the result of a genetic defect, such as Down's syndrome. Therapy can often aid the speech development of children with these conditions.

Emotional problems can also cause speech problems to develop or worsen. For example, children who are embarrassed about their speech may become very self-conscious in school and social situations. As a result, they sometimes develop emotional problems in addition to their speech problems.

Early detection of speech problems is important so that children can receive treatment before a problem worsens. Speech pathologists are specialists who work with speech and language problems. Because of the relationship between speech and hearing, many are also trained as audiologists, specialists in hearing problems. These health care professionals work closely with doctors and psychologists. Together, they can develop a special treatment program that best meets each child's individual needs.

◆ Being Bilingual

Being **bilingual** means being able to speak two languages. Many children in this country begin life speaking a language other than English. Then they learn English as a second language in preschool or elementary school. Often their parents want them to maintain their native language so they can converse with relatives and others who also speak that language.

Growing up bilingual has a number of advantages. Children learn languages very quickly. They are able to leap language barriers much faster than adults can.

Children who know two languages are often very competent in mathematics. This may be because mathematics requires abstract thinking, just as shifting from one language to another does.

Bilingual children may at first be slower than other children to develop speech because they are learning two words for each concept. However, in the long run, they often become very skilled in both languages. If they use both languages as they grow up, they will be able to communicate with more people throughout the world.

In the past, non-English-speaking children in the United States were placed in an English-speaking environment when they began school. All lessons were taught in English. Many of these children fell behind and struggled to catch up with their class-

Emphasize. Parents may be concerned that their child needs speech therapy because of mispronouncing words. Proper pronunciation is a maturation process. (The *L* sound is at a high level, so young children may say *yamp* instead of *lamp*.)

Discuss. How many of you are bilingual? What are the advantages and disadvantages of being bilingual? Have any of you been in other countries and not able to communicate with those around you? How did you feel?

mates. Not only their academic performance but also their self-esteem suffered. Now most schools offer bilingual programs if there are a sufficient number of children from a language group. In these programs, non-English-speaking children are taught the various school subjects in their native language while they also study English. Once the children have mastered enough English, they join the regular classes taught in English.

❖❖ Learning to Read

Among the language skills children are expected to acquire during the early school years is the ability to read. Some children feel—or are made to feel—that they are behind if they do not learn to read in first grade. This is unfortunate because some children are not ready to read in the first grade or even in the second grade. Their nervous system or visual thinking processes may not be sufficiently developed.

If children are pushed to read before they are ready, the immediate result may be failure. Once a child gets an early sense of academic failure, that self-concept can be carried over into the later school years.

Most children are ready to learn to read by second grade, when they are seven years old. Yet even then,

children's sense of language is gained mainly through their ears rather than their eyes. In the past, children were more likely to amuse and inform themselves by reading. Today, many children watch television instead, so they are more used to spoken language than to written language. If children are often read to when they are toddlers and preschoolers, however, they tend to become interested in reading despite the attractions of television.

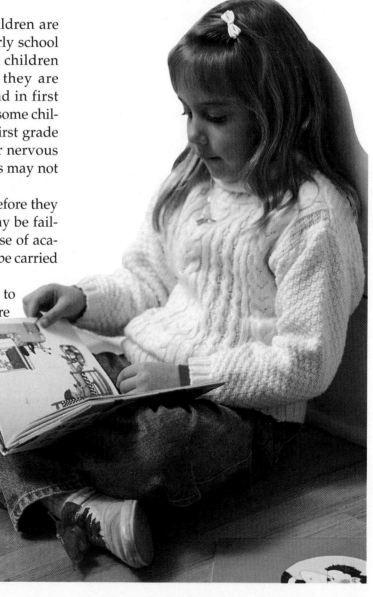

Receptive language includes the ability to understand written words. Some children begin reading at a young age. Other children are not developmentally ready to read until first or second grade.

Discuss. What stories do you remember being read to you when you were young? Why did you like them? What do you remember about the experience of having a parent or other caregiver read to you?

Activity. Have students research the phonics method of teaching reading to children. What are the advantages and disadvantages?

Stimulating Cognitive Development

Most psychologists agree that the environment in which a child grows up plays an essential role in the child's cognitive development. An environment that is rich in stimulation and offers a variety of experiences helps promote cognitive development. An environment that lacks stimulation hampers it.

At home and at school, children need to engage in activities that stimulate their cognitive abilities. They will not read if there are no books, and they will not draw if there are no drawing materials. Such materials do not have to be expensive to be useful to children. Books can be borrowed from public libraries. Drawing materials can consist of crayons and old newspapers or the blank back sides of letters and other paper. The important thing is that materials and activities be easily accessible so that children make use of them. In this way, children can find something cognitively worthwhile to do when there is "nothing to do."

❖ Exploring the Physical World

Each child starts out in a world that consists of his or her particular home and community. The child's first task is to explore that world. Without the help of parents or caregivers, the task is impossible. In the child's first years, these people can simply take the infant or toddler out in a stroller. Not only does this give the child a change of scenery, but it introduces the child to new people, plants, animals, buildings, and the weather.

Adults' questions and comments help the child learn to be an observer of the world. Allowing the toddler to explore—to see what is on the other side of a fence, for example—can teach important lessons about new sights and sounds.

On walks around the neighborhood, children can meet other people, see new sights, and hear different sounds. In this way, they learn more about their community and the world in general.

School field trips increase children's knowledge and make them curious about their world. For instance, on a trip to the local fire station, children learn about fire prevention and safety. They are reassured that fire fighters protect them night and day with all sorts of wonderful equipment.

❖ Learning New Words

Talking with children and listening to them are the best ways to help them develop language skills. With each new experience, children learn words that label and describe that experience. One of the easiest ways to help children increase their vocabulary is to describe activities that are taking place. On a shopping trip, parents can name each object that goes into the shopping cart. When Jean watches her father do household chores, he explains that he is vacuuming *under* the chair, dusting *over* the doorway, and putting an empty container *into* the garbage pail. Illustrating words with actions helps young children grasp their meaning.

It is necessary to use simple words and short sentences when giving instructions to toddlers. At other times, parents and caregivers should talk to them as they would to older children. This gives the toddlers a sense of the richness and flow of language.

Books, songs, and word games can enrich both listening and speaking skills. Pretend games, such as housekeeping or workshop play, encourage vocabulary development. Children who are not yet writing can dictate a letter or story that an adult writes down.

Parents should be sure to save the letter or story for later reference.

◆◆ Reading Books

Children enjoy having someone read books to them. Sitting on a parent's lap while listening to a bedtime story is one of the most treasured activities of a child's day. Parents or caregivers should encourage young children to think about and express what they know as they point out and name the objects they see in a book. For toddlers, books should have only a few items and only a word or two on each page. As children grow older, books can teach them about people, places, and situations that they may never experience firsthand.

Children also enjoy handling books and looking at them by themselves. Books made of cloth are especially useful for this purpose when children are very young. Books with hard cardboard pages are easy for toddlers to turn.

Unfortunately, some popular children's stories, fairy tales, and nursery rhymes send negative messages, often about male and female roles. Others can cause false expectations.

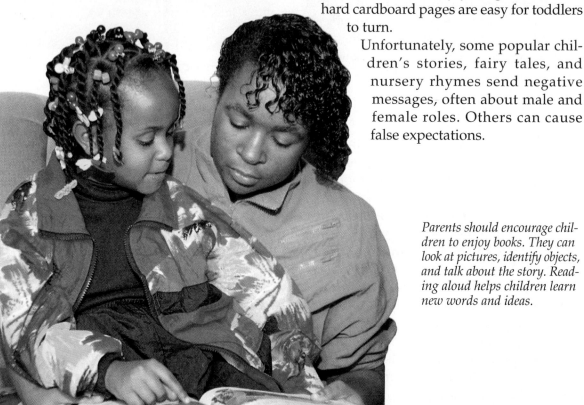

Parents should encourage children to enjoy books. They can look at pictures, identify objects, and talk about the story. Reading aloud helps children learn new words and ideas.

Activity. Invite a children's librarian to talk to students about the best books for toddlers and preschoolers. Have the librarian suggest helpful techniques to use when reading to children.

Activity. Ask students to volunteer to read to toddlers or preschoolers. Then have them discuss and compare their experiences.

Some of these myths are:

- Some day my prince will come.
- Princes are handsome, smart, and powerful; women are beautiful, charming, and helpless.
- Stepparents are evil.
- Men are rescuers; women need to be rescued.
- They lived happily ever after.

If parents and caregivers read such stories to children, they should point out the difference between fantasy and reality. They can help children develop realistic expectations about their own roles and abilities. Today, it is unrealistic for a woman to expect someone else to take care of her. Women can be smart, successful, and adventurous. Men can be sensitive, helpful, and caring. These traits are not limited to only one gender or the other. By talking with children about these messages, parents and caregivers can help strengthen children's self-esteem.

❖ Supervising Television

Television, too, can expand people's knowledge of the world. "Television is a marvelous educator and an awful curse," exclaimed one parent. "It is marvelous," he said, "because there are some worthwhile programs that teach my children things I never could. On the other hand, it takes time from the moments the family spends together."

It is important for parents to supervise and set rules limiting children's television viewing. Parents should acquaint themselves with the best in children's programs. Then they can select the programs worth watching and turn off the set at other times. Parents should not let the television set become a babysitter. That is, they should not allow a child to watch television just to keep the child occupied and out of their way.

Watching television is a passive activity. It requires children to sit and take in stimuli. Children do not learn well just by listening and watching. They need to get their hands on objects and to be with other people to understand their world. Television does not give children the opportunity to ask questions. It also moves too fast to allow children time to think about what they are seeing.

Parents should watch programs along with their children. Then they can discuss the programs and clear up any misunderstandings. They can also soothe any fears that may arise. Parents should be especially careful if they allow children to watch television beyond the family hour in the evening. After that time, programs with more violence are aired. Adults should turn off the set when violent or frightening programs come on when children are present.

DECISIONS ◆ ◆ DECISIONS

Dean and Nancy have two school-age sons. Lately, the boys keep pleading to stay up late in order to watch several popular television programs. They say all their friends watch the shows and talk about them at school. The boys feel left out if they have not seen the same shows. However, Dean and Nancy are concerned that their sons already watch too much television. They want them to get more physical exercise and to go to bed at a regular time. They discuss their problem with you. What advice do you give them?

❖ Using Computers

Increasingly, children have access to computers at home and at school. Special computer software programs can help children learn everything from art to zoology. Many of these software programs are designed to teach reading, mathematics, and perceptual skills for specific age groups. Being exposed

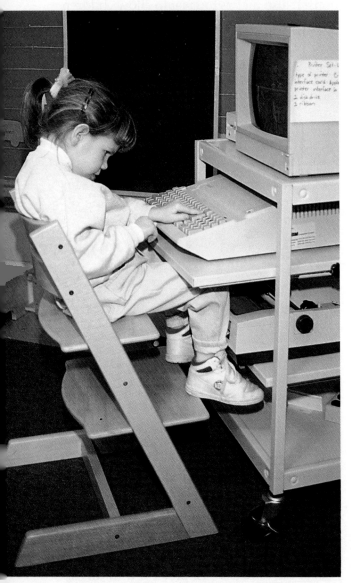

Special software programs can help children learn various cognitive skills, from classifying shapes to spelling words.

to computers at an early age enables children to develop computer literacy quickly.

Word processing on the computer is fascinating to children who are becoming interested in writing letters and stories. They enjoy seeing words appear on the screen and then moving them around or making them disappear.

Allowing children to experiment with a computer helps them become familiar with the alphabet and with directions. Young children enjoy dictating a story and seeing it produced in print for a book they can put together.

❖ Providing Extra Activities

Parents and caregivers can also stimulate cognitive development by providing a wide variety of activities for children. Most communities have concerts, plays, and museum exhibits especially for children and their families.

Trips are wonderful learning opportunities, whether they be a visit to an orchard at harvest time or a bus trip downtown. On a longer trip or vacation, parents can help children benefit from the experience by learning in advance something about the place they will visit. Library books and children's encyclopedias are good sources of information. If parents take the time to prepare the children and themselves in advance, the whole family will get the most out of the trip as a learning experience.

If possible, parents should take their children to see where they work and to spend a little time with them there. One five-year-old set up an "office" in her home after she visited her mother's office and watched her mother work for a morning. Being a worker is an important part of adult life, and parents should help children form some idea of what workers do.

Activity. Have students gather information about computer software programs that can help children learn. What are possible advantages and disadvantages of computer learning?

Activity. Ask students to describe a special vacation that they enjoyed with their family.

CHAPTER 19 REVIEW

Summary

- Intelligence is difficult to measure.
- According to Piaget, cognitive development proceeds in four stages: sensorimotor, preoperational, concrete operations, and formal operations.
- Children learn by arranging what they discover through their senses into general categories or concepts.
- Between the ages of two and six, most children learn concepts related to shape and size, number and quantity, and time.
- Memory, curiosity, imagination, creativity, reasoning, and problem solving develop cognitive abilities.
- Language development occurs in a gradual sequence.
- Parents and others can stimulate cognitive development by letting children explore their surroundings; by talking, listening, and reading to them; by watching worthwhile television programs with them; and by providing them with a variety of activities.

Questions

p. 358   1. Name the two halves of the brain and describe the functions of each.

p. 359   2. Name Piaget's four stages of cognitive development and list the characteristics of each stage.

p. 359   3. What is object permanence?

p. 363   4. How do children begin to learn the concept of size?

p. 367   5. Why should parents always listen to and answer children's questions?

p. 368   6. List the four steps in the reasoning process.

7. How do children develop productive language?   p. 369

8. What are the advantages of growing up bilingual?   p. 371

9. How can parents encourage children to read?   p. 374

10. Why should parents supervise and set limits on children's television viewing?   p. 375

Activities

1. In groups of three or four students, develop a learning game for one of Piaget's cognitive stages. Present your game to the class.

2. Using an audio cassette, record the productive language of one or more toddlers, preschoolers, and kindergarteners. Analyze your findings. Play portions of your tape for the class.

3. Plan three field trips in your neighborhood that would appeal to kindergarten children. Write a report describing each trip and explain what the children might learn from it.

4. Design a book for a toddler. Use cardboard for the pages and include a few words and lots of pictures. (Draw the pictures yourself or cut them out of old magazines.)

Think About

1. Why is imagination and creativity so important in all areas of life?

2. Your seven-year-old nephew tells you that watching television is more fun and more interesting than reading. What is your response?

CHAPTER 20

Value of Play

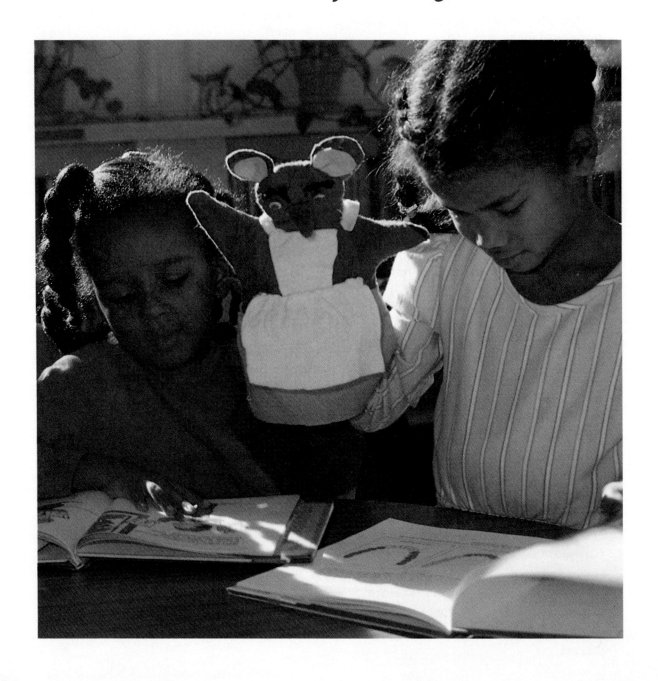

Objectives

This chapter will help you to:
- Relate the value of play to children's physical, emotional, social, and cognitive development.
- List factors to consider when choosing toys for children.
- Explain how different play activities can contribute to a child's learning.
- Discuss ways that parents and caregivers can guide children's play activities.

Vocabulary

play
solitary play
parallel play
cooperative play
exploratory play
dramatic play
collage

Ashley, an eight-month-old, sat on the carpet. She was put there by her mother, who had left the room for a few moments to wash her hands. On the floor near the baby were a number of colorful toys.

Ashley sat for only a moment, then she curled her right leg under her, leaned forward, and began crawling to a low table nearby. She used the table to pull herself up. Once standing, she discovered something—her mother's new magazine with its fresh, crisp cover. Ashley's chubby hand reached out and grasped the magazine. She plopped to a sitting position, pulling the magazine down with her. Then she crushed the paper and pulled it toward her mouth. The colorful cover came off the magazine. Ashley held it out triumphantly as her mother returned. "All your toys, and this is what you play with?" her mother laughed.

What Is Play?

When play is mentioned, most people typically think of toys. Yet an infant who is exploring a new world has not yet learned the difference between toys and other objects. Everything can be interesting to taste, hold, drop, watch, or carry. Infants investigate things by putting them in their mouth. They use their senses—taste, smell, sight, hearing, and touch—to explore their world.

Play is defined as any activity that individuals choose to do. It is fun and self-motivated. Often play is spur-of-the-moment activity that goes nowhere in particular and leads from one thing to another. Play may involve body movement, problem solving, and creativity. During play, a child often strives to use new physical and mental abilities. Psychologist Jerome Bruner suggests that through play, children extend their ability to move, think, reason, talk, and relate to other people.

Play uses energy and helps reduce tension. The difference between play and work becomes clear as you observe children.

Play Enhances Development

Healthy children are constantly learning. Parents and other caregivers can help this process by creating an environment that is stimulating and offers many opportunities for a variety of play. A child's age determines which activities are appropriate. Play aids all types of development: physical, emotional, social, and cognitive.

Play enhances children's physical, emotional, social, and cognitive development.

◆◆ Physical-Motor Development

Play activities that require use of the body are probably the most common. At an early age, children begin working on motor skills and seem to relish doing so. For a three-month-old, such play may mean reaching toward a mobile that is hung out of reach over the crib. A six-month-old may practice rolling over, and a five-year-old may go hand-over-hand on a trapeze swing. New motor skills make life much more interesting, and children naturally use these skills in their play.

Unfortunately, some parents and care-givers do not realize how important motor skills are in children's overall development. These individuals are inclined to limit children's active running and climbing because space is limited or because they fear the children will get hurt. Some parents are content if their children sit quietly for long periods in front of the television set. Others may not want to bother dressing children to go outdoors or do not want to go outside themselves to supervise play.

Some teachers in schools and child care centers do not consider activities that encourage physical development to be as important as those that promote cognitive development. They may prefer to keep children sitting at tables for long stretches playing learning games. Yet children can accomplish much of the same mental learning when they are running, climbing, and investigating outdoors.

Practicing motor skills is vital for both girls and boys. Children of both genders love and need to run and play, climb and jump. Very often, adult attitudes shape the way children behave. Some parents and caregivers feel that girls should not climb trees or play in an active, unrestrained way. Yet discouraging such activity may keep girls from developing strong, healthy bodies. It can also prevent them from exploring and learning about their environment. Both girls and boys must learn to work with and control their bodies.

Toys and Equipment for Practicing Large Motor Skills

As you learned earlier, large motor skills involve the control and use of large muscles, especially those in the arms and legs. These skills include walking, climbing, throwing, and catching. Most children practice these skills naturally if given the space, the time, and perhaps the friends to play with them.

Kiddie cars and wagons encourage walking skills in toddlers not yet ready for pedaling. Pull toys also invite a child to walk around the room or yard.

Balls are one of the oldest and most popular toys for stimulating large motor skills at all ages. Toddlers enjoy rolling balls along the floor. For them, balls should be large—8 to 10 inches in diameter—and made of soft material such as rubber, foam, or plastic. Finger holes or spaces in balls can make them easier for little fingers to grasp. Older children enjoy a whole range of ball games, starting with a simple game of catch.

A climbing gym with a slide and enclosed areas is popular in many yards, playgrounds, and child care centers. It invites children to climb stairs, sit and slide down, crawl under obstacles, and sit inside a hidden space. Similar but smaller climbing equipment can be purchased for the home. Indoors or outdoors, such equipment challenges children's large motor skills and balancing ability.

Games such as hide-and-seek, tag, and hopscotch can provide plenty of physical play, and they require no equipment. Tricycles, skates, and bicycles can encourage active play and help children develop good balance. These items can usually be obtained second-hand from friends, garage sales, or thrift shops.

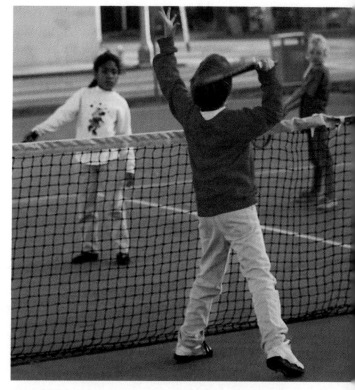

As children grow older, individual and team sports help them continue to develop their large motor skills.

School-age children enjoy activities such as bicycling, skating, jumping rope, gymnastics, jogging, or dancing. Many become involved in team sports such as soccer, softball, baseball, and basketball. Both individual and team sports help adolescents release energy and build physical fitness.

Toys for Practicing Small Motor Skills

Small motor skills involve the control and use of small muscles. Infants enjoy playing with blocks they can grasp in their hands. The blocks should not be so small that the infants can put them in their mouth and swallow them, however. Adults and older children can encourage a baby to pick up a block and drop it into their hand or into a plastic cup. All they need to do is hold out their hand or the cup and say, "Give me the block, please."

Activity. Have students plan three large motor skills activities for preschoolers. What safety precautions must be considered?
Activity. Ask students to create five games that could be played with a six-year-old and a large rubber ball.

Activity. Have students plan an obstacle course for children on three-wheeled bikes, using boxes, chairs, and cylinders. Have preschoolers try out the course. Discuss what concepts the children might have learned from the activity.

Puzzles allow children to practice eye-hand coordination. Toddlers' puzzles should have no more than six to nine large pieces. Nesting cans or cubes that can be placed inside each other or stacked to build a tower also provide a challenge that toddlers enjoy. Stacking rings that children can place over a spindle are another popular toy. Parents need not buy such toys but can collect different-sized tops from cottage cheese, yogurt, and margarine containers. Children enjoy sorting through these or putting them all in a box or can, then dumping them out again.

Parents can make other toys from items around the home that will help toddlers with small motor skills.

Other items appropriate for toddlers are large crayons, chalk, and paint brushes. Young children generally grasp these with a fist and take large, whole-arm strokes. Toddlers need large sheets of paper for their drawings.

All kinds of puzzles, blocks, erector sets, lacing kits, cars, and dolls stimulate the practice of small motor skills. Many of these objects are more appropriate for four-year-olds

◆◆ *Health & Safety* ◆◆

Protection from the Sun

As people grow older, their skin begins to wrinkle and sag. However, too much sun early in life can speed up the aging process. Ultraviolet rays from the sun can cause sunburn and damage to the layers of skin cells. Even worse, excessive sun exposure may result in skin cancer many years later.

All children should be protected from the sun, even those with dark skin. Although dark skin has extra melanin, which provides some natural protection from sunburn, people with a dark complexion can get wrinkles and skin cancer.

Here are some ways to protect children from the harmful effects of the sun.

• Use a hat with a large brim to protect the child's head, back, and shoulders. The hat will also help shade the child's eyes.

• Apply a sunscreen lotion or cream with an SPF (sun protection factor) of 15 or more to the child's skin. Sunscreens are rated by number from SPF 2 to SPF 50. The number indicates a sunscreen's

ability to screen out the ultraviolet rays. Choose a sunscreen recommended for children. Many babies have skin that is sensitive to fragrances and other additives used in products designed for adults. Reapply a sunscreen at least every two hours.

• Be particularly careful when the child is playing outdoors in water or snow. Ultraviolet rays are reflected upward from water, sand, and snow. Even on cloudy days, most of the ultraviolet rays can penetrate through the haze, fog, or clouds.

• See that the child relaxes in the shade—not the sun—at a beach or pool. Remember, however, that a beach umbrella or a leafy tree is no substitute for a sunscreen lotion or cream.

• Use an awning or hood on a stroller or carriage when taking a walk in the sun.

• If possible, keep the child out of the sun between 10:00 A.M. and 2:00 P.M. This is when the ultraviolet rays are strongest.

Discuss. What household items could toddlers play with safely that would encourage the development of their small motor skills? What activities would help them develop eye-hand coordination?

Activity. Ask students to create a puzzle for toddlers, using heavy cardboard.
Problem Solving. Have students discuss whether or not boys should be encouraged to play with dolls.

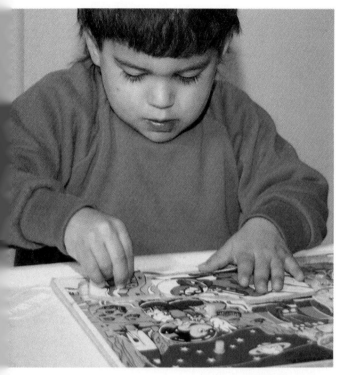

Picking up a puzzle piece and placing it in a specific position help children develop small motor skills.

because they demand greater skills than most three-year-olds possess.

Practicing small motor skills is important during the preschool years. These early skills form the basis for the useful skills of writing, drawing, cutting, and pasting at later ages.

◆ ◆ Self-Esteem ◆ ◆

As children play with others, they get to know themselves better. They form ideas about themselves by the way others play with them. They develop autonomy and a sense of self. Parents can help children develop good feelings about themselves by playing with them and in the process providing compliments and encouragement.

❖ Emotional-Social Development

Play can contribute a great deal to children's emotional and social development. The give-and-take of interacting with others is especially important during play. For example, a high school student makes friends and learns new ways to deal with people to make life more satisfying. Toddlers and young children are just getting started on the ladder of social development. They learn and develop socially and emotionally through play.

Learning to relate to others and learning how to handle the emotions involved in relating to others eventually become crucial parts of play. During their first two years or so, infants engage in **solitary play;** that is, they play by themselves. Babies play alone even when other babies are present, though they do seem to enjoy the presence of these others. At this age, babies play as if they were little satellites, each moving around in his or her own universe. If they do interact with others, it is quite by accident.

Between the ages of two and three, children begin to look forward to having another child around when they play. When they are together, they play side by side. This is known as **parallel play.** For instance, they may each zoom a truck around the room at the same time.

After age four, children engage in **cooperative play;** that is, their play actually requires them to do things together. In this kind of play, children make plans, talk things over, and pretend they are people they know from story books, television, or the neighborhood. Language development is obviously a big asset in such activities. Cooperative play helps children practice the social skills of sharing and taking turns. As children learn to share toys and take turns, they develop feelings of concern and respect for each another.

Activity. Have students list as many games and toys as they can on the chalkboard. Then ask them to label each as to which motor skills development would be strengthened most by its use.

Problem Solving. Have students describe how they think a playtime might go between a two-year-old and a four-year-old. What activities would be appropriate for both children?

Around the World

Games Around the Globe

Children all over the world play similar games. They swing, count on their fingers and toes, jump rope, bounce balls, play hide-and-seek, and clap in rhythm. Many of these games have rhymes to go with them. The words change to match the customs and folktales of the country, but the way the game is played is often the same.

- In the United States, small children love to play ring-around-a-rosy. Brazilian children play a similar circle game with several verses about a ring and a broken heart.

- Many babies in our country practice their eye-hand coordination by playing pat-a-cake with an older child or adult. Young Chinese children master the same skills with a clapping game called Little Ming, Little Ming.

- Toe- and finger-counting rhymes, such as this little piggy, make babies giggle with delight. Children in Denmark chant a song about a horse and a blacksmith. In France, a favorite finger-counting rhyme tells the story of a rabbit that was chased and eaten and a little boy who had none.

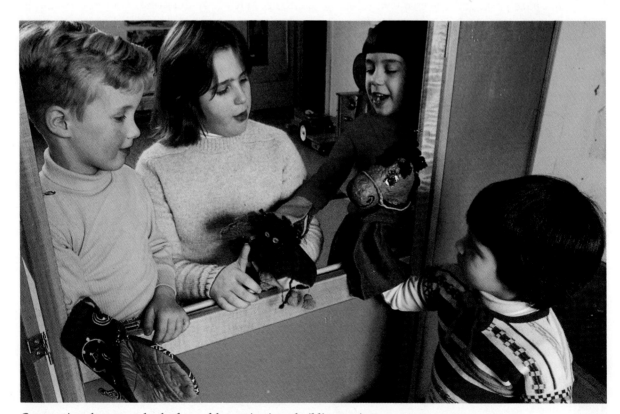

Cooperative play may take the form of dramatizations, building projects, or games.

Discuss. How can play help children learn to get along with others?
Emphasize. Parents should not let fear for the child's safety keep them from allowing the child to play without continual restraints.

Activity. Have students ask their parents and grandparents what games and toys were popular when they were children. Then have students identify which games and toys have been popular for several generations. Why might this be?

At about the same age, children try out different gender roles during play. Parents and caregivers should encourage all children to develop their individual interests and abilities. If girls are allowed only to play with dolls and boys are allowed only to play with tools, their ideas of what women and men can do will be sadly limited.

School-age children enjoy becoming members of scout, 4-H, and other groups. Many participate in team sports and learn the rules and skills of organized games. At this age, children often select best friends and expect always to play together. Hurt feelings arise when a friend prefers to play with another child. In moments such as this, play requires learning social and emotional lessons.

Through team sports, adolescents continue the ongoing process of interacting with other young people. They learn to cooperate, work toward group goals, develop strategies, and handle competition. Winning helps teach players to take success in stride, and losing teaches them to look ahead to the next challenge. In fact, many adults with successful careers claim that their experience in team sports contributed directly to their management skills.

❖ Cognitive Development

Children's play is also directly linked to cognitive development. Young infants respond to musical toys. When a little older, they look for a toy dropped from the high chair. Toddlers are fine explorers, curious about everything. Unfortunately, their ability to get around physically is superior to their ability to think about the danger they may get themselves into. Therefore, parents must supervise toddlers' play.

When children play, they also practice language skills as they communicate and solve problems. In this sense, play can contribute

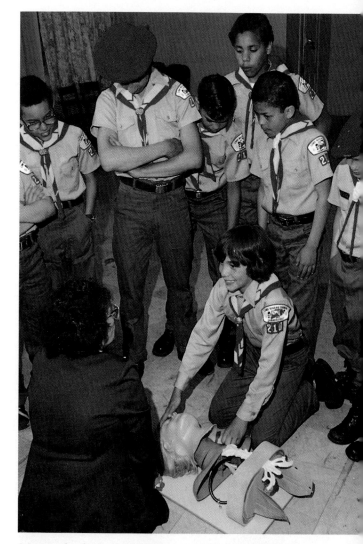

Many school-age children join organized groups such as a sports team or a scout troop. These experiences help children develop new skills while working together as a group.

both to social development and to language development.

Play can enhance cognitive development if parents and caregivers provide suitable space and stimulating materials for children to play with. For example, dominoes, lotto, and bingo are all good games for memory, word, and picture or number recognition. These games are suitable for children between the ages of three and six. Board games—such as checkers, backgammon, and chess—and numerous card games are favorites of school-age children. Though some games are mostly a matter of luck, others require considerable skill and contribute to cognitive growth.

Toy models also foster cognitive development, as do many hobbies, such as stamp and coin collecting, sewing, and cooking. Ryan, a sixth-grader, has always enjoyed helping his parents cook. He thinks this activity has sparked his interest in science. "Following a recipe for custard is like doing a chemistry experiment," he said. Cooking has also taught him about geography because his family prepares dishes from a variety of cultures around the world.

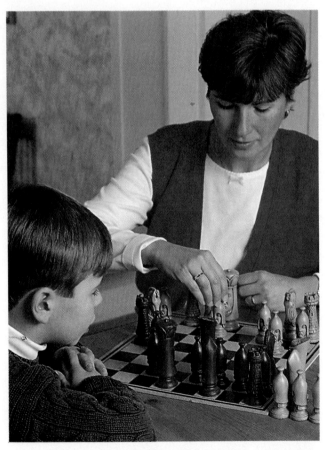

Games can help children develop their cognitive abilities. For example, chess requires considerable concentration and other mental skills.

Choosing Toys

Children's toys should be durable and strong, safe to use, and age appropriate. They should also be usable in different ways and in different places and reasonably priced.

- **Durable and strong.** Children may use many toys for several years. It is therefore important to choose toys that are tough enough to take the wear and tear.

- **Safe to use.** No matter how a toy is used, it should have no sharp corners that might cut someone. Toys for infants and toddlers should have no small parts that could come off and be swallowed. They should also have no paint that is poisonous if chewed, as are lead-based paints.

- **Age appropriate.** Children need toys that fit their age, body size, skills, and interests. For example, children should receive a two-wheeled bicycle only after their muscles and sense of balance have developed to the point where they can ride one safely. Children who are given a bicycle too early may get discouraged and refuse to try to ride when their muscles and balance are more mature.

- **Usable in different ways and in different places.** A good toy stimulates children to think of several ways to use it. For example, a toddler's small wagon may be a pull toy today. Tomorrow, the child may load it with other toys and then unload and sit in it. Later on, the wagon becomes a car and is parked in a garage that the toddler has built with blocks. This toy is more useful than one that serves only one purpose and is then forgotten. Most windup toys are single-purpose toys. Usually, a parent winds one up, and the child watches. When the child finds that there is nothing else to do with it, she or he loses interest.

- **Reasonably priced.** Parents need to consider the cost of a toy as well as its educational and enjoyment value. They can compare the costs of toys in terms of their durability and how long or often they will be used. For example, if a toy for one child falls apart in one year, its cost per year per child is much higher than that of a toy that is strong enough to be used by two children for two years. Blocks are an example of a low cost-per-child toy. Remember, however, a toy that falls apart from repeated use is more valuable than a toy that is never used.

A wooden spoon and metal pans, a cardboard box, and old magazines—all make good playthings.

Types of Play

Play is children's "work." Through play children grow in many ways. They develop their body and achieve control of their muscles. They explore their environment and become increasingly knowledgeable about it. They use their imagination and try out various adult roles. They develop creativity through music, dance, and art.

Quiet play—alone or with a parent or caregiver—is also essential. It helps children wind down before going to bed at night and when they have become overexcited. Reading to children or telling them a story is one way to provide quiet play. Leaving them to look at pictures or play with a doll on their own is another.

❖ Exploratory Play

Exploratory play enables children to discover how things work. Curious toddlers like to examine and handle many different objects. They may take a new toy and squeeze it, smell it, shake it, put part of it in their mouth, and pound on it. They discover that a musical toy makes a pleasant sound when they pull a string or press a button. Objects that can be taken apart and put back together—such as construction toys with parts that snap together—offer satisfaction as well as instruction.

Some of the most important learning takes place when toddlers appear to be playing aimlessly. At such times, they may be placing assorted objects on top of each other, trying to push a stool between the legs of a chair, or examining a shadow on the floor. Yet these activities are opportunities for children to explore their surroundings. Children do not need toys to be engaged in play.

◆ Dramatic Play

Dramatic play is imaginative, unrehearsed play in which children pretend to be other people or animals as they take part in make-believe events. Piaget called this *symbolic play.*

Often, several children will engage together in dramatic play around a theme they determine themselves. While doing this, they learn and practice cooperation. "Playing house" is a popular theme for cooperative dramatic play. Children create familiar scenes with fathers, mothers, and babies who are eating, sleeping, or just being fussy.

A supply of large cardboard blocks can contribute to housekeeping play. These versatile pieces of equipment can last six or seven years, making their cost per year quite low. With these blocks, children's imagination soars as they build homes, airports, and fire stations.

Dramatic play also occurs outdoors on the jungle gym, in the sandbox, and among wheeled toys and packing boxes. Children call packing boxes houses one day, corrals another, and submarines yet another day. Their ideas are limited only by how far their imagination will stretch.

Children most enjoy dramatic play when they are four to six years old. By this time, they have well-developed language skills. They have had broad experiences with people in the community. These give them ideas for roles, conversation, and action. They have also learned to cooperate with others in social situations. As a result, they have many ideas about resolving conflicts. They are not self-conscious and feel free to say what they feel.

Children enjoy acting out different roles through dramatic play. This type of play encourages children to use their imagination and language skills.

Activity. Ask students to describe in writing one type of dramatic play activity they enjoyed. They should tell where it took place, what props were used, how many playmates were involved, and whether any parents were involved.

Activity. Have students observe a group of preschoolers involved in dramatic play. They should record the theme and the roles that each child plays. How did the children cooperate with each other and resolve conflicts?

Benefits of Dramatic Play

Dramatic play benefits children in many ways:

- Provides an outlet for children's inner thoughts and feelings.
- Helps children who feel left out in other activities take a leadership role and make contact with other children.
- Teaches children about roles in families and in society.
- Helps children expand their mind by requiring them to use their imagination.
- Provides practice for language skills as children use new words and express ideas.
- Helps children learn and practice society's rules of courtesy, taking turns, sharing, and cooperating.

Role Playing

Dramatic play often involves dressing up in hats, jewelry, old clothing, and even makeup. This allows children to try out many different roles and identities. Children learn about some roles—such as king, queen, soldier, and Batman—from stories, television programs, and games. Other roles, such as mother, father, and doctor, are more familiar. Sometimes in dramatic play situations, who is the mommy and who is the daddy becomes a matter of convenience. Lisa and Marianne, with no boys present, take turns being the mommy and the daddy. Parents and caregivers should not direct girls into traditional female roles and boys into traditional male roles. Both boys and girls at this age enjoy pretending to be fire fighters or astronauts.

Children have plenty of ideas to act out. They can imitate grown-up activities by pretending to use the telephone or walking in high-heeled shoes. They can slay a dragon or heal a sick doll. True-to-life dramas often emerge, complete with verbal and social interaction.

Parents, caregivers, and teachers should observe dramatic play quietly from a distance rather than getting involved with it. They can help most by providing a few props to stimulate the spontaneous role playing that is at the heart of dramatic play. Even if conflicts arise, children can usually resolve them by themselves.

Imaginary Playmates

Some children have imaginary playmates. These playmates usually have names, certain clothing, and specific features. A child may carry on frequent conversations with the imaginary playmate. The child may even say to a parent, "Watch out! You almost stepped on Molly." Some playmates go everywhere with the child; others reside only in certain rooms.

Studies show that imaginary playmates occur mostly among bright children who are only children or the oldest in families with several younger siblings. Sometimes an imaginary playmate disappears with the birth of a brother or sister. Such a playmate almost always disappears when the child starts school. Then the child may explain, "Molly went to live in Chicago."

DECISIONS ◆ ◆ DECISIONS

Dana and Sam have a five-year-old only child named Courtney. She has several imaginary friends, both at home and at school. In addition, she holds conversations with her toys. Dana and Sam are concerned that Courtney may have an overly active imagination. They have mentioned their concern to you. What will you tell them?

❖ Art Activities

In art activities, the process, not the product, is important. Children try out creative ideas by drawing, painting, or modeling things important to them. Adults should not press children to represent what adults want to see. Children have their own vision and imagination.

Much of the time, art activity means simply experimenting with many colors, strokes, or shapes. Children may not be trying to represent any object that an adult would recognize. Hence, adults should avoid asking such questions as "Is that a cow?" The child may not have named the object yet or even be making something with a name. On the other hand, a child who is making a horse, not a cow, may be insulted by the adult's question. Children need to feel free to explore, to put things together, and to try using different materials.

Drawing and Painting

Scribbling is the first stage of drawing and painting. At first, children simply scribble all over the paper. Later on, between ages two and three, they may name the scribble, perhaps as mommy, baby, or truck. An adult will not be able to recognize the figure. However, the adult should still encourage such first attempts at representation by saying, "Oh, you used your red crayon to make the truck. Do you want to tell me about it?"

The second stage occurs between the ages

of three and four, when children begin to connect a circle to make a human face. Usually, early faces have eyes, a mouth, and perhaps a nose. Eyebrows and ears rarely appear until later.

In the third stage of drawing and painting, children begin trying to represent things they see around them. However, they may still scribble to fill in spaces. Sometimes children first draw something with a paintbrush and then fill the whole sheet with paint. A child who covers the whole sheet of paper with black paint may explain, "It's night now." Although adults may not want to see the first drawing disappear, they should remember that children paint for themselves, not for others.

Art activities help children express their thoughts and feelings. They can paint something they have seen or imagined. They can experiment with different colors, strokes, and shapes.

Discuss. Why is paper and a coloring medium better for young children than a coloring book?
Activity. Have students give a group of toddlers or preschoolers drawing materials and ask the children to draw a picture.

Encourage the children to talk about their drawings. Ask students to describe what they learned about children's imaginations and verbal abilities.

Scribbling, drawing, and finger painting provide important prewriting experience. Practice in drawing and painting helps children learn to control the tools of expression. Writing with pencils will follow naturally.

Drawing Supplies. Crayons are an art tool that parents can provide at home. They are also the most popular tools at school. Thick crayons are easiest for young children to handle. If the paper wrapping is removed, children can use the edges as well as the tips of the crayons.

Young children also love water-washable, felt-tipped colored markers. The colors are vivid, and the markers are large and easy to hold. Some have tips that do not dry out, even when the cap is left off. Permanent-color markers are not recommended because their dye will not wash out of clothing.

Pastels are soft pieces of chalk. They are about 1 inch in diameter and 3 inches long. Because they glide onto paper quickly, children find them very satisfying. Some children enjoy using pastels to make murals.

DECISIONS ◆ ◆ DECISIONS

Melanie is concerned about her toddler, Craig. She has noticed that Craig's drawings are unrecognizable scribbles. He calls one recent set of scribbles "Dee-Dee," his name for his older sister. The boy is very proud of his pictures, which contain unusual color combinations. How do you think Melanie should respond to them? Why?

Many types of drawing paper are available. Parents can purchase drawing paper in variety stores, stationery stores, or art supply stores. Used computer paper is also suitable for children's drawing.

Large rolls of brown wrapping paper make good drawing paper, especially for watercolor markers and pastels. Adults can roll out several feet of the paper and tape it to the floor or a large table. Then they can let three or four children work together. This is a good project for a rainy day.

Painting Supplies. Tempera paint can be purchased in either liquid or powder form. Adding liquid starch extends the paint and gives it a glossy look.

Younger children should begin painting with only one color. If they use several colors, they end up mixing them all together. As they gain experience, they can use two, then three colors. Some teachers and parents teach children to wash their brush in water, then wipe it on a sponge before changing colors. Others prefer to give children a separate brush for each color. Preschoolers need large brushes and large sheets of paper. Newsprint is the most common type of paper used. Children can paint either at an easel or at a table.

Finger Painting

Children can use commercial finger paints on slick-surfaced paper, such as freezer paper, or directly on washable tables. If the children paint on tables, adults can help them press a piece of newsprint onto the finger painting to pick up the design.

One mother lets her son finger paint in the bathtub. The child paints until he tires of the activity. Then both child and tub are easily washed. In other settings, children need smocks and aprons to protect their clothes while they finger paint. Most children enjoy the messiness of this activity.

Discuss. What other items besides brushes and fingers can be used for painting?

Activity. Hold an Art Day and have students enjoy activities such as finger painting, using pastels, and painting at an easel with tempera paints in the classroom.

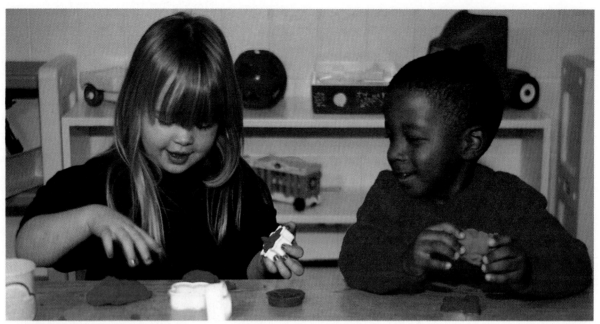

Working with clay and play dough gives children experience in creating three-dimensional shapes.

Collage

Many recycled or household materials can be used for cutting and gluing objects to form a collage. A **collage** (koh-LAHZH) is artwork made by pasting various materials onto a surface. The fun of this activity lies in the novelty and individuality that each child brings to it. The following items are good for cutting, sorting, arranging into designs, and then gluing in place.

- Holiday and greeting cards.
- Gift wrap and colorful shopping bags.
- Magazines.
- Fabric pieces.
- Wood scraps and shavings.
- Packing materials, corrugated cardboard, and excelsior.
- Computer paper, newsprint, and paper scraps from photocopy services.
- Natural materials, such as leaves, bark, twigs, seeds, cones, acorns, feathers, nutshells, and wheat straw.

- Common household items, such as toothpicks, frozen dessert sticks, and drinking straws cut in pieces.

White glue works best for attaching materials in collages. For some projects, the glue can be thinned with water and applied with a paste brush.

Clay and Play Dough

Children enjoy using clay and play dough to roll, pat, squeeze, and pound. In addition to using their fingers, children can use various objects as tools for shaping play dough and clay. The most popular are wooden spoons, tongue depressors, and cylindrical building blocks. However, at first children should use only their hands to experiment with the dough or clay. Later, they may make snakes, animals, and little bowls.

Woodworking

In woodworking, children learn to use tools such as rulers, hammers, saws, vises, and screwdrivers. The activity improves chil-

More About. Collage-making provides visual and tactile experiences and encourages small motor skills development. **Activity.** Have students make a batch of play dough and enjoy creating three-dimensional objects.

More About. Woodworking develops eye-hand coordination and promotes an understanding of spatial relationships.

dren's small motor coordination and offers them an outlet for creativity.

Children can do woodworking at home if parents have tools and a place to work. Of course, this activity needs close supervision to be safe. In class situations, generally only one child at a time is allowed at the workbench.

Children should choose what they want to make with wood. Three-year-olds may be content to hammer nails into a piece of wood or a tree stump. As they gain skills, they may want to make an object they call a boat or a radio. Obviously, their idea of a boat or radio will not be the same as an adult's.

❖ Music Activities

Children should be encouraged to listen and respond to music in spontaneous as well as planned music experiences. Anyone caring for young children should sing with them whenever possible. Nearly all children enjoy the fun of singing and moving to music. Many good musical recordings for children are available on cassettes and compact discs.

For young children, music is usually an active listening experience. They like to move, march, and dance to music or to accompany a song with rhythm instruments or clapping. A wooden spoon and a metal pot can serve as a drumstick and drum. It is interesting to play various types of music and see how children respond to each type. Having a parent or caregiver who plays a musical instrument often encourages children's interest in music.

❖ Computer and Electronic Games

Computer and electronic games are available for children of all ages. Such games' contribution to learning is not yet fully understood. Because these games are relatively new, long-term studies of children who

Many children enjoy playing a musical instrument. Such experiences help children express their feelings and entertain themselves and others.

have grown up with them have not been completed. Some people believe that many of the games consume time that would be better spent on reading or play activities with other children.

One advantage of using computer and electronic games is that children become familiar with the equipment and technology. As a result, they may be more interested in using computers at school or on the job.

Activity. Encourage students to share songs they learned at home, in preschool, or at camp. How many of the songs include actions? Repetition? Sounds? Have students learn the songs by singing along with a tape or with the group.

Discuss. How can musical activities enhance physical, emotional, social, and cognitive development? **Activity.** Have students make simple musical instruments (drums from coffee cans or oatmeal boxes, tambourines from plastic lids and bells).

Parent Involvement in Play

How involved should parents be in their children's play? It is important for parents to be very aware of and closely involved in their children's play activities. Parents can become involved by following these guidelines:

- **Provide age-appropriate toys, equipment, materials, and space.** By understanding physical, emotional, social, and cognitive development, parents can better choose suitable toys and activities when the child is at various ages.

- **Set aside time to enjoy playing with the child daily.** Parents should initiate simple play activities when their child is an infant They should be sure to talk and laugh with the child and to comment on the child's play even when they are involved with other activities.

- **Think about the meaning of the child's play.** As parents observe their child's play, it is important that they notice how the child is growing and developing physically, mentally, emotionally, and socially.

- **Provide a playmate for the child.** After the age of two, a child needs at least one other child to play with regularly. Parents should arrange for the child to have a playmate for several hours a week.

- **Encourage language use during play.** Children need to talk, explain, and express themselves while they are involved with play. Language development is closely related to all areas of learning. Parents should try not to worry about playtime noise. Laughter, squeals, and different sounds are an important part of play.

- **Avoid dominating the child's play.** Parents should follow the child's lead during play and not make the child practice skills that do not interest him or her. Sensitive parents know when their child needs them and when they should step back.

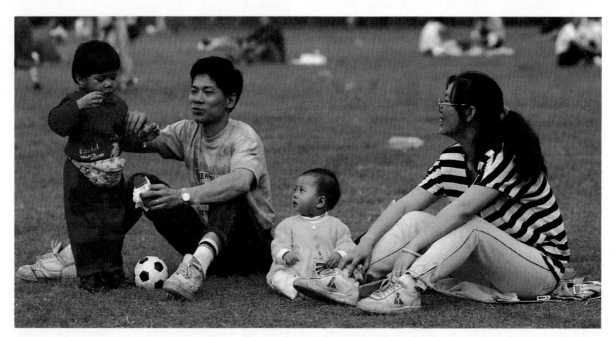

Parents should take time to play with their children. Through play children develop skills and learn how to relax and have fun.

Problem Solving. If you were employed as a nanny for two children, ages four and nine, what activities could you plan that would encourage learning, cooperation, and creativity? What activities could the children play together? Alone?

Discuss. How can parents and other caregivers encourage children's skill development? What effect does positive statements about a child's ability have? Negative statements? What guidelines should parents follow?

CHAPTER 20 REVIEW

Summary

- Play contributes to all forms of a child's development.
- Age-appropriate toys allow children to practice large and small motor skills.
- Children learn how to relate to others and how to deal with their emotions during play.
- As children grow older, they move from solitary play to parallel play to cooperative play.
- Various games, including board and card games, help children develop cognitive skills.
- Children's toys should be durable and strong, safe to use, age appropriate, usable in different ways and different places, and reasonably priced.
- Dramatic play encourages children to use their imagination and language skills.
- Art and music activities help children try out creative ideas.
- Parents should be involved in but not dominate children's play.

Questions

p. 379 1. What is play? Why is it important for children?

p. 380 2. How does play enhance children's development.

p. 381 3. Name at least five toys that allow children to practice large motor skills.

p. 381 4. What activities help children practice small motor skills?

p. 383 5. Define solitary play, parallel play, and cooperative play. At what ages do children engage in these types of play?

p. 386 6. List four factors to consider when choosing toys.

p. 389 7. In what ways can dramatic play benefit children?

p. 390 8. Describe the three stages of drawing and painting that young children go through.

p. 393 9. What is one advantage and one disadvantage of computer and electronic games?

p. 394 10. Should parents become involved in children's play? If so, how? If not, why?

Activities

1. Play at least one game with a toddler or preschooler. Describe what game you played, what happened during the game, and what skills were involved.

2. Observe a group of three- and four-year-olds at play. Describe examples of different kinds of play.

3. Visit a toy store and write a report on your findings.

   • Choose three toys for toddlers that meet the criteria for selecting toys and three toys that do not meet the criteria. Describe each toy and its cost. Explain why each toy is or is not suitable.

Think About

1. Write down whatever you can remember playing as a child. Which activity seemed to be the most fun? Why?

2. Are parents ever justified in insisting that children take art, music, or dancing lessons if the children are not interested in doing so? Explain.

Reference. See the Teacher's Manual in the front of the Teacher's Annotated Edition for complete answers to the chapter review questions.

395

Children with Special Needs

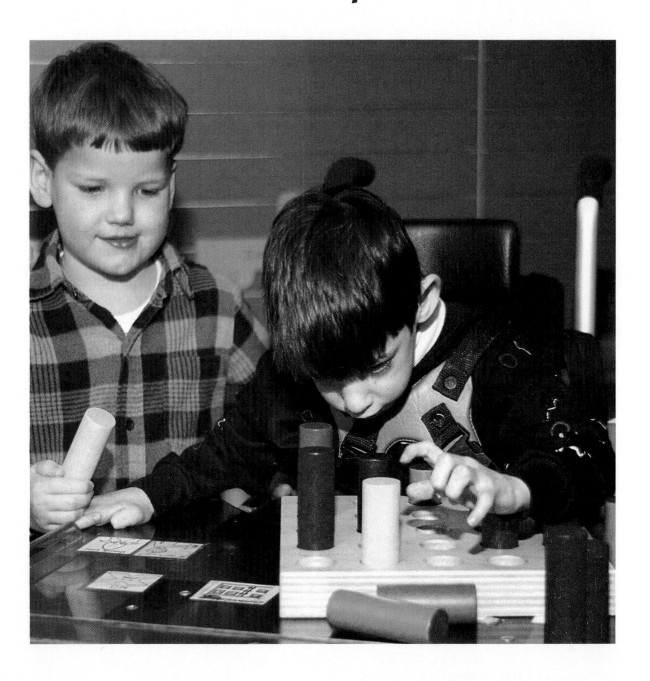

Objectives

This chapter will help you to:

- Identify different types of physical, emotional, cognitive, and learning disabilities.
- Discuss how parents and caregivers can meet the special needs of children with disabilities.
- Describe methods used to help educate children with special needs.
- Suggest ways to meet the special needs of gifted children.

Vocabulary

disabled
prosthesis
chronic
autism
mental retardation
attention-deficit hyperactive
   disorder (ADHD)
dyslexia

special education
inclusion
gifted children

"Joey, why are you in a wheelchair?" asked six-year-old Ervin.

"What happened to you, Joey?" asked Ramona.

"I broke my leg," Joey replied rather proudly.

Joey enjoyed being the center of attention for a change and gave each curious child in his class a chance to touch his wheelchair and feel his cast. After two days at home, Joey's life was back to normal—except for the cast on his leg.

Hundreds of children each year become **disabled,** or have a physical, mental, or emotional condition that limits their activity. Like Joey, some children become temporarily disabled. Others are permanently disabled.

Like Joey's friends, some children who have no disability are curious about children who do. Others may not react as positively. Many children with a disability feel the sting of discrimination as people respond negatively to them out of misunderstanding.

Types of Disabilities

Statistics show that approximately one family in ten has a child who is born with a disability or acquires a disability after birth. Some children are born with a genetic defect that affects their chromosomes. Others are exposed to drugs, alcohol, rubella, or sexually transmitted diseases when they are in the womb. After children are born, accidents such as falls or blows to the head can cause physical and mental disabilities. A high fever may cause brain damage.

Children with special needs may have a physical, emotional, cognitive, and/or learning disability. Each type of disability varies from slight to severe. For example, a person with a minor visual problem may wear glasses to eliminate the problem. A person who is blind, however, may need to rely on a companion or seeing-eye dog for help in some activities.

How children cope with their disability varies from child to child. The attitudes of

Chapter Opener. Ask students to read the opening scenario to the chapter. Ask these questions: What other questions might children have about people in a wheelchair? How might people react differently if Joe's disability was permanent, rather than temporary?

Discuss. What television shows include people with disabilities? What can viewers learn from these programs?

parents, caregivers, and others can help or hinder a child's adjustment. By demonstrating understanding, patience, and support, adults can help children with a disability deal with the challenges they face.

Children with a disability have the same needs, feelings, and wishes as other children. All children—regardless of their abilities—need to be recognized, accepted, and loved.

❖ Physical Disabilities

Physical disabilities include hearing and visual disorders, muscular disorders, spinal cord injuries, loss of limbs, and certain health impairments. Some children who are physically disabled need to use a special device such as a wheelchair, crutches, or braces. Other children have a disability that is less obvious, such as a heart defect or kidney disease.

By law, public buildings must now be accessible to people who are physically disabled. This helps them move about independently. All people who are disabled, young and old alike, benefit when public facilities are wheelchair accessible or barrier free.

Hearing Disabilities

Young children who are partially deaf are fitted with a hearing aid as soon as possible after their hearing impairment is discovered. Most children who are totally deaf learn to communicate through sign language, lip reading, or both. Some of these children can even learn to speak.

Visual Disabilities

Children who are visually impaired or blind are able to use their other senses to find their way around a home or a child care center. Eventually, they may learn to read Braille, a system of writing that consists of raised dots on a page. Many also learn by listening to cassette recordings of books.

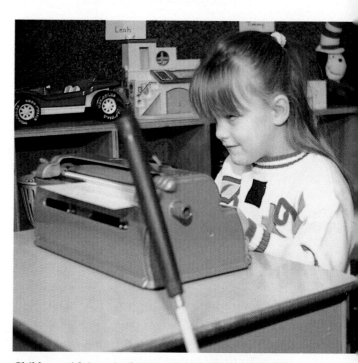

Children with impaired vision can learn to read Braille. They can also use a typewriter that prints the letters in Braille.

DECISIONS ◆ ◆ DECISIONS

Barbara is concerned about her four-year-old daughter, Kate. Recently Kate has been squinting and rubbing her eyes. She sometimes complains of headaches. Barbara wonders whether Kate has a vision problem. She plans to ask the pediatrician at Kate's scheduled checkup, but that is three months away. What should Barbara do now?

Children with muscular disorders are unable to control certain body movements. They may need assistance with some tasks.

Muscular Disabilities

Both muscular dystrophy and cerebral palsy affect the control of body movement. Muscular dystrophy involves gradual loss of the use of the muscles. This makes it difficult or impossible to move and maintain one's posture. The most common type of dystrophy in young children is genetic. It appears between the ages of two and six years in the muscles used in standing and walking.

Children with cerebral palsy usually have difficulty walking, balancing, remaining still, and speaking clearly. Cerebral palsy is caused by damage to the brain before or during birth or in the first few years of life. The part of the brain that is damaged involves the control of muscles. Most children with cerebral palsy are helped through physical therapy and training. Some may need to use braces or other walking aids.

Reference. See pages 125-126 for information about genetic birth defects.

Spinal Cord Defects and Injuries

Some children are born with spina bifida. This is a condition in which one or more of the vertebrae in the lower or middle back fail to fuse. If the spinal cord and membranes protrude from the spinal canal, the child may have partial or full paralysis of the legs. Bowel and bladder functions may also be affected.

Children whose spinal cord is injured may become physically disabled. Most spinal cord injuries are the result of automobile, motorcycle, diving, or sports accidents or physical abuse. If the injury occurs somewhere between the shoulders and the area below the waist, the legs may be paralyzed. Someone whose lower body is paralyzed is called a *paraplegic.* If the neck is injured, a person can be paralyzed from the neck down. Both the arms and legs are paralyzed. Someone with such an injury is called a *quadriplegic.*

Reference. See pages 164-170 for information about disabilities caused by alcohol, drugs, diseases, x-rays, and other conditions before birth, such as fetal alcohol syndrome.

Loss of Limbs

Some children lose part or all of a limb—that is, an arm or leg—through an accident or surgery. Others may be born without part or all of a limb. In many cases, these children can be fitted with a **prosthesis** (pross-THEE-suhs), which is an artificial arm or leg. With special training, such children can participate in many physical activities.

Health Impairments

A variety of health conditions can result in physical disabilities. These conditions are **chronic,** or continue over a long period of time. Children with a chronic condition can be affected both physically and emotionally.

Asthma affects up to ten percent of all children. It is characterized by difficulty in breathing, wheezing, and coughing. An asthma attack can last minutes, hours, or even days. Treatments includes trying to identify possible allergens, such as pollen, mold spores, dust mites, or animal dander. Then the allergens or irritants can be avoided. Medication can also be prescribed to help prevent asthma attacks. Fortunately, most children outgrow the condition by adulthood.

Some children are born with a congenital heart defect. This may affect a child's ability to grow or to play strenuously with other children. Many heart defects can be corrected or improved by surgery.

Kidney disorders interfere with the ability to eliminate body wastes. Many of these conditions can be treated with medication; others can be corrected by surgery.

Cystic fibrosis is an inherited condition in which the mucous glands, including those in the lungs, secrete very sticky mucus. This results in breathing and digestion problems. Children with this condition benefit from regular treatment given several times a day to help expel the mucus from the lungs. Parents can learn to perform the treatment technique on their children.

The most common childhood cancer is leukemia, any of several cancers of the bone marrow. Medical treatment for cancer may include chemotherapy, radiation, and surgery. Children undergoing cancer treatment may experience loss of hair, prolonged hospitalization, and absence from school. However, the survival rate for children with cancer is very good if the disease is detected early and treated properly.

❖ Emotional Disabilities

Emotional disabilities range from mild to severe. Generally, children with emotional disabilities have trouble getting along with others. They may be unable to develop a positive self-image. Their emotional problems often interfere with their behavior.

Some emotional problems arise from a traumatic event, such as the death of a loved one. Others may be caused by continuous abuse or neglect. The cause of some types of emotional disabilities is still unknown.

Failure to thrive is an early emotional condition. It is apparently caused when parents ignore and fail to bond with a child. As a result, the child does not grow or develop as he or she should.

Some children who are emotionally disturbed are severely withdrawn. They spend most of their time apart from the group and are often uncomfortable when others get too close. They may become frustrated when they do not know what to expect in a given situation. Other children who are emotionally disturbed may be very aggressive and destructive. They tend to hurt others without cause. They are often impatient and demanding and lack self-control. Children who exhibit either of these types of behavior usually benefit from professional counseling.

One special group of children with emotional disabilities are autistic children. **Autism** (AWH-tiz-ehm) is a severe disorder characterized by lack of communication, extreme concern with oneself, and detachment from reality. Most autistic children do not talk or communicate. Many engage in repetitive behaviors such as rocking or twirling an object. They retreat into a world of their own. They are either withdrawn and unemotional or become uncontrollable. Very little is known about the causes of autism. Special training can sometimes help autistic children live with their families and take care of themselves.

One of the greatest challenges for parents is to admit that their child may have an emotional disability. The parent who is able to talk about emotional problems is likely to be of greater help to the child than one who continues to deny that any problems exist. Children who are emotionally disturbed and also their families need support and encouragement from both professionals and friends.

◆◆ Cognitive Disabilities

Cognitive disabilities result from a genetic disorder, such as Down syndrome, or an environmental cause, such as fetal alcohol syndrome or a severe head injury. Children with a cognitive disability will not develop the learning and conceptual ability of the average person. Their cognitive development is slower and stops at a lower level. Cognitive disabilities range from mild to severe.

Mental retardation is a disorder characterized in varying degrees by low intelligence, abnormal ability to learn, and impaired social adaptation. Children who are severely mentally retarded are slow to learn even the most elementary concepts. Even when they become adults in terms of age, the degree of their cognitive development may be no more than that of an average three-year-old. These individuals require continual care throughout their lives. Fortunately, most people with mental retardation are only mildly retarded. With

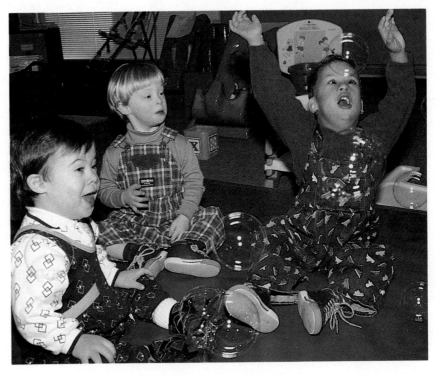

Children with Down syndrome are usually happy and friendly, but their development is much slower. Special programs that begin in infancy can help many of these children make the most of their abilities.

training, they can learn to take care of themselves and to hold repetitive jobs. Some work in sheltered workshops, which are special centers that employ the disabled. Many communities offer sheltered homes that provide supervised group living for adults who are mentally retarded.

Down syndrome is a genetic disorder that is the result of an extra chromosome. Children with Down syndrome are mildly to severely retarded. Special programs can help these children develop their learning potential. Many of these programs begin in infancy.

❖ Learning Disabilities

Children with a learning disability have difficulty processing and using information, especially when reading, writing, or doing math. Learning disabilities are often associated with a problem in the nervous system. Children with a learning disability can be very intelligent, but they are unable to learn in the same way most children learn. In fact, many brilliant people, including Thomas Edison and Albert Einstein, have had a learning disability.

There are many types of learning disabilities. Some children have a short attention span and are unable to concentrate on an activity for more than a minute or so. Others cannot listen to directions and then follow them. Some children have difficulty sounding out words, writing properly, expressing their thoughts in speech, or understanding simple number relationships. These children often try very hard to accomplish a task, but their brain does not process information from their senses in a normal way.

Unfortunately, children with learning disabilities are often considered difficult, lazy, or dumb by uninformed parents, teachers, and classmates. These children often become discouraged in school when they are unable to keep up with other students. Their failure to achieve or to get good grades may result in low self-esteem. It is important that students with learning disabilities be identified as early as possible so they can receive the help they need. Many schools have special programs that provide alternative methods of learning that benefit children with a learning disability. Two of the more common types of learning disabilities are attention-deficit hyperactivity disorder and dyslexia.

All children, regardless of abilities, have the same needs. They need to be recognized, accepted, and loved by their family and friends.

Attention-Deficit Hyperactivity Disorder (ADHD)

Children with **attention-deficit hyperactivity disorder (ADHD)** are inattentive, overactive, and impulsive. They are described as hyperactive because they are constantly on the move. Evidence of ADHD may appear quite early in life. Causes may be physical, emotional, social, or a combination of disorders.

Children with ADHD have difficulty sitting still and focusing their attention on any activity or task. As a result, they are not able to learn effectively in school without special instructional methods. Some ADHD children are treated with medication, although many experts believe this treatment should be used only after other treatments prove unsuccessful. Parents, caregivers, and teachers may need professional help in learning how best to handle children with ADHD.

Dyslexia

Children with **dyslexia** (dis-LEK-see-uh) have difficulty interpreting information they see and hear. They may confuse left and right, reverse letters and words, or be unable to spell a word they see often. As a result, dyslexia can severely affect children's ability to learn in school. They may have problems reading, writing, spelling, and doing math problems.

Many children reverse their letters and numbers until they are about six or seven years of age. This natural process of learning should not be confused with dyslexia, which can be diagnosed by specialists in learning disabilities.

Dyslexia is believed to be caused by a defect in the brain. Children with dyslexia can be taught how to overcome this condition, which has nothing to do with intelligence. Many successful people, including Vice President Nelson Rockefeller, have had dyslexia.

Around the World

What's In a Label?

The words used to describe a person with a learning disability can be very important. One interesting study shows how some parents misinterpreted the type of help their children needed because of the different meanings of the same word.

The parents in the study had immigrated to the United States from rural areas of Spanish-speaking countries. In their native cultures, there is a strong emphasis on the family as a group. These parents felt that if someone said there was something wrong with a child, it was the result of something that was wrong with the family. This is different from the attitude of the majority of Americans. As a culture, we tend to think of the family as a collection of individuals.

When school officials identified several of the children as having dyslexia, they used the term *retarded*. The parents and children then translated the English word *retarded* to the Spanish word *loco*. Their language does not include different words for the concepts of learning disabilities and mental illness. As a result, the parents thought the school officials were telling them that their children were insane. By the standards of their culture, the parents felt that the entire family was being labeled.

Misunderstandings such as this are not easy to straighten out. However, they do remind us to be careful about the labels we use for other people.

More About. Not all children with an attention deficit disorder are hyperactive.

Discuss. Why is the term *person with disabilities* preferred to the term *handicapped*? What other positive labels are being used to describe people with various disabilities?

Parenting Children with Special Needs

Parents and caregivers of children with special needs face various challenges, depending on the disability. Some children require special care or training at home. Other children need frequent medical treatment, therapy, or counseling at a hospital or clinic. Children with severe problems sometimes need special care throughout life.

❖ Dealing with Emotions

When a disability is discovered—whether at birth, due to an accident, or over a period of time—parents must deal with many emotions. According to professionals who help parents of children with a disability, such parents typically go through the following stages when they learn of the disability.

Stage 1: Shock. Parents report an overwhelming feeling of shock at the news that their child has a disability.

Stage 2: Denial. Parents try to avoid acknowledging the situation or receiving any information about it. When the disability is not visible, they deny its existence for a long time.

Stage 3: Sadness, anger, and anxiety. Parents face the reality that the child's problem will not go away. They grieve for the child as they might if he or she had died. They may express anger at the child, the other parent, or the child's doctor.

Stage 4: Adaptation. Parents admit the child has a disability and seek help. Those who are strong and have good coping skills are most effective at locating people and agencies that can help them care for and educate the child.

Stage 5: Reorganization. The family adjusts to its new life, which may include changes in the family structure, roles, style of living, and goals.

Parents must deal with their own emotions, as well as the emotions of their child. They should honestly examine their thoughts and feelings about the disability. Parents who value their children, whether disabled or not, can establish supportive and loving relationships with them. This helps parents shed feelings of guilt, resentment, and anger that may cause them to become discouraged or depressed. Those who view themselves positively and act in a positive way toward their child enhance their image as parents.

❖ Having a Positive Attitude

The attitude of parents and caregivers can greatly influence how well a child accepts and deals with a disability. If they see the child as a person who happens to have a particular limitation, such as deafness, they can focus on the many positive aspects of the child's entire being. They can view the disability in relation to the whole child.

Parents need to learn as much as possible about their child's disability. This will help them know what to expect of the child's development and behavior. In turn, parents

◆ ◆ *Self-Esteem* ◆ ◆

Parents and caregivers need to help children with disabilities feel self-confident. Then they are more likely to try new or challenging tasks. Focusing on their accomplishments rather than their failures helps inspire success.

Problem Solving. Divide class into small groups to identify and discuss the stresses that families with a special needs child face. How might these stresses affect a marriage relationship? Other parent/child relationships? What type of help or assistance would families need? What feelings might other children in the family have toward their brother or sister? What might be the impact of various crises (divorce, abuse, death) on the special needs child and the family? Have each group share their ideas.

by society. They need to develop their strengths and self-esteem. They need to develop independence and interdependence. Fortunately, special groups and agencies are available to help families deal with the challenges of having a child with special needs.

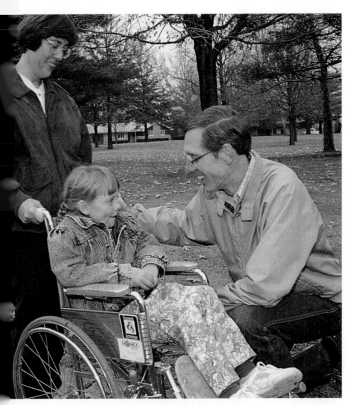

Parents need to help their child accept and deal with a disability. They should focus on the child's abilities and talents and help the child develop self-esteem.

can help the child gain an understanding of his or her special situation.

Children with special needs should never be hidden away, neglected, or abused. In the past, many of these children stayed at home or went to an institution. Today, professionals know that the earlier in a child's life the diagnosis is made, the more that medical attention and education can help the child reach his or her fullest potential. Most children with disabilities contribute joy and love to their family. They can lead rich and fulfilling lives. They can participate in many activities, go to school, and eventually hold a job, marry, and have a family.

Children with disabilities have the same basic needs as other children. They need to feel loved and accepted by their family and

❖ Identifying Children's Strengths

The challenge for parents, caregivers, and teachers of children with special needs is to focus on the children's potential strengths rather than their specific limitations. Do they have a special talent? Do they have a good sense of humor? Are they creative? Do they demonstrate motivation and determination? When children know that their parents, caregivers, and teachers care about them and have faith in them, they develop inner strength and self-confidence. For example, children who are blind may develop exceptional musical ability. Many children who have no arms learn to use their feet with great dexterity.

Above all, it is important for parents to accept their children as they are and not as the parents wish them to be. This enables parents to nurture and guide their children to become happy and confident adults.

❖ Promoting Independence

Moving toward independence is as important for children with a disability as it is for other children. Some children with a disability need extra help in learning to do tasks such as eating, bathing, dressing, or going to the bathroom. A parent who patiently teaches her son who is blind how to feed himself or tie his own shoelaces makes him less dependent. Later as an adult, he will be better able to use his alert mind, his sense of hearing, and sense of touch to take care of himself.

Activity. Ask students to write a "Bill of Rights" for children with disabilities.
Emphasize. Parents and caregivers should focus on the skills and abilities of children with special needs, rather than their limitations.

Problem Solving. Have children list and evaluate ten toys that would aid children with physical disabilities practice their large motor skills and small motor skills.

Clothing

Children with a physical disability often need clothing that they can put on and take off easily. Here are just a few examples:

- Clothes that fasten in the front.
- Pants and skirts with an elastic waistband.
- Clothing with large buttons, Velcro® fasteners, or zippers with large pull tabs.

Children who must wear a brace or cast need loose clothing that will fit over it easily. Children who are visually impaired can use small thread knots sewn inside their clothes to identify colors. For example, one knot might indicate red, two knots blue, and so on.

Living Space

Sometimes the home may have to be modified for a family member with a disability. This often involves installing the following items:

- Grab bars around the tub and toilet.
- Tub seat or hand-held shower head.
- Hallway handrails.
- Ramps in place of stairs.
- Low shelves, countertops, and light switches.

Common household objects can be marked with Braille labels for a child who is blind. For a child who is deaf, a special lighting system can signal when someone rings the doorbell or a smoke detector goes off.

Tasks and Responsibilities

Most children with a disability can help with tasks around the home. Depending on the disability, they may be able to set the table, fold laundry, or dust the furniture. Doing these things helps children feel useful and responsible and also improves their skills.

Most children with a disability want to be treated just like everyone else. They want to do the same things other people do, even when that is difficult. Parents should encour-

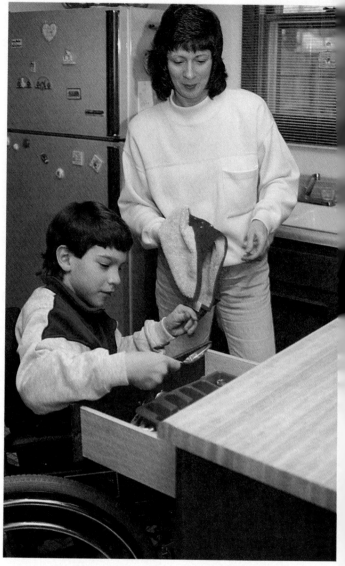

Children with disabilities should be given responsibilities for certain tasks and chores. This helps them develop skills and make a contribution to the well-being of the family.

age other children and friends to let the child with a disability do things on his or her own whenever possible. In turn, this child may at times be able to help a child without a disability. By interacting with each other in natural and spontaneous ways, children with and without a disability can enrich each other's lives.

Problem Solving. In small groups, have students identify specific adaptations that can be made to clothing or to living space that would aid children with various disabilities. What other family members might benefit from the same adaptations? Why?

Problem Solving. Ask students to discuss whether or not children with a disability should be "pushed" to assume responsibility for their own care and household tasks. How could conflicts between parents and child be overcome?

❖❖ Locating Resources

Rearing a child with special needs can be overwhelming at times. Parents can become discouraged, especially if the child is making very little progress in development.

When there are other children in the family, parents have to let them know they are important and loved, too. There is a tendency, especially for preschool children, to feel neglected. They think their parents love the child who is disabled more because they see the special attention that child receives. Parents should talk with these children about their concerns.

Parents also need time for themselves and for each other. It is important that they locate various resources that can help them meet the needs of both the child with the disability and the rest of the family.

Friends and Relatives

Many families have friends or relatives who are willing to spend some time with the child who is disabled. This allows a parent to have an afternoon, evening, or entire day free of caregiving responsibilities. Parents need this time to release stress and get relief from the work involved in the child's care. Occasional space between parent and child enables each to better enjoy the time they spend together.

Support Groups

Support groups for parents of children with a disability are available in many communities. These groups help parents explore and accept their situation and locate resources to help meet their children's needs. Some of these groups actively promote federal and

Children with disabilities benefit from special programs that provide a variety of learning experiences. These blind girls are able to learn about animals through their sense of touch.

Activity. Ask students to locate agencies, organizations, and support groups within or near your own community that provide support or resources to parents who have a special needs child. Have them create a list of all the resources.

Discuss. What careers would enable you to work with children or adults who have special needs?

◆◆ *Health & Safety* ◆◆

Animal Companions

Many people who are blind have a guide dog to help them navigate in a sighted world. Special organizations provide training for both the dog and its owner. Dogs chosen for such training must show qualities of intelligence, responsibility, good disposition, and physical fitness. They learn to obey verbal commands but also to disobey any command that might lead its owner into danger. For example, a guide dog will refuse to cross a busy street until the traffic has stopped.

Did you know there are also specially trained dogs to help people who are deaf? A hearing dog helps a deaf person deal with the routines of everyday life. The dog is trained to identify specific sounds. For example, the dog learns to recognize the sound of the doorbell, the ring of an alarm clock, and even the whistle of a teakettle. When the dog hears the sound, it can lead its owner to the source. This type of dog also obeys voice commands and hand signals.

Both dogs and monkeys are trained to aid people with physical disabilities. Dogs can open heavy doors, pick up items off the floor, and retrieve a cordless telephone. When fitted with a special jacket, dogs can carry schoolbooks or other items that are placed in the pockets. Monkeys are able to open cabinets and retrieve small objects. They can turn light switches and water faucets on and off. Some can even aid a person in dressing and grooming.

Animals can help people with disabilities become more independent in their daily lives. Perhaps just as important, they can also provide companionship, devotion, and love.

---

state legislation regarding people with special needs.

By meeting with others, parents begin to understand and accept their own feelings and overcome any guilt or self-blame. They also learn to be effective advocates for children with various disabilities.

National Organizations

Parents can contact national organizations for information and help. Among these organizations are the National Mental Health Association, March of Dimes Birth Defect Foundation, Muscular Dystrophy Association, United Cerebral Palsy Association, American Cancer Society, and Special Olympics. Many of these groups have state and local chapters, which are listed in the telephone directory.

Community Services

Federal and state legislation provides consultation services, assistance to parents, and educational opportunities for children with a disability. Most specialists agree that services should start at birth or as soon as the disability is recognized.

Unfortunately, medical costs for children with a disability can be tremendous. It is important for parents to find out who is helping special children in their community and to get in touch with them. For example, public libraries often have Braille books and cassette recordings of books for children who are visually impaired. Many communities offer special programs for children with Down syndrome or cerebral palsy. Many community hospitals and support groups provide special therapy or training for children and their fam-

Discuss. What are some laws that promote and protect the rights of the disabled in our society? (parking spaces, curb cuts, equal access to education, social security disability benefits)

Activity. Have students contact national organizations for information about the services they have available.
Activity. Ask students to gather information about programs that provide animal companions for people with disabilities.

ilies. School-age children can attend special programs designed for specific disabilities—physical, emotional, cognitive, or learning disabilities. Children who have severe disabilities and cannot be cared for by their parents may be placed in a nearby state or private facility.

Parents can obtain information on other sources of help from their child's pediatrician or clinic. The local school system has a variety of resource people on staff. These include the child's classroom teacher, special education teachers, the school psychologist, the school nurse, the librarian, and school administrators.

Human services agencies can usually refer parents to available resources within the community and state. Many of these resources answer questions, offer support, and provide services free of charge. These services are designed to benefit both children and families.

Educating Children with Special Needs

All children who have a disability are guaranteed the right to free and appropriate education in the least restrictive environment. Public Law 94-142, the Education of All Handicapped Children Act, guarantees this right. This act created **special education,** a program of individualized instruction for children with disabilities or exceptional needs. Parents should work closely with the schools to coordinate their efforts with those of teachers.

If a child does not progress, parents can ask for an assessment by a special education consultant. Public Law 94-142 states that parents should be involved in all decisions regarding their children with special needs.

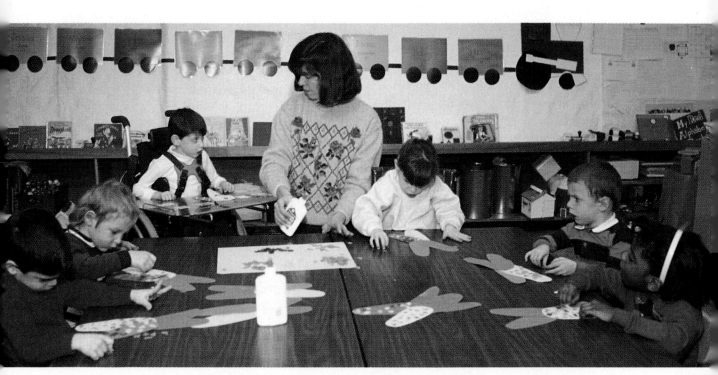

Many children with disabilities can be educated in a classroom with children who are not disabled. This process is called inclusion or integration, and it can benefit all children.

Activity. Invite a member of a community organization, such as the Lions Club, to talk about a program that aids people with disabilities.

Emphasize. Special education and related services are available from school districts in all states for children from the age of three through the age of twenty-one.

❖ Inclusion

Educating children with a disability in classrooms with children who are not disabled is called **inclusion** or integration. This process has also been called mainstreaming. Educators agree that children with disabilities develop their potential more rapidly when included as part of the regular program. Classroom teachers who have such children in their rooms receive advice and special teaching materials and aids from consultants who are trained to teach children with special needs.

Inclusion has several advantages:

- A regular classroom that includes children with disabilities is more like the community at large. It provides good preparation for all the children to function more effectively in society as they grow up.
- Children who are not disabled see the strengths of their special classmates and respond to them positively.
- Children with disabilities have the opportunity to observe and model the social behavior of their peers.
- Children and adults overcome their fear or uncomfortable feelings in the presence of special-needs children when they become better acquainted with and are helped to understand them.
- Parents of children who are disabled gain helpful support from sharing with other parents. They learn ways to deal with their children from other parents and teachers and feel less alone.

While children who are not severely disabled can be integrated, others are taught in small special groups or classes. Sometimes individual tutoring is given.

Children with disabilities deserve stimulating educational activities. They also need the opportunity to interact and learn with peers who are not disabled.

Discuss. How can students who are not disabled help students who have been included or mainstreamed into their classes?

DECISIONS ◆ ◆ DECISIONS

Danny, age five, was born with cerebral palsy. He has attended special schools since he was an infant. He can walk with a walker, and his mind is sharp. His caregivers recommend inclusion for Danny in public school next year. How can they and his parents prepare him for going to a new school with children who do not have a disability?

❖ Computer Technology

Computers are being used to educate children whose disability limits their communication or interaction with others. Children with poor motor skills and muscle tone, little or no speech, or minimal vision can use special computers. These are equipped with special keyboards, switches, speech synthesizers, or other electronic gear. This technology enables the children to demonstrate their abilities and learning potential.

For example, some children with Down syndrome are able to receive more information than they are able to respond to. With the use of a computer, these children are able to give back the correct answers to questions. Children with cerebral palsy can use special accessories with the computer. These enable the children to use limited motor skills as they learn.

Even children as young as toddlers are able to use computer programs with pictures and graphics instead of words. By demonstrating success at the computer, these children are able to focus on their abilities rather than their limitations. As a result, parents, caregivers, and teachers have a better understanding of each child's potential. Technology

Activity. Invite school personnel to talk to the class about the special services provided by your local school district.

is enabling children who are visually impaired, cannot talk, or cannot manipulate pencils and pens to communicate information and knowledge.

Special accessories permit children with a severe disability to use computers with whatever part of the body they control best. For example, large switches, touch windows with built-in sensors, and special power pads can be operated with a finger, a toe, or the head. With appropriate software, children with severe disabilities are able to build with blocks, dress dolls, and solve puzzles. Special communication boards and voice synthesizers allow children with speech disabilities to communicate their needs, wants, and ideas—often for the first time in their lives.

Computers also enable two or more children with special needs to play games together and thus develop social skills such as sharing and cooperation. These children have the opportunity to compete with each other and experience the feelings of winning and success.

In school, children with disabilities can use a computer for writing and a cassette recorder for recording notes that they listen to at home. This technology enables many children with a severe disability to function in a regular school program. At home, a computer can help children with disabilities study, play games, and operate other equipment, such as television sets and VCRs. These skills will enable some of them to hold jobs in the future.

Special resource groups, such as the Alliance for Technology Access, can help parents learn what technology is available and how to customize it for their children's needs. Every year, companies are manufacturing more special computer accessories and software programs to benefit people with special needs.

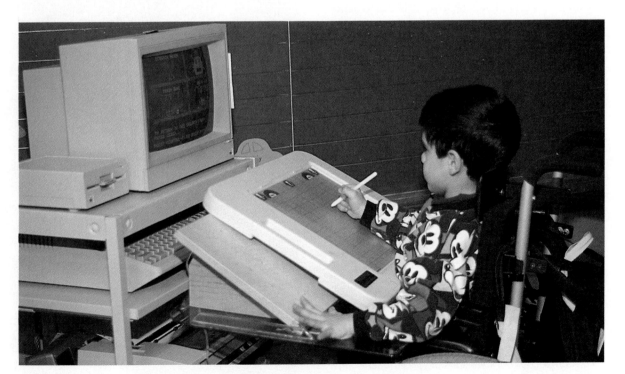

Specially equipped computers can help children with disabilities demonstrate their ability and knowledge. This child uses a special control board to operate the computer.

Activity. Ask students to look through computer catalogs or visit a computer store to get information about special equipment that can aid people with disabilities.

Gifted Children

Gifted children are also children with special needs. These children are very intelligent or show unusual talent in a particular area at an early age. For example, some gifted children have exceptional musical talent, while others have outstanding mathematical skills. Gifted children use abstract levels of reasoning long before their same-age peers. While other children are busy with a variety of activities, a gifted child may be totally absorbed in studying the stars or sketching pictures or playing the violin.

Although gifted children are cognitively advanced, they are not necessarily advanced in terms of physical, emotional, or social development. For example, the child who enjoys spending many hours practicing the piano may not enjoy playing outdoors with other children. As a result, the child may acquire the physical and social skills that develop naturally from group play later than other children do.

Some gifted children experience a great deal of emotional pressure because they set very high standards for themselves. They may repeat a task over and over until they achieve perfection. Others may worry excessively about problems, such as family finances or world peace, over which they have no control.

Gifted children need the same guidance, support, love, and affection that all children need. While they should be applauded for their special abilities, they should also be encouraged to develop a variety of interests and skills.

Gifted children may show a special talent, such as musical ability, at an early age. These children benefit from lessons or classes that provide stimulation and motivation.

Discuss. What social and emotional challenges might gifted children face with classmates and friends?

Activity. Have students research a gifted person, such as a musician or composer, who showed exceptional talent at a very young age.

✦✦ Parenting Gifted Children

Rearing a gifted child can present special challenges for parents and caregivers. Parents of a gifted child should learn as much as possible about their child's special abilities. This can help them make informed decisions about the child's development and education.

Parents of gifted children should provide them with activities that stimulate learning and motivate them. Some gifted children benefit from special lessons or classes in music, dance, art, languages, chess, reading, science, or mathematics. Visits to libraries, museums, theaters, and special cultural events provide added enrichment. Some parents of especially talented children find a scientist or musician with whom the children can study or work. Many gifted children enjoy spending time and energy helping others, such as tutoring other children.

Because learning comes easily to gifted children, they do not have to spend a great deal of time on routine learning. As a result, they can explore a topic, such as dinosaurs or electricity, in depth. Parents should provide opportunities for such children to read and write about their topic of interest and create drawings or models of it. Although parents should encourage gifted children to do their best, they should not pressure the children unreasonably.

In addition to activities that challenge their cognitive abilities, gifted children benefit from participating in a variety of activities with others of the same age. This helps both their social and emotional development, which are essential for their future happiness.

Like other children, gifted children need a combination of freedom and direction. They need freedom to develop their special talent. At the same time, they need direction to help them broaden their interests and make friends their own age. Most of all, gifted children need opportunities to share with other people the enjoyment and satisfaction they find in their special field.

If there are other children in the family, parents should take care to show as much love, pride, and attention to them as to the gifted child. Parents should never compare the intelligence or talents of siblings. One child may be a math whiz; another child may tell funny jokes. One child may be able to read at age three; another child may be a tennis star. Parents must remember that every child has special skills and abilities that should be nurtured.

Most parents have no way of evaluating how their child compares to others in intelligence or special talents. Nearly all believe that their child is "very bright." Thus parents should treat their child with the same special care and attention they would give a gifted child. Parents must realize that it is not test scores that will make the difference in their child's future but what the child does with his or her intelligence and talents.

✦✦ Educating Gifted Children

Educating gifted children involves providing for their needs as children as well as for their special talents. Differences of opinion exist regarding how gifted children should best be challenged. Some children benefit from enrichment; others benefit from acceleration.

Many schools provide enrichment programs for gifted children. If these children are in a class with average students, the teacher can give them special enrichment assignments to do in class or at home. Enrichment can also be given through special advanced classes in mathematics, science, foreign language, social studies, and language arts. Sometimes gifted students study special projects under the

Many schools offer advanced classes or after-school programs that provide enrichment activities for gifted children. These two students are monitoring vials in a science lab.

direction of a consultant who is trained to teach gifted and talented children.

Some states and large school districts have special high schools for gifted children. Here students enroll in a special program that focuses on their particular field of interest. Other states offer gifted students summer programs that are held on college or university campuses.

Most schools have special clubs and extracurricular activities that can provide enrichment experiences. Groups such as the debate team, orchestra, and chess club enable gifted students to sharpen their skills while interacting with other students.

Accelerated programs enable gifted children to gain their education at an accelerated, or faster, rate than normal. The children may skip grades in school and graduate from high school at a younger age than most other students. Some programs allow gifted students to take one or more college courses while still in high school or elementary school. Although accelerated programs promote cognitive development, they cause emotional or social problems for some children. Thus, many educators and parents prefer enrichment programs to accelerated programs for most gifted children.

Special education programs, as guaranteed by Public Law 94-142, apply to both gifted children and children with disabilities. Parents should find out from teachers and administrators what gifted programs are provided by their local school, school district, and state.

Discuss. What is the difference between enrichment and accelerated programs? What are the advantages and disadvantages of each for a student? If it were your decision, which would you prefer? Why?

CHAPTER 21 REVIEW

Summary

- About 10 percent of families have a child with one or more disabilities.
- Each type of disability—physical, emotional, cognitive, or learning—can vary from slight to severe.
- Children with disabilities have the same needs, feelings, and wishes as other children.
- Parents should focus on the child's abilities and talents rather than limitations.
- Children with disabilities should be encouraged to develop as much independence as possible.
- Friends and relatives, support groups, national organizations, and community services can help families who have a child with a disability.
- Inclusion is the name for placing students who have a disability in regular classrooms.
- Gifted children are very intelligent or very talented. They also have special needs.

Questions

p. 397 **1.** What environmental conditions can cause children to have a physical or cognitive disability?

p. 400 **2.** List three chronic health conditions that can result in physical disabilities.

p. 401 **3.** What is autism?

p. 402 **4.** What are two common types of learning disabilities? What are the characteristics of each?

p. 404 **5.** Why should parents learn all they can about their child's disability?

p. 405 **6.** How can parents promote the independence of a child with a disability?

p. 407 **7.** How can support groups help parents who have a child with a disability?

p. 410 **8.** What are three advantages of inclusion?

p. 412 **9.** Why do some gifted children feel strong emotional pressures?

Activities

1. Read about the lives of two famous people to find out how they overcame the limiting aspects of a disability. Some possibilities are Stevie Wonder, Ludwig von Beethoven, Ray Charles, Thomas Edison, Helen Keller, Itzhak Perlman, and Stephen Hawking.

2. Learn about the resources available in your community for families with children with special needs. What trained specialists are available? How can a family learn about these services? What are the costs of these services? Prepare a report.

3. Evaluate which public building and areas in your community are accessible to people in wheelchairs. How easy would it be for a person with a disability to attend your school, shop in local stores, or visit the library or courthouse? Share your findings with the class.

Think About

1. How would your life be changed if you had a physical disability that required the use of a wheelchair?

2. Why might gifted children not always get the best grades in school?

Guiding Children

CHAPTERS

Encouraging Children

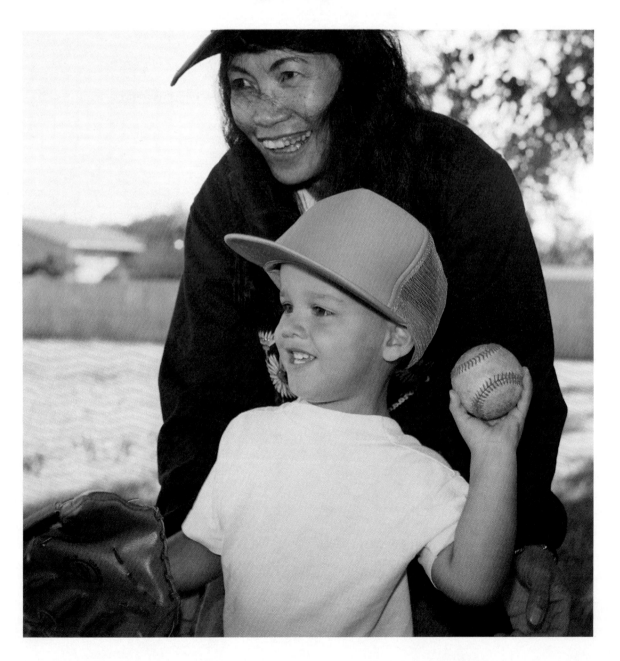

Objectives

This chapter will help you to:
- Explain the relationship between encouragement, motivation, and praise.
- Describe how parents and caregivers can provide guidance for children.
- List and give examples of effective communication skills.
- Discuss the importance of love for children.

Vocabulary

encouragement
motivation
communication
active listening

Terri and her father were at the playground in the park. She always enjoyed the swings. As she was swinging back and forth, she watched the other children climbing the slide and sliding down. As the swing slowed, Terri jumped off. She went to the slide but hesitated. Perhaps the children's shouts and their fast pace, along with the height of the slide, gave Terri a moment of fear.

Terri's father noticed her hesitation. He went near her but waited to see what she would do. She looked at him, then back at the slide. "I'll stand right here," said her father. He moved closer to the slide so he could reach Terri if necessary.

Her father continued, "You can hold on tight as you climb the steps. I know you can do it, and then you can slide down." He let her think about the situation for a moment. A few children passed her and climbed the steps.

At last Terri made her decision. She climbed up the stairs. At the top she said, "Look Daddy! See how high I am." Then she slid down and ran to the steps again. Her father had given her just the right amount of encouragement.

Providing Encouragement

All children need **encouragement**. This is a message of confidence and faith in another's ability. Encouragement is important for children at all stages of development. It gives them a sense of hope and self-confidence. Encouragement helps children feel important. It lets them know someone cares.

Encouragement is one of the most positive ways that parents and caregivers can help children develop into healthy and happy individuals. When adults provide encouragement, they nurture children's self-esteem. This encouragement leads to the development of a more positive self-concept and higher self-esteem. Encouragement also helps children develop self-confidence in their abilities.

❖ Motivation

Encouragement is especially important when children face new tasks. They enjoy trying new skills when they know others have faith and confidence in their abilities. They

Chapter Opener. Ask students to read the opening scenario to the chapter. Ask these questions: What conflicting feelings did Terri have at the playground? If her father had handled the situation differently, what might have been the result?

Activity. Ask students to tabulate how many times people say encouraging things to them in the next 24-hour period. Have them evaluate how each statement makes them feel.

Encouragement helps children learn new skills and nurtures their self-esteem.

want to do their best. Encouragement leads to **motivation**, an inner desire to act or behave in a certain way. It is like a driving force that makes a person work toward a particular goal. We speak of a person with such an inner drive as being motivated. Motivation affects children's learning and achievement, as well as their self-esteem.

Motivation gives direction to a person's behavior. It also determines the level of effort a person will put into an activity or task. For example, a two-year-old who wants a cookie will find a way to climb on a chair or countertop to get to the cookie jar. Even though the jar is out of reach, the child will exert much effort to get the cookie. The desire for a cookie motivates the child to do this. Can you think of times when children you know have made similar efforts? What motivated them? Did the strength of their desire influence their level of effort?

◆◆ Praise

Giving praise is an excellent way to provide encouragement. All children need adults to cheer their accomplishments.

Most parents find it easy to praise infants and take delight in their every accomplishment. Yet older children also need praise. At times, parents and caregivers are unsure of how to give such encouragement. Children of all ages like a smile, a hug, or a pat on the back. They respond warmly to comments such as "Good," "Fine," and "Well done."

In addition, children appreciate someone asking questions about their accomplishments. Such questions as "How did you do it?" and "Tell me about it" show sincere interest on the part of the listener. As children tell the story of what they did, they again experience the satisfaction of their accomplishment.

More About. Relate *motivation* to Erikson's stage of initiative (during the preschool years) and stage of industry (during the school-age years). See page 322.
Discuss. What is the difference between encouragement and praise?
Activity. Have students compile a list of phrases that parents and other caregivers can say to children when giving encouragement and praise.

Praising Efforts and Accomplishments

Praise is most effective when directed at children's efforts or accomplishments. This focuses on their attempts to succeed or to carry out certain tasks successfully. When praise is aimed at their personality, it has less impact.

For example, Tad's mother told him she liked the way he cleaned up the spill from the glass of milk he tried to pour. If she had told him he was a good boy for wiping up the spill, the result might have been different. Tad knows whether he was good or not. Maybe he was misbehaving when he spilled the milk. In that case, he might have become confused if his mother had told him he was a good boy for cleaning up the spill. He might even have misbehaved again to get future praise. Instead, Tad's mother praised his efforts, not him.

When children are praised for their efforts and accomplishments, they are encouraged to keep trying. For example, Isako's dad told her he was pleased that she tasted her broccoli even though she did not eat all of it. When Jake's mother told him he had really worked hard to tie his shoelaces, he beamed with joy. Even though he did not succeed, she praised his efforts.

A "high five" is one of many ways that parents can acknowledge childrens's efforts and accomplishments.

Praise can take many forms. It is up to parents to find the most effective approach in nurturing each child's confidence and self-esteem. Praising the child's efforts and accomplishments should be an important part of that approach.

Handling Mistakes and Failures

Sometimes children make mistakes or fail to achieve a task. Mistakes are a part of the process of trying various alternatives to see what works best. Children learn by experiencing the consequences of their actions.

DECISIONS ◆ ◆ DECISIONS

Clara, age three, uses her whole fist to grasp a spoon. She handles crayons and small blocks in the same way. She is adept at handling these objects, and her parents think she is ready for a more advanced level of coordination. How might Clara's parents encourage her to learn new skills?

Discuss. Why should parents and teachers praise a child's efforts along every step toward achieving a goal, rather than just praising the final accomplishment?

Emphasize. Children should be praised for their efforts and accomplishments, not for themselves.

Around the World

What's in a Name?

In some cultures, certain customs influence the name a parent chooses for a child.

Children in Burma are named for the day of the week on which they are born. Each day of the week is assigned a different set of letters from the alphabet. For example, if children were born on a Sunday, their name begins with a vowel. If they were born on a Monday, their name begins with *k, g,* or *ng*. If they were born on a Tuesday, their name begins with *s, z,* or *ny*. For Burmese children, the day of the week on which they are born is more important than the actual birth date. Many Burmese believe that a person's character is determined by the day of birth. People born on Sunday are thought to be stingy. Those born on Monday are considered jealous. Those born on Tuesday are supposedly honest.

In Venezuela, most of the people are Roman Catholic. Children are usually named after the saint whose feast day matches their birth date. This means that many children with the same name celebrate their birthday on the same day.

In the Jewish religion, children are named after a deceased relative or close friend of the family. The name does not have to be exactly the same, but it does have to start with the same letter of the alphabet. Jewish children usually have two first names. One is in the language of the country where they live, and the other is a Hebrew name.

When criticisms are directed at children's efforts or tasks rather than children's personality or character, their self-esteem is preserved. In this way, children learn that even though they have done something wrong, they are still loved as a person.

If parents and caregivers criticize the child rather than his or her actions, they make the child feel guilty and unworthy. Compare the following comments on the same incident:
"You really made a mess. Now you can help clean it up."
"How could you be so clumsy? Now look at what I have to do."

As children grow older, some do not always do well in school. Poor grades often bring discouragement and shame. A parent who nags, punishes, or threatens such a child will probably find that the child does worse instead of better. Rather than helping the child, the withdrawal of parental approval often has a discouraging effect.

At times like this, children need additional support and encouragement from parents as well as from teachers. When children know others are genuinely concerned about them, they have more self-confidence about trying again. They are able to direct their efforts toward learning rather than toward trying to compensate for their academic failures.

◆ ◆ *Self-Esteem* ◆ ◆

Parents and other caregivers should encourage children to try again when they experience failure. Adults should also recognize children's efforts when they succeed. Children who receive encouragement, guidance, and love usually develop a positive self-concept. Those who are neglected, rejected, and often punished usually develop a negative view of themselves.

Activity. Ask students to observe parents with their children at parks, ball games, grocery stores, and shopping malls. Have them tabulate how many times parents ignore "good" behavior and notice "bad" behavior. How many times do parents use the words *No* and *Don't?* How do the parents' attention and words influence their children's behavior? Have students share their findings.

Providing Guidance

Encouragement is a positive method of guiding children. Guidance refers to all the words and actions adults use to influence children's behavior. Guidance occurs whenever parents, caregivers, or teachers interact with children. Although some adults use rewards, fear, or punishment to try to motivate children, these are negative approaches. In contrast, encouragement helps children help themselves.

Providing guidance helps a child become self-guided or self-directed. A self-directed child is one who can make good decisions about behavior when adults are not around to reinforce rules. The child has learned what is meant by right and wrong.

The goals of guidance should be to help the child do the following:

- Develop a positive self-concept.
- Develop high self-esteem.
- Grow in independence.
- Learn to get along with others.
- Develop self-control.

❖ Being a Role Model

Being the kind of person parents would like the child to become is an effective form of guidance. Children learn quickly by watching others. If you study families, you will find striking similarities between children and their parents. Family members have similar mannerisms, attitudes, and ways of responding to situations.

Because children view their parents as the most significant people in their lives, they want to imitate them. Children also imitate caregivers and teachers. This places a great responsibility on adults for demonstrating the kind of behavior they would like to see the children imitate.

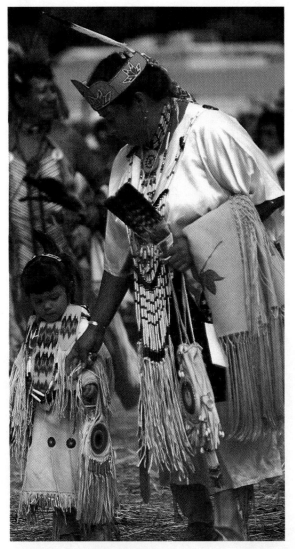

Children learn about their culture from the words and actions of their parents and other caregivers.

Parents, caregivers, and teachers are role models for children. They show through their behavior, attitudes, and actions how people act, talk, and behave. By setting good examples, role models help children learn appropriate behavior.

If adults model happy, calm, and generous behaviors, children will copy them. On the other hand, if children see adults being mean, bossy, or selfish, children will soon behave in the same manner. This modeling of behavior

Discuss. Many parents record a list of "firsts" in their child's baby book. Are baby books for other children in the family usually kept as diligently as the first child's? Why or why not? How might this make children feel when they grow older and ask to see their baby book?

Activity. Encourage students to examine some of their mannerisms or behavior. Can they identify the person or persons they are imitating?

is often seen when children play with other children. Some parents are surprised at how well their children imitate their own actions. Sometimes the imitated behavior is very negative—such as yelling, complaining, hitting, or cursing.

Children also treat their stuffed animals and dolls the same way their parents treat them or their younger siblings. When children love their dolls and handle them with care, they reveal that their own parent-child experiences are loving. When children spank their dolls, they usually do so because their parents spank them. They think this is the thing to do.

Children often develop an interest in a hobby from their parents or other relatives.

Of course, no adults can be perfect. All people—parents and children alike—have bad days. Children would form an unrealistic view of the world if they never saw adults get angry or behave unreasonably. Dealing with a certain amount of frustration and inconsistency probably helps children learn to cope. However, role models should take a long-range view of problem situations. They should recognize that harm may be done if they continually model inappropriate behavior.

❖ Participating with Children

Planning activities and routines that parents and children do as a family is very important. Children learn how to do many things by working along with a parent. They learn the various roles that family members have. They learn about relationships by watching what goes on between the mother and father and between parents and children in the family. Moreover, children learn attitudes toward work by watching the adults around them.

Sometimes a child develops an interest in a hobby from a family member. Many people have learned skills from relatives who let them help when they were children. Building models, gardening, sewing, cooking, and collecting items are interests that often develop in childhood.

❖ Acknowledging Feelings

Parents need to provide ways for children to express their feelings, both positive and negative. Children should feel free to let parents know when things are going well. For example, four-year-old Antonio came into the room with his arms wrapped tightly around himself. His father asked him what he was doing. Antonio replied, "Oh, Daddy, I like myself so much today I want to give myself a big hug."

It is just as important for children to be able to express negative or unpleasant feelings. Some parents try to teach children to avoid showing feelings such as pain, anger, and fear. This usually causes children to turn these feelings inward. Sometimes emotions are held inside so long that the children begin to feel a great deal of stress. This can result in outbursts such as crying, hitting others, or throwing things.

Sometimes children get confused as they try to express their feelings. Five-year-old Vanessa told her mother that she was feeling sad. Her mother asked, "Are you sure you are sad, or are you angry?" Vanessa quickly replied, "I'm angry. I'm mad because we're not going to the store like you promised."

Parents who understand emotional development can help guide children to express feelings in healthy ways. If parents spank and yell at children during spurts of anger, their children will learn to hit others and scream when they become angry. On the other hand, parents who talk about how they feel when they are angry help children learn to express such feelings in constructive ways. You will learn more about how to guide children's behavior in Chapter 24.

◆ *Health & Safety* ◆

Mental Health

Mental health is a measure of how one feels about oneself, relates to others, and deals with everyday challenges. People with good mental health like and accept themselves. They relate well to others. They are able to deal with the problems and frustrations of daily life without becoming overwhelmed.

During childhood, parents can help children be mentally healthy as well as physically healthy. Encouragement, praise, and love help children develop a positive self-image. Children who feel good about themselves tend to be more confident and self-assured. They are less likely to follow the crowd or give in to peer pressure just because "everybody's doing it."

Here are some suggestions for building children's confidence in themselves while guiding their behavior.
- **Work on one problem at a time.** Do not try to change too many things at once.
- **Be specific.** Saying, "I want you to keep your room neat" is too general for most young children. Instead, start with a specific task such as, "I want you to put your dirty clothes in the hamper."
- **Remember that big changes usually start small.** For some children, the task of sorting their dirty clothes and putting them in the hamper is a big one. Instead, they could start with just the underwear and socks.
- **Praise achievement.** If, at first, the only item children manage to put into the hamper is a dirty sock, be pleased and show it.
- **Criticize behavior but never the children.** Be sure children understand the difference between how you feel about their behavior and how you feel about them. "I love you even though you forget to put your dirty clothes in the hamper" is an important message to convey. Children who grow up feeling that love has to be earned by accomplishments and good behavior may become adults who never feel good about themselves.

Discuss. Many adults tell children "Big boys and girls don't cry." Do you agree with this message? Why or why not? How should parents teach children to show feelings of pain or sadness?

More About. Parents can help children learn to express their feelings by modeling the following statement: "*When* (describe the situation), I *feel* (name the feeling) *because* (give the reason)."

Communicating with Children

Parents and caregivers can use communication skills to guide children. **Communication** is the process of sharing information, thoughts, and feelings. Sometimes communication is accomplished with words. At other times, it involves smiles or frowns. It may be the most important factor in establishing good relationships between parents and children.

Effective communication strengthens parent-child relationships. When children can express their ideas, they feel important. This builds their self-esteem. They know that their thinking has value. In contrast, children feel rejected when their attempts to communicate are ignored or denied.

Communication with children begins in infancy. Babies can understand the meaning of a smile and a soft tone of voice before they can understand the words. As children grow older, parents and caregivers use communication to nurture and guide children. Through words and gestures, adults can communicate love as well as limits.

By developing good communication skills, parents and caregivers can help keep the avenue of communication open throughout childhood. Then adults and children can continue to share their thoughts and feelings during the teenage years. The rest of this section provides guidelines for developing good communication skills. Additional tips appear on pages 430–433.

❖ Getting on the Child's Level

Have you ever thought about how a child must feel, always looking up to others? When you kneel or sit on the floor, you can talk to the child face-to-face. You are better able to make eye contact, which brings a personal quality to any interaction. In this position, you help the child feel more at ease.

Getting on the child's level also means using words that the child understands. You can relate this principle to yourself. Do you understand the next sentence? "The magniloquence of his amplitude was supererogatory." Now imagine the child's frustration with words he or she cannot understand. Using simple words and short sentences helps children understand what you are saying.

Parents can communicate better with a child when they talk face-to-face with him.

Reference. See pages 501-505 for additional information on ways to communicate effectively and resolve conflicts.
Activity. Ask students to look up the words in the sentence, "The magniloquence of his amplitude was supererogatory." Have them write the sentence, using words that a preschooler could understand. (speaking in a grandiose style, mental capacity, greater than needed).

◆ Being Positive

Positive statements tell children what they should do. Negative statements leave children confused about how to behave. For example, "Come out of the pool as soon as I call" is much clearer than "Don't take so long to come when I call you." One should always emphasize the do's rather than the don'ts.

Saying "Please" and "Thank you" shows courtesy and consideration for others. Adults should use these words with children, not just with other adults. Compare these two statements: "Please close the door" and "How many times have I told you not to leave the door open?" Which statement is positive? Which statement encourages a child to take the requested action?

◆ Being Clear

Effective communication involves the use of action words. This helps children focus on the action parents and caregivers are requesting. Saying "Come over here" is much clearer to a child than "You're standing too close to that swinging door." Even young children understand simple statements that have action verbs near the beginning of the sentence. Action verbs include bring, come, put on, eat, drink, wash, turn off.

DECISIONS ◆ ◆ DECISIONS

Three-year-old Gregory accidentally spills his glass of milk. His mother yells, "Look at the mess you made! Why can't you be more careful? You're a bad boy!" Do you think Gregory's mother has handled the situation appropriately? Why or why not?

Young children should not be expected to remember instructions given to them far in advance. Also, they cannot remember a series of directions, such as put away your toys, put on your pajamas, wash your hands and face, and brush your teeth. Instead, adults should break the series into separate directions and give just one at a time. After the child has carried out the first direction, the adult can give the next one and so on.

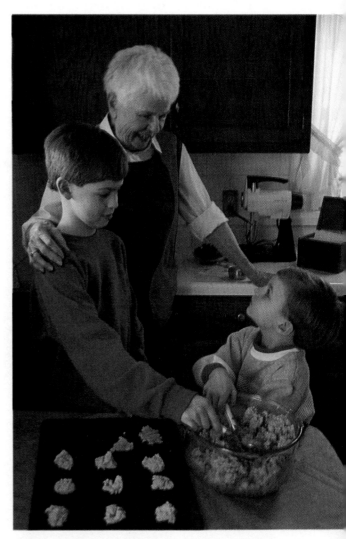

Adults should give children one direction at a time—at the place and time when they want the children to do it.

Activity. Ask students to write a list of negative statements that parents may tell children. Then have them rephrase each statement into a positive one. Have them underline each action verb.

Reference. See pages 430-433 for communication tips.
More About. Generally, give one direction at a time until age five, then an additional direction per year of age over age five. Limit directions to four at one time during school-age years.

❖ Using "I" Messages

When explaining the reasons for a direction, adults should use "I" messages. An example of such a statement is "I get upset when you throw your toys all around the room." This kind of statement helps a child know what bothers a parent. It clarifies that a certain action causes a problem for the parent. "I" messages can make reasons clearer and get more positive responses from children.

An "I" message usually describes three things:

1. *The undesirable behavior:* "When you come home late,"
2. *Your feelings:* "I get worried"
3. *The consequence:* "because I think something might have happened to you."

"I" messages are less threatening than "you" messages. A "you" message would be "You are very irresponsible when you come home late." This statement is filled with blame and accusation. It criticizes the other person and suggests that he or she is at fault. In contrast, "I" messages reveal how the speaker feels about the situation.

Adults can also give "I" messages when apologizing. No harm is done if a parent or caregiver is willing to say, "I'm sorry I yelled at you. I'm not feeling too well today, and what you did made me really angry—but I still shouldn't have yelled." In this way, the adult lets the child know that everyone has weak moments and everyone makes mistakes.

❖ Listening Actively

Active listening means giving full attention to what the speaker is saying and listening to the feelings behind the words. At best,

Adults should use "I" messages when explaining the reason for directions or rules. This father told his son, "I get upset when you don't put your toys away after playing with them."

Activity. Have students rephrase the following "you" messages to "I" messages:
. You never pick up your clothes.
. You always leave toys on the floor.
. You have to get out of bed on time.
. You always slam the door.
. You must stop teasing your sibling.
. You forgot to tell me where you were going after school.

tive communication also involves the exchange of thoughts and feelings by actively listening to and talking with each other.

❖ Avoiding Lectures

As children get older, they often resist conversations with their parents. Teenagers may feel they are receiving lectures or being criticized. They sometimes believe parents talk too much, ask too many questions, and pry into their lives. In turn, parents become frustrated because of the lack of communication with their children.

During adolescence, children become increasingly independent of their parents. They need to feel free to discuss their true feelings. One way that parents can create an atmosphere for this is to share their own feelings with teenage children.

Here are some guidelines for parents to follow when communicating with adolescents:

- **Express understanding.** Before giving advice or instructions, parents should state their understanding of the teenager's feelings. "I know you are unhappy, but we cannot allow you to go."

- **Avoid lecturing.** Parents should state their thoughts and feelings without needlessly repeating themselves. They should not insist that only they know exactly what is best for their teenage children.

- **Respect privacy.** Adolescents are developing their own sense of autonomy and identity and need time alone. Parents should not listen to their children's telephone conversations or open their mail.

- **Avoid imitating language and conduct.** Teenagers resent parents who use teenage slang and act in an immature manner.

You will learn more about communication among family members in Chapter 26.

Active listening helps parents better understand both the words and feelings that the child is trying to express.

when most people listen, they hear only the words that are being spoken. However, children often have difficulty finding the right words to express themselves.

Parents and caregivers who are good listeners will hear, see, and feel what the child is saying. Active listening means more than hearing the child's exact words. It means sensing the child's message and how the child feels.

If communication is to be meaningful, both parents and children must be good listeners. Children learn the art of listening from their parents. When parents pay attention to children as they speak, children learn to listen to what parents have to say when they speak.

Communication with children should not be limited to telling them what to do. Effec-

Discuss. Why is it important for parents to listen for the child's feelings as well as the words? How would a child feel when a parent seems to ignore what the child is saying? How do you feel when a person does this to you? Why?

Activity. Have students make a list of things parents should not do when communicating with children. Then have them list all the positive things that parents should do.

Communicating with Children

Here are some guidelines that can make communication with children more effective.

Get the child's attention. Be sure the child can see and hear you. Get down to the child's eye level and maintain eye-to-eye contact. Remember that your facial expression and tone of voice will communicate as much as your actual words.

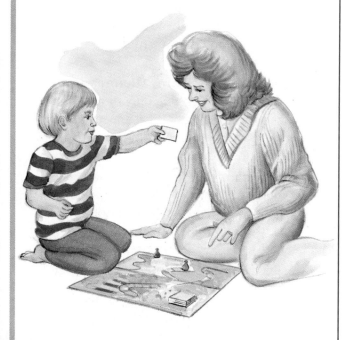

Be positive. Tell the child what you do want done rather than what you do not want done. A positive statement helps the child become self-directed. In contrast, a "don't" command may stick in the child's mind, and he or she may be unable to figure out what to do.

Positive Statements	Negative Statements
"Drink your milk."	"Don't blow bubbles in your milk."
"Bring the magazine to me."	"Don't play with the magazine."

Be clear. Use simple words and short sentences when talking to a young child. When giving directions, put the action part of the statement first. This helps the child focus on the action you want him or her to take.

Action Part First	Action Part Not Clear
"Come here."	"You might get hurt if you go over there."
"Put the book on the shelf."	"The book belongs on the shelf."

Be simple. Give only one or two directions at a time. Too many directions will make the child forget what he or she is supposed to do. After the child has successfully completed the first one or two directions, give a second or third direction.

One Simple Direction	Too Many Directions
"Put on your boots."	"Put on your sweater, find your raincoat, and bring me your boots."
"Put the plates on the table."	"Set the table, wash your hands, and then tell everyone that dinner is ready."

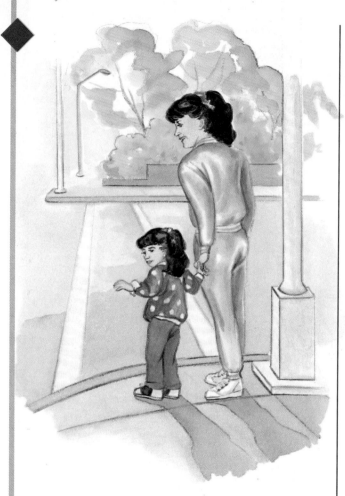

Give reasons. Giving reasons for a request helps the child see the point. Make your reasons honest and easy to understand. If a request does not have a good reason, perhaps you should not make it.

Reason Given	No Reason Given
"Turn off the television now. There are no more programs for children tonight."	"Turn off the television."
"I want you to go to bed early tonight because you have a cold. Extra sleep may help you feel better tomorrow."	"Put on your pajamas."

Be timely. Give a direction at the time and place you want the child to carry it out. Otherwise the child may not remember it.

Timely	Too Soon
"Hold my hand because we're going to cross the street now."	"When we go for a walk later today, be sure to hold my hand."
"Put the crayons away now that you've finished coloring."	"After you finish coloring, put the crayons away."

Listen. Stop and listen. Allow the child to express his or her ideas and feelings. Active listening helps you better understand what the child is trying to express. It also shows respect for the child and his or her opinions.

Use "I" messages. Tell the child how you feel about the situation rather than blame and criticize the child.

"I" messages	"You" messages
"I get upset when you don't pick up your toys."	"Can't you ever remember to pick up your toys?"
"I get worried when you don't let me know where you are."	"You are very thoughtless when you don't call to let me know where you are."

Importance of Love

Guidance should help children feel good about themselves. In part, this means letting children know that they are loved. Children who grow up feeling loved and wanted have a feeling of self-confidence and self-worth. They are able to develop positive attitudes and behaviors toward others. They learn from their parents' example to be kind and loving.

Children who feel loved usually are able to face most of life's challenges. They can handle disappointments and conflict that come their way. They can overcome stress and crises when they know there is a loving, caring family to support them.

❖ Communicating Love

Love is expressed in many ways. A parent expresses love for an infant by touching, holding, stroking, cuddling, kissing, or rocking the child. Such physical closeness is powerful. It

All children need to feel loved—even when they make mistakes or misbehave.

reinforces both the child's and the parent's feelings of joy, belonging, and security.

Parents also show their love in the way they talk with children. Using a kind tone of voice conveys love and caring. Playing with children is one of the best ways to show genuine interest. Tucking children into bed and telling them bedtime stories are simple ways to let children know they are loved. This type of behavior helps children learn that parents can be tender, gentle, and affectionate even though they are big and powerful. In turn, a loving attitude makes parents feel good about themselves.

Parents need to extend love to children even in times of stress and personal difficulties. For example, a father who comes home tired may not feel like playing with his children. Yet he can communicate a feeling of love by the way in which he greets them. He might pick them up, swing them around a couple of times, and give them a big hug. He could say, "I'm certainly happy to see you. Now I'm going to relax for a while because I'm feeling very tired. You'll need to play without me, but I'll be right here." This kind of communication helps children know that their parents care and are interested in them.

It is natural and easy to be loving when things are going well and the child is doing what pleases the parent. However, there are many times when children will make mistakes and misbehave as a part of growing and learning. Even in difficult situations, parents should remain calm and loving. Children should know they are always loved, not just when they are behaving to the parent's satisfaction.

When children receive encouragement, guidance, and love, they have a better chance of succeeding in life. They feel secure and valued as they go about the tasks of living and learning. These are important gifts that parents and caregivers can give to children.

Discuss. Should parents communicate their love in different ways to children at different age levels? Why or why not?

Reference. See chapter 24 for ways to handle misbehavior.

CHAPTER 22 REVIEW

Summary

- Encouragement helps children develop a positive self-concept and increased self-esteem and motivates them to take on new tasks with self-confidence.
- Praise should be directed at children's efforts and accomplishments rather than their personality.
- Parents provide guidance by acting as role models, joining in children's activities, and encouraging children to express their feelings.
- Communication skills are essential in building meaningful relationships with children.
- Knowing they are loved gives children feelings of security and self-worth. It helps them develop positive attitudes and behavior.

Questions

p. 419 **1.** Define *encouragement* and explain how it motivates children.

p. 421 **2.** Why is it better to criticize children's undesirable actions than the children themselves?

p. 423 **3.** What is guidance? Name four ways in which guidance can help children.

p. 423 **4.** What responsibilities do role models have?

p. 424 **5.** How can parents encourage children to express both positive and negative feelings? Why is this important?

p. 426 **6.** What does "getting on the child's level" mean in terms of communication?

p. 427 **7.** Why should parents use positive statements when telling children what to do?

p. 428 **8.** Why are "I" messages better than "you" messages?

p. 429 **9.** Name several ways in which parents can express love for their children.

Activities

1. Write a short essay on a parent's attitude of "Do As I Say, Not As I Do."
2. Visit a local park on the weekend and watch how parents relate to their children. Draw some conclusions about how the parents did or did not provide encouragement for their children.
   - How many parents participated in activities with their children?
   - How many parents praised their children for some action or behavior? How did they do this?
   - How many parents communicated love to their children? How did they do this?
3. For 24 hours, listen for negative statements in conversations. Then rephrase the statements to positive ones.

Think About

1. How can you tell when someone is actively listening to what you are saying?
2. Describe in detail the kind of role model you would like to be for a child and why.

Guiding Moral Development

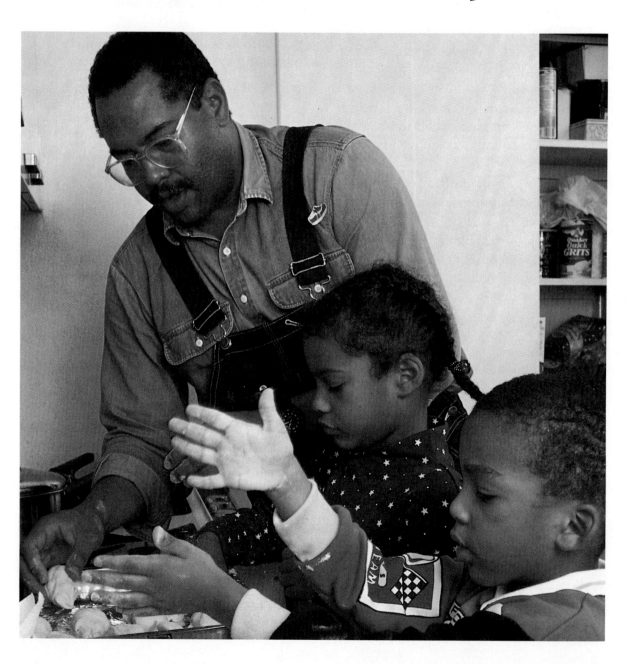

Objectives

This chapter will help you to:
- Compare the various stages of moral development.
- Discuss the importance of values.
- Explain how parents can help children develop responsibility.
- Describe how parents should handle questions about sexuality.

Vocabulary

moral development
conscience
principles
conventions
character
work ethic
allowance

Mike, age six, stands at the corner waiting to cross the street. It is snowing. Mike's parents have told him, "Always wait until you can't see any more cars before you cross the street." So Mike waits and waits.

The only cars in the street are two blocks away, and they are creeping slowly. Since Mike can still see cars coming down the street, he continues to wait on the curb. He remembers the safety rules for crossing streets that he has learned from his parents and teacher.

Mike's mother watches from the window. She guesses the dilemma that Mike faces. Every day when Mike leaves for school, she reminds him to cross the street only when every car is gone. Now she hurries outside to help him.

His mother says, "I'll help you cross the street today. The cars are moving very slowly because of the snow."

Mike replies, "I was afraid you'd be mad at me if I crossed the street when I could see a car coming."

Mike, like other children his age, has no real concept of rules. His main concern for doing or not doing something is to avoid punishment. This motivates his behavior.

Moral Development

Moral development is the process of learning standards of right and wrong. Parents need to help children develop a sense of morality that will guide their behavior. This process takes many years as children gradually go through different stages of moral development.

During early childhood, children begin to realize that certain behaviors are considered good or right. These behaviors are encouraged by parents and other caregivers. On the other hand, some actions are considered bad or wrong. These behaviors may result in criticism or punishment. Thus parents and caregivers help teach children what to do and what not to do. Children also learn by observing others.

As children grow older, they start to examine the standards and rules they have learned. They will test these against their own experience of what is right and wrong or good and bad. Eventually, they accept, modify, or reject each standard or rule. Then they use this sense of morality to guide and direct their future behavior.

Chapter Opener. Ask students to read the opening scenario to the chapter. Ask these questions: What thoughts and feelings did Mike have as he tried to cross the street? How else could his mother have handled the situation? Why?

Discuss. Why is moral development important? How does it relate to the other areas of growth and development?

Between the ages of five and seven, children begin to develop a **conscience** (KAHN-shens). This is an inner sense of what is right or wrong in one's own behavior. A person's conscience makes him or her feel obligated to do what is right or good. It helps the person control his or her behavior. A conscience also makes a person feel guilty for wrong or bad behavior.

❖ Kohlberg's Theory of Moral Development

Lawrence Kohlberg studied the development of moral reasoning in children. He believed that moral development is complex and continues over a long period of time. According to Kohlberg's theory, moral development occurs in a series of stages. The lowest stage is related to obedience. A child in this stage says, "I will not perform this action because I will be punished." The highest stage is related to conscience or principles. **Principles** are personal rules that form the basis of proper conduct. A person in the highest stage says, "I will not perform this action because it is morally wrong."

Kohlberg's theory of moral development is based on Piaget's theory of cognitive development (see Chapter 19). According to Kohlberg, one cannot proceed to the higher levels of moral reasoning until one has reached the higher levels of cognitive development. Kohlberg divides moral development into six stages grouped in three levels: the preconventional, conventional, and postconventional.

The Preconventional Level

Children's moral reasoning is at the preconventional level during their preschool and early school-age years. Kohlberg calls this level *preconventional* because children do not understand the **conventions**, or accepted standards, of behavior.

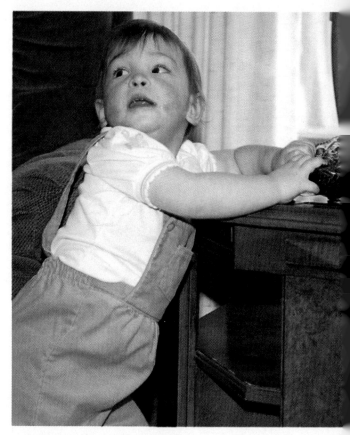

At the first level of moral development, young children have no sense of right or wrong. They obey rules to avoid punishment.

In Stage 1, children do not consider the point of view of others. They have no sense of right and wrong. Their main concern is avoiding punishment. In Stage 2, children learn how to receive rewards as well as avoid punishment. Children at this level help people who help them and hurt people who hurt them. They still evaluate actions in terms of the consequences.

The Conventional Level

Between the ages of nine and fifteen, children generally reach the conventional level of morality. They now understand the conventions of society. During Stage 3, there is a great deal of conformity. Children are sensitive to what other people want and think. A sense of

Discuss. What happens when a child does not develop a conscience? What actions or behavior might you expect the child to display?

Activity. Have students review Piaget's theory of cognitive development on pages 359-362. Ask them to explain why moral development is related directly to cognitive development.

Kohlberg's Stages of Moral Development
Stages and Reasons for Moral Decisions

LEVEL III: POSTCONVENTIONAL LEVEL (Adolescents and adults, though not everyone reaches Level III)

Stage 6: Principled. Decisions are made according to individual principles of conscience. Motivation is feeling right with oneself.

Stage 5: Autonomous. Decisions are based on upholding values of society and human rights. Motivation is community respect.

LEVEL II: CONVENTIONAL LEVEL (School age and young adolescent age)

Stage 4: Authority and Social Order-Maintaining Orientation. Right behavior consists of following fixed rules and respecting authority. Guilt occurs when authorities disapprove or punish.

Stage 3: Good-Boy, Nice-Girl Orientation. Reason for behavior is to maintain good relationships and approval of others. One conforms to notions of majority or natural behavior.

LEVEL I: PRECONVENTIONAL LEVEL (Preschool and early elementary-age children)

Stage 2: Naively Egoistic Orientation. Reason for behavior is to get rewards. People can do what they want to, even though their behavior conflicts with rights of others.

Stage 1: Obedience and Punishment. The reason for doing or not doing something is to avoid punishment. Being right means obeying an authority.

reciprocity, or mutual exchange between two people, now emerges. Children do the right thing not only to satisfy their own needs but also to satisfy the needs of others.

In Stage 4, children adopt a law-and-order kind of thinking. They realize that living by the rules wins praise or approval from others. Children begin to see more than one side to a situation. In Kohlberg's view, this ability to see another's perspective is the beginning of morality. Children no longer identify exclusively with their parents. They also begin to

identify with institutions of society, such as church or school. During this stage, children become increasingly sensitive to what others want and think. They generally abide by rules other people have made.

Between Stages 4 and 5 is an intermediate stage of morality. According to Kohlberg, this stage, unlike others, can be skipped. Those who experience this stage question the validity of general morality. They deeply question society's definition of right and wrong. Many omit the word *moral* from their vocabulary.

Activity. Have students relate Stages 3 and 4 of the conventional level to conformity and the power of peer pressure during the later school-age years and the teenage years.

Discuss. What is meant by a *sense of reciprocity*? What examples can you give?

The Postconventional Level

At about age sixteen, some young people reach the postconventional level. They have progressed beyond just following the rules. In Stage 5, they grasp the concept of human rights. They begin to understand the notion of the social contract. This is the idea that members of society must agree on rules to live together and settle disputes over competing rights.

Finally, in Stage 6, people develop universal ethical principles based on reciprocity and human equality. The development of a true conscience enables individuals to value behavior that respects the dignity of all other people as well as their own dignity. Most people do not reach this stage until adulthood, if ever. Some never reach this stage.

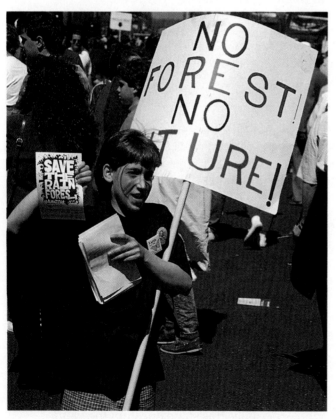

At the postconventional level, people become concerned about human rights and justice. They may work toward changing laws or behavior. They try to do what they deeply believe is right.

Problem Solving. Ask students to discuss ways that parents can help toddlers learn to develop self-discipline.

◆◆ Stages of Moral Development

How does Kohlberg's theory of moral development relate to children's behavior? Toddlers understand that there are certain things they must not do. However, they do not understand why these activities are wrong or undesirable. They do not have the language skills to grasp explanations or talk about their wishes instead of acting on them.

The word *no* is the easiest way to communicate to toddlers that they must control their impulses. However, toddlers do not have the self-discipline to control their own actions at all times. For example, two-year-old Maura has been told not to touch the flowers. She often repeats the rule aloud to herself: "Mustn't touch." At other times, she gives in to her urge. These failures of control are a normal part of the moral development process. It takes time for children to acquire their own sense of right and wrong.

Preschoolers learn to follow rules imposed on them by parents and other caregivers. The rules are enforced through reward and punishment. Children at this age tend to measure right and wrong in terms of the size of the misdeed or the amount of damage done. It makes no difference whether the act was accidental or intentional. For example, preschoolers think that the child who accidentally breaks several glasses deserves greater punishment than the child who intentionally breaks one glass.

◆ ◆ *Self-Esteem* ◆ ◆

Parents must nurture the moral development of their children. Such development builds a life-long foundation for children's character. Children learn respect, cooperation, and responsibility only if that is what they see in the behavior of adults around them.

Activity. Have students identify games that children play. What rules are followed for each type of game? How do school-age children change certain rules? Why?

School-age children begin to understand the rules of right and wrong made by adults. They know what they should do and what they should not do. By about age ten, most children begin to change their attitudes about rules. They no longer see rules simply as laws laid down by adults. For example, rules can be changed during a game as long as all the players agree. They grasp the concept of justice and equal treatment under the rules. This begins to mean more than the notion of adult authority.

At about eleven or twelve years of age, many children become aware of individual motives and circumstances. They begin to see another person's point of view. For example, Alberto said, "I understand, now that Dad explained why I shouldn't do it." Children of this age also begin to take into account such factors as age and experience. They will usually give a young child who is just learning a game an extra try or excuse the child's errors. Now they begin to think of right and wrong in terms of circumstances. When Nicole learned that her young brother accidentally broke some dishes, she responded, "Yes, but he didn't mean to do it."

Finally, some adolescents begin to develop their own personal standards of morality. They become concerned about the welfare of other human beings. At the highest level of moral development, individuals act morally because their own high standards demand it.

Moving from Stage to Stage

The ages at which children proceed from one stage of moral development to the next vary considerably. Parents and caregivers should not expect children to understand what they are not capable of understanding. For example, a four-year-old does not understand why lying is wrong. An eight-year-old is not capable of understanding human rights. Although moral guidance should begin in

DECISIONS ◆
◆ DECISIONS

A few days ago, Blair accepted a date with Charles for the big high school dance. Now she has learned that Brad is planning to ask her to the same dance. She has always wanted to go out with Brad, who is a popular senior. However, she knows that if she breaks her date with Charles it could damage their friendship. Blair is confused about what she should do. She has asked you for advice. What will you tell her?

early childhood, it will take years for children to develop a sense of morality.

In fact, some people never reach the highest level of moral development. Adolescents and adults who behave morally only because of rewards or punishment are still at the preconventional level. Adults who try to do what friends, family, and people in high positions expect of them are still at the conventional level. Only when individuals act morally because of their own principles have they reached the highest level of moral development.

Moral Development and Behavior

Both children and adults do not always behave according to their stage of moral development. For example, Janette believes that shoplifting is wrong. However, she is tempted to do it because she is being pressured by a group of friends. In the face of such peer pressure, it may take courage for Janette to stick to her own moral beliefs.

On the other hand, the development of moral beliefs and principles can help people make decisions about their own behavior. The motivation to act in a certain way comes from within themselves rather than from others.

Discuss. Why do some people never reach the postconventional level of moral development?
Activity. Have students list specific things that adolescents and adults may do only because of rewards and punishment

(preconventional level). Then ask students to make a second list of things adolescents and adults may do because of approval by peers and by authorities (conventional level). What does this tell you about behavior?

What Are Values?

Values are what people believe in. They are the beliefs that people stand up for or oppose. Values give meaning and direction to people's lives. They help people make decisions with which they are comfortable rather than yield to pressure to conform to the belief or behavior of others.

Values are individual and personal. However, there are certain qualities that most parents hope their children will come to value. Examples are honesty, integrity, genuine concern for others, responsible behavior, courage, and a sense of humor. Most parents also want their children to value family, friendship, education, and citizenship.

Certain values are important in almost all societies. For example, the writers of the Declaration of Independence believed that the values of life, liberty, and the pursuit of happiness are important. Other values of our society are listed in the Constitution and the Bill of Rights.

❖ Importance of Values

Values help develop a person's **character**, or moral qualities. Such qualities include honesty, cooperation, responsibility, and respect for others. Parents can nurture the development of these qualities in their children. When adults show that they care for others, children will learn to care for others, too. This helps establish a life-long foundation for children's character.

Values give meaning and direction to people's lives. The values that children see reflected by their family will influence their own set of values.

Activity. Ask students to read the Declaration of Independence and the Bill of Rights for the class. Have students list all the values they hear.

Activity. List common values on the chalkboard. Give each student "$500" to bid on the values they think are most important. The highest bidder tells why he or she feels the value is important.

Values help people make decisions. When people know what is important to them, they can make better choices. Some decisions are made quickly, such as choosing what to eat at lunch. Mary Kate values her health, so she tries to choose foods that are low in fat. Other decisions require more thought. Anthony has been trying to decide whether to stay in high school until graduation or drop out and get a job. He would like to have more money, but he also values education. He knows that getting his diploma will enable him to get a better job in the future. Thus his values help him decide to stay in school.

Values also form the basis of our society. When people value respect for others, there is less discrimination and intolerance. When people value the environment, there is less littering and pollution. As a result, values help people have more positive actions. Values also help the world to be a better place for everyone.

❖ Formation of Values

Parents begin soon after a child is born to set the stage for value formation. However, they cannot simply pass down a set of values to their children. Values are formed over a long period of time. Children do not fully acquire certain values until they are mature enough to think about what has meaning for them personally.

Influence of Family

Young children begin to learn values from their parents and other relatives. However, values differ from family to family. What is very important to one family may be unimportant to another. Values influence how families spend their time and money, guide their children, and even risk their lives.

Some values are communicated by words such as *should* and *ought*. Parents who teach

Children will learn to respect and care for others when they see this in the behavior of those around them.

children to say please and thank you are teaching the value of courtesy. Parents use direct communication when they say, "You should always tell the truth" or "You should not hit others." These are guidelines for behavior that parents want children to learn and value.

Parents also communicate values by their actions. Parents who show courtesy to others teach children more about courtesy than could be taught with repeated explanations. Young children, especially, like to model their parents' behavior. When parents demonstrate positive character traits, children learn to value those traits. On the other hand, some parents send mixed messages to children. If

Discuss. What values do children learn from parents that may be communicated in words? What values do children usually learn by example?

Emphasize. Parents cannot simply "teach" desired values to their children. They must also demonstrate their values through their behavior.

they tell children to do one thing but do another themselves, children become confused. For example, a parent may tell a child not to tell a lie. Later the child hears the parent telling lies to others. This child may not learn to value honesty.

Gradually, children learn to integrate many of the values of their family into their own personal value system. For example, how children feel toward others and toward society as a whole is influenced by their family's values. Some families do volunteer work and contribute to charities. Some attend weekly religious services and help their neighbors. Some are involved in civic organizations and community service projects. When children see activities such as these, they learn what is important to their family.

The values that children see reflected by their family will influence the kinds of values they will emphasize in their own families in the future. For example, children may carry on certain family traditions because those traditions are valued by family members. Thus parents and other family members have a lasting influence on the formation of children's values.

Influence of Peers

As children grow older, peers begin to have influence over one another. Peer influence often works because people want their friends to like them. They want to feel as if they belong to the group. For example, Ron was pressured by a group of high school friends to drink beer. Even though he felt uncomfortable about it, he hesitated to refuse because everyone else was drinking. To gain his friends' acceptance and approval, he gave in and drank some beer. Later he had to deal with his thoughts and feelings about his behavior.

Children who take on the values of their peers often do so by default rather than by choice. When family members are not available or do not show interest in a child's activities, that child may turn elsewhere for support and guidance.

However, parents can help children deal with negative peer pressure. When children can identify and express their values, they are better able to see their own actions in relation to their values. The following steps are helpful guidelines.

Step 1. Decide what values are important.

Step 2. Feel comfortable expressing those values to others.

Step 3. Behave in ways that are consistent with those values.

When Ron's parents helped him deal with peer pressure, they encouraged him to go through the three-step process.

Step 1. Ron listed the values that were important to him. He decided that health, acting responsibly, and obeying laws were more important to him than group approval. Since drinking could affect his health, could cause him to act irresponsibly, and was illegal, he now had good reasons to resist peer pressure.

Step 2. Ron practiced giving responses if his friends again tried to pressure him to drink. He felt comfortable talking about his reasons not to drink.

Step 3. Ron realized that his behavior reflects his values. Because he is now clearer about what he values, he knows what his actions will be if he is confronted with peer pressure again.

Other Influences on Values

Children are exposed to many influences through schools, churches and synagogues, community organizations, and the media. Many of these influences are very positive.

Discuss. What mixed messages do some parents send to children? (follow the law/break speed limit, be honest/cheat on taxes, don't hit/spank child) What influence does mixed messages have on a child's moral development?

Problem Solving. Have students discuss why membership in a gang is very important in certain communities. What positive and negatives pressures might gangs provide? Why? How can teenagers resist negative peer pressure from any group?

School-age children are influenced by their classmates, teachers, and course studies. These children are discovering an interest in science.

Children can learn about truth, knowledge, spirituality, and compassion. These values often reinforce the values taught by the family.

However, some standards and values expressed in the media may conflict with those taught by family, school, and religion. For example, some television programs and movies show violence. Some movies and song lyrics include profanity. Some advertising claims about products are misleading or deceptive. Children's role models are often popular personalities in the media. They may be athletes, movie stars, or entertainers who represent many and varying life-styles. Some of these personalities express ideas or show behavior that conflicts with many parents' values.

What happens to children who are presented with many different ways of life? Some are pulled in several directions and do not feel sure of which values to uphold. Parents need to talk to children about such value conflicts in our society. This helps children become aware of the different social and cultural pressures beyond the family. It also helps the family identify the values that are most important to them.

Parents cannot force children to accept certain values. However, they can help children decide what is right or wrong, just or unjust, true or false, significant or insignificant. They can do this by encouraging children to explore, question, and discuss their ideas and feelings. This fosters children's decision-making skills.

As children grow older, they make more decisions on their own. Parents are not always around to protect, influence, and guide them. Children must accept the responsibilities and consequences of their own decisions. By encouraging moral development throughout childhood, parents help children formulate their personal value system. This process gives children a sense of purpose and direction. It also helps them make choices that will promote their happiness and satisfaction in life.

Activity. Ask students to watch a children's program or a sitcom on TV and identify the values portrayed. Which values would you want your child to accept or reject?
Discuss. Who are current role models for children?

Activity. Ask students to write about a situation in which two values may be in competition or conflict. How could the person decide which value is most important?
Reference. See page 79 for the decision-making process.

Developing Responsibility

Parents and other caregivers can help children develop a sense of responsibility for their own behavior. Responsibility means seeing the relationship between what one says and does now and the results that will follow in the future. It also means acknowledging those results and carrying out related obligations.

Responsibility is attached to every area of life: family, schoolwork, friendships, career, and community. For example, responsibility means showing up for basketball practice even if the team usually loses. It means walking the dog every day even if it is raining.

When people act responsibly, they demonstrate maturity. In turn, they gain a sense of satisfaction from knowing that they are dependable. This knowledge can help increase their self-esteem.

Developing responsibility comes easily for some children and is difficult for others. What makes the difference? Often it depends on how much practice the child has in learning responsible behavior. Young children can practice feeding, dressing, and washing themselves. They can practice setting the table and putting away their toys. At the same time, they can learn the consequences of their behavior. For example, Erin is responsible for putting away her toys after play. One day, she left her toys on the floor. Her brother accidentally stepped on a toy and broke it. Erin's mother said to her, "When toys are left on the floor, people sometimes don't see them and they get stepped on and broken. I'm sure your brother did not mean to break your toy. This is one good reason for putting your toys away when you're finished with them." Erin learned the consequences of not being responsible.

Adolescence is a time when many children have opportunities to develop responsibility. Babysitting, dating, having a job, driving, and doing volunteer work in the community involve obligations that adolescents must fulfill over time. While parents may be available for guidance, it is important for adolescents to learn that they are responsible for certain decisions and actions.

When children are given certain tasks to do, they develop a sense of responsibility.

Discuss. How is developing responsibility and self-esteem related? How can parents help children increase self-esteem through household responsibilities? What might be the effect on self-esteem if parents always criticize the child's efforts?

Activity. Ask students to write about a specific responsibility that they have at home, at school, on the job, or in the community. Have them describe what they are learning from the experience and how it has influenced their self-concept.

❖ Household Responsibilities

Most preschoolers are able to assume some real household responsibilities. Picking up toys, emptying wastebaskets, and sorting the laundry are chores that help young children feel useful and important. They may work slowly, with many interruptions. However, they gain a sense of being a valuable, contributing member of the family when they can participate in household tasks.

As children grow older, they can set and clear the table, help wash dishes, and put items away. They can make their own bed and hang up their clothes. They may also help with cleaning jobs such as dusting and vacuuming.

Parents should assign chores that are appropriate for the child's developing skills. They should also show the child how to do a task, such as setting the table. Then they should allow the child to carry out the task in the way that the child is best able to complete it.

◆ ◆ *Health & Safety* ◆ ◆

Home Alone

When both parents work outside the home, the after-school hours can be a problem. This is especially true when children are too old for an after-school child care program but too young to be totally responsible for their own care.

When parents believe that their child is old enough to spend a few hours after school without adult supervision, they should establish some family guidelines. These help both parents and child feel more comfortable during the time the child is home alone.

- **Establish a check-in telephone call.** The child can call a parent at the workplace, or a parent should arrange to call the child at home at a specified time. Many parents feel more comfortable if they speak with their child several times during the course of the afternoon.

- **Instruct the child never to answer the door.** Even if the child knows the person at the door, the child should not let the person in without checking first with the parent.

- **Instruct the child never to tell a telephone caller that no adult is home.** When answering the telephone, the child should not say,

"My mother's not home." Instead, the child should say, "My mother can't come to the phone right now. Can I have her call you back?"

- **Discuss with the child what to do if certain situations arise.** For example, the child should know what to do if the house key is lost, the family pet gets loose, the electricity goes off, or the smoke alarm sounds. The child should also be told what to do if a parent does not arrive home at the expected time.

- **Set clear rules about snacks and meals.** The child should know what to eat if he or she gets hungry. While a parent may allow a child to use a microwave oven, many parents do not permit the use of the cook top or oven.

- **Post emergency numbers next to every telephone in the home.** Numbers for the fire department, police, ambulance, doctor, poison control center, and parents should be clearly written. Parents should also ask one or two nearby neighbors or friends to act as a resource that the child can turn to in case of an emergency.

Activity. Divide class into small groups. Have each group identify specific activities that preschoolers, school-age children, or adolescents can do to help in the preparation of a family meal. Have groups share their activities and identify safety considerations.

Sometimes children begin to resent being asked to do chores just when they are old enough to be of real assistance. Jayson, at age three, begged to be allowed to use the vacuum cleaner. At age seven he finds the activity not very appealing. When parents allow children to choose from several chores, children usually are more willing to do the task. Children also need to feel that they are making a definite contribution to the family. They should be able to take pride in the results of their efforts. Parents should express appreciation for children's efforts.

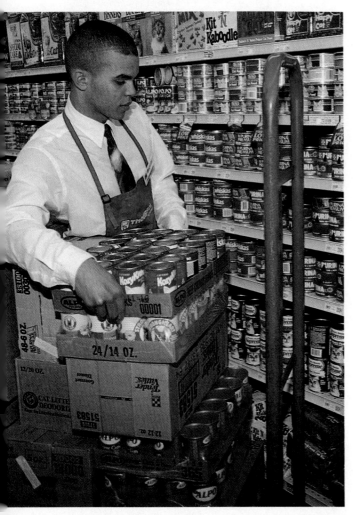

Part-time jobs can help teenagers learn about work responsibilities, as well as about their own interests, skills, and abilities.

◆◆ Work Responsibilities

Many teenagers hold part-time jobs. Besides learning a skill, teenagers can learn about responsibility, dependability, safety, and honesty. They often learn more about themselves and others. They may discover they enjoy working with their hands or meeting customers. They may also learn that they would prefer a career in another line of work.

Being employed can help teenagers learn the value and importance of work and its ability to strengthen one's character. This is called the **work ethic.** Work situations also provide opportunities for teenagers to learn to get along with employers and coworkers. Often teenagers work with people of different ages, races, and cultures. This helps them learn to respect people whose backgrounds are different from their own. In work situations, teenagers may find a good role model who helps them establish lifelong career goals.

A concern of many parents of teenagers working outside the home is the potential conflict between job responsibilities and schoolwork responsibilities. Some teenagers work so many hours at a job that they are unable to complete their homework or are too tired to attend classes. During the teenage years, education should take priority over work. However, learning to manage dual responsibilities can be a valuable lesson for later in life. By learning how to manage their time effectively, teenagers can accomplish all their responsibilities—at school, at home, and on the job.

◆◆ Money Responsibilities

An important part of teaching children to be responsible is helping them learn to manage money. Many parents do this by giving children a weekly **allowance.** This is a sum of money given on a regular basis for personal expenses.

Problem Solving. Ask students to design a young child's room so that he or she can be responsible for the care of clothing and toys. Include type and placement of storage areas, closet rods, hooks, shelves, light switches, tote boxes, and other items.

Discuss. How many of you hold part-time jobs? What are the benefits of being employed? What are the disadvantages? What is the greatest challenge you face when trying to balance the various responsibilities in your life? Why?

Young children may be given a small amount of money to spend on treats such as ice cream or inexpensive toys. This helps children plan ahead for a certain purchase, such as buying a small toy when they go shopping on Saturday. It also helps children learn to make choices about how to spend their money.

Children should be free to spend their allowance as they wish. This means they can occasionally waste it, if that is their choice. Otherwise, the money is not really theirs and the allowance does not serve as a teaching tool. Children should be permitted to learn from making poor choices as well as good ones.

As children grow older, their allowance can be increased to cover some of their regular expenses. These might include school lunches and supplies. This gives children a larger sum of money to budget and also helps them learn to comparison shop. Nine-year-old Tami pays for her own school notebook

Children need to learn how to manage money. They should be permitted to spend some money as they wish. They should also be encouraged to save for future goals.

DECISIONS ◆
◆ DECISIONS

Seven-year-old Russell receives a small allowance from his parents. They have encouraged him to use his money to buy items that he really wants. One day in the store, Russell suddenly insists on buying a small toy he has seen advertised on television. His father examines the toy and notices its poor quality. Thus he recommends that Russell buy something else. However, Russell insists that it is the only toy he wants. Later in the day, the toy breaks after Russell has played with it for only a few minutes. He begs his father to buy him another one. How do you think Russell's father should handle the situation?

paper and pencils. She has quickly learned to look around for the best buys.

Most child development experts believe that a child's allowance should not be dependent on good behavior or doing chores. An allowance should be a benefit of being a member of the family rather than a reward for obedience. If parents believe that children should be deprived of money when they fail to do assigned chores, they can offer a specific sum for these chores. This sum should be separate from the amount of the basic allowance. Children should understand that they will receive this additional money only if they do

Problem Solving. Have students debate how much allowance a child should receive at different ages. What expenses, if any, should the child pay for at each age? Should the child be required to save? Should money be paid or withheld for chores?

the work. Evan's parents, for example, give their ten-year-old son a basic weekly allowance. Out of this he pays for school supplies, school lunches, and trading cards. There is not much left over for extra treats. In addition, Evan receives another dollar a week if he sets the table for breakfast and dinner. He rarely fails to earn that extra dollar.

Around the World

Who Takes Care of the Baby?

In our culture, child care is primarily the responsibility of parents or other adult caregivers. In many other cultures, particularly those in less developed parts of the world, older children are responsible for the care of younger children. Even children under the age of ten are considered old enough to take care of a baby.

In many rural areas of Latin America, it is common to see a six-, seven-, or eight-year-old girl taking care of her two-year-old sibling. She might be carrying the tot on her hip or rocking the child in a hammock. Her culture considers this a proper job for an older sister.

In the North American culture, infants, toddlers, and school-age children are usually looked after by adults or teenagers. Most families consider a ten-year-old too young to be responsible for child care.

For most children in North America, childhood lasts longer than it does in Latin America. This gives North American children the advantage of more freedom. On the other hand, Latin American children can learn certain responsibilities and gain satisfaction from helping their family with child care.

Sexuality

Most young children are curious about their femaleness and maleness. Three-year-olds usually know whether they are boys or girls. Four-year-olds are curious about the differences. Undressing and doctor games are not uncommon.

At around this age, children start asking questions about how babies are born. They notice pregnant women and parents with babies. Children enjoy being close to new parents, hearing their personal stories. They get very positive feelings about such experiences.

This early interest in gender differences and sexuality is natural for children. Sexuality refers to everything about a person as a male or female. Children are exploring their own self-concept and identity. Unless adults teach them otherwise, children come to accept gender differences as a matter of fact. They are not overly concerned about them.

Sexuality Education During Early Childhood

Sound information about sexuality and reproduction adds to children's good feelings about themselves and their gender. Parents who name genital organs by their correct name, such as penis and vagina, help children develop accurate ideas about sexuality. However, education about sexuality should involve more than just factual information. It should convey values, standards, and attitudes.

Most children between three and five years of age ask questions about sex and sexuality. Some parents hesitate or are embarrassed to answer these questions. However children usually ask only the questions that concern them at the moment. Parents should answer only those questions, without going

Activity. On the chalkboard, have students list words used to describe human anatomy and reproduction. Discuss which words children would understand and which words might be confusing, such as stomach/uterus, egg/ovum.

Problem Solving. Ask students to describe how parents should react when they discover young children playing doctor games. Have them practice calm, factual statements that will redirect the children's play without showing disgust or shock.

into lengthy detail. For example, the child who asks where babies come from needs a simple, honest, and accurate answer. The parent can respond, "The baby grows inside the mother, in her uterus." The child may not ask anything else. There is no need to say anything more. Should the child ask another question, the response should again be frank and accurate. For example, if the child asks, "How does the baby get out?" the parent can say, "Through the vagina, between the mother's legs."

Parents can discuss picture books about reproduction and birth with their children. Children also benefit from stories and real instances of animal births. This helps them grasp the general idea of how birth occurs.

When children are free to ask questions and make comments about sex and sexuality, they develop a healthy attitude. If they do not get answers from their parents or if they are scolded for asking, they learn that these topics are different from all other topics. They look elsewhere for information—friends, magazines, television, and movies—and sometimes get misinformation. Most parents realize that information provided at home or at school is more accurate and age-appropriate than information the child learns from other children and elsewhere.

During the school-age years, parents should talk about relationships with their children. They should discuss their values and attitudes as they relate to popular television shows, movies, songs, and news stories. Children are exposed to many sexual messages through the media. Even commercials can convey sexual messages. This is a time for families to discuss how their own values may differ from those they see on the screen or in print. Parents should also prepare children for the changes that will happen to them during puberty.

Parents should talk about sexuality and reproduction with their children. Otherwise children will learn about these topics from other sources.

Activity. Bring to class children's books from the library that discuss reproduction and birth. Ask students to evaluate the books and decide which book they would want their own child to read.

Problem Solving. Ask students to discuss how parents can prepare their children for the changes that will occur during puberty. How did they learn about sex and sexuality? How would they want to inform their own child?

Many schools invite a police officer to talk to students about personal safety. The children learn what to do if they are lost, frightened, hurt, or molested.

◈ Sexuality Education During Adolescence

By the time children have reached adolescence, they have most of the facts about sex and sexuality. Now they need their parents' help with questions about relationships, love, marriage, commitment, responsibility, and parenting. This includes more than information about contraceptives and sexually transmitted diseases. Responsible decisions about sexuality involve self-esteem, values, and goals.

Teenagers who feel good about themselves and respect others can form relationships based on caring rather than sexual prowess. They can base their decisions on their personal values and not feel pressured to accept the values of their friends. Such adolescents are less likely to feel confused or guilty as they make decisions involving sexuality.

Parents should establish an environment where children feel free to ask questions about sexuality. Children need to know that their opinions and feelings are respected. At the same time, they want and need to hear their parent's values about sexual issues. Parents should always communicate with their children in a positive way—whether the topic is school, sports, or sexuality.

Problem Solving. Have students suggest ways that teenagers can improve communication about sexuality within their own family. How could hesitation or embarassment be overcome for parents and for teenagers?

Activity. Ask students to gather information about ways that parents and teachers can help inform children about personal dangers, such as sexual abuse or date rape. What precautions should be taken at various ages?

CHAPTER 23 REVIEW

Summary

- The process of moral development involves learning the standards of right and wrong that will guide and direct one's behavior.
- According to Kohlberg's theory, moral development occurs in a series of six stages in three levels: preconventional, conventional, and postconventional.
- People's values are what they believe in and are guided by. Values are influenced by one's family, peers, institutions, and society as a whole.
- Values expressed in the media sometimes conflict with values taught by family, school, and religion.
- Responsible people consider the consequences before doing something. They do what they say they will do.
- Children develop responsibility through practice.
- Children should feel free to ask questions about reproduction and sexuality; parents should answer these questions simply and accurately.

Questions

p. 437 **1.** What is moral development?

p. 438 **2.** How does a person's conscience control his or her behavior?

p. 439 **3.** List and summarize Kohlberg's three levels of moral development.

p. 442 **4.** Why are values important?

p. 443 **5.** How do parents communicate values to children?

6. How can parents help their children deal with peer pressure? p. 444

7. Explain how parents should help a child assume a particular household responsibility, such as setting the table. p. 447

8. How can holding a job outside the home help teenagers develop maturity? p. 448

9. Why should parents answer young children's questions about sexuality and reproduction simply and accurately? p. 450

Activities

1. List ten values that you hope would be important to your children. Which five do you think are most important? Why?

2. Use the three-step process to deal with other types of negative peer pressure, such as smoking, using drugs, cutting classes, or shoplifting.

3. List the household responsibilities that you had as a five-year-old, a ten-year-old, and now. Compare your list with your classmates' lists.

Think About

1. How might a knowledge of Kohlberg's stages of moral development help parents understand children's behavior?

2. Do you agree or disagree with some experts' belief that a child's allowance should not depend on his or her good behavior or doing chores? Defend your answer.

Reference. See the Teacher's Manual in the front of the Teacher's Annotated Edition for complete answers to the chapter review questions.

453

CHAPTER 24

Guiding Children's Behavior

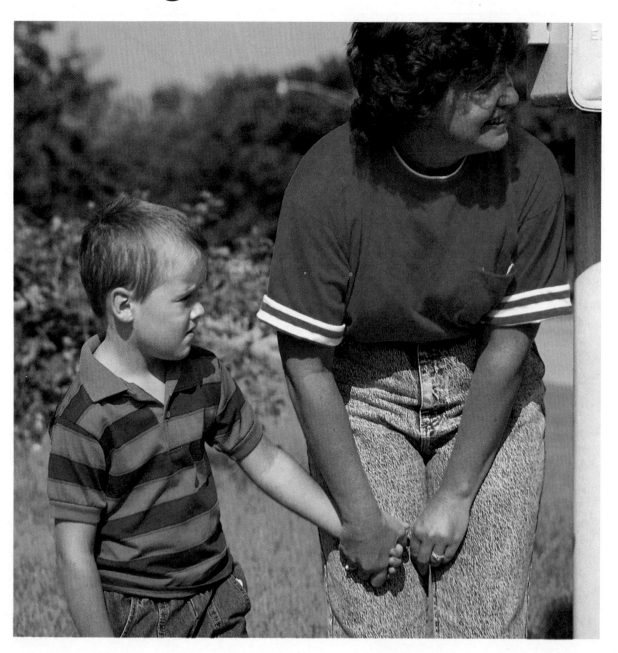

Objectives

This chapter will help you to:

- Explain why parents should have realistic expectations for children's behavior.
- Describe how parents can help children develop self-control.
- Compare the techniques used for indirect guidance and direct guidance.
- Discuss the causes and effects of child abuse.

Vocabulary

developmentally appropriate
positive reinforcement
limits
indirect guidance
direct guidance
physical guidance
verbal guidance
affective guidance
child abuse
child neglect
hot line

Ethan, age three and a half, and his mother, Melissa, walked along the street hand in hand. They were heading toward the neighborhood park. Melissa saw a puddle ahead. She knew children enjoy splashing in water. She considered whether it would matter if Ethan got wet from walking in the puddle. She decided he would damage his new shoes and probably get muddy. Also, she had planned for them to stop at the library on their way home.

Melissa began figuring out how to keep Ethan from walking in the puddle. "Ethan," she whispered, "there's a *giant* ocean ahead, so let's walk way over here along the side. Then we won't get in the d-e-e-e-e-p ocean." Ethan tiptoed around the puddle without a glance. "Whee! We made it!" Melissa exclaimed. Her guidance had worked.

Understanding Children's Behavior

Whether a child is seven months or seventeen years old, one of the most important responsibilities of parents is guiding their child's behavior. In many ways this begins early in the child's life. While the task is not easy, it can be very gratifying and rewarding for parents.

Children's behavior often goes through many changes daily. At one moment children can be happy and energetic. At another moment, they can be irritable or stubborn. The task for parents and other caregivers is to understand the meaning of children's behavior. Most things that children do are typical for their age. By learning about the developmental stages and typical kinds of behavior, parents and caregivers can interact more successfully with children.

The ultimate goal of guidance is to help children learn to control their own behavior. Par-

Children are not able to accomplish certain tasks, such as walking, until they are developmentally ready. When parents understand developmental principles, they know what to expect of children at various ages.

ents can encourage, direct, and reinforce behavior in a way that helps children learn self-control. As a result, children become self-guided or self-directed. Such children can make correct decisions about behavior when adults are not there to instruct them. They can deal with their feelings in acceptable ways. They have learned the skills needed to get along with other people. They know what is right and wrong. Guidance is an important part of emotional, social, and moral development.

❖ Influences on Behavior

Most adults know that the physical setting, the people involved, and the time of day all affect a child's behavior. On short outings, a toddler usually gets tired, hungry, and cranky far sooner than an older child.

Guidance is also affected by the child's stage of emotional and social development. Young children have not yet learned how to control their emotions. They act spontaneously and without regard for others. Young children are very self-centered. They are not yet able to understand other people's viewpoints. However, children can learn to control their emotions and behavior as they grow older.

Children also have different types of personalities. One child may be outgoing; another may be extremely shy. One may adapt easily to new situations; another may be upset by changes. Parents and caregivers have to use different types of guidance for different children at different times. No single approach is the correct one for every child at every moment.

❖ Age Expectations

Children are not able to accomplish certain tasks until they are developmentally ready. This means that children must reach a certain level of development before they can master a particular skill. It is very unfair of parents to expect their children to be able to perform a task when virtually no other children of their age can perform the same task.

Such an expectation sometimes occurs during toilet training, for example. However, children must have matured physically enough to be capable of controlling their bladder. When children wet themselves, parents who do not understand human development may wrongly yell at or punish them.

When parents and other caregivers understand developmental principles, they usually have realistic expectations of a child's behavior. They know what to expect at each developmental level and can anticipate how to help the child meet each developmental task. Then they can choose guidance strategies that are **developmentally appropriate**, or suitable for the level of the child's development.

❖ Reacting to Children's Behavior

Most children spend a good deal of time and effort in getting parents and other caregivers to notice them and their achievements. They try to get attention in any way they can. If they are not able to get attention with good behavior, they may misbehave. For example, they may jump on the furniture, make loud noises, act silly, or hit someone. If children get attention in this manner, they will be encouraged to do the same thing later.

Parents and other caregivers should respond to children's good behavior with **positive reinforcement**. This is action that encourages a particular behavior. Positive reinforcement rewards good behavior with attention and praise. This helps children feel good about themselves and associates their behavior with praise. Thus they have less motivation to seek attention in negative ways.

No matter how much positive reinforcement is given, all children sometimes misbehave. Parents and caregivers must be able to deal with these situations appropriately. The following questions are guidelines for helping parents evaluate the misbehavior.

- **How old is the child?** A one-year-old may hit another child without understanding the meaning of his or her actions. However, a four-year-old is capable of understanding that hitting is unacceptable behavior.

- **Was the behavior intentional or unintentional?** A two-year-old may cry if he or she is hungry and must wait for food at a restaurant. Similarly, a three-year-old may drop a breakable container that is too heavy to handle. These children are not deliberately misbehaving.

- **Does the child know right from wrong?** Children must learn the difference between acceptable and unacceptable behavior. This is especially important when they are two and three years old. During this period of rapid development, children naturally learn and explore. Mistakes are part of the learning process. Three-year-old Amanda marked on the wall with crayons. Her mother said to her, "Amanda, look what you've done to the wall!" Amanda replied, "Mommy, it will look pretty when I use the green crayon." She had never been told that it was wrong to draw on the walls.

- **Can the child learn from the consequences of the behavior?** When danger or harm is not present, children may learn more from an experience than from parental intervention.

Helping Children Develop Self-Control

Learning self-control or self-discipline is probably one of the hardest tasks for children to accomplish. Fortunately, some guidelines or rules for behavior can be taught directly. For example, parents can teach young children how to cross the street safely, when to wash one's hands, and when to say thank you.

However, many important rules are never stated clearly. Eventually, children are left on their own to figure out what is right or wrong. These are the rules that children learn by patterning their behavior after those around them. Children do this as part of their desire to grow, and adults should encourage it. As you learned in Chapter 22, this means that parents must be good models for children to imitate.

Parents must also be patient because it takes children many years to develop self-control. By using appropriate guidance techniques, parents can help children learn to control their own behavior. This enables children to become responsible individuals.

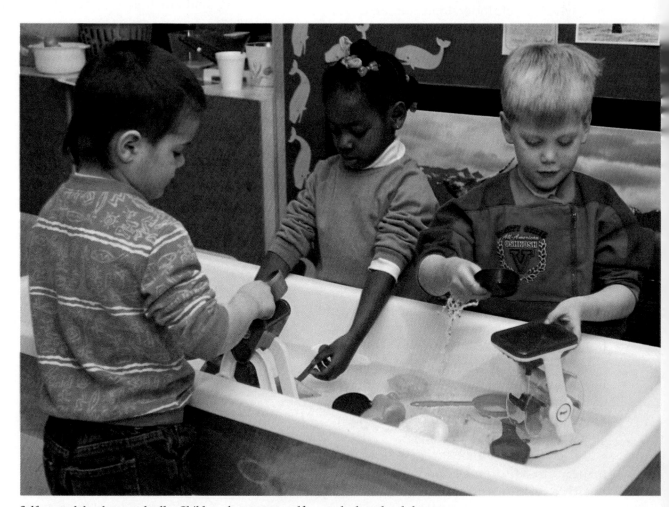

Self-control develops gradually. Children demonstrate self-control when they behave appropriately without being told by parents, teachers, or other caregivers.

Activity. Have students survey parents, relatives, and friends for ways that they use to maintain self-control. When do people find it hardest to retain self-control? Why?

Discuss. Why might learning to obey rules in games help children develop self-control?

❖ Offering Choices

Giving children opportunities to make choices can begin early in their lives. This helps them consider different alternatives and make decisions. For example, Kirsten's father has just seen Kirsten hit her baby brother. He says, "You seem to be angry with the baby. I will not let you hurt him. You may stay beside me while I change his diaper, or you may play with your toys. Which do you want to do?" This gives Kirsten an alternative to the anger.

Parents can help children develop responsibility by offering them reasonable choices. The following suggestions are helpful.

- **Offer a choice only when one is available.** Parents should think carefully before offering a choice. This will result in more reasonable alternatives. For example, if a parent asks, "Would you like breakfast?" the child may respond by saying, "No." If the parent asks, "What do you want for breakfast?" the child may say, "I want to go get a hamburger." A more appropriate question would be "Do you want hot oatmeal or cold cereal?" or "Would you like your eggs scrambled or boiled?" Here the child truly has a choice.

- **Be prepared to abide by the child's decision.** When parents give a child a choice, they must be willing to accept the child's decision whether or not they agree with it. For example, a parent may ask, "Which one of these shirts do you want to wear today?" If the child chooses one the parent would not have chosen, he or she should let the child wear it. This helps the child learn that decisions have meaning and value.

- **Allow children to experience the consequences of their choices.** Making decisions can result in pleasure or disappointment for children. Children who are disappointed are likely to seek ways of improv-

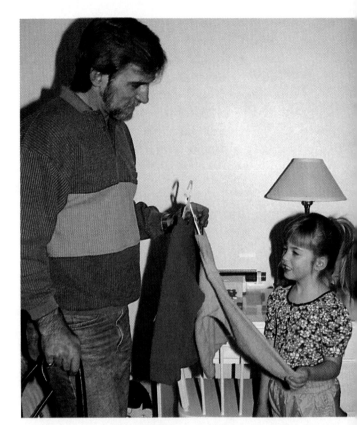

Giving children opportunities to make choices helps them develop decision-making skills.

ing their decision-making skills in the future. For example, a parent may say, "If you want to go outdoors, you must wear your hat and mittens. Otherwise, you will have to stay indoors." If the child refuses to put on the hat and mittens, he or she must stay indoors. This helps the child learn that choices are important and real.

- **Give children opportunities to succeed.** When children make good choices, they will be likely to repeat similar behaviors. Of course, the more help they can get in evaluating their choices, the less apt they are to make poor decisions.

- **Be consistent in giving and reacting to choices.** Children should know that certain actions or choices will always have a parent's approval. Other choices will always receive disapproval. Then child and parent know what to expect from each other when these choices are repeated. For example, when a child is allowed to throw a ball in the home some times but not at other times, he or she may become confused. This hinders the child from knowing what is acceptable and what is not.

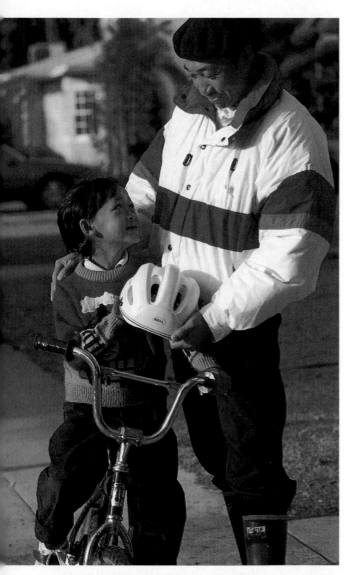

When parents set limits, they should use clear and simple language. This helps children understand which behaviors are allowed and which are not.

◆◆ Setting Limits

Since guidance should be positive rather than negative, how can parents let children know what they are not allowed to do? The answer is for parents to establish limits. **Limits** are guidelines and boundaries to which children must adhere.

Children need and want limits. They lack the experience and maturity to make good decisions about all that they do. They have difficulty in dealing with sudden impulses to do something. Limits help children learn what is acceptable and safe for them to do.

Children will usually cooperate when they do not have too many limits. They need some freedom to make decisions within the boundaries of certain restrictions. They also need to know that limits can change as they grow older.

Explaining Limits

Children must understand their limits in order to follow them. To explain these limits, parents need to state them clearly and consistently. Telling a school-age child to be home "before dark" can lead to confusion and disagreement. It is far better for parents to select a specific hour when the child is expected to be home.

At the same time, parents need to make clear which behaviors are allowed and which are not. This helps children learn the difference between appropriate and inappropriate behavior.

Changing Limits

Some behaviors may be prohibited at one stage of development and acceptable at the next stage. For example, a toddler may be forbidden to cross the street alone or use a sharp knife. However, a school-age child is usually allowed to cross certain streets and help slice vegetables for a meal.

Activity. Divide the class into small groups. Have students write specific limits for each age group for the following situations: bedtime, eating new foods, crossing the street, putting away toys, hanging up clothes, table manners, watching television. Have them give reasons for each limit. What limits are similar for several age groups? Why?

Thus parents need to change some limits as children grow older and gain independence. Too many restrictions will hinder their development. However, parents must be aware of children's individual capabilities. What one child may be ready to do at age five, another child may not be mature enough to do until age seven.

As children grow older, they often protest some of their limits. This is a time for parents and children to discuss their feelings and concerns. Parents must balance a child's desire for increased freedom with their own responsibility for the child's safety. Parents should never be pressured into allowing a child to do something just because "everyone else does it."

Some limits and rules should remain the same throughout children's lives. For example, health and personal safety guidelines apply to people of all ages.

❖ Enforcing Limits and Rules

Parents should enforce limits and rules consistently. Otherwise, children will be less likely to understand what behavior is expected of them. When parents fail to enforce an established rule, children learn that parents do not mean what they say.

If a child breaks a rule, some parents deprive the child of a privilege. This is effective if the privilege is related to the misbehavior. For example, a preschooler who purposely damages a toy may not be allowed to play with the toy for a day. However, taking away a privilege that is not related to the misbehavior is usually less effective. For example, a young child will not understand why he cannot watch his favorite television show because he spilled a glass of milk.

Teenagers sometimes try to test certain limits and rules. However, this is the time for parents to continue giving guidance. Teenagers should understand when they must come home, what household tasks they should do, and how they should behave toward others. Rules concerning driving, alcohol, drugs, and sexual activity can help teenagers make decisions that could affect their entire lives. At the same time, parents should let teenagers increasingly make more decisions in other areas of their lives. By establishing a balance between guidance and freedom, parents help teenagers learn to take responsibility for their actions.

As children gain independence, they may do things that endanger their safety. Parents should discuss the reasons for certain limits with their children. This helps prevent the temptation for children to go beyond the established limits.

Discuss. What limits need to be changed as children grow older? What limits need to remain the same? Why?
Discuss. What happens when parents or caregivers fail to follow through after a child violates clearly stated limits?

Problem Solving. Have students identify limits that parents might have for children. What should be the appropriate penalty for preschoolers, school-age, and adolescents who "break the rule"? How should the penalties differ for children of different ages?

Around the World

Changing Expectations

Throughout much of the world's history, children were treated as miniature adults. They were expected to work in the fields or factories along with their parents. At home, they were responsible for many household tasks. Children were expected to behave as adults, with proper manners and obedience to rules. They were also dressed in the same style clothing as adults.

For example, the typical outfit of a small girl in a well-to-do English family of the early eighteenth century was the same as her mother's. The girl would wear a dress made of silk and velvet. Her undergarments included a whale-bone harness and a hoop skirt. She wore high boots with high heels. These clothes did not allow a young child to run and climb as children do today.

Around the middle of the eighteenth century, new theories about child rearing and education began to emerge. These ideas were considered revolutionary because they stated that children should remain young as long as possible, both in spirit and in dress.

Today, children's clothing reflects a different attitude toward children. Clothes are now designed to meet the special needs of children, such as comfort for active play and Velcro® fasteners for self-dressing. Childhood is considered a time for physical, emotional, social, cognitive, and moral development. Parents are encouraged to nurture their children with love and care. Education tries to provide a variety of learning experiences. Child labor laws prevent children from working in most occupations. Criminal laws provide different sentences for children than for adults. Our society no longer considers children to be miniature adults.

Parents should always be consistent about enforcing limits and rules, even when the child reacts with anger and tears. Otherwise, children become confused about what they can and cannot do.

What happens when a child's behavior poses a risk to the child's health, disrupts the family, or breaks the law? Parents in this situation can get help from special groups and professionals in the community. Although parents may disapprove of the child's behavior, they can still provide emotional support and love. This may help their son or daughter overcome the problem and prevent a crisis.

Reference. See page 107 for a discussion of the three styles of parenting: authoritarian, democratic, and permissive.
Discuss. How would authoritarian, democratic, and permissive parents differ in the way they set and enforce limits and rules for children?

Emphasize. Parents should provide emotional support and love for their children, even when they disapprove of the child's behavior.

Guidance Techniques

When a child misbehaves, a parent or caregiver can react in different ways. Some people immediately think about disciplining the child. However, discipline is not the same as guidance. Discipline often implies punishment, which is a form of negative reinforcement. A child who is punished may learn to fear the punishment rather than change the behavior.

The guidance principles and approaches presented in this chapter are alternatives to punishment. They are positive rather than negative ways of guiding children. As such, they are ways of helping children move toward self-control and a clear sense of right and wrong. They also help children develop a positive self-concept and the ability to get along with others.

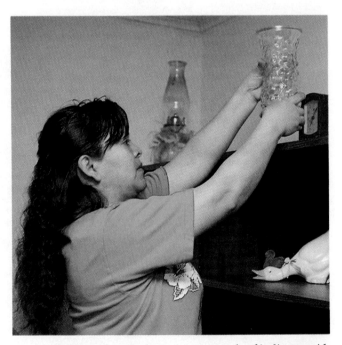

Childproofing the home is an example of indirect guidance. This enables children to explore and move about without parents having to tell them not to touch certain items.

Discuss. Do you agree or disagree with the saying, "Spare the rod and spoil the child"? Why?
Reference. See pages 276-279 for childproofing techniques.

◆◆Indirect Guidance

Indirect guidance is any method of arranging the environment to help children behave in an acceptable or desired way. Indirect guidance does not involve direct communication. Instead, parents and caregivers use other techniques to keep children safe and secure. Indirect guidance techniques include childproofing the home, arranging schedules, and planning children's activities.

Childproofing the Home

Childproofing the home and the space around it is important for children's safety. This is a form of indirect guidance because it influences safe behavior without dealing directly with the child.

Children need to explore and move about freely. Childproofing means arranging and storing toys, equipment, and other items so children can play safely. Then adults need not constantly step in to direct or control children as they play.

Arranging Schedules

Another technique of indirect guidance is organizing family schedules to influence children's behavior. Young children gain security from certain routines at mealtime and bedtime because they know what to expect. Such routines make decision making easier for both parents and children. Routines also promote habits that help children complete tasks, such as brushing their teeth.

Children also need some preparation before they must change from one scheduled event to another. This gives them time to finish what they are doing before moving on to a new activity. For example, parents can say, "Finish your breakfast because soon we must leave for nursery school." This helps prevent last-minute frustrations and struggles.

Activity. Have students describe how they would feel if their best friend walked up, shut the book they were reading, and said it was time to go to the store immediately. Have students relate this to children.

Planning Children's Activities

Planning children's activities is another indirect guidance technique. If there are many interesting things for children to do, they are more likely to become involved in their play. They will have less time to get into trouble or to seek attention through misbehavior.

Parents should see that toys and activities are appropriate for the age of their children. They can help children keep from becoming bored by rotating toys and play materials from time to time, putting some away for a while.

Since children have a shorter attention span than adults, children's activities should be adjusted to maintain their interest. Parents should also have special activities on hand when children must wait for some event. They can keep children occupied during the wait by playing guessing games, reading a story, or doing exercises.

✦ Direct Guidance

Direct guidance is any method of influencing children's behavior through face-to-face interaction. Direct guidance involves both actions and words. There are three kinds of direct guidance techniques: physical, verbal, and affective.

Physical Guidance

Physical guidance involves direct contact with children to guide their behavior. Most young children need physical guidance, such as showing, helping, and leading. Parents may give a hand as a two-year-old climbs a slide. However, a four-year-old wants to perform the task unaided. The challenge for parents and other caregivers is to know what kind and how much help each child needs.

Physical guidance is also used to control unsafe or unwanted behavior. For safety reasons, an adult should hold a toddler's hand when crossing the street. An adult may also want to carry a child having a temper tantrum outside the store. As children gradually grow more and more independent, they need less and less physical guidance.

Parents and other caregivers can use the following techniques to provide physical guidance.

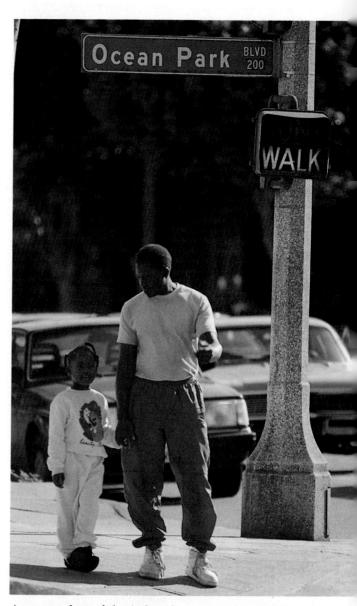

A common form of physical guidance is to hold a child's hand. This can be used to guide or restrain a child, as well as to provide reassurance.

Discuss. Why would toys that have been stored away for a period of time be challenging and exciting when reintroduced into the child's play environment?

Activity. Divide class into five groups. Ask each group to role play several examples of one type of direct guidance: demonstrating, restraining, ignoring, distracting, or removing.

- **Demonstrating.** One physical guidance technique is to demonstrate how to do something—use a spoon, put on a coat, toss a ball. Children, especially toddlers, are little mimics. They like to imitate adults. Parents and caregivers can encourage appropriate behavior by saying, "See, you do it this way" and "Now you try it."

- **Restraining.** Another common form of physical guidance is to hold a child's hand. Parents often do this to restrain their children. However, some toddlers react negatively to having their hand held. They like to feel they are independent. In fact, it may be uncomfortable to have one's hand pulled up for a long period of time. For these reasons, parents should reserve hand-holding for times when it is needed for the child's safety and when the child reaches out for reassurance.

- **Ignoring.** There are times when it is best to simply ignore a child's misbehavior. This is generally effective when a child deliberately misbehaves to get attention. When children see that they are not going to get attention by misbehaving, they usually stop what they are doing.

- **Distracting.** Sometimes a child can be distracted from a certain activity to avert a potential problem. A parent can often shift a young child's attention to a new activity. For example, if a toddler is climbing onto the countertop, he might be gently moved to another room. If a child is yelling, a parent might whisper softly in her ear.

- **Removing.** Sometimes a child needs to be removed from the presence of others or the center of activity. Having the child sit isolated for a short time gives him or her an opportunity to calm down. The parent can explain the reason for the time-out by saying, "I want to help you get yourself together. When you think you can play without hitting, you can go back. Let me know when you're ready." The amount of time should be very short, usually only a few minutes. This is long enough to give the child an opportunity to regain self-control before returning to play.

Having a child sit for a few minutes by herself gives her a chance to calm down and think about her behavior.

DECISIONS ◆
◆ DECISIONS

Four-year-old Luis climbs onto a low table and begins to walk back and forth. His mother ignores him and finally he gets down. When he begins to play with his blocks, she says, "Luis, I like the way you are playing now. You really know how to use those blocks." Do you think Luis's mother has handled his behavior in the best way? Why or why not?

Activity. Have students suggest types of demonstrations that parents and caregivers use as a method of physical guidance. **Discuss.** When is physical guidance required for the safety of a young child?

More About. Generally, an appropriate length of time-out is two minutes per year of age (4 minutes for a two-year-old; 10 minutes for a five-year-old). Setting a timer lets the child know when the time-out will be over.

As children grow older, verbal guidance becomes more effective because they can understand directions, limits, and rules. Parents can give a firm verbal command to stop a child's behavior, rather than using physical guidance.

Verbal Guidance

Verbal guidance is the use of words to influence children's behavior. As children learn to understand language better, verbal guidance becomes more effective. Most three-year-olds can understand simple words and phrases. Thus parents can use more verbal guidance with three-year-olds than with one-year-olds.

Once children are capable of understanding what is expected of them, parents and caregivers can give reasons why certain behaviors are appropriate. At the same time, they can help children understand why other behaviors may be unsafe or inappropriate. The emphasis switches from physical guidance to verbal guidance. Verbal guidance involves good communication skills. You learned about many of these in Chapter 22.

Reference. See pages 426-433 for information about communicating with children.
Activity. Have students write ten positive statements for giving verbal guidance to children.

Affective Guidance

Affective guidance involves expressing emotions or feelings to influence a child's behavior. The word *affective* has the same root as the word *affection*.

Affective guidance should help children feel good about themselves and raise their self-esteem. Parents use affective guidance when they give a child a smile, a hug, or a pat on the head.

Affective guidance also helps children understand their own feelings. For example, a parent might say, "You really feel good about building that block tower, don't you?" or "I know you feel sad because you wanted to play outside." The parent reflects the child's feeling and gives it a label. This helps children label their own feelings and deal with them in acceptable ways.

Discuss. What are some positive phrases that can be used with children as an affective means of guidance?

Combining Direct Guidance Techniques

Parents and caregivers often use all three types of direct guidance techniques with children. In the chapter-opening story, Melissa used physical guidance by holding Ethan's hand. She used verbal guidance as she spoke to Ethan about walking around the puddle. Her statement "We made it!" was affective guidance that told Ethan that she was pleased.

Ethan's behavior might have been different if Melissa had simply said, "Ethan, don't you dare step in this puddle" and offered no physical or affective guidance. Then he would have focused on the puddle rather than on tiptoeing around it as his mother had proposed.

The ultimate goal of guidance is to help children learn to control their own behavior. By using a variety of positive guidance techniques, parents and other caregivers can successfully reach this goal.

◆ *Health & Safety* ◆

Childhood Obesity

Surveys indicate that more than 50 percent of school-age children in the United States are overweight. Children are considered to be obese when they are 20 percent over what is considered to be their ideal weight.

Being overweight is not healthy, physically or emotionally, for a child. Although most health experts agree that heredity plays some role in a child's tendency to put on weight, it is not the only cause.

Parents should be alert to a child who continually weighs more than his or her ideal weight. Childhood is the time to establish healthy lifestyle habits. However, a child should never be put on a weight-loss program without the guidance of a doctor or dietitian.

Here are some guidelines for parents who have an obese child.

• **Take a close look at the family's eating habits.** Do family members eat large quantities of food? Do they eat many high-calorie snacks? Children learn by example.

• **Introduce more physical activity into the child's life.** Enroll the child in a sports or exercise program. Plan family outings that involve physical activity. Substitute walking for driving. Take the stairs instead of the elevator or escalator.

• **Reduce fat and sugar in the family's diet.** Use skim or low-fat milk. Select meats and poultry that are low in fat. Broil or bake rather than fry foods. Use margarine instead of butter. Serve unsweetened fruit juice. Purchase unsweetened cereal. Provide fresh fruit for snacks and dessert. Do not buy high-calorie snacks, such as chips or candy. Prepare popcorn with little or no margarine as a low-calorie snack.

• **Be supportive.** Do not nag, criticize, or make jokes about the child's size. This will only contribute to the child's poor self-image. Then the child may turn to food for comfort. The goal is to slow the rate of weight gain and allow growth to catch up. Then the child will be within his or her ideal weight range.

Problem Solving. Have students role play ways of combing direct guidance techniques for the following situations:
• A two-year-old is digging up your potted plants.
• A four-year-old does not want to share any toys with a friend.
• A seven-year-old does not want to go to bed.
• A twelve-year-old is using profanity.

❖ Unacceptable Methods of Discipline

When parents respond to children's behavior with harsh or highly emotional responses, children may not understand the message. On one hand, children are taught not to yell or hit. When parents use yelling or spanking as a form of discipline, the messages contradict each other.

Studies show that punishment is not effective in the long run in helping children become self-controlled and self-disciplined. It is ineffective because it often is not related to the behavior that caused it. As a result, children do not learn what they should do.

Unacceptable methods of discipline include withholding love, bribing, promising, threatening, and inflicting physical punishment.

Withholding Love

Withholding love from children is a cruel form of disciplining them. During infancy, children should become sure of their parents' love. If they learn they will not be loved unless they behave in a certain way, they may become insecure or frustrated.

Examples of statements that indicate the withholding of love are "I am not going to love you unless you clean up your room," "If you don't hurry and get dressed, I'll leave you home by yourself," and "If you don't stop hitting your brother, I'll give you away." These statements cause children to fear being rejected or abandoned.

Bribing and Promising

Some parents bribe children to get them to behave in certain ways. For example, a parent might say, "If you stop whining, I'll buy you an ice-cream cone." Later, the parent may be unable to follow through on the bribe. In some cases, parents even forget they made a promise or, worse, disregard it after the

desired behavior has been achieved. This kind of discipline breaks down the trust between the child and parent.

Other parents get children to make promises about their future behavior. However, statements such as "I want you to promise not to touch anything in the store" and "You must promise to keep your clothes clean while at the party" often result in dishonesty. If the promised behavior is not achieved, the child may deny the behavior, blame another child, or claim that he or she never made the promise.

Threatening

Parents who threaten their children to achieve desired behavior will have little success. Some parents make statements such as "If you do that one more time, I'm going to send you to your room."

Children often learn quickly that such statements are empty threats. They begin to disregard them. Sometimes they take the threats as challenges to defy the parent's control or authority. These children know just how far they can go with misbehavior before the parent takes action. On the other hand, if parents frequently do follow through on their threats, children can become afraid and insecure.

DECISIONS ◆ ◆ DECISIONS

Three-year-old Kara forgets to put away all the puzzle pieces. Her father yells, "If you don't pick those up right now, you'll get a spanking!" Do you think Kara's father is using the most appropriate guidance technique? Why or why not? How could he handle the situation in a different way?

Discuss. Why are these methods of discipline unacceptable? What others examples of unacceptable discipline have you observed in stores or malls? Why are positive methods of guidance more effective?

More About. Webster's definition of punishment is "to subject a person to pain, loss, confinement, or death as a penalty for some offense or fault."

Inflicting Physical Punishment

Most parents who physically punish a child think it will shape the child's behavior. It may indeed shape behavior, but not necessarily in the way the parents had in mind. Physical punishment, such as hitting or spanking, does not help children know what to do to improve their behavior. Sometimes it may even challenge children to repeat their misbehavior to get attention. More importantly, physical punishment damages a child's positive self-concept and self-esteem.

Still, some parents do use spanking as a form of discipline for young children. If a toddler runs into the street, a parent may give the child a swat on the buttocks. At the same time, the parent may tell the child in a firm tone of voice that he or she must not go into the street. The child will probably associate the spanking with the misbehavior. However, positive guidance techniques are more desirable and effective.

Sometimes parents spank children when they do not know what other method of discipline to use. This does not justify spanking. Even though it may relieve a parent's tension, it probably does not help the child learn how to correct the behavior that resulted in the spanking. Furthermore, the child may think it is all right to misbehave because the spanking pays for the misbehavior. Because the child no longer feels guilty, he or she may misbehave again.

Unfortunately, many spankings occur when parents lose control of their own emotions and behavior. They act on impulse and suddenly find themselves spanking the child. Then they may feel guilty or worried about their actions. Since children learn by example, parents who repeatedly use physical punishment should expect their children to resort to hitting and fighting as part of their behavior pattern.

Child Abuse Is Not Guidance

A tragic fact of life is that some parents abuse and neglect their children. **Child abuse** refers to physical, emotional, or sexual violence against children. **Child neglect** is failure to meet a child's physical or emotional needs.

More than two million cases of child abuse or neglect are reported in the United States every year. Experts agree that thousands of other cases go unreported and many deaths are disguised as accidents.

Children of all ages—infants through adolescents—are abused or neglected by people they know. These may be parents, stepparents, older siblings, or nonrelated adults living in the home or nearby. However, nine out of ten abusers are the children's own parents. Over half the time, the mother is the abuser.

Abuse and neglect occur in families from all income levels, racial and ethnic groups, and religions. They happen in urban, suburban, and rural areas. Both abuse and neglect tend to be repetitive and to increase in frequency and severity unless help is obtained.

- *Physical abuse* occurs when physical harm is done to the child. This may be caused by severe beatings, burns, bites, or other forms of torture. Sometimes the abuse can cause permanent injury to the child or even death.

- *Emotional abuse* occurs when unreasonable and excessive demands are placed on the child. It also occurs when love and affection are withheld from the child. Emotional abuse often involves verbal abuse, such as constant teasing, insulting, or belittling. As a result, the child usually feels humiliated, unworthy, and unloved.

Activity. Show a film or video about the causes and prevention of child abuse.

Activity. Have students research the current statistics on child abuse and neglect at the national, state, and local levels.

- *Sexual abuse* occurs when a child is molested for the sexual pleasure of an adult. If the abuser is a family member, the sexual abuse is called incest.
- *Neglect* occurs when a child's basic needs are not met. Some children may not be given adequate food, clothing, or medical attention. Others may be given little or no support or guidance.

◆ Effects of Child Abuse

Physical, emotional, and sexual abuse leave lasting impressions on children. Some children avoid situations where they must interact with others. Other children become violent themselves. The longer abuse continues, the more serious the problem becomes for both the child and the abuser.

The following are some warning signs of child abuse or neglect. None of the signs prove child abuse. However, when the signs appear repeatedly, they may be a good indication that abuse or neglect is occurring.

- **Repeated injuries.** The child has unexplained bruises, burns, bites, black eyes, or broken bones. The parent may deny that anything is wrong or give unlikely explanations.
- **Hunger, poor hygiene, inappropriate clothing.** The child is malnourished, dirty, or inadequately dressed. Medical or dental problems are not treated. The child is left alone or found wandering about the neighborhood at all hours.
- **Genital bruises, pain, itching, blood.** The child has difficulty walking or sitting or refuses to participate in physical education class. The child demonstrates unusual sexual behavior or a sophisticated sexual knowledge. STDs or pregnancy occurs.
- **Disruptive behavior.** The child is very aggressive or demanding. The child

"I can't stand this kid for one more minute!" is a feeling that many parents have at one time or another. It is a signal to stop for a moment, calm down, and find someone to help with the child. It should never lead to child abuse.

demonstrates negative behavior, disregards rules, or runs away.

- **Passive, withdrawn behavior.** The child is excessively shy and lacks friends. The child is wary of adults or is afraid to go home. The child attempts suicide.
- **Emotional problems.** The child has habit disorders, such as excessive sucking, rocking, or biting. The child shows signs of hysteria, obsession, or compulsion.
- **Talk about a "friend" who is abused.** The child tries to seek help or report an injury or sexual assault indirectly.

Unfortunately, the physical and emotional effects of abuse often remain with children for many years. Victims may suffer from low self-esteem, guilt, and fear. They may have problems forming close relationships with others.

Activity. Invite a professional counselor to talk to the class about the effects of child abuse on children, the causes of child abuse, and prevention methods.

Activity. Contact the human services or police department for suggestions for service projects that help abused children. For example, some collect teddy bears for officers to give to abused children when they must be removed from their home.

✥ Causes of Abuse

Why do parents abuse and neglect children? There are many reasons. Sometimes the parents were themselves the victims of child abuse. They may unthinkingly inflict on a child what they suffered in childhood. Some parents have alcohol or drug habits that make them lose control of their behavior. Some have personal problems, perhaps from their own childhood, that they have never resolved. Thus, when the child disobeys the parent, the parent explodes in uncontrolled anger and hurts the child.

Some parents are emotionally ill and need treatment and counseling to get well. Others feel very frustrated by some failure, such as a divorce or the loss of a job. Nervous and unhappy, they take out their frustration on a child who is too young, weak, or afraid to escape.

Many abusive parents know little about what to expect from children at various ages. They punish children for behavior that is in fact normal. For example, a parent may be irritated by a baby's repeated crying. Instead of comforting the baby, he or she may shake the baby vigorously, causing severe bleeding in the brain. Another parent may punish a toddler for touching items such as magazines or sunglasses, when it is natural for a toddler to explore everything within reach. A parent who understands the developmental levels of children will remove temptation from the toddler. An abusive parent may yell at or hit the child.

✥ Getting Involved

Child abuse is illegal. Teachers and health professionals are required by law to report any evidence of child abuse to authorities, such as the child welfare agency. In some cases, the court takes children away from abusive parents and places them with foster parents for protection.

Babysitters, friends, and neighbors may see evidence of child abuse. They, too, should report their suspicions to local authorities. The telephone numbers of the human services agency, welfare department, and child protective services are usually listed in the directory. The numbers can also be obtained by calling directory assistance. In cases of an emergency, the local police or hospital should be called. Information about child abuse and its prevention can be obtained from groups such as the National Committee for the Prevention of Child Abuse.

Occasionally, parents may suspect that a child is being abused by a babysitter or other caregiver. They should require the caregiver to explain any such harm. When in doubt, parents should remove their child from that person's care immediately. They should also report their suspicions to the authorities.

Sometimes people are hesitant to report their suspicions of child abuse or neglect. They may not have solid evidence or fear they may be invading family privacy. However, child abuse has very serious consequences. By recognizing abuse and becoming involved, others may help save a child's life.

◆ ◆ *Self-Esteem* ◆ ◆

Children who are constantly made to feel guilty about their misbehavior may develop low self-esteem. They may see themselves as unworthy, disliked, or rejected. They may choose not to do a task or play with others because they fear they will fail or be rebuffed. On the other hand, parents who accept their children and give them love even when they misbehave or fail will strengthen their children's self-esteem.

Emphasize. Child abuse is found in all strata of society: rich and poor; urban, suburban, and rural; all racial and ethnic groups; and all religions.

Problem Solving. Have students discuss what they should do if they suspect that a child in their neighborhood is being abused. What should they do if they suspect that a friend is being abused? If they are being abused?

❖ Finding Help

Most communities have programs to help abusive parents. Mental health centers offer counseling to help get to the source of the problem. Counselors try to help abusive parents understand that there are other, positive ways to deal with children.

Many groups that deal with child abuse prevention have a **hot line**. This is a telephone line that provides direct access to information or counseling. Parents can call a crisis hot line when they feel they are in danger of abusing a child. Often they can be helped just by being able to talk about their problems. They can call anonymously, without giving their name.

Some communities have self-help groups for abusive parents, such as Parents Anonymous. They meet regularly to discuss the problems, feelings, and frustrations that may cause them to abuse their children. The parents can offer support to each other, especially in times of crisis.

Some communities have homes or shelters where people can, on short notice, escape from abusive situations. Unfortunately, many child abuse cases also involve spouse abuse or other family violence.

Once children have been identified as having been abused, they need counseling by trained professionals. Parents, teachers, and foster parents may also need professional advice to find ways to help an abused child.

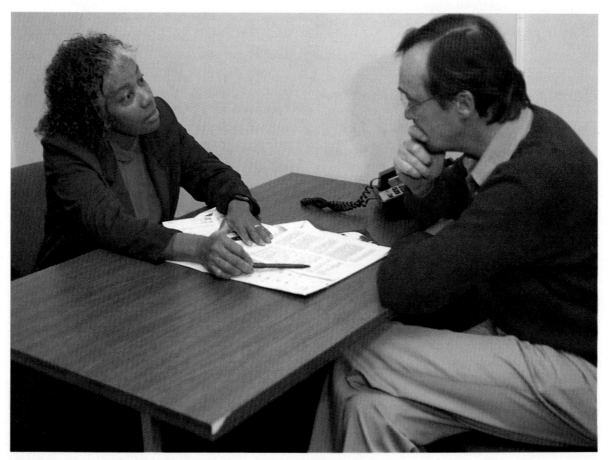

Counseling can help abusive parents understand and change their behavior.

CHAPTER 24 REVIEW

Summary

- The goal of guidance is to help children become self-directed.
- When parents understand what to expect of a child at each developmental stage, they are able to choose appropriate guidance strategies.
- Offering children choices, setting limits on what they may do, and enforcing limits and rules help children develop self-control.
- Indirect techniques for guiding children include childproofing the home, establishing certain routines, and providing stimulating activities.
- Direct guidance includes physical guidance (helping or leading), verbal guidance (explaining in words), and affective guidance (communicating feelings about the child's behavior).
- Millions of children in the United States are either neglected or physically, emotionally, or sexually abused each year.
- Anyone who suspects that a child has been neglected or abused should report his or her suspicions to the authorities.

Questions

p. 456 1. Why is understanding a child's developmental level important in deciding which guidance techniques to use?

p. 457 2. What is positive reinforcement? Why is it effective in guiding behavior?

p. 457 3. How can parents evaluate children's misbehavior?

p. 459 4. Why should children be given opportunities to make choices?

5. What are limits? Why are they necessary? p. 460

6. What is indirect guidance? How can parents use it? p. 463

7. Define and give examples of the three types of direct guidance: physical, verbal, and affective. p. 464

8. Why is punishment a poor technique for guiding children's behavior? p. 468

9. Name five potential signs of child abuse. p. 470

10. What should you do if you suspect a child is being abused or neglected? p. 471

Activities

1. Observe several parents and caregivers using various types of guidance techniques with children. Write down your observations and draw some conclusions about their effectiveness.

2. Make a list of activities to do with a young child while waiting in a dentist's office.

3. Find out what services are available in your community to prevent or stop child abuse. What kinds of help do they offer to parents and to children? Report your findings to the class.

Think About

1. If and when you have children, how will your guidance techniques differ from or be the same as those your parents used with you?

2. How is guidance beneficial to individuals and to society? What happens to an individual who has little or no guidance?

Handling Common Problems

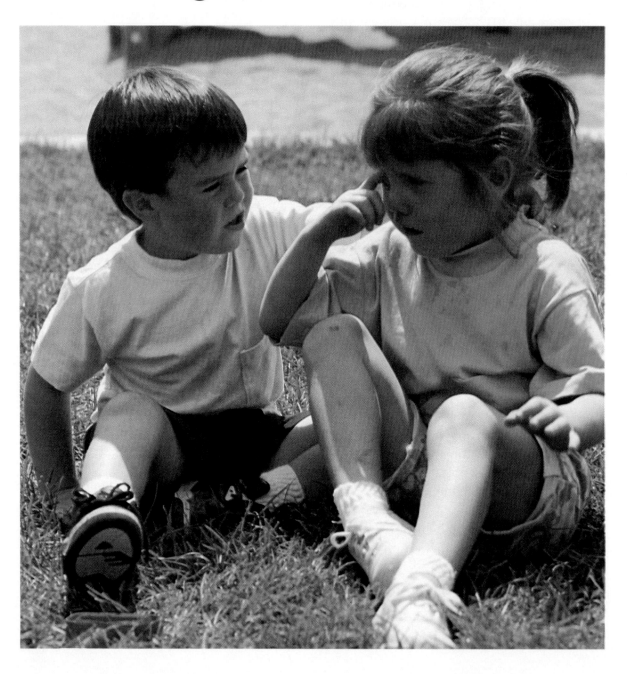

Objectives

This chapter will help you to:
- Explain why some behavioral problems should be discussed with a child and others ignored.
- Describe ways that parents can handle emotional problems such as temper tantrums, fears, sibling rivalry, and aggression.
- Discuss common problems associated with bedtime.
- Describe how parents should handle dishonest behavior.

Vocabulary

phobia
aggression
enuresis

Lauren and Ken have three children. Their youngest child, Kathleen, is six months old. At about four weeks of age, Kathleen developed colic. She would have crying spells that lasted for three or four hours. As the weeks passed and the colic ended, the baby was still fretful. Despite everything the doctor has recommended, Kathleen still cries several times during the night.

As a result, neither Lauren or Ken have been able to sleep through the night since Kathleen was born. They take turns getting up to comfort her and help her get back to sleep.

Neither of Lauren and Ken's other children were fretful or colicky babies. Both children began to sleep through the night when they were three or four months old. Although the parents know that children have different personalities, they were unprepared for Kathleen's fretfulness.

Lauren and Ken are relieved to know that nothing is seriously wrong with Kathleen. However, they become frustrated by not being able to comfort her when she cries. They occasionally leave Kathleen with a babysitter so they can go out, relax, and return refreshed. They know this difficult period will eventually end and everyone will be able to sleep through the night.

Preventing or Dealing with Behavioral Problems

All children go through trying times, and sometimes behavioral problems develop. Often these problems can be averted by the way parents handle situations that arise. Parents who can see many ways to deal with a problem are likely to succeed in helping their children work through the problem.

Chapter Opener. Ask students to read the opening scenario to the chapter. Ask these questions: What concerns might Lauren and Ken have? Why do they feel frustrated? What might help them during this difficult period? Where might they get advice or help?
Reference. See page 261 for information about colic.

Some behavioral problems result from the parents' lack of understanding of children's growth and development. The parents may have unrealistic expectations for their children. For example, parents may get upset because a toddler gets into many things around the home. However, toddlerhood is a stage of exploration. Perhaps the home has not been properly childproofed for a child of this age. Perhaps there are too many things the child is forbidden to touch or too few toys appropriate for the child's age.

Some behavioral problems are caused by inconsistent guidance from parents. For example, Rachel's father sometimes tells her it is all right to play with his hats. At other times, he scolds Rachel for playing with them.

Generally, there are several good ways to handle any problem. Parents who are calm and confident are more likely to be able to help their child than parents who are tense and insecure. The less anxiety a parent communicates, the more open the child will be to accept help and guidance.

Parents can help children with some behavioral problems by talking openly about the problem. This will help the child either overcome the problem or learn to live with it. Talking also helps gain the child's trust. Children are usually eager for help. However, they are too young and inexperienced to know how to go about getting help.

On the other hand, some behavioral problems come and go as part of normal growth and development. The problems may pass if little or no attention is paid to them. Only when parents become overly concerned about these problems, do they become bigger than they need to be.

Techniques for handling problems vary from one parent to another and from one child to another. What works for one family may not work for another. When a problem is handled well, parents will usually see a positive change in the child's behavior. However, parents should not hesitate to seek professional help when a problem becomes so serious that they cannot cope with it.

When parents understand the developmental stages of children, they are better able to handle certain behavioral problems. For example, infants and toddlers get tired, hungry, or cranky far sooner than older children and adults.

Discuss. What might be some common behavioral problems that develop during childhood? How might parents with different parenting styles (authoritative, democratic, permissive) handle the same problem?

Emphasize. Parents should never resort to physical punishment or abuse when dealing with children's behavioral problems. See pages 469–472 for information about child abuse.

Emotional and Social Problems

Some problems are emotional in nature. They affect the way children feel about themselves and others. They may also affect the way children get along with others.

Some common emotional problems in early childhood include crying and emotional outbursts, special fears, jealousy and sibling rivalry, and aggression.

◆◆ Crying and Emotional Outbursts

Crying and occasional emotional outbursts do not necessarily mean that a child has emotional problems. Part of growing up is learning to deal with frustration. Crying is a normal, healthy way for a child or an adult to relieve feelings of frustration or sadness.

Fatigue and hunger are two frequent causes of emotional outbursts in young children. Parents and other caregivers who want children to be happy try to keep them rested and well fed. Late bedtimes, late mealtimes, and long shopping trips often contribute to behavior problems.

Handling Crying

All babies cry, some more than others. Infants also respond to stress by crying. Thus the more stressful the situation, the longer and more intense the crying spell may be.

What should parents and other caregivers do when a baby cries? First, they should try to comfort the baby by meeting his or her needs. Is the cause hunger, wetness, fatigue, or illness? Does the baby want to be held and comforted? Once the need is met, most babies settle down.

However, some babies are more fretful than others. Some may be colicky. Others

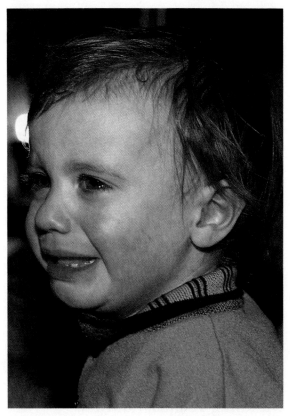

Crying helps a child deal with feelings of frustration. At the same time, a child's crying can make parents feel very frustrated. They may have to try a number of techniques before discovering how to best comfort their child.

seem to cry for no apparent reason. Many babies cry before going to sleep. Usually, if left alone, most fall asleep on their own within a few minutes. Others may cry for 20 minutes or so.

Parents can try a number of techniques to comfort a crying baby. However, techniques that work for some babies may not work for others. Thus parents may have to experiment to discover which techniques are most successful for their child. Some babies are comforted by sucking on a pacifier; others by being swaddled in a lightweight blanket. Some seem happiest when sleeping in a small space or up against a crib bumper. Many babies can be comforted by motion: walking,

Activity. Have students listen to an audio tape of a baby crying. Ask them to identify possible reasons for the crying. Then have them describe their own feelings as the crying continues. **Problem Solving.** Divide students into pairs. Have each "cou-

ple" role play various techniques to comfort their crying baby. What would they do if the baby was still crying after an hour? **Reference.** See page 258 for information about swaddling.

rocking, riding in a stroller or car. Others are comforted by listening to music, stroking a favorite blanket or toy, or sucking a thumb. Parents of babies who are unusually fretful may need to ask a friend or relative to care for the baby occasionally. This gives the parents a break from their caregiving responsibilities.

As babies grow older, their crying spells usually become shorter and less frequent. Then crying may be used to indicate a specific emotion, such as fear or anger.

Older children may learn to use crying to manipulate or control siblings or parents. For example, four-year-old Melinda often shrieked when her older brother approached her. At first, her parents assumed her brother was hurting her. After observing the children, they discovered this was not true. Instead, Melinda was using crying to gain attention. Her parents started helping her express her needs in words rather than by crying.

Handling Temper Tantrums

During the toddler and preschool years, children sometimes have temper tantrums. This is one way that they express their need for independence and control. Parents and other caregivers should respond calmly to a temper tantrum. This helps prevent the behavior from being repeated.

Generally, parents and caregivers should simply restate the decision that caused the tantrum. For example, an adult might say, "No, you can't play with the vase." Then the adult should ignore the child. Once the tantrum subsides, the adult can make a statement of encouragement and help: "I'll help you find a toy to play with when you're ready." This lets children know that the adult is not rejecting them but refuses to be part of the tantrum.

A child who has gone past the point of kicking and screaming and is throwing toys or trying to damage things must be physically restrained. The adult should do this as gently as possible. It also helps to take the child away from the site of misbehavior. For example, the child might be taken into another room or out of the store. Without an audience, the child may lose interest in the tantrum. As soon as possible, the adult should release the child. This prevents a long power struggle. When children are held still, they often resist and retaliate with greater force.

In some cases, a child may be so emotionally upset that the adult will have to alternate between restraining and releasing. For example, when a child is released, he or she may attempt to kick at the adult. Then the adult may have to hold the child again for a few seconds before releasing him or her. Each time the adult should tell the child, "I'm not going to hurt you. I want to help you settle down because you can't kick other people."

Some angry children hold their breath during a tantrum until they actually turn blue in the face. This behavior has also been observed in newborns. It is simply a way of expressing anger. No harm results when children do this. Parents should ignore it and follow the same steps recommended for other displays of temper.

Parents should give children permission to express their feelings or disappointment. For example, a parent might say, "I see you're upset and angry. It's all right for you to cry, but I will not allow you to climb on the furniture. You may jump on the floor but not on the sofa. Sofas are for sitting." This statement also gives a simple reason, "Sofas are for sitting," that a child can understand.

Above all, parents and other caregivers should avoid shouting or losing their own temper. This only makes the tantrum worse. It teaches children that they can, indeed, get attention by throwing tantrums.

Activity. Have students role play various ways (positive and negative) that parents can respond to a three-year-old child's temper tantrum. What might be the child's feelings after each situation? What might be the parent's feelings?

Problem Solving. Have students list situations that can cause temper tantrums in young children. For each situation, ask students to suggest two or three ways that parents might avoid or prevent the situation from occurring.

◆◆ Fears and Imagination

Young children have a variety of fears. Fear of separation and fear of strangers can produce real anxiety for children. They also have an active imagination and have not yet learned to distinguish the imaginary from the real. Objects, creatures, and situations—both real and imaginary—can cause special fears.

Handling Separation Anxiety

Separation anxiety occurs most frequently during infancy and early childhood. Some separations are short, such as when a parent goes shopping or to a movie. Other separations last all day, as when a parent must go to work. Occasionally, the separation can be longer. For example, a parent may be away on a trip, be hospitalized, or have moved out of the home because of separation or divorce.

Young children have little concept of time. They do not know how to anticipate the length of a parent's absence. They are not mature enough to understand the circumstances or the need for separating. Therefore, they feel uneasy until the parent returns.

Typically, children respond to separation with crying, anger, or withdrawal. Some preschoolers may be indifferent or resentful to a parent when they are reunited. Some parents misunderstand this behavior and think the child is not happy to see them.

Parents can help their children by talking with them about any separation. This is important even before they are old enough to talk. For example, a parent can say, "I know you don't want me to leave. I love you and I'll come back. You'll be all right while I'm gone." These statements should be short and simple. Children do not need long explanations. However, they do need to hear the parent's reassuring voice.

After making such statements, the parent should leave quickly. When a parent lingers,

Parents should never ignore or make fun of a child's fears. Instead, they should talk about the situation and reassure the frightened child.

separation becomes difficult for both the child and the parent. Parents should avoid statements such as "Aren't you going to tell me good-bye?" or "Aren't you going to miss me while I'm gone?" These statements indicate the parent's difficulty in separating from the child.

Parents should never slip away without preparing the child for the separation. They should not deceive the child about what will happen or where they are going. This only makes separation more difficult for the child.

When parents must be away for long periods of time, they can leave a picture of themselves or a tape recording with the child. They

Problem Solving. Divide students into small groups. Have each group decide the best way to prepare children for the following situations:
• A one-year-old for a parent's return to full-time employment outside the home.
• A three-year-old for a parent's five-day trip.
• A four-year-old for the parents' separation and divorce.

should also telephone or write to the child as often as possible.

Separation helps children develop independence and autonomy. Each time a parent and child experience a healthy separation and return, the task becomes easier.

Handling Stranger Anxiety

Until infants reach the age of seven or eight months, they respond to most people in a similar way. They look at a person's face and smile or coo or simply follow facial gestures.

By about eight or nine months of age, children are able to remember an image of a parent's face. They begin to compare the face of the parent with the faces of others. A parent's face brings a sense of comfort and security to babies. In contrast, less familiar faces evoke anxiety. Thus babies sometimes cry or scream when they see a person other than a parent or another very familiar person. Stranger anxiety often takes grandparents and friends by surprise. Previously, the baby may have responded to them with smiles and sounds of delight. Now the baby may cry or refuse to be held by them.

How should parents react? Some try to coax the baby to respond to the other person or hand the baby to that person. This usually causes the baby to scream louder. Instead, parents should comfort the baby and avoid forcing him or her to respond to others. Parents find it easier to accept the child's behavior when they know that this is a normal stage of the child's development.

Eventually, babies pass through the stage of stranger anxiety. Then they accept friends and relatives without fear or frustration.

Handling Imaginative Fears

As children grow older, they may develop certain fears. Such fears are normal and usually change with age. The causes of some of these fears could possibly happen. For exam-ple, a fear of wild animals or deep water can serve to protect young children. They should be taught never to pet wild animals or enter the water alone.

Other fears are based more on imaginary than on real dangers. Preschoolers, especially, have active imaginations. They can think about dangers that they have not actually experienced. They are also influenced by scary stories they may have seen on television or heard from others. Children this age often fear the dark, monsters, animals, and death.

Parents can talk to children about imagination and dreams. This sometimes helps children understand the difference between fantasy and reality. It also helps them recognize and admit their fears.

Parents should always be supportive and understanding of children's fears. Their fears are very real to them. Parents should not laugh at or argue with children. Above all, parents should never punish children for being afraid.

Instead, parents should talk about the situation and reassure a frightened child. Such a process may take weeks or months. For example, a child may be afraid of monsters under the bed. The parent could look under the bed with the child and show that there is nothing to fear. It may be necessary for the parent and child to do a "monster check" for several weeks until the child feels safe.

Another child may have a special fear of spiders. In this case, the parent and child could read some stories about spiders. Then they could look at some plastic toy spiders. Finally, they could see some real spiders in a park or zoo.

Children's fears should never be ignored. Otherwise, they are likely to remain and even grow. A **phobia** is a persistent, irrational fear of a specific object, situation, or activity. It may be a fear of snakes, heights, or flying in an airplane. Other phobias include claustrophobia, a fear of enclosed or crowded places, and agoraphobia, a fear of public places. Even though people often understand that their phobia is unrealistic, they are unable to control their emotional response. As a result, they go to great lengths to avoid the situation. If the phobia affects a person's ability to function at normal tasks, then professional treatment is needed.

DECISIONS ◆ ◆ DECISIONS

Jill, two-and-a-half years old, is beginning toilet training. She is excited about using the grown-ups' toilet, but she is afraid of the water flushing. How can Jill's parents help her become toilet trained despite this fear?

◆◆ Jealousy and Sibling Conflicts

As you learned earlier, a certain amount of sibling rivalry is normal in a family. During the preschool and early school-age years, however, there is likely to be more conflict between siblings than in later years. This is because children are still developing their personality. They are inclined to test their own ideas abut themselves. They compete with each other for attention from parents or from other siblings.

For example, the child who is confronted with a new sibling often fears that all the parents' love and attention will now go to the baby. A three- or four-year-old may be open about these feelings, saying, "I don't like the baby. Why don't you take it back to the hospital?" Older children may experience guilt over such feelings. As a result, they may try to cover up their feelings by constantly hugging and kissing the baby.

When young children are involved in the care of a new sibling, they are better able to overcome feelings of jealousy and rivalry. This gives them a sense of importance because they can see all the things they can do and the baby cannot do.

Activity. Ask students to view a television sitcom about families. Have them identify examples of sibling rivalry and describe how the caregivers handled the problem.

Problem Solving. Have students role play how parents should respond when an older sibling says, "Take the baby back to the hospital."

Although siblings usually feel love and affection for each other, they also have feelings of jealousy, insecurity, and anxiety. For example, two brothers are playing together.

Around the World

Massage for Infants

Massaging healthy babies is a custom that is seldom practiced in Western cultures. However, it is a common practice in other parts of the world, especially in Africa and Asia.

In Russia, both mothers and doctors believe that a massage should be an important part of a baby's daily routine. They believe that infant massage has several benefits.

- It makes the infant's body and limbs more supple.
- It strengthens and tones the skin and muscles.
- It accustoms the baby to regular physical activity.
- It contributes to the child's general feeling of well-being.
- It increases the bond between mother and infant.

New mothers in Russia are taught how to exercise and massage their infant as soon as he or she is a few days old. Massaging techniques are an important part of Russian books and films devoted to rearing a healthy baby.

In our culture, some child care experts are beginning to recommend gentle massage as a way of calming a crying baby. They believe parents can be taught to use massage techniques to relieve a baby's tension, constipation, and teething discomfort.

A third brother comes along and coaxes one of them to play with him. This can cause conflict if the child who is left alone feels rejected.

Siblings sometimes bicker with each other, especially if they are close in age. One may say to the other, "I'm bigger than you are. I can do things better than you can." Some tattle on each other to their parents or other siblings. Such behavior may indicate a child's desire for attention. Parents need to be sure that each child receives his or her fair share of affection, praise, and privileges.

Teasing is another way that siblings may test each other. Some types of teasing are good-humored. Others are insensitive and cruel. The latter can damage a child's self-esteem, and parents should take steps to end them. For example, a parent might say, "Hank, it upsets me when I hear you teasing your sister. Can you explain it to me?" Helping children express their feelings in more acceptable ways can help resolve conflicts.

Most sibling rivalry fades as children grow and develop their own self-identity. During the school-age years, siblings can often be very supportive of each other to people outside the family. They may also defend each other to their parents. However, some children never outgrow their rivalry and are jealous of siblings even as adults.

Handling Sibling Rivalry

Most parents are wise to stay out of their children's conflicts unless they involve destructive behavior. Then it may be necessary to step in. A parent can say, "I know you're having trouble playing together, but you must stop fighting. I'll hold the toy while the two of you decide what to do. You can play together or take turns, or I'll put the toy away and you can play with something else. Now what do you want to do?"

Parents should remain calm and not take sides in children's conflicts. Even when one child is wrong or misbehaving, the best approach is to remain neutral. Then the parent cannot be seen as playing favorites.

Here are some ways that parents can cope with jealousy and sibling rivalry.

- **Understand that jealousy between siblings is normal.** This helps parents cope with sibling rivalry.

- **Accept children's expressions of jealousy and help children feel comfortable with their feelings.** Saying, "I know you're feeling a little angry that the baby takes so much of my time" is more helpful than

"It's not nice to hate your little brother. You must love him." Children have a right to their feelings.

- **Realize that comparing children with each other fosters more jealousy.** Parents and other caregivers should not talk about one child being smarter, nicer, or more attractive than another.

- **Realize that encouraging competition between siblings also causes more jealousy.** Rather than saying, "Can you beat Sandy into the bathroom to wash your hands?" parents might say, "We'll be ready

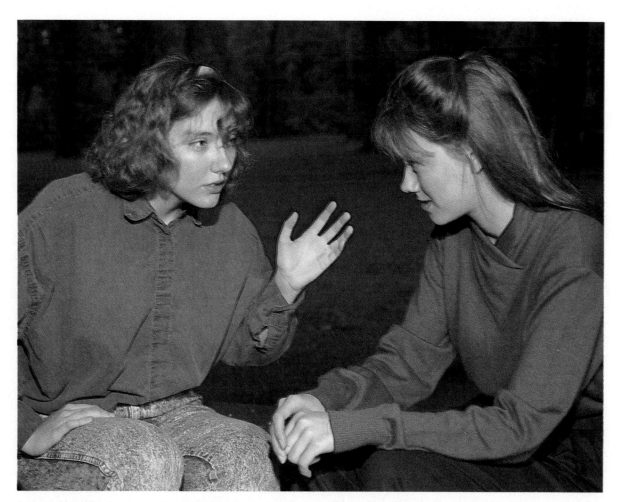

Parents should take care not to take sides in an argument between their children. Otherwise they will be seen as playing favorites, which causes more rivalry among siblings.

Problem Solving. Divide class into small groups. Have them write three responses to a child who expresses jealous feelings about a new sibling. Have each group role play their responses.

Discuss. In what ways do parents often encourage competition between siblings? Why might this cause more jealousy?

for dinner when both of you have washed your hands." Setting the stage for one sibling to win does not encourage children to like each other.

- **Give children the opportunity to continue friendships and activities.** Saying, "We have to stay home because of the baby" is sure to cause resentment.

- **Reassure children that they are loved.** The best way for parents to show love is for each of them to spend time with each child. Hugs, kisses, and saying, "I love you" are important, too.

- **Remember that each child is an individual and that equal treatment is therefore impossible.** Most parents understand their children's different emotional needs and deal with them accordingly. Children appreciate adults who recognize their individuality.

◆◆ Aggression

Aggression is an act marked by an attack on someone or something. Aggression can be positive or negative. For example, when soccer players are aggressive, they play hard to win the game. They show the positive side of aggression. Many people feel that a certain amount of assertiveness, or controlled aggression, is also good. It is part of a person's drive to work hard and succeed. However, aggression is negative when it is uncontrolled and hurts others.

Some parents encourage aggressive behavior in their children. Parents are naturally concerned when others pick on or take advantage of their child. They may want the child to learn how to defend himself or herself. For this reason, they may tell a child, "If anyone hits you, hit back." Unfortunately, this approach does not help children learn to work out their problems peacefully. It also does not encourage long-range social growth.

For example, if Tim hits Janice and Janice hits back, Tim must hit Janice again. The result is a fight.

Studies show that when parents or other caregivers permit aggression, children tend to act with aggression. Some parents permit their children to act aggressively toward other children but not toward them. This creates a problem for a child, who cannot see the logic in the rule. In addition, parents who punish children by slapping or hitting them are demonstrating aggression. Of course, there are more effective ways to control children than physically punishing them.

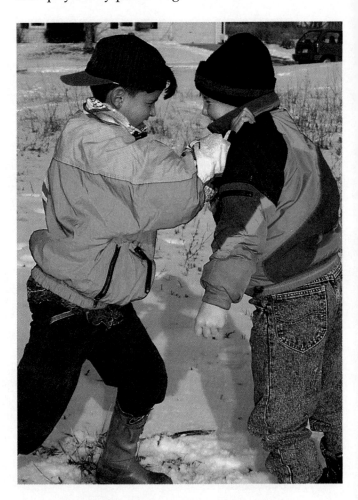

Aggressive behavior is often the result of anger. Parents should help children learn to express their angry feelings in ways other than hitting and fighting.

Problem Solving. Have students discuss what parents should say to a child instead of: "If anyone hits you, hit back."

Reference. See pages 458–462 for information about helping children develop self-control.

Handling Hitting and Fighting

Conflicts between young children usually occur over toys or other objects. One child may suddenly hit or begin fighting with another child over an object. Young children do not have the language skills to express their feelings in words. As a result, they may resort to physical acts such as hitting and kicking.

Parents and other caregivers need to accept children's feelings about a conflict. Physical aggression is usually the result of anger. However, adults should help children learn to express their angry feelings in ways other than hitting and fighting.

Parents and other caregivers should let children know that adults do not approve of physical aggression. For example, a parent may say, "Tim, it's all right for you to be angry with Janice, but it's not all right for you to hit her. When you're angry, stamp your foot or tell her you're angry." In turn, the parent could suggest ways for Janice to handle the conflict. "Don't let Tim hit you. Hold his hands, push him away, or walk away from him. If you prefer, tell Tim you don't like hitting, and it's against the rules." These approaches help children learn that they must express anger in more appropriate ways.

Everyone gets angry at times. However, parents and other caregivers should model nonviolent ways of expressing anger. Then children see how they can deal with their own anger. Adults should encourage children to talk openly about what bothers them. This helps prevent anger from growing into a long-lasting resentment. Adults should also praise children when they resolve their disagreements in positive ways without physical aggression. This helps reinforce positive behavior.

Unfortunately, some children continue to show aggressive behavior as they grow older. Their aggression becomes hostile, and their physical actions are meant to hurt other people. Some hit or fight with other children. Others turn to verbal aggression. They tease or insult others, often those who are younger or smaller. This form of aggression can be as emotionally damaging to another child as fighting can be physically damaging.

Children who are explosive and tend to hurt others usually have trouble developing good relationships. These children may benefit from professional help. Through counseling, they can develop a positive sense of self and learn how to develop self-control.

Handling Biting

When young children are angry or frustrated, they commonly resort to biting. However, parents and other caregivers should help children vent their anger or frustration in a more acceptable way.

Why do children bite? At first, biting may be simply a sensory experience. Children learn about objects by putting them in their mouth and biting on them. They bite toys, spoons, furniture, and a variety of nearby items. Some children watch others bite and then imitate the behavior. As children become toddlers, they may use biting to express aggression or frustration. Three- to five-year-olds use biting to get their way or a parent's attention.

When parents or other caregivers observe a child biting, they should use both words and actions to stop the behavior. They should immediately say, "The biting must stop." Then they should physically remove the child from the situation. Parents and caregivers should watch the child closely to see whether the behavior is repeated. If it is, they can step in quickly and stop the biting before it becomes a habit. Adults should never bite a child back. This only confuses the child as to what is appropriate and inappropriate behavior.

Problem Solving. Many conflicts among adolescents result in violence, including the use of knives and guns. Have students discuss possible causes of violence in our society. How can people learn to resolve their conflicts in nonviolent ways?

Discuss. How could parents encourage children to release anger or frustration in ways other than biting or hitting? **Problem Solving.** Ask students what they would do if another child is hostile or abusive toward their own child.

Bedtime Problems

Bedtime problems can be very frustrating. They occur at a time when parents may be least prepared to be patient and understanding. However, most sleep problems are short-lived. Problems with bedtime routines may last a little longer.

◆◆ Sleep Habits

In the early months of life, infants wake up during the night. After six months of age, most do so only occasionally. By the end of the first year, most babies sleep through the night.

Some babies fuss or cry when placed in bed. They may be bored or lonely. A few cuddly toys and comfort from a parent usually help babies fall asleep. Infants between five and eight months of age may wake up and cry for no apparent reason. This is about the time infants discover themselves. They may become startled when they find themselves alone in the dark. When this happens, a parent can spend a few minutes comforting and reassuring the child. Often a little stroking, cuddling, and gentle talking help the child fall asleep again.

Two- and three-year-olds require an average of about 12 hours of sleep a night. They also need a nap during the day. By the time children are four years old, most of them no

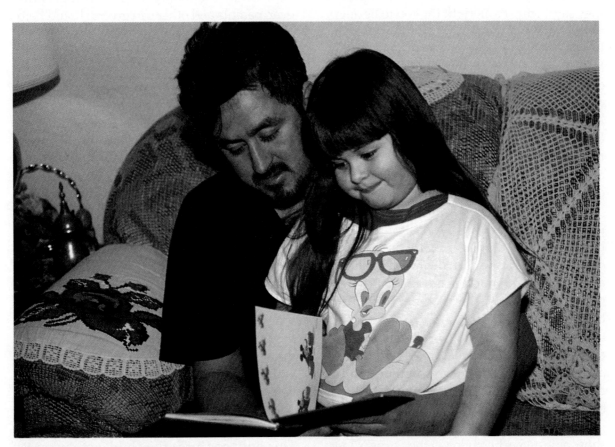

When children can spend some quiet time with a parents just before bedtime, it makes going to bed an enjoyable ritual.

Discuss. What bedtime routines did you have as a child? Did you take a favorite item to bed with you? If so, what was it?

Problem Solving. Some parents like to wrestle or play actively with a child before bedtime. Then the child is too excited to go to sleep. Have students list various activities that would help children settle down and relax before going to bed.

longer need a regular daytime nap. Short rest periods are usually adequate.

✦ Bedtime Routines

For many families, bedtime routines become an enjoyable ritual. They may include undressing, bathing, putting on pajamas, and reading or telling stories. They give parents and children the opportunity to talk together and hug and kiss each other good night.

Bedtime should be a calm and quiet time. Children need to settle down and relax. Parents encourage this by being calm and relaxed themselves. When it is time for children to get ready for bed, parents should let them know this in a cheerful, kind, yet firm, manner. For example, a parent may say, "It's almost bedtime. You may play a few minutes longer and then you must begin your bath." Children learn quickly how much they can get away with. Resisting bedtime is one of the areas in which most children push as far as they can. By establishing bedtime routines when children are babies, parents establish a habit that children continue for years.

Some children insist on taking a favorite doll, toy, or blanket to bed with them. This item provides comfort as a child goes to sleep. Parents and older siblings should never threaten to throw this item away because it gives the child a sense of security.

Handling Attention-Getting Bedtime Behavior

Parents usually know when children are trying to gain attention or control and when they are really troubled. When parents repeatedly run to a child's room at the first sound of a whimper, they establish a pattern. The child quickly learns that whimpering will get attention. Once this attention-getting pattern

is set, the child often cries louder when the parents do not quickly appear. Some children resort to screaming when the crying fails to get immediate results.

Handling such a problem takes time and patience. When a parent knows a child is merely seeking attention, the parent can say, "I'd like you to learn to stop whimpering and crying to get my attention. I'll be with you in the morning. Right now I'm tired and want to rest. You need rest too. You may go on crying, but I'm not going to pay attention."

Some children get up during the night and come to the parent's bed to get attention. Most experts say that allowing children to sleep with their parents will establish a hard-to-break routine. Instead, parents should talk to their children and state the limits. For example, a parent might say, "I know you want me to be with you, but it's time for sleeping. I'll play with you when you wake up in the morning. I love you and want you to rest now. Please go back to bed and go to sleep. Good night."

Parents should not allow children to get into a routine of making frequent bedtime requests. These include asking for a glass of water, asking for help in going to the bathroom, and requesting books or toys. Again, parents should talk with children and then enforce the limit.

Handling Fear of the Dark

Some children are afraid of being alone in the dark. They may need reassurance to help them feel secure.

Parents can help a child deal with this fear by going into the bedroom with the child. They can hold the child's hand and look around the room while the light is on. Then they can turn out the light and talk with the child. Sometimes it is a good idea to leave a very dim light on in the room so that it is not completely dark.

Problem Solving. Divide class into small groups. Have each group discuss ways to handle a child who is making bedtime requests, such as a glass of water or another toy. If desired, each group can role play the situation.

Activity. Ask students to write some helpful tips for a teenager who is babysitting a three-year-old who is afraid of the dark.

Some young children prefer to share a room with a brother or sister. Others may be comforted by having the family dog or cat sleep in the room.

Handling Nightmares

Nightmares, or frightening dreams, are fairly common during early childhood. Nightmares may be triggered by an illness or a scary daytime experience. Sometimes they are caused by tension or stress.

When some children experience a frightening dream, they become fearful and cry without fully waking up. The next day they may not even remember the dream. Others cry out, fully awake, and become very upset. Monsters and strange-looking creatures that appear in children's dreams can be very frightening. Often children think the monsters or creatures are in the room. When this happens, children may not want to go back to sleep.

As with all fears, parents should reassure the children. Comforting words and a hug may help them relax so that they can fall asleep again. Parents may say, "Oh, I know you must feel afraid when you dream about strange-looking creatures. I'm right here with you and everything's all right."

◆◆ Bed-Wetting

Generally, it takes a child longer to learn to stay dry during the night than to stay dry during the day. Although by age three some children remain dry at night, many do not. Boys frequently develop nighttime control later than girls.

By the time children are four or five years old, most no longer wet during the night. Those who do usually have not learned to control the reflex to urinate. The term for bed-wetting or lack of bladder control is **enuresis** (en-you-REE-sis).

Parents can often help children by following these guidelines.

- Be sure the child has urinated shortly before going to bed.
- Do not give the child large amounts of liquid after the evening meal.
- Encourage the child to get up during the night to go to the bathroom.
- Avoid punishing, scolding, or shaming the child.
- If bed-wetting continues to occur after age five or six, talk to the child's doctor. With professional help, the child can usually overcome the problem.

Parents should always provide reassurance and comfort for a child who has had a bad dream or nightmare. However, they should not allow a child to get into the habit of making frequent bedtime requests.

Activity. Have students write a description of a nightmare or frightening dream they had during childhood. Then ask them how a parent could reassure a child who experiences the same type of dream.

Emphasize. It is important that parents not eliminate all fluids for a child who has enuresis. The child should be offered small amounts of liquids in the evening, if requested, as water is needed for the proper functioning of the body.

Honesty and Dishonesty

Before the age of three, children are generally not dishonest. They may lie, but they do not do it intentionally. At about the age of four, children begin to realize they can say things that are not true. They may go through a period of exaggerating as their imagination becomes vivid. In most cases, they do not understand that making exaggerated statements may be interpreted as lying. Fantasy and distortion are simply ways for them to explore and test the world around them.

At about the age of five or six, most children begin to know when they are telling the truth. Still, they do not understand what a lie is. They think of a lie as words they must not say. By about age seven or eight, children come to know that a lie is an untruth. This progression is all part of their moral development.

✦ Lying

Why do children lie? They may lie for several reasons:

- To prevent punishment.
- To get what they lack in reality by creating fantasy.
- To express their fears and hopes, such as what they would like to be or do.
- To test their parents' perceptions. (Since parents are supposed to know everything, children expect them to know the difference between lies and true statements.)

Parents should always encourage children to tell the truth about their feelings and behavior. However, parents must be ready to listen to the truth even when it is unpleasant. Children learn whether or not "honesty is the best policy" from the reactions of others.

Children also learn about honesty from the words and actions of their parents and other role models. When children overhear adults telling someone something they know is untrue, they do not understand why adults may tell "little white lies." Instead, they often imitate the same behavior.

Parents should show understanding of a child's impulse to lie. For example, Anika's mother saw that her daughter's shoes were muddy. She said, "Anika, your shoes are all muddy." Anika replied, "Kathy pushed me." Her mother then said, "You would like me to think that Kathy pushed you in the mud. Then I wouldn't scold you for getting your shoes dirty, would I?" Parents should not hesitate, however, to let a child know that they know that what was said is untrue. Anika's mother told her, "I know you couldn't resist stepping in the puddles. Please clean your shoes now."

Parents can often prevent defensive lying by not asking questions that might cause the child to feel a need to lie. Children dislike being questioned when they suspect their parents already know the answers to the questions. Children usually respond more positively to statements of understanding than to questions about lying.

Young children gradually develop the ability to know the difference between what is real and what is not real. Parents can help

◆ ◆ *Self-Esteem* ◆ ◆

As children grow and develop, they need guidance and support to get through certain behavioral difficulties. Every child has special problems at one time or another. When parents are prepared and confident, they are able to help their children through these difficulties.

Discuss. What are some "little white lies" that children may hear adults say? Why are these confusing to children? How can parents handle these situations?

Activity. Ask students to share some of the consequences they have experienced after telling a lie.

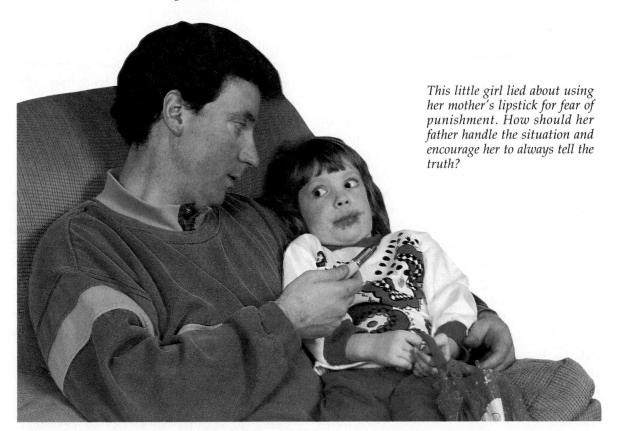

This little girl lied about using her mother's lipstick for fear of punishment. How should her father handle the situation and encourage her to always tell the truth?

them by distinguishing between fantasy statements and real ones. For example, Gary's mother responded to his story by saying, "Sometimes it's fun to pretend that you're a pilot and that you fly a plane. I know you enjoy making up stories when they help you talk about what you wish you could do."

When children lie, parents should not yell and preach at them. This is not the time to teach children what is right or wrong. Instead, parents should help children realize that there is no need to lie. They can do this by telling children that they will not be punished if they admit they made a mistake.

Parents should praise children when they are honest and tell the truth. Parents might also reward them by giving them more trust and privileges. Honesty is a value that parents hope their children will develop. Parents can promote honesty through encouragement and guidance.

Discuss. How can parents encourage children to be honest?

◆◆ Cheating

Young children usually cheat at one time or another. This is normal, especially for children between the ages of three and seven. Most young children cheat in order to win. They want to win because they have learned that it is good to be a winner. Winners get attention and are recognized for their achievements. Thus children may want to win even if it means changing the rules of the game.

In this sense, cheating is not a moral issue for children. Most of them do not know what the word *cheating* really means. Some may have learned that it means doing something wrong. When this is the case, they may deny having cheated to avoid punishment.

When children cheat in a game, parents can make a simple statement and then drop the subject. For example, a parent might say, "You didn't win because you placed a marker over

Problem Solving. Divide class into small groups. Ask each group to discuss ways that parents should handle dishonesty at a particular stage: preschool, school-age, or adolescence. Have each group share their ideas or role play specific situations.

the yellow square before it was called. Next time you must wait until the shape is named." In this way children get the message about appropriate and inappropriate behavior.

As children grow older, they gradually learn that cheating is a form of dishonesty. If they cheat on homework or an exam, they are being dishonest. They may feel guilty and fear getting caught.

When children cheat in schoolwork, parents must talk with them in a way that conveys understanding but disapproval. For example, a parent may say, "I'm sorry you copied your friend's math problems. You must learn to do your own work, even if you have trouble with it. When you copy someone else's work, there's no way to know whether or not you can do the work yourself. Next time, tell the teacher you're having a hard time with your work so you can get help. Tell me and I'll help you, too."

Most children learn that cheating is wrong and are motivated to achieve on their own. However, some children see their peers cheating and feel pressured to do the same thing. Parents may need to repeatedly convey that they disapprove of cheating and that it is unacceptable behavior. At the same time, they need to offer guidance about what is acceptable behavior.

◆◆ Health & Safety ◆◆

Teenage Drinking

Although drinking alcoholic beverages before the age of twenty-one is illegal in the United States, many young people begin drinking long before that age. Surveys have shown that the average age at which children begin drinking is twelve. Consumption of alcohol often increases dramatically during the high school years.

One danger of alcohol consumption is that it reduces a person's ability to think clearly and respond quickly. As a result, alcohol is frequently involved in other forms of drug abuse, automobile accidents, and sexual activity.

Another danger of teenage drinking is that it can lead to addiction. More than half of all adult alcoholics started drinking heavily as teenagers. Although it may take an adult many years to become addicted to alcohol, a teenager can become addicted in only months.

There are many reasons why children drink. Some are influenced by advertising. Others see parents and other role models using alcohol. Still others bow to peer pressure in order to feel accepted by the group.

Parents and schools need to work together to prevent the abuse of alcohol in families and communities. Parents should learn about alcohol, its short-term and long-term effects, and its appeal to young people. Then they can help their children understand the dangers of alcohol and learn how to resist peer pressure to drink. Parents also need to learn the signs of alcohol abuse and where they can get help for a child.

Two important factors can help young people resist the pressures to drink. These are high self-esteem and good communication with parents. Parents can encourage both of these throughout childhood. Then adolescents will be better prepared to face special challenges such as teenage drinking.

Problem Solving. Have students identify reasons why children cheat on homework or tests. What pressures encourage some children to cheat? How can parents and teachers motivate children to always do their own work?

Activity. Ask students to gather additional information about the dangers of alcohol abuse. Have them create a pamphlet, poster, or short video that would encourage young people not to drink alcohol.

❖ Stealing and Shoplifting

A young child may take a toy that belongs to another child or an item from a store. The item may be something that the child has wanted for a long time. At a young age, children do not understand about property rights. They may be confused about ownership because the toys and equipment at a child care center are used by all the children.

As with other kinds of misbehavior, stealing should be dealt with as quickly as possible. If parents discover that their child has taken an item from another child or a store, they should go with the child to return the item. This helps children learn how to correct a misdeed and to distinguish between what is theirs and what belongs to others. They begin to understand that people cannot have everything that they want.

During adolescence, children may be tempted to shoplift. The reasons why teenagers shoplift are many. Some steal because of peer pressure. Others want items they cannot afford. Still others shoplift simply for the thrill or challenge. They want to see whether they can get away with something without being caught by authorities.

Shoplifting is illegal. Stores and other businesses take special measures to prevent the stealing of merchandise. Special merchandise tags, mirrors, cameras, and security guards are being used to prevent shoplifting. Employers are also taking measures to prevent stealing by employees.

When people are arrested for shoplifting, they can suffer both short-term and long-term consequences. Because shoplifting is a crime, the shoplifter can be imprisoned, fined, or required to perform community service. He or she acquires a criminal record, which can affect getting and keeping a job.

When older children steal or shoplift, parents must make it very clear that the behavior is unacceptable. They should also emphasize that the children face stiff penalties if they commit illegal acts. Parents should be suspicious if they see their children with objects they probably did not purchase. This is the time to talk with children about the possible reasons for their actions. In such situations, parents need to offer support and help so that children will not repeat the behavior.

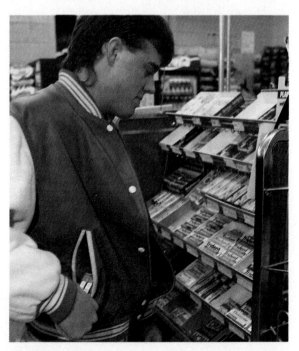

Stealing and shoplifting are considered crimes and can result in arrest, prosecution, and a criminal record.

DECISIONS ◆ ◆ DECISIONS

Erik is six years old. On the way home from the store, his mother discovers Erik playing with a toy car. She does not remember having seen the car before. When she asks him about it, he replies, "My friend Joey gave it to me." Erik's mother does not know whether to believe him or not. What should she do?

Activity. Have students research the financial costs of shoplifting and employee theft for stores and other types of businesses. Who ends up paying for these costs?

Problem Solving. Have students identify reasons why some teenagers shoplift. Ask them to create an advertising campaign that would inform teens about the consequences of stealing and motivate them to change their behavior.

CHAPTER 25 REVIEW

Summary

- Parents can usually prevent or successfully deal with children's behavioral problems by being flexible in dealing with trying situations, remaining calm and confident, and understanding each child's developmental stage.
- Generally there are several good ways to handle any behavioral problem.
- When dealing with crying or temper tantrums, parents should avoid shouting or losing their own temper.
- Parents should be supportive and understanding of children's fears.
- Jealousy and sibling rivalry are normal, and parents should reassure each child that he or she is loved.
- Parents should help children understand that negative or physical aggression is unacceptable behavior.
- Among children's common bedtime problems are sleep disturbances, fear of the dark, nightmares, and bed-wetting.
- Parents should explain why it is unacceptable and unnecessary to lie, cheat, or steal.

Questions

p. 476 **1.** Why should parents ignore some childhood behavioral problems?

p. 477 **2.** How should parents handle a crying baby?

p. 478 **3.** When should parents *not* ignore a child's temper tantrum? What should they do instead?

p. 479 **4.** Why should parents never slip away from their child without saying good-by?

5. List five ways in which parents can cope with sibling rivalry.   p. 483

6. How can parents handle a child's fear of the dark?   p. 487

7. What is enuresis? How can parents help children overcome it?   p. 488

8. How can parents promote honesty in their children?   p. 489

9. How should parents deal with an older child's stealing?   p. 492

Activities

1. Select a common behavior problem of children. Read two current magazine articles that suggest ways of handling the problem. Share your findings with the class.

2. Suggest ways that parents might avoid temper tantrums in a supermarket or toy store.

3. Research various kinds of phobias and make an alphabetically arranged "handbook of phobias." Include the names of at least eight phobias, the definition of each, and either a sketch or a sentence illustrating each.

Think About

1. Recall at least three things you were afraid of as a young child. How did your parents deal with these fears?

2. What does a child's stage of moral development have to do with how parents should handle his or her dishonest behavior?

Reference. See the Teacher's Manual in the front of the Teacher's Annotated Edition for complete answers to the chapter review questions.

493

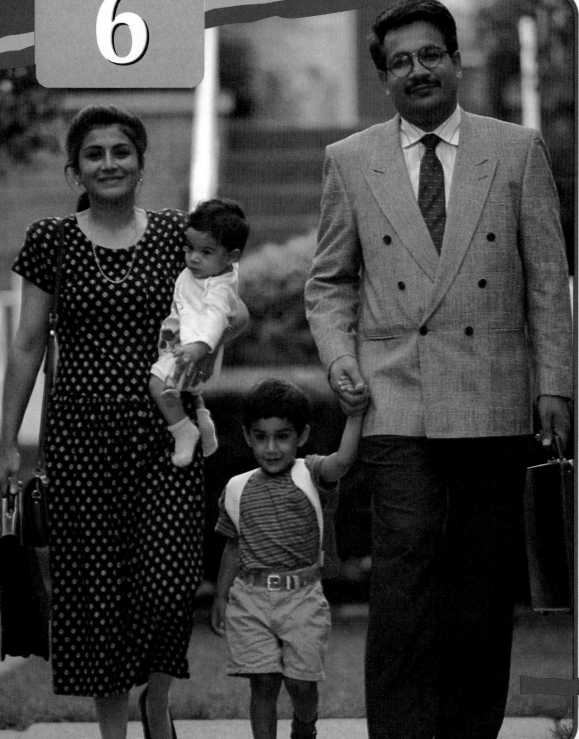

UNIT

6

Family Resources

CHAPTERS

Strengthening Families

Objectives

This chapter will help you to:
- Describe ways that parents and children can enrich family life.
- Explain how family members can communicate more effectively.
- List community resources for families.
- Discuss how families can develop support groups.

Vocabulary

quality time
respect
consensus
compromise
accommodation
resource
general equivalency
    diploma (GED)

"Dad, when's Thanksgiving?" asks seven-year-old Jamel.

"It's always the fourth Thursday in November," responds his father, Mr. Jackson.

"Are we going to have Thanksgiving at Grandma's like we always do?" asks Jamel.

"Yes," his mother answers, "and all your aunts and uncles and cousins are going to be there this year. You haven't seen your Uncle Raymond and his children for several years."

"Will we have turkey and mashed potatoes and lots of pies?" asks five-year-old Canisha.

"We sure will," replies Mrs. Jackson. "Do you remember how everyone in the family loves Grandma's pies? She made them just as good when I was a young girl like you."

Thanksgiving Day is a time when many families gather together to celebrate and give thanks for their blessings. The day is celebrated with big dinners and joyous reunions. Relatives from far away may telephone their greetings. This is just one way that family members help strengthen their ties with one another.

Enriching Families

The family is an important influence in children's lives. Although there are several types of family structures, each family functions in its own unique way. A strong, vital family is able to provide love and support to its members most of the time. Of course, there are times when every family may be less supportive. However, a healthy family works hard at nurturing its members.

A strong, vital family does not come about automatically. Both parents and children contribute to family relationships. By spending time together, showing respect and trust, expressing appreciation and understanding, and establishing traditions, they can enrich and strengthen family life.

❖ Spending Time Together

Time is limited for many parents today, just as it was for parents who worked long days on farms and in factories many years ago. The amount of time a family spends together is less important than the quality of the time. Parents who spend a few minutes listening, reading a story, or tossing a ball to a child usually develop better relationships than families who spend hours watching television without talking to each other. Spending **quality time** means focusing on the individual interests and needs of the child.

Family life is enriched when parents and children take time to do activities together.

Problem Solving. Have students identify ways that parents can spend quality time with each child in a family.

When there are several children in a family, it is sometimes harder for parents to spend quality time with each child. Parents may think of their children as a group and fail to remember the importance of giving each child individual attention. This is a mistake. Both fathers and mothers should plan how they can provide quality time for each child.

Some parents feel that spending quality time with children must involve special activities. Yet children enjoy just being together with family members. By going on a walk, playing a game, or washing the car together, parents and children can enjoy each other's company. Even when doing chores together, they can talk, laugh, tell jokes, and sing songs. Children will long remember times that are fun.

❖ Showing Respect and Trust

Family members need to show **respect** for one another. This means being considerate and polite to other people because you find them worthy. When you respect others, you

DECISIONS ◆
◆ DECISIONS

Three-year-old Jon goes to a child care center five days a week while his mother, Yvette, is at work. Yvette is pleased with Jon's growth and development, but she feels guilty about being away from him each day. In the evenings, she has to do household tasks, but she always manages to talk to Jon about his day and to read him a bedtime story. On the weekends, they do errands together and then go to a nearby park for an hour. Yvette is worried that she is not spending enough time with Jon. She has asked you for advice. What will you tell her?

Discuss. What activities did you share with family members that have the most meaning for you? What activities would you want to share with your own children?

◆ ◆ Self-Esteem ◆ ◆

When parents and children spend time together, the children feel important and valued. On the other hand, when parents ignore their children, the children feel that their parents do not care about them. The children's self-esteem is diminished. They begin to see themselves as less and less important.

do not make fun of their opinions that are different from yours. You are considerate of their possessions and privacy. Respecting others also means paying attention to them and showing concern for them. Children should show respect for their parents and grandparents. In turn, parents should show respect for their children.

Trust involves confidence. When you trust other people, you have confidence in their ability or honesty. Trust usually takes time to develop, but it can quickly be shattered. Young children trust their parents to take care of them. When parents make promises and follow through, the children's trust is reinforced. However, when parents fail to keep their promises, children lose confidence in the parents' word.

The reverse is also true. When children are honest, dependable, and truthful, they earn the trust of their parents. By remembering to do tasks and follow rules, children show that they can handle more responsibilities.

◆◆ Expressing Understanding and Love

Strong, vital families demonstrate understanding and love for family members. They appreciate each other and say thank you for help or favors. They praise each other's successes and comfort each other in times of disappointment. They know they are accepted

A strong, healthy family should provide love and support for all family members.

Discuss. How would you like your child to treat you if you were a parent? How do you show respect for your parents now? What are the similarities and differences?
Reference. See pages 238 and 322 for information about trust.

Activity. Have students list ways that parents shatter their children's trust. Then list things that children do to shatter the trust of their parents. How can trust be reestablished between parents and children?

for themselves, whatever their strengths and weaknesses.

When children receive understanding and love, they develop positive self-concepts and high self-esteem. These traits give them the confidence to explore new interests and discover new opportunities.

❖ Establishing Traditions

Every family develops certain traditions. Often, these are based on their ethnic or cultural background. Some families prepare certain foods, such as a special cake, for birthdays. Others read a certain story or poem on holidays. Many families look forward to special times when family members gather for picnics, reunions, weddings, or anniversaries.

Traditions create a special identity for family members. They can look forward to an occasion, enjoy its familiarity, and remember it with pleasure. Families can also establish new traditions to hand down to their children.

Family traditions help strengthen the links between generations.

Activity. Ask students to write about a special tradition in their family that they would like to continue with their own children. Discuss. What are some other characteristics or traits of healthy families?

Reference. See pages 45–46 for a discussion of the functions of families.

Around the World

Kwanzaa

Kwanzaa is an African-American holiday that honors black people and their history. It lasts for seven days, from December 26 through January 1. People gather to eat and to celebrate their history and their future.

At Kwanzaa time, homes are decorated in red, green, and black. These are the colors of the bendera. This is a flag that was created in the early 1900s by Marcus Garvey, a leader of black people. Its red bar stands for the struggle for fairness and freedom. Its green bar stands for the future. The black bar in the center stands for unity among blacks.

Many of the words used for the symbols of Kwanzaa are taken from Swahili, an African language.

- The *mkeka* (mm-KEH-kah), a woven placemat, is the symbol for history. The other symbols stand on the placemat the way today stands on yesterday.

- The *kikombe cha umoja* (kee-KOM-beh chah oo-MOH-jah) is the cup of togetherness. Everyone sips juice or wine from this cup.

- *Mazao* (mah-ZAH-oh) are the fruits and vegetables of the harvest.

- One ear of *muhindi* (moo-HIN-dee), or corn, is put on the placemat to represent each child in the family.

- The *kinara* (kee-NAH-rah) holds seven candles. It stands for the people who lived in Africa many years ago. The candles, called *mishumaa saba* (mee-shoo-MAH SAH-bah), light the way in the modern world. They are lighted by a child, one on each of the seven days. During the lighting, the child talks about one of the seven reasons for, or principles of, Kwanzaa. There is one principle for each day.

- *Zawadi* (zah-WAH-dee) are gifts for the children. These are opened on the last day of the feast.

Communicating Effectively

Communication is the exchange of information, thoughts, and feelings. Family communication occurs in many ways. It is heard through the words and laughter of conversations around the dinner table. It is seen in smiles and frowns as games are played. It is felt through a comforting hug and a joyous embrace.

Communication between parents and children begins when children are infants. Toddlers and preschoolers ask endless questions of family members as they explore the world. They love to talk about their ideas and activities. Most school-age children continue to use communication to maintain a close relationship with the family. During the teenage years, communication between parents and children can become more difficult. Questions such as "What did you do in school today?" seldom result in meaningful discussions. However, parents should continue to encourage young people to share their feelings and experiences. The following situation illustrates this point.

The front door bangs, announcing that thirteen-year-old Caitlin is home from school. A jacket sails through the air in the general direction of the closet and lands on the floor. Caitlin hops over it and heads for the kitchen.

Family members communicate their thoughts and feelings both verbally and non-verbally with each other.

"Hi, Mom, what's for supper?"

"Tuna casserole. How was school?"

"Okay. Need any help?"

"Not just now, thanks."

Caitlin turns toward the living room, where the television set is waiting.

"No more news?" her mother asks. "Did you do anything special today?"

"Not really." Caitlin snaps on the television set. A moment later, she reappears in the kitchen doorway. "Oh, by the way, Mom," she says casually, "we did have a math test today."

"A math test?" Her mother's tone is neutral. She is not sure whether to expect a report of success or of failure. "How did you do?"

"Well, somehow or other, I didn't make a single mistake!" her daughter informs her,

pride breaking through at last. "My score was the best in the whole class!"

By developing good communication skills when children are young, families are strengthened. They are better able to maintain effective communication between family members, even when the children become teenagers.

Family members use two different types of language to communicate with each other: verbal and nonverbal language.

◆ Verbal Messages

Verbal messages consist of words that are spoken or written. However, verbal communication includes more than just words. The tone of a speaker's voice, or how the speaker

Reference. See pages 426–433 for effective ways to communicate with children.
Activity. Have four students stand in front of the room blindfolded. Give each a piece of construction paper. Tell them how to fold the paper in 3–5 steps, being very specific. Then show how many of the papers look the same. Ask students to relate this to verbal communication.

says the words, can influence the message. For example, when four-year-old Raul showed his father his drawing, Mr. Lopez exclaimed, "Raul, I really like it! You sure have used lots of bright colors. Tell me about it." What message might Raul have received if his father had replied in a flat or sarcastic tone of voice?

Verbal communication can be used to express ideas and feelings. Both words and tone of voice can indicate politeness or rudeness to others. Try saying the following sentence in different tones of voice: "How are you today?" How does the message change?

❖ Nonverbal Messages

Nonverbal messages are expressed through appearance and actions, not words. Facial expression, eye contact, posture, and body movements can send powerful nonverbal messages. Many feelings and attitudes are conveyed, consciously or unconsciously, through such nonverbal communication. Here are some examples.

- **Facial expressions.** A smile indicates happiness and friendliness; a downturned mouth shows sadness. A raised eyebrow indicates surprise; a frown shows disappointment.
- **Eye contact.** Looking directly at another person shows interest, friendliness, and warmth. Averting the eyes conveys disinterest, shyness, or nervousness.
- **Posture.** Standing erect shows a positive attitude. Sloping shoulders and slumped posture are signs of discouragement and disappointment.
- **Body movements.** Outstretched arms and open hands demonstrate welcome and friendliness. Arms held at the sides and clenched fists reveal anger and discomfort. Tapping fingers or foot can indicate ner-

vousness, impatience, or boredom. Patting a back conveys encouragement. Tapping the back of the hand signals a no-no.

These examples of body language send strong messages during any face-to-face interaction. Smiling is a powerful gesture that strengthens relationships. A smile sends such unspoken messages as "I like you," "You're okay," and "I am pleased that you are my child."

❖ Listening Skills

To achieve effective communication, family members must be good listeners. Listening with understanding shows interest and concern for the other person.

Children often have difficulty finding the right words to express themselves. Parents who are good listeners will hear, see, and feel what the child is trying to say. Good listening means more than hearing a person's exact words. It means sensing the person's message and how the person feels about it.

❖ Resolving Conflicts

Families are made up of individuals who have their own needs, desires, and goals. Thus potential conflicts often arise between family members. By taking time to discuss and solve problems, families can eliminate the stress that is caused by conflict.

When parents develop a positive way of resolving conflicts, they can model or teach it to their children. This will help the children in the future when they form their own families.

Here are steps to follow in dealing with family conflicts.

1. **Identify the problem.** Conflict may arise over issues such as doing household chores, spending money, or having a child. It is important to focus on the problem and identify conflicting feelings.

Family discussions can help solve conflicts by allowing members to express their opinions.

2. **Talk it over**. The ability to talk over issues and really listen to the other person's point of view is essential to resolving conflicts. Statements should contain "I" messages to get more positive responses. Saying, "I'm upset because I always have to do the dishes" will get a different response than saying, "You never do anything to help out!"

3. **Keep calm.** Becoming angry or upset will not help resolve the problem. Being sarcastic or blaming the other person can only aggravate the situation. Comments such as "That is ridiculous!" or "It's your fault!" can quickly end the discussion.

4. **Keep to the point.** The discussion should stay focused on the problem. When other issues are brought up, the problem is less likely to be resolved quickly.

5. **Seek outside help if necessary.** Sometimes a neutral third party, such as a counselor, can help family members resolve conflicts. A professional counselor can help the family develop better communication and conflict-resolution skills. Often, the problem can be resolved before it becomes a major crisis.

There are a number of ways that families make decisions to ease their conflicts. These include consensus, compromise, accommodation, and deciding not to decide.

Consensus

One way families resolve conflicts is by reaching a **consensus** (kahn-SEN-suhs). This means that they come to an agreement after talking things over. To make good decisions, family members need to try to come up with clear alternatives. They can then discuss the probable outcome of each alternative. Next, they can evaluate their choices before agreeing on the best solution to the problem. In this method, all family members support the decision.

Compromise

Sometimes, family members must **compromise** (KAHM-pruh-myz) before they can reach a consensus. This means that each person gives up something in order to come to an agreement that satisfies everyone. Perhaps one parent wants to spend the family vacation with relatives. The other parent wants to

Discuss. What types of conflicts may need to be resolved in families? What are some common conflicts between parents? Between parents and children? Between two or more siblings? **Problem Solving.** Divide class into small groups. Have each group identify a family conflict that could be resolved through compromise. Ask each group to role play the situation. In what other ways could the family members resolve the conflict successfully?

rent a cabin on a lake. One compromise would be to spend a few days visiting the relatives before going to the lake. Another compromise would be to vacation at the lake and invite the relatives to join the family. In this method, each person gives up something in order to gain something else. Compromise is also known as give-and-take.

Accommodation

Another conflict-resolution method families use is **accommodation.** In this process, some family members must adjust or adapt if the problem is to be resolved. They may feel that further discussion will not change anyone's mind.

Deciding Not to Decide

At times, one family member may refuse to participate in the decision-making process. By choosing not to decide, that person avoids taking responsibility for trying to resolve a conflict. Some families do not give much thought to their family functions or goals. This is rarely an adequate method of resolving family conflicts.

DECISIONS ◆ ◆ DECISIONS

Rebecca, age fourteen, has been arguing with her parents about her curfew. She says her friends can all stay out later on weekend nights than she can. She feels embarrassed because she has to be home earlier than others. Her parents, however, are concerned about her safety when she is out at night. They fear she and her friends might go to parties where older teenagers are drinking. They also want her to get enough sleep each night. How can Rebecca and her parents resolve their conflict?

Discuss. Why is "deciding not to decide" usually not an effective method of resolving family conflicts?

Community Resources

Various community resources are available to families. A **resource** is something that individuals or families can use to accomplish a goal. There are many different kinds of resources.

- *Human resources* are people. They can provide knowledge, skills, and energy to help families.
- *Material resources* are objects used to provide or make things. They include money and possessions.
- *Community resources* are services that can help individuals and families. They include schools, libraries, places of worship, various agencies, and volunteer organizations. Communities also offer the services of police officers, doctors, dentists, child care providers, and professional counselors.

❖ Types of Support and Services

Let's take a look at the variety of resources available for individuals and families. Some resources are free; others have a fee. Sometimes the fee is based on a family's ability to pay. Thus families with a lower income pay a lower fee, while families with a higher income pay a higher fee.

Educational Services

Nearly every community has access to educational services. These range from local schools and libraries to colleges and universities.

- **Elementary and secondary schools.** Public education for school-age children is available free of charge in nearly every community in the United States. For the

Reference. See page 79 for the decision-making process.

◆ ◆ *Health & Safety* ◆ ◆

Help Is at Your Fingertips

When a crisis occurs, it helps to get expert outside assistance. Many organizations, both public and private, operate toll-free numbers to assist families in times of trouble. Some of these numbers are listed below. Others may be grouped together in the telephone directory under "Community Services Numbers."

Against Domestic Violence	1-800-892-3375
AIDS Hotline	1-800-243-2437
Alcohol & Drug Abuse Testing Center	1-800-942-3784
Alcohol & Drug 24 Hour Hotline	1-800-562-1240
Alcoholism Council	1-800-521-5140
Child Abuse Reporting Line	1-800-233-5437
Child Find	1-800-426-5678
Cocaine Abuse Hotline	1-800-COCAINE
Drug Prevention & Education	1-800-342-3691
National Council on Alcoholism	1-800-622-2255
National Domestic Violence Hotline	1-800-333-SAFE
National Runaway Switchboard	1-800-621-4000
National Support Center for Persons with Disabilities	1-800-426-2133
Parental Stress Telephone Counseling Service	1-800-632-8188
Parents Anonymous	1-800-421-0353
Poison Control Information Center	1-800-452-7165
Rape Crises Center	1-800-637-7273
Suicide Prevention Center	1-800-352-7873
Youth Crises Hotline	1-800-422-0009

few places without schools, bus service to schools in another community is usually available. In some secondary schools, students can take vocational courses. These provide training in skilled trades such as child care, food service, carpentry, and auto mechanics. Schools also provide counseling and health services.

- **General equivalency diploma.** Individuals who do not graduate from high school can take special classes and an examination to earn a **general equivalency diploma,** or **GED.** This qualifies them for jobs requiring a high school diploma or for entrance into a community college.
- **Colleges and universities.** Higher education is available in every state and most large cities. Community colleges and four-year colleges and universities offer a wide variety of courses. Potential students can obtain catalogs and class schedules by calling or visiting the school's admissions office.

- **Special education programs.** Special education programs for children and adults are available free in most communities. Some of the programs serve children with disabilities. Others focus on adult literacy. That is, they help people learn to read, write, and speak English. Information about these programs is available through the public school system or a human services agency.

Activity. Have students gather additional names and toll-free numbers of organizations that can be a resource for families.
Activity. Invite a GED instructor to discuss course content presented to students in preparation for the GED exam.

Activity. Have students write a letter requesting information from a college or university they might want to attend.
Activity. Ask students to research if your community offers an adult literacy program.

- **Adult education programs.** Many large school systems offer adult education. Members of the community can take a wide variety of courses at minimum cost. Some courses focus on career skills, such as accounting or word processing. Others help develop skills such as preparing gourmet meals, refinishing furniture, or speaking a foreign language.

- **Cooperative Extension Service.** Every state offers cooperative extension programs. These are given by county agents and supervised by a land-grant university. Some programs deal with parenting and home management skills. Others focus on agriculture and business concerns. The Cooperative Extension Service also sponsors 4-H programs for youths.

- **Libraries and Library Services.** Many communities have free public libraries. Here books, tapes, and videos can be borrowed for a certain period of time. Often a special section of the library is set aside just for children. The children can choose from a variety of colorful, easy-to-read books. Many libraries also sponsor special programs and movies for young children or families. In some areas, families may be able to call a local or toll-free number and have books sent to them by mail.

Youth Groups and Organizations

Many communities have organized groups for young people. Such groups include the Boy Scouts, Girl Scouts, 4-H, and boys' and girls' clubs. The groups provide recreational and skill-building activities. These range from camping to raising animals. Adult leaders also encourage the development of leadership and citizenship skills.

Team sports, such as soccer, basketball, football, and softball or baseball, are popular

Public libraries are a community resource that can be used by all family members. Many libraries have special programs for children and families.

in many communities. Recreation departments and service clubs may sponsor Little League teams for various age groups. Both schools and community groups may sponsor youth programs that present concerts or plays. By participating in these activities, children can develop a variety of interests and skills.

Health Services

Community health services are essential for families. Many state and county departments of health provide clinics for prenatal care, vision and hearing screening, and alcohol or drug abuse. Children may receive free

Activity. Invite an adult education teacher or an extension agent to talk to the students about their programs.
Activity. Have students visit the public library, research the various services, and obtain a library card if needed.

Discuss. Have you been a member of a youth group or organization? If so, what activities were offered? Which groups encourage parent involvement? What groups would you want your own children to join at various ages? Why?

Human services agencies offer a variety of services for families, ranging from counseling to economic assistance.

immunizations. Adults may receive free testing for blood pressure, cholesterol level, and cancer. These services are often offered at a hospital, health clinic, or community center.

Some communities offer a special educational program called Women, Infants, and Children (WIC). This program provides nutrition and parenting information for mothers of young children.

Health departments are also responsible for maintaining pure water supplies and sanitary garbage, trash, and sewage disposal. These services are usually paid for by taxes or user fees. Because of high standards, people can travel across the United States and get clean water wherever they go. This is not the case in many other countries.

Human Services

County and state departments of human services are responsible for many services to families. In some states they regulate the licensing of child care programs. They may supervise foster care and adoption programs, as well as programs for people with disabilities. Human services agencies can help families with economic assistance for housing, food, and other essentials. Many of these programs aid families in times of difficulty or crisis.

Mental Health Services

In many larger communities, counseling services are available for individuals and families. These include counseling for marriage and family relationships, alcohol or drug abuse, and psychological problems. Some of the services are government funded and cost the family little or nothing.

Religious Organizations

Most communities have a number of religious groups that offer both worship and fellowship programs. Individuals need not be members of a particular religion to take part in many of the programs. Most are free to those who participate.

Many religious groups sponsor activities for children. These include choirs, athletic teams, and teen programs. Family activities such as movie nights, picnics, and holiday festivals are offered. In addition, many religious groups are actively involved in programs to aid those who are ill, disabled, elderly, or homeless.

Recreation Services

Many communities provide parks and recreational activities for their residents. Playgrounds, ball fields, bicycle paths, and swimming pools offer opportunities for individuals and families to enjoy recreational activities.

Community recreation departments often sponsor lessons or team competitions. Some offer supervised programs for school-age children during the summer. For example, children might be involved in daily art projects, games, and competitive events. Other programs are aimed at older members of the community. They might meet daily or weekly at a local community center for recreation, companionship, and fun.

Crises Hot Lines

Volunteers at crises centers have been trained to help people with problems. Many of these centers have a hot line, a telephone line that provides direct access to information or counseling. By calling a toll-free 800 number, people can get immediate help in a variety of situations. For example, some crises hot lines are available for the prevention of child abuse or suicide. Others offer aid to runaways and drug abusers. Still others give factual information about pregnancy, STDs, and AIDS.

Emergency Shelters

Emergency shelters can provide warmth, food, clothes, and security for individuals and families. Some shelters aid people who have lost or been evicted from their homes. Others provide safety for victims of family violence or abuse. The location of a shelter for abused women and children is usually not made public. This is done to prevent the abuser from locating the shelter.

❖ Finding Assistance and Programs

Most community resources are listed in the local telephone directory. Some directories have a special section that lists local, county, and state government services. These sections are usually set apart by means of special colors or tabs. Telephone companies give their customers local directories. Directories are also available in public libraries.

Most agencies have local offices where people can stop by to get information. At times, one agency may refer an individual or family to another agency. Many state agencies have toll-free 800 numbers. Friends, relatives, medical professionals, and school administrators can also recommend agencies that provide needed services.

Large communities offer a variety of resources for families. Parents in smaller communities may have to search farther from home or help organize their own resources within the community. Unfortunately, it can take a great deal of time and effort to find the information and services a family needs. Parents should not hesitate or apologize when asking for help. Community resources are designed to provide needed support.

Many organizations, agencies, and crisis centers have a toll-free 800 number for people to call.

Activity. Ask students to make posters promoting hot lines that provide information or counseling. Display the posters throughout the school.

Problem Solving. Divide class into small groups. Have each group locate information about different types of resources available in your community. Ask groups to compile the information into a single listing or booklet.

Personal Support Groups

In the past, the extended family provided assistance and support for family members. Today, the extended family is often too far away to give immediate help. Instead, families may have to turn to friends and neighbors for advice or aid. They can talk to friends who have children the same age as their own. They can ask a neighbor to stay with the children for an hour. They can form an informal support group with other parents in their community.

Often families need support in handling the everyday situations of parenting. Working parents may have a sick child. A teacher calls about a school-related problem. A teenager rebels against limits and curfews. At such times, parents can benefit from having a personal support system. Besides offering advice or aid, others can provide understanding and comfort in times of stress.

To help develop a support system, families need to reach out to others. By sharing information, asking for advice, and donating

their time, parents can develop supportive relationships. "To have a friend, be one" is a good motto to follow.

Support groups for families dealing with certain situations are available in many communities. For example, Parents Without Partners is a support group for single parents. This group sponsors programs and activities for the parents, as well as for the children and parents together. Another group, Tough Love, provides support for parents who are having difficulty in guiding and disciplining their children. Other support groups are available for families dealing with alcoholism, drug abuse, or violence.

Support groups can help families deal with large and small problems. They can also provide guidance and support for strengthening family relationships.

Relatives, neighbors, and friends can be part of a family's support group. Parents can turn to these people for understanding, advice, and aid in times of stress.

Discuss. What support groups would be helpful for families with preschool children? School-age children? Adolescents?

More About. Parents who have no personal support system are four times more likely to abuse their children during a crisis situation.

CHAPTER 26 REVIEW

Summary

- Parents and children enrich family life by spending time together, showing respect and trust, expressing understanding and love, and establishing traditions.
- How effectively family members communicate with each other depends on the verbal and nonverbal language they use and on their listening skills.
- Families can resolve conflicts through consensus, compromise, accommodation, or deciding not to decide.
- Human, material, and community resources are available to help families overcome a problem or reach a goal.
- Although locating specific community resources takes time and effort, such resources can provide the information and services a family needs.
- It is important that families reach out to relatives, friends, and neighbors for personal support and mutual aid.

Questions

p. 498 **1.** How can family members show respect for each other?

p. 500 **2.** Of what value are family traditions?

p. 503 **3.** What are nonverbal messages? Give four examples of how such messages can be communicated.

p. 503 **4.** List five steps to follow in dealing with family conflicts.

p. 504 **5.** What is compromise?

p. 508 **6.** What kinds of assistance do county and state departments of human resources provide?

p. 509 **7.** How can people locate community resources and programs?

p. 510 **8.** How can families develop a personal support system?

Activities

1. Survey friends and neighbors about family traditions. As a class, create a booklet on family traditions for new parents.
2. Find out what groups and organizations are available in your community for children and families.
   - What activities or benefits do they provide?
   - What specific age-groups may participate?
   - What is the cost, if any?
3. Research the program known as Tough Love. In a short report, explain the type of support it provides for parents who are having trouble guiding their children.
4. Check the telephone directory for listings of crises hot lines.

Think About

1. In what kinds of situations might only the adults in a family decide how to resolve a family conflict? Is it fair that children are not allowed to participate in making these decisions?
2. How much help do you think people who answer a crisis hot line can give a caller? Defend your answer.

Family Challenges

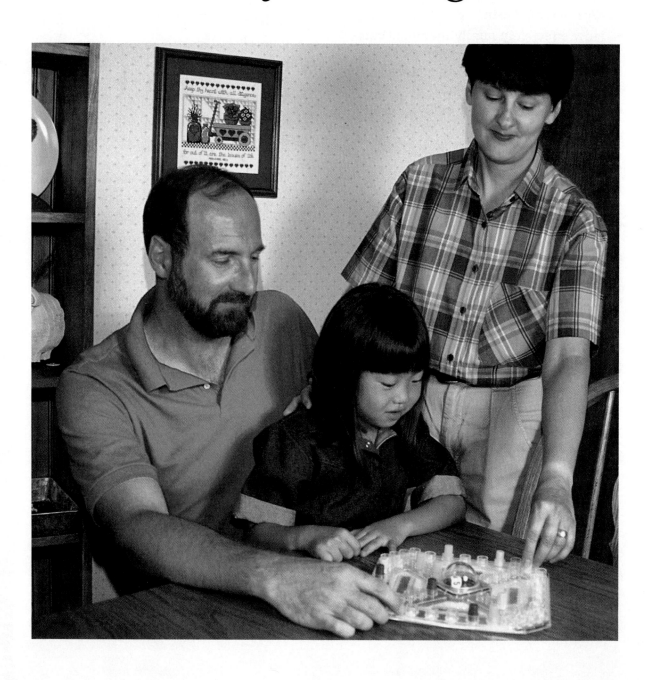

Objectives

This chapter will help you to:

- Discuss how parents can balance work and parenting responsibilities.
- Describe how changes in life-style can affect family members.
- Explain how divorce, remarriage, and adoption can affect children.
- Suggest ways that parents can help children cope with family crises.

Vocabulary

flextime
custody
joint custody
addiction
grief

Six-year-old Christina never had trouble sleeping before. Now, every time she falls asleep, she pictures her parents pointing at her and shouting, "It's your fault; it's your fault." She sits up in bed and cries. When Christina's mother comes into the bedroom to comfort her, Christina asks, "Mom, why can't Daddy live here anymore?"

More than a million children each year are caught in families that are breaking apart because of separation or divorce. Young children do not understand much of what is going on. However, they do know that the home is filled with tension and unhappiness.

The Challenges of Life

There are times when families are faced with challenges. These include a mother returning to full-time work, moving to a new community, separation and divorce, and illness or death in the family. These situations can create stress for both parents and children.

Parents are the ones that children depend on most for support and guidance. This is especially true in times of crisis. Parents are often faced with the responsibility of helping their children when they themselves are involved in the same crisis situation. This places a heavy burden on parents.

When parents are under stress, the children generally feel some of the stress too. Children are very sensitive, especially to those who are closest to them. When parents avoid talking with them about what is happening, the children may think they are the source of the problem. Some children feel sad and helpless. Others take their frustrations out on other children or adults. Being open and honest with children helps them deal with the reality of a crisis in a way that is healthy for both parents and children.

In challenging times, parents may feel the need for help from others. They may feel overwhelmed and even angry that so many things seem to go wrong. At such times, they should seek advice or assistance from family members, friends, a member of the clergy, or a professional counselor.

Children and parents are often drawn closer as a result of facing a stressful situation together. A major advantage for parents is that children look to them for help. Children have confidence in their parents. They want them near when they feel sad, hurt, or ill. When children are worried or anxious, they want reassurance and love from parents. Parents may be encouraged to know that a crisis situation will not usually change a child's life provided there is at least one person to provide sustaining care.

This chapter explores some of the challenges that families experience. A number of these challenges may result in positive change for the family, such as successfully balancing work and parenting responsibilities. Other challenges may stem from negative changes, such as unemployment, critical illness, and death. This chapter describes how parents can help children deal effectively with such challenges.

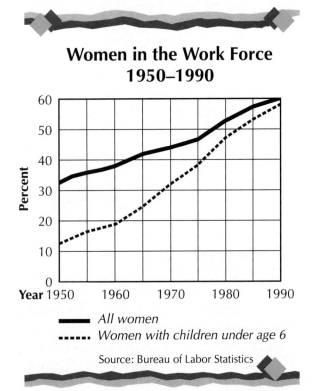

Women in the Work Force 1950–1990

— *All women*
----- *Women with children under age 6*

Source: Bureau of Labor Statistics

Reference. See pages 223–224 and pages 333–334 for information about stress, stress management, and depression.
Activity. Stress has become a leading health issue. Ask students to report on current articles about stress management.

Balancing Work and Parenting

When parents work outside the home, they must make many decisions about how to balance their responsibilities for work and family life. Some families are headed by a single parent who works full-time. In other families both parents may work outside the home.

❖ Parents' Need to Work

In many two-parent families, both parents must work outside the home to make enough money to pay basic expenses. Although some couples would prefer to have one parent stop working to care for the baby, they may not be able to afford this option.

In most single-parent families, the parent must work outside the home for the same reason. An increasing number of families are headed by a single parent. The divorce rate is almost one divorce for every two marriages. Moreover, an increasing number of mothers have never been married.

Sometimes the reason why parents work is not based solely on the need for money. Some parents work to keep their skills up-to-date and to maintain their place in the job market. If they take several years off from their career for child care, they may jeopardize that career. When they reenter the job market, they might have to return to school or take a lower-paying job. With the high cost of child care, a working parent may have very little salary left at the end of the week. Many people reason, however, that they are keeping their job skills intact and maintaining their contacts with the work world.

Still other parents work for personal fulfillment. They want to use their creative talents. These parents often feel unfulfilled and dissatisfied away from their job. They prefer

Activity. Have students research current statistics on the number of mothers of infants, preschoolers, and school-age children employed full- and part-time outside the home. Ask them to prepare a chart showing the statistics.

to work at a job they enjoy and hire someone to help care for their children.

❖ Investigating Options

Parents need to consider various options in deciding how they can best balance the demands of work and family. These include work options and child care options.

Work Options

In many communities and workplaces, parents have more work options than were available in the past. Numerous companies and industries have tried to become more "family friendly" in their policies. Some organizations offer options such as flexible hours, part-time work, job sharing, and at-home work. Parents must assess their financial and personal needs to decide which option is best for their family.

- **Flexible schedules.** Some companies have various work shifts. Thus one parent can work during the day and the other parent at night. This enables one parent to be home with the children at all times. Other companies offer **flextime,** a system that allows workers to arrive earlier or later than the standard starting hour. Some employees may work from 7:00 A.M. to 3:00 P.M., while others prefer to come in later and stay later. Flextime makes it possible for some parents to manage their own child care. Still other companies offer options to the standard five-day workweek. For example, employees may work four ten-hour days. Flexible working hours allow many parents to spend more time with their children.

- **Part-time work.** Working part-time is an option for some parents. Parents of school-age children may want to work only during school hours. One drawback to part-time work is that few, if any, benefits

such as health insurance are provided. Job sharing is a special form of part-time work available in a few businesses. Two employees handle one job. One person generally works mornings and the other afternoons. Occasionally, two people who share a job also share child care.

- **Working at home.** Some companies permit employees to work at home for pay. Jobs such as sales, writing, designing, and computer programming are frequently

Many parents have to balance responsibilities for work and family life. Good management skills can help parents and children manage more successfully.

done at home. Employees communicate with the office via telephone, computer, and fax machine. Some parents choose to start their own at-home business. Many provide a service, such as typing reports or caring for children. Others make a product, such as decorated cakes or home furnishings. Working for pay at home enables parents to earn income and also be with their children. However, some parents find that they still need some child care services even though they work at home.

- **Postponing work.** Some families who can afford it choose to have one parent stay home while the children are young. When the children are older and more independent, the parent then returns to the work force.

Child Care Options

Parents who work outside the home usually have to make important decisions about child care. One option is to have the child cared for at home by relatives or a paid caregiver. Another option is to have a relative, friend, or paid caregiver care for the child in that person's home. A third option is to take the child to a child care center. Some businesses provide child care at the work site. You will learn more about various child care options in Chapter 28.

Having one parent remain at home to care for the children is an option only for some families. Before the 1970s, many mothers stayed at home and focused on caring for the children and the household. Today, a majority of mothers are working full- or part-time in the labor force.

Most families realize that there are advantages and disadvantages to each option. Some working mothers feel guilty about leaving young children in the care of others for many hours each week. Some at-home mothers are criticized by others because they do not have a paying job.

Parents who can afford to stay home and care for their children gain great satisfaction from seeing the children grow and develop. They are there for the child's first step, first sentence, and first day of school. They feel it is important for a parent to nurture and guide children through each stage of development. Some parents who remain at home enjoy being involved in special hobbies. Others participate in volunteer activities in the community. Most enjoy spending time with other parents and relatives.

Some people argue that children are better off when their mother stays at home, especially when the children are very young. Research conducted by reputable psychologists disputes this argument. What is important is that parents make sure their children receive high-quality care—whether from their mother, their father, or another caregiver.

Ways to Balance Work and Parenting Responsibilities

To juggle the demands of work and family successfully, parents need to develop strong management skills. Here are some tips to help parents manage more successfully.

- **Do lots of preplanning.** Sudden emergencies create severe pressures on working parents. For example, a child may wake up ill in the early morning, when caregivers are not available. Therefore, while children are well, parents must plan how to care for them if illness strikes. Perhaps one or the other parent can take time off from work in an emergency. Maybe a relative or friend can help out.
- **Simplify tasks.** Working parents need to find ways to simplify household tasks. By setting priorities, they will know which

Discuss. What might be some disadvantages of working at home for parents of infants or preschoolers?
Discuss. What effect would inadequate child care arrangements have on a working parent?

Activity. Divide class into small groups. Ask each group to list the advantages and disadvantages for two different families in which both parents of a three-month-old work full-time. One family needs two incomes; the other is financially well-off.

tasks are most urgent and should be done first. Others can be postponed and done at another time. Children can help with many chores, giving parents and children the opportunity to talk and share as they work.

- **Share responsibilities.** All family members can help around the home. Even young children can help set the table, fold laundry, or put away their toys. Both father and mother can share responsibilities for shopping, cooking, cleaning, and child care.

- **Learn to compartmentalize.** When at home, parents should focus on the needs of the family and not worry about work. When at work, they should not have to worry about the children. When parents make good child care arrangements, they have more energy for work.

- **Schedule special time for children.** When parents get home from work, they should spend a few minutes with the children. This allows the family to gather together before beginning chores and homework. Parents also should schedule a special time to spend with each child every week.

- **Build a support system.** A support system is very important for working parents. In times of stress or emergency, others can help out. A family support system can include relatives, friends, neighbors, and community groups.

- **Minimize stress.** Working parents can be overwhelmed by the stress of balancing work and family responsibilities. They need to take time to relax, exercise, and enjoy the pleasures of life. A working mother of young children said, "The best advice I ever got was from an elderly neighbor. She told me that this was the time of my life to enjoy my children and family. I shouldn't feel guilty when choosing to spend free time playing with my children rather than doing household chores. Later, when the children are grown, I'll have time to do all the tasks I've postponed."

Parents and children can talk, laugh, and enjoy each other's company as they do chores together. By sharing responsibilities, they can spend time together.

Activity. Divide class into small groups. Have each group list 12 jobs that must be done every week in a typical family. Then have each group assign responsibilities to different members in the following families:
- a two-parent family with a toddler
- a single mother with a toddler and a preschooler
- a two-parent family with a four-year-old and a seven-year-old
- a single father with a ten-year-old.

Changes in Family Life-Style

Family life-style changes can affect both parents and children. Events such as moving to a new community or suffering a financial loss require adjustments by family members. Children may be confused when they hear parents discuss various options for the family. They may fear that their parents will abandon them. Parents need to reassure children and help them learn how to cope with change.

When a family moves, all members experience stress. Parents can help their children by letting them pack some belongings and talking to them about the move.

Activity. Survey students for family mobility. How many have lived in the same home since birth? Same neighborhood or town? Same state? Who has moved the most? Who has lived in the most states? Who has lived in another country?

❖ Moving

Our society is very mobile, and many families move every year. Often the move is due to a parent's job change. Moving to a new community is a big adjustment for all family members. They must get used to a new home, new friends, and new schools.

Moving creates stress for children. They may be afraid that they will not make any new friends. They may be nervous about going to a new school. Parents can help make the adjustment easier for children by talking about the move beforehand. If possible, they can show the children a picture of the house or apartment where the family will be living. They can describe the schools, stores, and parks in the area. Older children want information about various sports and youth groups in the community.

Parents should encourage children to ask questions about the move. Some look forward to moving and making new friends. Others get angry and make statements such as "I won't go. I want to stay here. I want my room, and I want you to stay here with me." In either case, parents should talk honestly about what will take place.

Letting children help pack and get ready for the move helps to reduce anxiety. It gives them an opportunity to ask questions and express concerns or excitement about the new experience.

After moving, parents need to help children make new friends. If the weather is warm and children are playing outside, parents can take walks with their children to meet families in the neighborhood. Many families enroll their children in community activities so they can meet other children. If the children go to school or to a child care center, parents can encourage them to invite a child to come over to play.

Activity. Ask students to compile a list of helpful tips for making a move to a new community or school easier for children. Have students create posters that illustrate their suggestions for display in the school or community.

❖ Financial Loss and Unemployment

A major responsibility of parents is providing economic support for the family. Employment provides income and often additional benefits, such as health insurance. Today many families depend on two paychecks to meet monthly expenses or to save for long-term goals, such as purchasing a home.

When parents are under financial stress or worried about losing their job, they may have less time for their children. Young children who sense that their parents are preoccupied sometimes misbehave to get attention. The children may even think they have done something to upset their parents.

At times like these, parents should be honest with children and talk about the frustrations. Parents can let children know why they are upset without going into detail about work or finances. For example, a parent can say, "I love you very much. I am not upset with you or anything you've done. I'm upset only because things haven't been going well at work."

When parents talk things over with their children, everyone in the family usually feels better. Above all, parents should never blame the children for their unpleasant feelings or misfortunes.

When parents lose a job, they sometimes feel rejected and depressed. If the job provided the main or only income for the family, they may face a financial crisis. Financial assistance may be available from various community services and organizations. However, some families must move in with relatives or seek refuge in a community shelter. Being without a home creates tremendous stress for both children and parents. In this situation, parents need to reassure their children continuously and seek assistance wherever possible.

When parents are under stress, they should talk to their children about the situation. Otherwise the children may believe they are the cause of the parent's worries or unhappiness.

◆ ◆ *Self-Esteem* ◆ ◆

During times of crisis, parents especially need to give children attention and love. Parents should talk honestly with children and let them express their thoughts and feelings. This will help the children face the challenges ahead.

Discuss. How might unemployment or financial loss affect children at different stages: toddler, preschool, school-age, and adolescent?
Activity. Have students provide a party for children in a community shelter.
Activity. Ask students to describe ways that family members can help reduce expenses during times of financial problems. Encourage as many creative ideas as possible.

Changes in Family Structure

Family structures can change for many reasons. Separation and divorce result in one parent no longer living in the home. However, parent-child relationships still need to be encouraged. If parents remarry, children face the task of becoming a part of a new family. They must develop relationships with a stepparent and perhaps with stepbrothers and stepsisters. Family relationships also change when a child is adopted.

❖❖ Separation and Divorce

Regardless of the reasons for separation or divorce, children are affected. Both parents still need to make decisions about their child or children. No matter how tired, worried, or anxious parents might be, the children's need for love, care, and guidance continues.

Many divorced parents are able to sustain a strong relationship with their children.

DECISIONS ◆ ◆ DECISIONS

Tanya's parents have been separated for several months. Tanya has just spent the weekend at her father's apartment. As her father is taking her back to her mother's home, he says, "I'll see you on Tuesday night. I'm coming over to fix your brother's bicycle." Six-year-old Tanya replies, "Dad, if you can fix Tommy's bike, why can't you fix your marriage with Mommy? Then we can live together again." If you were Tanya's father, how would you respond?

These are the people who work at maintaining good communication with their children. They put long hours and much energy into caring for their children. They also give the children ongoing attention that helps them feel secure and loved.

Different children respond in different ways to separation and divorce. Some parents are able to help their children cope with this change in the family so that the children experience little or no trauma. Others, however, are unable to help their children and may even make the situation worse.

How Children Deal with Separation and Divorce

Young children do not understand the reasons for divorce. They cannot yet think abstractly. That is, they cannot think of something becoming different than it is at present. Their feelings range from depression (they believe the absent parent rejected them) to anger and hostility (the parents broke up the children's home). Even when parents attempt to explain the causes of the divorce, young children often fail to understand.

Children older than two years of age understand that the absent parent still exists (object permanence). Thus they may long for the return of the absent parent. Some children think the parent is only on a trip and will return. They may watch for the parent longingly, even awaken at night wondering whether he or she has returned. As time goes by and the absent parent does not return, children may become even more confused.

Young children cannot reason well enough to explore the various visiting and living arrangements offered to them. They become confused about being with one parent on weekends and living with the other parent during the week. They just know that the security they felt when their parents were together is disturbed.

Children need lots of comfort when a family experiences separation or divorce. They may not understand the parents' explanations and may be confused about new living arrangements.

Older children, ages six to twelve, may respond with shock when told of an impending divorce. For a long time they may deny the reality of it to their friends and teachers. They may worry about the causes and the effects but feel there is no one to whom they can talk. When parents fail to answer their questions, the children quickly sense that the divorce is a forbidden topic and do not discuss it. They may fake cheerfulness, and their schoolwork often suffers. Some school counselors hold rap sessions with children of divorce, helping them relieve their tensions by sharing feelings and frustrations with each other. By talking about mutual problems, the children come to realize they are not different or bad because their parents are divorced.

Self-blame is common among children whose parents are divorcing. Like Christina in the chapter-opening story, many children think they are the cause of the separation or divorce. This is understandable because divorcing parents usually fight about their children as well as many other things. It helps to reassure children that both parents love them and will continue to love them.

Sometimes children become pawns in a struggle between their hurt and angry parents. One parent may attempt to get the children on his or her side in the dispute. Another parent may use the children to carry messages to and from the other parent. These tactics place the children in an awkward and confusing situation.

When parents live in constant conflict, the entire family is affected. Children sense the tension between their parents even when they do not hear them arguing. Sometimes children are relieved when a divorce occurs because violence or mistreatment of family members ends.

After a divorce, a parent may feel a greater sense of commitment to the children than he or she did before. The parent may make a special effort to go places and do things with the children. When this interaction continues throughout childhood and adolescence, both the parent and the children are likely to benefit.

Custody and Support Arrangements

The matter of custody usually arises early in divorce discussions. **Custody** is a legal arrangement in which one parent becomes the guardian of the children. The parent who gets custody has the main responsibility for the children. However, both parents are still considered responsible.

Joint custody is an arrangement giving both parents roughly equal time with the children and equal responsibility for them. The children may spend a week with one parent and then a week with the other. When distances prohibit an equal-time arrangement, other sharing arrangements must be worked out.

The financial support of a child is an issue in many divorce cases. Parents who do not meet their financial responsibility can be brought to court and forced to do so. Some divorced parents find themselves in court periodically trying to collect the child-support payments due from the other parent. These conflicts may continue until the child is eighteen years old and longer if the divorce decree indicates the parent should pay for the child's college education. This struggle over money affects the two former partners for many years. It also affects any new families they form.

Helping Children Cope

There is no easy way to help children adjust to a separation or divorce. Each couple must deal with their children's particular feelings and reactions to their past and present lives. Children usually long for the absent parent and hope that their parents will get back together.

Parents who are successful in helping children deal with separation and divorce share certain characteristics.

- Successful parents are honest with themselves. They acknowledge the reality of the situation.

- Both parents give the children lots of love and understanding. Both treat the children with respect and dignity.

- Both parents talk honestly and frankly with the children. They do not hide the fact they will not be living together.

After a divorce, parents should help their children continue a positive relationship with both parents.

Activity. Have students describe how roles and responsibilities may change for newly divorced parents in the following situations: mother has custody, father has custody, and parents share custody of children.

Activity. Invite an attorney or family service worker to talk about specific custody and child-support laws in your state. What happens to parents who do not provide regular financial support for their children?

- Both parents encourage the children to ask questions and express their feelings.
- Each parent encourages the children to continue a positive relationship with the other parent. Neither parent criticizes the other in front of the children.
- Both parents talk openly with the children about what to expect, such as living and visiting arrangements. They allow the children to express their concern, disappointment, or anger over these arrangements.
- Neither parent uses the children to send messages to the other parent. Above all, each parent avoids using the children to get revenge or make threats against the other parent.

Parents must give their children time and attention as well as love and care during this difficult period. Children need to know that their parents love them and want them. They also need help in understanding why their parents may be angry or sad. This helps the children cope with changes in parent behavior as well as family structure.

❖ Remarriage and Blended Families

After a divorce becomes final, one or both parents may remarry. At this point the children must give up any secret hope that their parents will get back together. For some children, this is a very difficult time.

When a parent remarries, the children must face the task of becoming part of a new family. They may be living with a stepparent and his or her children in a blended family. They may also be expected to form new relationships with step-grandparents and other relatives in the new extended family.

When children are with an unmarried parent, they are reminded of their former family life. When they are with a remarried parent, they are expected to accept a new family situation. When children resent a stepparent, they often play one household against the other. For example, they may say, "Our real mother doesn't make us do that."

It takes time and patience to ease the blending of two families into a new family unit. New household routines and family traditions have to be established. Blended families often argue about simple tasks, such as who does the dishes or where to place the Christmas tree. Good communication skills can help blended family members solve their differences. A willingness to compromise is also important in blended families. Experts say that it can take between four and seven years for a blended family to establish a truly integrated family unit.

When parents remarry, children are faced with many changes and adjustments. A blended family means new relationships, new household routines, and new family traditions.

Discuss. What role can grandparents play in the lives of grandchildren that have been touched by divorce?
Discuss. What are the positive and negative aspects of remarriage on children of different ages?

Activity. Have students identify specific adjustments in routines and traditions that must be made in blended families. What compromises might be made to resolve various conflicts?

Stepparents

Stepparents and stepchildren need time to adjust to each other. The biological parent should help both the children and the stepparent adapt to the new relationship.

Children can become very confused over loyalties to parents and stepparents. They may agonize over which ones to invite to watch their games or to attend parents' night at school. They may feel that by being nice to a stepparent they are being disloyal to their parent. This can result in feelings of guilt and stress.

Experts agree that it is important for parents to reassure children that loving a stepparent does not mean taking love away from a biological parent. Children should also understand that stepparents and stepchildren do not have to love each other. However, they should always treat each other with kindness and respect.

Conflicts often arise as to the authority that stepparents have over stepchildren. In families where two sets of children live together, discipline problems abound. Sometimes there are "his kids," "her kids," and "our kids" to consider. Most stepparents express frustration over disciplining their stepchildren, especially in matters of dress, language, and behavior. The husband and wife should agree on how discipline will be handled in a blended family.

Parents in a blended family should try to treat all the children the same way. They should not give special favors or privileges to a biological child and not to a stepchild. Children in a blended family should also be encouraged to remain close to their absent parent and other relatives. A blended family should enable children to have a wider circle of relatives, without having to choose one set over the other.

After their parents married, these stepbrothers began sharing a room. What adjustments might they have had to make?

Stepchildren

When two families merge, step-siblings may not get along. They may lose their previous identity. For example, a child may no longer be the oldest or the youngest. The only boy may suddenly have one or more stepbrothers.

If the children have to share rooms, they must learn to respect each other's possessions and privacy. Often stepchildren have feelings of resentment and jealousy. They may not want their natural parent to pay so much attention to the new stepparent and his or her children. As a result, they often compete for the attention of their biological parent.

Parents must try to understand each child's feelings about the other members of the new family. In some cases, the family may need professional counseling to deal with these feelings. It takes time and patience to help step-siblings develop warm, supportive relationships with each other.

◆ Adoption

Most experts agree that families who adopt children should tell them at the age of two or three years that they are adopted. It is better that they learn this from their family rather than someone else. Parents can explain that adoption is one special way a child comes into a family.

As adopted children get older, they usually have many questions about their biological parents. They wonder why their birth parents gave them away and where they are. The answer should not be that the birth parents did not want or love them. A better answer is that the birth parents could not take care of them and made arrangements for someone else to do so.

The children also need reassurance that the adoptive parents will never give them away. The parents can emphasize how much they wanted the children. They also can help the children realize that those who care for, nurture, and guide them are truly their parents.

Around the World

Adopting a Child from Another Country

Because adoptable babies are in short supply in the United States, some couples consider adopting a baby from another country. People often think that this is an easy way to adopt a child. It can be very exciting and rewarding to adopt a child from another culture. However, a couple who are considering an international adoption must be prepared to be very flexible parents.

- The children offered for adoption are frequently born to extremely poor parents. These children may have medical problems that are the result of malnourishment and a lack of prenatal care. Often there is no way of knowing about a child's background. Even the child's birth date may be unknown. In addition to medical problems, the child may have emotional or psychological problems that require special care.

- The laws and regulations regarding adoption are different in every country. A couple must follow the laws of the country where the child is born, as well as the laws of the United States and of the state where they live. In addition, the U.S. Department of Immigration and the agency that handles the adoption have requirements that must be met. The legal fees alone can make this a very expensive form of adoption.

- Many international adoptions are handled by agencies that specialize in such adoptions. Because it can be faster, some people search for a child on their own. This usually involves traveling to the other country. Once an available baby is found, it may not be easy to get him or her out of that country. Sometimes the baby and one or both of the adoptive parents end up living in the foreign country for a few weeks or a few months.

- It is sometimes easier to adopt a toddler or an older child than it is to adopt an infant. However, if the adoptive parents and the child do not speak the same language, the first months together as a family can be very difficult.

Activity. Bring books from the library that explain adoption to a young child. Have students evaluate the books and select the one they would want their own adopted child to read.

Reference. See page 95 for information about open adoptions.

Most families make happy adjustments to adopted children. Occasionally, when a baby is born into an adopted child's family, the adopted child feels displaced. However, feeling displaced is not uncommon among biological children either. Parents should reassure the child of their love and help the child feel secure in the family.

When adopted children become teenagers and adults, many of them try to find their birth parents. Some birth parents are willing to be found; others are not. Adoption was once a secret process, and the children were unable to learn even the names of their birth parents. Today, the legal system allows some adoption information to be made available to an adopted child. Special associations have been formed to help adopted children locate their birth parents.

Adopted children may ask many questions about their birth parents and cultural heritage.

Family Crises

Sometimes families face crises that disrupt family life. These may involve substance abuse, family violence, or serious illness or death of a family member.

Alcohol and Drug Abuse

Some children live with parents who are addicted to alcohol or drugs. An **addiction** is a strong physical or psychological need for a substance. The children may live in constant fear of being abused or neglected when their parents are out of control.

Because children love their parents, they often try to protect them by not asking for help. Some children even feel responsible for a parent's problems. Children of addicted parents often feel isolated in their own home. One child whose mother was an alcoholic had to tell anyone who came to the door that his mother was "taking a bath." The child could never invite a friend to his home.

Alcohol and drug abusers need professional care. Organizations such as Alcoholics Anonymous (AA) and drug treatment centers help these individuals by providing counseling, therapy, and support. Other organizations offer assistance to members of an abuser's family. For example, Al-Anon is designed to help family members and friends of alcoholics. Alateen helps teenagers and preteens whose parents abuse alcohol. These organizations are usually listed in the telephone book. Similar programs are available to help drug abusers and their families.

Family Violence

Too often, family violence is a family's best-kept secret. Feelings of shame and anxiety over what will happen keep family members from telling anyone else about the violence. However, the violence will not end until a member of the family reveals the problem and seeks help from an outside resource.

Spouse abuse is usually inflicted by the man in the family. In rare instances the man is the abused person. Many abused women were also abused as children—by their father or another man. They have come to believe that they have to bear the abuse. Of course, this is untrue. The first step an abused woman should take is to call the police or a crisis hot line and move out of the abusive situation. Many communities have shelters where women can go with their children to escape family violence.

◆ ◆ Health & Safety ◆ ◆

Codependency

Codependency is an extreme concern about other people's behavior and problems. When a person has an alcohol or drug dependency, close relatives and friends may show the traits of codependency.

Codependents feel responsible for the addicted person's behavior and happiness. They believe they can solve the person's drinking or drug use problem. They try to protect the person from facing the consequences of his or her addiction. For example, codependents may make excuses or lie for the person. They may lend the person money, which often is used to purchase more alcohol or drugs. Codependents ignore their own needs in an attempt to help the other person. However, their efforts to help actually harm both the person and themselves.

When there is alcohol or drug abuse in a family, all members are affected. The unhealthy demands and behavior of the addicted person force the other family members to develop various coping skills. They adjust their own needs, emotions, and behaviors to those of the addicted person. Some scream, cry, beg, nag, or threaten. Others withdraw, hoping the problem will go away. Still others deny there is a problem.

There are many ways that families can help the addicted person and themselves get well. First, they need to admit the problem. Then they need to get ouside help. Just as people can recover from addiction, family members can recover from codependency.

- **Information.** Different organizations and agencies can provide information about alcohol and drug abuse. Some of these are listed on page 506, others are listed in the telephone directory.

- **Intervention.** With the help of a counselor, family members can confront the addicted member with a plan for treatment. They also present the person with a list of consequences if he or she does not go for treatment.

- **Counseling.** Professional counselors can provide help for codependents. Sometimes family therapy is recommended, even if the addicted member refuses to participate.

- **Support groups.** People involved in the lives of alcoholics can seek help from groups such as Al-Anon and Alateen. Support groups such as Nar-Anon and Coc-Anon help relatives of narcotics and cocaine addicts.

- **Family programs.** Most drug rehabilitation and treatment centers offer programs for family members. They learn about addiction and codependency. They also learn how they can aid the recovery of all members of the family.

Activity. Invite a law enforcement official to discuss family violence and how it is handled when the abuse is reported to officials.

Activity. Have students gather information about local resources that deal with family violence.

A crisis, such as substance abuse or family violence, can seriously disrupt family life. Counseling can help both individuals and family members deal with the problem.

Child abuse may occur separately from or along with spouse abuse. Child abuse, which is discussed in Chapter 24, can be physical, emotional, or sexual. Teachers and medical personnel who recognize signs of child abuse are required by law to report them to authorities.

If family members are to recover from acts of family violence, they must first get out of the abusive situation. Then the abuser must be helped to solve his problems and change his habits. Those who have been abused may need professional counseling to help them rebuild their self-esteem.

Reference. See pages 469–472 for more information on child abuse and neglect.

◆◆ Serious Illness or Accident

When a family member becomes seriously ill or disabled, the family experiences different types of stress. Caring for an ill person takes much time and energy. Emotions may range from extreme worry to feelings of helplessness or even resentment as the family deals with the situation. Long-term illnesses or disabilities can create large medical bills. These often put a severe strain on family finances.

Often the illness or accident occurs without warning. Because such a crisis cannot be

Problem Solving. Have students suggest ways that family members can help children cope with a long-term illness or disability of a parent.

anticipated, it may seem mysterious to children. When a parent or other family member becomes ill, children often think they will become ill in the same way. Their logic is, "If it happened to _____, it will happen to me." Parents can relieve children of such fears and worries by talking about the situation with them. This is especially true for children between three and seven years of age. These are years when children's imaginations are extremely active.

When children see someone who has a physical disability, they often ask questions. Rather than saying, "Shh, it's not nice to ask" or "I'll tell you another time," parents should give a clear, simple answer. For example, Jimmy asked his mother why his aunt was using a wheelchair. She replied, "Aunt Carol is using a wheelchair because her legs are not strong enough to walk. The wheelchair helps her move around."

During a time of illness, family members need to share their feelings with one another. Children should be encouraged to talk about their worries and fears as often as necessary. Families also can seek help and support from friends and relatives.

DECISIONS ◆ ◆ DECISIONS

Brett, age five, visited his father in the hospital almost every day. Mr. Morgan was seriously injured in an automobile accident and his legs are permanently paralyzed. Now he is home, and Brett keeps asking when his father will walk again. Brett also refuses to ride in a car. If you were Brett's parents, how would you handle the situation?

◆◆ Dealing with Death

The death of a loved one is upsetting to a person of any age. Even infants sometimes go through a period of excessive crying and searching for a parent who has died. If a prolonged illness precedes the death, all family members feel the pressure. If the death is sudden, people are shocked and may react in unforeseen ways. In either case, some parents try to protect young children from learning about the death. This is unwise.

When someone dies, children should be told about it in an honest way. Adults should not tell children that the person is "just away" or "has gone on a trip." For example, Jamie's father explained, "Grandpa died last night. We won't see him again, but we can look at pictures of him and talk about the good times we've had with him." Children can accept honesty far better than a cover-up of the facts. Then parents can encourage them to talk about their feelings and answer their questions directly. Even very young children may be allowed to take part in the funeral or memorial service.

Older children often react differently to death than very young children do. Understanding how children of different ages respond to death helps parents and caregivers provide the most meaningful support.

- Children under the age of three view death as a separation or absence. They react to death just as they react to a week's separation.
- Children between the ages of three and five do not understand that death is permanent. They believe it is like sleep. First you are dead, then you are alive again.
- Children from ages five to nine do not see death as something that happens to everyone. They can, however, accept the idea that a particular person is dead and will not return.

- Children of nine or ten begin to understand that everyone eventually dies. They worry that their parents will die and leave them. As a result, they may ask for repeated assurances that their parents will live a long time.

- Between the ages of ten and twelve, children come to terms with their fears and worries. They may need help from parents to put death in its proper perspective.

Young children are often confused about death because of what they have seen on television. Some TV movies contain flashbacks showing dead characters at a time when they were still alive. News broadcasts announce the death of famous people and then show film footage of events they took part in before their death. Children who do not understand that these events took place at an earlier time naturally wonder about the finality of death. Parents and teachers can take these opportunities to clarify information about death for children.

When a parent dies, children have some of the same concerns that children of divorced parents have. They may experience intense feelings of abandonment, loneliness, anger, or guilt. At this time, children need emotional support and reassurance from the surviving parent and other relatives. They may especially need reassurance that the remaining parent will not die, too.

After a death occurs, children often act as though nothing has happened. They continue to play even though they feel the loss. Parents and caregivers should assume that children have more questions and concerns than they express. Adults should encourage children to grieve for the loved one. **Grief** (GREEF) is a great sorrow caused by a loss. By expressing their feelings of grief rather than being afraid of them, children learn how to cope with death.

Several weeks after her mother's death, five-year-old Emily said, "I'm mad because Mom died and left me. She doesn't care what happens to me. Why doesn't she come back? How long is she going to stay in heaven?" Emily's father realized he would have to spend more time helping his daughter adjust to her mother's absence. Father and daughter grew closer to each other as they began to work through this heartbreaking reality.

Many schools have begun crisis counseling for students whenever a tragedy occurs within the family, school, or community. The tragedy may be a death resulting from a fire, tornado, hurricane, suicide, or murder. Helping children cope with death is a difficult but important task for parents and other caregivers.

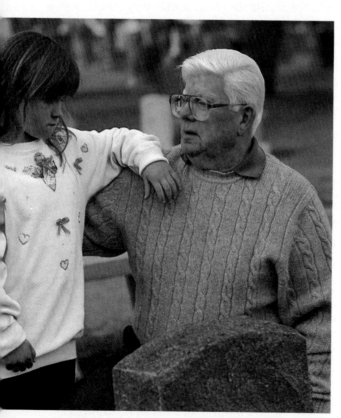

When a family member dies, children should be encouraged to talk about their feelings and concerns. This helps them learn how to cope with loss and grief.

Activity. Have students review several books on death and discuss their value for various age groups, from young children to adults.

Problem Solving. Have students suggest ways that parents can answer a five-year-old's questions about the death of a grandparent. For example: How long will grandma be gone? Will I see her again? Where did she go?

CHAPTER 27 REVIEW

Summary

- In times of family crisis, parents should talk openly and honestly with children.
- Parents who work outside the home need to explore work and child care options so they can successfully balance work and child care responsibilities.
- Among the life-style changes many families face are moving to a new area and experiencing financial setbacks or unemployment.
- Changes in family structure stem from separation and divorce, from remarriage and the formation of a blended family, and from having or adopting a child.
- The children of parents who are addicted to drugs or alcohol may be constantly afraid of being abused or neglected.
- In cases of family violence, family members must get out of the abusive situation. The abuser must be helped to solve his or her problems and change the violent habits.
- Serious illness or injury of a family member or the death of a loved one can cause stress, worries, and grief.

Questions

p. 515 1. Name three work options that "family friendly" companies may offer their employees.

p. 516 2. How can parents successfully balance work and parenting responsibilities?

p. 518 3. Explain what parents can do to make moving less stressful for children.

p. 520 4. What are some of the reactions of children to divorce?

p. 522 5. Suggest at least five things successful parents do to help children deal with divorce.

p. 523 6. Why does it take a long time for a blended family to become a family unit?

p. 525 7. How might parents explain adoption to their adopted child?

p. 526 8. Why is family violence often kept a secret?

p. 529 9. How do young children of various ages view death?

Activities

1. Read three articles on ways that parents can balance work and family life. Compile a list of recommendations.

2. Find out what organizations are available in your community to help alcohol and drug abusers or their families. What kind of assistance does each group provide?

3. Read one issue of a local newspaper. Note the following:
   - How many articles pertain to a family crisis?
   - What kind of crisis does each article describe or mention?
   - How is each family dealing with their crisis?

Think About

1. What do you think might be the advantages and disadvantages of joint custody over sole custody of a child?

2. Why do you think there are more reported incidents of child abuse today than there were, say, 25 years ago?

Reference. See the Teacher's Manual in the front of the Teacher's Annotated Edition for complete answers to the chapter review questions.

531

Selecting Child Care

Objectives

This chapter will help you to:

- Discuss the need for supplemental child care.
- Compare home-based child care and center-based child care.
- List the characteristics of a high-quality child care program.
- Describe the concerns that parents may have regarding child care.

Vocabulary

nanny
au pair
family child care
child care center
latchkey children
National Association for the Education of Young Children (NAEYC)
staff-child ratio

Michelle, age three, holds her father's hand tightly as they approach the Little Kids Child Care Center. Michelle has attended the center for almost a year. As they reach the door, Michelle sees Tamara and Kurt, two of her friends. Michelle's serious look gives way to joy as she says, "Hi, Tamara! Hi, Kurt!"

The teacher, Mr. Martinez, greets Michelle and her father. He remembers Michelle's first days in the two-year-old group. She had been unhappy, not wanting her father or mother to leave her. Separation, like it is for many children, was not easy for Michelle.

However, within a few days Michelle had made an adjustment to her new surroundings. Now she enjoys participating in the many different activities. Her favorites seem to be painting at the easel, building with blocks, and climbing the outdoor jungle gym. She is a happy child who has made friends with other children in the center.

As Michelle and her father say good-bye, he reminds her that her mother will pick her up at six o'clock. Other children continue to arrive at the center. Mr. Martinez and the other teachers, along with the child care aides, have a busy day ahead.

Supplemental Child Care

Michelle's parents have used supplemental child care since she was six months old. First, she was cared for by relatives at home. Last year her parents enrolled her in a new child care center in their community.

Supplemental child care usually means care that a child receives from someone other than his or her parents during each working day. However, the parents still maintain control of most aspects of their child's life. Child care is an important part of a community's support system for families.

Chapter Opener. Ask students to read the opening scenario to the chapter. Ask these questions: How has Michelle adjusted to child care? How can child care providers help children's growth and development? What should parents look for when selecting child care services?
Activity. Survey students in class to determine whether their parents had supplemental child care for them when they were young. What type of supplemental care was provided?

❖ Increased Need for Child Care

As you read in Chapter 27, a greater percentage of parents than ever before need supplemental child care for their infants and young children. Good care is essential if children are to grow and develop properly.

In an earlier era, women dropped out of the work force when they had children. Today, because of the increasing number of working mothers, many families need child care support. About half of the children of working parents are cared for by the parents themselves or by relatives. Some parents can juggle work schedules so they do not have to pay for care. Others who cannot be at home to care for their children must find supplemental child care.

Many groups and individuals are responding to the needs of parents who work by offering a variety of child care programs. Today, child care centers, early childhood education programs, and programs for school-age children are an answer for families of all income levels.

❖ Qualities of Child Care

When parents begin their search for child care, they generally want to find care that is suitable, affordable, and dependable.

- **Suitable.** Child care should be appropriate to the child's developmental level. It

Many parents need supplemental child care for their children. Some are cared for in their own home or a caregiver's home. Others attend a child care center.

More About. Current statistics show that more than 50 percent of mothers with children under age five are in the work force.

Discuss. What would be your goals if you were seeking child care services for your child? How would you prioritize those goals?

should be suited to the child's individual needs and interests. Care must be of high quality and the surroundings healthful and safe.

- **Affordable.** Cost of the child care should be within the family's financial means. The cost should be clearly spelled out and include any extra charges for food, diapers, or transportation.

- **Dependable.** Child care should be reliable. Parents must be able to depend on the caregiver to provide consistent, high-quality care. Undependable child care puts great stress on both children and parents.

Parents fill the need for supplemental child care in a variety of ways. The most common arrangements are listed in the chart below.

Primary Child-Care Arrangements for Children Under Age 15

Type of Child-Care Arrangement	Birth to 5-Year-Olds		5- to 14-Year Olds	
	Number	Percent	Number	Percent
Care in child's home	2,728,076	29.9%	2,681,648	13.6%
By father	1,395,972	15.3%	1,321,106	6.7%
By grandparent	465,324	5.1%	295,770	1.5%
By other relative	301,092	3.3%	788,720	4.0%
By nonrelative	565,688	6.2%	276,052	1.4%
Care in another home	3,248,144	35.6%	1,045,054	5.3%
By grandparent	793,788	8.7%	374,642	1.9%
By other relative	410,580	4.5%	177,462	.9%
By nonrelative	2,043,776	22.4%	492,950	2.5%
Child care center	1,468,964	16.1%	335,206	1.7%
Preschool/nursery school	757,292	8.3%	118,308	.6%
Kindergarten/grade school	91,240	1.0%	14,019,498	71.1%
Child cares for self	18,248	.2%	808,438	4.1%
Mother cares for child at work	812,036	8.9%	709,848	3.6%
TOTAL:	9,124,000	100%	19,718,000	100%

These children represent about 94 percent of all children under 15 years of age of employed women (30.6 million children).

Source: U.S. Bureau of the Census, *Current Population Reports,* Series 0-70, No. 20 and U.S. Department of Commerce, *Statistical Abstracts of the United States 1991,* lll Edition.

Activity. Ask students to gather the latest statistics on child-care arrangements in the United States.

Discuss. What advantages might there be for children attending a child care center or preschool compared to being cared for at home?

Home-Based Child Care

Home-based child care includes care either in the child's home or in the home of the caregiver. About 30 percent of children of working mothers are cared for in the child's own home. A slightly larger number of children—35.6 percent—are cared for in the homes of others.

❖ Relatives and Neighbors

Many parents who work outside the home leave their children in the care of relatives or neighbors. Relatives, such as grandparents, may care for a child either in the child's home or in their own home. In the case of neighbors, the child is usually taken to the neighbor's home.

There are many advantages to having a relative or neighbor care for the child. The child already knows and feels comfortable with the caregiver. When cared for at home, the child is among familiar surroundings and playthings. Then the parent does not have to take the child out in the morning or pick the child up at night. Often a relative will care for the child for little or no pay.

However, some older relatives and neighbors may not have enough energy to care for a young child on a daily basis. They may not be familiar with appropriate learning activities or encourage the child to play with other children. Some parents find it difficult to ask a relative or neighbor to alter his or her parenting techniques.

❖ Nannies and Au Pairs

Some parents who can afford it hire someone other than a relative or neighbor to care for the child in their own home. Such a caregiver either lives with the family or comes to the family's home each day.

A **nanny** is a live-in caregiver. Nannies are generally on call 24 hours a day, although they have regular days off. Some have

A nanny or au pair lives with the family or comes to the family's home each day to care for the children.

Discuss. What would be the advantages and disadvantages of having grandparents care for children on a regular basis?

Activity. Have students gather information about nanny schools in the United States. Addresses may be obtained from guidance counselors, the yellow pages, or the classified section of newspapers.

received special training to prepare them for the position of nanny. They are paid a weekly salary and given free room and board.

An **au pair** (oh PARE) is a young person who comes from one country to live with a family in another country. Au pairs agree to care for the child and do light housework in exchange for being able to live with the family. Like nannies, au pairs are usually on call 24 hours a day with regular days off.

A hired, full-time caregiver offers both advantages and disadvantages for families. On one hand, in-home care is very convenient for both parents and children. However, this type of care can be expensive. If the caregiver lives with the family, separate living quarters are usually required. Also, the family must adjust to having a new person live with them.

Parents should interview prospective caregivers extensively and check their references carefully. Parents need to make sure that a caregiver has the qualifications necessary for working with children. Has the person received training in child care? Has the person cared for other children? For infant care particularly, the parent may want to remain at home for a few days to see that the caregiver knows how to handle the baby properly.

Many nannies and au pairs are recruited by agencies who specialize in child care services. If the caregiver is from a foreign country, it is important that he or she has the necessary immigration and working papers. Written contracts should be developed for in-home employees, stating responsibilities, hours, pay, and benefits.

❖ Family Child Care

Another type of home-based child care is **family child care.** This type of care is usually provided by a mother in her own home. She makes money caring for three or four children in addition to her own children. A variation on this arrangement is group child care in one's home. In group child care, the provider may care for as many as ten children and hire a worker to help.

In many communities family child care homes must be licensed. To obtain a license, owners have to see that their home meets certain requirements such as a specified amount of space. Usually owners must also adhere to strict health and safety guidelines.

Family child care homes are usually less expensive than child care centers. Other advantages include a home environment and a small group of children. Often the home is located in the family's own neighborhood. This is convenient for school-age children who walk to the caregiver's home after school.

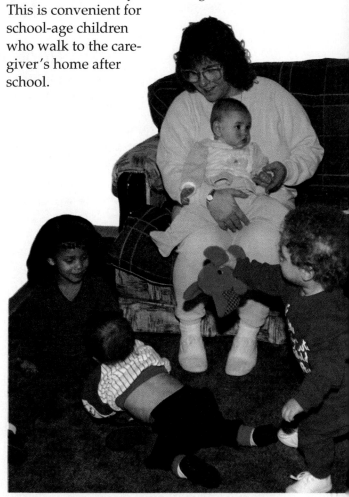

A family child care provider cares for children in her own home. Many communities and states require a family child care provider to be licensed.

Activity. Have students obtain licensing requirements for family child care homes in your community and state.

Activity. Ask students to gather information about family child care homes in your community. Are they licensed? How many children are cared for in each home? What is the cost?

On the other hand, the family child care provider may not have an educational background in child development and early childhood education. Some caregivers allow the children to watch television for many hours instead of providing them with meaningful learning activities. Some caregivers care for more children than they can safely supervise.

Generally, licensing helps eliminate any potential caregiver who has committed a crime, such as child abuse. Although licensing helps protect the child from known offenders, parents must still be alert to their child's health and safety. Using an unlicensed family child care provider can be very risky.

When evaluating family child care, parents should look for a caregiver who has the same basic childrearing philosophy that they do. At its best, family child care can offer a warm, homelike atmosphere for young children. It may be an attractive alternative for parents who feel that their child is too young to spend as many as ten hours a day in a child care center.

◆◆ *Health & Safety* ◆◆

Hiring a Caregiver

Unless a parent is responsible for hiring people at work, hiring a caregiver may be the first time he or she has to interview someone for a job. Here are some tips to help parents find out what they need to know about a potential in-home caregiver:

- A brief telephone conversation can help determine whether it will be worthwhile to interview the person. Introduce yourself, describe your child, and briefly state your needs. Mention any special requirements, such as having a car or being a nonsmoker. If you are pleased with the answers to your questions, arrange a date and time for an interview.

- Begin the interview with casual talk to help put both of you at ease.

- Be sure the child is with you during the interview. This will give you a chance to see how the child responds to the person.

- Ask open-ended questions so you can find out whether you and the caregiver have similar ideas and values about parenting. For example, ask, "What will you and the child usually do in the afternoon?" This

question will draw out more information than "Will you take the child for a walk in the afternoon?" Questions concerning naps, bottles, pacifiers, snacks, spanking, and toilet training can provide valuable insight. What does the person like best about taking care of children? What is the most difficult? Avoid expressing your own opinions during the interview. Otherwise, the person may give you the answers you want to hear.

- Describe your needs to the person. Clearly state the exact days and hours that she or he would be needed. Mention any added responsibilities, such as doing some household tasks. Discuss salary and how often the person would be paid.

- Ask for references. Check all references carefully before hiring anyone.

- If you have any doubts about hiring the person, end the interview politely. You might say, "Thank you for coming, but I don't think this would be the right arrangement for me."

Discuss. What health and safety conditions should parents look for when evaluating a family child care home?
Activity. How would you want your child to spend time while in a family child care home? How can parents learn about activities?

Problem Solving. Ask students to prepare a list of questions that would help parents determine a caregiver's philosophy about parenting practices. Then have them prioritize the questions according to importance.

Center-Based Child Care

Throughout the United States there are several types of nonhome child care options. In this chapter you will learn about child care centers that have designed programs to meet the needs of working parents. A **child care center** is a facility that provides full-day, supervised care and education for children. It is staffed by professionally trained teachers and caregivers. In Chapter 29, you will learn about other types of early childhood education programs.

About 16 percent of working parents use child care centers. Most centers are open nine or more hours a day, five days a week throughout the year. For example, many centers open at 6:30 A.M. and close at 7:00 P.M. Some centers near medical facilities and military bases offer extended hours to accom-

modate the unusual schedules of parents who work there.

Some centers provide care for children of all ages. Others specialize only in infants, toddlers, or preschool children. Because of their developmental needs, infants and toddlers require the most specialized care. The greatest increase in child care enrollment has occurred in centers devoted to infants and toddlers. In fact, the demand is so great and the spaces so few that high-quality centers often have waiting lists.

Directors and teachers in child care centers have received professional training in child development and child care. Many have a degree from a four-year college or technical school. Some centers have assistant teachers who work with the children under the direction of the professional teachers. Assistant teachers usually have a two-year degree from a college or technical school. Child care aides assist the teachers with various tasks. Theirs

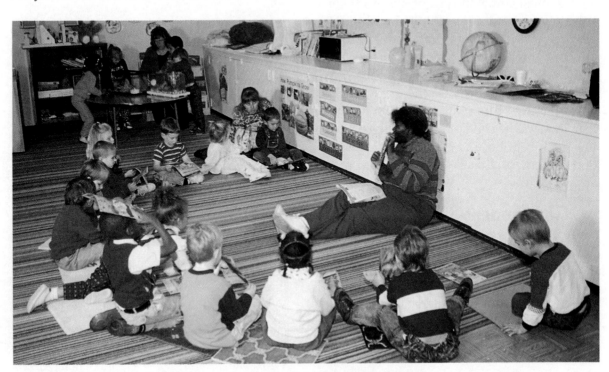

A child care center provides full-day, supervised care for children. The children are able to participate in a variety of activities and learning experiences.

is an entry-level job and usually requires a high school diploma. Some states set educational and training requirements for child care workers.

Fees for center-based child care vary. Nonprofit centers and those supported by community or business groups can offer lower fees than for-profit centers. Infant care is generally more expensive than care for toddlers and preschool children. Because infants need individual attention throughout the day, one caregiver can legally care for only four infants.

Large communities usually offer a wide range of center-based child care programs; rural communities may have only a few. The rest of this section describes various types of nonprofit and for-profit child care centers.

❖ Organization-Sponsored Child Care Centers

The most common type of nonprofit center is one located in or affiliated with a religious or charitable organization. Institutions such as churches, synagogues, and YMCA/YWCAs often provide space for a child care center. Because the organization charges little or no rent, the tuition fees are usually low. The child care center uses the fees to pay for supplies and teacher salaries. Some of these centers also offer religious instruction and services.

❖ Government-Sponsored Child Care Centers

Some nonprofit child care centers are funded by government agencies. Fees for public, tax-supported centers are most often based on the family's ability to pay. Additional costs for running the center are paid by the state or local government. In many states, children are not eligible for this service if the family income exceeds a certain amount.

Discuss. Why can nonprofit child care centers offer lower fees?
Problem Solving. What types of support might be offered by organizations or business groups for child care centers in your community?

❖ Employer-Sponsored Child Care Centers

Some corporations, hospitals, and government departments operate or sponsor child care programs for their employees. Such programs are usually inexpensive because they are subsidized by the employer. The child care center may be located at the work site or conveniently nearby.

Businesses are finding that on-site centers help their employees in several ways. Parents no longer have to worry about finding high-quality child care. They work more effectively on the job and miss fewer work days. New parents take shorter parental leaves because they are able to feed and play with their infant during work breaks. Some centers even have special rooms where children with minor illnesses can rest. This enables parents to come to work instead of staying home with a child who has a cold, for example.

A work-site child care center enables working parents to spend time with their children during lunch time or breaks.

Activity. Have students investigate whether any local employers operate or sponsor child care programs for their employees in your area.

❖ School-Sponsored Child Care Centers

Some high schools have established an on-site child care center for teenage parents. This allows students to attend classes knowing that their baby is well cared for by teachers and student aides. The young parents are enrolled in a parenting course during the school year. As a result, they are able to complete their high school education.

School-sponsored child care centers also serve as laboratories for students taking parenting and child care courses. These students observe infants and toddlers, practice parenting skills, and learn about careers in the child care field.

❖ Privately Owned Child Care Centers

Many private owners of child care centers are former teachers or child care workers. Privately owned centers are almost always more expensive than nonprofit centers. Tuition fees must cover the costs of rent or mortgage, insurance, equipment, food, and salaries. Such centers must also make a reasonable profit for their owners.

❖ Franchised Child Care Centers

A number of franchised child care centers are located throughout the country or in a large geographic region. A central organization usually operates these centers and oversees their standards of quality. Such organizations often advertise widely as they increase the number of centers in their chain. Fees are usually higher at these for-profit centers than at nonprofit centers sponsored by organizations, government agencies, and businesses.

School-Age Child Care

Some parents of school-age children must leave for work before school begins and cannot be at home when their children get out of school. Many of these children must take care of themselves before and after school. Such children are often called **latchkey children** because they carry a key to their home. Estimates indicate that there are 4.1 million latchkey children between the ages of five and fourteen in the United States.

Many parents attempt to ease their children's fears and loneliness by telephoning them after school (See "Home Alone" on page 447.) . However, police and fire departments report that many accidents and fires occur during the hours when children are home alone.

Some schools provide "Home Safe" learning materials to their students. These materials help prepare older school-age children to take care of themselves when their parents are still at work. Children learn about safety procedures for different situations, such as answering the telephone and doorbell.

Many communities now have child care programs for school-age children. These programs are available before and after school and during vacation periods to meet the needs of working parents. The children spend one to three hours in the program before or after school. They can participate in sports, art, dance, or music or do their homework. In some communities, the program is offered in the school building. In other communities, the children are transported by bus to a separate care center.

Some family child care homes also accept school-age children. Parents must make arrangements for their children to travel safely from school to the home of the child care provider.

Activity. Ask students to identify programs, either before or after school, that are available for school-age children in your community.
Problem Solving. What simple snacks could parents allow

school-age children to make without supervision?
Problem Solving. Have students identify emergency situations that latchkey children might face when home alone. What guidelines should parents establish for these situations?

Evaluating Child Care Services

When choosing a family child care provider or a child care center, parents should take time to study their choices and compare services. They should find a facility that provides adequately for the physical and social needs of their child. Nutritious food and attention to the child's health, rest, safety, and educational needs are very important. The setting should promote development of the total child.

◆◆ What Is a High-Quality Child Care Program?

An ideal child care program provides both care and educational activities for children. For infants and toddlers, the routines of eating, sleeping, and playing are individualized. Careful attention is given to the health, comfort, cleanliness, and happiness of the children.

Standards and Accreditation

Each state has regulations that help define standards of quality for child care programs. Centers must meet minimum standards for health, safety, and staff requirements. Information on these standards may be obtained by calling the state human services or public health department. Centers must also be licensed by the state licensing authority.

The **National Association for the Education of Young Children (NAEYC)** has established an accreditation system for child care centers. The NAEYC is an association of nearly 80,000 teachers, caregivers, and parents who work for improved quality in all early childhood programs. Child care centers that meet NAEYC standards are eligible for the association's accreditation. This is a recogni-

tion of high standards of care and education. Accreditation is also available to high-quality, early childhood education programs, which you will learn about in Chapter 29. You can obtain information about accredited centers and programs in your locality by calling the NAEYC at 800-424-2460.

Staff-Child Ratio

Another factor to consider in assessing the quality of group child care is the **staff-child ratio.** This is the number of adult caregivers per number of children. NAEYC accreditation requires that the infant care room should always have at least two staff people. In addition, there should be no more than eight infants for every two caregivers. If a group contains both infants and toddlers, there should be no more than two infants and no more than six toddlers for every two caregivers.

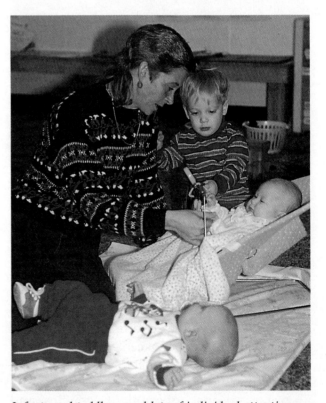

Infants and toddlers need lots of individual attention from caregivers.

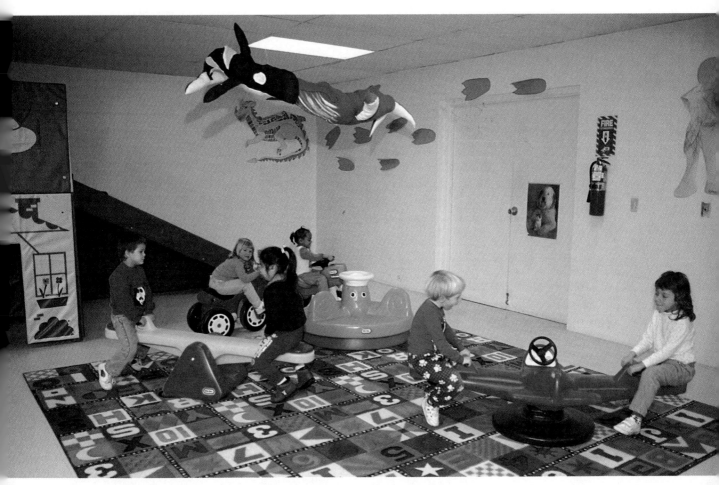

A quality child care center has equipment and space—indoors or outdoors—for active play. This enables children to exercise and develop their motor skills.

Activities and Equipment

If you drop by a high-quality child care center, you might see some children playing with toys, others sleeping, and still others eating or being diapered. The atmosphere will be relaxed. The caregivers know that loud voices and hurried or fast-paced activities can overstimulate and tire young children.

You should observe activities that are developmentally appropriate for the children. This means that the activities are planned to fit not only the particular ages of the children in the group but also the special needs and interests of each individual child.

A good child care center has color and beauty, for children need things to see, touch, and wonder about. It has objects to climb over and under and to hide in and crawl through. The center has plenty of items to play with so that the children progress in all areas of development: physical, social, cognitive, and emotional. Toys are durable, strong, safe, and usable in different ways and places.

With a variety of equipment, supplies, and activities, children find it easy to have fun. In addition, such variety encourages children to explore independently, which is an essential activity in the early childhood years.

Activity. Divide class into small groups. Have each group role play a situation in which a child care provider must meet the needs of several children at the same time. How difficult is the task if the children are infants, toddlers, or preschoolers?

Activity. Have students visit a child care center and observe the various activities and equipment. What different activities and equipment are available for different age groups? How many of these could be duplicated in a family child care home?

DECISIONS ◆
◆ DECISIONS

Five-year-old Kara has been attending kindergarten during the school year. Her mother, Valerie, has been working part-time during the hours that Kara is in school. However, summer is approaching and school will soon be out. Valerie must make child care arrangements for the summer months. What are some options that she might consider?

Communication with Parents

Quality child care centers maintain strong links with the children's parents. Caregivers take time to talk to parents about the children's activities and development. Parents also share the pleasures and problems they have had with their children during the night or weekend. This communication helps both parents and caregivers better meet the needs of each child—whether at home or at the child care center.

◆◆ Guidelines for Parents

The following guidelines can help parents decide on the child care services that will best meet the needs of their family.

1. Make a needs list describing the child care services that you want.
2. Start the search for child care several weeks before it will be needed. Call city or town offices and ask for the name of the agency that licenses family child care homes and group child care centers.
3. Call the licensing agency. Ask what standards child care facilities must meet in order to be licensed in your town and state. Request a list of licensed child care providers in your area.

4. Call the NAEYC (800-424-2460) and ask which centers in your area are accredited. Also request a brochure on choosing child care.
5. Call several of the licensed caregivers or centers. Ask what days and hours they are open. What is the staff-child ratio? What are the qualifications of the staff or caregiver? What is the cost? Is there an opening for another child right now?
6. Visit several of the homes or centers unannounced. Observing the staff when they are not expecting visitors provides better information about the normal routine.
7. On the day of the visit, leave the child with someone else if possible. Having the child along can be distracting and prevent a careful look at details.
8. Check the information that you received over the phone with the director or caregiver. Write it down. Discuss family needs with that person.
9. Observe the caregivers and children. If possible, stay at least one hour. Take notes. Are children enjoying their activity? Have constructive, worthwhile activities been planned for them? Do caregivers seem to know what comes next? Are children addressed by name? Is there very little crying? Are children's arguments settled in a way that helps them learn? Are plans made for fire safety? Are healthful foods served? Can children draw, sing, read, pretend, and run? How would a child feel in this place for eight or more hours a day?
10. Compare at least two centers or homes. Take time to consider carefully the advantages and disadvantages of each.
11. After making a choice, take the child to visit the site if possible. This lets the child get used to the rooms, the play area, and the bathroom. Make plans for the child's

Discuss. What health and safety conditions should parents look for when evaluating a child care center?

Reference. See page 546 for a parents' checklist for evaluating a child care center.

first day at the home or center. Talk enthusiastically about the fun the child will have there.

12. Plan to stay with the child for at least short periods for the first few days. When the teacher or caregiver thinks the child will be all right without you, leave promptly. Say something such as, "Now I have to leave. I'll come back for you. Bye-bye." Never slip away without saying goodbye. Don't worry if the child starts to cry; the teacher or caregiver is experienced in handling such situations.

DECISIONS ◆
◆ DECISIONS

William, who has custody of his four-year-old son, has accepted a new job in another state. The two will soon be moving. William must seek child care arrangements for his son in their new community. He has asked your advice on ways to locate suitable child care. What will you tell him?

Parents should take time to evaluate child care services in their community. This helps them make the best choice for their children and their family.

Discuss. How might a high-quality child care program for infants and toddlers differ from a high-quality program for preschoolers?

Activity. Have students visit a child care center and observe the different guidance techniques used for different ages of children. See pages 463–467 for information about indirect, direct, and affective guidance techniques.

Parents' Checklist for Evaluating a Child Care Center

Rating:

High	Medium	Low
3	2	1

Emotional and Social Climate

3 2 1 Children appear happy and content.
3 2 1 Caregivers seem pleasant and calm.

Caregivers' Attention to Children

3 2 1 Groups have at least two staff members present at a time.
3 2 1 Infants have a staff/child ratio of 1:4.
3 2 1 Toddlers have a staff/child ratio of 1:6.
3 2 1 Preschoolers have a staff/child ratio of 1:9.
3 2 1 Experience of teachers and aides.
3 2 1 Education of teachers and aides.
3 2 1 General attitude of caregivers toward children.

Program of Children's Activities

3 2 1 Planned activities for week are posted.
3 2 1 Total program fits children's needs.
3 2 1 Motor skills activities are encouraged.
3 2 1 Social development needs are met.
3 2 1 Affection and nurturing needs are met.
3 2 1 Intellectual learning is stimulated.
3 2 1 Language expression is encouraged.
3 2 1 Pre-reading activities are encouraged.
3 2 1 Creative activities are encouraged.
3 2 1 Musical activities are encouraged.

Safety of Children and Caregivers

3 2 1 Rooms are tidy without potential safety hazards.
3 2 1 Children are always supervised by caregivers.
3 2 1 Children's belongings have a specific space.
3 2 1 Fire exits are unobstructed.
3 2 1 Emergency routines are posted.

3 2 1 Emergency numbers are posted by telephones.
3 2 1 A feeling of security exists in building.
3 2 1 A feeling of security exists on play yard.
3 2 1 Strangers cannot enter unchecked.
3 2 1 Transportation is well organized for safety.

Health of Children and Caregivers

3 2 1 Children appear healthy.
3 2 1 Children are required to have all immunizations.
3 2 1 Arrangements are made for a sick child.
3 2 1 Caregivers wash hands after diapering and wiping noses.
3 2 1 Playrooms and bathrooms are clean and sanitary.
3 2 1 Sanitation procedures are followed for food handling and service.
3 2 1 Meals and snacks are nutritious.
3 2 1 Caregivers appear healthy.

Administration

3 2 1 Friendly.
3 2 1 Organized.
3 2 1 Reputation of honesty and integrity.
3 2 1 Up-to-date accreditation certificate.
3 2 1 Up-to-date state licensing certificate.

Parental Involvement

3 2 1 Parents are permitted to visit at anytime without advance notice.
3 2 1 Parents are encouraged to talk with staff members.
3 2 1 Parents are encouraged to talk with other parents.
3 2 1 Activities are planned for parents.

Activity. Have students suggest additional characteristics that parents might want to consider when evaluating a child care center.

Discuss. How can parents be sure that a child care program maintains a certain level of quality on a continuing basis?

Concerns of Parents

When parents locate suitable, affordable, and dependable child care, they and their child usually fall into a pleasant routine. The parents find that the child is happy. In a high-quality center, there are many interesting friends and activities. Teachers and caregivers work hard to provide for the children's needs on an individual basis. Children greet their parents at the end of the day describing what they have done. Parents feel relieved and fortunate when their selection matches their family's needs.

However, parents must continue to monitor their child's care. They should keep their eyes open wide, observing both their child and the other children for signs that the program is—or is not—serving children's needs. It is useful to become acquainted with other parents in order to share any comments or concerns.

❖ Dealing with Separation

It is very helpful to the child and to the caregivers if the child can be introduced gradually to the child care center. The ideal is for the child to attend with a parent for only a couple of hours the first few days. However, this procedure is frequently too expensive in terms of time and money to be practical for many working parents. Thus, many parents must leave the child without much time for introductions. In this case, the caregiver must plan to help relieve any separation anxiety the child may experience.

Although children may appear not to like a child care center or home at first, parents should not worry too much about the first few days. Even if the child cries for a time, the caregivers are usually successful in enticing the child into interesting activities. If parents

Reference. See pages 479–480 for ways to handle separation anxiety in young children.

Around the World

Child Care on a Kibbutz

In Israel, some children are being brought up very differently. These children are born to parents who live on a kibbutz (kib-BOOTS). A kibbutz is a community of people who live together as one big family, even if they are not related. These small settlements are mainly involved in the business of agriculture. All property belongs to the community. The members of the community work together to provide what everyone needs. Because the women are needed as workers, the community assumes the responsibility of rearing the children. About 4 percent of all Israelis live on kibbutzim.

On the kibbutz, newborns move into a special children's house when they are about four days old. All the babies are raised together. A member of the kibbutz serves as caregiver for the entire group. Each mother nurses her baby at the children's house until the baby is about six months old. Both mother and father visit the baby at the house. Then, when the baby is about one year old, he or she goes to the parents' home for visits.

When an infant starts to crawl, he or she is put in a large playpen with the other infants. They are left alone to play together for hours at a time. Nobody interferes when two babies want the same toy or when one baby annoys another. The infants learn how to accommodate each other's needs and to help each other. The infants are often more attached to each other than to their parents or caregiver.

This system develops a very strong sense of group identity and cooperation in the children. These two traits are important in special communities such as the kibbutz. Everyone is equal, and all are expected to work together for the common good.

Emphasize. Parents should never slip away at a child care center without preparing the child for the separation.

were to return, they would probably find that the child had stopped crying and was playing contentedly.

As the strangeness of the new environment wears off, the child usually adjusts very well. Frequently, the parting is actually harder on the parent than on the child. However, if the child continues to be unhappy, parents may have to reconsider their choice of child care services.

Parent-Caregiver Relationships

Many parents feel guilty about leaving their child to go to work. Some worry that the caregivers may try to compete with them for the child's affection. It is the responsibility of the center to be aware of such feelings and to support the most important relationship—the one between the child and the parent. Caregivers should not be thought of as replacements for parents but as supplements who support the parent-child relationship. Although the child is in the center for about 8 hours a day, the parents still have 16 hours

◆ ◆ *Self-Esteem* ◆ ◆

Young children may feel anxiety when going to a child care center for the first time. They are leaving the security of their home and the protection of their parents. To help children understand what will take place, parents should talk about the new experience beforehand. Parents should also reassure children that they will return home after their day at the center.

a day plus weekends to continue the bonding and attachment process.

High-quality child care centers encourage communication between parents and caregivers. Most caregivers will take time to talk with parents about their child. If they do not, parents should ask them for comments on the child's progress.

The selection of child care services is one of the most important decisions that parents make. The right choice can result in very positive experiences for both parents and children.

Parents should talk with caregivers daily about their child's activities and development.

Discuss. Why might parting at a child care center be more difficult for the parent than for the child?

Problem Solving. Have students suggest ways that parents can help children adjust to a new child care arrangement.

CHAPTER 28 REVIEW

Summary

- More parents than ever before need supplemental child care for their children.
- Child care should be suitable for a child's level of development, affordable, and dependable.
- About two-thirds of all children of working mothers are cared for in their own home or someone else's home by a relative, neighbor, live-in caregiver, or family child care provider.
- Some center-based child care programs are sponsored by organizations, government, employers, and schools. Others are privately owned or franchised.
- Parents should compare child care services and evaluate their options.
- High-quality child care programs are licensed, have a high staff-child ratio, offer a variety of activities, and communicate regularly with parents.
- Parents should monitor their child's care to ensure it is meeting the child's needs.

Questions

p. 534 1. Why is the need for supplemental child care greater today than it was in the past?

p. 534 2. What are three qualities of child care that parents generally seek?

p. 536 3. Give two advantages and two potential disadvantages of having a relative or neighbor care for the child in the child's home.

p. 536 4. What is a nanny?

p. 537 5. What is family child care?

p. 540 6. Why do some businesses sponsor child care programs for their employees?

7. What are latchkey children? What alternatives are available for school-age children in some communities? p. 541

8. List at least four characteristics of a high-quality child care program. p. 542

9. How should parents go about selecting a child care service? p. 544

10. How can parents and children best deal with separation? p. 544

Activities

1. Research the types of child care programs available in your community. Gather information about cost, staff-child ratio, licensing, accreditation, activities, parent involvement, and possible waiting list. Share your findings with the class.

2. Interview a parent who has a child in a child care program. Ask: Why did you choose this program? What benefits does your child get from it? Which activities does your child enjoy most? How often do you talk with your child's caregiver? Are you satisfied with the program?

3. Write a set of guidelines for latchkey children that would be helpful for both children and parents.

Think About

1. If you had your choice, what type of supplemental child care described in this chapter would you choose for your own child? Why?

2. Do you think more businesses will provide on-site child care centers for their employees in the coming years? Why or why not?

chapter 29

Early Childhood Education

Objectives

This chapter will help you to:

- Compare various types of preschool facilities and programs.
- Describe the types of activities offered in kindergarten.
- Discuss the advantages and disadvantages of enrichment activities.
- Explain how parents can become involved in their children's early education.

Vocabulary

parent cooperatives
Head Start
Montessori method
kindergarten
learning centers

"Mommy, are you going to be in school today?" asks four-year-old Nicholas. About once a month his mother assists the teacher in his nursery school class. The children attend the morning program three times a week.

"Not today," Mrs. Graham responds, "but next week I'll go to school with you. What do you want me to see?"

"I can climb the jungle gym! And I can paint lots of pictures! You can hear the songs! And we have a new fish!" Nicholas tells his mother excitedly.

Nicholas always looks forward to the days when his mother or father can visit the preschool. Although parents are there to assist the teacher, they can also observe their child's activities and behavior.

Most early childhood education programs are designed to help children in all areas of development. They encourage children to learn through play, to experience the arts, to use their imagination, and to develop communication skills. Emphasis is placed on developing high self-esteem and learning to get along with others.

The Need for Early Childhood Education

Programs called early childhood education provide supervised activities for young children. These are short programs that are offered for a few hours one or more days a week. For example, a nursery school may offer programs for three- and four-year-olds. Sessions may be held in the morning or afternoon for two to five days a week, from September through May.

Many parents want their child to have an early childhood education experience before entering first grade. Perhaps they want the child to learn how to interact with other children, to experience activities in areas such as art and music, or to develop certain skills. Many parents enroll their child in a preschool program to improve the child's motor skills, language skills, and social skills.

Such educational programs serve the needs of families in which one parent is at home at least part of the time. The parent must be able to drop off and pick up the child at the designated time and care for the child when the program is not being held. Parents who work full-time outside the home usually need a full-day child care program, as described in Chapter 28. However, children of working parents may attend an early childhood education program along with a home-based or center-based child care program.

Both preschool and school-age children often become involved in enrichment activities outside the classroom. They may take piano or dancing lessons, join a sports team, or become involved in a youth program. These activities also provide opportunities to develop skills and interact with other children.

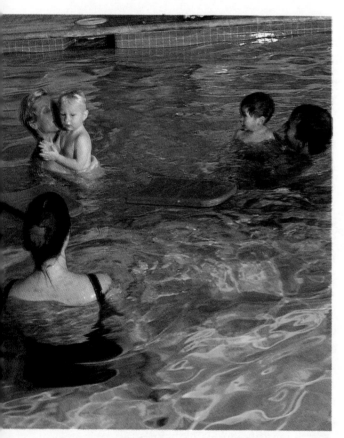

Special programs, such as Water Babies, provide opportunities for parents to interact with their children. The parents take turns supervising the children and their activities.

More About. There are two basic philosophies found in early childhood education programs. Some are instruction-oriented. Others are discovery-oriented.

Types of Early Childhood Education

A variety of early childhood education programs are available to meet the needs of various age groups. For example, parents of infants may join a class where they can participate in activities with their baby. Parents of toddlers may form a play group so their child can have playmates of the same age. Parents of preschoolers may seek a program that offers varied learning experiences, such as a nursery school. Special programs also are available for disadvantaged families. These programs provide children with an enriched environment that may not be available at home. Most public school systems offer half-day or full-day kindergarten classes that introduce children to elementary school.

❖ Infant-Parent Classes

Infant-parent classes provide opportunities for parents to interact with their baby during the class period. Some classes deal with infant care and parenting skills. Others focus on activities such as exercise, swimming, or stimulating play.

The instructors encourage parents to ask questions about their infant's development. Parents also get acquainted with other parents who have a child of the same age. This allows them to share various experiences and exchange information.

Infant-parent classes may be sponsored by recreation centers, religious organizations, YMCA/YWCAs, schools, or neighborhood groups. The Cooperative Extension Service also offers classes that help parents of young children. Some classes focus on infant care. Others discuss topics such as nutrition, budgeting, and job training.

Activity. Have students gather information about infant-parent classes that are available in your community. How might parents and children benefit from each program?

Many parents form informal play groups for their children. The parents take turns supervising the children and their activities.

◆◆ Play Groups

Some parents set up informal play groups with friends or neighbors. The parents take turns supervising the children for two or three hours on specified days. The children play together indoors or outside during nice weather. Although these groups provide children with playmates, the groups should be kept small. There should be no more than four children per caregiver. Most informal play groups involve no fees.

◆◆ Preschools

Many preschools, also known as nursery schools or prekindergartens, provide half-day programs two or more days a week. Some, however, are now offering full-day programs.

Some preschools are funded by participating families through tuition fees. Other preschools are funded by community groups or the federal government. The preschool staff usually includes one or more qualified teachers. Often these teachers are assisted by classroom aides or parents.

Parent Cooperatives

Some preschools provide opportunities for parents to be actively involved in the program. **Parent cooperatives** are nursery schools in which parents take turns assisting in the classroom. They are supervised by a preschool teacher or other qualified caregiver who directs the program and organizes the activities.

Cooperatives allow parents to participate in the preschool experience along with their child. Parents gain valuable information about child development as they work with the teacher, the children, and other parents. Because parents participate in the program, their tuition costs are lower than those for most other preschool programs.

Many parent cooperatives are sponsored by religious organizations or community cen-

In cooperative nursery schools parents assist the preschool teachers. Besides providing a valuable service to the school, the parents have the opportunity to observe and interact with their children.

ters that have available space for preschool use. Most cooperatives offer half-day programs for two to five days each week during the regular school year.

Each family in a cooperative usually assists in the program about once a month. Fathers and grandparents, as well as mothers, can participate in the classroom and accompany the children on local trips. Parents who work part-time or have flexible hours are often able to arrange their schedule in order to participate. Parents who are unable to assist during the day can fulfill their obligation in other ways. Many cooperatives have special work nights or weekends when parents clean the rooms, paint furniture, and repair equipment. Working parents can also serve on various committees throughout the school year. For example, they may be involved in fund-raising activities to supplement the cooperative's budget.

Discuss. What might the title "Head Start" mean for a child in terms of school readiness?

Head Start

Head Start is a form of early childhood education funded by the federal government for low-income and disadvantaged preschool children. Funded since 1965, Head Start provides a variety of activities to enrich the lives of young children. Its programs are free for three- and four-year-olds who qualify. Some programs are half-day; others are full-day to meet the needs of working parents.

Research shows that children enrolled in Head Start programs are more successful later on in school than children who were not in a preschool program. The learning experiences provided by Head Start aid all areas of the children's development. The children receive nutritious meals, as well as medical and dental care.

Parents have many opportunities to assist in a Head Start program. They learn about child development and parenting, as well as human services available for their family. Both parents and children benefit from parental participation in the program.

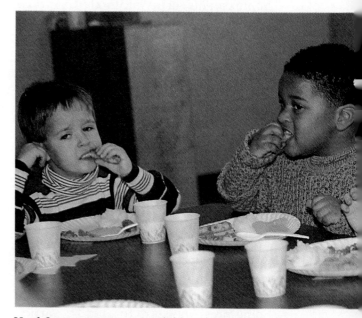

Head Start programs serve children from low income and disadvantaged backgrounds. The children are encouraged to develop their skills and are given nutritious meals and health care.

Activity. Have students visit a Head Start program and learn about the activities and services provided.

Public Education Preschools

Some states fund special preschool classes for three- and four-year-olds considered to be at-risk of school failure. At-risk children may speak a language other than English or have developmental problems. The children are involved in learning activities to help them become better prepared for elementary school. Many of the activities are academically oriented, such as learning the letters of the alphabet.

These preschools are designed for children who are not being served by Head Start. Like all public education, the programs are free for qualified children. Some states offer the programs to all children.

Child Development Laboratories

A number of high schools and colleges have a child development laboratory, or preschool program, for children three to five years of age. In such laboratories, individuals studying child development get practical experience in working with young children. They observe children's behavior and often help plan and lead activities for the children.

At the university level, laboratory programs serve a variety of needs. Students

Around the World

Preschools in Other Countries

The most important part of a preschool teacher's job is to take good care of the children. This is true all over the world. However, the experiences that children have in preschool are not the same in every culture.

- In Denmark, nearly 70 percent of children between the ages of three and six attend preschool. Most of the cost is paid by the government, but parents also pay a small monthly fee. Usually there are two teachers and one assistant for every 20 children. The teachers have received three years of training at a teacher's college. Most preschools do not teach the children to read and write. The Danes feel that this would give the children who attend preschool an unfair advantage over the children who do not. They believe that early childhood should be a time for playing.

- In Kenya, about 30 percent of children between the ages of three and six attend preschool. Most of the preschools are organized by the community. Activities such as raffles and dances are used to raise money to pay for the teachers and the school. Parents donate the necessary supplies. Although some of the teachers receive formal training, most are middle-aged women with a primary school education. There are approximately two teachers for every 30 children. Since space is limited, children who have some reading and math ability usually have a better chance of getting in a preschool.

- In Japan, there are two types of preschools. One type, called *yochien*, is for children of mothers who do not work. Children between the ages of three and six attend the school four hours a day. The other type, *hoikuen*, provides all-day care for children of working parents. This type of preschool also cares for infants and toddlers. In both types of schools, classes may have as many as 30 children. Japanese educators believe that large classes are the best way to teach children to function as part of a group.

majoring in early childhood education can practice their teaching skills. Research can be conducted on children's behavior and effective teaching methods. The programs provide low-cost care for the children of university employees and others in the community.

Montessori Schools

Montessori (mon-tuh-SOHR-ee) schools are based on the philosophy of Maria Montessori, an Italian medical doctor and educator. She developed a method of teaching that provides structured learning for preschool and school-age children. Montessori schools do not separate children by age for the purpose of learning. The **Montessori method** is a system of teaching children to be motivated learners. Special emphasis is placed on using the five senses to develop cognitive and social skills. Often these skills are combined in learning games.

Authentic Montessori schools differ from other schools for young children in several ways. The method focuses on independent learning, using the specific learning materials that Montessori designed. It also places less emphasis on group projects and activities than other programs do.

DECISIONS ◆
◆ DECISIONS

Li-ming is three years old. Her parents want to send her to a preschool program next fall. Some friends have recommended the parent cooperative nursery school that their children attend. Other friends have praised a Montessori school. The two preschools have different philosophies and programs. How can the parents decide which program would be best for Li-ming and their family?

Types of Preschool Activities

A high-quality preschool offers a variety of activities to stimulate all areas of development: physical, cognitive, social, and emotional.

Play. Children may creatively build with blocks, use art materials, or dress up in the housekeeping corner. After experimenting with scribbles, preschoolers begin to paint and draw recognizable forms and faces.

Literacy Activities. During the preschool years, children are gaining knowledge and skills that will eventually help them write and read effectively. They use crayons, pencils, and markers to write their names.

Children are encouraged to express their ideas as they talk among themselves. This fluency in language is essential for learning to read later on. Children need to know many words in order to understand the words they read. Preschoolers especially enjoy poetry and songs that have rhyming words.

Books are readily available in preschools, and listening to stories is a favorite activity for almost everyone. Literacy skills are emerging even as the child turns the pages of a book or tells about a home event from memory.

Science activities. Some preschool activities build on the children's growing curiosity about the world around them. They often do simple science projects such as planting seeds or beans and watching them sprout.

Physical activities. Except in very bad weather, the children go outdoors for part of each day. There is a variety of equipment on the playground for developing large motor skills. Running, climbing, and other vigorous activities are encouraged.

Caring for oneself. Children in preschools become quite self-sufficient in caring for themselves when eating, drinking, going to the toilet, and washing their hands. They gain self-esteem by taking care of their own needs "all by myself," as they frequently say.

Understanding others. A preschool program offers opportunities for interacting and learning how to get along with others. Interpersonal skills are practiced every day. Social conversation is extensive. If a conflict occurs, children are helped to develop negotiating skills to solve the problem through verbal rather than physical means.

◆ ◆ *Self-Esteem* ◆ ◆

When a child continues to be upset and fearful about going to preschool, the child may lack self-confidence and a feeling of independence. If the parents scold or belittle the child, he or she may become more insecure. Instead, parents should encourage the child to develop skills that will lead to greater confidence and independence.

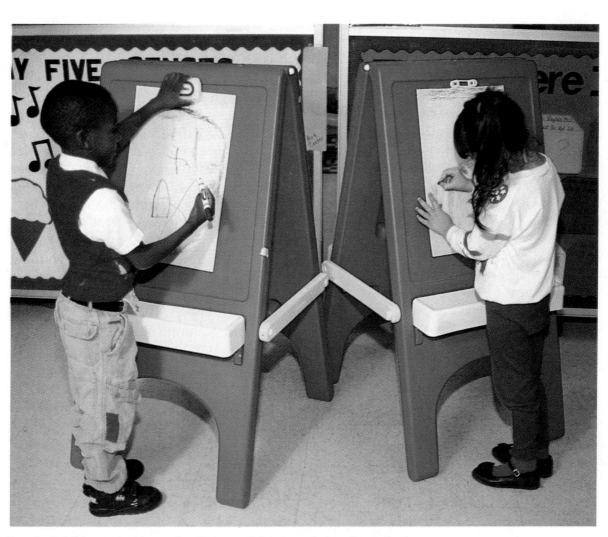

Preschool children enjoy expressing their creativity through drawing and painting activities.

Activity. Divide class into small groups. Have each group prepare an activity or game in one of the following areas: creative play, literacy, science, physical activity, caring for oneself, or understanding others. Have groups present their activity or game to the class.

Discuss. What concepts could preschoolers learn from having one or more animals in the classroom?

❖ Kindergartens

Kindergarten is a class or school for children who are about five years of age. In most states, kindergarten is not compulsory. The earliest age of compulsory school attendance is usually seven years. States differ on exactly when the fifth birthday must fall to permit children to enroll in kindergartens in public schools. In some states, children must be five by September 1. In others, the deadline is as late as January 1. This means that some children are able to start kindergarten when they are four years old. Private kindergartens set their own age requirements.

More than 95 percent of all children attend kindergarten, even in states where attendance is not compulsory. Each state sets its own educational requirements for teachers. Generally, kindergarten teachers have the same teaching certificate that elementary teachers have.

For many years, the standard kindergarten held half-day sessions. Children went either in the morning or in the afternoon. In many communities, the kindergarten schedule is now similar in length to that of the elementary grades. Such a regular school-day schedule gives kindergartners opportunities for more learning experiences. It also helps parents who work full-time because fewer hours of supplemental child care are necessary.

The Kindergarten Classroom

In a high-quality kindergarten, the classroom bulletin boards and shelves are arranged with interesting things to look at and wonder about. Books are prominently displayed and regularly read aloud. Experience charts on the wall tell of recent trips, projects, or science experiments. Stories that children have dictated to the teacher appear on the chalkboard. Children's drawings, paintings, collages, and other works are also posted around the room.

Much of the learning in a high-quality kindergarten takes place in **learning centers** set up around the classroom. Each center contains supplies and enough room for a few children to work independently or together. For example, the children may work with computers, finger paints, or building blocks. Experimenting with various materials encourages children's curiosity and creativity.

Children are usually free to move in and out of the different learning centers. They direct their own exploration and learning within each center. Teachers are close by to answer questions and increase understanding. They also ask questions to encourage thinking skills.

Types of Kindergarten Activities

In a high-quality kindergarten, planned activities contribute to all areas of development: physical, cognitive, emotional, and social. Many of the activities are the same as those enjoyed by children in preschool. However, these activities are altered to match the children's increasing growth and development.

Kindergartners work both in groups and alone. However, the solitary play in kindergarten is different from that in younger groups. Now children have skills for group play, yet they sometimes choose to work or play alone. They have longer interest spans and can concentrate on projects for a longer period of time.

Show-and-tell. In the activity known as show-and-tell, children bring something to class and relate their experience with it or describe it to classmates. In this activity, children develop skills in speaking and in listening to others.

Social interaction activities. Children practice interpersonal skills as they engage in dramatic play and talk over their interests and concerns. In the course of such play, they learn to be leaders and followers. They also practice getting along with each other in a friendly environment.

Literacy activities. Literacy activities include reading, writing, and speaking activities.

- Using many books for information and for fun helps motivate children to learn to read.
- Seeing words grouped in phrases or sentences begins training the eyes to read.
- Relating pictures to the words on a page helps children recognize the relationship between the two.
- Recognizing names on pictures, name tags, and charts gives children practice in reading their own names and those of their friends.
- Recognizing shapes, sizes, likenesses, and differences in art and other activities helps children identify letters. During reading activities, the teacher points out letters that are large or small, curved or straight, the same or different.

- Writing their names on artwork in manuscript or print letters encourages the development of writing skills.
- Orally relating their experiences builds a speaking vocabulary. This helps children understand the written vocabulary in stories.

Mathematics activities. Mathematics is an important part of many kindergarten activities. Children can keep their own height and weight charts. They can count the number of cartons of milk needed for a snack or the number of sandwiches needed for a picnic. Numbers are related to the calendar, temperature, time, and money.

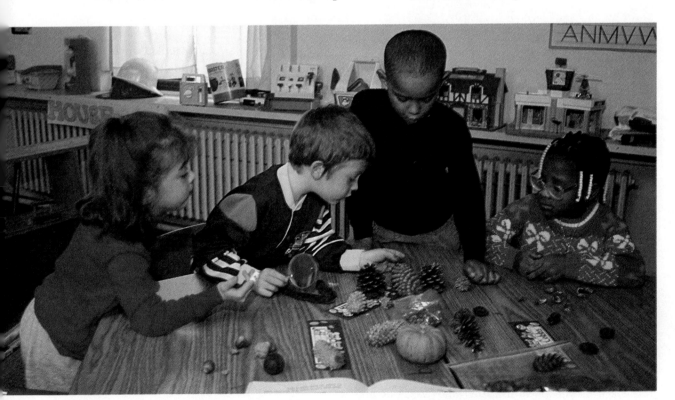

These kindergartners are learning about pine cones and other items from nature in their science learning center.

Discuss. Why do preschool and kindergarten programs change activities frequently in their daily schedule?
Activity. Divide class into small groups. Have each group create a folder game which would teach a math concept to kinder- gartners. (using coins to buy a 50c item; matching written and numerical numbers such as four=4; placing 1, 2, 3, 4 scoops of ice cream on a cone)

Blocks help children discover mathematical relationships and equivalents. For example, as they build something, they discover they need to use just the right blocks to fit their structure. Blocks can also be used for measuring.

Science experiments. Kindergartners love to grow plants. They may grow pots of beans or flowers. In the spring, they can plant outdoor vegetable or flower gardens. In the fall, children can notice leaves change color and pick dry weeds for bouquets.

Other science projects often involve animals. Children can learn how to be gentle with small animals. They may learn what foods animals like to eat and how animals

enjoy exercising. Children can observe animals on field trips to zoos and farms.

Additional science activities often center around physical forces or machinery. Air, wind, gravity, magnetism, temperature, and weather can be explored through observations and experiments.

Kindergartners enjoy using hand tools such as hammers, pliers, and screwdrivers. They also like to watch street repairs and building construction. They enjoy visits to airports, railroad and bus stations, and boat docks.

Understanding oneself. By age five, children have a concept of self and know that they are different from others. They are developing their self-esteem as they participate in school activities and make friends. Teachers and parents can work together to help children achieve success and develop high self-esteem.

Caring for oneself. Gradually, kindergartners are expected to take care of their personal needs and their belongings. Some activities relate to personal hygiene and health. Others involve learning to use zippers, tie shoes, pull on boots, and dress themselves.

The children also learn about safety in the home, school, streets, and car. They may have safety drills for fire, tornadoes, and earthquakes. They practice reciting their address and telephone number. They learn to dial 911 or the operator for help in an emergency.

Understanding the community. The community, including its people, workers, institutions, and celebrations, provides many opportunities to teach children about the culture in which they live. Kindergarten children often take field trips to various places in the community. There they become acquainted with workers in the fire station, post office, gas station, grocery store, or health clinic.

A visit to the fire station enables young children to learn about the equipment that firefighters use. This helps children learn about their community, its workers, and the jobs they do.

Activity. Have students plan a workbench project for kindergartners. What safety rules and supervision would be needed? **Problem Solving.** Have students suggest activities that would help kindergartners develop an understanding of themselves and others.

Activity. Divide class into small groups. Have each group plan a local trip for a kindergarten class that would help children learn more about your community.

Enrichment Activities

Many schools offer enrichment in the form of extracurricular activities. Families, community centers, libraries, and religious organizations also provide enrichment activities. Some of these activities help children develop athletic or musical skills. Others focus on group involvement and leadership skills.

Following are some of the activities available in many communities.

- **Swimming.** Swimming is a survival skill that everyone should learn. Many communities offer free or low-cost lessons for kindergarten and school-age children at a local pool or lake. Classes are sometimes available for three- and four-year-olds. The Red Cross and YMCA/YWCAs sponsor many swimming programs.

- **Little League and other sports.** Most communities have sports programs for boys and girls, starting in elementary school. These often include soccer, baseball and softball, football, basketball, wrestling, and ice hockey. Registration fees are usually required. The goals should be to have fun and develop motor skills.

- **Music lessons.** Music lessons must usually wait until children learn to read. Musical notes are symbols similar to the letters of the alphabet. Early experiences with listening to music and singing songs prepare children for taking music lessons. Although schools often offer some music activities, private music lessons must be paid for by parents.

- **Gymnastics.** Gymnastics is offered in some community centers at minimum cost. Classes are often available for children of all ages. Private gymnastics schools also offer programs in many communities.

Many communities offer sports programs for boys and girls. These programs should emphasize skill development and sportsmanship, rather than winning.

- **Dance lessons.** Preschool and school-age children can be involved in dance programs offered by community groups or private dance studios. Lessons in ballet, tap, and modern dance are usually available. Fees vary widely. Many programs end the year with a dance recital for parents, relatives, and friends.

- **Scouts and 4-H Club.** Youth groups, such as scouts and 4-H, exist in most communities. They provide opportunities for a wide variety of activities for both boys and girls. These organizations also develop citizenship and leadership skills. Most troops and clubs meet once a week during the school year. Many offer special summertime activities, such as camping or visits to county fairs. Generally, these organizations are for children eight years of age and older. Most have modest membership fees.

✦ Avoiding Overscheduling

Some children are so busy going from activity to activity that they have little time to explore on their own. On Monday, it is piano lessons. Tuesdays are for a computer class. Scouts meet on Wednesday. Thursday is reserved for gymnastics. On Friday the soccer team practices for Saturday's game.

◆ *Health & Safety* ◆

Safe Play

For young children, a playground is an adventure. It is a place for them to have fun, explore new skills, and use their boundless energy.

Unfortunately, a playground is not always a safe place. Each year more than 250,000 children are treated in hospital emergency rooms for playground injuries. Parents, teachers, and other caregivers should always supervise young children on a playground. Adults should also check on the safety of the playground.

The U.S. Consumer Products Safety Commission has established some guidelines to help one judge the safety of a playground.

- Playground equipment should never be placed on a hard surface, such as asphalt or cement.

- All equipment should be installed at least 6 feet from any fences or walls.

- Equipment should have no sharp edges or open S-type hooks. These can catch on children's clothing.

- Rings, tubes, and similar round spaces should be smaller than 5 inches or larger than 10 inches. Otherwise, children might get their head caught in the space.

- Swing seats should be made from soft materials, such as rubber or canvas. Ideally, the swings should be in their own fenced-in enclosure.

- If a slide is more than 4 feet high, there should be a barrier at the top that is at least 30 inches high. This will help prevent falls. Slides that are more than 10 feet tall should be avoided. Serious injury could result if a child fell from a slide this high.

- Seesaws should be used only when both riders are closely matched in weight. Children should be taught not to jump off the seesaw until their partner is ready.

Activity. Have students gather information about enrichment activities for children that are available in your community. Ask them to prepare a brochure or chart listing the activities, location, sponsor, age groups, and fees.

Discuss. What are the pros and cons of team sports during the school-age years?

Although parents may want to provide many enrichment activities for their children, overscheduling can be very stressful. Children who are experiencing stress may develop anxiety, feelings of inadequacy, or stomachaches.

Child development experts say that children need time to play and enjoy life. They need to daydream over a book, kick a ball around, make mud pies, or whistle a tune. Although children should be encouraged to explore new activities, they should not be pushed too hard to achieve success. Childhood ought to be a time of exploration rather than achievement.

For parents who work outside the home, organized after-school activities are usually a better alternative for children than returning to an empty home and watching television. However, parents should monitor their children's activities. They should check to be sure the children are benefiting emotionally, as well as physically and socially, from their activities. If a child feels too hurried or over-scheduled, cutbacks are in order.

DECISIONS ◆ ◆ DECISIONS

Todd is eight years old. He has always been outgoing and enthusiastic about many activities. He is involved in basketball and swimming. He is taking piano lessons and a drama course. Lately, however, Todd has been complaining of being tired and having stomachaches. Yesterday, he refused to go to basketball practice. Today, when his parents talked with him about taking a special computer course, Todd ran out of the room. Do you think Todd's parents should be concerned about his behavior? Why or why not?

Parental Interest and Involvement

Parents can enjoy and share in their child's experience with early childhood education. This sharing makes the child's own experience even richer.

All high-quality schools welcome parental involvement. Parents should feel welcome to visit their child's classroom at any time. If a school will not permit parents to visit without an appointment, parents should ask, "What is going on that you don't want us to see?"

❖ Showing Interest

Parents can make their child's learning experience more enjoyable by showing a genuine interest in what the child is doing. When asked, "What did you do today?" some children answer, "Nothing." Others say, "We just played." Still others may tell about something that happened several days earlier or perhaps about something that did not happen at all. Parents will learn more if they relax and let things come out during the course of the evening. Children need practice in describing experiences, so parents need to be patient with early attempts that often seem sketchy.

Parents can arrange a special bulletin board or space on the wall or refrigerator for hanging drawings and paintings their child brings home from school. All children feel proud when parents display their artwork.

❖ Becoming Involved

High-quality early childhood education programs make efforts to involve parents in a variety of ways. They may ask all parents to join a parents' organization. In parent cooperatives, parents are usually involved in mak-

Activity. Have students write a short essay on the advantages or disadvantages of organized after-school activities for children. **Reference.** See pages 333–334 for more information about stress and children.

Discuss. Did your parents display any of your artwork or schoolwork in your home? If so, where? Can you remember how you felt seeing your work on display?

Most schools have teacher-parent conferences once or twice during the school term. Because parents and teachers often see different aspects of a child's personality, such conferences sometimes help both understand the child better.

❖ Easing Transitions

Most children go through a transition stage between schools from time to time. The first major transition comes between preschool and kindergarten. Many kindergartens hold an exploration day in the spring. The children visit the kindergarten classroom and meet the teacher. They learn where materials are kept and the location of the bathroom. The visit helps to ease any concern or fear the children may have about starting kindergarten. However, many children, lacking the understanding of time, believe that they will start kindergarten immediately after the visit.

Near the end of the kindergarten year, children look forward to visiting the first-grade classroom. The teacher describes the many new activities that the children will participate in during first grade. Parents may also be invited to meet with the first-grade teacher. They can discuss the expectations and goals for first grade.

During the summer, parents can help ease the transition from preschool to kindergarten or from kindergarten to first grade. One way of doing this is by helping the child feel ready for a new level of experiences. A parent can give compliments such as "You know how to take care of your clothes, so I think you're ready to go to school."

During times of transition, parents should not stress what children must know or what they can and cannot do in school. This can worry children unnecessarily about how to act and how other children will treat them. Teachers are trained to help children adjust to the school routine.

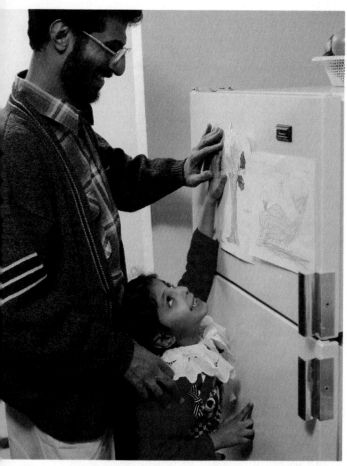

Children enjoy seeing their art work on display in their home. This encourages their self-esteem and lets them know that their activities are recognized by the family.

ing decisions about school policy. Boards of directors of some schools include parents as either voting or nonvoting members.

Attending school events is another way to become involved in children's activities. Sometimes parents are invited to attend a special program with the children. At other times parents can volunteer to assist the teacher on field trips.

Many schools hold parents' workshops once or twice a year. In such workshops, parents come to the classrooms and actually work with the children's materials. Teachers explain what kinds of learning they expect children to gain from these materials.

Emphasize. Parents should set aside a regular time when their child can talk about his or her activities. This might be while going for a walk or ride, having a snack, or getting ready for bed.

Reference. See page 518 for information about helping children adjust to a family move.

CHAPTER 29 REVIEW

Summary

- Most early childhood education programs are offered for a few hours one or more days a week.
- Types of early childhood education programs include infant-parent classes, play groups, various types of preschools, and kindergartens.
- Preschools and kindergartens provide a variety of activities ranging from play, literacy, science, and mathematics activities to caring for oneself and learning about others.
- Enrichment activities help children develop skills in athletics, music, dance, leadership, and citizenship.
- Parents should show an interest in their children's early childhood education experiences and become involved in some way in the activities.

Questions

p. 551   1. For whom are early childhood education programs most appropriate? Why?

p. 553   2. Name four types of preschools. What is one advantage of each?

p. 554   3. What is Head Start?

p. 556   4. How might children develop literacy skills in a preschool or kindergarten program?

p. 558   5. What are learning centers?

p. 562   6. Why should parents not overschedule children in enrichment activities?

7. How can parents become involved in their children's early childhood education experiences?   p. 563

8. How might parents ease a child's transition from preschool to kindergarten?   p. 564

Activities

1. Research early childhood education programs that are available in your community. Gather information about infant-parent classes and preschools, such as type of program, cost, and location. Report your findings to the class.

2. Plan a science activity for a kindergarten program.

3. Determine what percentage of your classmates attended a kindergarten. What do they remember most about the experience?

Think About

1. Why do you think kindergarten attendance is not mandatory in most states? Why do most children attend such programs anyway?

2. In what kinds of extracurricular or other enrichment activities have you participated? What benefits do you feel you have gained from them?

Reference. See the Teacher's Manual in the front of the Teacher's Annotated Edition for complete answers to the chapter review questions.

565

Exploring Careers in Child Care and Other Occupations

Objectives

This chapter will help you to:

- List some advantages and disadvantages of child care careers.
- Identify ways to learn more about various occupations.
- Describe the steps involved in finding and applying for a job.
- Discuss the personal characteristics that contribute to success on the job.

Vocabulary

entrepreneur
parent helper
resume
references
fringe benefits

Astrid Blake has worked as a child care aide in an infant care center for over a year. Although the work can be tiring, she loves taking care of the children in her charge. She has seen them grow and develop over the months. Some are learning to sit up; others are learning to crawl. One child started walking at eleven months of age, while a fourteen-month-old took his first steps yesterday. Every day brings something new!

Astrid is taking courses in child care and business management at a community college. She hopes someday to open her own child care center.

Now Astrid sees eight-month-old Ellen arriving at the center with her mother. Ellen's eyes light up when she sees her caregiver. Ellen has been in Astrid's infant group since she was three months old. She smiles and wiggles in anticipation as Astrid welcomes her warmly and takes her in her arms.

Astrid spends a few minutes talking with Ellen's mother, exchanging information about Ellen's development. Ellen's mother kisses the baby good-bye and leaves for work. She is confident of the nurturing that Astrid will give Ellen throughout the day.

Opportunities for Caregivers

The demand for caregivers and teachers of infants and young children has been growing. It is expected to continue to grow in the years ahead. Much of this demand is a result of economic reality: more than 50 percent of mothers of one- through five-year-olds are presently employed outside the home. A growing proportion of these women are heads of one-parent households. They include divorced, widowed, and unmarried mothers.

Much of the growing demand for care of young children will be filled by center-based programs, as described in Chapter 28. These centers will need teachers and aides. Child care aides assist the teacher in carrying out the day-to-day activities that help children grow and develop.

Other parents will prefer family care for their children, as in family child care homes. About 22 percent of children of working parents are cared for in such homes.

Many communities are developing school-age child care programs. These are held in schools, child care centers, and family child care homes. The programs provide care for school-age children whose parents must be at work during hours when schools are not in session.

Many school systems are extending their kindergartens from half to full days. Such a change increases the demand for kindergarten teachers nearly 100 percent.

In addition, some school districts are initiating prekindergarten programs for four-year-olds. These programs are similar to Head Start, the federally funded program for economically disadvantaged young children. Some of these preschools are for at-risk children who are developmentally delayed or economically deprived. Head Start itself is expected to continue and perhaps even to grow because of its nationwide popularity.

Public schools are now required to provide education to children with a disability and those with other special needs. (Previously, these children were often excluded from public schools.) This increases the demand for people trained to work with such children. It also increases the need for entry-level workers who can give one-on-one attention to these children.

Many parents are willing to pay for other services as their children grow older. These services include music or art lessons, sports training, and tutoring.

Some occupations offer opportunities to be an **entrepreneur** (ohn-truh-pruh-NUR). This is a person who starts and manages his or her own business. Being an entrepreneur can be exciting and rewarding. As your own boss, you set your own goals and standards. You may also establish your own hours. You get to keep the profits that the business makes. However, being an entrepreneur also involves many challenges and risks. You need to know how to manage a small business. This requires financial planning. You are

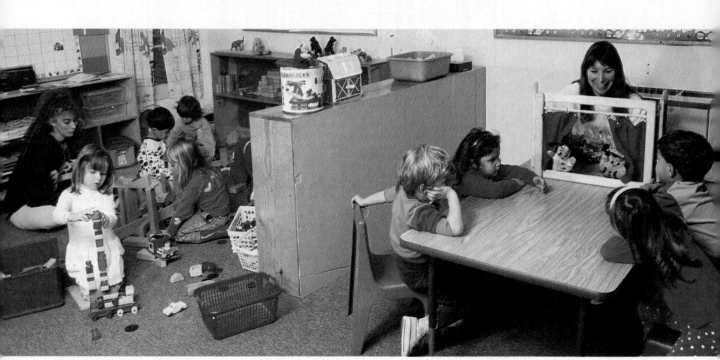

Job opportunities in the field of child care are expected to grow in the coming years.

Activity. Invite one or more people in some type of child-related career to talk about their job responsibilities, their educational background and training, and the positive and negative aspects of their job.

Activity. Have students compile a list of recent books and magazine articles that discuss careers in child-related areas.

responsible for the daily operation of the business. If the business is not successful, you can lose all the money you have invested.

Clearly, the opportunities for working with children are numerous and varied. All prospects indicate that the demand for such services will continue to grow in the years ahead.

Every career will have certain advantages and disadvantages. It helps to ask, "What can I expect in a career that serves children?"

◆◆ Advantages of Child Care Careers

Here are just some of the advantages of child care careers.

- **On-the-job learning.** You can continue to learn about children and their development while actually working with them, their parents, and other child care professionals.
- **Never boring.** Children change from moment to moment. Challenging situations present themselves constantly.
- **Opportunity to fill a real need.** Many parents rely on child care services for their children. Without such services, these parents would be unable to hold a job.
- **Daily interaction with people.** You can communicate on a person-to-person basis with staff members, parents, and children every day.
- **Practical application of knowledge.** You are able to apply your knowledge and understanding of physical, cognitive, emotional, and social development to daily interactions with children.
- **Opportunity to strengthen families.** By working with both children and parents, you can help promote understanding and communication within families.

- **Flexible schedule.** Many jobs offer flexible work schedules, enabling you to attend classes or care for your own children.
- **Opportunity for advancement.** Many jobs provide opportunities to move from an entry-level position to positions with increasing responsibilities.
- **Application of job experience to your own family life.** You can gain valuable skills to use with your own children and family.
- **Worldwide professional opportunities.** Professional organizations such as the National Association for the Education of Young Children (NAEYC) are active in the United States and other countries.

◆◆ Disadvantages of Child Care Careers

Along with the many advantages of careers in child care, there are some potential disadvantages.

- **Low paying.** Many of the jobs, especially entry-level ones, are low paying. This is true despite the fact that the workers have many responsibilities.
- **Physically demanding.** Working with active children all day requires a great deal of physical energy.
- **Limited interaction with adults.** Some jobs involve working almost exclusively with children and thus offer little contact with parents or other adults.
- **Need for patience.** Dealing with children and solving problems require a great deal of patience.
- **Lack of appreciation.** Unfortunately, some people consider child care workers to be babysitters. Such people do not understand or appreciate the responsibilities and skills involved in high-quality child care.

Activity. Have students use the *Occupational Encyclopedia* to research entry-level salaries for the careers that interest them most. What might be possible stages of advancement? Ask students to compile their findings in a report or chart.

Activity. Have FHA sponsor a Career Day and invite numerous people to talk with students about their careers.

Career Possibilities with Children

Education-Related Careers

Aide or assistant in
    Child care centers
    Infant care centers
    Elementary schools
    Recreation centers
    YWCAs and YMCAs
    Public libraries
Infant caregiver
Babysitter
Family child care provider
Nursery school teacher
Child care center teacher
Kindergarten teacher
Elementary school teacher

School music teacher
Special education teacher
Religious education director
Social worker
Librarian in school or children's library
Children's storyteller or puppeteer
Home economics teacher
4-H agent
Children's art instructor
Children's music teacher
Children's swimming instructor
Children's gymnastics or dance teacher
Recreation coach
Recreation center director
School principal
Superintendent of schools
College teacher of child development, child psychology, or early childhood education
College teacher of elementary education, secondary education, home economics education, or special education
Researcher in child development, psychology, or education

Health-Related Careers

Receptionist in hospital, clinic, or doctor's office
Nurse's aide in pediatrics
Registered pediatric nurse
Maternity nurse or nurse-midwife
Medical technician
Family physician
Pediatrician
Hospital playroom teacher
Physical therapist
Nutritionist
Dietitian for child care program
Dentist
Dental assistant
Researcher in health
Food and nutrition researcher

Art- and Design-Related Careers

Writer or artist of children's books
Children's photographer
Designer of children's clothing
Designer of toys
Designer or architect of child care centers
Architect of school designs
Designer of equipment for schools and child care centers
Designer of playgrounds and recreation centers
Architect of home designs
Production worker, writer, or consultant for children's television programming
Children's theater worker
Singer or writer of songs for children
Director of children's museum

Mental Health-Related Careers

Camp counselor
Aide to children with disabilities
Foster parent
Probation officer
School social worker
Child care licensing officer
Friend-of-the-court counselor
Houseparent in halfway house or
    institution
Occupational therapist
Mental health aide
Child psychologist or psychiatrist

Business-Related Careers

Salesperson or owner of toy store
Salesperson or owner of children's
    clothing store
Salesperson or owner of children's
    bookstore
Doll maker
Children's party caterer
Toy builder or repairer
Developer of baby food
Entertainer for children's parties
Maker of children's clothing
Children's television director or producer
Children's hairstylist

Food-Related Careers

Child care center cook
School lunchroom worker
School dietitian
Camp cook
Caterer for children's parties
Hospital pediatric dietitian

Volunteer Jobs

Religious organization aide
4-H junior leader
Scout patrol leader or troop leader
Hospital or clinic volunteer
Big Brother or Big Sister volunteer
Children's museum guide
Head Start aide
Preschool aide
Children's library aide
Little League coach
Children's tutor

Thinking About a Career

Choosing a career requires planning and decision making. Getting a good education is the important first step. It also helps to gain work experience in a variety of part-time jobs while you are still in high school. These can allow you to find out what you really enjoy and do well. On-the-job experience also helps you develop important work habits such as punctuality and dependability. You learn how to follow directions and complete tasks. Doing volunteer work is still another way to discover your interests and talents and learn about various careers.

◆ Discovering Your Interests and Talents

Knowing what your interests and talents are will help you find work you will enjoy and can perform successfully. Start by taking an inventory of yourself. Make a list of things you like doing in your spare time. End this list with things you think you would like to do but have not yet had a chance to try.

Make another list of your personality traits. Do you prefer working alone or on a team? Do you enjoy making decisions? Are you patient? Do you work well under pressure? Would you like to work in an office or outdoors?

A third list should focus on your talents. Among these may be writing, working with your hands, solving puzzles, settling disputes, or encouraging others to talk. You may even have some talents you have not yet discovered. One way to find out about these is to try new activities.

Look over your lists carefully to see if you can spot any patterns. For example, if you enjoy being with people and can communicate your ideas well, you might enjoy teach-

ing, public relations work, or management. Think about the kinds of skills you have rather than the ways you may be using them right now. This is a good exercise whether you plan to look for a job right after high school or to go on for further education.

Show your lists to a teacher, a guidance counselor, your parents, or a friend. Your guidance counselor is there to discuss your future with you and perhaps suggest ideas that may be new to you. Your school's guidance office probably has tests that can help you identify your strong points. Ultimately, though, you are the one to decide what your strengths are and what you enjoy.

◆ Learning About Various Occupations

The next step is to find out about occupations that match your interests and abilities. Your school's guidance office or library may have books and pamphlets about careers. Ask your guidance counselor or librarian to help you find these and other resources. The *Occupational Outlook Handbook* and *Encyclopedia of Careers and Vocational Guidance* are two books that can aid you in your search.

Public libraries usually have numerous publications on various careers, including those in child care. Bookstores sell many inexpensive paperback books about children, child care, child psychology, and education. Popular magazines and newspapers often carry articles on children, too.

If you think a child care career may be right for you, discuss ideas from books and articles with your friends, parents, teachers, supervisors, and the parents of young children. Talk to people who work in child-related occupations. Ask them about their daily activities on the job, the requirements for getting the job, and the opportunities to advance. Many schools and communities

Activity. Ask students to identify the characteristics they perceive to be their strengths and weaknesses from the "ABCs of a Capable Caregiver" on page 578. Encourage them to begin to work on any weaknesses, preferably one or two at a time.

Activity. Have students look up the following terms in the dictionary: *entry-level*, *paraprofessional*, and *professional*. Ask them to relate the terms to careers in child care.

DECISIONS ◆ ◆ DECISIONS

Julio has been studying music for several years. He sings and plays the piano and guitar. He likes his job at the local Head Start program, but he would also like to put his other talents and interests to work. What are some options for Julio that include both music and the care and education of children?

sponsor a career day, when representatives of various career areas are on hand with information for students.

You may find that you will need more education or training to pursue a career in your chosen field. Some child-related occupations require only minimal training. Others require college or higher-level degrees. For example, a child care aide usually needs a high school diploma. A teacher needs a college degree and a teaching certificate. A pediatrician needs a medical degree plus an internship and residency in a hospital.

◆◆ Trying out the Role of Caregiver

Many part-time jobs and volunteer activities allow you to learn more about a career while working with a trained professional. With such experience, you will be better able to decide whether a career in child care is right for you. This may also give you a firmer basis for making decisions about parenting.

Here are some possible ways to get experience in caring for children.

- Play with or read to children whenever an opportunity arises.
- Volunteer to help in a children's library, recreational program, or hospital pediatric ward.
- Become a teacher of young children in your church or synagogue. Volunteer to help in the nursery during religious services.
- Volunteer to help an elementary or early childhood education teacher after school.
- Babysit with children of friends and neighbors.
- Tutor a child who needs special help in developing physical or academic skills.
- Get a job in the toy department or the children's clothing section of a store.

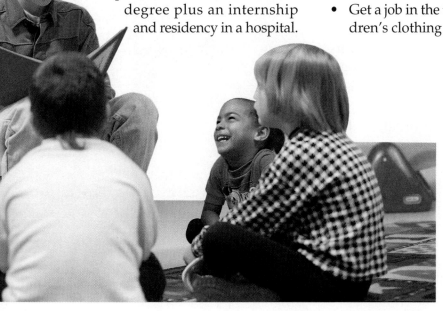

Volunteer jobs can help you learn whether you like working with children.

Discuss. Why is it important to have some hands-on experience with children before preparing for a career in a child-care field? **Activity.** Have students find out what organizations or agencies in your community have volunteers who work with children.

Problem Solving. Divide the class into small groups. Have each group make a list of all the ways that teenagers in your community can gain experience with children. Have groups share their lists.

As you work with children, take every opportunity to learn more about them. Ask parents and caregivers questions. Learn about the sponsoring organizations for which you work. Each agency or organization offers a future career opportunity to work with children.

Be sure to keep records of your part-time jobs and volunteer activities. These can give future employers a sense of your ability to do certain work, follow schedules, assist coworkers, and give of yourself.

Babysitters and Parent Helpers

If you work as a babysitter or parent helper, you can gain valuable child care experience. A **parent helper** does work similar to a babysitter's, but the work is usually done while a parent is in the home.

When you begin working for a family, try to get to know the children ahead of time. If you will be babysitting, ask the parents if you can come to their home once or twice while they are there. If this is not possible, try to arrive a half-hour early the first few times you babysit. Get to know the parents as well as the children. Understand and respect the parents' ideas about child rearing, and follow their instructions.

When you babysit, make sure you ask a parent to write down the following information:

- The telephone number or numbers where a parent can be reached.

- The number of the doctor or hospital to call in case of an emergency.

- A signed note from the parent giving permission for the children to receive emergency medical care in the parent's absence.

- The telephone number of a close relative or friend, in case a parent cannot be reached.

- The approximate time the parent or parents expect to be home.

- The routine the parent would like you to follow with the children at mealtime, bath time, and bedtime.

- Whether the children are allowed to watch television, how long each child may watch, and what each one's favorite stories and games are.

Be sure your own parents know where you are and have the telephone number and name of the people for whom you are babysitting. Then they can contact you if there is an emergency or can check if you do not return when they expect you. It is not a good idea to have your friends telephone or visit you on the job. They will distract you from your child care responsibilities.

Babysitting jobs provide valuable child care experience. Whether caring for a baby or a school-age child, you are responsible for the child's welfare and safety.

Child Care Center Aides

If you are taking a child care course, you may observe and assist in a child care center or early childhood education program as part of your course work. As a child care aide, you will follow the teacher's instructions in working with the children. The teacher will probably need your help in planning the program and conferring with parents. In fact, an effective aide extends the teacher's time and energy.

The following suggestions can help you become a successful aide.

- Spend some time with the lead teacher. Ask that person to explain whenever possible what she or he is doing, step-by-step. Listen carefully, watch closely, and take notes. The opportunities for such discussion and demonstration may be few, but they will be very helpful.

- Watch and listen to how the teacher directs the children's activities and behavior. Follow her or his example. Remember that children get confused if different caregivers handle them in different ways. Then they may end up feeling uncomfortable during the time they are at the center.

- Get acquainted with the children, and show that you enjoy their successes and progress. In your position, you will have a front-row seat for watching young lives unfold. You will notice that each child is special and different from the others.

- Apply what you know about child development in interpreting the children's behavior and working with them. Practice encouraging the children to try to do a task independently. Perhaps you can think of new games to play with them.

- Give warm, affectionate hugs. Be available when a child wants to sit on your lap to rock or to listen to a story.

- Be calm and professional when the going

Aides assist teachers in child care centers and early childhood education programs.

gets rough—when all at once one child throws a tantrum, another spills milk, and still another needs a diaper change. A professional caregiver is cool under pressure, helping everyone feel confident.

- Practice communicating with children in a positive way. Keep learning how to deal effectively with parents and coworkers.

- Be prepared to become tired and frustrated at times. Discuss any difficulties openly with your coworkers. Together you can probably find the causes of most problems and some possible solutions.

- Share with parents their children's progress and successes. Remember that many things parents discuss with caregivers should be kept confidential.

Discuss. What characteristics would help a teenager be a successful aide in a child care program?

Activity. Divide class into small groups. Have each group create a game or activity to play with children in a child care center. Ask each group to demonstrate their activity.

ABCs of a Capable Caregiver

Each day, a successful caregiver needs many of the personality characteristics listed below.

Alert to all children for whom one is responsible and alert to the tasks that need to be done.

Bright, using fast thinking and sound reasoning.

Calm and not easily flustered when conflicts or competing tasks arise.

Dependable in following rules and directions.

Enthusiastic about working with children and parents.

Fun-loving, enjoying children and laughing easily with them.

Generous with love, ideas, and energy, sharing them readily with children, parents, and coworkers.

Healthy in both mind and body, with energy to work steadily for the hours required.

Industrious, working energetically at tasks and doing them willingly without prodding or pressure.

Just and fair to all children, parents, and coworkers regardless of race, religion, gender, age, income level, or disability.

Knowledgeable about the developmental stages of children.

Loving to children in one's care.

Mature for one's age and experience.

Neat and clean in appearance.

Organized on the job and at home so work gets done with a minimum of stress and confusion.

Punctual in arriving at work and in keeping activities on schedule.

Quick to respond to the needs of children, parents, and staff.

Resourceful, able to figure out solutions to problems and to find creative uses for materials.

Strong in body, with stamina for the required work.

Thoughtful of others, seeing the children's point of view and responding to their feelings and needs.

Understanding of children's emotions and self-esteem.

Venturesome in new ideas and new approaches to working with children.

Witty, using humor in dealing with children and others.

(E)**X**cited and optimistic about the future.

Yearning to be helpful to others.

Zealous for children's rights and causes.

Finding Job Openings

Finding the right job is not always easy. It takes a planned strategy plus self-confidence, enthusiasm, hard work, know-how, and sometimes luck. When you are seriously looking for a job, you should follow every possible lead.

Contact every person you can think of who might know of a job opening in your area of interest. Talk to relatives, friends who are working, members of any clubs or groups to which you belong, your school counselor, and your teachers.

Look in the classified section of local newspapers. Sunday newspapers usually have the largest number of "help wanted" ads. Do not limit your search to one job title. There may be several names for one position.

A good advertisement lists the type of work, the location, the wage or salary, the qualifications needed, and an address or a telephone number. Answer such ads quickly because many people may be applying for the same opening.

Check to see whether your school has a job placement service. Employers sometimes contact schools when they are trying to fill an open position. Visit the placement service at a local college. It may have a bulletin board with job listings. Similar listings can sometimes be found on library and supermarket bulletin boards.

Many cities have established child care resource and referral services. Some list jobs for caregivers and teachers, especially substitute jobs. Call them to see whether they will put your name and address on a list of potential employees.

Employment agencies match people to job openings. Find out what you can about an agency before you visit it. Most agencies charge a fee if you accept a job they have

The help wanted section of the newspaper may list child-related job opportunities under several different titles.

found for you. Before you sign anything, make sure you know who pays the fee—you or your new employer. This is important, because the fee may be as much as 15 percent of the yearly starting salary. Remember, you are under no obligation to go to an interview or accept a position the agency has found for you if the job does not interest you.

Government agencies, such as state employment offices and the federal Civil Service Commission, have a wide range of job listings. For more information, look in the telephone book in the special sections that give state government and U.S. government listings. You can also write to the U.S. Civil Service Commission, Washington, D.C. 20415.

Finally, you do not have to wait for a job opening before you approach a prospective employer. You may contact employers directly whether or not they have any positions immediately available. Your first contact can be a letter, a telephone call, or a visit. Make your inquiry to the supervisor in charge of the area in which you are interested. If you do not know that person's name, ask for the person by title—for example, the director of the center. Sometimes you may be referred to the personnel office.

Around the World

Education and Our American Neighbors

Have you ever thought about what it would be like to go to school in another country? Some things would seem very familiar, while others would seem very different.

In Canada, each province and territory is responsible for its own schools. In some provinces, such as Ontario and Alberta, most students attend public schools. These schools are much like the schools in the United States. The money to run the schools comes from local taxes and taxes paid to the provincial government. The schools are governed by local school boards. In other provinces, such as Quebec and Newfoundland, there are very few public schools. Most schools are operated by religious groups. In some parts of Canada, particularly in areas populated by Native Americans and Inuits (Eskimos), the schools are operated by the federal government.

In Canada, everyone must go to school until the age of fifteen or sixteen. In some areas, the French language is used in the schools. In other areas, English is used and French is taught as a second language.

In Canadian high schools, students can choose an academic course that will prepare them for college. Students who are not planning on college usually choose a combination of academic and vocational classes. The literacy rate in Canada is 99 percent.

In Mexico, there is a law that says all children must attend school until they are fifteen years old. However, many children only attend school for three or four years. These children usually live in areas where there are few schools or teachers. Sometimes they must leave school to earn a living because their families are too poor to support them.

In some rural areas, Mexican schools have only the first three or four grades. In cities, children go to kindergarten and then to elementary school for six years. Only about 25 percent of all Mexican students go on to secondary school, which is similar to our high school. The literacy rate in Mexico is 88 percent.

In the Caribbean countries, there are not enough schools and teachers for the number of children. Many students attend only the first few grades. Only a small number of students graduate from high school. In the last decade, many Caribbean countries have worked very hard to improve the education of their people. For example, in 1980, less than half the people in Nicaragua could read and write. By 1991, the literacy rate had been raised to 87 percent. In Jamaica, the literacy rate is 76 percent. However, in Guatemala, the literacy rate is only 51 percent. In Haiti, less than 25 percent of the people can read and write.

Discuss. Where in your community can people find information about possible job opportunities?

Emphasize. When seeking a job, you should follow every possible lead. Many people find jobs through personal networking.

Applying for a Job

When you apply for a job, you should follow certain procedures. By being aware of these, you will be better prepared to respond quickly to an opening.

❖ Resume

A **resume** (REHZ-oo-may), or personal data sheet, is a detailed summary of your education, work experience, and job-related volunteer activities. Resumes are used mainly in applying for professional, technical, managerial, clerical, and some service jobs. They are not usually needed to apply for factory work, the craft trades, or manual labor. If you are looking for a job in which a resume is expected, be sure to take one with you to each interview.

There are many different ways to organize a resume. Your library has books that present several different resume formats. The resume should be neatly typed and single-spaced and preferably only one page long. Accuracy is important, so check the resume carefully and correct any errors. When you have a perfect original, duplicate it. Resumes do not have to be originals. Just make sure that your copies are of high quality.

❖ Letter of Application

If you are answering an advertisement that gives only an address, you will have to write a letter of application. You also will have to write such a letter if you are approaching an organization without knowing whether it currently has any openings.

Type your letter on plain white, high-quality paper. Follow a standard business style in placing the date, your address, the organization's address, closing, and signature.

In the first paragraph, explain why you are writing. If someone has suggested this contact, mention the person's name. Then describe as specifically as you can the type of position you want and why you want it.

In the second paragraph, briefly list your qualifications for the position. Include your education, work experience, and other activities that are relevant to the job you are seeking. Your aim is to show the employer how you can benefit the organization.

In the last paragraph, ask for a specific response. For example, you might ask for a personal interview, an application form, or additional information. If you have a resume, enclose it with your letter of application.

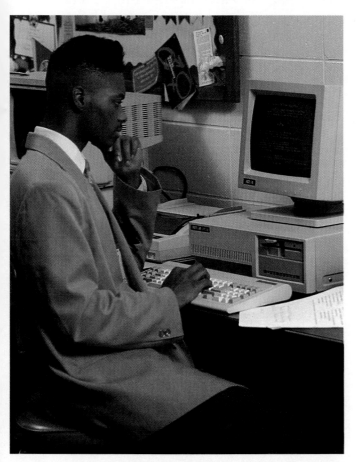

Before beginning a job search, take time to prepare a resume that lists your educational background, interests and activities, and work experiences.

Proofread the letter several times to be sure there are no errors. Correct any mistakes, and retype the letter or reprint it if you prepared it on a computer. The letter should be no longer than one typed page.

❖ Application Form

At some point in your job search, you will be asked to fill out an application form. You may have requested one by mail, or you may be asked to complete one when you arrive for an interview. Most employers rely heavily on the information you provide on their application forms, so complete them carefully. Neatness, accuracy, and correct spelling and grammar are essential. Fill in every space on the form. If a question does not apply to you, put a dash or "N/A" (for not applicable) in the space after the question to show that you did not overlook it.

Since most application forms ask for the same basic information, you might want to put this information on a card to use when you fill out applications.

- **Social security number.**

- **Education.** Include names and addresses of schools and dates attended, courses taken, and diploma or degree and honors received.

- **Employment.** Include employers' names, addresses, and telephone numbers; names of supervisors; positions held; employment dates; and, possibly, salaries.

- **References.** Include full names, addresses, occupations, and telephone numbers of **references.** These are people who will recommend you for the job. They can be former employers, teachers, or supervisors of volunteer activities. They should know

◆ Health & Safety ◆

Good Health for All

Good health habits are important for adults and for children.

- Get plenty of rest. Small children are very active and demanding. It is hard to do your job well and keep your sense of humor when you are tired.

- Wash your hands before and after feeding or changing a baby. This prevents the spread of harmful germs and bacteria. Toddlers and young children need to wash their hands before eating and after using the bathroom. If they forget, remind them.

- Walking is wonderful exercise for both adults and children. Infants can ride in a stroller or carriage. Older children should

be encouraged to walk as much as possible, even if they prefer the stroller. Everyone will benefit from the fresh air, change of scenery, and exercise.

- Avoid poor health habits. Children learn by example and like to imitate parents, caregivers, and teachers. Snack on fruits and low-fat crackers instead of junk foods. Join the children in drinking milk, juice, or water.

- Smoking is harmful to your health and to the health of those around you. Do not expose children to the dangers of secondary smoke.

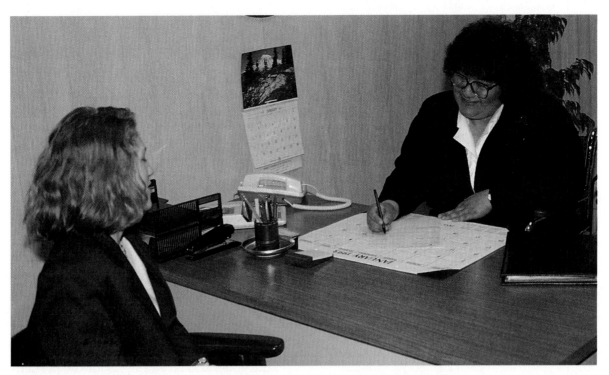

An interview helps you learn about a job—and helps the interviewer learn about you.

you and be interested in your career advancement. Always ask for permission before you list someone as a reference. You can help the people you ask to be your references by supplying them with a copy of your resume or a list of your accomplishments and goals.

◆◆ The Interview

Employers talk to you because they want to find out more about you. However, you should find out more about the organization, too. In reality, you and the employer are interviewing each other. Yet it is only natural to feel somewhat nervous about a job interview.

Make sure you know exactly where and when the interview is to take place. Then prepare for it. Review your skills and other relevant qualities. Find out about the company and its goods or services. Do your own research to become as knowledgeable as possible about the organization and the position for which you are applying.

Sample Interview Questions

Be ready to answer questions such as the following during the interview.

- Why did you apply for a position with this organization?
- What type of work do you like best? Why?
- What do you plan to be doing five years from now? What about ten years from now?
- With what kind of people do you find it difficult to work?
- What jobs have you held? What have you learned from them?
- Why should you be hired for this job?

Interview Tips

The following tips can be helpful to you on the day of the interview.

- **Dress appropriately.** No matter what position you are applying for, you want to look businesslike. Avoid wearing too much makeup, perfume or aftershave cologne, and jewelry. Do not wear clothes that are extreme in style. Be sure your clothes are clean and neatly pressed and your dress shoes are polished.

- **Go to the interview alone.** If you take family or friends along, you give the impression that you cannot function well on your own. If others must accompany you, ask them to wait outside.

- **Arrive a few minutes early.** If there is a receptionist, state your name and the person you wish to see.

- **Be positive, interested, and enthusiastic about the position.** Try not to appear pushy, insincere, or bored. Do not speak negatively about other employers for whom you have worked.

- **Sit comfortably in the chair and speak slowly and clearly.** Do not fidget or play with your hands. Avoid using slang expressions.

- **Use complete sentences to answer questions.** Do not answer with a simple yes or no. Add a few words of explanation.

◆ ◆ *Self-Esteem* ◆ ◆

People who have a positive self-concept tend to get along well with other people. When they see themselves in a positive light, they see others in a similar way. They are able to interact with confidence and self-assurance at home, at school, or on the job.

- **Be prepared to answer questions about your past record.** For example, if the interviewer has questions about your attendance record or any conflicts with former employers, be brief but honest in your response. It is better to give your version than to have the interviewer find out about a possible problem from someone else.

- **Ask questions.** Asking questions indicates interest and preparation on your part. You might ask about the specific responsibilities of the job in which you are interested. It is also a good idea to ask about opportunities for advancement within the organization.

- **Wait for the interviewer to bring up the subject of salary.** If the interviewer does not mention salary within a reasonable amount of time, you should ask about it. However, try to find out in advance what the general salary range is for the particular position. Also ask what benefits the company offers.

- **Thank the interviewer.** As the interview draws to a close, thank the interviewer for meeting with you. If the interviewer extends his or her hand, be prepared to shake it firmly. Remember that job offers are seldom made during an interview. If you feel the interview has gone well and you are interested in the job, however, ask when the employer expects to fill the position.

After the Interview

After the interview, the employer may contact your references and past employers. You may be asked to take some tests.

In the meantime, write a short follow-up note again thanking the interviewer. This is a courtesy that will help him or her remember you. In this note, you may want to offer information you did not mention before.

Finally, telephone the interviewer if you are interested in the job and have not heard from the organization after one or two weeks.

Activity. Have students take turns videotaping each other as they practice interviewing for a job. Then have them view the video, evaluate their skills, and suggest ways they can improve their techniques.

Activity. Ask students to practice shaking hands with a classmate. Discuss handshakes such as the limp dishrag, the pump handle, and the clincher.
Activity. Have students write a follow-up letter to an interview.

◆◆ Deciding on a Job

If an employer offers you a job, you may be given a day or two to think it over. Consider what your level of satisfaction would be if you took the job. Are you prepared to meet the demands of the job? Some positions require unusually long or irregular hours.

Make a list of the advantages of each job you are considering. Then make a list of the disadvantages. Try to get more information about each place of possible employment. For example, you might talk to someone who has worked in each organization. Still, the decision is yours to make. You are the one who will be performing the job.

Do not be discouraged if it takes you a long time to find the right job. Your search may require several months of serious effort. If few jobs are available, you may have to take a job that is less than ideal. In this way, you will gain the experience you need to qualify for a better job in the future.

Fringe Benefits

Fringe benefits are incentives other than wages that an employer may provide as part of the job compensation. Here are some of the fringe benefits you may be offered.

- Paid vacation.
- Medical and life insurance.
- Pension plan, which is based on funds put aside and paid to employees at retirement.
- Disability insurance, which provides income during any short-term absence from work due to illness or injury.
- Bonuses that an organization may distribute to employees when it has had a profitable year.
- Tuition-refund program for employees who take job-related courses.
- Recreational facilities.

Discuss. Would you accept a job you didn't like if it offered $5,000 more a year than your current job? $10,000 more a year? Why or why not? How much additional income would the job provide after taxes?

Success on the Job

Approach your new position with a positive attitude. You will have to learn the operating procedures and techniques of your employer. Most organizations have employee handbooks or posted rules. You must also become familiar with a new group of people. Remember that everyone likes to be treated with respect. You probably will not like everyone, but you do have to find ways of cooperating with all your coworkers.

Once you are on the job, remember that many of the qualities employers look for in a job applicant are the same qualities they expect throughout a person's employment.

- **Be responsible.** Do all your assignments willingly and complete them on schedule. Follow directions and ask questions if you do not understand.

- **Cooperate with others.** Getting along with others is essential for job success. Be friendly and helpful with customers, clients, and fellow employees.

- **Be punctual.** It is essential that you arrive on time and work the stated number of hours. Take lunch and other breaks during the specified time periods.

DECISIONS ◆ ◆ DECISIONS

Marla is about to start a new job at a child care center. She got the job through a study program in her high school. Marla is confident about working with children because she is the oldest of five. Her job begins next week, and she has not done anything to prepare herself for it. She says her personal experiences have trained her for this job. What do you think?

Activity. Ask students to talk to their parents about the fringe benefits, if any, that are provided by their employer. If they employ other people, what fringe benefits do they offer their employees?

One of the most important qualities for job success is a positive attitude toward your work. If you have a positive attitude, you will seek satisfaction in your work and in getting along with others on the job.

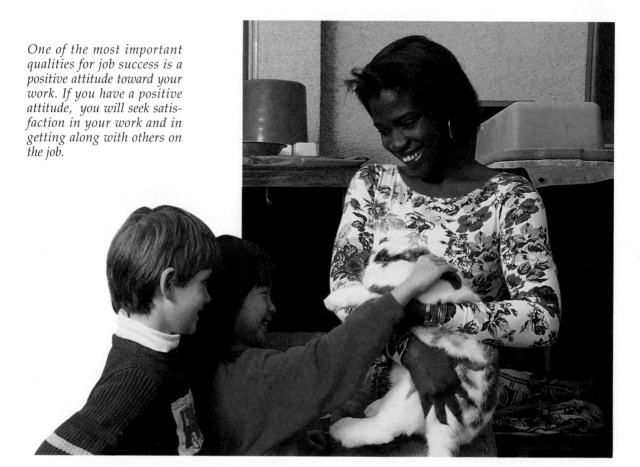

- **Use good communication skills.** Carefully consider your words and how they will affect others. Edit all written work for accuracy and rehearse oral presentations.
- **Be courteous.** Use good manners when interacting with others in person and on the telephone.
- **Maintain a good appearance.** Always be clean and well groomed.
- **Follow rules and procedures.** All organizations have certain regulations related to health, safety, and business procedures. Be sure you know these regulations so you can follow them at all times.
- **Be honest and trustworthy.** Honesty and integrity are important in any job. People must be able to trust you in every respect.

- **Set high standards.** Be professional on the job. Ask for advice about improving your performance and learning new tasks.
- **Always try to do your best.** Work hard every day. Manage your time and other resources efficiently. Be willing to learn and improve your skills. Maintain a positive attitude toward your work, coworkers, customers, and employer. Then you will gain satisfaction from your success on the job.

Your work is only part of your identity, but it is an important part. Be aware that in terms of your working life, your ambitions and needs may change. Think of each stage of your work experience as preparation for the next and as an opportunity for growth.

Discuss. What are similarities and differences between getting ready for the first day of school and for the first day of a new job? **Activity.** In small groups, have students practice good telephone procedures to use in the workplace.

Problem Solving. Often the biggest challenge of any job is getting along with coworkers. Ask students why this is so. **Activity.** Have students write an essay on the characteristics they would want an employee to have if they owned a business.

Summary

- The demand for caregivers and teachers of young children is expected to continue to grow in the years ahead.

- As is true of every career, a child care career has both advantages and disadvantages.

- Getting a good education and on-the-job experience, doing volunteer work, and taking a personal inventory can help a person choose a fulfilling career.

- Part-time jobs and volunteer activities allow teenagers to get experience in working with children.

- Finding the right job requires planning, self-confidence, hard work, and know-how.

- A resume is a personal information sheet that outlines an individual's education, work experience, and job-related volunteer activities.

- It is often necessary to write a letter of application and fill out an application form when applying for a job.

- A job interview is a two-way conversation in which each person is trying to learn something from the other.

Questions

p. 568   1. What is an entrepreneur?

p. 569   2. List at least four advantages and four disadvantages of a career in child care.

p. 574   3. Why should a person take a personal inventory when thinking about a career?

p. 575   4. List four ways that young people can gain experience in caring for children.

5. What telephone numbers should parents leave with a babysitter?   p. 576

6. How can a person find job openings?   p. 579

7. What is a resume? When is it needed?   p. 581

8. What information is usually requested on an application form?   p. 582

9. Suggest six tips to follow when interviewing for a job.   p. 584

10. What are five qualities that employers expect employees to have on the job?   p. 585

Activities

1. Take a personal inventory of things you like to do or would enjoy doing, your personality traits, and your talents. Review the lists to see whether you can spot any patterns. Then discuss the lists with your school guidance counselor.

2. On a 5" × 7" card, write down your social security number and your background information that would be required on most job application forms. Keep this card in a safe place and update the information when appropriate.

3. Prepare an oral or written report on a career in child care.

Think About

1. Which of the careers related to children listed on pages 570–573 appeals to you the most? Why?

2. If you had to give an employment agency three references tomorrow, whom would you ask to be your references? Explain the reasons for your answers.

Reference. See the Teacher's Manual in the front of the Teacher's Annotated Edition for complete answers to the chapter review questions.

587

Glossary

A

abstinence (AB-stuh-nuns). Refraining from sexual intercourse. (5)

accommodation. When one or more family members adjust or adapt so the problem can be resolved. (26)

acquired immunodeficiency syndrome (AIDS) (im-yoo-noh-dih-FISH-uhn-see). Disease caused by the HIV virus which can destroy the immune system of a pregnant woman and the developing fetus. (9)

active listening. Giving full attention to what the speaker is saying and listening to the feelings behind the words. (22)

addiction. A strong physical or psychological need for a substance. (27)

adoptive parent. A person who legally becomes the parent of a child and raises the child as his or her own. (1)

affective guidance. Involves expressing emotions or feelings to influence a child's behavior. (24)

aggression. An act marked by an attack on someone or something. (25)

allergy. Sensitivity to a substance that causes reactions such as a skin rash, itching, sneezing, or coughing. (15)

allowance. A sum of money given on a regular basis for personal expenses. (23)

ambidextrious (am-beh-DEK-struhs). Ability to use both hands equally well. (16)

ambivalence (am-BIV-ah-lahns). Being drawn both toward and away from something. (3)

amniocentesis (am-nee-oh-sen-TEE-sis). A technique that enables doctors to check for abnormal chromosomes in the fetus that might cause birth defects. (8)

anemia. A condition caused by a shortage of red blood cells. (8)

anesthetic (an-ehs-THET-ik). A medication used to eliminate pain. (11)

Apgar scale. A quick evaluation of the neonate which calls attention to the need for any emergency steps. (11)

artificial respiration. Forcing air into and out of the lungs of someone who is not breathing by using mouth-to-mouth or mouth-to-nose rescue breathing. (15)

attachment behavior. When babies recognize the people who most frequently attend to their needs and become excited when these people appear and show distress when they leave. (13)

attention-deficit hyperactivity disorder (ADHD). A type of learning disability in which children are inattentive, overactive, and impulsive. (21)

au pair (oh PARE). A young person who comes from one country to live with a family in another country and care for the children. (28)

authoritarian. Parenting style in which parents are generally strict in rearing their children. (6)

autism (AWH-tiz-ehm). A severe disorder characterized by lack of communication, extreme concern with oneself, and detachment from reality. (21)

autonomy. Independence. (17)

B

bilingual. Being able to speak two languages. (19)

biological parent. One of the two people who conceive a child; also called a birth parent. (1)

birthing room. A specially designed labor and delivery room located in a hospital or an alternative birth center that has many of the comforts of home. (10)

birth order. Relationship to other siblings in terms of time of birth. (17)

blended family. Consists of two parents, one or both of whom have children from a previous relationship. (2)

bonding. The attachment between a parent and child that establishes the basis for their ongoing relationship. (11)

Bradley method. Breathing and relaxing techniques which stress the role of a coach during labor and delivery; similar to the Lamaze method. (10)

breech delivery. When a baby is born with the feet or buttocks appearing first. (11)

C

cardiopulmonary resuscitation (CPR) (kard-ee-oh-PUL-muh-nehr-ee reh-suhs-uh-TAY-shuhn). A technique for reviving a person or keeping that person alive until an emergency team can take over by breathing into the victim's lungs and applying pressure to the victim's chest. (15)

caregiver. A person who loves, cares for, and guides a child. (1)

cervix. The narrow lower end of the uterus leading to the vagina. (8)

cesarean section (sih-ZAIR-ee-uhn). An operation to deliver the baby through an opening cut in the mother's abdominal wall and uterus. (11)

character. A person's moral qualities. (23)

child abuse. Physical, emotional, or sexual violence against children. (24)

child care center. A facility that provides full-day, supervised care and education for children. (28)

child neglect. Failure to meet a child's physical or emotional needs. (24)

chlamydia (kluh-MID-ee-uh). The most common STD which, if untreated, can damage the reproductive organs of both men and women. (9)

chorionic villus sampling (CVS) (KOR-ee-ahn-ik). A technique to test for genetic abnormalities by analyzing tissue that covers the developing cells. (8)

chromosomes (KROH-muh-sohms). Long, threadlike particles in the reproductive cell nucleus. (7)

chronic. A condition that continues over a long period of time. (21)

circumcision (sur-kuhm-SIZH-uhn). A procedure in which the foreskin is cut away from the head of the penis. (11)

classification. The result of sorting or arranging items by common qualities or traits. (19)

cognitive development. Growing ability to perceive, remember, think, reason, and solve problems; also called mental or intellectual development. (13)

colic (KAHL-ik). Pain in baby's abdomen for which no cause can be found, resulting in loud and prolonged crying. (14)

collage (koh-LAHZH). Artwork made by pasting various materials onto a surface. (20)

colostrum (kuh-LAHS-trum). Fluid present in the breasts after birth and before breast milk becomes available. (11)

communication. Process of sharing information, thoughts, and feelings. (22)

compromise (KAHM-pruh-myz). Each person gives up something in order to come to an agreement that satisfies everyone. (26)

conception (kahn-SEP-shuhn). The moment when the male and female reproductive cells unite; also called fertilization. (7)

concepts. General categories of objects and ideas formed by mentally combining their characteristics. (19)

concrete operations. The third stage of cognitive development when children can think about real objects or experiences without physically doing them. (19)

condition. Affect. (4)

conscience (KAHN-shens). An inner sense of what is right or wrong in one's own behavior. (23)

consensus (kahn-SEN-suhs). Coming to an agreement after talking things over. (26)

consequences. Results or outcomes. (5)

conservation. Properties of objects remain the same, even though other characteristics may change. (19)

contraception (kahn-truh-SEP-shuhn). Deliberate prevention of conception or pregnancy by any of various drugs, devices, or techniques. (7)

contractions. Rhythmic tightening and relaxing motions of the muscles of the uterus. (11)

conventions. Accepted standards. (23)

convulsion. A series of strong, involuntary contractions of muscles. (15)

cooperative family. Consists of nonrelated people who get together to rear their children in one household. (2)

cooperative play. Type of play in which children do things together. (20)

coping (KOHP-ing). Being able to deal with responsibilities and problems with some degree of success. (12)

cradle cap. Dirty-looking, patchy scalp condition. (14)

creativity. The ability to produce something original and unique. (19)

croup (KROOP). A condition marked by a loud, barking cough and difficult breathing. (15)

custody. A legal arrangement in which one parent becomes the guardian of the children. (27)

D

delivery. The process of birth. (10)

delivery room. A sterile hospital area that is specifically used for delivering babies and equipped for surgery and emergency procedures. (10)

democratic. Parenting style in which parents consider both the child's needs and their own point of view when making decisions; also called authoritative. (6)

depression. A prolonged feeling of sadness marked by helplessness and an inability to enjoy life. (12)

development. An increasing skill in one or a combination of abilities. (1)

developmentally appropriate. Suitable for the level of the child's development. (24)

dexterity (dek-STER-ih-tee). Skilled use of the hands. (16)

diarrhea (dy-ah-REE-ah). Extremely loose bowel movements. (14)

dilate. Widen. (11)

direct guidance. Any method of influencing children's behavior through face-to-face interaction. (24)

disabled. Having a physical, mental, or emotional condition that limits activity. (21)

dramatic play. Imaginative, unrehearsed play in which children pretend to be other people or animals as they take part in make-believe events. (20)

dyslexia (dis-LEK-see-uh). A type of learning disability in which people have difficulty interpreting information they see and hear. (21)

E

egocentric. Very self-centered. (17)

embryo (EM-bree-oh). The ball of rapidly multiplying cells during the second stage of prenatal development which lasts from the end of the second week of pregnancy through the eighth week. (8)

emotional development. Growing ability to express feelings. (13)

empathy. The ability to understand and share another person's feelings. (17)

encouragement. A message of confidence and faith in another's ability. (22)

eneuresis (en-you-REE-sis). Bedwetting or lack of bladder control. (25)

entrepreneur (ohn-truh-pruh-NUR). A person who starts and manages his or her own business. (30)

episiotomy (ih-PIHZ-ee-OTT-uh-mee). A small incision made at the back of the woman's vagina to prevent tearing of the vaginal opening during birth. (11)

exploratory play. Type of play in which children can discover how things work. (20)

extended family. Consists of all the immediate relatives of a family, such as grandparents, aunts, uncles, and cousins. (2)

eye-hand coordination. Coordinating vision and small motor skills. (16)

F

family child care. Type of home-based child care provided usually by a mother in her own home who cares for three or four children in addition to her own children. (28)

family life cycle. A series of stages that families go through. (2)

fertilization (fert-uhl-uh-ZAY-shuhn). The union of the sperm and ovum; also called conception. (7)

fetal alcohol syndrome (FAS). Serious birth defect caused when a female drinks large amounts of alcohol during pregnancy. (9)

fetal monitor. A device which records contractions and fetal heartbeat. (11)

fetus (FEE-tus). The unborn child during the third and final stage of prenatal development. (8)

first aid. Emergency treatment given to a person who is injured or ill. (15)

flame retardant. Not easily set on fire and does not burn quickly. (16)

flextime. A system that allows workers to arrive earlier or later than the standard starting hour. (27)

fluoride (FLUR-eyed). A mineral that makes tooth enamel resistant to cavities. (16)

fontanels (fahn-tuh-NELZ). Soft spots between the bone plates in a baby's head. (13)

Food Guide Pyramid. Tells how many servings a person should eat from each of the main food groups. (9)

forceps. An instrument for reaching into the birth canal and pulling out the baby. (11)

formal operations. The fourth stage of cognitive development when individuals can perform mental operations that involve abstract or hypothetical objects or experiences without the help of real objects. (19)

formula. A commercially prepared mixture of milk or milk substitute, water, and added nutrients. (10)

foster parent. A person who provides a home to children in times of emergency. (1)

fracture. A break in a bone. (15)

fringe benefits. Incentives other than wages that an employer may provide as part of the job compensation. (30)

G

general equivalency diploma (GED). Earned by individuals who do not graduate from high school but take special classes and pass an examination. (26)

genes (JEENZ). Chromosome parts that determine inherited traits. (7)

genetic counseling. Expert information and explanation about heredity, especially about the risks for disorders passed along to children through the genes. (7)

gifted children. Children who are very intelligent or show unusual talent in a particular area at an early age. (21)

grief (GREEF). A great sorrow caused by a loss. (27)

growth spurt. When parts of the body grow at different rates. (16)

guidance. The words and actions that adults use to influence children's behavior. (1)

gynecologist (gyn-uh-KAHL-uh-juhst). Doctor who specializes in the health of the female reproductive organs. (7)

H

Head Start. A form of early childhood education funded by the federal government for low-income and disadvantaged preschool children. (29)

hormones. Body chemicals that stimulate growth. (5)

hot line. Telephone line that provides direct access to information or counseling. (24)

I

identity. A sense of who one really is. (17)

immunizations (im-yoo-nih-ZAY-shuhns). Vaccines that are given in shots or taken by mouth to protect children from certain diseases. (15)

inclusion. The process of educating children with a disability in classrooms with children who are not disabled; also called integration or mainstreaming. (21)

indirect guidance. Any method of arranging the environment to help children behave in an acceptable or desired way. (24)

indulgence. The practice of giving children more of everything, such as attention, toys, or food, whether they want it or not. (6)

infatuation. An intense but usually short-term feeling of love for someone. (4)

infertility (in-fur-TIL-eh-tee). Inability to have children. (7)

initiative (in-NISH-ee-eh-tiv). The readiness and ability to start something on one's own. (17)

irreversible thinking. Inability to go back in the thought process and think about things as they were. (19)

J

joint custody. A legal arrangement giving both parents roughly equal time with the children and equal responsibility for them. (27)

kindergarten. A class or school for children who are about five years of age. (29)

labor. Contractions of the uterine muscles that gradually push the baby out of the mother's body. (10)

Lamaze method (lah-MAHZ). Special breathing and relaxation techniques for women in labor which stress the helpful role of a coach. (10)

large motor skills. Those involving the control and use of large muscles, especially those in the arms and legs. (16)

latchkey children. Children who must take care of themselves before and after school. (28)

layette (lay-ETT). A collection of baby clothing and equipment. (10)

learning centers. A special area in a classroom that contains supplies and enough room for a few children to work independently or together. (29)

legal guardian. A person appointed by a court to provide parenting for a child. (1)

life-style. How individuals and families choose to live. (2)

limits. Guidelines and boundaries to which children must adhere. (24)

low birth weight. A weight of less than 5½ pounds at birth. (5)

malnutrition. A physical condition due to a poor or inadequate diet. (16)

maturation. The process of reaching full growth and development. (13)

maturity. The condition in which a person's body is fully developed and he or she thinks and acts reasonably, responsibly, reliably, and independently. (4)

mental retardation. A disorder characterized in varying degrees by low intelligence, abnormal ability to learn, and impaired social adaptation. (21)

miscarriage. The body's way of expelling the embryo or fetus before it can fully develop. (8)

Montessori method. A system of teaching children to be motivated learners developed by Maria Montessori, an Italian medical doctor and educator. (29)

moral development. Process of learning standards of right and wrong. (23)

motivation. An inner desire to act or behave in a certain way. (22)

motor skills. The ability to use and control the muscles of the body. (13)

nanny. A live-in caregiver. (28)

National Association for the Education of Young Children (NAEYC). An association of teachers, caregivers, and parents who work for improved quality in early childhood programs. (28)

negativism. A tendency to resist suggestions and commands. (17)

neonate (NEE-oh-nate). A newborn baby. (11)

nuclear family. Consists of a mother, a father, and one or more biological or adopted children. (2)

nurse-midwife. Registered nurse trained in obstetrics and prenatal care. (7)

nurture. To support and encourage. (1)

nutrients (NOO-tree-unts). Chemicals the body must have in order to function, grow, repair itself, and produce energy. (9)

O

object permanence. Objects continue to exist even when they are out of sight. (19)

obstetrician (ahb-stuh-TRISH-uhn). Doctor who specializes in delivering babies. (7)

open adoption. Allows the birth and adoptive parents to share information about themselves and the child. (5)

orthodontist (OR-thuh-DON-tist). A specialist in straightening and realigning teeth. (16)

ovaries (OHV-uh-rees). The female reproductive glands. (7)

ovum. The female reproductive cell. (7)

P

pacifier. A nipple-shaped device for babies to suck. (14)

Pap smear. A test used to detect the early stage of cancer of the cervix. (8)

parallel play. Type of play in which children play side by side. (20)

parental leave. Time away from a job that a parent is allowed to take after the birth or adoption of a child. (10)

parent cooperatives. Nursery schools in which parents take turns assisting in the classroom. (29)

parent helper. Work similar to a babysitter's but usually done while a parent is in the home. (30)

parenting. Providing care, support, and love in a way that leads to a child's total development. (1)

parenting style. The particular way that a parent consistently behaves toward children. (6)

pediatrician (PEE-dee-uh-TRISH-un). A doctor who specializes in the treatment of infants and young children. (10)

peer pressure. The strong influence of friends or others of the same age to make someone do whatever the group does. (18)

peers. People of the same age. (18)

permissive. Parenting style in which parents generally permit a wide range of behavior. (6)

personality. The sum total of a person's emotional, social, cognitive, and physical characteristics as seen by others. (17)

phobia. A persistent, irrational fear of a specific object, situation, or activity. (25)

physical development. Increasing ability to control and coordinate body movements. (13)

physical guidance. Involves direct physical contact with children to guide their behavior. (24)

physiological (fiz-ee-ah-LAHJ-eh-kahl). Refers to the functioning of the body. (6)

placenta (pluh-SENT-uh). A flat disk-shaped organ formed from the tissue connecting the embryo to the uterine wall. (8)

play. Any activity that individuals choose to do; activity that is fun and self-motivated. (20)

positive reinforcement. Action that encourages a particular behavior, such as rewarding good behavior with attention and praise. (24)

postnatal. After childbirth. (12)

postpartum blues. Feelings of frustration and a letdown after childbirth. (12)

pregnancy induced hypertension (PIH). A potentially serious condition of pregnancy that involves high blood pressure; also called toxemia or preeclampsia. (9)

prejudice (PREJ-uh-dis). An opinion or feeling formed without knowledge about someone or something. (18)

premature (pree-muh-CHOOR). A baby born before his or her development is complete. (5)

prenatal care. Regular medical care and supervision prior to the baby's birth. (5)

preoperational stage. Second stage of cognitive development when children begin to take more interest in the people and things around them. (19)

prepared childbirth. When expectant parents understand the birth process, can control the pain through breathing and relaxation techniques, and take an active part in the birth process. (10)

principles. Personal rules that form the basis of proper conduct. (23)

priorities. Tasks that are most urgent and should be done first. (12)

prioritize. To rank in order of importance. (4)

prosthesis (pross-THEE-suhs). An artificial arm or leg. (2l)

psychological (sigh-keh-LAHJ-eh-kahl). Refers to a person's mental and emotional states.(6)

puberty. The beginning of adolescence; the stage of growth and development when males and females become physically able to reproduce. (5)

quality time. Focusing on the individual interests and needs of the child. (26)

reasoning. The ability to think logically, to make judgments, and to form conclusions. (19)

references. People who will recommend you for the job. (30)

reflexes. Automatic, or involuntary, responses to stimulation of some kind. (13)

resource. Something that individuals or families can use to accomplish a goal. (26)

respect. Being considerate and polite to other people because you find them worthy. (26)

resume (REHZ-oo-may). Personal data sheet containing a detailed summary of one's education, work experience, and activities. (30)

reversibility. The ability to think about an object and change one's mind about it without having to manipulate it physically. (19)

Rh factor. A substance present in the blood of 85 percent of the population. (8)

role models. People who show children how to talk, act, and behave through their own words, attitudes, actions, and behavior. (3)

roles. Parts one plays when interacting with others. (2)

rubella (ruh-BELL-uh). A disease, commonly known as German measles, which can cause mental and physical disabilities in a fetus during the first trimester of pregnancy. (9)

self-actualization. Achievement of one's full potential. (6)

self-concept. The image of oneself. (1)

self-demand feeding. Feeding babies when they seem to be hungry rather than according to a fixed schedule. (14)

self-esteem. A person's opinion, belief, or judgement about one's worthiness as a person; the feelings about oneself. (1)

sensorimotor stage. First period in cognitive development when children learn to use their senses and to manipulate and control their muscles. (13)

separation anxiety. The fear of being away from familiar people or a familiar environment. (13)

seriation (SEER-ee-AY-shun). The ability to arrange items in order according to size, number, or date. (19)

sexuality. A person's concept of himself or herself as a male or a female. (5)

sexually transmitted disease (STD). A disease that is transmitted by sexual contact. (5)

sibling. A brother or sister. (10)

sibling rivalry. Competition among brothers and sisters for parents' attention; a form of jealousy. (17)

single-parent family. Consists of only one parent and one or more children. (2)

small motor skills. Those involving the control and use of small muscles, especially those in the fingers and hands. (16)

social development. Growing ability to relate to other people. (13)

socialization. The process by which people acquire the attitudes, beliefs, and behavior patterns of a society. (18)

solitary play. Type of play in which children play by themselves. (20)

special education. A program of individualized instruction for children with disabilities or exceptional needs. (21)

sperm. The male reproductive cell. (7)

sphincter muscles (SFINK-tuhr). Muscles in the bowel and bladder regions that control elimination. (16)

staff-child ratio. Number of adult caregivers per number of children. (28)

stepparent. A person whose spouse has children from an earlier relationship. (1)

stereotype. A standardized mental picture of a person or group held by many people. (18)

sterilizing. Bringing an item to a high temperature, usually by boiling, to destroy any germs. (14)

stimuli. Any things that arouse thoughts, feelings, or actions. (19)

stranger anxiety. The fear of people one does not know. (13)

stress. Tension caused by important events or changes in one's life. (12)

sudden infant death syndrome (SIDS). When a seemingly healthy baby is put to bed and later is found dead; also called crib death. (15)

temperament. The intensity and duration of a person's emotional response. (13)

temper tantrum. A fit of anger that may be expressed through screaming, hitting, and kicking. (17)

testes (TES-tees). The male reproductive glands. (7)

theory. An organized set of suggestions about facts or events that is developed through study and observation. (1)

ultrasonography (ulh-truh-suh-NOG-ruh-fee). A procedure in which high-frequency sound waves are bounced off the developing fetus to produce a video image, or sonogram. (8)

umbilical cord (uhm-BILL-ih-kuhl). Cord that attaches the embryo to the placenta. (8)

uterus (YOOT-uh-russ). Pear-shaped organ in which the future child develops; also called womb. (7)

vagina (vuh-JY-nuh). An elastic, tubular organ that leads from the uterus to the outside of the female body; the birth canal. (8)

values. Beliefs about what is right, worthwhile, or desirable. (3)

verbal guidance. Use of words to influence children's behavior. (24)

weaning. Getting baby to drink milk from a cup rather than from a bottle or a breast. (14)

wellness. Achieving and maintaining a state of good health. (15)

work ethic. Understanding the value and importance of work and its ability to strengthen one's character. (23)

zygote (ZY-goht). New cell formed after sperm and ovum unite. (8)

Photo Credits

AP/Wide World Photos   26
Archive Photos   26, 27
Arnold & Brown Photographers   16, 32, 42, 58, 75, 85, 86, 91, 93, 97, 98, 105, 106, 112, 116, 123, 125, 139, 170, 174, 178, 179, 192, 217, 248, 273, 274, 276, 282, 283, 286, 288, 292, 309, 318, 341, 343, 354, 356, 373, 401, 429, 446, 459, 465, 466, 470, 476, 479, 484, 486, 488, 537, 554, 583
Roger B. Bean   7, 9, 19, 21, 22, 38, 63, 82, 124, 156, 167, 168, 183, 208, 211, 212, 218, 230, 231, 240, 254, 255, 258, 259, 262, 265, 266, 281, 283, 298, 344, 374, 393, 420, 421, 424, 427, 438, 443, 449, 451, 455, 462, 463, 472, 512, 533, 576
Keith M. Berry   34, 92, 100, 127, 130, 134, 146, 150, 151, 162, 163, 165, 172, 188, 216, 219, 220, 228, 294, 299, 302, 304, 308, 310, 336, 418, 483, 564, 566
The Bettmann Archive   26, 27
Bradley University/Saint Francis Medical Center, Peoria, IL/Roger B. Bean   88
Comstock, Inc.
    Russ Kinne   190, 200
Leo de Wys
    Bill Bachmann   338, 349
    Per Erikson   561
    Bill Grimes   210
    Robb Kendrick   560
    Bob Krist   385
    Randy G. Taylor   108
    Bob Thomason   414
    Steve Vidler   412
David R. Frazier Photolibrary Inc.   136, 250
Linda Henson   477, 481, 490, 492
The Image Bank
    David J. Maenza   442
    Roger Miller   176, 195
Index Stock International Inc.
    Wallace Garrison   456
    John Wood   205
Thomas Jefferson School, Peoria, IL/Roger B. Bean   25, 376, 396, 402, 411, 559
Jones Metropolitan High School/Mishima   77, 581
James Marshall Photography   5, 8, 10, 11, 29, 47, 50, 59, 68, 80, 89, 102, 104, 145, 177, 184, 256, 295, 307, 323, 331, 339, 342, 347, 358, 359, 378, 380, 394, 423, 436, 440, 452, 461, 500
McGraw YMCA Evanston, IL/Mishima   550
Mishima   14, 20, 24, 28, 30, 37, 52, 54, 55, 64, 66, 70, 72, 84, 118, 154, 159, 164, 182, 222, 224, 233, 238, 241, 243, 245, 251, 252, 253, 264, 290, 314, 316, 317, 319, 321, 324, 325, 329, 330, 332, 333, 351, 352, 368, 372, 387, 390, 416, 474, 494, 510
Murray Language Academy/Mishima   361, 365, 370
Cristin Nestor Photography   386, 426, 428, 434, 445
Photo Options
    Bill Bachmann   36, 40, 399, 502, 517
    Sylvia Caswell   316
    Lee Issacs   226
    Ed Malles   206

Photo Researchers
    John Carter   234
    Larry Mulvehill   194
    Petit Format/Nestle   138
    SIU   198
PHOTOTAKE
    Ann Chwatsky   214
    Mitch Kezar   521
    Maurtius GMBH   201
    Ken Sherman   202
Saint Francis Medical Center, Peoria, IL   175, 221
Carol Spengel/Circle Design   120, 122, 140, 141, 142, 143, 197, 199, 236, 237, 278, 279, 285, 300, 301, 326, 327, 430, 431, 432, 433, 570, 571, 572, 573
Thompson Food Basket/Arnold & Brown Photographers   448
U.S.D.A.   158
Westlight
    Adamsmith   1, 39, 340
    Dennis Degnan   13
    Fotografia, Inc.   12, 160
    Walter Hodges   6
    Julie Houck   18, 180
    Warren Morgan   2, 61, 312
    Pete Saloutos   114
West Surburban Hospital, Oak Park, IL/ Mishima   268
Dana White - Dana White Productions, Inc.   43, 45, 46, 94, 110, 271, 297, 346, 366, 367, 381, 388, 460, 464, 496, 498, 499, 504, 506, 508, 509, 515, 518, 519, 522, 523, 524, 526, 528, 530, 534, 536, 540, 545, 548, 552, 553, 554, 568, 579, 586
YWCA Lakeview, Peoria, IL
    Arnold & Brown Photographers   542
    Roger B. Bean   348, 363, 383, 392, 411, 458, 539, 543, 557
    Keith M. Berry   575, 577
Zephyr Pictures
    Melanie Carr   186, 260
    Morris   270
Frank Zosky   56

Special thanks to the following for their support and contributions:
Laura Corpuz

John Adams Middle School
Maternity Center Association, NY, NY
Martin Minkardo
Santa Monica High School
Santa Monica YWCA
Venice Family Clinic
Natalie, Michael, and Andrew White
Windward School

Cover Photo: Nicole Katano/Tony Stone Images

Index

Q

R

Rubella, 167-168

S